Housing law

An adviser's handbook

Diane Astin is a solicitor specialising in housing law, with many years' experience in private practice and in the voluntary sector. She regularly trains and lectures in housing law, community care and asylum support for organisations including Legal Action Group, the Law Centres Federation, the Red Cross and the Refugee Council. Diane was previously a part-time visiting lecturer at London Metropolitan University and was a member of the Law Society Housing Law Committee from 1997 to 2006.

Available as an ebook at www.lag.org.uk/ebooks

The purpose of the Legal Action Group is to promote equal access to justice for all members of society who are socially, economically or otherwise disadvantaged. To this end, it seeks to improve law and practice, the administration of justice and legal services.

Housing law

An adviser's handbook

SECOND EDITION

Diane Astin

Legal Action Group
2012

This edition published in Great Britain 2012
by LAG Education and Service Trust Limited
242 Pentonville Road, London N1 9UN
www.lag.org.uk

First published 2008
Reprinted 2010

British Library Cataloguing in Publication Data
a CIP catalogue record for this book is available from the British Library.

This book has been produced using Forest Stewardship
Council (FSC) certified paper. The wood used to produce
FSC certified products with a 'Mixed Sources' label comes
from FSC certified well-managed forests, controlled sources
and/or recycled material.

Print ISBN   978 1 903307 87 8
ebook ISBN   978 1 903307 96 0

Typeset by Regent Typesetting, London
Printed in Great Britain by Hobbs the Printers, Totton, Hampshire

Preface

'It is, inevitably, money.' An unusual way to begin a Court of Appeal judgment but Lord Justice Ward wasted no time identifying the issue in *SA v A Local Authority*.[1] The case concerned the way local authorities provide accommodation and care for children in need. Not surprisingly, the local authority maintained that it was acceptable to exercise its duties in a way that would require it to pay the carer £83 per week less than the alternative way. The Court of Appeal held that, as a matter of law, the authority was bound to pay the higher rate.

Much housing advice, in common with other types of social welfare law, is about the battle between public bodies responsible for allocating scarce resources and individuals seeking access to those resources. In housing cases, the resource people are seeking is usually no more than a secure and affordable home.

Sadly, many of the recent developments and the forthcoming changes described in this book will mean that homes for the poor will become both less secure and less affordable. Under the Localism Act 2011, which received royal assent as this book went to press, local authorities will be able to grant the disingenuously named 'flexible tenancy' which, being for a fixed period only, offers less security than secure periodic tenancies which have been granted by local authorities for decades. And under the downright dishonestly named 'affordable rent tenancy' other social landlords will be able to charge rents that are much higher than those currently paid by social tenants and will be encouraged to use similar fixed term agreements instead of periodic assured tenancies.

Developments since the first edition

Since 2008, when the first edition of this book appeared, there has been a flurry of activity in both the Supreme Court and the European

---

1   [2011] EWCA Civ 1303, 10 November 2011.

Court of Human Rights in relation to the application of public law and article 8 of the European Convention on Human Rights to possession proceedings. Thankfully, the issue is now reasonably settled: in principle tenants with no security of tenure can ask the county court to review the proportionality of a decision by a public body to evict them. Such cases are likely to be exceptional and the burden will be on the tenant to convince the court that they have an arguable defence. This is a welcome development but the proposed changes to legal aid are likely to mean that fewer tenants are represented in possession claims and it remains to be seen how these exceptional and complex human rights arguments will be identified in the busy county courts.

The Equality Act 2010 has now come into force. The Act extends protection from discrimination to all those with protected characteristics: age, disability, gender reassignment, marriage and civil partnership, pregnancy and maternity, race, religion and belief, sex and sexual orientation. It also redefined indirect disability discrimination to resolve the problem caused by the House of Lords' decision in *Lewisham LBC v Malcolm*.[2] In addition, the public sector equality duty, which is re-enacted in the 2010 Act, has been considered by the Court of Appeal in two cases specifically about housing and it is now clear that public bodies are bound by the duty not only when devising policies but also when making decisions affecting individual homeless applicants and tenants.[3] Doubtless this is an area that will see further consideration in the near future.

As these developments illustrate, public law is increasingly relevant to housing advice and this shift in emphasis will continue when the Localism Act comes into force, making yet more tenants dependent on administrative decision making and giving local authorities more discretion as to how they allocate housing and the types of tenancies they grant.

The changes to the benefit system are also likely to have a major effect on housing rights. The capping of housing benefit was introduced in April 2011. This will have a significant effect on the availability of private rented accommodation to low income families, particularly in London and the South East. It applies to new claims made after April 2011 and to existing claims on the first annual review, so the full effect has not yet been felt. Moreover, it is likely

2   [2008] UKHL 43, 25 June 2008.
3   See *Pieretti v Enfield LBC* [2010] EWCA Civ 1104, 12 October 2010 and *Barnsley MBC v Norton* [2011] EWCA Civ 834, 21 July 2011.

to take some time before those claimants whose benefits have been reduced fall into significant rent arrears and start to be evicted. The likely effect of the proposed Universal Credit on housing costs is not yet known.

The Localism Act 2011

The changes this Act will make to housing rights are set out in relatively few sections but have the potential to bring about fundamental change. Under the Act the homelessness duty will no longer be an indefinite duty to provide suitable accommodation, ended only by a specific event. Instead the duty will end when the authority arrange for a private sector accommodation offer to be made to the applicant. Local authorities will have more power to decide who can be allocated social housing and when providing accommodation to those who qualify they will be able to offer tenancies for a limited period, instead of long term secure tenancies. Other social landlords will be encouraged to do the same and to charge rents of up to 80 per cent of market rents.

How the Act will work in practice, however, is uncertain. It is questionable whether the proposals for the homelessness duty are even workable. The use of the private sector accommodation offer to end the duty depends on private landlords being willing to grant 12-month fixed-term agreements to homeless applicants. This will involve checks on the standard of the accommodation as well as a 'fit and proper person' test applied to the landlord. And since there will still be a right to challenge the suitability of the offer, provision will need to be made for those cases where the property is found to be unsuitable after the tenancy has started. Whether there will be sufficient numbers of private landlords willing to work with local authorities in this way, particularly given the new restrictions on the amount of housing benefit payable, is doubtful.

Changes to legal aid

Probably of more significance than the Localism Act 2011 to the world of housing law will be the Legal Aid, Sentencing and Punishment of Offenders (LASPO) Bill whose only virtue is a pronounceable acronym. This bill will remove legal aid from the areas of law that affect the most vulnerable: debt, welfare benefits, employment, non-asylum immigration and most family disputes about finance and children. Housing law escapes relatively unscathed as most cases about the loss of a home will remain eligible for legal aid. This covers possession proceedings and homelessness cases which comprise the bulk of housing advice work. However, claims for possession made against trespassers will not be eligible for legal aid and legal aid will be restricted in cases which concern disrepair and illegal eviction and harassment. Essentially, legal aid will not generally be available for claims for damages where lawyers will be expected to work under Conditional Fee Agreements. Judicial review claims will also remain 'in scope'. The fact that people will be unable to get help with their debt problems and their welfare benefit or employment issues is likely to lead to an increase in people facing the loss of their homes which may mean a greater need for housing advice than ever. But many legal aid firms and law centres will be unable to operate when most social welfare law is taken out of the scope of legal aid, not to mention the proposal to funnel all legal aid cases through a mandatory telephone call centre which will decide whether face to face advice is justified.

So, yes, it is inevitably money. And in the current climate when those who have so little of it are being penalised, asserting housing rights and challenging public bodies is more important than ever. I hope that this book helps those who are still committed to doing both of those things.

I remain grateful to all of the people who helped me with the first edition. In addition, I would like to thank Chessie Aeron-Thomas and Justin Leslie for commenting on the drafts of some new material. As with the first edition I owe particular thanks to John Gallagher who read yet more drafts and fielded my incessant questions about the Localism Act with patience and thoughtful consideration.

I would also like to thank Esther Pilger at LAG for her support and help throughout this process and Lesley Exton at Regent Typesetting for sorting out the messy proofs.

I have endeavoured to describe accurately the law in England and Wales as at 1 November 2011. Given the extent of the powers of the Welsh Assembly it is increasingly the case that the detail of certain provisions differs in England and Wales. Given this, and for reasons of space, in some cases I have only been able to highlight that the provisions in Wales are different to those in England and to provide the relevant references. It may be that at some time in the future a Welsh version of this book will be needed.

Diane Astin

November 2011

This book is dedicated to my mother, who taught me to type, as well as many other even more valuable things.

Contents

Table of cases

Table of statutes

Table of statutory instruments

Table of European legislation

Directives

Abbreviations

ADR	alternative dispute resolution
AIA 1999	Asylum and Immigration Act 1999
AJA 1970	Administration of Justice Act 1970
AJA 1973	Administration of Justice Act 1973
AOG	Adjudication Officers' Guide
ASBA 2003	Anti-social Behaviour Act 2003
ASBI	anti-social behaviour injunction
ASBO	anti-social behaviour order
BA 1984	Building Act 1984
CA 1989	Children Act 1989
CCA 1974	Consumer Credit Act 1974
CDA 1998	Crime and Disorder Act 1998
CFA	conditional fee agreement
CLA 1977	Criminal Law Act 1977
CLRA 2002	Commonhold and Leasehold Reform Act 2002
CPA 2004	Civil Partnership Act 2004
CPR 1999	Civil Procedure Rules 1999
CSDPA 1970	Chronically Sick and Disabled Persons Act 1970
CTA	Common Travel Area
DCLG	Department of Communities and Local Government
DDA 1995	Disability Discrimination Act 1995
DFG	disabled facilities grants
DHP	discretionary housing payment
DoH	Department of Health
DPA 1972	Defective Premises Act 1972
DPS	Deposit Protection Services
DRO	displaced residential occupiers
DWP	Department for Work and Pensions
EA 2010	Equality Act 2010
ECHR	European Convention on Human Rights
ECtHR	European Court of Human Rights
ECJ	European Court of Justice
EEA	European Economic Area
EFTA	European Free Trade Association
EHO	environmental health officer
EHRC	Equality and Human Rights Commission
ELR	exceptional leave to remain
EPA 1990	Environmental Protection Act 1990
FACS	Fair Access to Care Services

FIA 2000	Freedom of Information Act 2000
FIT	family intervention tenancies
FLA 1996	Family Law Act 1996
FOS	Financial Ombudsman Service
FSA	Financial Services Authority
HA 1980	Housing Act 1980
HA 1985	Housing Act 1985
HA 1988	Housing Act 1988
HA 1996	Housing Act 1996
HA 2004	Housing Act 2004
HAT	housing action trust
HB	housing benefit
HB Regs 2006	Housing Benefit Regulations 2006
HBRB	Housing Benefit Review Board
HGCRA 1996	Housing Grants, Construction and Regeneration Act 1996
HHSRS	Housing Health and Safety Rating System
HHSRS Regs 2005	Housing Health and Safety Rating System Regulations 2005
HIA	Home Improvement Agency
HMO	house in multiple occupation
HOS	Housing Ombudsman Service
HRA 1998	Human Rights Act 1998
H&RA 2008	Housing and Regeneration Act 2008
HRT	habitual residence test
HSE	Health and Safety Executive
HSPHA 1968	Health Services and Public Health Act 1968
IA 1971	Immigration Act 1971
IA 1988	Immigration Act 1988
IAA 1999	Immigration and Asylum Act 1999
ILR	indefinite leave to remain
IPO	interim possession order
IS	income support
JSA	jobseeker's allowance
LASSA 1970	Local Authority Social Services Act 1970
LGA 2000	Local Government Act 2000
LGO	Local Government Ombudsman
LHA	local housing allowance
LOTR	leave outside the rules
LPA 1925	Law of Property Act 1925
LRA 1967	Leasehold Reform Act 1967
LRA 2002	Land Registration Act 2002
LRHUDA 1999	Leasehold Reform, Housing and Urban Development Act 1993
LSC	Legal Services Commission
LSCT	large scale voluntary transfer
LTA 1954	Landlord and Tenant Act 1954
LTA 1985	Landlord and Tenant Act 1985
LTA 1987	Landlord and Tenant Act 1987
LVT	Leasehold Valuation Tribunal
MCA 1973	Matrimonial Causes Act 1973

MCA 2005	Mental Capacity Act 2005
MCOB	Mortgage Conduct of Business Rules
MHA 1983	Mental Health Act 1983
MR(PT)A 2010	Mortgage Repossessions (Protection of Tenants) Act 2010
NAA 1948	National Assistance Act 1948
NASS	National Asylum Support Service
NHSA 1977	National Health Service Act 1977
NHSCCA 1990	NHS & Community Care Act 1990
NIA 2002	Nationality, Immigration and Asylum Act 2002
NOSP	notice of seeking possession
NSP	notice seeking possession
ODPM	Office of the Deputy Prime Minister
OFT	Office of Fair Trading
PEA 1977	Prevention from Eviction Act 1977
PHA 1997	Protection from Harassment Act 1997
PIO	protected intending occupier
PPO	postponed possession order
PR	personal representative
PRP	private registered provider
PSL	private sector leasing
PST	protected shorthold tenancy
RA 1977	Rent Act 1977
RMO	responsible medical officer
RSL	registered social landlord
SJE	single joint expert
SSCBA 1992	Social Security Contributions and Benefits Act 1992
SSCSA	Social Security and Child Support Appeal
TFEU	Treaty on the Functioning of the European Union
TLATA 1996	Trusts of Land and Appointment of Trustees Act 1996
TSA	Tenant Services Authority
UKBA	UK Border Agency
UTCCR 1999	Unfair Terms in Consumer Contracts Regulations 1999
YOI	young offenders institution

Occupiers' rights: basic principles

continued

Key points

- In English law land is not 'owned'. Rather a person may have an estate or interest in land.
- A tenancy is an interest in land.
- A tenancy is distinct from a licence, which is a personal right.
- A tenancy may be created without a written agreement.
- The 'hallmarks of a tenancy' are: the grant of exclusive possession of premises; for a period of time; in return for the payment of rent.
- If these features are present an agreement will be a tenancy unless it falls into a specific category of recognised exceptions.
- A tenancy can be for a fixed term or periodic. A periodic tenancy runs automatically from one period to the next.
- Security of tenure is about the restriction on a landlord's right to evict. It may be 'procedural' (the landlord must follow a certain procedure to evict) or 'substantive' (the landlord cannot evict unless there are grounds).
- In the private sector, only tenants can enjoy substantive security of tenure.
- Licensees will enjoy procedural security of tenure unless they are 'excluded occupiers' as listed in the Protection from Eviction Act 1977.
- Excluded occupiers can be evicted without a court order.
- A tenant can end a tenancy either by serving notice to quit or by surrender. Notice to quit only operates to end a periodic tenancy. Surrender brings any sort of tenancy to an end but all parties must agree to a surrender.
- A notice to quit served by one joint tenant ends the joint tenancy.
- A person who does not have a legal interest in land may nevertheless have an equitable interest.

Introduction

1.1   Most of this book deals with the rights of those who occupy accommodation as a home. This is largely governed by statute. In some cases the statutory rights are in addition to rights set out in the agreement to occupy; in other cases the statutory rights override the agreement. The statutory intervention largely protects occupiers and restricts the rights of landlords. However, some occupiers fall outside statutory schemes of protection, which means that the parties' rights, such as the right to end an occupation agreement, are not restricted by statute. A significant part of the relationship between an occupier and a landlord is therefore governed by the occupation agreement or the general legal principles applying to rights over land.

1.2   This chapter examines some of these basic legal principles. The nature of a tenancy is examined and the different levels of security enjoyed by occupiers are explained, with particular reference to occupiers who are excluded from any protection. In addition, some difficult situations are explored, for example hotel and bed and breakfast accommodation and premises that are let for both business and residential use. Finally, the relevance of the law of trusts and equity to occupiers' rights is briefly explained.

Security of tenure

1.3   Before giving housing advice to any occupier it is necessary to identify the nature of the person's right to remain in occupation, in other words whether the person has 'security of tenure'. There are two levels of security of tenure. At the higher level a tenant may have the right not to be evicted unless the landlord can prove a statutory ground for possession; at the lower level an occupier may have the right not to be evicted unless the landlord follows a certain procedure (serving notice and obtaining a possession order).[1] These will be referred to as 'substantive security of tenure' and 'procedural security of tenure' respectively.

1.4   Whether an occupier has any security of tenure and, if so, whether this is procedural or substantive, depends on the status of the occupier. This involves an understanding of both:

- the common law principles concerning rights over land; and
- the statutory rights enjoyed by occupiers.

Common law

1.5   The 'common law' refers to the legal principles and rules established by previous decisions of the courts. These have developed to regulate relationships, such as that between a landlord and tenant, or between neighbouring occupiers. The system of law in England and Wales is

---

1   The lower level of security of tenure is often referred to as 'basic protection' or 'protection from eviction'. However, such occupiers are sometimes also referred to as having 'unprotected tenancies' which causes confusion.

a common law system. The law is interpreted by judges and the decisions of the higher courts are binding on the lower courts.

1.6 Until the beginning of the twentieth century the relationship of landlord and tenant was almost entirely governed by the common law. It was determined by the principles of 'land law' and 'contract law' as they had developed through decided cases. Land law is the law relating to the creation and transfer of legal interests in land. A tenancy is a legal interest in land. Contract law refers to the principles governing legally binding contracts, which can be enforced through the civil courts. A tenancy agreement is both an agreement creating an interest in land and a contract. An understanding of some of the principles of both land law and contract law is necessary before giving housing advice.

Statutory law

1.7 Statutory law refers to legislation made by Parliament. It includes 'primary legislation' which means statutes or Acts of Parliament and 'secondary legislation' (also called delegated or subordinate legislation). Secondary legislation is authorised to be made by primary legislation (known as enabling legislation). Most secondary legislation is made by way of a statutory instrument. In some cases secondary legislation merely sets out the detail of a requirement contained in primary legislation. In other cases the secondary legislation sets out the substance of a provision. An example of the former are the requirements for a notice seeking possession. The primary legislation provides that notice must be in 'prescribed form' and contain certain information but the detail of the prescribed form is set out in a statutory instrument: see para 6.29 below. An example of the latter would be the provisions about eligibility for homeless assistance, the substance of which is predominantly found in the relevant statutory instruments: see para 14.3 below.

1.8 Statutory law takes precedence over the common law but statutory rights are enforced through the courts and so judges must interpret the statutes. A court's decision about the interpretation of a statute will be binding on lower courts.

1.9 Since 1915 there has been extensive statutory interference in the relationship of landlord and tenant. Mostly, statutes protect the rights of tenants.

1.10 Occupiers who are not tenants may also enjoy some statutory rights. For example, the eviction of many residential occupiers can be carried out only by using the civil courts.

1.11   The particular rights enjoyed by tenants depend on which statute applies to the agreement. The main statutes governing different
types of tenancies are: the Rent Act (RA) 1977, the Housing Act (HA)
1985 and the Housing Act (HA) 1988. These are dealt with in chapter
2. This chapter describes some of the important legal principles that
apply generally in relation to occupiers' rights and to the relationship
of landlord and tenant.

Interests in land

1.12   Although land and premises are 'bought' and 'sold', technically English law does not recognise the 'ownership' of land. It is said that the
only true owner of land is the Crown. Rather, a person may have an
'interest' or 'estate' in land and the nature of the interest will determine how much control the person has over the land. Different
'interests' may exist in relation to the same land. This may sound
artificial but it is important to understand the nature of an 'interest'
in land. The chart below sets out the recognised legal interests and
the rights that flow from the interest.

Interest	Rights
Freehold	This is the nearest thing to outright ownership – it is an interest or estate for unlimited duration. A freeholder may sell the freehold or may grant lesser interests to others, such as a lease or tenancy.
Legal charge/ mortgage	A person who lends money to another may secure the loan by taking a charge on property owned by the borrower. This entitles the lender to take possession if the borrower defaults.
Leasehold	A lease is a 'term of years', ie the grant of exclusive possession for a limited period of time. A person with a long lease may grant a shorter lease or may assign the remaining period of the lease to another person.
Tenancy	The terms tenancy and lease mean the same but the term tenancy is commonly used to refer to a lease granted for a short period only.

Commonhold	Commonhold is a new kind of interest created by statute: it enables those 'owning' parts of a building or estate to 'own' the common parts through a commonhold association. It is an alternative to a lease being held by one party and the freehold by another.

1.13 All of the above are 'legal interests' in land. This means that they can be transferred to another person.

1.14 The same land may be subject to a number of different interests at the same time. For example, a house 'owner' may have a mortgage and may grant a long lease to another person who in turn may grant a tenancy to another person. In such a case there will exist a freehold, a legal charge, a long lease and a short-term lease, all in respect of the same land.

1.15 People may occupy premises without any legal interest but because they are permitted to do so, ie they have a 'licence' to occupy. They are known as 'licensees'. A licence is a personal interest and cannot be transferred to another person. Sometimes it can be difficult to ascertain whether a person occupies as a tenant or a licensee.

What is a tenancy?

1.16 A tenancy or lease is an interest in land for a period of time. The terms tenancy and lease mean the same but 'tenancy' is usually used to refer to short-term tenancies whereas the term 'lease' is commonly used to describe a tenancy granted for a longer period of time.

1.17 The period of time for which a tenancy may be granted is either:

- fixed; or
- periodic.

1.18 A fixed-term tenancy is created where, for example, the tenancy is granted for a period of six or 12 months. A periodic tenancy is created where no fixed period is identified or the tenancy is expressed to run from week to week or month to month, or to be a 'weekly tenancy' or a 'monthly tenancy'.

1.19 At common law a tenancy for a fixed period ends at the end of the period or 'term'. A periodic tenancy continues from one period to the next until one party serves notice (a notice to quit) that he or she does not want the tenancy to continue beyond the end of the next complete period. However, if the tenant enjoys security of tenure, this means either that the tenancy continues or that the landlord cannot evict the tenant without following a certain procedure.

1.20   A person may occupy accommodation under a tenancy or simply with the permission of the owner. An occupier who does not have an interest as a tenant but is permitted to occupy is a 'licensee', ie he or she has a 'licence' to occupy. The person who grants the permission is a 'licensor'.

1.21   The statutory protection, first introduced in 1915 and continuing throughout the twentieth century, was enjoyed only by tenants. To avoid an occupier having statutory protection many landlords sought to create licences instead of tenancies. This practice led to a number of cases in which the courts considered the difference between a tenancy and a licence, the most important of which are discussed below at paras 1.23 and 1.57.

1.22   Much of this case-law is still important in understanding the nature of a tenancy. However, because most tenancies in the private sector now offer very limited rights to tenants, there is little incentive for landlords to try to avoid creating a tenancy. Since 1997 almost all new private tenancies are assured shorthold tenancies and it is less common for advisers to come across 'sham licences'. Nevertheless, the difference between licences and tenancies still has some practical importance.

Difference between a tenancy and a licence

1.23   If a tenancy is created, regardless of the provisions of the agreement, additional statutory rights may be enjoyed by the tenant. Examples of these rights are:

- the right not to be evicted unless there are grounds (the grounds being set out in the statute);
- the right to have repairs carried out by a landlord;
- the right to pass on the tenancy to a family member on death.

1.24   These rights are not given to licensees. Usually the most a licensee will enjoy will be some protection against summary eviction.[2] A licence is a personal permission to occupy. It may be withdrawn by the licensor and cannot be transferred to another person.

1.25   Frequently landlords would attempt to avoid the statutory protection given to tenants by simply describing the agreement as a

---

2 One exception to this is the 'secure licence' which is discussed at paras 3.106–3.108. However, such licences are very rare.

licence agreement or including terms that suggested it was a licence rather than a tenancy. Prior to the House of Lords decision in *Street v Mountford*[3] in 1985, the courts' approach had been to examine the terms of a disputed agreement and if, on balance, they suggested a licence rather than a tenancy the agreement was construed as a licence. However, in *Street v Mountford* the House of Lords rejected this approach.

In *Street v Mountford* a house was divided into furnished rooms. Mrs Mountford signed an agreement entitled a 'licence agreement' to occupy the top floor. The landlord conceded that she had exclusive possession of this part of the house. However, the agreement she signed included rules limiting the way the accommodation was to be used. The agreement referred to a licence fee and included a statement signed by Mrs Mountford stating: 'I understand and accept that a licence in the above form does not and is not intended to give me a tenancy protected under the Rent Acts'.

The owner sought a declaration that Mrs Mountford did not have a tenancy. The county court held that she did and the owner appealed successfully. The Court of Appeal examined all of the express terms and decided that many were inconsistent with the grant of a tenancy. Furthermore, it held that the statement signed by Mrs Mountford was a clear indication of the parties' intentions. In the absence of misrepresentation, undue influence or mistake, the burden was on the occupant to displace the express statement of intention by showing that it was either a deliberate sham or at least an inaccurate summary of the true substance of the real agreement.

The House of Lords allowed Mrs Mountford's appeal: it is the substance of the agreement and not the label attached to it that matters. In the words of Lord Templeman: 'The manufacture of a five pronged implement for manual digging results in a fork even if the manufacturer, unfamiliar with the English language, insists that he intended to make and has made a spade'.[4] To examine the terms to see which suggested a tenancy and which a licence was not the correct approach. Rather, if the 'hallmarks of a tenancy' were present, the agreement would be a tenancy agreement unless it fell within a class of recognised exceptions.

3 (1985) 17 HLR 402, HL.
4 (1985) 17 HLR 402 at 411.

The hallmarks of a tenancy are:

1) the grant of exclusive possession;
2) for a period of time;
3) in return for the payment of rent.

If these features are present, the agreement will be a tenancy unless it is of a type previously recognised by the courts as being exceptional. These exceptional kinds of agreements are:

1) tied accommodation – accommodation occupied by employees;
2) acts of charity and family arrangements – where there is no intention to enter into legally binding relations; and
3) cases in which there is a legal relationship, but not that of landlord and tenant.

What is a lodger?

1.26   A lodger is someone who occupies part of a house but whose occupation is under the control of a landlord or his or her representative who resides in or retains possession or control over the house.[5]

1.27   In most cases a hotel occupier will also be a lodger or licensee.[6] However, exceptionally, it is possible for a person to occupy a 'dwelling' within a 'hotel' as a tenant, see paras 1.128 and 3.14 below.

1.28   A lodger is a licensee and will not enjoy long-term rights. Furthermore, if accommodation is shared with a landlord, he or she may be subject to eviction without a court order, see para 1.102 below.

Hallmarks of a tenancy

Exclusive possession

1.29   The grant of 'exclusive possession' is essential to a tenancy. If an occupier does not have exclusive possession he or she cannot be a tenant.

1.30   Exclusive possession means more than being the only occupier. Exclusive 'possession' means being the person in control of the premises. A tenant can exclude the whole world, including the landlord. In contrast, someone in exclusive 'occupation' can exclude the whole world, except the landlord. 'Possession' is distinct from

---

5   *Thompson v Ward* [1906] 1 KB 60.
6   *Luganda v Service Hotels* [1969] 2 Ch 209.

'occupation': a hotel guest may have exclusive occupation of a room but does not have exclusive possession because the hotel management retains control of the room.

1.31   Landlords sometimes include in a tenancy agreement terms which suggest that the occupier does not have exclusive possession. Examples include terms reserving a right of unlimited access and terms stating that the landlord has the right to move other occupiers into the premises or to move into the premises him or herself. Such terms may be 'pretences' or 'shams'. This is explained at paras 1.46–1.48 below.

1.32   It should be noted that a landlord's right of access for the purpose of inspection and repair does not mean that the tenant does not have exclusive possession. In fact, the inclusion of a term reserving such a right suggests that it is the tenant not the landlord who has control of the premises.

For a period of time

1.33   This may be expressly indicated in the tenancy agreement. In most fixed-term tenancies the period will be expressly stated in a written agreement, although it is possible to create a fixed-term tenancy for less than three years orally.[7] If there is no such agreed term, or perhaps no written agreement at all, the tenancy will be a periodic tenancy. The period will be implied by reference to the 'rental period'. If it is stated that 'the weekly rent is £x' or that the rent is '£x per week' the tenancy will be a weekly periodic tenancy. This is different from an agreement about the way in which rent is paid. For example, if a tenancy agreement states that 'the rent is £x per week, payable four weekly in advance', the period of the agreement is weekly, not four weekly.[8]

At a rent

1.34   In *Street v Mountford* the House of Lords suggested that the payment of rent was essential to a tenancy agreement. However, it is theoretically possible to create a tenancy without the payment of rent.[9] In fact, where no rent is payable this will often suggest that a legally binding tenancy has not been created. Furthermore, such agreements have

---

7 Law of Property Act 1925 s54(2).
8 *Ladies Hosiery and Underwear v Packer* [1930] Ch 304, CA.
9 *Ashburn Anstalt v Arnold* [1988] 2 WLR 706, CA.

always been outside statutory protection[10] and, since 1989, occupiers who pay no rent have been excluded from any sort of security and can be evicted without a court order (see para 1.112).

Exceptions

1.35   If there is no exclusive possession there can be no tenancy. However, there are some situations in which an occupier may apparently enjoy exclusive possession but not be a tenant. These are (see paras 1.36–1.45):

- service occupiers;
- no intention to enter into a legal relationship;
- legal relationship but no tenancy.

Service occupiers

1.36   This is also known as 'tied accommodation'. Service occupation arises where:

- accommodation is provided by the occupant's employer; and
- it is a term of the employment contract that the employee occupies the accommodation in order to carry out the employment duties, or to better perform those duties.

1.37   Although an employee may enjoy exclusive occupation under such an agreement, this is deemed to be on behalf of the employer and the occupier is a licensee rather than a tenant.[11]

1.38   If there is a term in the employment contract stating that the employee is required to live in the premises, it is sufficient that this is for the better performance of the employment duties. If a requirement to occupy is not an express term of the contract, the court may imply such a term but will only do so if it is necessary, ie the job cannot be performed without the employee living in the premises.[12]

1.39   Service occupiers have procedural security of tenure (unless they are also 'excluded occupiers', as listed at para 1.101). This means that a court order must be obtained by the landlord before the occupier can be evicted.

---

10   Tenancies for no rent, or at a low rent, are excluded from the Rent Act 1977 and the Housing Act 1988.

11   *Mayhew v Suttle* (1845) 4 El & Bl 347: the possession and occupation of the 'servant' is treated as being that of the 'master'.

12   *Glasgow Corporation v Johnstone* [1965] AC 609, HL.

No intention to enter into a legal relationship

1.40 In a number of cases where the agreement was between family members or where the agreement was considered to be an 'act of charity' the courts have held no tenancy was created. In *Street v Mountford*[13] the House of Lords held that these cases had been decided on the basis that there had been no intention between the parties to enter into a legally binding agreement.

Family arrangements

1.41 It is presumed that when an agreement is between family members there is no intention to create legal obligations. This presumption can, however, be overturned if there is sufficient evidence of an intention to be legally bound by the agreement, for example the drawing up of a formal tenancy agreement at a market rent.

1.42 The fact that the landlord and the occupier are related does not automatically prevent a tenancy arising.[14] However, the closer the relationship is, the stronger will be the presumption that the parties do not intend to be legally bound.

Acts of charity

1.43 Similarly, where the agreement has come about through an act of charity or generosity there is a presumption that no legal relationship was intended. It is not always easy to identify such situations. A person may offer to allow a friend to live in a property 'as a favour'. The surrounding circumstances will be relevant to decide whether a tenancy is created or the agreement is, exceptionally, an act of charity. Relevant factors will be the amount of 'rent' agreed and whether any kind of agreement is drawn up. The fact that a landlord may wish to gain possession at will does not mean that a tenancy has not been created. When deciding whether parties intend to be legally bound the question is not whether the parties intended to create a tenancy but whether they thought they were bound by the arrangement, ie that one party was obliged to pay rent in return for which he or she had the right to live in the property. Cases in which the courts found that no tenancy was created include the following:

> *Booker v Palmer*,[15] in which an owner of a cottage agreed to allow a friend to place an evacuee in a cottage for the duration of the war.

13 (1985) 17 HLR 402, HL. See para 1.25 above.
14 *Nunn v Dalrymple* (1989) 21 HLR 569, CA.
15 [1942] 2 All ER 674, CA.

Marcroft Wagons Ltd v Smith,[16] where the tenant died and her daughter claimed to be entitled to succeed to the tenancy. The landlords expressly denied that she was so entitled but, while they considered their position, allowed her to remain in occupation paying rent. The landlords indicated that, if they decided to take possession, the monies paid would be treated as 'mesne profits' (a form of damages for unlawful occupation) and, if they accepted her claim, as rent.

When they did claim possession the Court of Appeal held that there had been no intention to enter into contractual relations during that period.

Heslop v Burns,[17] in which an owner allowed friends to stay in a property rent free.

Legal relationship but no tenancy

1.44   In some cases the parties do intend to be legally bound by the agreement but the relationship is not that of landlord and tenant. An example is *Sopwich v Stuchbury*[18] in which a man selling a property let the prospective purchaser into occupation prior to the sale. This was held not to amount to the creation of a tenancy.

1.45   A tolerated trespasser would also have fallen into this category. He or she had exclusive possession but the tenancy had ended by virtue of a court order. Tolerated trespass has now been abolished, see para 6.125.

Shams and pretences

1.46   *Street v Mountford* re-asserted three principles:[19]

- parties to an agreement cannot contract out of statutory protection;
- in the absence of special circumstances, the enjoyment of exclusive possession for a term in return for periodical payment, creates a tenancy; and

---

16 [1951] 2 KB 496.
17 [1974] 1 WLR 1241.
18 (1984) 17 HLR 50, CA.
19 See also *AG Securities v Vaughan, Antoniades v Villiers* (1988) 21 HLR 79, Lord Templeman at 91.

- where the language of the agreement suggests a licence rather than a tenancy, the facts prevail.

1.47 A court may decide that a term or a whole agreement is a 'sham' or 'pretence'. A sham is a term included in a contract which does not reflect the true agreement and which is intended to mislead a third party.[20] Where both parties do not intend to deceive another, the term will not be a sham but, if it does not reflect the true agreement, it may be a pretence.

1.48 It is usually the case that the landlord draws up the occupation agreement and those seeking accommodation will rarely be in a position to negotiate.[21] The occupiers may not read or understand the terms. If, however, a term is included that neither party ever intended would really apply, the term may be held to be a 'pretence'. It is sufficient that, if the parties had been asked at the time whether a particular term would apply, they would have indicated that it would not. In deciding the issue, it is the intention of the parties *at the time the agreement was made* that is relevant. However, in deciding what that intention was, account may be taken of the way the parties have subsequently behaved. An example would be a term that permitted the landlord to move an occupier from one room to another. The fact that the landlord has never exercised the right does not, of itself, mean that the term is not genuine but may be relevant when deciding what the parties intended when they made the agreement. In such a case, the nature of the accommodation will also be relevant. A social landlord running a special needs hostel is more likely to need such control than a private landlord letting rooms in an ordinary house in multiple occupation (HMO).

Shared accommodation

1.49 In cases where accommodation is shared, it can be difficult to decide whether the occupiers are tenants or licensees. In such a case the legal arrangement may be:

- a joint tenancy of the whole of the premises;
- individual tenancies of rooms with shared use of common parts, such as living room, kitchen and bathroom;

---

20 *Snook v London and West Riding Investments Ltd* [1967] 2 QB 786.

21 In such a case the Unfair Terms in Consumer Contracts Regulations 1999 may also be relevant. See paras 4.163–4.173.

- a tenancy granted to one or more occupants, with others occupying as subtenants or lodgers of the tenant(s); or
- individual licensees.

Joint tenancies

1.50   For a joint tenancy to be created the 'four unities' must be present:

- unity of title;
- unity of time;
- unity of interest; and
- unity of possession.

1.51   This means that each tenant claims his or her right to occupy under the same act or document (unity of title); that the interest of each tenant commences at the same time (unity of time); that the interest of each tenant is the same in extent, nature and duration (unity of interest); and each tenant is as much entitled to possession of the premises as any of the others (unity of possession).

1.52   Joint tenants jointly occupy the whole of the premises. One tenant cannot exclude another tenant from part of the premises.[22] Joint tenants are 'jointly and severally' liable for the rent and other obligations under the agreement. This means that a landlord is entitled to sue one or all of the joint tenants for the whole of the rent.

1.53   A joint tenancy will be created when more than one occupier signs the same tenancy agreement at the same time and together they occupy the whole of the premises. The fact that the joint tenants may choose to occupy different parts of the premises and agree individual contributions to the rent will not alter the nature of the agreement between the landlord and the tenants.

Individual tenancies of parts of the premises

1.54   In this case, each tenant must have an agreement with the landlord under which he or she has exclusive possession of part of the premises, for example, a particular room. In the private sector there is specific provision for such a tenant to have security of tenure even where other accommodation is shared with other tenants.[23]

---

22 This can only be done by virtue of a court order made under the Family Law Act 1996 because of domestic violence or relationship breakdown, see chapter 11.

23 RA 1977 s22 and HA 1988 s3.

Tenancy with subletting

1.55   Where a tenancy of the whole of the premises is granted by the landlord to one or more tenants, the tenant(s) may then sublet parts of
the premises to others. This would be the case, for example, where
two joint tenants of a four-bedroom house sublet the unoccupied
bedrooms to two others. In such a case, there will be no legal relationship between the two subtenants and the landlord. In fact the
'subtenants' are more likely to be licensees (lodgers) if living as part
of the same household as the tenants. In any event, if there is sharing
of accommodation the subtenants/lodgers will have little protection
as against the tenants, who may evict them without a court order
(see para 1.102 below). Subtenancies are described in more detail in
chapter 4.

Individual licensees

1.56   While it is possible to have a tenancy of a room with shared use of
other parts of the premises, sometimes the arrangement is so fluid
that this cannot be established. Unless there is a joint tenancy, it
will be necessary for each occupier to have an agreement with the
landlord for the letting of a specific room. In the absence of such an
agreement, there can be no tenancy.

1.57   The following cases, heard together by the House of Lords, illustrate the correct approach to shared accommodation and the identifi-
cation of genuine or sham terms.

> In *AG Securities v Vaughan*[24] four men occupied a four-bedroom
> property with two living rooms, kitchen and bathroom. Each had
> signed a separate agreement with the landlord, at different times
> and at different rents. When a room became vacant the remaining
> occupiers would move so that the best rooms were occupied and
> the least attractive offered to the newest occupier.
>
> The House of Lords rejected the occupiers' argument that they
> had a joint tenancy, because the four unities essential to a joint
> tenancy were not present. Furthermore, none of the occupiers had
> an agreement with the landlord identifying a specific room; therefore
> they could not be tenants of individual rooms. The occupiers were
> therefore licensees.

24 [1988] WLR 1205.

The House of Lords considered at the same time, in *Antoniades v Villiers*,[25] the case of a co-habiting couple who occupied a small furnished flat comprising a bedroom, sitting room, kitchen and bathroom. When they moved in, each signed a separate 'licence agreement', which stated that neither enjoyed exclusive possession and that the landlord had the right to take up occupation or to nominate other occupiers to share with them. The identical agreements were signed on the same day at the same time. The occupiers also indicated that they would like a double bed to be provided rather than two single beds.

The House of Lords held that there had been no genuine intention that the occupiers would be required to share with anyone else: the term was included by the landlord solely to avoid the protection of the Rent Act 1977 and the reality of the agreement was that the couple together enjoyed exclusive possession and were therefore joint tenants.

Termination of a tenancy

1.58   For tenants with security of tenure there are statutory limits on the landlord's right to end the tenancy and take possession: see chapters 3, 6 and 7. However, some tenancies fall outside the statutory provisions and termination is governed solely by the common law.

1.59   Under the common law a tenancy may be brought to an end in the following ways:

- Periodic tenancies may be ended by either the landlord or the tenant serving notice to quit.
- Fixed-term tenancies end automatically at the end of the agreed period (by 'effluxion of time').
- A periodic or a fixed-term tenancy may be ended by an agreement between the landlord and the tenant that the tenancy is surrendered.
- A landlord may 'forfeit' (end) a fixed-term tenancy if the tenant breaches the agreement, provided the agreement permits this. This is usually drafted as a clause that allows the landlord to 're-enter' the premises.

25 [1988] WLR 1205.

1.60 The fact that legislation intervenes to protect residential tenants means that in most cases there are restrictions on the landlord's right to serve notice to quit and to forfeit a tenancy. Also, at the end of a fixed term, a tenant who remains in occupation may automatically become a 'statutory periodic tenant'. This is because it is provided by statute that a periodic tenancy arises in such a situation. These restrictions, however, apply only to a landlord's right to terminate a tenancy.

1.61 There is no restriction on the termination of a tenancy by way of:

- tenant's notice to quit; or
- surrender.

Termination by the tenant

Tenant's notice to quit

1.62 A periodic tenancy can be ended by the tenant by service of notice to quit on the landlord. A notice to quit is a notice indicating that the tenant intends to quit and give up possession to the landlord. At common law the minimum period of a notice to quit is a complete period of the tenancy. The notice can expire on either the last or the first day of the period. However, Protection from Eviction Act (PEA) 1977 s5 provides that a valid notice to quit, including one served by a tenant, must be at least 28 days long. Shorter notice may be accepted by the landlord but this will take effect as a 'surrender' – the ending of the tenancy by agreement between the landlord and the tenant.

1.63 A tenant's notice to quit unilaterally ends the tenancy. The landlord need not agree: a valid notice to quit brings the tenancy to an end regardless. A fixed-term tenancy cannot be ended by notice to quit. However, the agreement may contain a 'break clause' allowing either party to serve notice to end the tenancy within the fixed period, see para 1.81 below.

1.64 A precedent for a tenant's notice to quit is included in the appendix to this chapter.

Notices to quit and joint tenancies

1.65 Where there is a joint periodic tenancy, one tenant can end the tenancy by serving notice to quit.[26] This is the case even if the other joint tenant does not want the tenancy to end, and even if he or she is unaware of the notice. The notice to quit must be served on the

26 *Hammersmith and Fulham LBC v Monk* (1991) 24 HLR 206, HL.

landlord not the other tenant(s).[27] The failure of one joint tenant to consult the other(s) before serving notice is not a breach of trust.[28]

1.66 After expiry of the notice any person remaining in occupation is technically a trespasser, although in most cases the landlord cannot take possession without obtaining a possession order.[29] If the landlord is a public authority, consideration must be given to the right of the remaining occupier to respect for his or her home under the European Convention on Human Rights (see paras 7.120–7.144).

1.67 If a sole tenant serves notice that is technically deficient, for example not being for the required period, a landlord may nevertheless accept and act upon the notice, and the tenancy will end. However, this is not the case if the notice is served by one joint tenant. To terminate a joint tenancy, the notice must comply strictly with the legal requirements and, in particular, must be for the correct period, ie 28 days or a complete period of the tenancy, whichever is longer.[30]

Surrender

1.68 A surrender is an agreement between the landlord and the tenant that the tenancy shall come to an end. It can either be express or implied 'by operation of law'. Surrender is effective to end a periodic or a fixed-term agreement.

1.69 Because surrender is an agreement between the parties, all the joint tenants must agree to the surrender if the tenancy is a joint tenancy.[31]

Express surrender

1.70 Express surrender must be by deed.[32] A deed is an agreement in writing, clearly expressed to be a deed and which is properly executed, ie signed by all parties who intend to be bound by the provisions of the deed and whose signatures are witnessed.[33]

---

27 Clearly, however, it would be good practice to send a copy of the notice to all affected parties.
28 See *Crawley BC v Ure* [1996] 1 All ER 724, CA and *Frank Brackley v Notting Hill Housing Trust and Julie Brackley* [2001] EWCA Civ 601, the latter case being decided after the Trusts of Land and Appointment of Trustees Act 1996 came into force.
29 See PEA 1977 s3.
30 *Hounslow LBC v Pilling* (1993) 25 HLR 305, CA; PEA 1977 s5.
31 *Leek and Moorlands Building Society v Clarke* [1952] 2 All ER 492, CA.
32 Law of Property Act 1925 ss52–53.
33 Law of Property (Miscellaneous Provisions) Act 1989 s1.

Implied surrender

1.71 In certain circumstances surrender may take effect by operation of law. This is also known as 'implied surrender'.

1.72 For surrender to be implied it is necessary that there is conduct by **both** parties that unequivocally amounts to an acceptance that the tenancy has ended. This may be either:

- relinquishment of possession and its acceptance by the landlord; or
- other conduct by both parties consistent only with the ending of the tenancy; as recently summarised by the Court of Appeal: 'where both parties act on the basis that the tenancy has ended, the result will be that the tenancy has ended'.[34]

1.73 In each case, it is a question of fact for the court to decide whether these conditions are met.

Handing in the keys

1.74 If keys are returned and accepted by the landlord as ending the tenancy with immediate effect this will be an implied surrender. However, a tenant may give keys to the landlord for a reason other than wishing to surrender. Furthermore, a landlord is not bound to accept the return of keys as ending the tenancy.

> In *Laine v Cadwallader*[35] the tenants put the keys through the landlord's letter box. The landlord later made a claim against the tenant for four weeks' rent on the basis that the tenants had been required to give notice to terminate the agreement.
>
> The Court of Appeal held that the dropping in of keys cannot constitute more than an offer to surrender which a landlord is free to accept or reject. The landlord was entitled to treat the act as the giving of informal notice to quit or terminate the tenancy and the tenants were liable for the four weeks' rent following the delivery of the keys.

It should be noted that in *Laine v Cadwallader* the landlord would have been entitled to treat the tenancy as continuing indefinitely, in which

---

34 *QFS Scaffolding Ltd v Sable & Sable* [2010] EWCA Civ 682, 17 June 2010, Morgan J at [14]. See also *Proudcreed Ltd v Microgen Holdings plc* (1995) 72 P&CR 388 and *Bellcourt Estates Ltd v Adesina* [2005] EWCA Civ 208, 18 February 2005, see para 1.75 below.

35 (2000) 33 HLR 397, CA.

case, the tenant would have had a continuing obligation for rent. If a tenant wishes to terminate a periodic tenancy, he or she must serve a formal notice to quit that complies with the common law and statutory requirements (see para 1.62 above). Such a notice operates unilaterally and does not depend on the landlord's agreement.

Tenants 'abandoning' premises

1.75   The fact that a tenant appears to have abandoned premises does not mean that the tenancy has been surrendered.

> In *Bellcourt Estates Ltd v Victoria Adesina*[36] a tenancy agreement was entered into for premises that comprised both residential and business units. The tenant paid part of the agreed deposit but no rent and subsequently complained about the state of the premises. She ceased to occupy the premises about three months after the start of the tenancy and asked the landlord to return the money she had paid. The landlord was aware that she had ceased to occupy and did not make any demand for the next rent payment. However, the landlord did inform the local authority's business rates department that Ms Adesina was the tenant and liable for the rates.
>
>   The county court judge held that the landlord's awareness that the tenant had left the premises, together with the failure to demand rent, amounted to surrender. However, the Court of Appeal upheld the landlord's appeal, holding that the landlord's conduct could not be held to be unequivocal conduct inconsistent with the continuation of the tenancy. All that the landlord had done was to omit to demand rent, service charges or arrears and to have failed to continue the correspondence with the tenant. This was not sufficient to establish surrender.

1.76   Many social landlords have procedures to take possession of dwellings they believe have been 'abandoned' by the tenants. However, the term 'abandonment' has no specific legal meaning and, even if a property has apparently been abandoned by the tenant and the landlord wishes to take possession, this is not enough to establish that the tenancy has ended.

> In *Preston v Fairclough*[37] the tenants of a local authority house invited another person to live in the house and then moved out, leaving

36   [2005] EWCA Civ 208, 18 February 2005.
37   (1982) 8 HLR 70.

arrears of rent. When the local authority became aware of this a claim for possession was made against the occupier.

The Court of Appeal held that the authority was not entitled to possession. It had taken no steps to end the tenancy and the abandonment by the tenants plus the arrears of rent were insufficient to establish surrender.

Conduct over a period of time

1.77 If there is an unequivocal act indicating a wish to surrender, the acceptance of the surrender by the landlord may be established by the landlord's conduct over a period of time rather than by a single act.

In *Brent LBC v Sharma and Vyas*[38] the sole tenant had lived in her home with her partner. She moved out and was granted a council tenancy elsewhere, following which she wrote to her landlords stating that she was no longer sharing the flat with her partner and would not object to a transfer of the tenancy into his name. At this stage there were rent arrears of £4,000. On receipt of the letter the landlords closed the rent account and served notice to quit, requiring the tenant's partner to leave. It was later held that the notice was ineffective. Several months later a claim for possession was made. A possession order was made on the basis that the tenant's letter was an unequivocal act showing that she wished to surrender and that this had been accepted by the landlords. The tenant and her partner appealed, arguing that there was no evidence of unequivocal conduct by the landlord to treat the tenancy as at an end and that the service of the notice to quit was only consistent with the continued existence of a tenancy.

The Court of Appeal dismissed their appeal, holding that the court was entitled to look at the whole of the landlord's conduct before the claim for possession was made. The combination of no longer charging rent to the tenant and the service of the notice (a 'belt and braces effort by the council') clearly showed that from the expiry of the notice the landlords were treating the tenancy as at an end. By the time the proceedings were issued the landlords had unequivocally shown that the tenancy no longer existed.

38 (1992) 25 HLR 257.

1.78   A landlord who believes that premises have been abandoned by a tenant is not entitled to possession until the tenancy has ended. If surrender can be established, this ends the tenancy. If surrender is not established, but the tenant is no longer residing in the premises, a landlord may be able to end the tenancy by serving notice to quit. However, it should be noted that a tenant may be considered still to be resident even during an extended absence (see para 4.5).

Liability for rent

Fixed-term agreements

1.79   Where a tenant enters into a tenancy agreement for a fixed period, he or she is liable for the rent for the whole period, unless the agreement contains a 'break clause' (see para 1.81 below). Where a tenant wants to leave and end the tenancy early the landlord has no obligation to accept a surrender. Furthermore, if the tenant quits the premises and stops paying the rent, the landlord has no duty to treat the tenancy as at an end or to find another tenant in order to 'mitigate loss'. The landlord can sue the tenant for the whole of the rent for the remainder of the term.[39]

1.80   A tenant who wants to end a fixed-term tenancy early would be well advised to find someone who wishes to take on the tenancy. The landlord may then be more likely to agree to a surrender.

Break clauses

1.81   A break clause is a term that gives either party the right to end a fixed-term agreement early. The break clause will specify the length of notice that must be given and may be conditional on the tenant having complied with the obligations of the tenancy. This would mean that a tenant in rent arrears would be unable to trigger the break clause. If there is more than one tenant, all must agree to serve notice under a break clause unless the agreement specifies otherwise.

Periodic agreements

1.82   If a tenant serves notice to quit, the tenant's rent liability ends when the notice expires. If the tenant simply leaves the premises without

---

39 *Reichman & Dunn v Beveridge & Gauntlett* [2006] EWCA Civ 1659, 13 December 2006. A person claiming damages for breach of contract has a duty to mitigate (minimise) his or her losses. However, where a fixed-term tenancy is concerned, the landlord has no obligation to terminate the tenancy because if the tenancy was terminated the landlord would lose the right to seek rent for the remaining term or damages for loss of future rent.

serving an effective notice to quit, liability for rent continues. This is the case even if the landlord is informed that the tenant wants to end the tenancy or is moving out. The landlord is not obliged to treat the tenancy as at an end and may sue the tenant for unpaid rent until the date the tenancy is formally ended, see *Laine v Cadwallader* at para 1.74 above. If, however, the landlord takes possession or lets the premises to someone else, this would be taken as an acceptance of the tenant's surrender and the tenancy and rent liability would come to an end.

Subtenancies

1.83 Many tenants rent accommodation from landlords who are them- selves tenants of higher landlords. For example, a long-leaseholder may let a flat to a tenant or a local authority may let a house to a tenant who then sublets a room to a subtenant. In such cases, the middle tenant is known as the 'mesne tenant'; he or she is both a tenant and a landlord. A mesne tenant cannot grant a subtenancy for a period that is longer than the tenancy he or she has. There may be more than one subtenancy in relation to the same premises.

1.84 The issues that arise when subtenancies are created are explained at para 4.93.

Statutory intervention

1.85 The legislation that governs residential tenancies means that the statute that applies and the type of tenancy will depend on the date the tenancy was granted and the identity of the landlord. The parties cannot contract out of the statutory protection given to tenants. So, regardless of the express terms of the tenancy agreement, certain stat- utory provisions will apply. For example, the tenancy agreement may state that a landlord can forfeit (end) the lease and take possession if the tenant is in arrears of rent. However, if the tenant has statutory protection, a landlord cannot enforce this right and take possession. The only way to take possession is to follow the procedure set out in the relevant statute. In relation to rents, under the Rent Act 1977 the parties could agree a certain contractual rent but the tenant could immediately apply for a fair rent to be registered, which would then become the maximum rent that could be charged.

Private sector

1.86   Since the Increase of Rent and Mortgage Interest (War Restrictions) Act 1915 there has been extensive statutory intervention restricting the right of landlords to evict residential tenants.

1.87   The 1915 Act was introduced as an emergency wartime measure to prevent private landlords exploiting the shortage of rented accommodation in certain areas of the UK. The Act introduced for the first time security of tenure and rent control: tenants could not be evicted unless they failed to pay their rent or otherwise breached the tenancy agreement and landlords' rights to increase rents was restricted.

1.88   Clearly, security of tenure and rent control operate in tandem. Unless there is a restriction on a landlord's right to evict a tenant, there is no point in restricting the right to increase the rent. Otherwise, the landlord would be able to evict the tenant and enter into a contract with a new tenant at a higher rent.

1.89   The controls were intended only to last during the First World War. However, the scarcity of rented accommodation continued and successive governments found it impossible to remove the restrictions entirely. Various Rent Acts and Housing Acts were passed between 1914 and 1977 all providing differing levels of security of tenure and rent control. The Rent Act 1977 still governs tenancies granted in the private sector before 15 January 1989. Under the Rent Act 1977 tenants have a high level of security of tenure and rent is controlled by being limited to a 'fair rent' set by an independent rent officer (see para 4.178).

1.90   The Housing Act 1988 made it possible for landlords to grant short-term tenancies by way of the assured shorthold tenancy. The assured shorthold tenancy is now the main form of tenure for private tenants. It gives only limited security and a landlord may obtain a possession order as of right, following service of two months' written notice. However, the courts will not make a possession order to take effect before the end of six months from the start of the tenancy or before any fixed period has ended, whichever is longer. The Housing Act 1988 also effectively abandoned rent control for private tenants. While there are some limited rights to challenge very high rents and rent increases, the presumption is that rents should be 'market rents' as opposed to 'fair rents' as under the Rent Act 1977. Fair rents are set by deducting from the market rent any element deemed to be attributable to the scarcity of accommodation. Market rents are, by definition, set by the market, taking full account of the scarcity of accommodation. Rent control for different kinds of tenants is explained chapter 4.

Social housing

1.91 Social housing is accommodation provided by local authorities and other social landlords. Non-local authority social landlords were previously known as registered social landlords (RSLs). RSLs were not-for-profit housing providers, mainly housing associations and housing trusts, registered and monitored by the Housing Corporation. The Housing and Regeneration Act 2008 abolished the Housing Corporation and set up the Tenants Services Authority (TSA). The term RSL was replaced by the term 'registered provider of social housing' (RPSH). Non-local authority registered providers are known as private registered providers (PRPs). At the time of writing the TSA regulates PRPs much as the Housing Corporation regulated RSLs. However, the Localism Act 2011 will abolish the TSA and future regulation will be by the Regulation Committee of the Homes and Communities Agency which will regulate all social landlords, including local authorities. Local authorities will then also be registered providers (RPs) but will be distinct from PRPs. PRPs include 'for profit' providers as well as not-for-profit providers of low-cost rented accommodation and home ownership schemes. The government is promoting the use of the so called 'affordable rent' tenancy within social housing, under which rent will be fixed at 80 per cent of market rents, see para 4.197. In this book the term RSL is sometimes used to refer to not-for-profit PRPs as much of the legislation still refers to RSLs and the two terms, though not identical, are used interchangeably.

1.92 Before 1980 the tenants of local authorities and housing associations did not enjoy statutory security of tenure. The tenants' rights were governed by the tenancy agreement which usually provided that the landlord would not take possession except in certain circumstances. These included failure to pay rent and other breaches of the tenancy agreement. Housing association tenants had rent control through the fair rent mechanism of the Rent Acts.

1.93 The Housing Act 1980 provided that the tenants of local authorities and housing associations would be 'secure tenants' with similar security of tenure to that of most private tenants. Secure tenants could only be evicted if one of the grounds for possession was proved. Additional statutory rights, including succession on the death of the tenant and the right to mutual exchange, were also granted to secure tenants. The secure tenants of local authorities also had a right to buy their home from the authority. The rights of secure tenants are now set out in the Housing Act 1985.

1.94   The Housing Act 1988 took new housing association tenancies outside the provisions of the Housing Act 1985. From 15 January 1989 they have been under the same regime as the tenancies created by private landlord.

1.95   Chapter 3 provides for a summary of the different kinds of tenancy and the relevant statutes.

Security of tenure: levels of protection

1.96   As indicated above (para 1.3), there are two levels of security of tenure: substantive security of tenure and procedural security of tenure. Some residential occupiers have no security of tenure at all and can be evicted without a court order being obtained, although not forcibly.

1.97   The main statutes applying to residential tenancies are: the Rent Act 1977, the Housing Act 1985 and the Housing Act 1988. These Acts and the types of tenancies they govern are discussed in detail in chapter 2. Each Act sets out the conditions for a tenancy under which the tenant enjoys substantive security of tenure. In each Act the tenancy has a different name: under the Rent Act 1977, a 'protected' or 'statutory' tenancy (also known as a 'regulated' tenancy); under the Housing Act 1985, a 'secure' tenancy; and under the Housing Act 1988, an 'assured' tenancy (as distinct from an assured shorthold tenancy).

1.98   In addition, there are tenancies under which a tenant has more limited rights such as the 'restricted contract' under the Rent Act 1977 and the assured shorthold tenancy under the Housing Act 1988, see paras 3.93 and 3.57. More recently, in the public sector, under anti-social behaviour provisions, the 'introductory' tenancy and the 'demoted' tenancy give tenants no substantive security of tenure but nevertheless impose some limits on the landlords' right to evict. These types of tenancy are explained in detail in chapter 3.

1.99   In addition to specific tenancies giving limited rights, some agreements simply fall outside the scope of statutory protection and the tenancy is referred to as, for example, a 'non-secure' tenancy or a 'contractual' tenancy.

1.100   A tenant who does not have substantive security of tenure may nevertheless have procedural security of tenure. The right to procedural security of tenure originates in the Protection from Eviction Act (PEA) 1977.[40] PEA 1977 s3 provides that certain occupiers can be

---

40   The provisions of PEA 1977 are described in detail in chapter 8.

evicted only by bringing possession proceedings in the county court. The occupiers protected by section 3 are those who, when a tenancy or licence comes to an end, are lawfully residing in premises, where the letting was neither 'statutorily protected' nor 'excluded'. This means that a tenant who does not have substantive security of tenure but who is not an 'excluded occupier' will have the right to a court order before being evicted. PEA 1977 s3A lists the agreements that are excluded from the requirement to obtain a possession order. These are set out below (paras 1.101–1.121).

Excluded occupiers

1.101 Excluded occupiers can be lawfully evicted without the landlord obtaining a possession order. The list following are excluded occupiers:

- resident landlords with shared accommodation;
- licences granted to trespassers;
- holiday lets;
- rent-free accommodation;
- licensees of hostel accommodation;
- accommodation provided to asylum-seekers.

Resident landlords with shared accommodation

Sharing accommodation with the landlord

1.102 A tenancy or licence is excluded if the following conditions are met:

- under the terms of the agreement the occupier shares any accommodation[41] with the landlord; and
- immediately before it was granted, and at the time when it comes to an end, the landlord was a resident landlord (ie he or she occupied the premises of which the shared accommodation forms part as his or her only or principal home).[42]

Sharing accommodation with a resident landlord's family

1.103 A tenancy or licence is also excluded if the following conditions are met:

- under the terms of the agreement the occupier shares any accommodation with a member of the family of the landlord; and

---

41 'Accommodation' means any accommodation other than storage areas or means of access: PEA 1977 s3A(5).
42 See paras 4.13–4.25 for a detailed explanation of resident landlords.

- immediately before it was granted, and at the time when it comes to an end, the landlord was a resident landlord and the family member also occupied the premises as his or her only or principal home.

1.104   'Member of the family' is defined in HA 1985 s113. It includes the following: spouse, civil partner, co-habitees (those living together as spouse or civil partner), parent, grandparent, child, grandchild, brother, sister, uncle, aunt, nephew or niece. Relationships of marriage or civil partnerships are treated as relationships of blood, half-blood relationships are treated as whole blood relationships, stepchildren are treated as children and illegitimate children are treated as the legitimate children of the mother and reputed father.

1.105   The situation in para 1.103 is rare. It will arise only where there is a resident landlord in a different part of the building and a sharing of accommodation with a member of his or her family.

1.106   It should be noted that it is necessary for the landlord (and family member, if relevant) to occupy the premises at the beginning and at the end of the letting. It is not necessary that the landlord intends the occupation to be permanent or long-term and, where a landlord does not intend to continue to occupy after evicting the occupier, this does not change the status of the occupier.[43]

1.107   Before 1989 those who were lodging as part of the household of another were termed 'bare licensees' with no security of tenure. Since 1989 anyone sharing a person's home will necessarily be sharing accommodation with the landlord (or licensor) and will be an excluded occupier.

1.108   Advisers should always be aware of the possibility of agreements that are 'pretences', ie they do not reflect the reality of the situation. An agreement that states that the landlord resides in the premises and shares accommodation with the tenant will not make the occupier an excluded occupier if this is a pretence (see paras 1.47–1.48 above).

Licences granted to trespassers

1.109   A tenancy or licence granted as a temporary expedient to someone who entered the premises as a trespasser is excluded.

1.110   This would be the case where a landlord discovers that an empty property is occupied by trespassers and agrees to allow the trespassers to stay on a temporary basis, paying a weekly fee, or rent, until the landlord needs possession.

43   *Sumeghova v McMahon* [2002] EWCA Civ 1581, 24 October 2002.

Holiday lets

1.111 Where a tenancy or licence gives to a person the right to occupy premises for a holiday only, it is excluded. Again, advisers should be alert to the possibility that the agreement may be labelled a holiday let but that this may be a pretence (see paras 1.47–1.48).

Rent-free accommodation

1.112 A tenancy or licence granted otherwise than for money or money's worth is excluded.

1.113 The term 'money's worth' includes anything of value given or performed in return for the right or permission to occupy. A person who agrees to perform services, for example, cleaning, in return for 'rent-free' occupation would not be excluded, regardless of the value of the services.

Licensees of hostel accommodation

1.114 A licence is excluded if it grants the right of occupation in a public sector hostel.[44]

1.115 A 'hostel' is defined as

> ... a building in which is provided, for persons generally or for a class of persons:
> (a) residential accommodation otherwise than in separate and self-contained sets of premises, and
> (b) either board or facilities for the preparation of food adequate to the needs of those persons, or both.[45]

1.116 To be excluded therefore the following conditions must be met:

- the landlord must be of a specified type;
- the agreement must be a licence agreement; and
- the premises must be a 'hostel' as defined above (para 1.115).

1.117 The mere fact that an accommodation provider describes the building as a 'hostel' or the agreement as a 'licence' does not determine

---

44 The public bodies that can grant excluded agreements are local authorities, development corporations, New Town Commissions, urban development corporations, housing action trusts, the Housing Corporation, the secretary of state under the Housing Associations Act 1985 s89 and a housing trust which is a charity or an RSL. Other bodies can be specified by order made by the secretary of state. To date orders have been made in favour of the London Hostels Association Ltd (1991 SI No 1943), the Shaftesbury Society (1999 SI No 1758) and Royal British Legion Industries Ltd (2003 SI No 2436).

45 HA 1985 s622.

the issue. An occupier may be able to establish that he or she is in reality a tenant, having been granted exclusive possession of a room. If this is the case, he or she will not be excluded. The key issue is whether the occupier or the landlord retains control of the room (see paras 1.29–1.32 above). Many public sector hostels are for those with special needs and additional support may be provided. This does not of itself mean that the occupier will be excluded but makes it more likely that the landlord will genuinely retain overall control of an occupier's room.

Accommodation provided to asylum-seekers

1.118 Since April 2000 support and accommodation for asylum-seekers has been provided by the Home Office. Initially this was arranged by the National Asylum Support Service (NASS). Although NASS no longer exists and asylum support is arranged by the UK Border Agency (UKBA – a part of the Home Office), the term 'NASS support' is still commonly used. Such accommodation is provided under Immigration and Asylum Act (IAA) 1999 Part VI and any tenancy or licence granted under these provisions will be excluded.

1.119 In fact, the providers of the accommodation are mostly private individuals and voluntary sector agencies under contracts with UKBA. Regardless of the identity of the provider, occupiers will be excluded if the arrangements are made under IAA 1999 Part VI.

1.120 Some asylum-seekers are accommodated by local authority social services departments because they have community care needs or they are children and such arrangements are not governed by IAA 1999 Part VI.

1.121 Asylum-seekers who are granted leave to remain in the UK cease to be asylum-seekers and become eligible for homeless assistance and social housing. Former asylum-seekers who are accommodated as homeless or allocated social housing have the same rights as others with the same type of tenancy or licence.

Evicting excluded occupiers

1.122 Excluded occupiers can be evicted without a court order. The tenancy or licence must first be brought to an end by giving either the notice specified in any agreement or, if there is no such agreement, reasonable notice.[46] After the notice has expired the occupier may be peaceably excluded from the premises, ie the locks may be changed.

46 *Smith v Northside Developments Ltd* (1988) 55 P&CR 164.

However, it is a criminal offence to use or threaten violence to gain entry to premises when there is someone inside who is opposed to entry.[47] This includes violence to property so could cover breaking a window or door. See paras 8.40–8.45.

Reasonable notice

1.123 What is considered reasonable is to be determined according to the circumstances. Because the minimum period of a notice to quit is 28 days, this is usually deemed to be sufficient notice. However, shorter notice may be reasonable if, for example, the occupier has not been in occupation for long or if he or she has behaved violently. Conversely, a longer period of notice may be appropriate in certain circumstances.

> In *Mehta v Royal Bank of Scotland*[48] it was held that an occupier of a room in a hotel was a contractual licensee and that the agreement between the parties was that the licence could be determined on 'reasonable notice'. Mr Mehta was bringing a claim for unlawful eviction and the court had to decide what reasonable notice would have been. Taking into account the references by the hotel owners to Mr Mehta being a 'long-term occupier' the court held that a period of four months would have constituted reasonable notice.

1.124 Where a person is excluded because he or she is sharing another person's home, enforcing a right to 'reasonable notice' may be impossible: a court will be reluctant to order someone to allow another person to occupy his or her home for a further period of time when the relationship has clearly broken down.

Trespassers

1.125 The term 'trespasser' means any person in occupation of land unlawfully. It includes a person who was at one time lawfully occupying but whose right to occupy has ended. This would include a subtenant when his or her landlord's (the mesne tenant's) interest is brought to an end or a joint tenant when the tenancy is ended by a tenant's notice to quit.

---

47 Criminal Law Act 1977 s6.
48 (2000) 32 HLR 45, QBD.

1.126   Those who were occupying lawfully when a tenancy or licence is brought to an end usually have procedural security of tenure (unless they are excluded occupiers). However, trespassers who entered as trespassers have no security of tenure. They can be evicted without a court order, but not forcibly. Special provision is made for the eviction of trespassers who are preventing a person from residing in the accommodation. This is described at paras 8.44–8.53. Such trespassers are often referred to as 'squatters' but the term squatter has no specific legal meaning.

Difficult situations

Hotels

1.127   A hotel is, according to the *Oxford English Dictionary,* 'an establishment providing accommodation and meals for travellers and tourists'.

1.128   Some people 'live' in hotels. It is possible that accommodation occupied within a hotel can constitute a letting of a 'dwelling' and attract security of tenure.[49] More likely a hotel occupier will be a licensee with no more than procedural security of tenure, as in *Mehta v Royal Bank of Scotland* at para 1.123 above). If the letting is for the purpose of a holiday only, the occupier will be excluded from any sort of protection (see para 1.111 above). So, depending on the circumstances surrounding the 'letting' an occupier of hotel accommodation could be a tenant with long-term rights, a licensee with procedural rights only or an excluded occupier.

'Bed and breakfast' establishments

1.129   Many hotels provide accommodation on a 'bed and breakfast' basis. Those occupying such accommodation for a holiday are excluded occupiers. Some owners of bed and breakfast establishments have arrangements with local authorities to provide emergency accommodation for those to whom the authority has a statutory accommodation duty. Such a duty may be owed by the homeless persons department or the social services department. Where the accommodation is

---

49   See *Uratemps Ventures Ltd v Collins* [2001] UKHL 43, 11 October 2001, discussed at para 3.14.

provided on an emergency basis the occupier will not gain any security of tenure, whether substantive or procedural.[50]

1.130 Because it is possible to evict a person placed in bed and breakfast accommodation by a local authority without a court order, some accommodation providers designate all accommodation, including self-contained dwellings, 'bed and breakfast'. However, as is the case when identifying tenancies and licences, what determines the nature of a letting is the factual situation, not the label applied. Advisers should be alert to the possibility that describing accommodation as 'bed and breakfast' may be a pretence, and that occupiers may have a tenancy. While the tenancy is unlikely to attract substantive security of tenure, the occupier may have the right not to be evicted without a court order.

Hostels

1.131 Licensees in hostels run by specified public bodies are excluded occupiers. However, this only applies to licensees and not tenants. A person who has exclusive possession of a room in a hostel will usually be a tenant. If the hostel is run by an RSL, he or she will be an assured shorthold tenant (see para 3.57). If the hostel is run by a local authority he or she will be a secure tenant only if the premises let are self-contained, ie include cooking facilities (see paras 3.103–3.105).

1.132 If the hostel is not run by one of the specified bodies or does not satisfy the definition of 'hostel', as explained above (para 1.115), a licensee will have procedural security of tenure.

Mixed business and residential use

1.133 The Landlord and Tenant Act (LTA) 1954 Part II applies to 'any tenancy where the property comprised in the tenancy is or includes premises which are occupied by the tenant and are so occupied for

---

50 In *Mohammed v Manek and RLBC Kensington & Chelsea* (1995) 27 HLR 439, the Court of Appeal decided that those occupying bed and breakfast accommodation while awaiting a decision on a homeless application did not enjoy any procedural security of tenure. *Roma Desnousse v (1) Newham LBC, (2) Paddington Churches HA, (3) Veni Properties Ltd* [2006] EWCA Civ 547, 17 May 2006, went further. The court held that any licensee awaiting a homeless decision was in the same position – he or she could be evicted without a court order. See para 8.1. Although both of these cases concerned a duty owed by the housing authority, it is likely that those placed in similar accommodation by social services would be held to have no procedural security of tenure.

the purposes of a business carried on by him or for those and other purposes'.[51]

1.134   If LTA 1954 Part II applies to a tenancy the tenant cannot be a protected or statutory tenant under the Rent Act 1977 and cannot be secure or assured. This is the case even if the premises include residential accommodation. However, the business use must be significant; if it is incidental to the use of the premises as a home, the tenant will not be excluded from residential security.

Is business use significant or incidental?

1.135   This is a question of fact to be determined by a court if at issue. The following two cases were heard at the same time by the Court of Appeal:[52]

> In *Cheryl Investments Ltd v Saldanha* a businessman rented residential premises but almost immediately began to use them for the purposes of his business. The business had no other premises, stationery was printed and a business telephone and other office equipment were installed at the premises. The court held that the tenancy was governed by the LTA 1954 Part II and not the Rent Act 1977.
>
> A different conclusion was reached in *Royal Life Saving Society v Page* in which a doctor took a lease of residential premises and, with the consent of the landlord, installed a consulting room where he occasionally saw patients. His principal practice and consulting rooms were elsewhere. The court held that the degree of business user was insufficient for the LTA 1954 to apply as the letting was residential.

1.136   Although a change of use may bring the tenancy within the Landlord and Tenant Act (LTA) 1954, spare time activities, even for financial reward, do not necessarily change the character of the user from residential to business.

> In *Gurton v Parrot*[53] the main purpose of the tenant's occupation was to reside in the premises as his home and it was found that the running of a kennel business from the premises was incidental to that purpose.

51 LTA 1954 s23(1).
52 [1978] 1 WLR 1329, CA.
53 (1990) 23 HLR 418, CA.

Occupying for the purpose of a business

1.137 The above cases concerned residential premises also used for business purposes. The courts examined whether the business use was significant or incidental to the residential use. Where the stated purpose of a lease is for business use, the LTA 1954 will apply, even if the premises also include residential accommodation.

> In *Broadway Investments Hackney Ltd v Grant*[54] the lease stated that the permitted use for the ground floor was for sale and catering for fish and the upper part was for residential purposes only. The tenant was obliged to keep the premises open as a shop throughout the year during business hours. Initially it had not been possible to conduct business because of the need for substantial works to the shop premises. In a claim for possession, the tenant argued therefore that the purpose of the letting had been residential.
>
> The Court of Appeal held that, even if that had been the case initially, by the time the issue came to be determined the tenant was using the premises for the purpose of a business in accordance with the terms of the lease. The tenancy was governed by the LTA 1954.

1.138 However, the fact that tenants of mixed business and residential premises may not enjoy long-term security does not mean that they can be evicted without a court order.

> In *Patel v Pirabakaran*[55] the Court of Appeal held that premises, including both business and residential premises, were 'let as a dwelling' for the purpose of the Protection from Eviction Act 1977. The landlord was required to obtain a possession order to evict the tenants lawfully.

Trusts and the law of equity

Trusts

1.139 A trust exists where one person holds property for the benefit of another person. The person who holds the property is the trustee and the person for whom the property is held is the beneficiary. Trusts

---

54 [2006] EWCA Civ 1709, 20 December 2006.
55 [2006] EWCA Civ 685, 26 May 2006.

are used for a variety of purposes, for example when a person wants to leave or transfer property for the benefit of a child or wishes to control the way property is used by another person. In such a case an express trust may be created, the terms of the trust and the powers of the trustees being set out in a deed of trust.

1.140　　In addition to express trusts, certain circumstances result in the creation of a trust by implication of law. For example, where two people purchase property in the sole name of one but contribute equally to the purchase price, intending both parties to benefit equally, a trust is created, despite the absence of an express deed of trust. While the 'legal' ownership of the property is in the name of one party, the law implies a trust whereby the legal owner holds the property on trust for the benefit of both parties. The parties are joint 'equitable' owners, see paras 12.96–12.104.

1.141　　Furthermore, under English law, jointly owned property is always owned under a 'trust of land'. The joint owners own the legal interest for the benefit of themselves. Such trusts are now governed by the Trusts of Land and Appointment of Trustees Act (TLATA) 1996. The fact that jointly held property is held by way of a trust enables one party to apply to a court for an order for sale. The presumption is that, if one trustee no longer wants the property to remain in joint ownership, the property should be sold and the 'equity' divided between the parties.

1.142　　The matters that must be considered by the court when considering an application for sale are set out in TLATA 1996 s15 and are:

- the intentions of those who created the trust;
- the purposes for which the property is held;
- the welfare of any child who lives in the property or might reasonably be expected to;
- the interests of any secured creditor; and
- the circumstances and wishes of each of the beneficiaries who are entitled to occupy the property.

The law of equity

Implied trusts

1.143　Trusts are a creation of the 'law of equity'. The law of equity is a system of rules and principles which developed alongside the common law. It evolved through the decisions of the Court of Chancery (originally a court of equity) to remedy some of the defects of the common law.

1.144 Other equitable principles have been developed so as to achieve fairness between parties. Where parties intend to create a certain legal relationship but fail to take the correct legal steps or there is some obstacle to the legal relationship intended, the law of equity may intervene to ensure a fair (equitable) outcome. An example is where a tenancy is granted to a minor. A minor cannot hold a legal tenancy but if a person purports to grant a tenancy to a minor the law of equity ensures a fair result by providing that the tenancy will be held on trust for the minor until he or she becomes an adult. The doctrine of 'implied' trusts is closely linked to the doctrine of 'estoppel': a party is prevented ('estopped') from denying his or her acts or representations where this would be unfair to the other party.

> In *Alexander-David v Hammersmith & Fulham LBC*[56] the Court of Appeal considered the effect of a local authority granting a tenancy to a 16-year-old child. The local authority used its standard form for granting a non-secure tenancy to a homeless applicant. Alleging breaches of the tenancy agreement, the authority served notice to quit to end the tenancy and a possession order was obtained.
>
> The Court of Appeal held that the TLATA 1996 applied. This provides that where 'a person purports to convey a legal estate in land to a minor ... the conveyance – (a) is not effective to pass the legal estate, but (b) operates as a declaration that the land is held in trust for the minor ...'.[57] This meant that the legal tenancy was held on trust by the local authority; the service of the notice on the minor was a breach of trust; and, moreover, the notice was ineffective as the tenancy was held not by the minor but by the local authority as trustee.

Estoppel

1.145 The following are examples of the operation of estoppel in landlord and tenant law:

- *Estoppel by conduct* (known as *'estoppel in pais'*) means that a tenant who has accepted a lease cannot dispute the landlord's title.

56 [2009] EWCA Civ 258, 1 April 2009. The court suggested that local authorities should instead grant licences to minors, ensuring that they did not enjoy exclusive possession by including terms giving social workers a right to inspect the premises as part of their general duty to provide support.
57 TLATA 1996 Sch 1 para 1(1).

- *Promissory estoppel* refers to a situation in which a person makes unequivocal representations to another (whether by words or conduct), on which the other person relies to his or her detriment. The 'promissor' may be estopped from denying the representations. A tenant may raise such an argument against a landlord who represents that he or she will accept less than the full contractual rent but subsequently seeks possession on the ground of rent arrears.

- *Proprietary estoppel* prevents a person from denying another person's rights in property. An example would be where a person relies on another person's representations (whether by words or conduct) that he or she will have some interest in property. Where that person, relying on the representations, has spent money on the property he or she may gain an equitable interest in it, see paras 12.96–12.104.

The court's discretion

1.146   One central feature of the law of equity is that remedies granted by the courts are discretionary. A person who relies on equity must come to the court with 'clean hands', which means that a person who has not behaved well or honestly in the transaction may be refused relief.

1.147   At one time claims based on the law of equity had to be brought in the Court of Chancery but an equitable claim can now be brought in any civil court.

APPENDIX

Tenant's notice to quit

NOTICE TO QUIT

To: [LANDLORD'S NAME AND ADDRESS]

I, [TENANT'S NAME], of [TENANT'S ADDRESS]

Give you Notice that I intend to quit and to deliver possession of the premises at [ADDRESS OF THE PREMISES]

On [INSERT DATE – should be the last or the first day of a period of the tenancy] or on the day on which a complete period of my tenancy expires next after the end of four weeks from the service of this notice.

Date:

Signed: [by tenant]

CHAPTER 2

Public law and housing

continued

Key points

- The Human Rights Act 1998 means that rights under the European Convention on Human Rights can be enforced in UK courts.
- There is a difference between 'public law' and 'private law'. Public law is about decision-making by public bodies. Private law is about disputes between individual legal persons.
- A public body, such as a local authority, is generally governed by public law when acting in its capacity as a public body (eg in relation to homeless applications) and by private law when acting in a private capacity (eg when carrying out repairs as a landlord).
- Most arguments about 'public law' duties will be brought by way of judicial review.
- It is, however, possible to raise some public law arguments, including under the Human Rights Act, by way of a defence to a claim for possession.
- Most other social landlords will also be classed as public bodies and and be bound by the Human Rights Act and subject to judicial review.
- An alternative way of challenging 'public law' decisions by local authorities and RSLs is by making a formal complaint to the body and, if not resolved, to the appropriate Ombudsman.
- Important information about a public body's decision-making may be obtained under the Data Protection Act 1998 and the Freedom of Information Act 2000.

Public law and private law

2.1   Housing law involves both private law and public law. Although the distinction between private and public law is becoming less distinct, broadly speaking, private law is about the legal relationship between private individuals, including landlord and tenant. Public law is the law governing the exercise by public bodies of public functions. A local authority is a public body but not all of its activities are public functions. For example, a local authority may enter into an employment contract or a tenancy agreement and when it does so it has the same rights and obligations as private individuals who are employers and landlords. Nevertheless, even in these spheres a local authority may be subject to additional obligations as a public body. For example, it must act in accordance with the Human Rights Act (HRA) 1998 and must, under the Equality Act 2010 have due regard to the need to combat discrimination and promote equality of opportunity for protected groups.

2.2 Housing law has become more about public law and less about private law over recent years. This is due to a number of factors, including the erosion of the rights of private tenants, the increase in the number of public sector tenants whose rights depend on the exercise of administrative discretion and, not least, the incorporation of the European Convention of Human Rights (ECHR) into domestic law by the Human Rights Act 1998.

2.3 Chapters 13 to 17 deal in detail with local authorities' duties in relation to homeless assistance and the allocation of accommodation. Such functions have always been public law functions and public law principles apply. Similarly, chapters 18 to 20 describe social services functions, again functions that fall clearly within the realm of public law. However, in addition to these areas of housing law, public law is increasingly relevant to activities that would previously have been identified as private law functions, most particularly those exercised by local authorities as landlords, including decisions to evict tenants. The application of public law and the Human Rights Act to possession claims is examined in chapters 6 and 7. This chapter seeks to summarise other key public law duties relevant to the housing adviser. This chapter examines the following:

- public law principles and judicial review;
- the effect of the Human Rights Act 1998;
- the effect of the Equality Act 2010;
- complaints and non-legal regulation of social landlords;
- rights of access to information held by public bodies and landlords.

Judicial review and public law principles

2.4 Judicial review means a claim to review the lawfulness of:

- an enactment; or
- a decision, action or failure to act in relation to the exercise of a public function.[1]

---

1 Civil Procedure Rules (CPR) 54.1(2)(a).

2.5 It is the means by which the courts exercise scrutiny over 'administrative action' and claims are brought in the Administrative Court, a branch of the High Court. Claims may only be brought against bodies exercising public functions, including the government and local authorities. Many decisions relating to housing made by local authorities are challenged by judicial review.[2] Furthermore, when hearing homeless appeals the county court is exercising a power akin to that of judicial review.[3]

2.6 In judicial review the courts are exercising a supervisory function. A claim for judicial review is not an appeal or a challenge to the merits of a decision. The fundamental principle is that Parliament has given to certain bodies the power to make decisions and the court will intervene only if that body acts unlawfully.

2.7 Judicial review is only available to challenge public law decisions. However, the distinction between public law and private law decision-making is becoming blurred at the edges. The county courts now exercise judicial review functions in relation to homeless appeals and can consider public law and proportionality defences to claims for possession. And judicial review can now encompass primary fact finding (see *R (A) v Croydon LBC*,[4] below at para 2.59).

Grounds for judicial review

2.8 In its scrutiny of administrative decision-making, judicial review focuses on the process rather than the substance of decision-making.

2.9 Below is a summary of the grounds for judicial review, ie the reasons a decision, action or failure to act may be unlawful.

2.10 The House of Lords has suggested that the various grounds can be classified under three heads:[5]

- illegality;
- irrationality; and
- procedural impropriety.

2 See paras 15.13–15.14 and 17.59–17.61.
3 *Nipa Begum v Tower Hamlets LBC* (1999) 32 HLR 445, CA.
4 [2009] UKSC 8, 17 February 2010.
5 *Council of Civil Service Unions v Minister for the Civil Service* [1985] 1 AC 374, HL (the 'CCSU' case).

Illegality

2.11   This includes the following:

- a decision based on an incorrect interpretation of the law or a mistake of fact;
- a decision made when relevant matters have been ignored, or irrelevant matters taken into account;
- a decision taken by a body not authorised to make the decision, for example a body exceeding its powers or a decision unlawfully delegated to another person or body;
- fettering discretion, ie a decision taken in accordance with a rigid policy rather than being a true exercise of a discretion.

Examples

2.12   Cases regarding a local authority's duties under homelessness legislation abound with examples of decisions based on an incorrect understanding of the law or taken without regard to relevant matters (see, eg, paras 13.194 and 13.277).

2.13   In relation to unlawful delegation, a number of priority need decisions have been found to be flawed on the basis that the decision was effectively taken by a medical adviser rather than the housing authority. The authority may take advice from a medical adviser but may not delegate the ultimate decision to the medical adviser.

2.14   The question of fettering discretion has often arisen in cases concerning the allocation of accommodation. In *R v Westminster CC ex p Nadhum Hussain*[6] a policy to suspend applicants from the waiting list for two years for unreasonably refusing an offer was challenged. The policy did not, in most cases, allow for exceptions, and was held to be an unreasonable fetter on the discretion of the authority.

Irrationality

2.15   This is often referred to as '*Wednesbury* unreasonableness' after the case in which the concept was elaborated.[7] It is also referred to as 'perversity' and has been said to apply to 'a decision which is so outrageous in its defiance of logic or of accepted moral standards that no sensible person who had applied his mind to the question to be decided could have arrived at it'.[8]

---

6   (1998) 31 HLR 645, see para 17.75 below.

7   *Associated Provincial Picture Houses Ltd v Wednesbury Corporation* [1948] 1 KB 223, CA.

8   Lord Diplock in the CCSU case (see para 2.10 above) [1985] 1 AC 374, HL at 410G.

2.16　　More recently it has been suggested that the scope of *Wednesbury* unreasonableness is too narrow and that the court's power to intervene should not be limited to such extreme degrees of unreasonable decision-making. When applying the Human Rights Act 1998 the courts are required to apply the test of proportionality, see paras 7.120–7.144 below. The proportionality test requires flexibility in the court's approach, depending on the nature of the rights that are at issue. The House of Lords has held that 'The depth of judicial review and the deference due to administrative discretion vary with the subject matter'.[9] So, in cases where fundamental rights are at issue the courts will be more willing to intervene in administrative decision-making and will apply a greater degree of scrutiny.

2.17　　It is, however, rare that a challenge to an administrative decision succeeds on the ground of irrationality alone. More commonly, where a decision appears to be unreasonable it may also be found to be unlawful for another reason, for example, for failure to take account of relevant matters or to give adequate reasons for the decision.

Procedural impropriety

2.18　　This includes a failure to act in accordance with specific procedural rules as well as a failure to observe the basic rules of natural justice.

2.19　　An example of the former would be an authority that fails to follow the statutory procedure when carrying out a homeless review (see paras 15.33–15.34).

2.20　　The term 'rules of natural justice' refers to the general duty to act fairly. The extent of this duty varies according to the nature of the decision-making. It is generally held that two matters are fundamental to a fair process:

- the right to an unbiased decision-maker; and
- the right to be informed of and to comment on adverse information.

2.21　　A decision taken in bad faith would clearly be unlawful as would a decision taken by an officer who was 'biased'. Such challenges, however, are rare and 'bias' usually refers to the existence of a personal interest in the decision rather than the general perception, sometimes alleged by clients, that the particular officer is biased or has approached the decision with a closed mind. In *Feld v Barnet LBC, Ali Pour v Westminster CC*,[10] the Court of Appeal rejected allegations of

---

9　*R (Daly) v Secretary of State for the Home Department* [2001] UKHL 26.
10　[2004] EWCA Civ 1307, 18 October 2004.

bias or lack of impartiality where the same reviewing officer conducted a second review following the quashing of the first review decision. Similarly, the court rejected alleged bias where the officer who made a negative homeless decision was also responsible for making the decision on whether interim accommodation should be provided pending a review of that decision.[11]

2.22   The duty to disclose adverse information often arises in the context of homelessness decision-making. Before making a decision an authority must offer an applicant the opportunity to comment on adverse information[12] and if the authority is unable to disclose the information it must be disregarded.[13]

Legitimate expectation

2.23   Legitimate expectation is an aspect of the duty of fairness. 'Where a public authority has made a promise or adopted a practice which represents how it proposes to act in a given area, the law will require the promise or practice to be honoured unless there is good reason not to do so.'[14] This is known as 'legitimate expectation'.

2.24   See *R on the application of Weaver v LQHT*[15] at para 2.71 below for an example of an unsuccessful attempt to rely on legitimate expectation in challenging the decision to evict a tenant using the mandatory rent arrears ground.

Reasons

2.25   In addition, a decision may be challenged on the ground that the decision-maker has failed to explain adequately the reasons for the decision. In homelessness decision-making there is a statutory duty to give reasons for any adverse decision.[16] Such reasons must be 'proper, adequate and intelligible and enable the person to know why they have won or lost'.[17]

2.26   There is no general duty to give reasons for administrative decisions. However, even where there is no express duty to give reasons,

11 *Abdi v Lambeth LBC* [2007] EWHC 1565, 26 June 2007.

12 *R v Tower Hamlets LBC ex p Rouf* (1989) 21 HLR 294.

13 *R v Poole BC ex p Cooper* (1994) 27 HLR 605, QBD.

14 See *R (Nardarajah and Abdi) v Secretary of State for the Home Department* [2005] EWCA Civ 1363, 22 November 2005, Laws LJ at [68].

15 [2009] EWCA Civ 587, 18 June 2009.

16 Housing Act (HA) 1996 s184(3). There are also specific decisions made in relation to allocations which require reasons to be given. See chapter 17.

17 *R v Brent LBC ex p Baruwa* (1997) 29 HLR 915, CA at 920.

in certain circumstances a particular decision may call for an explanation, for example where a decision-maker is rejecting an expert opinion or an account of events given by the person concerned. In *R v Westminster CC ex p Nadhum Hussain*, a further reason for quashing the decision was the authority's failure to offer any reasons for not following the recommendation of its social services department (see para 17.86). While it was open to the authority not to follow the recommendation, the decision was unlawful because the assessment appeared to have been ignored completely.

Judicial review remedies

2.27   The court can make one of the following orders:
- a mandatory order – requiring a body to carry out some act;
- a prohibiting order – prohibiting a body from carrying out some act;
- a quashing order – an order cancelling a decision.

2.28   In addition, the court may grant an injunction to restrain a person from acting in any office in which he or she is not entitled to act.

2.29   Damages can also be awarded but a claim for judicial review cannot be based on a claim for damages alone.

2.30   The most common order is a quashing order. This means that the body must make a new decision, since the original decision no longer stands. This reflects the court's role: not to substitute its own finding but to review the lawfulness of the decision.

Which bodies can be challenged by judicial review?

2.31   Local authorities are clearly public bodies and may be challenged by a claim for judicial review when making public law decisions.

2.32   Most registered providers of social housing will also be public bodies for the purposes of judicial review, depending on the nature of the provider and the particular decision under challenge, see *R on the application of Weaver v LQHT*,[18] at para 2.71 below.[19]

---

18   [2009] EWCA Civ 587, 18 June 2009.
19   The tests for whether a body is subject to judicial review and whether it is bound by the Human Rights Act 1998 are not identical but they are very closely linked.

Who may bring a claim for judicial review?

2.33   The claimant must have 'sufficient interest' in the matter to which the application relates. Usually this will mean the person directly affected by the decision. However, it is possible for campaigning organisations to bring claims or to intervene in claims already before the court, particularly where they have access to information useful to the court or represent a particular interest group.

Procedure

2.34   In all but the most urgent cases a pre-action protocol letter must be sent before the claim is issued, see appendix 2 to chapter 18.

2.35   Unless urgent relief is sought, the first step will be to apply for permission to bring the claim. After issuing the application for permission, the papers must be served on the respondent, who should file an acknowledgement of service within 21 days indicating whether the claim is to be contested and attaching summary grounds of defence. In urgent cases these time limits can be shortened.

2.36   The permission application is considered by a single judge, without a hearing (a 'paper application'). If permission is refused, an application may be made for reconsideration at a hearing. If permission is again refused the applicant may appeal to the Court of Appeal.

2.37   In urgent cases the claimant may be seeking an interim injunction. If so, a certificate of urgency must be completed and the papers will be referred to a judge for urgent consideration within a specified period. If necessary a judge can consider an application for an injunction by telephone before the claim has been issued.

Time limits

2.38   A claim must be brought promptly, and, in any event, within three months from the date when grounds first arose.[20] This is usually the date of the decision that is being challenged.

2.39   The court has the power to extend the time limit where there is good reason to do so. The parties cannot extend the time limit by agreement.

---

20 CPR 54.5(1).

Legal aid

2.40 Subject to the applicant's means and the merits of the claim, public funding is available for judicial review proceedings and will remain available when the Legal Aid and Sentencing of Offenders Bill becomes law, see paras 22.156–22.168.

Human Rights Act 1998 and housing law

2.41 The Human Rights Act (HRA) 1998 came into force on 2 October 2000. It incorporated into UK law most of the rights contained in the European Convention on Human Rights (ECHR or 'the Convention'). The Convention is an international treaty of the Council of Europe, ratified by the UK in 1951. The human rights protected by the ECHR are referred to as Convention rights and the Human Rights Act 1998 means that those rights can be enforced in UK courts. Previously, Convention rights could only be enforced by application to the European Court of Human Rights (ECtHR) in Strasbourg.

Effect of the Human Rights Act 1998

Enforcement of Convention rights in UK courts

2.42 The Human Rights Act 1998:
- lists the Convention rights which are made part of UK law;
- makes it unlawful for any 'public authority' to act in a way that is incompatible with Convention rights;
- enables a person alleging a breach of a Convention right to bring a claim in the UK courts against the relevant public authority; and
- allows such a person to claim compensation for a breach of Convention rights.

UK law must be compatible with the Convention

2.43 The Human Rights Act 1998 provides that:
- the courts are public authorities and must not act in a way that is incompatible with Convention rights;
- UK courts and tribunals must take account of decisions made by the ECtHR when making decisions about Convention rights;

- legislation must be interpreted in a way that is compatible with Conventions rights 'so far as it is possible to do so';[21] and
- if this is not possible, higher courts can make 'declarations of incompatibility', stating that legislation is not compatible with Convention rights.[22]

Convention rights that are part of UK law

2.44   The following Convention rights are now part of UK law:[23]

article 2: the right to life

article 3: the prohibition on torture and inhuman or degrading treatment or punishment

article 4: the prohibition on slavery and forced labour

article 5: the right to liberty and security

article 6: the right to a fair trial

article 7: protection from punishment for acts that were not offences at the time they were committed

article 8: the right to respect for private and family life, home and correspondence

article 9: freedom of thought, conscience and religion

article 10: freedom of expression

article 11: freedom of assembly and association

article 12: the right to marry and found a family

article 14: the prohibition of discrimination in relation to the enforcement of Convention rights.

Under Protocol 1 to the Convention:

article 1: the right to property

article 2: the right to education

article 3: the right to free and fair elections.

Under Protocol 13 to the Convention:

article 1: the abolition of the death penalty and prohibition on condemnation to death.

---

21 HRA 1998 s3(1).

22 HRA 1998 s4(2).

23 Articles 1 and 13 of the Convention have not been incorporated. Article 1 is an obligation on the state to ensure that everyone within its jurisdiction has his or her rights safeguarded and article 13 is an obligation to ensure that there is a way of enforcing Convention rights in the state's own courts or institutions. The reason these articles have not been incorporated is that the very purpose of the HRA 1998 is to secure those rights.

How Convention rights work

Absolute and qualified rights

2.45   Some Convention rights are 'absolute' and others 'qualified'. What this means is that, in relation to qualified rights, individual rights are balanced against collective rights. The state may be justified in restricting the exercise of qualified rights in the interests of other people. Article 3 is an absolute right: there can be no justification for subjecting a person to torture, inhuman or degrading treatment. Article 8 is a qualified right: it is the right to 'respect' for private and family life, home and correspondence. The state may interfere with article 8 rights if necessary in certain circumstances.

Derogation and reservation

2.46   A state may enter a 'reservation' about particular Convention rights and may, in times of war or public emergency 'derogate' from the Convention. It can do this only if the situation 'strictly requires' the suspension of the rights. Reservation and derogation are not possible in relation to absolute rights.

Convention rights and housing

2.47   The Convention rights most relevant to housing law are articles 6, 8, 14 and article 1 of the 1st Protocol. In addition, article 3 has been used to challenge the government's policy of refusing housing and subsistence to asylum-seekers and failed asylum-seekers, thereby causing destitution, see chapter 20 and para 2.51 below.

2.48   These Convention rights are examined below (paras 2.49–2.67) with reference to case-law.

Article 3

2.49   Article 3 provides:

> No one shall be subjected to torture or to inhuman or degrading treatment or punishment.

2.50   Torture is deliberate inhuman treatment which causes very serious suffering.[24] Inhuman treatment or punishment is less severe than torture and need not be deliberately inflicted. The threat of torture and very poor conditions of detention may amount to inhuman treatment. Degrading treatment is that which 'grossly humiliates' or

24 *Selmouni v France*, ECtHR AG0000970, 28 July 1999.

'debases' the victim. To establish a breach of article 3 the treatment must reach a minimum level of severity.[25]

> In *Pretty v UK*[26] the ECtHR considered the types of 'treatment' that fell within the scope of article 3 holding that it is:
>
> ... ill-treatment' that attains a minimum level of severity and involves actual bodily injury or intense physical or mental suffering. Where treatment humiliates or debases an individual showing a lack of respect for, or diminishing, his or her human dignity or arouses feelings of fear, anguish or inferiority capable of breaking an individual's moral and physical resistance, it may be characterised as degrading and also fall within the prohibition of article 3.[27]

Treatment

2.51 As a general rule the withholding of a service, such as benefits or housing, does not amount to 'treatment'. However, if it is part of a system under which people are prevented from fending for themselves it may amount to treatment that constitutes a breach of article 3.

> *R on the application of Limbuela and Others v Secretary of State for the Home Department*[28] concerned the Nationality, Immigration and Asylum Act (NIAA) 2002 s55. This applies to asylum-seekers who, in the opinion of the Home Office, did not make their claim for asylum as soon as reasonably practical; section 55 prevents them from being provided with any accommodation or support pending consideration of the asylum claim. This is subject to the proviso that support should be provided if necessary to avoid a breach of Convention rights. Asylum-seekers cannot work and are ineligible for benefits or homeless assistance.
>
> The House of Lords determined that although the withdrawal of support does not of itself amount to treatment that is a breach of article 3, it will do so 'once the margin is crossed between destitution [as defined in the asylum support legislation] and the condition that results from inhuman or degrading treatment'.[29]

25 *Ireland v UK* (1979–80) 2 EHRR 25 at para 162, 18 January 1978.
26 ECtHR (2346/02), 26 April 2002.
27 At [52].
28 [2005] UKHL 66, 3 November 2005.
29 Lord Hope at [57].

> The fact that the asylum support system prohibited asylum-seekers from working and claiming mainstream benefits meant that the provision did not just amount to the refusal of a service but was 'treatment' under article 3.
>
> The question was whether the degree of suffering endured or about to be endured imminently reached the severity prohibited by article 3. The threshold is high but the court held that to place asylum-seekers in a situation of having to endure the indefinite prospect of being without shelter or money for food and clothing was both inhuman and degrading.

2.52 In contrast, in *Bernard v Enfield LBC*[30] the claimant failed to establish a breach of article 3 (though she succeeded in establishing a breach of article 8) where a local authority had failed to provide suitable disabled-adapted accommodation after accepting a duty to do so.

Article 6

2.53 Article 6(1) provides:

> In the determination of his civil rights and obligations or of any criminal charge against him, everyone is entitled to a fair and public hearing within a reasonable time by an independent and impartial tribunal established by law.

Internal reviews

2.54 There are many cases in which civil rights are determined by tribunals other than courts. Indeed, since 1996 the role of the courts in challenging decision-making by local authorities has been reduced. Instead, for many decisions there is a right to request an internal review by the authority. This applies to most decisions about the homelessness duties and the allocation of housing. Similarly, introductory and demoted tenants may challenge a decision to seek possession by requesting an internal review.

2.55 In relation to a decision about accommodation offered to a homeless applicant, the House of Lords has determined that the availability of a procedure akin to judicial review to challenge the lawfulness and/or fairness of the review means that the process, considered as a whole, complies with article 6:

---

30 [2002] EWHC Admin 2282, 25 October 2002. See para 18.24.

In *Runa Begum v Tower Hamlets LBC*[31] the House of Lords considered a challenge to a decision that accommodation offered under HA 1996 Part VII was suitable. The applicant argued that the review of the decision on suitability did not satisfy the requirement under article 6(1) for an independent and impartial tribunal.

The House of Lords held that the reviewing officer was not an independent tribunal but that it was necessary to consider the composite procedure for this kind of administrative decision-making. The fact that an appeal lay to the county court, albeit on a point of law only, meant that the requirements of article 6 were satisfied. The scope of conventional judicial review (which is what the jurisdiction of the county court in homeless appeals is based on) was sufficient to comply. It was not necessary for there to be independent fact finding or a full appeal. As the court decided that the review and appeal taken together satisfied the requirements of article 6, it was not necessary to decide if 'civil rights' were at stake in such cases.

2.56   However, whether judicial review provides an adequate safeguard 'for the resolution of sensitive factual questions' has been doubted by the ECtHR[32] (see para 2.58 below).

2.57   In housing cases article 6 is closely connected with article 8: an interference with rights under article 8 may be justified (proportionate) but, if there is no forum for an occupier to have the proportionality of the decision considered by an independent and impartial decision-maker, the rights under both articles 6 and 8 may be breached. A recognition of the limits of traditional judicial review is reflected in two recent developments. First, it is now accepted that article 8 and public law defences to claims for possession must, in principle, be considered by the county courts (see paras 7.120–7.144). Second, the extent of the court's role in considering claims for judicial review has been expanded to involve making determinations of fact in certain cases.[33]

2.58   These developments reflect the decisions of the ECtHR, which has, in a number of cases, been called on to examine the extent to

31 [2003] UKHL 5, 13 February 2003.

32 See *McCann v UK* ECtHR App No 19009/04, 13 May 2008 and *Tsfayo v UK*, para 2.58 below.

33 Specifically, in relation to age disputes concerning unaccompanied asylum-seeking children, see para 2.59.

which judicial review in the UK is sufficient to cure the inadequacies of an internal review process.

> In *Tsfayo v UK*[34] the ECtHR considered a decision by a housing benefit review board that an applicant had failed to establish good cause for a late claim.
>
> The ECtHR decided that the review board was not independent and impartial. The issue was a simple question of fact and the board not only lacked independence but was directly connected to one of the parties to the dispute. Furthermore, the availability of judicial review did not correct the deficiency because the issue went to the credibility of the applicant and the Administrative Court had no jurisdiction to rehear evidence or substitute its own finding on the applicant's credibility.

2.59   Housing benefit appeals are now heard by the independent First-tier Tribunal (Social Security and Child Support). However, the UK courts have held that, in many other areas of decision-making affecting housing rights, the 'rights' at issue are not civil rights for the purpose of article 6.

> In *R (A) v Croydon LBC; R (M) v Lambeth LBC*[35] the Supreme Court considered challenges to decisions by social services that certain asylum-seeking children were not, as a matter of fact, children.
> It held that in cases of dispute the issue must be determined by the court: since the authority's statutory powers depended on the establishment of a factual situation, the courts must be the ultimate arbiters of whether those facts existed. The Administrative Court can therefore operate as a fact-finding tribunal in such cases. Having found that the court's role on judicial review was wide enough to encompass fact finding, the Supreme Court held that, as in *Runa Begum*, the lack of an independent decision-maker was cured by the availability of judicial review and declined to determine whether the rights to accommodation and support under the Children Act 1989 were civil rights. The court did, however, suggest that if the rights were civil rights at all they were on the periphery of such rights.

34   ECtHR (60860/00), 14 November 2006.
35   [2009] UKSC 8, 17 February 2010.

In *Tomlinson v Birmingham City Council*[36] the Supreme Court held that a decision about whether or not the homelessness duty had ended was not a determination of civil rights. The issue between the parties was whether the appellants had received a crucial letter informing them of the consequences of refusing offers made under HA 1996 s193. The council maintained that it had sent the letters but both applicants claimed not to have received the letters. The appellants sought a review but the reviewing officer found, as a matter of fact, that they had received the letters. Their appeals to the county court were rejected on the basis that there was no 'point of law' that justified interfering with the reviewing officer's decision.

The Supreme Court held that the appellants' cases were outside the scope of article 6: this was not a determination of civil rights. Having reviewed the relevant ECtHR judgments, Lord Hope held:

> I would be prepared now to hold that cases where the award of services or benefits in kind is not an individual right of which the applicant can consider himself the holder, but is dependent upon a series of evaluative judgments by the provider as to whether the statutory critera are satisfied and how the need for it ought to be met, do not engage article 6(1). In my opinion they do not give rise to 'civil rights' ... for the purpose of article 6(1).[37]

Article 8

2.60   Article 8 is the Convention right most directly relevant to housing. It provides:

(1) Everyone has the right to respect for his private and family life, his home and his correspondence.

(2) There shall be no interference by a public authority with the exercise of this right except such as is in accordance with the law and is necessary in a democratic society in the interests of national security, public safety or the economic well-being of the country, for the prevention of disorder or crime, for the protection of health or morals, or for the protection of the rights and freedoms of others.

Recent developments regarding article 8 and possession proceedings are summarised at paras 7.120–7.144.

2.61   Article 8 is relevant to many of the issues that arise in relation to the provision of accommodation as well as decisions to evict a person.

36 [2010] UKSC 8.
37 At [49].

See, for example, *Bernard v Enfield LBC*, above, para 2.52, and summarised at para 18.24.

2.62 Where the person seeking accommodation is subject to immigration control, and thereby prevented from having access to social housing, benefits or employment, the effect of a refusal to provide 'safety net' community care services is more likely to breach the person's rights under article 8. And it must be remembered that article 8 is about respect not only for a person's home but also for his or her private and family life. In cases concerning people subject to immigration control, the focus has tended to be on the rights of the parents of children and the balancing of their rights under article 8 with the state's right to operate a system of immigration control. In a landmark judgment about the removal of a parent whose children were British nationals, the Supreme Court focused instead on the rights of the children, not only to family life but also their rights as British citizens.

> In *ZH (Tanzania) v Secretary of State for the Home Department*[38] the Supreme Court considered a challenge to a decision to remove a woman whose immigration history had 'rightly been described as "appalling"'.[39] She had been in the UK since 1995 and had made a number of unsuccessful claims for asylum, two using false identities. She had had a long-standing relationship with a British man, which ended in 2005, with whom she had two children. The children, aged 9 and 12 at the date of the hearing, had been born in the UK to a British father and were therefore also British. They had lived all their lives in the UK. The Immigration Tribunal had held that a decision to remove the mother and children to Tanzania would be a breach of article 8. However, the question was whether it would be proportionate. The tribunal held that the removal of the mother would not represent a disproportionate interference with the children's family life because they could either remain in the UK with their father or return to Tanzania with their mother, and their father could visit them there.
>
> The Supreme Court considered not just the family's rights under article 8 but also the general principles of international law and in particular article 3 of the UN Convention on the Rights of the Child (UNCRC) which provides that:
>
> > In all actions concerning children, whether undertaken by public or private social welfare institutions, courts of law, administrative

38 [2011] UKSC 4, 1 February 2011.
39 Baroness Hale at [5].

authorities or legislative bodies, the best interests of the child shall be a primary consideration.

This is a binding obligation in international law and is translated into national law under Children Act 2004 s11.

The Supreme Court held that, although nationality is not a 'trump card', it is of particular importance in assessing the best interests of any child. The children in this case

> ... are British children; they are British, not just through the 'accident' of being born here, but by descent from a British parent; they have an unqualified right of abode here; they have lived here all their lives; they are being educated here; they have other social links with the community here; they have a good relationship with their father here.[40]

Furthermore, in relation to their rights under article 8:

> In making the proportionality assessment under article 8, the best interests of the child must be a primary consideration.[41]

The tribunal had failed to consider what was in the children's best interests and to appreciate the importance that should have been attached to their citizenship:

> The fact of British citizenship does not trump everying else. But it will hardly ever be less than a very significant and weighty factor against moving children who have that status to another country with a parent who has no right to remain here, especially if the effect of doing this is that they will inevitably lose those benefits and advantages for the rest of their childhood.[42]

Article 14

2.63   Article 14 provides:

> The enjoyment of the rights and freedoms set forth in this Convention shall be secured without discrimination on any ground such as sex, race, colour, language, religion, political or other opinion, national or social origin, association with a national minority, property, birth or other status.

---

40 [2011] UKSC 4, Baroness Hale at [31].
41 Baroness Hale at [33].
42 Lord Hope at [41].

2.64 The right not to be discriminated against under article 14 is not free-standing. Article 14 is engaged only if there is discrimination in relation to Convention rights and freedoms.

2.65 *Mendoza v Ghaidan*[43] provides a good example of the operation of article 14 and of the courts' duty to interpret domestic law in accordance with the Convention. It also illustrates the way in which articles 8 and 14 may be engaged in a dispute between individuals, as opposed to one between an individual and a public authority.

Mendoza v Ghaidan concerned a claim by a same-sex partner to succeed to a Rent Act (RA) 1977 tenancy. RA 1977, at the time, provided that the right of succession was enjoyed by a spouse or a person living with the deceased tenant as husband or wife. Cases determined prior to the Human Rights Act 1998 had held that a same-sex partnership could not fall within this definition.

The House of Lords held that, although the dispute was between two private individuals, once the state has chosen to intervene in a factual area involving those rights protected by article 8, article 14 is engaged if there is relevant discrimination in the mode of that intervention. The question was whether the discrimination could be justified. The landlord argued that the discrimination fell within the legitimate ambit of the state's discretion to arrange its housing schemes and the disposition of its housing stock. Alternatively it was argued that the policy of distinguishing between heterosexual and homosexual couples was legitimate and reasonable.

The court held that once discrimination has been demonstrated it is for the discriminator to establish an objective and reasonable justification for that discrimination. It is not enough to claim that what has been done falls within the permissible ambit of Parliament's discretion.

The House of Lords rejected the argument that the policy of the Rent Act was the protection of the family or that the exclusion of homosexuals from succession to a statutory tenancy would, in any event, be necessary to pursue such a policy.

To remedy this breach of the Convention the court must, if it can, interpret the Rent Act so that its provisions are rendered compatible with the Convention rights of the survivors of same-sex partnerships. That duty can be properly discharged by reading the words 'as his or her wife or husband' to mean 'as if they were his

43 [2004] UKHL 30, 21 June 2004.

or her wife or husband'.[44] This included a same-sex partner of a relationship that had the characteristics of a marriage.

Article 1 of the 1st Protocol

2.66   Article 1 of the 1st Protocol provides:

> Every natural or legal person is entitled to the peaceful enjoyment of his possessions. No one shall be deprived of his possessions except in the public interest and subject to the conditions provided for by law and by the general principles of international law.
>
> The preceding provision shall not, however, in any way impair the right of a state to enforce such laws as it deems necessary to control the use of property in accordance with the general interest or to secure the payment of taxes or other contributions or penalties.

2.67   The term 'possessions' includes both the interest of a tenant and the landlord's interest in the premises let.

In *Chapman and others v UK*[45] the applicants wanted to live in caravans on their own land but were refused planning permission by the local authorities. Their complaints included that there had been a violation of their rights under article 8 and Protocol 1 article 1.

Their claims were dismissed. The ECtHR held that the decisions to refuse planning permission were in accordance with the law and pursued the legitimate aim of protecting the rights of others through the preservation of the environment. Domestic authorities must be given a wide margin of appreciation in the case of planning decisions. The interference with the claimants' right to respect for the home under article 8 and the right to peaceful enjoyment of their property under Protocol 1 article 1 was proportionate and struck a fair balance between individual rights and the public interest.

---

44 In fact the Rent Act 1977 has now been amended by the Civil Partnership Act 2004 to provide specifically that partners living together as if they were civil partners are entitled to succeed, see para 4.31.

45 (2001) 33 EHRR 18, 18 January 2001, ECtHR.

Public authorities

2.68 The Human Rights Act 1998 applies to the decisions and actions of public authorities. Under HRA 1998 s6(6) a public authority includes:[46]

- a court or tribunal; and
- any person certain of whose functions are functions of a public nature.

2.69 But, in relation to a particular act, a person is not a public authority by virtue only of this provision if the nature of the act is private.[47]

Registered providers of social housing (formerly registered social landlords)

2.70 Local authorities, when making decisions about homelessness and the allocation of accommodation, or about community care services, are clearly public authorities. However, whether other providers of social housing are public authorities for the purpose of the Human Rights Act (HRA) 1998 is a more complex issue. This will depend on the nature of the provider and the particular function being performed.

In *Poplar Housing and Regeneration Community Association Ltd v Donaghue*[48] the Court of Appeal considered a claim for possession against an assured shorthold tenant. The claimants had become the defendant's landlords following a stock transfer of accommodation by the local authority. The defendant had been granted the tenancy by the authority, originally as interim accommodation pending a homeless decision. On the stock transfer her tenancy became an assured shorthold tenancy. Following a finding by the authority that she was intentionally homeless the claimants served notice under the Housing Act 1988 s21 and sought possession. The defendant argued that the provisions of section 21(4) were incompatible with articles 6 and 8 of the ECHR, that the association was a public authority for the purpose of the HRA 1998 and therefore under a duty to act in a way compatible with Convention rights.

---

46 HRA 1998 s6(6).
47 HRA 1998 s6(5).
48 [2001] EWCA Civ 595, 27 April 2001.

The Court of Appeal held:

1) HRA 1998 s6 requires a generous interpretation of what is a public authority and is inspired by the approach previously developed by the courts in relation to those bodies that are susceptible to judicial review. The emphasis on public functions reflects the approach adopted in judicial review cases.

2) When the authority transferred its housing stock to the association it did not transfer its primary public duties. The association was no more than the means by which the authority sought to perform those duties.

3) The act of providing accommodation for rent, without more, is not a public function for the purpose of HRA 1998 s6.

4) The fact that a body is a charity or not-for-profit organisation means it is likely to be motivated by what it perceives to be the public interest but that does not point to the body being a public authority. Even if such a body performs functions that would be considered to be of a public nature if performed by a public body, such acts may nevertheless remain of a private nature.

5) It is a feature or combination of features that gives 'public character' to the act so as to make it public when it would otherwise be private. Statutory authority for what is done can help to mark the act as being public, as can the extent of control over the function exercised by a public authority. The more closely the acts are enmeshed in the activities of a public body, the more likely they are to be public. However, the fact that acts are supervised by a public regulatory body does not necessarily mean the acts of of a public nature.

6) In this case, the closeness of the relationship between the authority and the association was relevant: the association was created by the authority to take a stock transfer; five of its board members were also members of the authority; and it was subject to the guidance of the authority in the way it acted towards the defendant.

7) The fact that the defendant was a sitting tenant of the authority before the transfer and was advised that she would be treated no better or worse as a result of the stock transfer was also relevant. While she remained a tenant the association stood, in relation to the defendant, in much the same position as that previously occupied by the authority.

The Court of Appeal held that in the circumstances the association was a public authority. However, the operation of HA 1988 s21, notwithstanding its mandatory terms, did not conflict with the defendant's rights under article 6 or article 8. Section 21(4) is necessary in a democratic society in so far as there must be a procedure for recovering possession of property at the end of a tenancy. The question is whether the restricted power of the court is legitimate and proportionate.[49] This is the area of policy where the court should defer to the decision of Parliament.

2.71   The issue was again considered by the Court of Appeal in relation to a trust that was not the recipient of a large scale stock transfer.

In *R on the application of Weaver v London and Quadrant Housing Trust*[50] the applicant was an assured tenant of the trust which sought to evict her using Ground 8 (the mandatory ground). She argued that trust was acting unlawfully in that she had a 'legitimate expectation' that, in accordance with Housing Corporation guidance referred to in the tenancy terms and conditions, it would pursue all reasonable alternatives before resorting to a Ground 8 claim for possession. Furthermore, she argued that the decision was in breach of her rights under article 8 and Protocol 1 article 1 (A1P1, see para 2.66 above). As a preliminary issue it was necessary for the court to decide whether the trust was amenable to judicial review and whether it was a public authority for the purposes of the Human Rights Act (HRA) 1998.

It was held that the management and allocation of housing stock by the trust is a function of a public nature and that it should be regarded as a public authority under HRA 1998 s6(3)(b). Although the court had rejected the tenant's arguments on the facts, the trust appealed to the Court of Appeal on the issue of whether or not it was exercising public functions for the purposes of the HRA 1998. The trust argued that although it was a hybrid authority (a body, certain of whose functions are of a public nature), the act in

---

49   See, however, the developments described at paras 7.100–7.144: an assured shorthold tenant would now, in principle, be able to defend a claim for possession on the grounds that the decision was disproportionate or otherwise unlawful on public law grounds.

50   [2009] EWCA Civ 587, 18 June 2009.

question, the termination of the tenancy, was an act of a private nature and therefore not within the scope of the HRA 1998.

The Court of Appeal held that the key question in a case such as this, where the body in question was a hybrid authority, was whether the act in question was a private act. The starting point was to consider both the source and the nature of the activities of the body before deciding whether a function was public or private. The issue was fact specific. The following factors were relevant: the extent to which the body was publicly funded, the extent to which it was exercising statutory functions, or taking the place of central government or local authorities or was providing a public service. Here, the trust relied significantly on public funding and while not taking the place of local government operated in close harmony with it. Providing subsidised housing was a government function. The trust was providing a public service, it was acting in the public interest and had charitable objectives. It was also subject to regulations designed in part to ensure that the government's objectives regarding a vulnerable group were fulfilled. All of these factors brought the provision of social housing by the trust within the realm of a public function. The grant and termination of a tenancy were part and parcel of determining who should be allowed to take advantage of the public benefit of social housing. Accordingly, the act of terminating the tenancy did not constitute an act of a private nature and was in principle subject to human rights considerations.

2.72   So, while it cannot be said that all registered providers of social housing are public authorities for the purposes of the Human Rights Act 1998, it now seems likely that almost all not-for-profit providers will be treated as public authorities for the purposes of the Human Rights Act and judicial review and in relation to the Equality Act public sector duty (see para 2.84 below).

Contracting out social services functions

2.73   The Court of Appeal reached a different conclusion in considering whether a registered social landlord providing long-term residential accommodation for disabled residents was a public authority for the purpose of the Human Rights Act 1998.

In *R on the application of Heather v Leonard Cheshire Foundation and another*[51] a decision was made to close a residential home so that it could be operated as a high dependency unit and the the long-term residents moved into community homes. The appellants had been placed in the Leonard Cheshire Foundation (LCF) home by local authorities acting under the National Assistance Act (NAA) 1948 s21. The residents challenged the decision claiming that they had been promised a 'home for life' and that the decision breached their rights under ECHR article 8.

The Court of Appeal upheld the decision that the defendants were not a public authority:

> If the authority itself provides accommodation, it is performing a public function. It is also performing a public function if it makes arrangements for the accommodation to be provided by the LCF. However, if a body which is a charity, like LCF provides accommodation to those to whom the authority owes a duty under section 21 ... it does not follow that the charity is performing a public function.[52]

The appellants continue to enjoy article 8 rights in relation to the local authority. The local authority cannot divest itself of its article 8 obligations by contracting out to a voluntary sector provider its obligations under section 21:

> In our judgment the role that LCF was performing manifestly did not involve the performance of public functions. The fact that LCF is a large and flourishing organisation does not change the nature of its activities from private to public.[53]

2.74　A similar approach was applied by the House of Lords in relation to the rights of a resident placed in a private care home by a local authority under NAA 1948.

In *YL v Birmingham CC*[54] the House of Lords held (by a majority of three to two) that the Human Rights Act 1998 did not apply to a private care home, Southern Cross Healthcare, even though the home was providing accommodation under arrangements made

51　[2002] EWCA Civ 366, 21 March 2002.
52　Lord Woolf CJ at [15].
53　Lord Woolf CJ at [35].
54　[2007] UKHL 27, 20 June 2007.

under NAA 1948. The company carried on a socially useful business for profit but was not a charity; it entered into private law contracts with the residents in its care homes and with local authorities with whom it did business. It did not receive public funding and had no statutory powers and, subject to discrimination laws, could choose to accept or reject residents and to charge whatever fees it thought appropriate. Residents placed in the home retained their rights under the Convention in regard to the provision of care and accommodation against the local authority but could not assert those rights against the company.

Declarations of incompatibility

2.75   Where an action is brought against a public authority for breach of a Convention right, it is a defence if the public authority can show that it was bound to act the way that it did because of primary legislation.[55]

2.76   In such a claim the issue then becomes whether the legislation is incompatible with the Convention and the government would be joined as defendant. In *R on the application of Morris v Westminster City Council*[56] the Court of Appeal declared that the Housing Act 1996 s185(4) was incompatible with article 14 of the Convention to the extent that it required that a dependent child subject to immigration control be disregarded when deciding whether a British citizen had a priority need for accommodation: it was discrimination on the grounds of nationality.

2.77   The legislative amendments to resolve this incompatibility are set out at paras 14.141–14.148.

Remedies

2.78   Human Rights Act 1998 s8(1) provides that:

> ... in relation to any act (or proposed act) of a public authority which the court finds is (or would be) unlawful, it may grant such relief or remedy, or make such order, within its powers as it considers just and appropriate.

In other words, the court may grant any remedy it considers appropriate provided the court already has the power to grant such a remedy.

55   HRA 1998 s2.
56   [2005] EWCA Civ 1184, 14 October 2005, and see para 14.141.

2.79 Most of the housing cases in which Human Rights Act 1998 has been used have been possession cases in which the occupier argued that an eviction would involve an unjustified breach of article 8. In such a case the remedy sought is the refusal of a possession order.

2.80 In judicial review proceedings the court can quash (cancel) any decision deemed to be in breach of the Act and, to avoid a breach, can order a public authority to do something or to refrain from doing something.

2.81 It is also possible to claim damages from a court that has the power to award damages.[57] A court can only award damages if satisfied that such an award is necessary 'to afford just satisfaction to the person in whose favour it is made'. In arriving at its decision the court must take into account:

> ... all the circumstances of the case, including:
> (a) any other relief or remedy granted, or order made, in relation to the act in question (by that or any other court), and
> (b) the consequences of any decision (that or any other court) in respect of that act.[58]

Equality Act 2010

2.82 The Equality Act (EA) 2010 has brought into a single Act the provisions relating to equality and discrimination regarding race, gender and disability and has expanded equality duties to encompass other 'protected characteristics'. Most of the Act came into force in April 2011. In relation to equality duties on public bodies, the key feature is that it is not enough that public bodies avoid direct and indirect discrimination; public bodies must, in all their functions, have due regard to the need to promote equality of opportunity and combat discrimination and harassment. A failure to do so may make their decisions and policies unlawful. This is known as the general or public sector equality duty.

The new protected groups

2.83 The old public sector equality duty applied only in relation to race, gender and disability.[59] The new duty applies to 'protected characteristics':

57 HRA 1998 s8(3).
58 HRA 1998 s8(3).
59 Under Sex Discrimination Act 1975, Equal Pay Act 1970, Race Relations Act 1976 and Disability Discrimination Acts 1995 and 2005.

age, disability, gender reassignment, pregnancy and maternity, race, religion or belief, sex and sexual orientation. In relation to disability, the duty may mean treating disabled persons more favourably than others.

The public sector equality duty

2.84   The duty is found in EA 2010 s149. This provides that in relation to all protected groups:

> (1) A public authority must, in the exercise of its functions, have due regard to the need to –
>   (a) eliminate discrimination, harassment, victimisation and any other conduct that is prohibited by or under this Act;
>   (b) advance equality of opportunity between persons who share a relevant protected characteristic and persons who do not share it;
>   (c) foster good relations between persons who share a relevant protected characteristic and persons who do not share it.

2.85   In relation to advancing equality of opportunity, this means having due regard to the need to remove or minimise disadvantage suffered by protected groups, taking steps to meet their needs, where different, and encouraging participation in public life where such participation is disproportionately low. And, in relation to disabled people, it means taking steps to take account of disabled people's disabilities.

2.86   The duty applies to public authorities[60] and to other bodies that exercise public functions. This would include most registered providers of social housing. Similar factors will be relevant as under the Human Rights Act 1998, see paras 2.70–2.72 above, including: the extent of public funding the organisation has; whether it is exercising statutory powers; whether it is doing things that a public body would otherwise have to do; and whether it is providing a public service.

2.87   There is extensive case-law on the nature of the general equality duty and the extent of the duty to have 'due regard'. Information and guidance is available on the website of the Equalities and Human Rights Commission (EHRC): www.equalityhumanrights.com. The statutory Codes of Guidance which should be followed by public bodies are also available from the commission's website.

---

60   EA 2010 Sch 19 provides a list of public authorities subject to s149. In addition to the general duty set out in s149, the listed public authorities also have specific equality duties set out in regulations.

2.88   Most of the cases in which the courts have considered the duty have concerned the development of policies and decisions regarding such issues as the funding of services and voluntary organisations by local authorites and other public bodies. However, the courts have recently made clear that the disability equality duty applies equally to decisions about individuals, such as decisions on homeless applications and decisions to evict.[61]

> In *Pieretti v London Borough of Enfield*[62] the Court of Appeal considered the public sector equality duty in the context of a homeless application. When completing the application forms there had been an indication that Mr and Mrs Pieretti were disabled. They were found to be intentionally homeless as their private landlady stated she had evicted because of rent arrears. They requested a review of the decision which was unsuccessful. At the county court appeal they argued that Enfield had been in breach of the public sector equality duty (then under the Disability Discrimination Act 1995 s49A). The general rule is that a person can only raise an issue at the county court appeal if it has been raised in the review. The county court judge dismissed the appeal on this basis. A further appeal was made to the Court of Appeal. Enfield argued that the duty to have due regard to the need to take steps to take account of a person's disability did not apply to the decision that the applicants were intentionally homeless for three reasons: (1) the duty only applies to the general formulation of policy and not to its decision on individual cases; (2) Part VII of the Housing Act 1996 addresses the rights and needs of the disabled comprehensively though the priority need categories, the 'good faith' provision under intentionality and the suitability of accommodation provisions; and (3) when making such a decision a local authority is not carrying out 'functions' to which the duty applies.
>
> The Court of Appeal rejected all of these arguments holding that:
>
> 1) The duty applies both when a local authority is planning its services and drawing up criteria and also when applying them in individual cases. While the duty does not create new individual rights it is designed 'to secure the brighter illumination of a person's disability so that, to the extent that it bears upon his rights under other laws, it attracts a full appraisal'.

61 See *Barnsley MBC v Norton* [2011] EWCA Civ 834, 21 July 2011.
62 [2010] EWCA Civ 1104, 12 October 2010.

2) Section 49A was clearly intended to apply in relation to Part VII, the section being set out verbatim in the statutory guidance [para 11 of the Introduction]. When enacting s49A Parliament intended that there be 'a culture of greater awareness of the existence and legal consequences of disability, including the fact that a disabled person may not be adept at proclaiming his disability'.

3) The authority's duties of inquiry and review, prior to the discharging of the accommodation duty, are also 'functions' to which s49A applies. The s49A duty under (d) – to have duty regard to ... the need to take steps to take account of disabled persons' disability – applies to local authorities carrying out *all* of their functions under Part VII Housing Act 1996.

The reviewing officer was in breach of the duty as she failed to take the appropriate steps to take account of the disability; she failed to make further inquiry into the evidence that suggested that the applicant was disabled in a way relevant to whether he was acting 'deliberately' as is necessary for a person to be found intentionally homeless. The review decision was quashed.

Complaints

Local authorities

2.89   The statutory complaints procedures operating in relation to social services duties to adults and children are described in chapters 18 and 19.

2.90   There is no statutory complaints procedure in relation to housing decisions by local authorities but all local authorities operate general complaints procedures and some may have procedures specific to the particular department. Most local authority complaints procedures follow a similar pattern, beginning with informal resolution, formal investigation and a final appeal or panel hearing.

Regulation of other social landlords

2.91   At the time of writing the arrangements for the regulation of social housing are changing. Until December 2008 registered social landlords (RSLs) were regulated by the Housing Corporation, a government agency set up under the Housing Act 1996. The Housing and Regeneration Act 2008 abolished the Housing Corporation and replaced it with the Tenants' Services Authority (TSA) which in turn is to be abolished in 2012 and its functions transferred to the Homes and Communities Agency.

2.92 Whereas the Housing Corporation regulated only not-for-profit providers, the TSA regulates all registered providers of social housing, which includes both not-for-profit providers and private providers. The government aims to encourage private providers to invest in social housing by permitting them to set 'affordable' rents at 80 per cent of local market rents, see para 4.197.

Ombudsman complaints

2.93 Currently the Local Government Ombudsman (LGO) deals with complaints about local authorities and the Housing Ombudsman Service (HOS) with complaints about other registered providers. The Ombudsmen investigate complaints about maladministration. The Localism Act 2011 provides that there will be a single Ombudsman who will deal with complaints regarding all registered providers of social housing, including local authorities and private providers. It will also require that a complaint to the Ombudsman must be made in writing by a designated person, ie an MP or local councillor, or a 'designated tenants' panel' (which will be set up under the Act). So, an individual will no longer be able to submit a complaint directly but must refer the complaint to the designated person. These provisions are intended to be implemented in April 2013.

2.94 Information about the current Ombudsman services can be downloaded from the respective websites, as can the complaints forms. The website of the HOS is: www.ihos.org.uk and the website of the LGO is: www.lgo.org.uk.

2.95 The following are common to both Ombudsman schemes:

- Complaint can usually only be made after the authority or RSL's own complaints procedure has been exhausted.[63]
- Complaints must be made within 12 months from the date the complainant first had notice of the relevant matters. The Ombudsman can extend this time limit if he or she considers it reasonable to do so.
- The service is free.

---

63 There are exceptions however: the LGO will investigate complaints by homeless persons without requiring them to exhaust the authority's complaints procedures and will 'fast-track' complaints from children and young people, see para 19.56.

- The Ombudsman may decline to deal with a complaint if there is a legal remedy available to the complainant or the issue is one of legal interpretation. However, there is some overlap and complaints are frequently made to the Ombudsman about such issues as disrepair or a failure to accept a homeless duty when the complainant has a clear right to issue legal proceedings.
- The Ombudsman can recommend compensation but this will usually be much less than a court would award where there is a legal remedy.
- The Ombudsman may make other recommendations, for example, that the particular body changes a policy or ensures that staff are properly trained.

2.96   The main disadvantage of the complaints and Ombudsman procedure is that there is usually considerable delay before the complaint is resolved and effective action taken. Also, the Ombudsman accepts only a very small proportion of complaints for full investigation. The advantage is that it is free and legal representation is not necessary.

Obtaining information

2.97   There are two statutes under which information can be obtained from a public body such as a local authority:

- the Data Protection Act 1998 concerns information held about an individual;
- the Freedom of Information Act 2000 concerns other information held by a public authority.

Data Protection Act 1998

2.98   The Data Protection Act 1998 governs the holding and processing of personal data (information) by businesses and organisations in the public and private sector. Under the Act an individual has the right to be informed whether data is being held on him or her and to have communicated 'in an intelligible form' the information held and the source of the information.[64] Such information must be given provided the following conditions are satisfied:[65]

---

64 Certain information is exempt, for example information that may cause distress to the recipient or that may disclose the identity of a third party who does not consent.

65 Data Protection Act 1998 s7(1)–(3).

- the request is made in writing;
- sufficient information is provided as to the identity of the individual concerned; and
- the fee (currently a maximum of £10) is paid.[66]

2.99 If the request is made on behalf of another individual that person's consent must also be provided. A model letter requesting information under the Data Protection Act 1998 is contained in the appendix to this chapter.

2.100 Provided those conditions are satisfied, the information (usually in the form of photocopies) must be provided no later than 40 calendar days after the request is received.[67] This does not mean that organisations should routinely take 40 days to provide the information: Data Protection Act 1998 s7(8) provides that: '... a data controller shall comply with a request under this section promptly and in any event before the end of [the 40-day period].'

2.101 Complaints about breaches of the Data Protection Act 1998 may be made to the Information Commissioner's Office, website: www. ico.gov. uk. An application may also be made in the county court for an order compelling an organisation to comply with its obligations under Data Protection Act 1998.

Freedom of Information Act 2000

2.102 The Freedom of Information Act 2000 gives a person the right to obtain information from a public authority.

2.103 Public authorities include:

- central and local government;
- the health service;
- schools, colleges and universities;
- the police; and
- many other non-governmental organisations, committees and advisory bodies.

2.104 Most requests are free but a person may be asked to pay a fee for photocopies or postage. However, if the public authority thinks it will cost more than £450 to comply with the request (or £600 if the request is made to a central government department) the request can be refused.

---

66 Data Protection (Subject Access) (Fees and Miscellaneous Provisions) Regulations 2000 SI No 191 reg 3. Different fees apply in relation to credit agencies and health records.
67 Data Protection Act 1998 s7(8) and (10).

2.105   A request under the Freedom of Information Act 2000 must be made in writing and should identify the person making the request and give an address for reply. It is not necessary to identify the request as one made under the Act but it is usually helpful to do so. It is also not necessary to state why the information is required. The public body has 20 working days to respond to the request, so it is important to ensure that the request is dated. Usually a request to a local authority will be sent to the relevant department (addressed to the director of the department) or it could be sent to the Chief Executive. However, many large local authorities have Freedom of Information Departments and requests can be made online.

2.106   The information required should be identified as precisely as possible, for example, requesting copies of minutes of meetings or internal policies and guidance on a specific issue rather than requesting all information held in relation to that issue. A request that is too vague may be impossible to respond to or a public body may argue that it would be too expensive to do so. A precedent letter is contained in the appendix to this chapter.

2.107   A public body may refuse a request because, for example, the information is already in the public domain (much information can now be found on the websites of public authorities) or because it may prejudice national security or damage commercial interests.

2.108   If there is a dispute about whether information should be provided or not, an internal review should be requested. If this does not resolve the issue (or if the body does not offer an internal review) complaint may be made to the Information Commissioner.

The Information Rights Tribunal

2.109   If complaint to the Information Commissioner does not resolve the issue and/or the person wishes to challenge the decision of the commissioner, an appeal can be made to the the First-tier Tribunal (Information Rights). The tribunal's website is at: www.justice.gov.uk/guidance/courts-and-tribunals/tribunals/information-rights. The tribunal deals with both Data Protection Act 1998 and Freedom of Information Act 2000 disputes.

APPENDIX

Request under Data Protection Act 1998

Dear Sir or Madam,

Re: Mr/Ms Client (DOB: ....)

Request under Data Protection Act 1998

We are advising the above named with regard to [............].

On his/her behalf we request that you provide to us a complete copy of [his/her housing/social services file].

We enclose our client's signed authority for the release of this information together with a cheque in the sum of £10.

We look forward to receiving the information as soon as possible [include any reason for needing the information urgently, eg required for homeless submissions] and in any event within the statutory period of 40 days.

Yours faithfully,

A.N. Adviser

Request under Freedom of Information Act 2000

To: A Local Authority [depending on the subject area, address to either Chief Executive/Director of relevant department or, if appropriate the Freedom of Information Officer]

Dear Sir or Madam,

Request under Freedom of Information Act 2000

We request that you supply the following information:

Copies of the minutes of the Cabinet meetings since [date] at which the new [housing allocations policy/homeless prevention strategy etc] was discussed;

Copies of any internal policies or guidance regarding the implementation of the [....] policy/strategy.

Please acknowledge this request.

We look forward to receiving the information as soon as possible and, in any event, within the statutory period of 20 working days.

Yours faithfully,

A.N. Adviser

Different kinds of tenancies

continued

Key points

- The type of tenancy a person has will be determined by the identity of the landlord and the date the tenancy started.
- Each of the main schemes operates in a similar way. For a tenant to have long-term rights he or she must live in the premises as a home.
- In each scheme certain kinds of tenancies cannot be protected. These include tenancies for a very high or very low rent, licensed premises and tenancies where there is a resident landlord. For local authorities this also includes tenancies granted to homeless applicants.
- A tenant who has long-term rights ('substantive security of tenure') cannot be evicted unless there is a reason (ground for possession). The landlord must apply to the court for a possession order.
- The majority of private lettings are now assured shorthold tenancies where the tenant has no long-term rights. In most cases the tenant can be evicted after the first six months. The landlord must obtain a possession order but does not need a reason to evict.
- Legislation aimed at controlling anti-social behaviour has led to three new kinds of tenancy under which a tenant does not have long-term rights: the introductory tenancy, the demoted tenancy and the family intervention tenancy. Introductory tenancies are very common, demoted tenancies less so and family intervention tenancies are very rare.
- The Localism Act 2011 introduces a new type of local authority tenancy with limited security of tenure: the flexible tenancy.

Introduction

3.1   Different schemes of statutory protection apply to residential tenancies depending on whether the landlord is a private or social landlord and the date the tenancy commenced. In each scheme certain conditions must be met for the tenant to enjoy substantive security of tenure and there is a list of tenancies that fall outside statutory protection. The main Acts and types of tenancies granted under each are summarised in the chart opposite. The new local authority fixed-term tenancy which authorities will be able to grant in the future under the Localism Act 2011 is described at paras 3.195–3.203.

The Act	Type of tenancy	Type of landlord and date of grant
Rent Act 1977	Protected tenancy and statutory tenancy – both also known as regulated tenancies	Tenancies granted by private landlords before 15 January 1989.
Housing Act 1985	Secure tenancy	Tenancies granted by local authorities whenever granted; and tenancies granted by housing associations before 15 January 1989.
Housing Act 1988	Assured tenancy and assured shorthold tenancy	Tenancies granted by private landlords and housing associations on or after 15 January 1989.
Housing Act 1996	Introductory tenancy	Probationary tenancies granted by local authorities.
Anti-social Behaviour Act 2003	Demoted tenancy	Previously secure tenancies granted by local authorities but demoted by the court.
Housing and Regeneration Act 2008	Family intervention tenancy	A tenancy granted by a social landlord in order to provide behaviour support. Available only where tenants guilty of anti-social behaviour.

Housing Act 1988: assured and assured shorthold tenancies

3.2   The Housing Act (HA) 1988 introduced a new regime in the private sector. Most tenancies granted by private landlords on or after 15 January 1989 will be either:

- an assured tenancy; or
- an assured shorthold tenancy.

3.3   The Housing Act 1988 also brought non-local authority social housing within the private sector regime. The tenancies granted by registered social landlords (RSLs), now known as registered providers of social housing (see para 2.91) are also assured and assured shorthold tenancies if granted on or after 15 January 1989. Before that date housing associations could grant secure tenancies and housing association tenancies granted before that date remain secure tenancies.

3.4　　An assured tenant enjoys substantive security of tenure whereas an assured shorthold tenant has security only for an initial period of six months. For both types of tenancy there is very limited rent control. In practice, there are few assured tenancies in the private sector; most are granted by Registered Providers to tenants who have been nominated for an allocation of social housing (see chapter 17). However, Registered Providers also use assured shorthold tenancies, mainly when operating a 'starter' or 'probationary' tenancy scheme, or when accommodating homeless applicants by arrangement with a local authority.

3.5　　Initially there were certain formal requirements for the creation of an assured shorthold tenancy. If a landlord failed to comply with these formalities an assured tenancy would be created by default. The Housing Act 1996 changed this: from 28 February 1997 any new tenancy created by a private landlord or a registered provider will be an assured shorthold tenancy unless it is expressly stated that it is not an assured shorthold tenancy.

3.6　　An assured shorthold tenancy is a type of assured tenancy. If a tenancy cannot be an assured tenancy it cannot be an assured shorthold tenancy. This section is therefore in three parts:

- the necessary conditions for the creation of any assured tenancy, including an assured shorthold;
- the specific characteristics of assured tenancies (as distinct from assured shorthold tenancies);
- the specific characteristics of assured shorthold tenancies.

Conditions for all assured tenancies

3.7　　To create an assured tenancy the following conditions must be satisfied:[1]

- The tenancy must be of a dwelling-house 'let as a separate dwelling'.
- The tenant must be an individual, or if there are joint tenants all must be individuals.

1　HA 1988 s1.

- The tenant must occupy as his or her only or principal home. If there are joint tenants at least one must occupy as his or her only or principal home.
- The tenancy must not be one excluded by HA 1988 Sch 1.

3.8   In all cases there must be a tenancy. An occupier who does not have exclusive possession of at least some part of the premises cannot be a tenant, see paras 1.29–1.32.

'Dwelling-house let as a separate dwelling'

3.9   Housing Act 1988 s1(1) provides that there must be:

A tenancy under which a dwelling-house is let as a separate dwelling.

3.10   This condition contains two separate elements.

A 'dwelling-house'

3.11   This includes part of a dwelling-house.[2] Whether a particular letting is of a dwelling-house depends on the facts of the case. A caravan was held to be a dwelling-house where the wheels had been raised and it had been connected to mains services.[3] However, if a caravan is let as moveable property it cannot be a dwelling-house.[4] A houseboat does not have sufficient degree of attachment and annexation to the land to become part of it and cannot be a dwelling-house.[5] Even where a houseboat had been placed on a wooden platform it was held not to have become annexed to the land so as to become a dwelling-house.[6] In any particular case, the relative degrees of permanence and mobility will be relevant.

'Let as a separate dwelling'

3.12   This means that the main purpose of the letting must be to provide a home for the tenant.

3.13   The requirement that for a tenant to have substantive security of tenure the premises must be let as a separate dwelling is well established in the statutory schemes. It was originally intended to prevent a tenant who shared accommodation with his or her landlord from having long-term security. However, express provision is now made for the following situations:

2   HA 1988 s45.
3   *R v Guildford Area Rent Tribunal ex p Grubey* (1951) (unreported), DC.
4   *R v Rent Officer of Nottingham Registration Area ex p Allen* (1985) 17 HLR 481, QBD.
5   *Chelsea Yacht and Boat Co Ltd v Pope* [2001] 2 All ER 409.
6   *Mew & Just v Tristmire Ltd* [2011] EWCA Civ 912, 28 July 2011.

- a tenant sharing accommodation with a landlord, see para 1.102;
- a tenant sharing accommodation with other tenants, see paras 3.52–3.54 and 3.83.

3.14 The early case-law is therefore of limited relevance and more recently the issue of whether a tenant occupies 'a dwelling-house let as a separate dwelling' has been considered in the context of accommodation in hotels and hostels. The phrase 'let as a separate dwelling' had previously been interpreted by the courts as meaning that the premises let had to be capable of being lived in and that the absence of a kitchen meant that premises were not let as a separate dwelling.[7] However, in *Uratemps Ventures Ltd v Collins*[8] this approach was rejected.

> In *Uratemps* Mr Collins occupied a hotel room which was basically furnished and did not include any cooking facilities, although there was a power point. Breakfast had initially been available in the restaurant and included in the rent. Mr Collins brought in a pizza warmer, a toasted sandwich maker, a kettle and a warming plate. The landlords sought possession, arguing that that Mr Collins could not be an assured tenant under the Housing Act 1988 as there was no 'letting of a dwelling-house as a separate dwelling'.
>
> The House of Lords held that the word 'dwelling' is not a term of art with a specialised legal meaning. It is 'the place where [an occupier] lives and to which he returns and which forms the centre of his existence ... No doubt he will sleep there and usually eat there; he will often prepare at least some of his meals there.'[9]
>
> However, there is no legislative requirement that cooking facilities must be available for premises to qualify as a dwelling. In deciding whether an occupant has security of tenure:
>
> > The first step is to identify the subject-matter of the tenancy agreement. If this is a house or part of a house of which the tenant has exclusive possession with no element of sharing, the only question is whether, at the date when proceedings were brought, it was the tenant's home. If so, it was his dwelling ... The presence or absence of cooking facilities in the part of the premises of which the tenant has exclusive occupation is not relevant.[10]
>
> The House of Lords held that Mr Collins was an assured tenant.

7 This is in contrast to the sharing of facilities such as bathroom and toilet which did not prevent there being a letting of a separate dwelling.
8 [2001] UKHL 43, 11 October 2001.
9 Millet LJ at [31].
10 Millet LJ at [58].

Tenant(s) must be individual(s)

3.15   A letting to a company cannot be an assured tenancy.

Tenant(s) must occupy as only or principal home

3.16   It should be noted that this condition is stricter than under the Rent Act 1977 where the equivalent requirement is that the tenant occupies the premises as a residence. For an assured tenancy to exist the premises must be the tenant's only or main home. Under the Rent Act 1977 it was possible for a person to reside in more than one place and to be a statutory tenant of two homes at the same time.

3.17   The residence condition may still be met even during the tenant's absence provided that there remains:

- an intention by the tenant to return; and
- some physical sign of that intention.[11]

3.18   This issue is discussed in detail at paras 4.2–4.7.

Agreements that cannot be assured

3.19   Schedule 1 of HA 1988 sets out those agreements that cannot be assured tenancies. They are listed below at paras 3.20–3.37.

Tenancies entered into before HA 1988: para 1

3.20   A tenancy entered into before 15 January 1989, or pursuant to a contract made before that date.

High value tenancies: para 2

3.21   Any tenancy entered into on or after 1 April 1990 under which the rent is more than £100,000 a year.[12] 'Rent' does not include any sum expressed to be payable in respect of rates, council tax, services, management, repairs, maintenance or insurance.

3.22   The threshold was increased from £25,000 as from 1 October 2010 but applies retrospectively to tenancies granted after 1 April 1990 in England. This means that a tenancy that was outside the Housing Act 1988 by virtue of a rent in excess of £25,000 will have become an assured tenancy provided the rent does not exceed £100,000. If it was granted on or after 28 February 1997 it will be an assured shorthold

---

11   *Brown v Brash* [1948] 2 KB 247.

12   For tenancies entered into between 15 January 1989 and 31 March 1990 the test is set by the rateable value. If the rateable value was in excess of £1,500 in Greater London or £750 elsewhere, the tenancy cannot be an assured tenancy.

tenancy which means that any deposit held by the landlord should be protected (see paras 4.142–4.162).[13]

Tenancies at a low rent or no rent: para 3

3.23 This means either:

- a tenancy under which, for the time being, no rent is payable; or
- a tenancy entered into on or after 1 April 1990 under which the rent for the time being payable is £1,000 or less if the premises are in Greater London, and £250 or less elsewhere.[14]

3.24 Where services are provided in return for the accommodation, the tenancy will not be a 'no rent' tenancy provided the value of the services is capable of quantification. If capable of quantification, the value of the services must exceed £1,000 per year for the tenancy to be an assured tenancy. If the nature of the services means that the value cannot be quantified, this will mean that the tenancy cannot be assured.

3.25 If no rent is paid or services provided, the tenancy will also be an 'excluded tenancy' which means that the tenant can be evicted without a court order.[15]

Business tenancies: para 4

3.26 A tenancy of premises occupied primarily for business purposes is governed by the Landlord and Tenant Act 1954 and not the Housing Act 1988. See paras 1.133–1.136 regarding premises occupied for mixed business and residential use.

Licenced premises: para 5

3.27 A tenancy of premises or part of premises licensed for the sale of intoxicating liquor for consumption on the premises.

Tenancies of agricultural land: para 6

3.28 A tenancy under which agricultural land, exceeding two acres, is let together with the dwelling-house.

---

13 See Assured Tenancies (Amendment) (England) Order 2010 SI No 908. The Assured Tenancies (Amendment of Rental Threshold) (Wales) Order 2011 SI No 1409 will increase the threshold in Wales and comes into force on 1 December 2011.

14 For tenancies entered into between 15 January 1989 and 31 March 1990, the tenancy is a low rent tenancy if the rent for the time being payable is less than two-thirds of the rateable value on 31 March 1990.

15 Protection from Eviction Act 1977 s3A and para 1.112.

Agricultural holdings: para 7

3.29   A tenancy under which the dwelling-house is comprised of:

- an agricultural holding occupied by the person responsible for the control of the farming of the holding; or
- a holding held under a farm business tenancy occupied by the person responsible for the control of the management of the holding.[16]

Specified student lettings: para 8

3.30   A tenancy granted to a student pursuing or intending to pursue a course of study, provided by a specified educational institution, and which is granted either by that institution or by another specified institution or body of persons. 'Specified' means specified by regulations.[17]

Holiday lettings: para 9

3.31   A tenancy the purpose of which is to give the tenant the right to occupy for a holiday. Such tenancies are also 'excluded tenancies' and a landlord need not obtain a court order to evict.

Resident landlords: para 10

3.32   Tenants with a resident landlord. See paras 4.13–4.27 below for the definition of resident landlord and the conditions that must be satisfied.

Crown tenancies: para 11

3.33   A tenancy under which the landlord is Her Majesty or a government department or where the premises are held in trust for Her Majesty for the purpose of a government department.

Local authority and other tenancies: para 12

3.34   A tenancy under which the landlord is one of the following bodies:

- a local authority;[18]
- the Commission for the New Towns;

---

16 The term 'agricultural holding' is defined in the Agricultural Holdings Act 1986 and the terms 'farm business tenancy', and 'holding' are defined in the Agricultural Tenancies Act 1995.

17 The current regulations are the Assured and Protected Tenancies (Lettings to Students) Regulations 1998 SI No 1967 which have been amended several times to add specific private providers of student accommodation.

18 Local authorities include the London Fire and Emergency Planning Authority and police authorities.

- an urban development corporation established by an order under Local Government, Planning and Land Act 1980 s135;
- a development corporation within the meaning of the New Towns Act 1981;
- a 'waste disposal authority' established under Local Government Act 1985 s10;
- a residuary body, within the meaning of the Local Government
- Act 1985;
- the Residuary Body for Wales;
- a fully mutual housing association; or
- a housing action trust established under HA 1988 Part III.

Accommodation for asylum-seekers: para 12A

3.35 A tenancy granted by a private landlord under arrangements made for the provision of support for asylum-seekers and their dependants under Immigration and Asylum Act 1999 Part VI. Such tenancies are also excluded tenancies and the occupiers can be evicted without a court order.

Accommodation for people with temporary protection: para 12B

3.36 A tenancy granted by a private landlord under arrangements for the provision of accommodation for people with temporary protection made under the Displaced Persons (Temporary Protection) Regulations 2005.[19]

Transitional cases: para 13

3.37 The following tenancies are not assured because they are governed by different statutes, all of which are explained below:

- a protected tenancy, within the meaning of the Rent Act 1977;
- a housing association tenancy granted before 15 January 1989;
- a secure tenancy;
- a protected occupier under the Rent (Agriculture) Act 1976.

---

19 SI No 1379. These regulations bring into force a European Directive (2001/55/ EC) that requires member states to apply minimum standards for giving temporary protection to persons in the event of a mass influx of displaced persons. In the event that such persons had to be accommodated, any tenancy granted by a private landlord would not be capable of being an assured tenancy.

Features of an assured tenancy

Security of tenure

3.38   An assured tenant (in contrast to an assured shorthold tenant) has substantive security of tenure: he or she can be evicted only if the landlord obtains a possession order and an order will be made only if one of the grounds for possession is proved. A landlord cannot terminate an assured tenancy other than by obtaining a possession order; it is the possession order that brings the tenancy to an end.

3.39   HA 1988 s5(1) provides that:

- an assured tenancy cannot be brought to an end by the landlord except by obtaining an order of the court; and
- the service by the landlord of a notice to quit shall be of no effect in relation to a periodic assured tenancy.[20]

3.40   In the case of a fixed-term tenancy containing a power for the landlord to determine the tenancy,[21] the landlord can bring the tenancy to an end by exercising that power. However, HA 1988 s5(2) provides that where a fixed-term tenancy comes to an end, other than by an order of the court or the tenant's surrender, the tenant is entitled to remain in possession as a 'statutory periodic tenant'.

3.41   This means that when an assured fixed-term tenancy ends, either by the landlord exercising a right to end the tenancy or by 'effluxion of time' (ie, the fixed period expires), a tenant who remains in occupation automatically becomes a statutory periodic tenant.

3.42   The only way a landlord can end a periodic assured tenancy (including a statutory periodic tenancy) is by obtaining a possession order, and HA 1988 s7 provides:

> ... the court shall not make an order for possession of a dwelling-house let on an assured tenancy except on one or more of the grounds set out in Schedule 2 to this Act.

3.43   So, although a landlord may end a fixed-term assured tenancy under the agreement, the statutory periodic tenancy that then arises can only be brought to an end by obtaining a possession order.

3.44   The grounds for possession are explained in detail in chapter 6.

---

20 Note, however, that this does not prevent a tenant, including a joint tenant, ending a tenancy by serving notice to quit.

21 This does not include a power of re-entry or forfeiture: s45(4). Re-entry and forfeiture are explained at paras 5.7–5.22.

Periodic assured tenancies

3.45 An assured tenancy may be a periodic tenancy from the outset. This will be the case if it is expressed to be a weekly or monthly tenancy. If no term is specifically agreed, the period will be implied from the 'rental period'. The rental period is not the same as the way rent is paid. The rental period refers to the way rent is calculated, not the way rent is actually paid, although in most cases these will be the same.[22] So, if the tenancy agreement states that the rent is a certain amount per month the tenancy will be a monthly periodic tenancy. This is regardless of the fact that the rent may actually be paid, for example, four weekly in arrears (as is usual when a tenant relies on housing benefit).

3.46 If the tenancy was originally a fixed-term tenancy it becomes a statutory periodic tenancy on the expiry of the fixed term. It is deemed to be granted by the same landlord to the same tenant in relation to the same dwelling-house as under the fixed-term agreement.[23]

3.47 Registered providers usually grant periodic assured tenancies. Fixed-term agreements are more common in the private sector.

The terms of a statutory periodic assured tenancy

3.48 Housing Act 1988 s5(3) provides:
- The statutory periodic tenancy takes effect immediately on the coming to an end of the fixed-term tenancy.
- The periods of the tenancy are the same as those for which rent was last payable under the fixed-term tenancy.
- The other terms are the same as under the fixed-term tenancy.[24] However, any term that makes provision for the landlord or tenant to end the agreement is of no effect while the tenancy remains assured.

3.49 A statutory periodic tenancy does not arise if a new tenancy of the same or substantially the same dwelling-house is granted at the end of the fixed-term tenancy.

---

22 See para 1.33.
23 HA 1988 s5(3)(a)–(c).
24 Though any rent review clause within the fixed period will not be a term of the periodic tenancy, which means that HA 1988 s13 will apply to rent increases under the statutory periodic tenancy: *London District Properties Management Ltd and Others v Goolamy & Goolamy* [2009] EWHC 1367 (Admin), 16 June 2009, see paras 4.186–4.190.

3.50   Ascertaining the correct period of the statutory tenancy may be crucial when considering the validity of a possession notice served by a landlord.

> In *Church Commissioners for England v Gisele Meya*[25] the fixed-term agreement, prior to the statutory periodic tenancy arising, had been for a term of one year less a day. Rent had been expressed to be a certain amount per annum, payable by equal quarterly payments in advance on the usual quarter days.
>
> At common law a periodic tenancy arising by implication would be an annual tenancy. However, the Court of Appeal held that HA 1988 s5(3)(d) meant that, in respect of a statutory periodic assured tenancy, the period was to be calculated by reference to the way rent was *payable*, not to the way rent was calculated. The statutory tenancy which arose at the end of the fixed term was therefore a quarterly periodic tenancy and not, as the tenant contended, an annual tenancy.

3.51   Possession notices are discussed in more detail in paras 6.23–6.81.

Tenant sharing accommodation with others

3.52   Even if a tenant shares accommodation with others, he or she may still be an assured tenant. However, there must be some accommodation of which the tenant has exclusive possession.

3.53   HA 1988 s3(1) provides that a person may have an assured tenancy of 'the separate accommodation' (ie, the room(s) of which exclusive possession is granted) despite the fact that the agreement provides for the sharing of other accommodation with other people, not including the landlord.[26]

3.54   Furthermore, as long as the tenant remains in possession of the separate accommodation, any term of the tenancy modifying or terminating the right to use the shared accommodation will be of no effect.[27] However, a term permitting variation or increase in the number of people with whom the tenant shares accommodation is enforceable.[28]

---

25 [2006] EWCA Civ 821, 21 June 2006.
26 For the position of tenants who share accommodation with their landlords see para 1.102.
27 HA 1988 s3(3).
28 HA 1988 s3(4).

Tenant subletting part of the accommodation

3.55 Where a tenant has sublet part of his or her premises to another person this will not prevent the tenancy from remaining an assured tenancy even though the tenant now shares accommodation with others.[29]

3.56 However, subletting is prohibited in most assured tenancy agreements. Subletting could therefore lead to the landlord claiming possession on the grounds that the tenant has breached the tenancy agreement. See paras 4.108–4.121.

Features of an assured shorthold tenancy

Security of tenure

3.57 Unless granted for a fixed term of longer than six months, after the first six months the assured shorthold tenant has no substantive security of tenure: the landlord is entitled to a possession order but must serve notice and obtain a possession order. No ground or reason for requiring possession is needed. The procedure for obtaining possession of premises let on an assured shorthold tenancy is described in chapter 6.

Formalities prior to 28 February 1997

3.58 On or after 28 February 1997 all new assured tenancies will be assured shorthold tenancies unless it is expressly provided that the tenancy is not an assured shorthold tenancy. In contrast, to create an assured shorthold tenancy before 28 February 1997 the following conditions had to be satisfied:[30]

- the tenancy had to be for a fixed term of not less than six months, with no provision for the landlord to end the tenancy within the first six months;[31] and
- notice in a prescribed form must have been served by the landlord on the tenant before the tenancy was entered into.

3.59 If these conditions were not met, the tenancy was an assured tenancy and the tenant had substantive security of tenure.

---

29 HA 1988 s4.
30 HA 1988 s20.
31 This does not include a term for re-entry or forfeiture, see paras 5.7–5.22 below.

3.60   In most cases where it was argued that there had been a failure to comply with the formalities, the issue was the validity of the pre-scribed notice, known as the 'section 20 notice'.

HA 1988 section 20 notice

3.61   The notice served by the landlord had to be in a 'prescribed form' (HA 1988 s20(3)). 'Prescribed' means prescribed by regulations.[32]

3.62   It is sufficient that the notice is in 'a form substantially to the same effect' as the prescribed form.[33] This means that if there is an error or omission on the form itself, or it is completed incorrectly, it may nevertheless be valid provided it is 'substantially to the same effect' as a properly completed prescribed form.

3.63   In some of the early cases about section 20 notices, the test applied by the courts was whether the error was obvious to the tenant so that he or she did not suffer detriment as a result of the error. It was held that such an error did not invalidate the notice.[34]

3.64   However, where important information for the tenant was missing it was held that the notice was invalid.

> In *Manel v Memon*[35] the notice had omitted bullet points with instructions and advice to the tenant. The Court of Appeal held that the bullet points, in particular the exhortation to take legal advice and the statement that the giving of the notice did not commit the tenant to take the tenancy, were part of the substance of the notice. Without them the notice was not 'substantially to the same effect' as the prescribed form. The notice was defective and a possession order made by the district judge was set aside.

3.65   However, the Court of Appeal has since rejected the approach that focuses on whether an error is obvious and whether it has caused detriment to the tenant. Rather, it has been held that there is only one question: whether the notice accomplishes the statutory purpose

---

32 Assured Tenancies and Agricultural Occupancies (Forms) Regulations 1988 SI No 2203 contain a schedule of prescribed forms, including that under section 20.

33 Regulation 2.

34 *Brewer v Andrews* and *York v Ross & Casey* (1998) 31 HLR 209, CA.

35 (2001) 33 HLR 24, CA. This case was recently approved in relation to a tenant's notice converting an assured tenancy into an assured shorthold tenancy; see *Kahlon v Isherwood* [2011] EWCA Civ 602 at para 3.74 below.

of warning the tenant of the special nature of an assured shorthold tenancy.[36]

In *Osborne & Co Ltd v Dior and Marito Holdings SA v Deneche and Lundborg*[37] the Court of Appeal considered two notices challenged by the tenants.

In the first case the notice was signed by an employee of the managing agents and the space for the landlord's details left blank. In the second case the notice was also signed by the agent. In the box for the landlord's details the name of a company was entered but the company was not, in fact, the landlord.

The Court of Appeal held, following *Ravenseft*, that the test which the court must apply is whether, notwithstanding any errors or omissions that have been demonstrated, the notice is 'substantially to the same effect' as a notice in the proper form which has been duly completed. In reaching its conclusion, the court must bear in mind the statutory purpose of the notice, namely that of telling the proposed tenant of the special nature of an assured shorthold tenancy.[38] Both notices were held to be valid and the tenancies were assured shorthold tenancies.

Service of the notice

Joint landlords and tenants

3.66 The section 20 notice must have been served by one of two or more joint landlords.[39] The notice must have been served on all the joint tenants.[40]

Agency

3.67 It is common for landlords to instruct agents to manage properties. A section 20 notice may be signed and served by a landlord's agent. Even where an agent fails to indicate the identity of the landlord, or gives incorrect details for the landlord, this will not necessarily invalidate the notice (see *Osborne & Co Ltd v Dior* at para 3.65 above). This,

---

36 *Ravenseft Properties Ltd v Hall* [2001] EWCA Civ 2034, 19 December 2001.
37 [2003] EWCA Civ 281, 22 January 2003.
38 Arden LJ at [37].
39 HA 1988 s20(6).
40 HA 1988 s45(3).

however, is a different issue from the tenant's right to be informed of the identity of the landlord which is dealt with at paras 4.131–4.138.

3.68   A section 20 notice can also be served *on* an agent acting for the tenant.[41] However, this will only be in circumstances where the tenant has instructed an agent to act on his or her behalf in relation to the tenancy, which is unusual.

Timing

3.69   The notice must be served before the tenancy is entered into. This is a question of fact in each case.[42] A landlord who failed to serve notice at the appropriate time may seek to remedy this by delivering a back-dated notice to the tenant. The simple production of a copy notice that apparently complies with section 20 is not determinative. In a possession claim the burden is on the landlord to satisfy the court 'on balance of probabilities' that any necessary conditions were satisfied. A tenant who disputes this must state this in the reply or defence and will be able to give oral evidence about what happened when the tenancy was granted; if the court cannot decide who is telling the truth, the claim should be dismissed.

Understanding the notice

3.70   In a case concerning the service of notices of rent increase and possession the Court of Appeal held that it was not necessary that the notice was understood by the tenant; serving the notice simply means delivering it to the tenant.[43] However, that case was decided before important developments in disability discrimination law. In a case where the landlord knows of a tenant's disability or incapacity it may be argued that a landlord cannot rely on simply delivering an important notice to someone incapable of understanding or dealing with it. See paras 7.145–7.175.

New tenancies granted to existing tenants

Existing assured tenants

3.71   Where a tenant is already an assured tenant the drawing up of a new assured shorthold tenancy will be of no effect. This is the case even if the landlord grants the tenant a tenancy of different premises.

41 *Yenula Properties Ltd v Naidu* [2002] EWCA Civ 719, 23 May 2002.
42 *Bedding v McCarthy* (1993) 27 HLR 103.
43 *Tadema Holdings v Ferguson* (2000) 32 HLR 866, see para 6.40.

3.72 Housing Act 1988 s20(3) provides that if:

> ... immediately before a [new] tenancy is granted, the persons to whom it is granted or, as the case may be, at least one of [them], was a tenant under an assured tenancy which was not a shorthold tenancy, and the new tenancy is granted by the person who, immediately before the beginning of the tenancy, was the landlord under the assured tenancy ... the new tenancy cannot be an assured shorthold tenancy.

3.73 Therefore, a landlord cannot remedy a failure to follow the proper procedure after the start of the tenancy. Simply getting the tenant to sign a new tenancy agreement that is a shorthold agreement will not 'convert' an assured tenancy into an assured shorthold tenancy. However, the circumstances may be such that the old tenancy is deemed to have ended before the commencement of the new tenancy.

> In *Dibbs v Cambell*[44] it was held that tenants who signed a deed of surrender one day and entered into a new tenancy agreement the following day, were not tenants immediately before the grant of the new agreement. This was the case even though the tenants had not vacated the premises.

Tenant's notice that a new tenancy is shorthold

3.74 An exception to the rule that a new tenancy granted to an existing assured tenant cannot be a shorthold is where the tenant serves on the landlord a notice in prescribed form (or form substantially to the same effect) stating that the new tenancy is to be assured.[45] Despite being a notice served by a tenant, the form begins with bullet points warning the tenant that he or she is giving up rights as an assured tenant and includes an exhortation to take advice if in doubt about whether to sign the form.

> In *Kahlon v Isherwood*[46] the Court of Appeal considered a case in which an assured tenant had entered into a consent order in possession proceedings. The agreed terms were that the landlord would waive the rent arrears, that the parties would enter into a new

---

44 (1988) 20 HLR 372, CA. This case was about similar anti-avoidance provisions to prevent a landlord converting a protected tenancy into a protected shorthold tenancy. Protected shorthold tenancies are described below at paras 3.185–3.189.

45 HA 1988 s19A and Sch 2A para 7(2). The prescribed form is Form 8 and is set out in Assured Tenancies and Agricultural Occupancies (Forms) Regulations 1997 SI No 194.

46 [2011] EWCA Civ 602, 19 May 2011.

12-month assured shorthold tenancy, and that the landlord would not claim any rent in excess of the tenant's housing benefit.
The parties did enter into such an agreement but when the landlord sought possession at the end of the term the tenant argued that the tenancy was not an assured shorthold tenancy because he had not served on the landlord notice in prescribed form.

The Court of Appeal rejected the landlord's argument that the schedule to the order, setting out the terms of the agreement, was effectively a form substantially to the same effect as the prescribed form. Although commenting that the tenant's defence was 'deeply unattractive', the court held that, as in *Manel v Manon* (see above, para 3.64) the bullet points were crucial and furthermore there was nothing corresponding to paragraph 4 of the form which confirms that the tenant understands the nature of the tenancy he or she is giving up and the limited rights under an assured shorthold tenancy. The notice is 'the means of providing a clear record that the tenant has been appraised of his rights and the loss of security which the new arrangements will entail'.[47] The new tenancy was not an assured shorthold tenancy.

Existing assured shorthold tenants

3.75   Where an assured shorthold tenant simply remains in occupation after the end of the fixed term he or she becomes a statutory periodic assured shorthold tenant. It is not necessary for the parties to enter into a new agreement (or, in a case where the tenancy commenced before 28 February 1997, to be served with a new section 20 notice). However, it is common for an assured shorthold tenant to be given a succession of fixed-term agreements by a landlord.[48]

Existing Rent Act tenants: HA 1988 s34

3.76   As described below (paras 3.80–3.98), tenants under the Rent Act 1977 have the strongest rights: the grounds for possession are the most restrictive and rents are controlled by the fair rent system. A landlord would have a strong incentive for wishing to 'convert' a Rent Act tenancy into an assured or assured shorthold tenancy. There is no express protection in terms similar to HA 1988 s20(3) (see para 3.72 above). Rather, the position is governed by HA 1988 s34(1) which

---

47   Patten LJ at [24].
48   Many local authorities insist, incorrectly, that housing benefit cannot be paid unless a new tenancy agreement is drawn up.

provides that tenancies entered into on or after 15 January 1989 cannot be protected (under the Rent Act 1977) except in certain circumstances. These circumstances include a tenancy which 'is granted to a person (alone or jointly with others) who, immediately before the tenancy was granted, was a protected or statutory tenant and is so granted by the person who at that time was the landlord (or one of the joint landlords) under the protected or statutory tenancy'.[49]

3.77   Although the terms of HA 1998 s34 suggest only that it is *possible* to create a new protected tenancy in such a situation, the courts have held that any new tenancy *will* be a protected tenancy, provided the landlord and tenant are the same, even if the tenancy is of different premises.[50]

In *Rajah v Arogol Co Ltd*[51] the defendant had been a Rent Act tenant of a room on the ground floor of a property since 1982. In 1990 he moved to the entire floor. In possession proceedings the landlord argued that he was no longer a protected tenant. The county court made an order for possession, holding that there had been a surrender of the protected tenancy when the parties entered into a tenancy for the whole floor.

The Court of Appeal upheld the tenant's appeal: the protection of HA 1988 s34(1)(b) was not limited to the same or substantially the same premises. The move did not constitute a surrender and the defendant retained the protection of the Rent Act.

3.78   It is, however, always necessary that the tenant is a protected or statutory tenant 'immediately before the [new] tenancy was granted'.

In *The Governing Body of Rugby School v Edwards*[52] the defendant had been a protected tenant of the claimants. Possession proceedings were brought on the grounds of substantial rent arrears. The proceedings were compromised by a consent order which provided that the defendant give up possession in consideration for the claimants agreeing not to enforce payment of the agreed rent arrears of £7,885. It was also agreed, although not part of the consent order, that the claimants would grant to the

49 HA 1998 s34(1)(b).
50 *Laimond Properties Ltd v Al Shakarchi* (1998) 30 HLR 1099.
51 [2001] EWCA Civ 454.
52 July 2004 *Legal Action* 17, Mayors & City County Court.

defendant a three-year assured tenancy of a smaller property. Rent arrears accrued in the new property and a claim for possession made. The defendant argued that he was a protected tenant as HA 1988 s34(1) applied; as such, his case was that rather than being in arrears of £4,500 he had overpaid rent of about £15,000.

The district judge, however, found that the tenant had surrendered his previous tenancy as part of the agreement *before* being granted a new tenancy of the smaller property. He was not therefore a protected or statutory tenant immediately before the grant of the new tenancy and section 34 did not apply. The decision was upheld by a circuit judge.

3.79　Housing Act 1988 s34 also enables new protected tenancies to be granted when a possession order is made on the ground that suitable alternative accommodation is available to the tenant. However, such a tenancy is not automatically protected; rather, section 34(1)(c) permits the court to order that a new tenancy be protected if that is necessary for it to constitute a suitable alternative to the existing accommodation. See paras 7.75–7.86.

Rent Act 1977: protected and statutory tenancies

3.80　The Rent Act (RA) 1977 governs tenancies granted by private landlords before 15 January 1989. A contractual tenancy which gives a tenant substantive security of tenure under Rent Act 1977 is known as a 'protected tenancy'.

3.81　The Rent Act 1977 has a similar structure to the Housing Act 1988: the Act sets out the conditions for a protected tenancy and a schedule lists the types of tenancy that cannot be protected. However, the way security of tenure operates is different. Under the HA 1988 a landlord cannot bring an assured tenancy to an end except by a court order. Under the Rent Act there is no restriction on the landlord's right to bring the tenancy to an end but, when the protected tenancy ends, a 'statutory tenancy' comes into existence, provided the tenant is residing in the premises. This is why, under the Rent Act 1977 the tenancy is known as 'protected' during the contractual term and 'statutory' after the contractual term has ended. Both kinds of tenancy are called 'regulated tenancies'.[53]

Conditions for protected tenancies

3.82 The tenancy must be one 'under which a dwelling-house (which may be a house or part of a house) is let as a separate dwelling'.[54] See paras 3.9–3.14 above for a discussion of the case-law on this condition which also applies under HA 1988.

Sharing with other tenants

3.83 As with assured tenancies, there is specific provision that the sharing of accommodation with other tenants does not prevent the tenancy being protected. RA 1977 s22 provides that where a tenant has exclusive occupation of separate accommodation but the terms of the agreement include the use of other accommodation in common with others, not including the landlord, the separate accommodation shall be deemed a dwelling-house let on a protected or statutory tenancy. Any term terminating or modifying the right to use the shared living accommodation shall be of no effect but the terms may provide for a variation and/or increase in the number of persons with whom the tenant must share.

Ending the protected tenancy

3.84 As the Rent Act 1977 places no restriction on a landlord's right to end a tenancy, the service of a notice to quit ends a periodic protected tenancy.

3.85 A fixed-term protected tenancy ends when the fixed term expires ('by effluxion of time').

3.86 Whether the tenancy ends by notice to quit or at the end of a fixed period, a tenant who remains in residence becomes a statutory tenant and can be evicted only if a possession order is obtained. A possession order will be made only if one of the statutory grounds is proved.

---

53 RA 1977 s18(1). Under RA 1977 s18A and Sch 17 tenancies governed by previous Rent Acts, known as 'controlled tenancies' were converted into regulated tenancies.
54 RA 1977 s1(1).

3.87   Furthermore, a notice of rent increase operates to convert a periodic protected tenancy into a statutory tenancy.[55]

3.88   Even where a tenant serves notice to quit on a landlord this only ends the protected tenancy; the tenant who remains in residence becomes a statutory tenant. There is, however, a ground for possession where the landlord has relied on the tenant's notice and contracted to sell or let the premises or is otherwise prejudiced.[56]

The statutory tenancy

3.89   Rent Act 1977 s2(1)(a) provides that:

> ... after the termination of a protected tenancy of a dwelling-house the person who, immediately before that termination, was the protected tenant of the dwelling-house shall, if and so long as he occupies the dwelling-house as his residence, be the statutory tenant of it.

Security of tenure

3.90   A protected or statutory tenant cannot be evicted by a landlord unless either:[57]

- one of the grounds for possession is proved to a court; or
- suitable alternative accommodation is available to the tenant.

3.91   As is the case under the Housing Acts 1985 and 1988 security of tenure is enjoyed only if a person is occupying the premises as a home. Under the Rent Act 1977 the statutory tenant must be occupying premises as his or her residence[58] and under the Housing Acts the assured or secure tenant must occupy premises as his or her only or principal home. The residence condition is discussed in detail below at paras 4.2–4.12.

Exceptions to Rent Act protection

3.92   The Rent Act 1977 lists those tenancies that cannot be protected:

---

55 RA 1977 s49(4).
56 RA 1977 Sch 15, Case 5, see appendix to chapter 7.
57 RA 1977 ss98 and 99.
58 It is not necessary that a protected tenant resides in the premises. It is unlikely that many Rent Act tenancies are still protected. This will only be the case if the original contract is still in existence and no notice to quit or notice of rent increase has been served since the tenancy started.

- tenancies with a high rateable value (s4);[59]
- tenancies under which no rent or a low rent is paid. A low rent is a rent of less than two thirds of the rateable value (s5);[60]
- dwelling-houses let with more than two acres of agricultural land (ss6 and 26);
- tenancies which include payments for board or attendance, provided the payment forms a substantial part of the rent (s7); board means the provision of food (as in 'board and lodgings'), attendance means the provision of services personal to the tenancy, such as room cleaning and the supply of clean linen;
- certain tenancies granted to students by specified educational institutions (s8); the conditions are the same as under the Housing Act 1988, see para 3.30 above;
- holiday lets (s9);
- tenancies of agricultural holdings and farm business lets (s10), see paras 3.190–3.194 below;
- tenancies of licensed premises (s11);
- tenancies where there is a resident landlord (s12); this is discussed in detail at paras 4.14–4.29;
- Crown tenancies (s13);
- business tenancies (s24); mixed business and residential tenancies are discussed at paras 1.133–1.136;
- tenancies granted by exempt landlords such as local authorities, housing associations and housing co-operatives (ss14, 15 and 16).

In most cases, even if a tenancy cannot be protected for one of the above reasons, it will be a contractual tenancy and the tenant's rights will depend on the agreed terms. In most cases the tenant will be protected from eviction without a court order, see paras 8.11–8.18.

Restricted contracts

3.93   Under the Rent Act 1977 some tenancies were 'restricted contracts' under which tenants had limited rights: the possible postponement of a notice to quit and some rent control. A restricted contract was created in two situations:

---

59 What constitutes a high rateable value depends on when the tenancy was granted and whether the property is in Greater London or elsewhere. See RA 1977 s25. Rates on domestic premises were abolished in 1990. Few local authorities keep old ratings lists but archived lists may be held by local libraries.

60 Again, the relevant rateable value depends on when and where the tenancy was granted and it may be necessary to consult archived ratings lists.

- where there was a resident landlord; and
- where the tenant made payments for board but where the payments were not substantial.

The majority of restricted contracts were granted by resident landlords. No new restricted contracts could be granted after 15 January 1989 and any change in the terms of the agreement, including a rent increase, after that date will mean that the tenancy is no longer a restricted contract but is governed by the Housing Act 1988 (or, more correctly falls outside HA 1988 and is simply a contractual tenancy).

Fair rents

3.94 Under the Rent Act 1977 all protected and statutory tenants have the right to have a 'fair rent' registered. This is the maximum rent that can be charged. The fair rent system is explained below at paras 4.178–4.179.

'Sitting tenants' and being 'bought out'

3.95 The term 'sitting tenant' refers to a tenant who is entitled to remain in occupation of premises so that if ownership of the premises changes the new owner takes the premises subject to the tenant's interest. Tenancies, being interests in land, bind a purchaser.[61] A landlord cannot evict a tenant simply because he or she wishes to sell, or because he or she has just purchased the premises and wishes to obtain vacant possession.

3.96 Clearly, some tenancies can be ended more easily than others; an owner with an assured shorthold tenant in occupation can evict the tenant by serving two months' notice and obtaining a possession order before selling with vacant possession. Alternatively, a purchaser can obtain possession in the same way following completion of the purchase. Because a statutory tenant under the Rent Act 1977 has the strongest rights possible, the term 'sitting tenant' is usually used to refer to such tenants. An owner of premises subject to a statutory tenancy may wish to pay the tenant a sum of money to give up his or her tenancy. The question arises: how is such an interest valued?

3.97 There is no statutory formula for determining the value of a tenant's interest. Any agreement will depend on how much the landlord is prepared to pay and how much the tenant is prepared to accept. A tenant who wishes to move in with family members may accept less than

61 Land Registration Act 2002 Schs 1 and 3.

someone who needs to secure alternative accommodation. If the tenant is elderly the landlord may prefer to keep the property until the tenant dies rather than pay a substantial sum to gain vacant possession.

3.98 If negotiating such an agreement, the tenant may wish to obtain expert valuation evidence because the increased value of the property with vacant possession is often underestimated. However, agreement always depends on reaching a compromise and if a landlord is unwilling to pay the amount asked by the tenant, the tenant will remain in occupation as a statutory tenant. Advisers should be aware, however, that a possession order may be made by a court if suitable alternative accommodation is available to the tenant. A landlord may choose to offer alternative accommodation to obtain vacant possession rather than pay the tenant to leave. Suitable alternative accommodation as a ground for possession is discussed at paras 7.75–7.89.

Local authority tenancies

3.99 Tenancies under which the landlord is a local authority may be one of the following:

- a secure periodic tenancy;
- (from the coming into force of the Localism Act 2011) a secure 'flexible' (fixed-term) tenancy;
- an introductory tenancy;
- a demoted tenancy;
- a family intervention tenancy; or
- a non-secure tenancy – a tenancy which is excluded from being secure.

Housing association secure tenancies

3.100 Before 15 January 1989 housing associations also granted secure tenancies, governed by the Housing Act 1985. Tenants of housing associations whose tenancy started before that date remain secure tenants, while tenants whose tenancy was granted on or after that date will be assured tenants.

3.101 The secure tenants of housing associations have the same rights as the secure tenants of local authorities with two main differences: (1) secure tenants of housing associations do not have the 'right to buy' and (2) secure tenancies of housing associations are subject to the fair rent scheme under the Rent Act 1977; this is described at paras 4.178–4.180.

Conditions for secure tenancies

3.102   The Housing Act 1985 Part IV sets out the conditions for creating secure tenancies and the rights of secure tenants. The conditions for the creation of a secure tenancy are that:[62]

- the premises are 'let as a separate dwelling';
- the landlord condition is satisfied;
- the tenant condition is satisfied; and
- the tenancy is not excluded by HA 1985 Sch 1.

Separate dwelling

3.103   HA 1985 s79(1) provides that the tenancy must be one 'under which a dwelling-house is let as a separate dwelling'.

3.104   As in all of the statutes that provide for security of tenure this is a condition that must be met for a secure tenancy to exist, see paras 3.9–3.14 above.

3.105   Unlike tenancies in the private sector there is no provision for a secure tenancy where a tenant has possession of a room only, with shared use of other accommodation. Such a letting cannot be a secure tenancy because there is no letting of a separate dwelling.

Secure licences

3.106   HA 1985 s79(3) provides that the rights of secure tenants, not including the right to buy, apply also to licensees of dwelling-houses (except those granted to trespassers as a temporary measure, see para 3.109 below). So, under the Housing Act 1985 there is the possibility of a 'secure licence'.

3.107   One situation in which a secure licence may be granted is when a right to occupy is granted to a person under the age of 18 years. A minor cannot legally hold a tenancy but there are two possible ways of granting a right to occupy to a child. Either a secure licence can be granted until the child reaches the age of 18 when it will become a tenancy, or a secure tenancy can be granted, to be held on trust by some other person for the benefit of the child, until he or she reaches the age of 18, see paras 1.139–1.144 for an explanation of such trusts.

3.108   In addition, an occupier of a single room who shares facilities with others may have a secure licence provided he or she has exclusive possession of the room.[63]

62 HA 1985 ss79–81.
63 *Westminster CC v Clarke* (1992) 24 HLR 360, HL.

3.109 A licence may also be granted to a trespasser as a 'temporary expedient' pending the recovery of possession. Such a licence will not be secure and the trespasser/licensee is an excluded occupier, who can be evicted without a court order after the licence is ended.[64]

Landlord and tenant conditions

3.110 In addition, a tenancy will be secure only if the landlord and the tenant conditions are satisfied. HA 1985 s79 provides that the tenancy will be secure 'at any time when' those conditions are satisfied. The same tenancy may therefore be at one time secure and at another time not secure if the conditions are not met, for example, there is a change of landlord or the tenant ceases to live in the premises.

Landlord condition

3.111 HA 1985 s80 provides that the landlord must be one of the following specified authorities or bodies:

- a local authority;
- a development corporation;
- a housing action trust;
- an urban development corporation;
- the Homes and Communities Agency or Welsh Ministers; or
- a certain kind of housing co-operative (see para 3.113 below).

3.112 In addition, before 15 January 1989 most housing trusts and housing associations could grant secure tenancies. A secure tenancy granted by such a body before that date will remain secure and the following paragraphs therefore apply also to the secure tenants of housing trusts and housing associations.

3.113 Housing co-operatives are sometimes employed as agents by local authorities to manage their accommodation.[65] Most housing co-operatives are 'fully mutual' associations registered under the Industrial and Provident Societies Act 1965.[66] Such organisations cannot themselves grant secure tenancies and the tenants of such co-ops do not enjoy any substantive security of tenure. They are non-profit-making organisations run by the members who are also the tenants of the

---

64 HA 1985 s79(4) and Protection from Eviction Act 1977 s3A, and see paras 1.101–1.122.

65 See HA 1985 s27.

66 The registering authority for such societies is currently the Financial Services Authority (FSA) whose website, www.fsa.gov.uk, gives information about the registration requirements.

co-op. The tenants' rights will be set out in the tenancy agreement and the rules of the association.

3.114 However, where a housing co-operative is an agent for a local authority, the tenancies can be secure because the landlord is the local authority and not the co-op. The tenancy agreement should make this clear but, in cases of doubt, a tenant is entitled to be informed of the identity of his or her landlord, see para 4.131 below.

Tenant condition

3.115 HA 1985 s81 provides that the tenant must be an individual who occupies the dwelling-house as his or her only or principal home. If there are joint tenants each must be an individual and at least one of them must occupy the premises as his or her only or principal home.

3.116 If at any time the tenant condition is not met, ie, the tenant is not occupying the premises as his or her only or principal home, the tenant stops being a secure tenant. He or she enjoys only a non-secure contractual tenancy at this time. However, the secure status can be regained if the tenant resumes occupation as his or her only or principal home, provided there has not been a subletting or parting with possession of the whole of the premises, see paras 4.11 and 4.108.

Exceptions which cannot be secure

3.117 Certain tenancies cannot be secure. These are set out in HA 1985 Sch 1 and are as follows.

Long leases: para 1

3.118 A 'long tenancy' is defined in HA 1985 s115 and includes a lease granted for a fixed period of more than 21 years and any lease granted under the right to buy or right to acquire provisions.[67]

Introductory tenancies: para 1A

3.119 Introductory tenancies are governed by HA 1996 Part V, see paras 3.151–3.165 below. Also excluded are tenancies that have ceased to be introductory following the death of the tenant or where the tenant is not occupying as his or her only or principal home.

---

67 The 'right to buy' enjoyed by secure tenants is set out in HA 1985 Part V. The 'right to acquire' for assured tenants of RSLs is set out in HA 1996 ss16–17. Both schemes are outside the scope of this book.

Demoted tenances: para 1B

3.120 See paras 3.166–3.173 below.

Tenancies granted to employees: para 2

3.121 Tenancies granted to employees of the landlord or certain specified bodies where it is a condition of the employment contract that the employee occupies the dwelling-house for the better performance of his or her duties.[68]

3.122 Those who are required to occupy accommodation owned by an employer for the better performance of the employment duties will, under the common law, be licensees and not tenants (see chapter 1). However, this exception to secure status extends to those who are employed by one specified body and accommodated by another. The specified bodies are:

- local authorities;
- new town corporations;
- housing action trusts;
- urban development corporations; and
- the governors of an aided school.

3.123 In all cases the employment contract must specify that the employee must live in the particular accommodation.

3.124 This exclusion also deals specifically with rent-free accommodation provided to the police and fire authority employees.

3.125 Where the landlord is a local housing authority the tenancy does not become secure unless the authority notifies the tenant that it is secure. Where the landlord is not a local housing authority the tenancy will become secure automatically if the conditions are not met for a period of three years in aggregate.

Short-life tenancies on land acquired for development: para 3

3.126 Tenancies granted to provide temporary accommodation on land acquired for development, pending the development. Development is defined by the Town and Country Planning Act 1990 s55: 'the carrying out of building, engineering, mining or other operations in, on, and over or under land, or the making of any material change in the use of buildings or other land.'

---

68 HA 1985 Sch 1 provides that the employment contract may be express or implied and an express contract may be an oral contract. However, a term requiring occupation will only be implied into the employment contract if occupation is necessary in order for the employee to do the job: *Hughes & Hughes v Greenwich LBC* (1993) 26 HLR 99.

3.127　Although the provision is for 'temporary' accommodation the occupiers may be in occupation for long periods, and even under long fixed term lettings, provided development is pending. The exception applies even if the identity of the landlord changes. However, if the development plans are rejected or abandoned and no alternative development plan is pending the exception will cease to apply and any tenants will become secure.[69]

Homeless accommodation: para 4

3.128　Tenancies granted to homeless applicants under HA 1996 Part VII. This includes accommodation pending inquiries and accommodation provided under HA 1996 s193 following acceptance of a housing duty.

Family intervention tenancies: para 4ZA

3.129　See paras 3.174–3.176 below.

Asylum-seekers: para 4A

3.130　Accommodation provided to asylum-seekers under the Immigration and Asylum Act 1999 Part VI (ie, by arrangement with the UK Border Agency). However, the landlord may notify the tenant that the tenancy is to become secure. This will only happen if the asylum-seeker is granted some form of leave and becomes entitled to an allocation under HA 1996 Part VI (see chapter 17).

Accommodation for people with temporary protection: para 4B

3.131　See para 3.36 above – this provision is the same as for tenancies excluded from the Housing Act 1988.

Temporary accommodation to people taking up employment: para 5

3.132　This exception applies to schemes under which an authority offers temporary accommodation to those taking up employment in the district or surrounding area. The tenant must be informed in writing, before the grant of the tenancy, that the exception applies. Unless the authority is a local housing authority the tenancy will automatically become secure one year after the start of the tenancy. In the case of a local housing authority the tenancy will only become secure if the authority notifies the tenant. In practice, such schemes are now rare.

---

69 *Lillieshall Road Housing Co-operative Ltd v Brennan & Brennan* (1991) 24 HLR 195, CA.

Short-term subleasing schemes: para 6

3.133 Where the accommodation has been leased to the landlord for use as temporary housing accommodation, with a provision that vacant possession will be given back by the landlord after a certain period. This exception covers 'private sector leasing' arrangements in which private landlords let vacant property to a local authority or housing association who then sublet the accommodation on a temporary basis to homeless applicants.

Temporary accommodation during works: para 7

3.134 Where a tenancy is offered to a person on a temporary basis to enable works to be carried out to the tenant's home. This exception does not apply if the tenant was already a secure tenant of the home being repaired. In such a case the tenant will become a secure tenant of the temporary accommodation but there is a discretionary ground for possession available to the landlord to compel the tenant to return to the repaired property.

3.135 This provision enables an authority to offer to a non-local authority tenant temporary accommodation to facilitate the landlord carrying out major works. In the past some authorities had a policy of doing this when serving repair or improvement notices on private landlords where vacant possession was needed to complete the major works. However, given the shortage of local authority accommodation such policies are now rare.

Agricultural holdings: para 8

3.136 Tenancies granted to tenants who are also engaged in farming land where the accommodation is part of an agricultural land. Such tenancies are governed by the Agricultural Holdings Act 1986 and the Agricultural Tenancies Act 1995 (see paras 3.190–3.194 below).

Licenced premises: para 9

3.137 A tenancy of premises or part of premises licensed for the sale of intoxicating liquor for consumption on the premises.

Specified student lettings: para 10

3.138 A tenancy granted to a student to enable the tenant to attend a designated course at a university or further education establishment is not a secure tenancy. In this case a written notice must be served on the tenant before the tenancy is granted, stating that the tenancy falls within this exception and specifying the proposed educational establishment.

3.139   Unless the landlord is a local authority the tenancy will automatically become secure six months after the tenant ceases to attend the designated course (or, if the tenant fails to take up the course, six months from the date of grant). If the landlord is a local authority the tenancy will only become secure if the landlord notifies the tenant.

Business tenancies: para 11

3.140   A tenancy of premises occupied primarily for business purposes is governed by the Landlord and Tenant Act 1954. See paras 1.133–1.136 for the issues arising when there is mixed business and residential use.

Almshouses: para 12

3.141   A licence to occupy an almshouse dwelling will not be a secure tenancy. Almshouse occupiers are licensees and not tenants because the grant of the right of occupation is a charitable act.[70] The licence must have been granted by or on behalf of a charity which is authorised to maintain the dwelling-house as an almshouse and which has no power to grant a tenancy of the dwelling-house.

Becoming a secure tenant of a local authority

3.142   It should be noted that where there is provision for tenancies to become secure by default, after a certain period (under HA 1985 Sch 1 paras 2, 5 and 10), if the landlord is a local authority the tenancy will only become secure if the authority notifies the tenant. This is to ensure that only those who qualify for an allocation of accommodation under HA 1996 Part VI become local authority tenants.

Features of a secure tenancy

Security of tenure

3.143   HA 1985 s82 provides that a secure tenancy can only be ended by a landlord by obtaining a possession order. The tenancy ends on the date on which the tenant is to give up possession in pursuance of the order.

3.144   HA 1985 s84 provides that a possession order will only be made on one of more of the possession grounds set out in HA 1985 Sch 2.

3.145   The grounds for possession are set out in the appendix to chapter 7. They include grounds in which it is alleged the tenant is at fault, which

70 *Gray v Taylor* [1998] 1 WLR 1093 CA.

are all discretionary. In addition, there are grounds which depend on the landlord making available suitable alternative accommodation for the tenant. Some of these grounds are discretionary and some mandatory. These grounds enable public sector landlords to exercise control over the occupancy of accommodation designed for those with special needs and to forcibly re-house tenants to facilitate development.

Other statutory rights

3.146 Secure tenants also have the following additional statutory rights:

- succession – the right to pass the tenancy to a partner or family member after death;
- transfer of the tenancy – in limited circumstances;
- mutual exchange – the right to 'swap' the tenancy with another tenant of a social landlords;
- the right to take in lodgers;
- the right to make improvements;
- the right to buy the property.

HA 1985 s110 provides that the county court has the power to deal with all disputes regarding the rights of secure tenants.

Variation of secure tenancies

3.147 A feature peculiar to the secure tenancy regime is that the landlord has the right to vary the terms of a periodic secure tenancy. The general rule is that once a contract has been entered into, both parties are bound by the agreed terms and can only vary the terms by agreement. However, the Housing Act 1985 provides that a landlord can unilaterally vary the terms of the tenancy agreement by following the procedure set out in section 103. This requires the landlord to serve notice of variation on the tenant in advance and to invite comment. The variation cannot take effect sooner than four weeks from the date of the notice.

3.148 The right to buy is outside the scope of this book. The other rights are discussed in chapter 4.

Introductory tenancies

3.149 The 'introductory tenancy' was created by the Housing Act 1996.[71] Local authorities and housing action trusts (HATs) may adopt a

---

71 The introductory tenancy scheme is set out in HA 1996 Part V and came into force on 12 February 1997.

scheme whereby all new tenancies, which would otherwise be secure, are 'probationary' tenancies for an initial period of one year. If an authority operates an introductory tenancy scheme it must grant introductory tenancies to *all* new tenants.[72] An authority cannot offer introductory tenancies to particular tenants or types of tenants and unless a scheme has been adopted it has no power to grant any form of introductory or probationary tenancy.

3.150   An exception is where a new tenancy is granted to someone who was already a secure tenant or an assured tenant of an RSL of the same or another dwelling.[73] In such a case he or she will not become an introductory tenant.

Conditions of an introductory tenancy

3.151   If a housing authority or HAT has elected to operate a regime of introductory tenancies, every periodic tenancy entered into shall, if it would otherwise be secure, be an introductory tenancy.[74] So, if a tenancy could not be a secure tenancy, because the necessary conditions are not met, it cannot be an introductory tenancy. The conditions for a secure tenancy are described at paras 3.99–3.114 above.

Features of an introductory tenancy

3.152   An introductory tenant has limited security of tenure; the landlord may serve notice that it has been decided to apply to the court for a possession order. The notice must give reasons and advise the tenant of the right to request a review of the decision by the authority (see para 5.65). The conduct of the review is governed by regulations (see para 5.78).

3.153   If no review is requested or the decision is confirmed on review, an application may be made for a possession order. It has been held in a number of cases that the court cannot entertain a defence to a claim for possession based on an allegation that the review process was not conducted fairly. However, recent cases in the House of Lords/Supreme Court and the European Court of Human Rights suggest otherwise (see para 6.81 and chapter 7).

3.154   Introductory tenancies were introduced as part of a raft of measures to tackle anti-social behaviour. However, most introductory tenancies are terminated because of rent arrears.

---

72   HA 1996 s124(2).
73   HA 1996 s124(2)(a) and (b).
74   HA 1996 s124(2).

Licences[75]

3.155 Where an authority or HAT has made an election to use introductory tenancies, any licences granted will be subject to the same rules. However, this does not apply to licences granted to trespassers as a temporary expedient. Such licensees remain excluded occupiers (see paras 1.109–1.110).

The 'trial' period

3.156 The tenancy will remain an introductory tenancy until one year has passed unless:[76]

- the circumstances are such that the tenancy would no longer be secure, for example, the tenant no longer lives in the dwelling-house as his or her only or principal home;
- a person or body other than the authority or HAT becomes the landlord;
- the election (to operate a scheme of introductory tenancies) is revoked;
- the tenant dies and there is no one entitled to succeed:
- the period of the introductory tenancy is extended by the authority (see para 3.160 below);
- the landlord starts a claim for possession (see chapter 6).

3.157 At the end of the one-year period, if none of the above has happened, the tenancy automatically becomes secure. The one-year period is calculated from:

- the date the tenancy is entered into; or
- if later, the date on which the tenant becomes entitled to possession; or,
- if the tenancy is adopted by the authority or HAT, from the date of the adoption.[77]

Previous probationary tenancies

3.158 Any time immediately prior to a new tenancy during which the tenant was an introductory tenant of another landlord or another property,

---

75 HA 1996 s126.
76 HA 1996 s125(5).
77 A tenancy is adopted if the landlord changes because of a disposal or surrender and the new landlord is a local authority or HAT that operates an introductory tenancy scheme. Such a tenancy will only become an introductory tenancy if it was not a secure or assured tenancy granted by an RSL. See HA 1996 s124(2) and (4).

or an assured shorthold tenant of a registered social landlord,[78] will count towards the trial period, provided there is no interruption in the cumulative period.[79]

3.159   Where the introductory tenants are joint tenants the trial period starts at the earliest date when any of the joint tenants was a probationary tenant under a previous tenancy agreement.[80]

Extending the trial period

3.160   A landlord may extend the introductory tenancy for six months. Notice must be served on the tenant giving reasons and the tenant has the right to seek a review of the decision.[81]

Statutory rights of introductory tenants

3.161   Introductory tenants have rights similar to those of secure tenants in relation to succession but more limited rights of assignment. These are described at paras 4.85–4.86. No specific provision is made regarding lodgers and subletting. Introductory tenants also have the same rights to have repairs carried out as all other short-term tenants. These are dealt with in chapter 10.

Information about introductory tenancies

3.162   Authorities or HATs operating introductory tenancies must from time to time publish information about such tenancies, in whatever form it considers most suitable, and 'so far as it considers it appropriate' to explain in simple terms:[82]

- the express terms of its introductory tenancies;
- the law relating to introductory tenancies;
- the implied repairing obligations.

3.163   This information should be supplied to introductory tenants together with a written statement of the terms of the tenancy. This should be given to the tenant on the grant of the tenancy, 'or as soon as practicable afterwards'.

---

78 RSLs cannot grant introductory tenancies. If they wish to operate 'probationary' or 'starter' tenancies they may do so by granting assured shorthold tenancies for an initial period. However, such tenancies do not automatically become assured after the initial period: the landlord must serve a notice indicating that the tenancy is no longer an assured shorthold tenancy or a new assured tenancy agreement must be entered into.

79 HA 1996 s125(3).

80 HA 1996 s125(4).

81 HA 2004 s179 see HA 1996 ss125A and 125B.

82 HA 1996 s136.

Consultation

3.164 An authority or HAT that lets dwelling-houses on introductory tenancies must maintain arrangements to consult introductory tenants regarding matters of housing management likely to substantially affect such tenants.[83]

Powers of the county court

3.165 As is the case for secure tenancies, a county court has the power to determine questions arising under the provisions of HA 1996 Part V.

Demoted tenancies

3.166 A demoted tenancy is one that was previously secure but that has been 'demoted' by the court, on the landlord's application. Demotion is often sought as an alternative to possession, see chapter 6. A demotion order has the effect of bringing to an end a secure tenancy and replacing it with a demoted tenancy.

3.167 The nature of a demoted tenancy is similar to an introductory tenancy.

Features of a demoted tenancy

3.168 A demoted tenancy remains demoted for 12 months before becoming secure again, unless during the 12 months the landlord applies for possession.[84]

3.169 There is a right to succeed to a demoted tenancy if the tenant dies, but the conditions are slightly different from those applying to secure or introductory tenancies,[85] see para 4.33. A demoted tenant may only assign the tenancy pursuant to a court order made in the event of relationship breakdown or for the benefit of children.[86]

3.170 A demoted tenant does not have substantive security of tenure: a landlord need not prove a statutory ground for possession in order to obtain a possession order.

---

83 HA 1996 s137.
84 HA 1996 s143B(1). The tenancy also ceases to be a demoted tenancy if the landlord or tenant conditions are not met, if the demotion order is quashed, or if the tenant dies and there is no one to succeed to the tenancy: HA 1996 s143B(2).
85 HA 1996 ss143H–143J.
86 HA 1996 s143K.

3.171   A landlord may decide to seek a possession order against a demoted tenant for any reason. A notice of intention to seek possession must be served setting out the reasons and informing the tenant of the right to request an internal review of the decision. The review procedure is governed by regulation.[87]

3.172   If the review confirms the decision, or the tenant fails to request a review, the court must make a possession order against a demoted tenant unless the proper procedure has not been followed by the landlord. However, this does not prevent a tenant raising a public law or article 8 defence, see paras 7.100–7.144.

3.173   The procedure for seeking possession of a demoted tenancy is discussed at paras 6.75–6.81.

Family intervention tenancies

3.174   A family intervention tenancy (FIT) may be offered by a local housing authority or a registered provider of social housing to:

- anyone who is a secure or assured tenant and is subject to a possession order on the grounds of anti-social behaviour or domestic violence;
- anyone who is a secure or assured tenant who could be subject to such a possession order;
- anyone who (if they were a secure or assured tenant) could have such a possession order made against them.

3.175   The landlord's purpose in offering the FIT must be the provision of behaviour support services. A notice must be served on the prospective tenant containing prescribed information about the reasons for offering the FIT and the terms of the tenancy, in particular any requirements concerning behaviour support services. The notice must inform the tenant that he or she is not obliged to accept the tenancy and set out what the landlord is likely to do if the tenancy is refused. Although FITs have been available to social landlords for more than two years, at the time of writing, few, if any, have been granted.

3.176   A tenant with an FIT has rights similar to those of introductory and demoted tenants, ie no substantive security of tenure but the right to be given reasons for a decision to evict and (if the landlord is

---

87 Demoted Tenancies (Review of Decisions) (England) Regulations 2004 SI No 1679 and Demoted Tenancies (Review of Decisions) (Wales) Regulations 2005 SI No 1228, W86.

a local authority) the right to an internal review of the decision. The actual notices that must be served are dealt with in para 6.24.

Non-secure tenancies

3.177 A tenancy that is 'non-secure' is nevertheless still a contractually binding tenancy. Non-secure tenants enjoy the rights that are implied into all tenancy agreements such as the right to have repairs carried out by the landlord and the right to peaceful enjoyment of the premises. Non-secure tenants do not have substantive security of tenure. However, unless the letting is 'excluded' from the Protection from Eviction Act 1977, see para 1.101, a landlord who wishes to evict must serve notice to quit to end the tenancy and obtain a possession order.

3.178 A non-secure tenancy must have ended *before* a claim for possession can be made. Once the tenancy has come to an end the landlord has a right of possession and need not prove any grounds.

Other types of tenancy

3.179 Most residential tenancies fall into one of the categories described above. However, advisers may also come across the following types of tenancy:

- assured tenancies created under the Housing Act 1980; and
- protected shorthold tenancies.

3.180 'Old style' assured tenancies created under the Housing Ac 1980 will have automatically become 'new style' assured tenancies under HA 1988.[88]

3.181 Protected shorthold tenancies are described briefly below (paras 3.185–3.189).

3.182 In addition there are different statutory schemes that govern tenancies of agricultural land and agricultural holdings. These are also described briefly below (paras 3.190–3.194).

---

88 These tenancies were introduced to encourage the expansion of private sector lettings. They were modelled on the business code and a market rent was payable. HA 1988 ss1(3) and 37 provide that such tenancies were converted into 'new style' assured tenancies when HA 1988 came into force.

'Unprotected tenancies'

3.183   Many tenancies cannot be any of the main types of tenancy because they fall outside the provisions of the Rent 1977 and the Housing Acts 1985 and 1988. The most common reasons for this are:

- the tenant does not reside in the premises (see paras 4.2–4.4);
- the tenant has a resident landlord (see paras 4.13–4.27);
- the tenant has been granted a 'non-secure' tenancy by a local authority following a homeless application;
- the tenancy is excluded for some other reason, such as, for example, a very low or very high rent, or because the premises are licensed for the sale of alcohol.[89]

3.184   Such tenancies are sometimes referred to as 'unprotected tenancies' or 'contractual tenancies'. The tenant has only the rights under the tenancy agreement. He or she does not enjoy substantive security of tenure: the landlord can end the tenancy and is entitled to possession when the tenancy ends. However, it will be necessary to bring a claim for possession in order to evict the tenant unless the tenancy is an excluded letting (see para 1.101).

Protected shorthold tenancies

3.185   The protected shorthold tenancy (PST) was an early attempt to enable private landlords to grant short-term tenancies. They are now very rare. Under the Housing Act 1980 the following conditions must have been met in order to create a PST:[90]

- The tenancy was for a fixed term of not less than one year and not more than five years.
- There was no provision for the landlord to end the tenancy before the expiry of the fixed term.[91]
- Before the grant of the tenancy, the landlord must have given to the tenant a notice in prescribed form, stating that the tenancy was to be a protected shorthold. However, on a claim for possession the court has the power to waive this requirement if it is just and equitable to make a possession order.[92]

---

89   All of the exceptions under the various statutes are listed above at paras 3.19–3.37, 3.92 and 3.117–3.141.
90   HA 1980 s52(1).
91   Excepting a right of forfeiture or re-entry.
92   See appendix to chapter 7.

- If there was not already a registered rent, the landlord must apply for rent to be registered no later than 28 days after the beginning of the period of the tenancy.

3.186 If those conditions were not met, the tenancy created will have been a protected tenancy, provided the relevant conditions were satisfied. Such a tenancy is likely now to have become a statutory tenancy. Under HA 1980 s55(2) the court has a discretion to waive the conditions if it is 'just and equitable' to do so.

3.187 A landlord cannot grant a PST to a tenant who, immediately before the grant, was a protected or statutory tenant.[93] So, a tenancy cannot be 'converted' into a PST if the initial requirements were not met.

A PST becoming an assured shorthold tenancy

3.188 The Housing Act 1988 provides that no new PST can be created on or after 15 January 1989.[94] Furthermore, if a tenancy is entered into after that date by the same landlord and tenant as at the coming to an end of the PST, the new agreement will be an assured shorthold tenancy regardless of whether the conditions under HA 1988 s20 were met.[95]

Claiming possession of a PST

3.189 If a tenancy is still a PST there is a mandatory ground for possession but the landlord must serve notice on the tenant before bringing a claim for possession. The notice must be served within three months of the anniversary of the end of the PST.[96]

Occupiers of agricultural land

3.190 A distinction is made between those who occupy agricultural land by virtue of their employment in agriculture (farm workers) and those who occupy agricultural land as farmers or farm managers. The occupation rights of farm workers are governed by statutory schemes similar to Rent Act 1977 and Housing Act 1988 while the rights of farmers and farm managers are similar to those of business tenants.

93 HA 1980 s52(2).
94 HA 1988 s34(1).
95 HA 1988 s34(3).
96 RA 1977 Sch 15 Case 19.

Farm workers and former farm workers

3.191   The key features of the statutory schemes are as follows:

- Special protection is given to tenants and licensees who work in agriculture and forestry. Such occupiers are referred to as 'agricultural occupiers'.
- An agricultural occupier may be protected even though he or she pays a low rent, or no rent at all.
- The rights of most agricultural occupiers whose agreement began before 15 January 1989 are governed by the Rent (Agriculture) Act 1976 which is similar to Rent Act 1977. Protected agreements are called 'protected occupancies' and 'statutory tenancies'.
- For those whose agreement began on or after 15 January 1989, HA 1988 Part I Chapter III applies. Sections 24–26 provide that an assured tenancy, other than an assured shorthold tenancy, will be an 'assured agricultural occupancy'.
- Many agricultural occupiers are required to live in the premises as a condition of their employment for the better performance of their employment duties. Under the common law such an occupier cannot be a tenant, see paras 1.36–1.39. However, under both the Rent (Agriculture) Act 1976 and the Housing Act 1988 protection extends to agricultural licensees (ie service occupiers), provided they have exclusive possession.
- Under both Acts certain conditions must be met regarding the employment of the occupier in agriculture or forestry for a minimum period.[97]
- Protection may continue even after the agricultural occupier has retired. However, to facilitate efficient management of agricultural land, the landlord will have a right to possession if suitable alternative accommodation is available, provided either by the landlord or the local authority.
- Special provision is made for unprotected agricultural occupiers in the Protection from Eviction Act 1977 s4: a court may suspend the execution of a possession order for up to six months.

Farmers and farm managers

3.192   Protection under the Rent (Agriculture) Act 1976 and under HA 1988 ss24–26 is given to a person who is employed in agriculture. The tenants of agricultural holdings, who are in control of the holding, do

---

97 See Rent (Agriculture) Act 1976 s1(1) and HA 1988 Sch 3.

not enjoy this protection. They are excluded from the Rent Act 1977 and the Housing Acts 1985 and 1988.

3.193   Such agreements will usually be governed by the Agricultural Holdings Act 1986 or the Agricultural Tenancies Act 1995; these operate on a similar basis to the Landlord and Tenant Act 1954, which applies to business tenancies.

3.194   In addition, under RA 1977 and HA 1988 a tenancy cannot be protected or assured if it includes more than two acres of agricultural land, even if the main purpose of the letting is to provide a home.

The 'flexible tenancy'

3.195   The stated aim of the Localism Act 2011 is to devolve power to local authorities and this includes decisions about the nature of the tenancies it grants. Instead of all long-term tenancies granted by local authorities being secure periodic tenancies with substantive security of tenure, a local authority will instead be able to operate a policy of granting secure fixed-term tenancies which must be for a period of at least two years, at the end of which there will be an option for the landlord to grant a further fixed-term tenancy or to claim possession.

3.196   Local authorities will be required to prepare and publish a 'tenancy strategy' setting out the matters to which registered providers of social housing in the area (including the local authority itself) must have regard when formulating policies about the kinds of tenancies they grant, the circumstances in which they will grant particular kinds of tenancies and, if they grant fixed-term tenancies, the lengths of the terms and the circumstances in which they will grant a further tenancy at the end of the initial tenancy.

3.197   The strategies must be published no later than 12 months from the date on which this part of the Act comes into force; this is expected to be at some point after April 2012. In devising a strategy, certain matters must be taken into account (for example, the existing allocation scheme and homelessness strategy) and certain bodies must be consulted, for example, the private registered providers in the area.

3.198   This fixed-term tenancy will be a type of secure tenancy: the so-called 'flexible tenancy' which must be for no less than two years (there is no upper limit). The government has recently issued a revised draft directive to the social housing regulator, stating that flexible tenancies should normally last for at least five years. Flexible tenants will not have substantive security of tenure: at the end of the fixed period the landlord will be able to obtain a possession order as of right, provided the correct notices have been served.

3.199   The first notice, which should be served six months before the end of the tenancy, is a notice stating that no new tenancy will be granted when the tenancy ends, and giving reasons for the decision. The tenant will have a right to request a review. The second notice, which may be served at any date up to the end of the tenancy, is a notice stating that possession is required. This will give at least two months' notice before the possession claim is issued. This will not be a notice of seeking possession and no reasons need be given.

3.200   On a claim for possession, the court will have a limited powers: it will only be able to refuse an order if a review has been requested and the landlord has not carried out the review or if the decision made on the review is 'otherwise wrong in law', which will encompass the public law and human rights defences (see paras 7.100–7.144).

3.201   The landlord will, during the fixed term, be able to recover possession if there are statutory grounds (for example, non-payment of rent, nuisance etc). However, as the tenancy will be a fixed-term tenancy, it will be necessary for the agreement to include a forfeiture clause (see para 5.7).

3.202   For tenants of other social landlords (private registered providers),[98] the same end is achieved via the mechanism of the assured shorthold tenancy. Where an assured shorthold tenancy is granted by a private registered provider of social housing and is for a fixed term of at least two years, an additional notice requirement is added: in addition to the HA 1988 section 21 notice, notice must also be served at least six months before the end of the tenancy stating that the landlord does not propose to grant a new tenancy. The notice will inform the tenant where to obtain help or advice about the notice but there will be no right to a review (as is the case currently in respect of 'starter' tenancies that are assured shorthold, in contrast to introductory tenants of local authorities).

3.203   Provision is made for flexible tenancies to be granted in relation to demoted tenants and family intervention tenants. For introductory tenants, the tenant will have been notified in advance that at the end of the introductory tenancy the secure tenancy that arises will be a flexible tenancy and the term of that tenancy.

---

98 The Localism Act 2011 also introduces a system of regulation for 'public registered providers of social housing' (local authorities) and 'private registered providers of social housing' which will include both non-profit making and profit-making providers, see para 21.2.

Right of review

3.204 Where a landlord offers to grant a flexible tenancy (whether on the coming to an end of an existing tenancy or not) or serves notice on an introductory tenant that on the coming to end of the introductory tenancy it will become a flexible tenancy, the prospective flexible tenant has a right to request a review about the length of the term that is proposed. This review may only be requested on the basis that the length of the term does not accord with the landlord's policy. The request must be made within 21 days of receipt of the notice.

3.205 In relation to the request for a review of the decision not to grant a new tenancy at the end of the fixed term, this is not so limited and will presumably be broad enough for the tenant to challenge any of the reasons given for not granting a new tenancy.

3.206 Regulations will provide for the conduct of the reviews and are likely to mirror the requirements of the existing review procedures for decisions about homelessness and allocations and seeking possession of introductory and demoted tenancies.

3.207 In all cases, the decision-making of the authority when deciding on the length of the fixed term to grant and whether or not to grant a further tenancy when the initial tenancy ends, will be subject to public law principles. Unlawful decisions may be challenged by judicial review and, if the decision subject to challenge is a decision to evict, by raising a public law defence to the claim. See paras 7.100–7.144.

3.208 The Localism Act 2011 received royal assent in November 2011 and it is intended that the provisions regarding flexible tenancies will come into force in the spring of 2012. However, before offering flexible tenancies local authorities will need to have adopted a housing strategy on which they must consult. It is likely therefore that local authorities will not be in a position to use the flexible tenancy until late 2012.

Common issues for tenants

continued

Key points

- To enjoy substantive security of tenure a tenant must satisfy a residence condition: he or she must live in a dwelling as his or her home. During an extended absence a person may continue to satisfy the residence condition provided there is an intention to return and physical evidence of this.
- Tenants with resident landlords do not enjoy substantive security of tenure but the landlord must be resident when the tenancy starts and continuously throughout.
- If a tenant dies the tenancy may be passed to a family member who lives with the tenant by succession. Each scheme of protection has different conditions for succession.
- Assignment of a tenancy means transferring it to someone else. Mostly this is prohibited except in specific circumstances.
- Subletting is when the tenant grants a tenancy to someone else but retains his or her tenancy. Subletting is mostly prohibited in short-term residential tenancies.
- There is statutory provision for a tenant to obtain information about the identity of his or her landlord. Failure to provide information may be a criminal offence.
- Since 6 April 2007 there has been a mandatory scheme for the protection of rent deposits paid in respect of assured shorthold tenancies. A landlord who fails to protect the deposit in one of the prescribed schemes cannot serve a possession notice until the deposit is protected. Furthermore, the court can award the tenant a sum equivalent to three times the deposit.
- Terms in tenancy agreements that are unfair may be unenforceable. Only a court can declare a term to be unenforceable.
- Tenants with assured tenancies have little rent control: rents are set at market levels. Tenants under the Rent Act and housing association secure tenants have strong rent control: fair rents are set by the rent officer. For local authority tenants the authority must set a 'reasonable rent'. These tend to be much lower than market rents.

Introduction

4.1   This chapter examines issues that commonly arise in relation to residential tenancies and explains how the rules apply to each type of tenancy. The following issues are considered:

- the tenancy condition – residing in the premises;
- resident landlords;
- succession (the tenancy passing to another on the death of the tenant);
- assignment (transfer of the tenancy);
- subletting;
- obtaining information about a landlord;
- rent deposits;
- unfair contract terms;
- rent control.

The tenancy condition – residing in the premises

4.2   At common law a tenant is not required to live in the premises let. However, statutory security of tenure is to protect a tenant's home; only a tenant who resides in premises can enjoy security of tenure.

4.3   Under the Rent Act (RA) 1977 it is provided that after the (contractual) tenancy ends the tenant remains a statutory tenant if and so long as he or she occupies the premises as a residence. A statutory tenant can be evicted only if a possession order is made and an order will be made only if a statutory ground for possession is proved. The Housing Acts 1985 and 1988 provide that a tenancy is only secure or assured when the tenant is occupying the premises as his or her only or principal home; the only way a landlord can end a secure or assured tenancy is by obtaining a possession order; and, an order will only be made if a statutory ground for possession is proved.

4.4   The condition under the Rent Act 1977 is not so strict as under the Housing Acts: occupation as *a residence* is required as opposed to occupation as the tenant's *only or principal home*. In several cases concerning Rent Act tenants it has been held that a person can occupy more than one dwelling as a residence. Under the Housing Acts the dwelling must be the person's only or main home to enjoy security of tenure.

Absence of the tenant

4.5 Clearly, a tenant need not be physically present at all times to be residing in premises. It is recognised that a tenant may continue to be resident in premises even during an extended absence. In such a case the tenant may continue to reside in or occupy premises as a home provided that:

- the tenant intends to return; and
- there is some physical evidence of that intention.[1]

> In *Amoah v Barking and Dagenham*[2] a secure tenant was sentenced to 12 years' imprisonment. He left items of furniture in his flat and appointed a relative to act as a 'caretaker' in his absence. The council served notice to quit and obtained a possession order on the basis that the tenant had lost his secure status.
>
> On appeal it was held that he had retained his secure status. The correct approach was that a prolonged absence raised a presumption that a tenant no longer occupied. That presumption must be rebutted by the tenant who must establish:
>
> 1) an intention to return;
> 2) a practical or real possibility of fulfilment of the intention within a reasonable time; and
> 3) some outward and visible sign of the intention.
>
> In this case, in spite of the length of the expected absence, the tenant had continued to reside in the premises as his only or principal home and could only be evicted if a ground for possession could be proved.

4.6 It is common for those who are imprisoned to lose their tenancies but this is usually because the tenant cannot ensure that rent is paid during the absence: housing benefit can only be paid for a limited period during a tenant's absence (see paras 9.42–9.49). Subletting the whole of premises let on a secure tenancy will result in the loss of security (see para 4.108 below) and an arrangement between family members will only be possible if the family member looking after the premises for the tenant can pay the rent without reliance on housing benefit.[3]

1 *Brown v Brash* [1948] 2 KB 247.
2 (2001) 82 P&CR DG6, CA.
3 This is because housing benefit will not normally be paid where the occupier is a family member of the 'landlord': see para 9.19 below.

4.7   Another common situation is when an elderly tenant becomes unwell and is absent in hospital or a residential home for respite care. Provided the tenant intends to return home he or she should be considered to be continuing to reside there.[4] However, a problem may arise when the tenant's physical or mental health deteriorates so that return becomes unlikely or impossible. When the intention to return ends the tenant can no longer be said to reside in the premises. However, care must be taken to ascertain the tenant's enduring intention.

> *Hammersmith & Fulham LBC v Clarke*[5] concerned a frail, elderly tenant who since 1981 had lived in council accommodation that was adapted for her needs. In 1997 her grandson and his wife moved in to look after her and in 1998 a joint right-to-buy application was submitted. The tenant was subsequently admitted to a nursing home suffering from depression and physical disabilities. While at the nursing home she signed a note prepared by a council social worker stating that she had decided to become a permanent resident of the nursing home and that she no longer intended to return home. The next month the authority served notice to quit and sought possession. The tenant returned home before the trial. Her evidence was that she had gone to the nursing home intending to return home and had signed the note at a time when she was depressed and when her medication had just been sorted out. The claim for possession was dismissed.
>
> The authority appealed, arguing that the tenant's earlier intention was irrelevant, that the material date was the date of the expiry of the notice to quit and that the social worker's note was the best evidence of this. The Court of Appeal accepted that the relevant time for determining the tenant's intention was the date of the expiry of the notice but held that the court should focus on 'the enduring intention of that person' and not 'fleeting changes of mind'. This was particularly true of an elderly tenant in poor health whose intentions may have fluctuated from day to day. The judge was entitled to find that the note did not represent the tenant's more general and enduring intention which was borne out by her evidence, the continuing presence of her family and furniture and all the other circumstances.

4 See para 9.37 for an explanation of housing benefit entitlement during such an absence.
5 (2002) HLR 37, CA.

4.8 Secure tenants can assign a tenancy to a person who would be entitled to succeed to the tenancy in the event of the tenant's death (see below at paras 4.31 and 4.79). However, such an assignment will only be effective to transfer a secure tenancy if, at the date of the assignment, the tenant is still secure, ie still occupying the premises as his or her only or principal home. If assignment is only considered after the tenant has been absent for some time and no longer intends to return home the tenancy will no longer be secure.

Statutory tenancies

4.9 A statutory tenancy arises when a protected tenancy ends provided the tenant is in occupation. Such a tenant 'shall, if and so long as he occupies the dwelling-house as his residence, be the statutory tenant of it'.[6]

Assured tenancies

4.10 The same wording is used in the Housing Act (HA) 1988: a tenancy is only assured 'if and so long as' the conditions, including occupation as only or principal home, are met.[7]

Secure tenancies

4.11 A secure tenant is secure 'at any time when' the relevant conditions are met, including the condition that the tenant occupies the dwelling as his or her only or principal home.[8] This means that a tenant who has lost secure status by moving out may regain the status of a secure tenant by resuming occupation. A tenancy that is no longer secure can be ended by a landlord's notice to quit but if a tenant resumes occupation before a notice to quit expires, it will have no effect; the tenant will have again become a secure tenant and a secure tenancy can only be ended by a court order.[9] However, if a secure tenant sublets the whole of the premises the tenancy ceases to be secure and cannot subsequently become a secure tenancy.[10]

---

6 RA 1977 s2(1)(a).
7 HA 1988 s1(1).
8 HA 1985 ss79(1) and 81.
9 *Hussey v Camden LBC* (1995) 27 HLR 5, CA.
10 HA 1985 s93(2), see para 4.108 below.

Occupation by spouse/civil partner

4.12 The occupation of the spouse or civil partner of the tenant is sufficient to satisfy the tenant condition. This is the case whether the
tenancy is assured, statutory or secure. However, this ceases to be the
case after the termination of the marriage or civil partnership. If the
tenant is out of occupation, it is therefore essential that any transfer
of the tenancy takes place before the decree absolute or dissolution of
the civil partnership (see chapter 12).

Resident landlords

4.13 Under both the Rent Act 1977 and the Housing Act 1988 tenants
who have a resident landlord, as defined below (paras 4.14–4.20), do
not have substantive security of tenure: they cannot be protected or
assured. Under Rent Act 1977 such a tenant had a 'restricted contract', see below (paras 4.26–27), which gave the tenant very limited
rights. Under Housing Act 1988 there is no specific provision; the
tenancy cannot be assured and is therefore an unprotected or basic
contractual tenancy. In both cases, although the tenant does not have
substantive security of tenure, he or she cannot be evicted without a
court order, unless the agreement was made on or after 15 January
1989 *and* the landlord and tenant share accommodation (see para
1.101).

Meaning of 'resident landlord'[11]

4.14 A tenant has a resident landlord where:
- the premises let form part of a building, and that building is not a
  purpose-built block of flats;
- the landlord lives in other premises in the same building; and
- he or she has done so since the tenancy began and continuously
  throughout the tenancy.

The premises

4.15 A landlord may be a resident landlord even if the premises he or
she occupies are completely separate from those occupied by the
tenant, if they are in the same building. Only purpose-built flats are
excluded, and so a landlord residing in a converted house may be a

11 The conditions are set out in RA 1977 s12 and HA 1988 Sch 1 para 10.

resident landlord, regardless of when the conversion was completed and even if the premises have separate entrances.

Landlord's residence

4.16   The landlord must be a resident landlord when the tenancy commences; a landlord who begins to reside in the building after the tenancy started does not become a resident landlord for these purposes. The occupation by any one of joint landlords is sufficient to retain the resident landlord status.[12]

4.17   A tenant who is already protected, statutory or assured, who is granted a new tenancy by the same landlord (whether of the same or different premises in the building) will remain a protected, statutory or assured tenant.[13]

4.18   The residence condition is different under the Rent Act 1977 and the Housing Act 1988: under the 1977 Act the landlord must 'occupy the premises as a residence'; under the 1988 Act the landlord must occupy the premises as his or her 'only or principal home'. A landlord who has more than one home may qualify as a resident landlord under the Rent Act 1977 whereas under the Housing Act 1988 the premises in the shared building must be the only or main home of the landlord.

4.19   If a landlord ceases to satisfy the residence condition, the tenancy will no longer be excluded from the provisions of the Rent Act 1977 or the Housing Act 1988, see below para 4.27.

4.20   However, as for tenants, physical absence alone does not mean that a landlord no longer resides in premises. A landlord may continue to satisfy the residence condition provided he or she intends to resume occupation and there is physical evidence of the intention (see para 4.5 above).

Transfer of ownership

4.21   If ownership of the premises changes, certain periods of time are disregarded for the purposes of determining continuous residence. These are known as 'periods of disregard'.[14]

---

12 *Cooper v Tait* (1984) 15 HLR 98, CA and HA 1988 Sch 1 para 10(2).
13 RA 1977 s12(2) and HA 1988 Sch 1 para 10(3).
14 See RA 1977 Sch 2 and HA 1988 Sch I Pt III.

Lifetime transfer

4.22   Where ownership of the premises changes during the resident land-lord's life, the new owner has 28 days in which to take up occupation. This can be extended to six months if the new landlord gives notice in writing that he or she intends to reside in the premises. This notice must be given within the 28-day period.

4.23   A new landlord cannot serve a notice to quit during this period unless he or she takes up residence. If he or she fails to take up residence within the 28 days, or six months if extended, the tenancy ceases to be excluded from the protection of either the Rent Act 1977 or the Housing Act 1988.

Death of resident landlord

4.24   Where the landlord dies and the property passes to personal repre-sentatives (PRs)[15] the residence requirement is deemed to be satis-fied for a period of up to two years, commencing with the death of the landlord.

4.25   The difference between a lifetime transfer and a transfer on death should be noted: the PRs of a deceased resident landlord may serve notice to quit to end the tenancy within the two-year period of dis-regard.[16] If there is a lifetime transfer, the new landlord must actually take up occupation to retain the resident landlord status. Notice to quit cannot be served by a non-resident landlord during the period of disregard: during this period the tenant may only be evicted on a statutory ground, as if he or she were a statutory or assured tenant.

Restricted contracts

4.26   No new restricted contracts may be granted after 15 January 1989. Most will now have ceased to be restricted contracts and become unprotected tenancies, outside the scope of the Housing Act 1988.

---

15   Personal representatives means executors named in the will or, where there is no will, anyone who applies, as next of kin, for authority to deal with the estate (known as 'letters of administration').

16   The situation is more complicated under RA 1977 in that if the landlord's interest is vested in trustees (including the trustee in bankruptcy) or the Public Trustee (as happens if the landlord dies without a will) up to two years is disregarded, during which no notice to quit can be served. If the premises then pass to PRs appointed to deal with the estate, there is a further period of up to two years during which the resident landlord condition is deemed to be satisfied so that notice to quit can be served.

HA 1988 s36(2)(a) provides that if there has been an increase of rent (other than by reference to the rent tribunal), the agreement is treated as though made at the date of the increase and therefore ceases to be a restricted contract. Similarly, a fundamental variation of other terms would mean that a new agreement was entered into at the date of the variation.

Landlord ceasing to be resident

4.27   If the resident landlord condition ceases to be met, the tenant is no longer excluded from the provisions of the relevant Act. However, one issue remains unclear: whether the type of tenancy is determined by the date of the commencement of the original tenancy or the date it ceases to be excluded. This will be significant if the tenancy commenced between 15 January 1989 and 28 February 1997 and the landlord ceases to be resident after 28 February 1997. If the date of commencement of the tenancy is decisive it will be an assured tenancy unless the landlord complied with the relevant formalities to create an assured shorthold tenancy when the tenancy was granted. However, it is unlikely that a landlord would have done so as, at the date of the grant, the tenancy would have been excluded from the HA 1988 and therefore could not have been an assured shorthold tenancy.

Succession

4.28   Succession means one person becoming entitled to something after another person's entitlement ends, for example inheriting the property of someone who dies. A tenancy, being an interest in land, is property that can be inherited. However, each statutory scheme provides that a person can succeed to a tenancy with security of tenure only if certain conditions are satisfied.

4.29   Under the Rent Act 1977 more than one succession was permitted and currently it is still possible for there to be two successions although the second can only be to an assured and not a statutory tenancy. Under the Housing Acts 1985 and 1988 there can be only one succession. Under the HA 1988 only the spouse, civil partner or co-habitee can succeed whereas under RA 1977 and HA 1985 other family members may also succeed.[17] In all cases the person

---

17 The Localism Act 2011 will restrict statutory succession for future secure tenants in the same way. See paras 4.57–4.58.

succeeding to the tenancy must be residing in the premises at the date of death.

4.30 Succession happens by 'operation of law' and is not something that is 'granted' by a landlord. However, it is often the case that there is a dispute between a landlord and a tenant about whether the necessary conditions are satisfied. Unless agreement can be reached any dispute must be resolved by a court. This may happen when the landlord claims possession against the occupiers. Alternatively, an occupier may seek a declaration from the county court to confirm that he or she is a tenant by succession.

Summary of succession rights

4.31 The following chart sets out the rules relating to succession for tenancies granted before the coming into force of the Localism Act 2011. After the Act comes into force, statutory succession to secure tenancies will be limited to spouses, civil partners and co-habitants but local authorities will have the power to grant more generous succession rights through the tenancy.

	Rent Act 1977[18]	Housing Act 1985[19]	Housing Act 1988[20]
Type of tenancy	Protected and statutory tenancies.	Secure and introductory tenancies.	Assured tenancies, including assured shorthold tenancies.
Who can succeed?	Spouse, civil partner, co-habitee, member of family (not defined).	Spouse, civil partner, member of family (defined, and includes co-habitee).	Spouse, civil partner, co-habitee.

18 RA 1977 Sch 1 Pt 1.
19 HA 1985 ss87–89.
20 HA 1988 s17.

	Rent Act 1977	Housing Act 1985	Housing Act 1988
Conditions	Spouse/civil partner/co-habitee must be residing in premises immediately before death. Family member must be residing in premises for two years before death.	Spouse/civil partner must be occupying as only or principal home at the time of death. Co-habitee/family member must have been residing with the deceased for 12 months before death and be occupying premises as only or principal home at time of death.[21]	Must be occupying as only or principal home immediately before death.
What kind of tenancy does successor get?	Spouse/civil partner/co-habitee gets statutory tenancy. Family member gets assured tenancy.	The tenancy of the deceased: secure or introductory tenancy.	The tenancy of the deceased: assured or assured shorthold tenancy.
Number of successions	Two are possible only if first succession (to a statutory tenancy) is by spouse/civil partner/co-habitee and second succession (to an assured tenancy) is by a person who is a family member of both original and the successor tenant.	One only. Joint tenancy becoming sole tenancy = one succession. If there has been an assignment to a potential successor no 'further' successions possible.	One only. Only a sole assured tenancy carries a right of succession.

---

21 It is not necessary that the 12 months' residence is of the premises occupied at the time of death. This means that there can be succession to a tenancy granted less than 12 months before the death of the tenant providing the successor was living with the deceased tenant for at least 12 months before the death: *Waltham Forest v Thomas* (1992) 24 HLR 622.

4.32   In the table the term 'co-habitee' refers to a person who is living with the tenant as the tenant's husband or wife or as if they were civil partners.

Demoted tenants and succession

4.33   There is a right of succession to a demoted tenancy. However, the conditions are different from the conditions for succession to a secure or introductory tenancy. Any family member (including spouse or civil partner) who occupies the premises as his or her only or principal home at the time of death may succeed to the tenancy but he or she must have resided with the tenant for a period of 12 months ending with the tenant's death.[22] If there is more than one potential successor, the spouse or civil partner is preferred; if there is no spouse or civil partner, a co-habitee (defined as one who lived with the deceased as a couple in an enduring family relationship, whether of the opposite or same sex) is preferred. Family members are defined in the same way as for secure tenants (see paras 3.39–3.40 below).[23] If the potential successors cannot agree who shall succeed the landlord will select the successor.[24]

Joint tenancies

4.34   Under the Housing Acts 1985 and 1988 it is specifically provided that where a joint tenant has become a sole tenant he or she is treated as a successor and no further succession is possible. When a joint tenant dies the other tenant becomes the sole tenant not by succession but by 'survivorship' (ie he or she was already a joint tenant and becomes a sole tenant simply by having survived the other joint tenant). This is not a succession but the surviving sole tenant is treated as a successor.[25] However, this is not the case if a secure tenancy became a sole tenancy before the Housing Act 1980 came into force.[26] This means that whenever there is a joint tenancy there is no possibility of a statutory succession. However, some local authorities and registered social landlords operate policies whereby, in certain circumstances, they will grant a 'non-statutory succession' to another family member. In reality this takes effect as the grant of a new tenancy to the family member (see below at paras 4.48–4.51).

22   HA 1996 s143H(1).
23   HA 1996 s143P.
24   HA 1996 s143H(5)(b).
25   HA 1985 s88(1)(b); HA 1988 s17(2)(b).
26   *Birmingham CC v Walker* [2007] UKHL 22, 16 May 2007.

4.35   Under RA 1977 there is nothing to prevent a succession to a sole statutory tenancy where the deceased tenant had previously been a joint statutory or protected tenant with another person.

Meaning of 'residing with' the deceased tenant

4.36   'Staying with' the deceased tenant or being physically present in the premises is not sufficient: 'residing with' means making a home with the deceased tenant.

> In *Freeman v Islington LBC*[27] the person claiming the right of succession was the tenant's daughter. She had owned her own flat for many years but had let it out from time to time and when her father became ill she started staying with him to care for him, initially three nights a week but eventually she was staying with him full time. For most of the year before her father died she had left her own flat unoccupied but let it out on an assured shorthold tenancy shortly before he died. Despite finding that the daughter had stayed with her father full time for the year before his death a possession order was made on the basis that she had not established that she was 'residing with' him during that period.
>
> She appealed to the Court of Appeal which upheld the judge's decision: residing with a person meant making one's home in the premises, and '... the retention of another home, whilst not fatal, can be a significant factor in deciding that a person was not making their home in the premises in question'.[28] Although it was accepted that by the time of her father's death the appellant has made the premises her home, it was held on the facts that she could not establish that it had been her home for the previous 12 months. Her appeal was dismissed and the possession order upheld.

Common problems

Evidence of residence

4.37   When a tenant dies the potential successor should notify the landlord and he or she will be asked for evidence of residence. For family members, a specific period of residence with the tenancy is necessary: for secure and introductory tenancies this is 12 months and for statutory

27 [2009] EWCA Civ 536, 11 June 2009.
28 Jacob LJ at [22].

tenancies it is two years. Landlords sometimes indicate that only certain kinds of documentary evidence will be accepted. However, the issue is a factual one and any evidence confirming a person's residence should be obtained and submitted. Letters and witness statements from neighbours and friends may be obtained although evidence from more neutral and/or official sources, such as doctors or teachers, the Department for Work and Pensions (DWP) or HM Revenue and Customs (HMRC), are likely to be more persuasive.

4.38 Occupiers in receipt of housing benefit are required to declare who is in occupation of the premises. Because this usually results in a reduction of benefit some occupiers falsely declare that they live alone. Local authority landlords with access to this information may suggest that this is decisive and proves that the potential successor was not living in the property. Obviously, such evidence is relevant but there may be other evidence strong enough to persuade an authority (or a court) that the declaration was untrue and that the succession conditions are satisfied. In *Freeman v Islington LBC*, above, para 4.36 above, the fact that the deceased tenant had stated in his housing benefit application that he lived alone was one of many factors that led to the finding that his daughter had not, at that time, made her home with him despite staying with him on a regular basis.

Relationship between successor and deceased tenant

4.39 Where the relationship is that of spouse or civil partner, documentary evidence of identity and marriage or civil partnership will be required. In relation to secure and introductory tenancies, the family members are defined in HA 1985 s113. They are: a person living with the tenant as husband and wife or as civil partner; parents, grandparents, children and grandchildren; brothers and sisters; uncles, aunts, nephews and nieces. 'Children' does not include foster children.[29]

4.40 Relationships of marriage or civil partnership are treated as relationships of blood. This means that the relative of a person's spouse or civil partner is treated as a relative of that person. Half (blood) relatives are included, step-children are treated as children of the step parent and illegitimate children are treated as the legitimate children of the mother and the reputed father.

4.41 Disputes may arise with regard to 'co-habitees'. It is not enough to be residing in the premises and to be in an intimate relationship with

---

29 *Sheffield CC v The Personal Representatives of June Wall, Steven Wall, Robert Ingham & Theresa June Butler* [2010] EWCA Civ 922, 30 July 2010.

the deceased tenant; the quality of the relationship must be similar to that of marriage or civil partnership.

> In *Nutting v Southern Housing Group*[30] the gay partner of a deceased assured tenant claimed he was entitled to succeed to the tenancy. The case was heard before the Civil Partnership Act 2004 was in force but it had been established that gay couples could live together as if they were husband and wife and thereby qualify for succession.[31] However, the court rejected the claim on the basis that the relationship did not have the necessary characteristics such that it could be said that they were living together as if they were husband and wife. The two men had lived together for just over two years before the tenant's death. The relationship was characterised by alcohol abuse and the tenant had obtained a non-molestation order at one point against the appellant. However, it was accepted that the appellant was living with the tenant immediately before his death.
>
> On appeal by the tenant the court upheld the decision. The tests applied by the judge, and approved by the appeal court, included: whether the relationship was one of mutual lifetime commitment rather than one of convenience, friendship, companionship or the living together as lovers; and whether the relationship was one that had been presented to the outside world openly and unequivocally so that society considers it to be of permanent intent. The appeal was dismissed, the judge had been entitled to find that the appellant had failed to demonstrate that the relationship displayed a sufficient commitment to permanence to meet the test.

More than one potential successor

4.42   It is possible for more than one person to be qualified to succeed to a tenancy. In such cases, the way the successor is selected is different in each Act.

HA 1985: secure and introductory tenancies[32]

4.43   The tenant's spouse or civil partner is preferred over other members of the family. If there is no spouse or civil partner the family members should agree who will be the successor and, if no agreement is possible, the landlord may select the successor.

---

30   [2004] EWHC 2982 (Ch).
31   *Mendoza v Ghaidon* [2004] UKHL 30, 21 June 2004.
32   HA 1985 s89(2).

HA 1988: assured and assured shorthold tenancies[33]

4.44 The issue is determined by agreement between the potential successors and, in the absence of agreement, by the county court. The problem is unlikely to arise under the Housing Act 1988 as it would require a spouse or civil partner *and* a co-habitee to be living with the deceased at the time of death.

RA 1977: statutory tenancies[34]

4.45 The tenant's spouse or civil partner is preferred over other members of the family. If there is more than one person entitled to succeed, the potential successors should agree who will be the successor and, if no agreement is possible, the issue will be determined by the county court.

Succession by children

4.46 A child can succeed to a tenancy provided the relevant conditions are satisfied. If the deceased tenant leaves a will appointing a personal representative or trustee, the tenancy is held on trust by that person until the child becomes an adult. The child holds an equitable tenancy that automatically becomes a legal tenancy when he or she reaches the age of 18. Where no person is expressly appointed as trustee the tenancy will usually be held on trust by the landlord until the child reaches the age of 18. See para 1.139 for an explanation of trusts and legal and equitable interests.

> In *Kingston upon Thames RLBC v Prince*[35] the tenant of a three-bedroom house died, leaving in occupation his adult daughter who had lived with him for six months and his 13-year-old granddaughter who had lived with him for three years. The local authority served notice on the daughter requiring her to vacate. Possession proceedings were issued against the daughter and a possession order made. An application was made to join the granddaughter and to set aside the possession order. The application was granted and the circuit judge dismissed the authority's appeal, making a declaration that the tenancy was held by the daughter on trust for the granddaughter until she reached the age of majority; further, the tenancy had been so held since the death of the tenant. The

33 HA 1988 s17(5).
34 RA 1977 Sch 1 Pt 1 para 2.
35 (1999) 31 HLR 794.

authority appealed, arguing that a minor could not hold a legal estate and there was no provision in the 1985 Act for the creation of secure equitable tenancies.

The Court of Appeal held that a minor can hold an equitable tenancy of any property, including a council house. Property law provided that where a legal estate in land was granted to or devolved to a child it operated as a trust, with the legal estate held by a trustee for the benefit of the child and that there was nothing to stop a local authority granting to a child a tenancy effective in equity.[36] The authority's appeal was dismissed.

Succession and rent arrears

4.47   Where the tenant dies owing rent arrears these do not become the responsibility of the successor.[37] The debt is, however, owed by the deceased tenant's estate and it may be the case that the successor is also the personal representative and beneficiary of the estate as next of kin. If so, he or she is responsible for paying the arrears from the estate. A landlord cannot make it a condition of succession that arrears are paid as the succession takes effect as a matter of law and is not 'granted' by the landlord. However, if a suspended or postponed possession order is in existence and it is a condition of the order that the arrears are cleared by instalments, the successor tenant is bound by the order and may be evicted if the instalments are not paid and the arrears cleared.

Succession and housing benefit

4.48   Even where there is a dispute about whether the conditions for succession are satisfied, as a matter of law, if the conditions are satisfied, the tenancy vests in the successor automatically on the death of the tenant. Those claiming a right to succeed who qualify for housing benefit should ensure that an application is submitted as soon as possible. Where the succession is disputed the application may be

---

36   The tenant had died before the Trusts of Land and Appointment of Trustees Act 1996, which now governs such trusts, was in force. However, the Court of Appeal held that this did not change the previous position. See also *Alexander-David v Hammersmith & Fulham LBC* summarised at para 1.144 which deals with the position when an authority expressly grants a legal tenancy to a minor.

37   See *Tickner v Clifton* [1929] 1KB 207.

suspended but, if the right to succession is subsequently established, benefit will be payable from the date of the application.[38]

'Non-statutory' succession

4.49 Some social landlords operate what are usually called 'non-statutory' succession schemes. This means an agreement or policy that 'succession' will be allowed in certain circumstances even where the 'successor' does not qualify under the relevant statute. Some local authorities operate such policies in relation to the children of deceased tenants who would be entitled to succeed if the original tenancy had not been a joint tenancy.

4.50 Furthermore, under large scale voluntary transfers of local authority properties to non-local authority providers, tenants who were originally secure become assured with less generous succession rights. Most such tenants are given enhanced rights by way of 'non-statutory' succession to those family members who would have been entitled to succeed to the secure tenancy. Despite the name a tenancy granted to such a person is not 'succession' at all; it is the grant of a new tenancy.

4.51 Where local authorities operate such policies they must be reflected in the allocation policy since the grant of a new tenancy is an allocation governed by HA 1996 Part VI (see chapter 17).

Disputes about non-statutory succession

4.52 To benefit from a non-statutory succession scheme a person will have to satisfy the conditions of the particular scheme. As is the case for statutory succession, a dispute may arise about whether the conditions are met. The way such disputes are resolved will depend on whether the right to non-statutory succession is part of a policy or is a term of the tenancy agreement.

4.53 Where the concession is operated as a policy by a local authority, and is part of the general allocation scheme, a refusal to grant a tenancy could be challenged by way of judicial review.[39] However, the issue may arise in possession proceedings and the occupier may assert the entitlement to non-statutory succession as a defence to the claim.

---

38 Housing benefit should be paid regardless of whether the succession is established, where the 'successor' occupies the premises as a home. Such an occupier has a liability to make payments equivalent to rent even if in unlawful occupation, see paras 9.10–9.11.

39 See *R v Lambeth LBC ex p Trabi* (1997) 30 HLR 975, QBD.

4.54   If the scheme is part of a non-local authority landlord's policy, judicial review will only be possible if the landlord is deemed to be a public authority (see para 2.72).

4.55   An alternative remedy would be to make a formal complaint followed by an Ombudsman complaint.

4.56   If, instead of a policy, the provision for non-statutory succession is contained in the tenancy agreement, a problem may arise as to whether the agreement can be enforced by a person who was not party to the agreement. If the tenancy agreement was entered into on or after 11 November 1999 this should not be a problem: the person claiming the tenancy can rely on the Contracts (Rights of Third Parties) Act 1999 which provides that a person may enforce a contract if the contract 'purports to confer a benefit' on him or her.

Localism Act 2011: changes to succession for secure tenants

4.57   The Act will limit statutory succession of secure tenancies, including flexible tenancies (see paras 3.195–3.208), to a spouse or civil partner (including someone living with the tenant *as if they were* a spouse or civil partner) living in the premises, as only or principal home, with the deceased tenant at the time of death. Succession to other family members will be possible only where there is no spouse or civil partner in occupation and there is an express term of the tenancy making provision for a person other than the spouse or civil partner to succeed.

4.58   This will only apply to tenancies which came into being on or after this provision of the Localism Act 2011 comes into force, which is likely to be a date sometime after April 2012. The above provisions will therefore still apply to succession to tenancies which started before that date.

Assignment

4.59   An assignment is the transfer of the tenancy during the life of the tenant. The person who transfers the tenancy is the 'assignor' and the person to whom the tenancy is transferred is the 'assignee'. The effect of an assignment is that the assignee becomes the tenant of the landlord under the same tenancy agreement. For this reason, in most well drafted leases assignment is permitted only with the landlord's consent.

4.60   An assignment is the transfer of a legal interest in land and to be valid must be done by deed.[40] An attempt to assign by deed that does not comply with the relevant formalities may, however, still be effective between the parties to the assignment although it will not bind the landlord.[41] References in this section to assignor and assignee refer to the parties to a valid assignment by deed.

4.61   The general rule is that tenancies, as legal interests in land, are capable of being assigned. However, that does not necessarily mean that the statutory security of tenure enjoyed by the tenant can also be assigned. Each Act specifies the limited situations in which a tenancy can be transferred to someone else so that that 'statutory security' is also transferred.

Rent Act 1977

4.62   A protected tenancy is capable of assignment but, if assignment is prohibited under the terms of the tenancy, the landlord may have a ground for possession against the assignee.

4.63   A statutory tenancy, being personal to the statutory tenant, is not capable of assignment, other than in matrimonial proceedings, see paras 12.73 and 12.79.[42]

Housing Act 1985

4.64   The Housing Act 1985 provides that a secure tenancy is not capable of assignment save in three situations.[43] These are set out in HA 1985 s91(3):

- assignment by way of mutual exchange;
- assignment made pursuant to a court order in certain matrimonial, civil partnership or Children Act proceedings;
- assignment to a potential successor.

4.65   Any assignment in circumstances other than those expressly permitted under HA 1985 s91(3) will be ineffective to transfer the secure tenancy; the assignee will become the tenant but the tenancy will no

---

40 Law of Property Act 1925 s52.
41 Law of Property (Miscellaneous Provisions) Act 1989 s2: if evidenced in writing it may take effect as an enforceable contract for the assignment.
42 RA 1977 also makes provision for the transfer of a statutory tenancy by written agreement with the landlord: Sch 1 para 13. However, it is impossible to imagine why a landlord would enter into such an agreement.
43 HA 1985 s91(1).

longer be secure. The assignee will have a contractual tenancy only which the landlord can terminate by service of notice to quit. Furthermore, as the original secure tenant will have parted with possession of the whole of the premises he or she cannot regain secure status by taking back possession of the premises assigned (see para 4.108).

Mutual exchange

4.66   It is a term of every secure tenancy that the tenant has the right to exchange his or her tenancy with another secure tenant or with an assured tenant of a social landlord provided both parties have the written consent of their respective landlords, see paras 4.67–4.73.

Consent

4.67   The landlord can only withhold consent to an assignment of a secure tenancy on certain grounds which are set out in HA 1985 Sch 3. If the landlord withholds consent for reasons not set out in HA 1985 Sch 3, consent is deemed to be given.[44] The grounds upon which consent can be refused are:

1) either tenant is obliged to give up possession under a court order;
2) proceedings have been commenced under Grounds 1 to 6, or notice of seeking possession under one or more of those grounds has been served (Grounds 1 to 6 are the 'tenant's fault' grounds, see appendix to chapter 7);
3) the accommodation is substantially more extensive than is reasonably required by the assignee;
4) the extent of the accommodation is not reasonably suitable to the needs of the assignee and family;
5) the accommodation was let to the tenant in consequence of employment, relating to non-housing purposes;
6) the assignment would conflict with the purposes of a landlord who is a charity;
7) the premises are adapted for a disabled person;
8) the assignment would conflict with the purposes of a landlord who is a specialist housing association or trust;
9) the accommodation is sheltered accommodation;
10) the property is managed by a housing association and the assignee refuses to become a member of the housing association.

---

44 HA 1985 s92(3).

4.68 If consent is sought and the landlord wishes to withhold consent the landlord must give notice to the tenant stating the ground upon which consent is withheld and giving particulars. This notice must be served within 42 days of the tenant's application. If no notice is served within the 42 days the landlord loses the right to withhold consent on any of the specified grounds. However, in the absence of any response, consent is not deemed to have been given. The tenant must therefore persuade the landlord to give consent, on the basis that the landlord has lost the right to refuse consent, or apply to the court for an order that the landlord must give consent. The tenant cannot simply proceed as if consent had been given.

4.69 The county court has jurisdiction to resolve issues regarding secure tenancies, including issues about the giving or withholding of consent under HA 1985 Sch 3.[45]

4.70 Where the tenant is in arrears of rent or is otherwise in breach of the tenancy agreement the landlord can give conditional consent, requiring the tenant to pay the outstanding rent or remedy the breach: HA 1985 s93(5). A landlord can give such conditional consent even after the 42-day period has expired: HA 1985 s93(6). Otherwise, the landlord is not entitled to impose a condition on the giving of consent and any condition imposed can be disregarded by the tenant.

4.71 So a tenant can proceed if:

- the landlord gives written consent;
- consent is withheld for reasons other than those specified in HA 1985 Sch 3;
- consent is given subject to conditions other than relating to arrears of rent or the remedying of a breach of the tenancy agreement;
- conditions attached relating to rent arrears or other breach are met.

4.72 In all cases the other tenant must also have the written consent of his or her landlord.

4.73 The tenant cannot proceed if the landlord has failed to respond to the request for consent.

Rent arrears

4.74 Landlords will always insist that rent arrears are cleared before an exchange can proceed. It is sometimes the case that the exchanging tenant is so keen to move that he or she will offer money so that the other tenant can clear his or her arrears. Advisers should be aware that if payment is made by either tenant as part of the agreement to

45 HA 1985 s110.

exchange this provides the landlord with a ground for possession. The ground is a discretionary one and where a landlord has been aware of the transaction made to clear arrears the court is unlikely to grant a possession order.

Matrimonial or Children Act assignment

4.75   In divorce or judicial separation proceedings the court can, under the Matrimonial Causes Act 1973, order one party to assign a tenancy to the other party, see chapter 12. It is more usual now for a transfer of tenancy to be ordered under the Family Law Act 1996. Under Family Law Act 1996 it is the court order that actually transfers the tenancy. Under Matrimonial Causes Act 1973 the transfer happens when the parties enter into a deed of assignment and if they fail to do this the tenancy is not transferred.[46]

4.76   The Matrimonial and Family Proceedings Act 1984 also gives the court the power to order assignments where divorce proceedings take place abroad.

4.77   Under the Children Act 1989 Sch 1 a court can make orders for the assignment of tenancies for the benefit of children (see chapter 12).

4.78   Assignments pursuant to court orders made under these Acts are effective to transfer the secure tenancy into the name of the assignee.

Assignments to potential successors

4.79   It is possible to assign a secure tenancy to a person who would, if the tenant died, be qualified to succeed (see para 4.31 above). This enables a tenant who wishes to move out of the premises to transfer the tenancy to a family member before doing so. It is important that the assignment is done before the person moves out. The tenancy must be secure at the date of the assignment. If the tenant has ceased to occupy the premises as his or her only or principal home the tenancy will no longer be secure and this right will have been lost (see para 3.116 above).[47]

4.80   If an assignment to a potential successor is made there can be no succession when the assignee tenant dies.[48]

---

46   *Crago v Julian* (1991) 24 HLR 306, CA.
47   HA 1985 s95 specifically provides that the restrictions on assignment under HA 1985 s91 apply also to a tenancy that ceases to be secure because the tenant condition is not satisfied.
48   HA 1985 s88(16)(d).

Landlord's consent

4.81 Other than for mutual exchange, there is no requirement under HA 1985 that the tenant must obtain the landlord's consent to an assignment. However, the tenancy agreement itself may require that the landlord's consent be obtained. If so, an assignment without the landlord's consent will be effective to transfer the secure tenancy but will be a breach of the tenancy agreement. This will give the landlord the right to seek possession against the assignee. The ground is discretionary so the court would have to be satisfied not only that the assignment was in breach of the agreement but also that making a possession order was reasonable.

4.82 Where a tenancy agreement provides that consent must be sought, the landlord must not withhold consent unreasonably.[49]

4.83 If a secure tenancy has been assigned without the landlord's consent a request for consent can be made retrospectively. The landlord must still consider the request and, if reasonable, give consent. If a landlord refuses to respond to a request and seeks possession against the assignee, the court would take this into account when considering whether it was reasonable to make a possession order. The likely outcome is that the court would refuse to make an order if it found that the landlord would not have had any reasonable grounds on which to refuse consent.[50]

4.84 Even if the tenancy agreement prohibits assignment absolutely, if the necessary conditions are satisfied, the assignment will be effective to transfer the secure tenancy to the assignee. However, the landlord could claim possession against the assignee tenant for breach of the tenancy agreement.[51] Again, an order would be made only if the court considered it reasonable to make a possession order.

Introductory tenancies

4.85 Introductory tenancies cannot be assigned except in the following circumstances:[52]

- an assignment on relationship breakdown or for the benefit of children, as for secure tenancies;
- an assignment to a potential successor.

4.86 An introductory tenant does not have the right to mutual exchange.

---

49 Landlord and Tenant Act 1927 s19(1).
50 *Leeward Securities Ltd v Lilyheath Properties Ltd* (1983) 17 HLR 35, CA.
51 See *Peabody Donation Fund v Higgins* (1983) 10 HLR 82, CA.
52 HA 1996 s134.

Demoted tenancies

4.87   A demoted tenancy cannot be assigned except on relationship break-down or for the benefit of children.[53]

4.88   A demoted tenant does not have the right to mutual exchange or to assign to a potential successor.

Housing Act 1988

4.89   When advising an assured tenant about assignment the starting point is the tenancy agreement. Most written agreements will either prohibit assignment absolutely or permit assignment only with the landlord's consent. If the agreement is silent, or there is no written agreement, Housing Act 1988 may imply a term prohibiting assignment.

4.90   HA 1988 s15(2) provides that where a periodic tenancy agreement makes no provision about assignment it is an implied term that the tenant cannot assign the tenancy without the consent of the landlord. However, this does not apply if the tenant has paid a premium.[54] Where such a term is implied the landlord can refuse consent for any reason.[55]

4.91   So the situation for assured and assured shorthold tenancies is:

Terms of agreement	Result
Agreement prohibits assignment	Assignment not possible.
Agreement permits assignment with the consent of the landlord	Consent required and must not be unreasonably withheld.
Agreement is silent	Periodic tenancy (no premium paid): assignment not possible without landlord's consent and landlord may withhold consent for any reason. Fixed-term tenancy or periodic tenancy where premium paid: assignment is possible and the landlord's consent is not required.

---

53 HA 1996 s143K.

54 This is a payment made for the grant of the tenancy but also includes a deposit that is more than two months' rent: HA 1988 s15(4).

55 Under Landlord and Tenant Act 1927 s19 where the landlord's consent is required it is an implied term that such consent shall not be unreasonably withheld. However, this is specifically excluded by HA 1988 s15(2).

4.92 Even where assignment is absolutely prohibited a landlord may agree to an assignment. However, the landlord is entitled to refuse and need not have any reason.

Subletting

What is subletting?

4.93 Subletting is when a tenant creates a tenancy out of his or her interest, but remains in the position of tenant against a higher landlord. This is distinct from an assignment where the tenant transfers the whole of his or her interest to someone else. In an assignment the assignee becomes the tenant of the landlord. The relationship between the parties is shown in the diagram below:

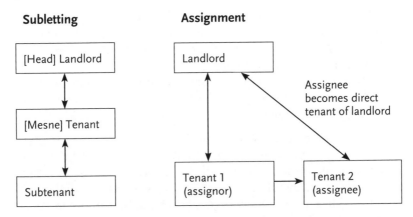

4.94 There is no limit to the number of subtenancies of the same premises so long as each subtenancy is shorter than the tenancy out of which it is created. There may also be joint tenants or joint landlords at each level.

4.95 Subletting must be distinguished from lodging (which creates a licence). For subletting the hallmarks of a tenancy must be present: the grant of exclusive possession, for a period of time, in return for rent (see paras 1.29–1.34). In situations where the tenant shares the accommodation with another person it is more likely to be an arrangement of lodging than subletting (see para 1.26).

4.96 For the purpose of this section it is assumed that there are three parties only: the head landlord; the mesne tenant;[56] and the subtenant.

---

56 'Mesne' means 'intermediate'. It is pronounced 'mean'.

The issues

4.97   The questions that arise are:

- Is a tenant allowed to sublet?
- What happens if a tenant who isn't allowed to sublet does so?
- What happens to a subtenant when the mesne tenancy ends?

4.98   The answers to these questions depend on the terms of the tenancy agreement and the statutory provisions that apply to the tenancy. There is a distinction between subletting part of the premises and subletting the whole of the premises.

Is the tenant allowed to sublet?

4.99   Apart from secure tenancies where the position is governed by statute, the starting point is the tenancy agreement:

- if the tenancy agreement permits subletting, it is allowed;
- if the tenancy agreement permits subletting only with the landlord's consent, consent must be sought but the landlord must not unreasonably withhold consent;
- if the tenancy agreement prohibits subletting, it is not allowed;
- if the tenancy agreement is silent (or there is no tenancy agreement) the answer depends on the type of the tenancy.

4.100   It should be noted that where a tenant sublets in breach of the tenancy agreement the landlord may 'waive' the breach if he or she, knowing of the breach, confirms the existence of the tenancy. This may make an unlawful subletting lawful. Waiver is generally only established by positive, intentional acts and not by a failure to act.

Rent Act tenancies

Subletting part

4.101   A protected or statutory tenant may sublet part of the premises. However, if subletting is prohibited or subject to the landlord's consent and consent is not obtained, it will be a breach of a term of the tenancy agreement. This gives the landlord a ground for possession but the ground is discretionary so the court would have to be satisfied that it is reasonable to make a possession order.

Subletting the whole

4.102   Subletting of the whole of the dwelling is only possible if the tenancy is protected, ie still within the contractual period. However, there is a ground for possession where a tenant has sublet the whole without the landlord's consent. This applies even if the tenancy agreement does not prohibit subletting, see appendix to chapter 7.

4.103　If the tenancy has become statutory, subletting the whole will result in the loss of the tenancy: a statutory tenancy lasts only if and so long as the tenant resides in the premises.

Secure tenancies

4.104　The right of a secure tenant to sublet is entirely governed by statute.

Subletting part

4.105　A secure tenant may take in lodgers without the consent of the land-lord[57] and has a right to sublet part of the premises with the written consent of the landlord.[58]

4.106　HA 1985 s94 sets out detailed provisions regarding consent and provides:

- consent cannot be unreasonably withheld: s94(2);
- consent cannot be given subject to conditions: s94(5);
- if the tenant applies in writing for consent and the landlord refuses consent, a written statement of reasons must be given: s94(6)(a);
- in deciding whether to give consent, relevant issues include whether the subletting would lead to overcrowding and any proposed works that would affect the subtenant's accommodation: s94(3);
- if the landlord neither gives nor refuses consent, or fails to reply within a reasonable time, consent is treated as being withheld: s94(6) (b);
- in contrast, if a landlord refuses consent unreasonably, or gives consent subject to a condition, consent is treated as being given unconditionally: s94(2) and (5).

4.107　Any issue regarding consent may be dealt with by a county court.[59] A tenant may apply for an injunction or declaration or the issue may arise in possession proceedings. If there is an issue as to whether consent was withheld unreasonably, it is for the landlord to show that it was not: HA 1985 s94(2).

57　HA 1985 s93(1)(a).
58　HA 1985 s93(1)(b).
59　HA 1985 s110.

Subletting the whole

4.108   HA 1985 s93(2) provides that a secure tenant who sublets or parts
with possession of the whole premises ceases to be secure and cannot subsequently become secure.[60]

Introductory tenancies

Subletting part

4.109   Whether an introductory tenant can sublet part of the premises will
depend on the terms of the tenancy agreement. In most cases it will
be prohibited or subject to the landlord's consent.

Subletting the whole

4.110   Although there is no specific prohibition on subletting for introductory tenancies HA 1996 s124(5) provides that an introductory tenancy
ceases to be an introductory tenancy if the circumstances are such that
a secure tenant would no longer be secure. Subletting of the whole
would therefore mean that the tenancy ceased to be introductory.

Assured tenancies and assured shorthold tenancies

4.111   Whether or not subletting is allowed depends on the terms of the tenancy agreement. If the agreement is silent, in most cases the Housing Act 1988 implies a term prohibiting subletting. The term is not
implied into fixed-term tenancies or to tenancies where the tenant
has paid a premium to the landlord for the grant of the tenancy.[61] In
most of those cases the tenancy agreement will make specific provision about subletting.

4.112   So for a periodic tenancy where there is no written agreement or
no specific provision, subletting is prohibited and a landlord may
refuse consent to subletting for any reason.[62]

4.113   For most assured and assured shorthold tenants, therefore, subletting, whether of part or the whole, will be prohibited, either expressly
in the tenancy agreement or by implication, under HA 1988 s15.

---

60   This is in contrast to a tenant who ceases to be secure because of not occupying
the premises as only or principal home. Such a tenant can become a secure
tenant again by re-occupying but a tenant who sublets the whole cannot regain
secure status.

61   HA 1988 s15(3).

62   HA 1988 s15(1)(b) and (2).

What happens if a tenant who is not allowed to sublet does so?

4.114   If a tenant is prohibited from subletting this does not mean that a subtenancy created by the tenant is invalid or void. The subtenancy will create the relationship of landlord and tenant between the mesne tenant and the subtenant. However, if it is in breach of the mesne tenancy agreement this will usually give the head landlord the right to end the mesne tenancy and take possession. In most cases the subtenant will have no right to remain in possession against the head landlord.

4.115   The positions of the tenant and the subtenant must be considered separately.

The tenant

4.116   A subletting in breach of the tenancy agreement gives the landlord a ground for possession: breach of a term of the tenancy agreement. Furthermore, for secure and assured tenants a subletting of the whole will mean that the mesne tenant no longer occupies the premises and thereby loses the secure or assured status. A landlord may therefore serve notice to quit on the mesne tenant and claim possession on the basis that the tenancy has ended following expiry of the notice to quit.

The subtenant

4.117   The fact that the subletting is in breach of the mesne tenancy agreement does not give the head landlord a right to possession against the subtenant without first ending the mesne tenancy. Landlords who discover that their tenant is no longer in occupation sometimes serve notice on the occupiers/subtenants, indicating that they are in unlawful occupation and must leave. This is not the case; the subtenant is lawfully occupying under the subtenancy until the point at which the mesne tenancy is brought to an end. A landlord cannot take any action, whether through the courts or otherwise, to take possession against a subtenant until the mesne tenancy is terminated.

4.118   Moreover, the fact that the subtenancy is in breach of the mesne tenancy agreement does not give the mesne tenant the right to possession against the subtenant. The mesne tenant has created a binding subtenancy agreement. Unless the subtenant agrees to give up possession the mesne tenant can only obtain possession by serving the appropriate notice and obtaining a possession order against the subtenant.[63] An attempt to gain possession forcibly will be unlawful under the Protection from Eviction Act 1977, see paras 8.23 and 8.81.

What happens to a subtenant when the mesne tenancy ends?

4.119   The general rule is that when a mesne tenancy ends, any subtenancies or licences also come to an end and the head landlord is entitled to possession of the premises.

4.120   However, for subtenants in this situation, there are two common law exceptions. A subtenant may become the direct tenant of the head landlord in the following situations:

- where the mesne tenancy is ended by surrender (see para 4.122);[64]
- where the mesne tenancy is ended by forfeiture (see paras 4.123–4.124).

4.121   In addition, the Rent Act 1977 and the Housing Act 1988 make specific provision for subtenancies and set out the circumstances in which a subtenant may become a direct tenant, with statutory protection, against a head landlord (see paras 4.125–4.128).

Surrender

4.122   Surrender is an agreement between a tenant and a landlord that the tenancy is given up, see paras 1.68–1.78. The landlord must agree to the surrender and, in doing so, takes back the premises subject to any rights and interests created by the tenant. For this reason when a mesne tenant surrenders the tenancy, the subtenant becomes the direct tenant of the head landlord. This applies whether or not the subtenancy is in breach of the tenancy agreement.

> The unusual case of *Basingstoke and Deane BC v Paice*[65] illustrates how this doctrine operates. The tenancy was of commercial premises owned by the local authority. The tenant of the commercial premises carried out works to create a dwelling within the premises which he then sublet. The authority subsequently accepted the

---

63   A subtenancy granted by a private individual to another private individual after 28 February 1997 will usually be an assured shorthold tenancy. See paras 6.43–6.54 for information about possession claims against assured shorthold tenants.

64   *Parker v Jones* [1910] 2 KB 32.

65   (1995) 27 HLR 433, CA.

surrender of the tenancy of the commercial premises, at which point the subtenant became the direct tenant of the authority. As the landlord and tenant conditions were satisfied the tenancy was a secure tenancy.

Forfeiture

4.123 Forfeiture is described in more detail at paras 5.7–5.23. It is a common law remedy giving the landlord the right to end a fixed-term tenancy if the tenant breaches the terms of the agreement. If the tenant is able to remedy the breach he or she may apply to a court for 'relief against forfeiture' which restores the lease. Subtenants may also apply for relief against forfeiture and the court may make an order effectively transferring the tenancy to the subtenant.

4.124 However, relief against forfeiture depends on the tenant or subtenant being able to remedy any breach. If the breach complained of is the unlawful subletting (as opposed to, say, rent arrears owed to the head landlord), relief will not be granted to the subtenant because the breach cannot be remedied by the subtenant.

Rent Act tenancies

4.125 RA 1977 s137 provides that if certain conditions are met a subtenant may become the protected or statutory tenant of the head landlord when the mesne tenancy ends. The conditions are that:

- the tenancy (ie, the agreement between the head landlord and the mesne tenant) must be a 'statutory protected tenancy';
- the subtenancy (ie, the agreement between the mesne tenant and the subtenant) must be a protected or statutory tenancy; and
- the subtenancy must be lawful.

4.126 These conditions will rarely be satisfied for the following reasons:

- if the head tenancy is a statutory tenancy under RA 1977 this will end if the statutory tenant no longer resides in the premises;
- if the statutory tenant shares the premises with the subtenant he or she will be a resident landlord which means that the subtenancy cannot be protected or statutory;
- most written tenancy agreements prohibit subletting so that the subtenancy will not be lawful.

Housing Act 1988

4.127 If there is a lawful subletting to an assured subtenant he or she becomes the assured tenant of the head landlord when the mesne tenancy ends.[66] If the subtenancy is an assured shorthold tenancy the subtenant will become the assured shorthold tenant of the head landlord.

4.128   It should be noted that the subtenancy must be a lawful assured subtenancy, ie one which is permitted under the mesne tenancy agreement.

Obtaining information about the landlord

4.129   Tenancies may be created with little formality; no documentation is necessary and negotiations are often conducted by agents. A tenant may therefore be in a legally binding relationship but have little information about the identity of his or her landlord.

4.130   Various statutory provisions assist a tenant who wishes to know the name and address of his or her landlord (paras 4.131–4.138). In addition, tenants have other wasys of obtaining information, see paras 4.139–4.141.

Requesting information

4.131   The Landlord and Tenant Act (LTA) 1985 s1 provides that a tenant of a dwelling can make a written request for the landlord's name and address to any person demanding rent or who last received rent, or to anyone acting as the landlord's agent. The person receiving the request must supply to the tenant a written statement of the landlord's name and address within 21 days.

4.132   If the landlord is a company the tenant may make a further written request to the landlord for the name and address of every director and the secretary of the company: LTA 1985 s2. The request may be made to the agent or the person who demands rent and must be forwarded to the landlord 'as soon as may be'. The landlord must provide this information within 21 days of receiving the request.

Change of landlord

4.133   If the landlord sells or otherwise transfers his or her interest the new landlord must inform the tenant of his or her name and address no

---

66   HA 1988 s18. This is not possible, however, if the tenancy is excluded by Schedule 1 to the Act.

later than two months after the transfer, or if rent is not payable within that two-month period, no later than the next day on which rent is payable: LTA 1985 s3.[67]

4.134 If the tenant is not informed of the new landlord's name and address the previous landlord remains liable for any breach of the tenancy agreement (for example, disrepair) up to the date when notice is given.[68]

Criminal penalties

4.135 The sanction for failure, without reasonable excuse, to give information to tenants about the identity of the landlord is that the landlord, or rent collector or agent, can be prosecuted. The penalty for offences under LTA 1985 ss1, 2 and 3 is the same: a fine, not exceeding level four, currently £2,500. Such cases are not prosecuted by the police but by local authorities.

4.136 It is often the case that a tenant is seeking information about the landlord because of complaints about disrepair. Local authorities' Environmental Health or Housing Standards departments may assist the tenant, but prosecutions are rare. The withholding of rent will often be sufficient to force a landlord to provide the information required but tenants must be advised clearly that any rent withheld becomes payable as soon as the landlord gives the information, see below, para 4.137.

Withholding rent

4.137 Under LTA 1987 s48 a landlord must provide a tenant with an address in England and Wales at which notices may be served on the landlord by the tenant. If the landlord fails to do so any rent or service charge otherwise due to the landlord shall be treated as not being due 'at any time before' the landlord complies. Advisers should note that the tenant's liability for the rent is not extinguished by the landlord's failure to give this information: the moment the landlord gives the information the whole of any unpaid rent or service charge becomes payable.

---

67 Some tenants have the 'right of first refusal' and must, under LTA 1985 s3A, be served with notice to that effect.
68 LTA 1985 s3(3A).

4.138   The information need not be given in a specific notice; it is sufficient if the information is stated in the tenancy agreement or in a
possession notice.[69]

The Land Registry

4.139   Most land in England and Wales is registered at the Land Registry.
The Land Registry records the name and address of the registered
proprietor and any registered charges (mortgages). It should be noted
that the registered proprietor may not be the landlord. Any member
of the public can request this information for any address by completing a form (form 313: Who Owns That Property?) available to
download from the Land Registry website at www. landreg.gov.uk.
The current fee payable is £4.00.

Data Protection Act 1998

4.140   For tenants of social landlords (or other large-scale landlords) useful
information may be obtained under the Data Protection Act 1998.
However, the Act covers information held on the 'data subject' rather
than on the landlord. See paras 2.98–2.101 and the appendix to
chapter 2.

Housing Act 1985 – housing applications

4.141   Under HA 1985 s106(5) a person may obtain information held by a
housing authority in relation to an application for housing.

Deposits

4.142   In the private sector most landlords insist that the tenant pays a
returnable deposit as well as rent in advance at the start of the tenancy. Because of the difficulty faced by many tenants in recovering the
deposit at the end of the tenancy, the Housing Act 2004 introduced a
compulsory scheme under which private landlords granting assured
shorthold tenancies must deal with deposits in a certain way. The
provisions are set out in HA 2004 ss212–215 and apply to any deposit
received on or after 6 April 2007.

---

69 *Rogan v Woodfield Building Services Ltd* (1994) 27 HLR 78; *Drew-Morgan v
Hamid-Zadeh* (2000) 32 HLR 316.

Tenancy deposit schemes

4.143   The Localism Act 2011 will amend the tenancy deposit scheme to counter the effect of the cases referred to below (paras 4.154–4.155). The amendments are indicated in brackets in the text. They are expected to come into force in early 2012.

4.144   The scheme provides that:

- the landlord must protect any deposit in a certain way; and
- the landlord must, within 14 days of receiving the deposit (the Localism Act 2011 will change this to 30 days), give to the tenant prescribed information and must comply with the requirements of the particular deposit scheme being used.

4.145   A landlord's failure to comply means that:

- an application may be made to a county court and the landlord ordered to pay a sum equivalent to three times the amount of the deposit (the Localism Act 2011 will change this to a sum between the amount of the deposit and three times that amount); and
- the landlord may not claim possession (unless there are grounds) until the requirements have been complied with.

Deposit paid by third party

4.146   The rights of tenants in relation to deposits are also given to 'any relevant person'. This is defined as 'any person who, in accordance with arrangements made with the tenant, paid the deposit on behalf of the tenant'.[70] This may include a local authority operating a tenancy deposit scheme whereby deposits are paid to landlords to facilitate the granting of an assured shorthold tenancy. Prescribed information must be given to such a person and an application to the county court may be made by such a person, even if the tenant does not wish to take action.

Protecting the deposit

4.147   'Tenancy deposit' is defined as 'money intended to be held ... as security for – (a) the performance of any obligations of the tenant, or (b) the discharge of any liability of his, arising in connection with the tenancy.'[71]

---

70 HA 2004 s213(10).
71 HA 2004 s212(8).

4.148　　　Any tenancy deposit paid to a person in connection with a short-hold tenancy must, as from the time when it is received, be dealt with in accordance with an authorised scheme.[72] Furthermore, the landlord must comply with the 'initial requirements' of the authorised scheme within 14 days from the date of receipt (the Localism Act 2011 will change this to 30 days).[73] There are two types of authorised scheme:

- *Custodial schemes:* the landlord pays the deposit into a deposit protection scheme. There is presently one such scheme – the Deposit Protection Services (DPS). The DPS is a government-authorised scheme that is free to use. Transactions can be made online.
- *Insurance based schemes:* the landlord keeps the deposit but pays a premium for an insurance policy against which the tenant can claim if the landlord fails to return the deposit.

4.149　Information about the options for landlords is available on the government website: www.directgov.uk.

Dispute resolution

4.150　The tenancy deposit schemes are intended to ensure that the tenant is able to recover the deposit at the end of the tenancy. Disputes may arise about whether the landlord is entitled to withhold the deposit or part of it because of damage caused by the tenant or unpaid bills. The authorised schemes also provide a dispute resolution mechanism to resolve such issues as between the landlord and the tenant.

Prescribed information

4.151　Within 14 days (the Localism Act 2011 will change this to 30 days) of receiving the deposit the landlord or agent must give certain prescribed information to the tenant and to any relevant person (ie, the person who actually paid the deposit, see para 4.146 above).[74] The prescribed information is:

- contact details of the scheme administrator where the deposit is held;
- information provided by the scheme administrator to the landlord explaining the requirements of the HA 2004 in relation to deposits;

72　HA 2004 s213(1).
73　HA 2004 s213(3).
74　HA 2004 s213(5) and (6); Housing (Tenancy Deposits) (Prescribed Information) Order 2007 SI No 797. In addition HA 2004 states that the landlord must comply with the initial requirement of the particular scheme being used, within 14 days. A particular scheme may require other information to be given to the tenant.

- the procedures for recovering the deposit at the end of the tenancy, including the procedures applying if either the landlord or tenant cannot be contacted;
- the procedures applying where there are disputes about the amount to be returned and the facilities available for resolving disputes;
- information about the tenancy and the deposit: the amount paid, the address of the property, and the contact details of the landlord and the tenant which will be used by the administrator of the scheme at the end of the tenancy;
- the circumstances in which all or part of the deposit may be retained by the landlord;
- confirmation by the landlord that the information given is accurate to the best of his or her knowledge or belief and that he or she has given the tenant the opportunity to sign to confirm that the information is accurate to the best of the tenant's knowledge and belief.

Sanctions for non-compliance

County court action

4.152 Where a deposit has been paid and any of the above requirements (paras 4.148–4.151) have not been met, or the scheme administrator has not confirmed that the deposit is being held in accordance with the scheme, an application may be made to the county court.[75] The application may be made either by the tenant or the person who paid the deposit.

4.153 If the court is satisfied that:

- the initial requirements of the particular scheme have not been complied with;
- the prescribed information has not be provided; or
- the deposit is not being held in accordance with an authorised scheme,

the court *must* make an order that:

- the person who appears to be holding the deposit either repay it to the applicant, or pay it into the designated account of an authorised custodial scheme; and
- that the landlord pays to the applicant a sum equal to three times the amount of the deposit within 14 days (the Localism Act 2011 will change the amount to a sum between the amount of the deposit and three times that amount).

75 HA 2004 s214.

4.154   Although HA 2004 s213 provides that the landlord must comply with the requirements within 14 days of receiving the deposit, for the purpose of a section 214 application Court of Appeal held that the relevant date is the date of the hearing, so a landlord can avoid the penalty of paying three times the deposit by complying before the hearing.[76]

4.155   Furthermore, the sanctions in HA 2004 s214 only apply during the life of the tenancy. A former tenant cannot make an application under section 214 after the tenancy has ended.[77] (the Localism Act 2011 amends HA 2004 s214 to provide that a former tenant can make an application after the end of the tenancy.)

Non-monetary deposits

4.156   It is unlawful for a person to require a deposit that consists of property other than money in connection with an assured shorthold tenancy.[78] However, if such a deposit is taken, the property is 'recoverable' from the person holding it.[79] There is no specific provision for a county court claim but a person seeking the return of such a deposit may bring an ordinary action in the county court. It is unclear whether a claim for three times the value of the non-monetary deposit may also be made.

Restriction on possession proceedings

4.157   No notice requiring possession, under section 21 of the HA 1988 (see chapter 6), may be given by a landlord 'at any time when':[80]

- the deposit is not being held in accordance with an authorised scheme;
- the initial requirements of the particular scheme being used have not been complied with;
- the prescribed information has not been given to the tenant; or
- a non-monetary deposit has been taken and not returned to the tenant.

---

76 *Tiensa v Vision Enterprises Ltd; Honeysuckle Properties v Fletcher, McGrory and Whitworth* [2010] EWCA Civ 1224, 12 November 2010.

77 *Gladehurst Properties Ltd v Hashemi & Johnson* [2011] EWCA Civ 604, 19 May 2011.

78 HA 2004 s213(7).

79 HA 2004 s214(5).

80 HA 2004 s215.

4.158 The Localism Act 2011 also provides that this restriction on the HA 1988 section 21 notice will not apply where the deposit has been returned to the tenant in full or with deductions agreed between landlord and tenant or where an application has been made under HA 2004 s214 and has been decided by the court, withdrawn or settled by agreement between the parties.

4.159 It is the *giving* of the notice that is prohibited during a period of non-compliance and so, if a notice has already been served, the landlord cannot make the notice good by subsequently complying with HA 2004 s213. The landlord will have to comply with the deposit requirements and then serve a fresh section 21 notice. The provisions do not prevent a landlord from serving a notice seeking possession where there are grounds for a possession order to be made (for example, rent arrears or nuisance).

4.160 The claim form used under the accelerated procedure (form N5B) requires a landlord to provide evidence that the deposit is safeguarded with an authorised tenancy deposit scheme. The tenant has the opportunity to dispute the landlord's statement in the defence form (form N11B).

4.161 If proceedings are brought under the accelerated procedure the court should refuse an order if it is satisfied that the landlord has not complied with the relevant requirements. If there is a dispute between the landlord and the tenant regarding compliance a hearing should be listed for the dispute to be resolved.

4.162 A tenant may wish to apply for an order under HA 2004 s214 (see paras 4.152–4.153 above) at the same time as disputing the claim for possession. Under the accelerated procedure the landlord cannot make a money claim so, arguably, the tenant's application cannot be brought as a 'counterclaim'. A tenant may indicate on the defence form that he or she wishes to apply for an order under section 214. However, given the consequences for the landlord (being ordered to pay three times the deposit) and the fact that the court has no discretion, the court may be unwilling to deal with a tenant's application in this way. A safer course of action would be to issue a separate claim against the landlord[81] and request that the court list the claim for consideration at the same time as hearing the claim for possession.

---

81 Such a claim must be brought under Part 8 of the Civil Procedure Rules. See paras 22.104–22.107.

Unfair contract terms in tenancy agreements

4.163   The Unfair Terms in Consumer Contracts Regulations (UTCCR) 1999[82] apply to contracts between 'suppliers' and 'consumers', including tenancy agreements. To apply, the following conditions must be met:

- The tenant must be an individual not acting in the course of a trade, business or profession.
- The landlord may be an individual or a company, but must be acting for purposes relating to his or her trade, business or profession, whether publicly or privately owned.
- The agreement or particular term must not have been individually negotiated. Where an agreement is in a pre-formulated standard contract the terms will always be regarded as not having been individually negotiated. However, if a particular term has been agreed expressly between the parties that term will not be subject to the regulations. If it is argued that a term was individually negotiated the burden is on the landlord to show that it was.

4.164   UTCCR 1999 apply to tenancies granted by registered providers and local authorities as well as private landlords.[83]

When is a term unfair?

4.165   Under the regulations: 'A contractual term ... shall be regarded as unfair if, contrary to the requirements of good faith, it causes a significant imbalance in the parties' rights and obligations arising under the contract to the detriment of the consumer.'[84] But, significant imbalance alone is not sufficient: the term must also be contrary to the requirements of good faith, for example a term that is expressed unclearly or where the consumer's inexperience or lack of understanding is exploited.

---

82   UTCCR 1999 SI No 2083 came into force on 1 October 1999. They replaced the 1994 Regulations SI No 3159, which applied to all contracts entered into on or after 1 July 1995. The purpose of the 1994 Regulations was to give effect to a European Community Directive, effective from 1 January 1995. There is therefore an argument that the 1994 Regulations (and the 1999 Regulations) apply to contracts entered into by emanations of the state, including local authorities, as from 1 January 1995.

83   *Newham LBC v Khatun, Zeb, Iqbal & OFT* [2004] EWCA Civ 55.

84   UTCCR 1999 reg 5(1).

UK Housing Alliance (North West) Ltd v Francis[85] concerned a sale and leaseback scheme under which the property was sold and a tenancy granted by the purchaser to the seller for a period of 10 years. 70 per cent of the purchase price was to be paid on completion with 30 per cent paid at the end of the tenancy. The tenant (consumer) argued that a term in which the final payment could be withheld if the tenancy ended early (because of the tenant's breach) was an unfair term.

The Court of Appeal held that the term was not unfair: it did not create a significant imbalance between the parties and as it was 'fully, clearly and legibly' expressed the tenant could not say that he had been taken advantage of unfairly.[86]

4.166   The assessment of fairness does not apply to:[87]

- the definition of the main subject matter of the contract (for example, the extent of the letting); or
- the 'adequacy of the price or remuneration, as against the goods or services supplied' – in the context of tenancy agreements this would exclude an argument that the rent is excessive. Other provisions may be used to challenge excessive rents, see below, paras 4.181–4.190.

Plain language

4.167   The landlord must ensure that any written tenancy agreement is expressed in plain, intelligible language. If there is any doubt about the meaning of a written term, the interpretation most favourable to the consumer shall prevail.[88]

Effect of unfair terms

4.168   An unfair term is not binding on the tenant. However, the remainder of the tenancy agreement continues to be binding provided it can operate in the absence of the unfair term.

---

85   [2010] EWCA Civ 117, 8 February 2010.
86   Longmore LJ at [29].
87   UTCCR 1999 reg 6(2), although such terms must be in 'plain intelligible language' and could be challenged under the regulations if not.
88   UTCCR 1999 reg 7.

Enforcing the regulations

4.169   The Office of Fair Trading (OFT) can take legal action to prevent the use of unfair terms. In September 2005 the OFT produced guidance on terms considered potentially unfair in assured and assured short-hold tenancies. The guidance can be downloaded from the OFT web-site at: www.oft.gov.uk. Complaint may be made to the OFT about particular agreements but the OFT cannot become involved in indi-vidual disputes.

4.170   For tenants it is more likely that the issue will arise in court pro-ceedings when a landlord is seeking to rely on the disputed term. The tenant must indicate in the defence that the particular term is alleged to be unfair. If the court finds that the term is an unfair term under UTCCR 1999, it is unenforceable.

Examples of unfair terms in tenancy agreements

4.171   In the following cases the courts have considered the application of UTCCR 1999 to tenancy agreements.

> In *Camden LBC v McBride*,[89] Central London County Court considered the application of the previous regulations to a 'nuisance' clause in a local authority tenancy agreement. The clause prohibited the tenant from doing anything which in the landlord's opinion might be or become a nuisance.
>
> The court held that the term was unenforceable and unfair because the question of its breach was to be determined subjectively by the landlord.

> In *Cody v Philps*[90] the tenancy agreement contained a clause that prevented the tenant from making any 'set-off' or deduction whatsoever against rent. The tenant had a claim for damages for disrepair and wished to set off the damages awarded against the agreed rent arrears.
>
> West London County Court found that the clause was contrary to good faith and caused significant imbalance between the parties. It was therefore unfair and unenforceable; the tenant was entitled to set off the damages against the arrears of rent.

89 [1999] 1 CL 284.
90 January 2005 *Legal Action* 28.

4.172 UTCCR 1999 Sch 2 sets out a non-exhaustive list of terms that may be regarded as unfair. Furthermore, the OFT guidance[91] suggests a number of terms in tenancy agreements that would be considered unfair. These include:

- clauses that allow the landlord to determine whether the tenant is in breach of contract;
- clauses that give the landlord the final decision as to whether repairs have been properly done, or whether work is rechargeable to the tenant;
- clauses that require the tenant to go through an arbitration process before he or she can go to court;
- clauses that give the landlord an excessive right of access to the property;
- clauses that require a tenant to pay a 'penalty' charge for breach that is in excess of the landlord's loss; this would include excessive interest charged on late rent;
- excessive restrictions on day-to-day use of the property.

4.173 However, the OFT cannot determine whether a term is or is not unfair. Only the courts can decide whether a term is unfair and therefore whether it is enforceable.

Rents

4.174 Under a tenancy agreement the amount of rent payable is agreed between the parties and, if there is a written agreement, the rent will be stated in the agreement. Provision may be made for rent to be increased in the future. This may be expressed to be by a fixed amount or to be calculated by a specific formula. Alternatively, the agreement may simply give the landlord the right to increase rent on a periodic basis, the amount to be determined by the landlord.

4.175 If the agreement provides that no rent is payable it is unlikely to be a tenancy. If a rent-free tenancy *is* created the tenant will have few rights (see paras 1.101 and 1.112–1.113).

4.176 In all cases where a tenant has substantive security of tenure it is a ground for possession that the tenant has failed to pay rent 'lawfully due'. It is therefore crucial to understand how rents are set and increased.

---

91 See the OFT Guidance on unfair contract terms in tenancy agreements published in September 2005 and available from the OFT website.

Rents in the private sector

4.177   Rent control was effectively abandoned by the Housing Act 1988: the rents for assured and assured shorthold tenancies are expected to be market rents. Although assured shorthold tenants have the right to challenge a rent that is significantly higher than the market rent, the fact that such a tenant has no long-term security means that such challenges are rare. Assured tenants may challenge rent increases only if the tenancy agreement makes no provision for rent increases, and any challenge will be on the basis that the proposed increase is in excess of a market rent.

Rent Act 1977: fair rents

4.178   Prior to 15 January 1989 private and housing association tenants enjoyed a high level of rent control. Under the Rent Act 1977, regardless of what was agreed between the parties, either the tenant or the landlord could apply for the rent to be 'registered' by a rent officer. The rent registered would be a 'fair rent', assessed by discounting from the appropriate market rent any sum deemed attributable to the scarcity of accommodation. The registered rent became the maximum rent a landlord could charge. Furthermore, the only way a landlord could increase the rent was by applying for a registered rent, or for an increase in a rent previously registered. Most remaining Rent Act tenants will already have a registered rent. If not, a Rent Act tenant can apply for a fair rent to be registered for the first time.

4.179   Both private tenants (protected or statutory) and housing association (secure) tenants whose tenancy began before 15 January 1989 have the right to fair rents under RA 1977 Parts III and IV. The features of fair rents are as follows:

- If there is a registered rent for a particular property, that is the maximum rent that the landlord can recover.[92] A rent registered in respect of a previous tenancy was binding even if the parties to a later tenancy were completely different.
- If there is no registered rent, the maximum rent the landlord can recover is the original contractual rent. The only way this can be increased is by an agreement complying with RA 1977 s51: see below, or by applying to the rent officer for a new (fair) rent to be registered.
- An agreement to increase the rent is only valid if it is in writing and complies with RA 1977 s51: it must include a statement that

92   RA 1977 s44(1).

the tenant's security of tenure will not be affected by a refusal to sign and that the agreement does not prevent a future application for a registered rent.[93]

- If a landlord purports to increase the rent, otherwise than under section 51 or by applying for a new rent to be registered, the tenant may recover from the landlord any rent overpaid over the previous two years.[94] Recovery may be made by deductions from future rent or by bringing a claim in the county court. Because of the limit on the period for which recovery can be made a claim should be made without delay.

- Where there is a registered rent the landlord can apply for an increase in the registered rent two years after it was last registered, unless there are other reasons justifying an increase, such as improvement works, or an increase in rates or service charges payable by the tenant. In such a case the landlord must still apply for a new rent to be registered and the decision as to the new rent will be made by a rent officer.

- Rent officers are employed by the Rent Service, a government agency. They value property both for the purposes of the registration of rents and for the setting of housing benefit levels. Usually a rent officer will inspect a property for the purpose of setting a fair rent or when asked to increase a fair rent. Information on the Rent Service and copies of relevant forms can be obtained from the Valuation Office Agency website: www.voa.gov.uk.

- Since 1999 there has been a cap on the level of increases to fair rents.[95] An increase cannot exceed a sum calculated as follows: the difference in the Retail Price Index at the date of last registration and the date of the current registration plus 7.5 per cent on the first increase after February 1999 and 5 per cent on any subsequent increase. However, this does not apply if repairs or improvements carried out by the landlord justify an increase in the rent.[96]

- If rent is increased following an application to a rent officer, the increased rent does not become payable until the landlord has served a valid notice of increase on the tenant in prescribed form.[97]

---

93 Furthermore, this information must be set out in 'characters not less conspicuous than those used in any other part of the agreement'.

94 RA 1977 s57. Where the overpayment of rent was because of a failure to comply with the technical requirement of section 51 the recovery period is one year: s54.

95 Rent Acts (Maximum Fair Rent) Order 1999 SI No 6.

96 Rent Acts (Maximum Fair Rent) Order 1999 art 2(7).

97 RA 1977 s45(2)(b) and (3).

4.180　The rents for tenancies granted by housing associations, housing trusts and the Housing Corporation that would have been protected tenancies, if it were not for the identity of the landlord, are also subject to the fair rent scheme.[98] Such tenancies must have been created before 15 January 1989.

Housing Act 1988: assured and assured shorthold tenancies

Challenging the agreed rent

4.181　An assured shorthold tenant can apply to a rent assessment committee for a determination of the rent.[99] An application can only be made in the first six months of the tenancy and must be made in prescribed form. If successive agreements are entered into by the same parties this does not revive the right to apply to the committee.

4.182　The assessment committee will make a determination only if:

- there are a sufficient number of similar dwellings let on similar tenancies in the locality; and
- the rent payable is 'significantly higher' than the market rent, having regard to the rents for those other dwellings.

4.183　If the assessment committee makes a determination, that becomes the maximum rent the landlord can recover.

4.184　Given that a landlord can evict an assured shorthold tenant as of right after six months, this right is seldom enforced.

4.185　An assured tenant has no right to challenge the agreed rent.

Rent increases and HA 1988 s13

4.186　HA 1988 s13 gives to some assured tenants[100] the right to refer proposed rent increases to a rent committee. It applies to:

- a statutory periodic assured tenancy; and
- any other periodic tenancy which is an assured tenancy, other than one in relation to which there is a provision, for the time being binding on the tenant, under which the rent for a particular period of the tenancy will or may be greater than the rent for an earlier period.[101]

4.187　So, HA 1988 s13 applies to a periodic tenancy that comes into being at the end of a fixed term. Any rent increase term in the fixed-term

---

98　RA 1977 s86.

99　HA 1988 s22.

100　This includes assured shorthold tenants but, because of their lack of security, is rarely used by such tenants.

101　HA 1988 s13(1)(b).

agreement does not become a term of the statutory periodic tenancy so as to displace section 13.[102] Where the tenancy has always been a periodic tenancy, section 13 applies only if there is no term in the agreement that provides for future rent increases.

4.188   It had often been argued that HA 1998 s13 was excluded only if there was a term that made provision for a specified increase at a future date. However, the Court of Appeal has held that this is not the case.

In *Contour Homes Ltd v Rowen*[103] the agreement was a periodic tenancy that included a term stating: 'The rent will be reviewed by the Association in April of each year. The Association shall give to the tenant no less than four weeks notice of the revised amount payable. The revised Net Rent shall be the amount specified in the notice of increase.' On receiving a notice of increase the tenant referred the notice to the Rent Committee under HA 1988 s13 but the committee decided that the notice was not in prescribed form, as required by section 13, and refused to deal with the referral. The landlords appealed against the decision to the High Court. Their appeal was dismissed, the court holding that section 13 applied being excluded only in relation to tenancies with a fixed agreed uplift and not to tenancies that simply reserved to the landlord the right to increase rent by serving notice.

The Court of Appeal upheld the landlords' further appeal: section 13 did not apply if there was *any* provision in the tenancy agreement for the rent to be increased if certain events occur, in this case the service by the landlord of a notice.

4.189   So, if the tenancy agreement makes provision for the landlord to increase the rent a tenant will have no right to challenge the increase on the basis that it exceeds a market rent. However, where a rent increase is imposed for the purpose of removing a tenant's security by taking the tenancy outside the provisions of the Housing Act 1988 it may be held to be unenforceable.[104]

4.190   If HA 1988 s13 does apply, a landlord must serve a prescribed notice on the tenant stating the proposed new rent. The increased rent cannot take effect before a certain date, being no earlier than

102 *London District Properties Management Ltd & Others v Goolamy & Goolamy* [2009] EWHC 1367 (Admin), 16 June 2009.

103 [2007] EWCA Civ 842, 26 June 2007.

104 *Bankway Properties Ltd v Pensfold Dunsford* [2001] EWCA Civ 528.

one year since the last increase. Furthermore, a certain period must elapse between service of the notice and the increase taking effect.[105] If the tenant wishes to object, he or she can refer the notice to a rent assessment committee. The referral must be made (ie, received by the committee[106]) before the increase takes effect. The committee will determine an open market rent which will be the maximum rent the landlord can charge. This may be done at a hearing. If a tenant wishes to challenge the rent as being in excess of a market rent he or she will need to provide evidence of market rents for similar properties in the locality.

4.191   Legal aid is not available for representation at committee hearings.

Varying the rent by agreement

4.192   A landlord and tenant under an assured tenancy agreement may agree a rent increase or any other variation of terms.[107]

Rents set by social landlords

Local authorities

Setting 'reasonable rents'

4.193   Local authorities may make such reasonable charges for the occupation of their dwellings as they determine and must from time to time review their rents: HA 1985 s24. Authorities therefore have a wide discretion as to how much rent to charge for their properties. However, the discretion is not absolute and an authority must act reasonably and take into account relevant considerations when deciding on rent levels. The 'relevant considerations' include the relevant legislation, the duty to balance the 'Housing Revenue Account' and the subsidies received. Section 24 also provides that an authority must have regard to the principle that rents of houses of any class or description should bear broadly the same proportion to private sector rents as the rents of houses of any other class or description. This does not mean that local authority rents should be similar to private sector rents but that the difference in market rents, say, for high rise flats, as compared to converted flats or houses, should also be reflected in local authority rents. In other words, the local authority rent for a desirable property should be more than for a less desirable property.

---

105 This varies, depending on the period of the tenancy, see HA 1988 s13(2)–(3).
106 *R on the application of Lester v London RAC* [2003] EWCA Civ 319, 12 March 2003.
107 HA 1988 s13(5).

4.194   In practice local authority rents remain substantially lower than private sector rents and are usually also lower than the rents charged by registered providers of social housing. The Localism Act 2011 will permit registered providers to charge rents to up to 80 per cent of market rents.

Increasing rents and challenging increases

4.195   Most local authorities increase rents on an annual basis. For secure and introductory tenancies rent can be increased by agreement between the parties or under the terms of the tenancy agreement. Furthermore, in respect of all periodic tenancies (which means almost all secure and introductory tenancies) a notice of variation may be served on the tenant to increase the rent. The increased rent cannot take effect before the end of a complete period of the tenancy, or four weeks, whichever is the longer period. A tenant who does not wish to pay the increased rent can serve notice to quit on the landlord to bring the tenancy to an end. However, the tenant would then lose his or her tenancy. Unlike other variations of terms the authority is not required to consult before increasing the rent (see para 3.142).

4.196   If an authority has acted unlawfully in setting the rent levels an application for judicial review may be made. A tenant has 'sufficient interest' to bring such an action. The decision must be shown to be unlawful under the usual principles of public law (see chapter 2). Alternatively, a challenge to the validity of a rent increase may be raised as a defence to possession proceedings.[108]

Registered social landlords

Setting rents

4.197   Housing association secure tenants have access to the fair rent regime under the Rent Act 1977, see above, paras 4.178–4.180. For the assured and assured shorthold tenants of registered providers the mechanism for challenging rents and rent increases is the same as for private tenants. However, they are regulated by the Tenant Services Authority (TSA).[109] The TSA has a 'Tenancy Standard' which covers allocations, rents and tenure, and registered providers are required to report on how they perform in relation to the Tenancy Standard.

---

108 *Wandsworth LBC v Winder (No 1)* [1984] UKHL 2, 29 November 1984.
109 The TSA replaced the Housing Corporation as the regulator of housing associations on 1 December 2008. However the TSA will be abolished in 2013 and its regulatory functions transferred to the Homes and Communities Agency.

The Tenancy Standard deals with rent increases and was revised in April 2011 to exempt the restrictions on rent increases for homes let on 'affordable rent terms', see para 4.200 below. It is available on the TSA website: www.tenantservicesauthority.org. Most social landlords (not-for-profit registered providers) will be amenable to a challenge by way of judicial review if they act unlawfully when making decisions about the rents they charge, see paras 2.68–2.74.

Rent increases

4.198   Registered Providers usually grant periodic assured and assured shorthold tenancies and most agreements will include a term providing for annual rent increases. In light of the Court of Appeal decision in *Contour Homes Ltd v Rowen*[110] (at para 4.188 above), it is not necessary for a landlord to serve a prescribed notice of increase under HA 1988 s13 and a tenant will have no right to challenge an increase by applying to a rent assessment committee.

4.199   If the agreement contains no provision for the increase of the rent, the landlord must follow the procedure set out in HA 1988 s13 and the tenant can challenge the proposed increase (see above para 4.190). However, it is unlikely that a rent assessment committee will uphold a challenge as the committee's remit is to set a market rent and rents for social housing tend to be much lower than market rents.

Affordable rents

4.200   Lettings by registered providers at so called 'affordable rents' have been possible since April 2010. An affordable rent can be set at up to 80 per cent of market rents. The Tenancy Standard requires that when a tenancy is offered on affordable rent terms the tenant must have an agreement of no less than two years. However, it is possible to grant a probationary tenancy for less than this period on affordable rent terms. Furthermore, there is no bar on periodic tenancies being offered on affordable rent terms. The current Tenancy Standard is an interim measure that will be in force pending a comprehensive review of the regulatory framework which will happen on the implementation of the Localism Act 2011, which will abolish the TSA and place regulation within the functions of the Homes and Communities Agency.

110 [2007] EWCA Civ 842.

CHAPTER 5

Leaseholders' rights

continued

Key points

- A 'long lease' for most purposes is a lease granted for a term of at least 21 years.
- A long lease may be ended (forfeited) by a landlord if the lease-holder breaches the lease. If the premises are residential the right of forfeiture can only be enforced by obtaining a posses-sion order.
- A landlord's right to forfeit the lease is restricted by statute: for-mal notice must be served and a lease cannot be forfeited for small amounts of arrears unless they have been outstanding for more than three years. Other breaches must be agreed or deter-mined by a court or tribunal before the landlord can start the forfeiture procedure.
- In all cases a leaseholder can apply to a court for relief against forfeiture.
- Long leases will set out the landlord's obligation to insure, repair and maintain the premises and the right to recover the cost of doing so from the leaseholder by way of service charges and administration charges.
- Leaseholders can challenge demands for service charges and administration charges. Only charges that are reasonable can be recovered.
- At the end of the lease a leaseholder may be able to remain in occupation as a statutory tenant.
- A leaseholder may also be able to extend the lease or force the landlord to sell the freehold.

Introduction

5.1 A 'lease' is an interest in land granted for a fixed period. The term 'lease' and the term 'tenancy' have the same meaning. The person who grants a lease may be referred to as the lessor or landlord and the person to whom the lease is granted, the lessee, leaseholder or tenant. In this chapter the terms 'landlord' and 'leaseholder' will be used.

5.2 A long lease is the same as any tenancy for a fixed period: the grant of exclusive possession for a specified period of time. How-ever, many of the statutory rights of periodic tenants or tenants with short fixed-term agreements (described in chapters 3 and 4) are not enjoyed by those whose tenancy or lease is for a long period of time.[1] Most of the rights and obligations of the landlord and the leaseholder are set out in the lease. However, long-leaseholders have some statutory rights over and above those contained in the lease. In most of the statutes that deal with these rights a long lease is defined as a lease for a fixed period of at least 21 years.

5.3   The rights of long-leaseholders are complex and contained in a number of different statutes. This chapter contains only an overview. Advice and information on leaseholders' rights may be obtained from LEASE, the Leasehold Advisory Service. LEASE is funded by the Department for Communities and Local Government, and the Welsh Government. Their website is at www.lease-advice.org and useful leaflets on different aspects of leaseholders' rights can be downloaded. In addition the website contains a list of solicitors and surveyors who claim expertise in leaseholders' rights.

5.4   This chapter examines briefly the following issues:

- forfeiture;
- service charges and administration charges;
- security of tenure at the end of the lease; and
- enfranchisement – the right to purchase the freehold or to extend the lease.

Key features of long leases

5.5   Some of the key features of a 'long lease', as distinct from a short-term tenancy, are summarised below:

- A fixed-term tenancy or lease for a period of three years or more must be created by deed.[2] See para 1.70 for the requirements of a deed.
- A long lease has a value and can be transferred (assigned) to another person (the assignee) in return for a sum of money (a premium).
- The 'rent' payable under a long lease is usually a nominal sum, often as little as £10 per year, referred to as 'ground rent'.

---

1   Such tenancies are excluded from the Rent Act 1977 and the Housing Act 1988 because they are at a low rent. They are expressly excluded from the Housing Act 1985.
2   Law of Property Act 1925 ss52 and 54.

- Most long leases will permit the assignment of the lease during the fixed term with the consent of the landlord. The landlord's consent must not be unreasonably withheld.
- Most long leases will also permit the leaseholder to sublet, again with the landlord's consent which must not be unreasonably withheld.
- The respective repairing obligations of the landlord and the leaseholder are set out in the lease. Section 11 of the Landlord and Tenant Act (LTA) 1985 (the landlords' implied repairing obligation (described in chapter 10)) does not apply to leases for a fixed period of seven years or more.
- A long lease will provide that the landlord carries out certain works of repair and maintenance and will also provide that the leaseholder must reimburse the landlord's costs by way of a service charge. Unreasonable service charges can be challenged by application to the Leasehold Valuation Tribunal (LVT).
- The main cost of a long lease is the purchase price or premium which will usually be funded by a mortgage and the lender will have the right to take possession if the terms of the mortgage are breached, see chapter 7.
- Leaseholders do not have statutory security of tenure during the term of the lease; their right to possession is by virtue the lease. However, at the end of the lease a statutory tenancy may come into being if the leaseholder is residing in the premises.
- Most long leases include a 'forfeiture' clause which entitles the landlord to end the lease and/or re-enter the premises if the leaseholder breaches the terms of the lease. The leaseholder has the right to apply to a court for 'relief against forfeiture' to have the lease re-instated.
- Many disputes between a landlord and a leaseholder can be determined by the LVT. However, claims for possession and relief against forfeiture are dealt with in the county court or the High Court.

Right to information

5.6 A leaseholder has the right to obtain information about the landlord in the same way as any other tenant. These rights include the right to be notified of the landlord's name and address and to be informed of a change of landlord. They are described in paras 4.131–4.136.

Forfeiture

5.7   A landlord only has a right to forfeit a lease if this is expressly provided in the lease. Most long leases contain a forfeiture clause. The
clause will usually state that if the tenant commits a breach of covenant or fails to pay rent the landlord may re-enter the premises and
the lease will come to an end. Alternatively, a lease may provide that
it is granted 'on condition that' or 'provided that' the tenant fulfils
certain obligations. This also gives the landlord a right of forfeiture.

5.8   At common law, the power of forfeiture was enforced by the landlord 're-entering' the land and taking possession. However, if there is
a residential occupier in the premises it is unlawful for a landlord to
re-enter without obtaining a possession order.[3] Furthermore, there
are now statutory restrictions on the right of forfeiture, described
below at paras 5.10–5.15.

5.9   A landlord may claim the right of forfeiture for the non-payment
of rent or for other breaches of the lease. The procedure for each
differs.

Forfeiture for rent arrears

Formal demand

5.10   The common law position was that a landlord who wished to forfeit
for the non-payment of rent must have made a formal demand for
payment. However, a lease could, and usually would, provide that
the landlord was exempt from this requirement. This loophole was
closed by the Commonhold and Leasehold Reform Act (CLRA) 2002
which provides that a long-leaseholder is not liable to pay rent unless
the landlord has served notice demanding payment.[4] The notice must
be in prescribed form and must state:

- the amount of the payment and the date by which it is payable;[5]
- the name of the leaseholder to whom notice is given;
- the period to which the rent demanded is attributable;

---

3 Protection from Eviction Act 1977 s2. If there is a residential occupier taking
   possession without obtaining a court order is both a civil wrong and a criminal
   offence. A further criminal offence would be committed under Criminal Law
   Act 1977 s6 if a landlord forcibly takes possession while a person is in the
   premises. These offences are described in paras 8.2–8.11 and 8.40–8.43.
4 CLRA 2002 s166(1).
5 The date payment is due must be no sooner than 30 days and no later than 60
   days after the notice is served and cannot be earlier than payment is required
   under the lease: CLRA 2002 s166(3).

- the name of the person to whom payment is to be made and the address for payment;
- the name of the landlord who is giving notice and the landlord's address;
- the information for landlords and tenants contained in the prescribed form.[6]

Restriction on forfeiture for small arrears

5.11 CLRA 2002 also provides that a landlord cannot forfeit a lease for unpaid rent, service charges or administration charges unless the total amount exceeds a prescribed sum, currently £350[7] or unless the total amount includes a sum that has been outstanding for more than a prescribed period, currently three years.[8]

Unpaid service charges and administration charges

5.12 Further protection is given by the Housing Act (HA) 1996 s81 which prevents a landlord from exercising a right of re-entry or forfeiture of premises let as a dwelling for the non-payment of service charge demands unless the amount claimed is either agreed or determined by a court or tribunal.[9]

Forfeiture for unpaid rent – tenant's rights

5.13 Where the landlord is applying to the court to enforce a right of re-entry or forfeiture for non-payment of rent, the County Courts Act 1984 s138 provides that the tenant has the following rights:

- The tenant can pay all of the rent arrears and costs into court at least five days before the first hearing date. If this is done the lease continues as if proceedings had not been issued.
- At the hearing the court must delay possession for at least four weeks during which the tenant has the opportunity to pay the

---

6 See CLRA 2002 s166 and Landlord and Tenant (Notice of Rent) (England) Regulations 2004 SI No 3096 and Landlord and Tenant (Notice of Rent) (Wales) Regulations 2005 SI No 1355.

7 This sum excludes any 'default' charge imposed for a failure to pay on time: CLRA 2002 s167(3).

8 CLRA 2002 s167(1) and Rights of Re-entry and Forfeiture (Prescribed Sum and Period) (England) Regulations 2004 SI No 3086 and Rights of Re-entry and Forfeiture (Prescribed Sum and Period) (Wales) Regulations 2005 SI No 1352.

9 The provision applies to all proceedings started on or after 24 September 1996.

arrears and costs. If the tenant pays in full, there is 'relief against forfeiture' and the lease continues.

- Within six months of the landlord actually taking possession, the tenant can apply to the court for relief against forfeiture.

Forfeiture for other breach

5.14   The Law of Property Act (LPA) 1925 s146 provides that before exercising a power of forfeiture for breaches other than the non-payment of rent a landlord must serve notice on the tenant, known as a 'section 146 notice'.

5.15   Under the Commonhold and Leasehold Reform Act 2002 s168 a landlord under a long lease cannot serve a section 146 notice unless:

- it has been finally determined on an application by the landlord to the LVT that the alleged breach has occurred; or
- the tenant has admitted the breach; or
- a court or tribunal has finally determined that the breach has occurred.

Section 146 notice

5.16   Where a landlord is claiming forfeiture for breaches other than the non-payment of rent the section 146 notice must:

- specify the breach complained of;
- if the breach is capable of remedy, require the leaseholder to remedy the breach;
- require the tenant to pay compensation to the landlord if required; and
- give the tenant a reasonable time to comply with the notice.[10]

Tenant's response

5.17   If the tenant remedies the breach within the specified period the landlord will be unable to exercise the power of forfeiture. Even if the tenant cannot remedy the breach or pay any compensation within the period, the tenant may still apply to the local county court for relief against forfeiture. However, if there is a residential occupier a claim for possession must be made in the county court, so it is more common for the leaseholder to make the claim for relief against forfeiture in response to the possession claim.

10 LPA 1925 s146(1).

5.18   The section 146 notice must be served on any subtenant who also has the right to seek relief against forfeiture.[11]

Relief against forfeiture

5.19   The right to relief is generally dependent on the leaseholder paying the arrears and the landlord's costs or otherwise remedying any breach.

5.20   However, the court's discretion when considering an application for relief against forfeiture is very wide and relief may be granted on terms. LPA 1925 s146(2) provides that:

> ... the court may grant or refuse relief, as the court, having regard to the proceedings and conduct of the parties ... and to all other circumstances, thinks fit; and ... may grant [relief] ... on such terms, if any, as to costs, expenses, damages, compensation, penalty, or otherwise, including the granting of an injunction to restrain any like breach in the future, as the court, in the circumstances of each case, thinks fit.

5.21   The courts have been generally reluctant to lay down principles to be applied in the exercise of the discretion.[12]

5.22   The court can order relief on terms that the lease be sold so that the leaseholder can benefit from the value of the lease and the landlord recover any monies outstanding.[13]

Waiver

5.23   A landlord may 'waive' the right to forfeit the lease by taking positive steps to confirm the existence of the lease while aware of the breach. However, this does not prevent a landlord from taking other action to enforce a covenant.

Service charges and administration charges

5.24   In addition to the payment of ground rent the lease will specify that the leaseholder must pay other sums as 'service charges' and 'administration charges'. Such charges are a common source of conflict

---

11 LPA 1925 s146(5).
12 See *Greenwood Reversions Ltd v World Environment Foundation Ltd and Madhav Mehra* [2008] EWCA Civ 47, in which the Court of Appeal dismissed the leaseholder's appeal against the refusal of relief.
13 *Khar v Delbounty Ltd* [1996] NPC 163, CA.

between landlords and leaseholders. Service charges and administration charges are only recoverable to the extent that they are reasonable and this may be determined by the LVT.

5.25   A landlord may only charge the leaseholder for costs incurred if the lease expressly provides this. A lease will usually set out a landlord's obligation for maintenance, repairs and other services and the right to be reimbursed by the leaseholder for the costs incurred. It will also set out how the charges are apportioned between different leaseholders in the same building or estate.

Service charges

5.26   A service charge is:

> an amount payable by a tenant of a dwelling as part of or in addition to the rent ... for services, repairs, maintenance, improvements or insurance or the landlord's costs of management, ... the whole or part of which varies or may vary according to the relevant costs.[14]

Administration charges

5.27   An administration charge is an amount payable by a leaseholder as part of or in addition to rent that is payable, directly or indirectly for costs relating to:[15]

- the consideration of and grant of approvals under the lease, for example, consent to alterations or subletting;
- the provision of information or documents by or on behalf of the landlord or a person who is party to the lease, other than between the landlord and leaseholder (for example, in connection with the sale of the leasehold);
- a failure by the leaseholder to make payments due under the lease;
- a breach or alleged breach of covenant or condition in the lease.

Demand for payment

5.28   Service charges and administration charges are not payable until a demand has been served on the leaseholder, accompanied by a summary of the rights and obligations of the leaseholder.[16] The demand

---

14 LTA 1985 s18(1).
15 CLRA 2002 Sch 11 para 1.
16 LTA 1985 s21B and CLRA 2002 Sch 11 para 4. The prescribed information is set out in the Service Charges (Summary of Rights and Obligations, and Transitional Provisions) (England) Regulations 2007 SI No 1257. The Welsh regulations are contained in 2007 SI No 3160.

must contain the name and address of the landlord. If the address is not in England or Wales an address in England or Wales must be given at which notices may be served on the landlord.[17]

Reasonableness of service charges

5.29 The Landlord and Tenant Act 1985 s19(1) provides that service charges can be recovered from the tenant:

(a) only to the extent that they are reasonably incurred; and

(b) where they are incurred on the provision of services or the carrying out of works, only if the services or works are of a reasonable standard;

and the amount payable shall be limited accordingly.

5.30 Furthermore, where a landlord can charge in advance of the costs being incurred, only a reasonable amount is payable and the landlord must make an adjustment after the costs have been incurred, including repayment where appropriate.[18]

5.31 In relation to a service charge demand the leaseholder may apply to an LVT for a determination as to:[19]

- whether costs incurred for services, repairs, maintenance, insurance or management were reasonably incurred;
- whether services or works for which costs were incurred are of a reasonable standard; or
- whether an amount payable before costs are incurred is reasonable.

5.32 In addition, either a landlord or a leaseholder may apply in advance to an LVT for a determination as to whether:

- costs for services, repairs, maintenance, insurance, or management of a specified description would be reasonable;
- services provided or works carried out to a particular specification would be of a reasonable standard; or
- what amount payable before costs are incurred would be reasonable.

5.33 However, no application to the LVT can be made in respect of a matter that has been agreed or admitted by the tenant, or which is subject to resolution by arbitration or where a court or tribunal has already made a determination.[20]

---

17 LTA 1987 s47.
18 LTA 1985 s19(2).
19 LTA 1985 s19(2A).
20 LTA 1985 s19(2C).

5.34   If the demand for payment includes a demand for costs incurred more than 18 months before the demand, those costs are not payable by the leaseholder.[21]

Information about service charges

5.35   Landlords must supply to leaseholders a statement of account for the charges made, no later than six months after the end of the accounting period.[22] This must be accompanied by an accountant's certificate and a summary of the leaseholder's rights and obligations (see para 5.28 above). Leaseholders may request facilities to inspect documents supporting the statement of account, such as receipts and estimates.

What is reasonable?

5.36   There is no definition of what is reasonable in the relevant legislation. Where the dispute is about whether works were necessary or about the standard of work carried out, expert evidence will usually be needed.

5.37   Costs are not necessarily unreasonable because it may have been possible to do works or provide services more cheaply. The question is whether the costs would have been incurred if the landlord had been responsible for bearing the cost. The issue of whether costs are reasonable is therefore decided from the landlord's perspective.

5.38   It should be noted that, even if it is decided that charges are unreasonable or the works not done to a reasonable standard, this does not mean that nothing is payable. The LVT will assess what is a reasonable amount.

Right-to-buy leases

5.39   There are additional restrictions on service charge demands for 'right-to-buy' leaseholders. During the right-to-buy process a landlord must provide information to the leaseholder about service charges including an estimate of the likely cost of repairs or improvements over the next five years.[23] For the five-year period the leaseholder cannot be required to pay service charges in excess of the estimated costs.

---

21 See LTA 1985 s20B(1) and *Paddington Walk Management Ltd v Governors of Peabody Trust* (2009) Central London County Court, 16 April 2009 and *Brent LBC v Shlum B Association Ltd* [2011] EWHC 1663 (Ch), 29 June 2011.

22 LTA1985 s21.

23 HA 1985 s125.

Right-to-buy leaseholders may also be entitled to a loan from the landlord if the service charges exceed a certain amount.[24]

Reasonableness of administration charges

5.40 The Commonhold and Leasehold Reform Act 2002 introduced similar controls in relation to administration charges. It provides that a variable administration charge is payable only to the extent that the amount of the charge is reasonable.[25]

5.41 A leaseholder can also apply to the LVT to vary the lease on the grounds that any administration charge specified in the lease is unreasonable or that any formula in the lease for calculating the administration charge is unreasonable.[26]

Consultation

5.42 Landlords must consult leaseholders before carrying out works above a certain value or entering into a long-term agreement for the provision of services.[27] If a landlord fails to consult in accordance with the regulations, the services charges recoverable may be capped.

> In *Daejan Investments Ltd v Benson & Others*[28] the landlords had failed to comply with the consultation requirements and the LVT held that it was not reasonable to dispense with the requirements. As a result the landlords could not recover the £270,000 they had spent on works to a block of flats, the amount recoverable being capped at £250 per leaseholder.
>
> The Court of Appeal dismissed the landlord's appeal. The landlord's argument that the financial effect of the grant or refusal of a dispensation was a relevant consideration was rejected by the Court of Appeal.

5.43 The consultation provisions are complex and different rules and costs thresholds apply depending on when the works were carried out. The requirements changed on 31 October 2003 in England and on 31 March 2004 in Wales.

24 HA 1985 s450A.
25 CLRA 2002 Sch 11 para 2.
26 CLRA 2002 Sch 11 para 3.
27 LTA 1985 s20 and Service Charges (Consultation Requirements) (England) Regulations 2003 SI No 1987.
28 [2011] EWCA Civ 38, 28 January 2011.

Unfair contract terms

5.44   Further protection for leaseholders may be found in the Unfair Terms in Consumer Contracts Regulations 1999. The regulations are described at paras 4.163–4.173 above.

Leasehold Valuation Tribunal

5.45   Disputes about the amount of service charges are mostly dealt with by the Leasehold Valuation Tribunal (LVT). The LVT is part of the Residential Property Tribunal Service. The forms used to make applications to the LVT are available online. Most cases are resolved at a hearing but the parties can agree to a determination without a hearing. The hearing will be before a three-person panel, and one of the panel will be a lawyer or a person experienced in land valuation. Hearings in London usually take place at the panel offices in central London. Outside London hearings are arranged near the location of the property in public buildings such as church halls and town halls.

5.46   Public funding is not available for legal representation at an LVT hearing but assistance to prepare for a hearing may currently be funded under the Legal Help scheme, see chapter 22.[29] As a general rule the LVT will not order a party to pay the legal costs of the other party but it can order a party to reimburse other fees incurred. It can also make an order to prevent a landlord from enforcing a term in the lease to recover legal costs incurred in taking or defending a claim in the LVT.[30]

5.47   An appeal from an LVT decision is made to the Upper Tribunal (Lands). Permission to appeal must be sought from the LVT within 14 days of the reasons for the decision being sent. If permission is refused an application may be made directly to the Upper Tribunal (Lands) for permission. Decisions of the Upper Tribunal are appealed to the Court of Appeal.

Security of tenure at the end of the lease

5.48   Subject to the landlord's right of forfeiture a leaseholder has exclusive possession and therefore a right of occupation during the term

---

29   Proposed changes to the legal aid scheme may mean that such help will not be available in the future.

30   LTA 1987 s20C.

of the lease. When the lease expires the leaseholder may continue to occupy under a statutory tenancy provided certain conditions are met. The main condition is that the leaseholder is occupying the premises as a 'home'. Whether the statutory tenancy is governed by the Rent Act 1977 or the Housing Act 1988 depends on when the lease commenced or expired. In each case the kinds of agreement that are excluded from the Act apply (see paras 3.19 and 3.92) save for the provision that excludes tenancies at a low rent.

5.49   If the lease expired before 15 January 1999 the tenant will be a statutory tenant under RA 1977.[31]

5.50   If the lease commenced after 1 January 1990 or expires after 15 January 1999 the statutory tenancy will be an assured tenancy under HA 1988.[32]

5.51   There are complex provisions regarding the service of notices by the landlord and the leaseholder. A landlord may serve notice either proposing the terms of a new assured tenancy or indicating an intention to seek possession. The leaseholder should respond by serving a counter notice. The leaseholder may wish to exercise the right to a lease extension or to purchase the freehold, see para 5.58 below. If so, it is essential that the relevant notices are served within the time limits otherwise the rights may be lost. Furthermore, if the landlord is proposing a new assured tenancy and the leaseholder fails to serve a counter notice, the leaseholder will be bound by the terms proposed by the landlord.

5.52   If no notice is served the lease continues on the same terms until the landlord does serve notice.

5.53   If the parties wish to enter into a new assured tenancy agreement but cannot agree on a new rent, an application can be made to the Rent Assessment Committee.

5.54   If the landlord wishes to obtain possession, an application must be made to the court and grounds must be proved before a possession order will be made.

Enfranchisement

5.55   Enfranchisement refers to the right of a leaseholder to force a freeholder to extend the lease or to grant a new one, or to sell the freehold. Rights of enfranchisement have developed and expanded over

31 LTA 1954 Pt X.
32 Local Government and Housing Act 1989 Sch 10.

the last 40 years and a number of different statutes apply. The qualifying conditions and procedures are extremely complex and outside
the scope of this book. A leaseholder who wishes to exercise the right
will need help from a specialist solicitor or surveyor. This section
contains only a brief summary.

Leaseholds of houses

5.56   Most long leases are of flats. However, it is also possible to hold a
long lease of a house and leasehold houses are common in some
parts of the UK. The rights of leaseholders of houses are set out in
the Leasehold Reform Act 1967. It gives leaseholders of houses the
following rights:

- the right to an extension of the lease for 50 years at no cost; or
- the right to purchase the freehold at an agreed price or a price
fixed by the LVT.

5.57   The Leasehold Reform Act 1967 applies to leases of 21 years or more
(when originally granted) and to some right-to-buy leases for a shorter
term.[33]

Leaseholds of flats

5.58   Most flats are held on long leases because they form part only of a
building. The Leasehold Reform, Housing and Urban Development
Act 1993 gives to the leaseholders of flats:

- the right to a new lease of 90 years for an agreed price or a price
set by the LVT; and
- the collective right of a group of leaseholders to purchase the freehold of the building – collective enfranchisement.

Collective enfranchisement

5.59   Where there are a number of leaseholders in a building, the right to
purchase the freehold depends on there being a minimum number
of 'qualifying tenants', a minimum proportion of whom must want
to exercise the right. The purchase will usually be made by a company formed by the leaseholders for this purpose.

5.60   Long-leaseholders may also rely on the rights in the Landlord and
Tenant Act 1987 Part I. This gives to qualifying leaseholders the right
of first refusal if the landlord proposes to dispose of the freehold. In

33 CLRA 2002 s76(2).

addition, under Part III of the Act there is a right to apply to a court for a compulsory 'acquisition order' if the following conditions are met:

- the freeholder is in breach of the obligations under the lease; or
- the freeholder cannot be found.

Commonhold

5.61   The Commonhold and Leasehold Reform Act (CLRA) 2002 created a new type of property ownership: commonhold. This allows for the ownership of individual commonhold units within a building or estate, the common parts being owned and managed jointly by the unit-holders through a commonhold association.

Right to manage

5.62   The CLRA 2002 also provides for a right to manage by way of a 'right to manage company' set up by leaseholders of flats. The leaseholders can force a transfer of the landlord's management functions to the company. The right is not dependent on the landlord being in default of the obligations under the lease.

Possession claims – procedure

continued

Key points

- Most residential occupiers cannot be evicted without a court order. Exceptions are 'excluded occupiers' and trespassers who entered as trespassers.
- In most cases formal notice must be given to the occupier before the claim can be issued. Some notices must be in prescribed form.
- Failure to serve valid notice may mean that the possession claim is struck out or dismissed.
- There are two types of ground for possession: mandatory grounds and discretionary grounds. Where the landlord is relying on a discretionary ground the court must be satisfied that it is reasonable to make a possession order.
- If the court makes an order on a discretionary ground it may also adjourn the claim, postpone possession or suspend enforcement when making the order or at any time up to the date of eviction.
- The enforcement of a possession order requires an application for a warrant. The warrant authorises court bailiffs to evict the occupiers.
- Even after eviction a warrant may be set aside on the grounds of fraud, abuse of process or oppression.

Introduction

6.1   Chapters 1 and 3 set out which tenants have substantive security of tenure, which occupiers have procedural security of tenure and which occupiers can be evicted without a possession order (see paras 1.101–1.121). Even occupiers with no substantive defence to a claim may nevertheless avoid eviction if the correct procedure has not been followed by the landlord. Furthermore, it is possible to use public law and the Human Rights Act 1998 to challenge evictions by public bodies, including registered providers of social housing. Such challenges are examined in paras 7.100–7.144. This chapter focuses on the procedural requirements, including:

- steps before serving notice;
- possession notices;
- issuing the possession claim;
- the hearing;

- the possession order;
- enforcing the order;
- possible action after eviction.

Steps before serving notice

6.2   A landlord who intends to take action against a tenant because of rent arrears or complaints of nuisance or who simply wants a tenant to leave the premises will usually contact the tenant before serving formal notice. There is no requirement that a private landlord contacts a tenant before serving formal notice but a failure to do so may be relevant if the court is considering whether it is reasonable to make a possession order. For social landlords, however, there are certain procedural requirements in relation to managing both rent arrears and complaints of nuisance.

Nuisance and anti-social behaviour

6.3   Social landlords usually have policies and procedures setting out the action they will take before deciding to seek possession. Under the Anti-social Behaviour Act (ASBA) 2003 social landlords must have a published policy stating how complaints of nuisance will be dealt with.[1] Usually this will include the investigations that will be undertaken before serving notice as well as the support that will be given to vulnerable tenants, both the perpetrators and the victims of anti-social behaviour. However, it should be noted that where serious anti-social behaviour is alleged, a claim for possession may be started at the same time as serving notice of seeking possession.

Rent arrears

Pre-Action Protocol

6.4   On 4 October 2006 a Pre-Action Protocol was introduced for possession proceedings brought by public sector landlords claiming possession on the grounds of rent arrears.[2] The Protocol can be downloaded

---

1   See Housing Act (HA) 1996 s218A inserted by ASBA 2003 s12, and the guidance, *Anti-social Behaviour: Policies and Procedure*, published in August 2004 and available at www.communities.gov.uk/documents/housing/pdf/138694.pdf

2   A similar Pre-Action Protocol for possession claims based on mortgage arrears was introduced in November 2008.

from: www.justice.gov.uk/civil/procrules. The Protocol sets out the steps that should be taken before serving notice and after serving notice but before the hearing.

6.5   The Protocol applies to all claims for possession of residential premises brought by social landlords (local authorities, registered providers and Housing Action Trusts) solely on the ground of rent arrears. It does not apply to claims in respect of long leases or where the occupier has no security of tenure (this would include assured shorthold tenants and non-secure tenants even if the reason for taking action is the existence of rent arrears). The Protocol has four sections, summarised below (paras 6.6–6.19).

(1) Initial contact

6.6   The landlord should contact the tenant when the tenant falls into arrears. The landlord and tenant should try to agree affordable sums for the tenant to pay towards the arrears. The landlord should provide quarterly rent statements and, if aware of difficulties in reading or understanding information, should take reasonable steps to ensure that the tenant understands any information given.

Tenants who are under 18 or vulnerable

6.7   If the landlord is aware that a tenant is under 18 or particularly vulnerable, the landlord should consider at an early stage:

- whether the tenant has capacity and, if not, an application for a litigation friend should be made;
- whether any issue arises under the Disability Discrimination Act 1995 (now the Equality Act 2010); and
- if the landlord is a local authority, whether there is a need for a community care assessment.

Housing benefit

6.8   The landlord should offer to assist the tenant in any claim the tenant may have for housing benefit. The landlord should not start possession proceedings against a tenant who can demonstrate that he or she has provided the authority with all evidence required to process the claim, that he or she has a reasonable expectation of eligibility and has paid other sums due not covered by housing benefit.

6.9   The landlord should make every effort to establish effective ongoing liaison with housing benefit department, and should, with the tenant's consent, make direct contact with the housing benefit department prior to taking enforcement action.

6.10   The landlord and tenant should work together to resolve any housing benefit problems.

6.11   The landlord should arrange for arrears to be paid by the Department for Work and Pensions (DWP) if the criteria are met.

(2) After service of statutory notices

6.12   After service of notice but before issue of proceedings the landlord should make reasonable attempts to contact the tenant to discuss the amount of arrears, the cause of the arrears, repayment of the arrears and the housing benefit position.

6.13   If the tenant complies with an agreement the landlord should agree to postpone court proceedings as long as the tenant keeps to the agreement.

6.14   If the tenant fails to comply with the agreement the landlord should warn the tenant of the intention to bring proceedings and give the tenant clear time limits within which to comply.

(3) Alternative dispute resolution

6.15   The parties should consider whether it is possible to resolve the issues by discussion and negotiation without recourse to litigation. The parties may be required by the court to provide evidence that alternative means of resolving the dispute were considered. Courts take the view that litigation should be a last resort, and that claims should not be issued prematurely when a settlement is still actively being explored.

(4) Court proceedings

6.16   No later than ten days before the hearing, the landlord should:

- provide to the tenant up to date rent statements;
- disclose what the landlord knows about the tenant's housing benefit.

6.17   The landlord should inform the tenant of the date and time of any court hearing and the order applied for. The landlord should advise the tenant to attend the hearing and should record such advice.

6.18   If the tenant complies with an agreement made after the issue of proceedings the landlord should agree to postpone court proceedings so long as the tenant keeps to the agreement.

6.19   If the tenant ceases to comply with the agreement, the landlord should warn the tenant of the intention to restore the proceedings and give clear time limits within which to comply.

Sanctions for non-compliance

6.20 The protocol states that, if the landlord unreasonably fails to comply with the terms of the protocol, the court may:

- make an order for costs;
- adjourn, strike out or dismiss claims (except where the claim is brought solely on a mandatory ground).

6.21 However, it should be noted that, if a social landlord fails to comply with the protocol in a claim based on the mandatory rent arrears ground, the tenant could raise a public law or proportionality defence to the claim for possession, see paras 7.100–7.144.

6.22 If the tenant unreasonably fails to comply with the terms of the protocol, the court may take such failure into account when considering whether it is reasonable to make a possession order.

Possession notices

6.23 If a possession order is required there is usually some form of notice that must be given to the occupier before the claim can be issued. The type of notice depends on the type of tenancy or agreement. The Housing Acts (HA) 1985 and 1988 provide that a landlord can terminate certain kinds of tenancy only by obtaining a possession order. For such tenancies the relevant Act sets out the kind of notice that must be served before applying for an order. For tenancies that fall outside the Housing Acts and for Rent Act 1977 tenancies, the common law applies: a periodic tenancy must be ended by service of a notice to quit. A 'notice to quit' is a common law instrument that ends a contractual periodic tenancy so as to give the landlord the right to possession. However, there are some statutory requirements as to the content and length of a notice to quit. A notice to quit that does not comply with these requirements will not be effective to end the tenancy.

Summary of possession notices

6.24   The table below summarises the notices applicable to each type of tenancy or agreement under the Housing Acts 1985, 1988 and 1996, Protection from Eviction Act (PEA) 1977 and common law.[3]

Type of occupier	Notice	Authority	Requirements	Length of notice
Assured tenancy	Notice seeking possession	HA 1988 s8	Prescribed form or form substantially to the same effect.	Depends on grounds: if nuisance ground proceedings can start immediately. Otherwise, either two weeks or two months.
Assured shorthold tenancy	Notice requiring possession	HA 1988 s21	Must be in writing. Not a prescribed form. If tenancy is periodic must require possession after last day of a period of the tenancy.	At least two months.
Secure tenancy	Notice of seeking possession	HA 1985 s83	Prescribed form or form substantially to the same effect.	Depends on grounds: if nuisance ground proceedings can start immediately. Otherwise, at least 28 days.

3 In addition, family intervention tenancies (see paras 3.174–3.176) require both a notice of an intention to serve a notice to quit, giving reasons and informing the tenant of the right to seek a review, followed by the service of a notice to quit. These notices are not dealt with in any detail as such tenancies are extremely rare, if indeed any at all have been granted since they were introduced in January 2009.

Type of occupier	Notice	Authority	Requirements	Length of notice
Introductory tenancy	Notice of proceedings	HA 1996 s128	Notice not in prescribed form but must contain certain information.	At least 28 days. Notice informs tenant of right to seek a review and review must be completed before claim started.
Demoted tenancy	Notice of proceedings	HA 1996 s143E	Notice not in prescribed form but must contain certain information.	At least 28 days. Notice informs tenant of right to seek a review and review must be completed before claim started.
Rent Act periodic tenancy (protected or statutory)[4] and other contractual tenancies not governed by HA 1985 or HA 1988 and not excluded letting	Notice to quit	Common law and PEA 1977 s5	Notice not in prescribed form but must be in writing and contain prescribed information.	A complete period of the tenancy or 28 days, whichever is longer.
Contractual licensee (not 'excluded occupier')	Notice to quit	Common law and PEA 1977 s5	Notice not in prescribed form but must be in writing and contain prescribed information.	What the contract provides or 28 days, whichever is longer.

4 A periodic protected tenancy is ended by a notice to quit but a tenant who remains in occupation becomes a statutory tenant.

6.25   In the case of notices to quit and notices served on assured shorthold tenants, a failure to serve valid notice means the claim must be dismissed. For statutory 'notices seeking possession' served on assured and secure tenants the court has the power to hear a claim for possession even where no notice has been served and can permit the landlord to amend the notice (see below at paras 6.36–6.39).

6.26   The detailed requirements for each kind of notice are set out below at paras 6.27–6.81.

Secure and assured tenants – notices seeking possession

6.27   Secure and assured tenants have substantive security. This operates in the same way for both types of tenant: a landlord can bring the tenancy to an end only by obtaining a possession order. Before a claim for possession can be brought a statutory notice must be served. The notice must:

- be in prescribed form, or form substantially to the same effect;
- state the ground(s) on which the court will be asked to make a possession order;
- give particulars of the ground(s) (ie, an explanation of why each ground is being is relied on); and
- state the earliest date on which the claim can be commenced.

6.28   The prescribed forms give information about the procedure to be followed, the requirements of particular grounds and the tenant's rights. The particular prescribed form is different for each type of tenancy and there are some differences in the time limits. In both cases the court has the power to waive the notice requirement if it is 'just and equitable' and can permit the landlord to amend the notice.

Secure tenants

6.29   The prescribed form for a secure tenant is a notice of seeking possession[5] (referred to as an NSP or NOSP). The general rule is that the earliest date the proceedings can commence is no earlier than the tenancy could be ended by a notice to quit, ie a complete period of the tenancy, or four weeks, whichever is longer. However, if the landlord is relying on the nuisance ground (Ground 2) proceedings can be started immediately though the tenant cannot be required to give

---

5   See Secure Tenancies (Notices) Regulations 1987 SI No 755 and Secure Tenancies (Notices) (Amendment) Regulations 1997 SI No 71.

up possession earlier than the tenancy could be ended by a notice to quit. The notice expires 12 months after the date specified as the earliest date on which proceedings can commence.

Assured tenants

6.30   The prescribed form for an assured tenant is a notice seeking possession (NSP).[6] The earliest date on which proceedings can commence depends on which grounds are relied on. If the nuisance ground (Ground 14) is relied on proceedings may be commenced immediately. Otherwise, the proceedings may be commenced two weeks or two months after service of the notice. For all of the grounds relying on rent arrears or some other breach of the tenancy agreement two weeks' notice must be given. The notice expires 12 months after the date it is served (not, as with secure tenants, 12 months after the date proceedings can be commenced).

Challenging notices seeking possession

Errors in the notice

6.31   The notice must be in prescribed form or in a form substantially to the same effect. A notice that is completed incorrectly may nevertheless be held by a court to be 'substantially to the same effect' as a properly completed notice. The cases regarding errors in notices served under Housing Act 1988 s20 (see paras 3.64–3.65), suggest that where the prescribed information for tenants is omitted the notice will be held to be invalid. Whether the notice is 'substantially to the same effect' as a properly completed notice will depend on the nature of any error or omission. While the court has a discretion to waive the requirement to serve notice and to permit amendments, a notice that is not properly completed or is not in the prescribed form may be held to be invalid and the proceedings struck out. Much will depend on the merits of the claim. Where there is evidence of serious and continuing nuisance a court will be more likely to exercise its discretion than in a claim involving less serious allegations or alleging a low level of rent arrears.[7]

6.32   If the grounds relied on are summarised incorrectly this may invalidate the notice.

---

6 See Assured Tenancies and Agricultural Occupancies (Forms) Regulations 1997 SI No 194.
7 See *Kelsey Housing Association v King* (1995) 28 HLR 270, CA, and para 6.36 below.

In *Mountain v Hastings*[8] a private landlord was seeking possession on Ground 8. Ground 8 required there were arrears of rent of at least three months at the date of the notice and at the date of the hearing.[9] However, in the notice the ground was summarised in the following terms: 'at least three months rent is unpaid'. Although other grounds were also specified, because Ground 8 is mandatory the court made an order for possession at the first hearing on the tenant admitting the level of arrears. The tenant appealed.

The Court of Appeal held that the notice was invalid as the purpose of the notice

> ... is to give to the tenant the information ... to enable the tenant to consider what she should do and, with or without advice, to do that which is in her power and which will best protect her against the loss of her home.[10]

The failure of the notice to specify that the ground requires the level of arrears to exist at the date of the hearing meant that it was not substantially to the same effect as a notice that correctly set out Ground 8. The possession order was set aside and the case remitted to the county court.

6.33   Similarly, insufficient particulars of the allegations against the tenant may mean the notice is held to be invalid:

In *Torridge District Council v Jones*[11] the rent arrears ground was correctly set out. However, the only particulars given were: 'the reasons for taking this action are non-payment of rent'. A possession order was made, the judge holding that the tenant had suffered no injustice or embarrassment because of the failure to set out the amount of the arrears.

The Court of Appeal upheld the tenant's appeal: 'nothing short of a specification of the amount which is claimed as being in arrear could ... amount to a proper particular of the ground upon which possession was sought'. What is required is 'a specification sufficient to tell the tenant what it is he has to do to put matters right before the proceedings are commenced'.[12]

8   (1993) 25 HLR 427.
9   The requirement is now only two months' rent arrears.
10   (1993) 25 HLR 427, Ralph Gibson LJ at 433.
11   (1985) 18 HLR 107.
12   Oliver LJ at 114.

6.34   However, this does not mean that if the figure given is incorrect, the notice will necessarily be invalid.

> The notice in *Dudley MBC v Bailey*[13] stated that the tenant was in arrears of a certain amount as at the date of the notice. Subsequently, the local authority accepted that the figure stated included arrears of rates and water rates as well as rent.
> The Court of Appeal held that an error in the particulars made in good faith would not invalidate the notice providing there is a statement in summary form of the facts which the landlord intends to prove to support the claim for possession.

6.35   Furthermore, it has been held that even if the arrears at the date of the notice are not specified, the notice will be valid if the figure can easily be ascertained by the tenant.

> In *Marath v MacGillivray*[14] the particulars stated only that 'at a meeting between the landlord and tenant on 24 July 1994 the arrears were agreed at £103.29 ... Since that date no payments of rent have been made'. The total arrears at the date of the notice were not stated.
> The Court of Appeal held that the notice was valid and that HA 1988 s8 was satisfied provided
>
> > ... it is made clear ... that more than three months' rent is at the date of that notice unpaid and due and provided also that in some way or other that notice makes it clear either how much, or how the tenant can ascertain how much, is alleged to be due.

Courts' power to waive notice

6.36   For both secure and assured tenants it is provided that 'the court shall not entertain proceedings' for possession unless notice has been served on the tenant, or 'the court considers it just and equitable to dispense with the requirement of such a notice'.[15]

---

13 (1990) 22 HLR 424.
14 (1996) 28 HLR 484, CA.
15 HA 1985 s83 and HA 1988 s8. For assured tenants it is also stated that the proceedings must be begun within the time limits stated in the notice.

In *Kelsey Housing Association v King*[16] the defendants were alleged to have been violent, abusive and threatening towards neighbours and there had been a conviction for actual bodily harm. The housing association served a notice to quit in February 1994 when they should have served a notice seeking possession. The case was commenced in May 1994 and possession was claimed on Grounds 12 and 14 of HA 1988. The allegations were detailed in an appendix to the summons. A defence was served denying the allegations. In November 1994 the defendants applied for the summons to be dismissed because of the failure to serve notice seeking possession. The court refused, holding that it was just and equitable to waive the requirement. The defendants appealed.

The Court of Appeal dismissed the appeal holding that: 'in deciding whether the requirement should be waived the court should weigh all of the factors, taking into account the view of the landlord and the tenant'. Even if the failure to give notice created prejudice to the tenant that was not itself decisive. The court was entitled to take account of things that occurred after the proceedings had commenced and was right to conclude that the defendants had suffered no prejudice; by the time of the hearing the defendants had had time to put things right. Furthermore, an application to dismiss a claim for possession must be made promptly, at about the same time as serving the defence or even before.

Assured tenants: Ground 8

6.37   It should be noted that the court does not have the power to waive the notice requirement when possession is sought against an assured tenant on HA 1988 Ground 8.[17] The ground is only made out if the arrears of rent exist at the date of the notice and at the date of the hearing, see para 7.30 below.

Courts' power to allow amendments

6.38   The court can only make an order for possession on any ground if that ground and particulars of it are specified in the notice. However, the court may give permission for the specified grounds to be altered

16   (1995) 28 HLR 270.
17   HA 1988 s8(5).

or added to.[18] This includes a power to add or amend the particulars of the ground.[19]

6.39 Whether a court will exercise its discretion will depend on the nature and extent of the proposed amendment or addition. Moreover, the time at which the application is made will be relevant. A court may permit a minor amendment at a late stage but is less likely to do so if the amendment significantly changes what is at issue between the parties. An application for permission to amend at an early stage, before the defence has been filed, is more likely to succeed.

Service of the notice

6.40 No special method of service is required but the burden is on the claimant to satisfy the court, on balance of probabilities, that the notice was received by the tenant.

> In *Tadema Holdings v Ferguson*[20] the Court of Appeal held that notice of rent increase and notice of seeking possession were both validly served on a tenant who did not have capacity to either understand the notice or to defend a claim without the appointment of a litigation friend.
> The Court of Appeal held that service under both s8 and s13 of the Housing Act 1988 simply meant delivering the notice and that it was not necessary that the notice was understood by the tenant.

6.41 The Disability Discrimination Act 1995 was not argued in that case and it seems likely that had it been raised the outcome would have been different. See *Haworth v HMRC*[21] at para 7.161. Furthermore, under the Rent Arrears Protocol, where a social landlord is aware that a tenant has difficulties in reading or understanding information, the landlord must take reasonable steps to ensure he or she understands any information given (see para 6.8).

6.42 It should be noted that a social landlord will be bound by the general disability equality duty under the Equality Act 2010 s149 (see para 2.84) and under that Act must make reasonable adjustments in relation to disabled people to ensure that they do not suffer disadvantage by virtue of its policies and procedures (see paras 7.156–7.163).

---

18 HA 1985 s84(3); HA 1988 s8(2).
19 *Camden LBC v Oppong* (1996) 28 HLR 701, CA.
20 *Tadema Holdings v Ferguson* (2000) 32 HLR 866.
21 [2011] EWHC 36 (Ch).

Additionally, the Rent Arrears Protocol expressly provides that a social landlord who is aware that a tenant may be vulnerable must consider whether a litigation friend should be appointed, see para 6.7. Moreover, the tenant's understanding of a notice will always be relevant if the court is considering whether it is reasonable to make a possession order.

Assured shorthold tenants – notice requiring possession

6.43 The possession notice for an assured shorthold tenant is not a pre-scribed notice. The requirements are set out in HA 1988 s21 and the notice is commonly referred to as a 'section 21 notice' or 'notice requiring possession'.

6.44 An assured shorthold tenancy is a form of assured tenancy and, as such, cannot be ended by a landlord other than by obtaining a court order (see para 3.57). HA 1988 s21 sets out the conditions that must be satisfied for the court to make a possession order, including that the landlord must have given notice to the tenant. The requirements are different for a notice given within a fixed term and one given in respect of a periodic tenancy.

6.45 Before 28 February 1997 an assured shorthold tenancy had to be for a fixed period of at least six months. Since that requirement was abandoned, the tenant's protection for the initial period is found in the provision that a possession order made against an assured shorthold tenant under section 21 cannot take effect earlier than six months after the start of the tenancy.[22]

Notice within fixed term

6.46 If notice is served before the end of the fixed term, including the last day of the fixed term, the requirement is simply that the landlord, or at least one joint landlord, 'has given to the tenant not less than two months' notice in writing stating that he requires possession of the dwelling-house'.[23] The requirement is for at least two months' notice but a landlord may give notice at the commencement of the tenancy that possession is required at the end of the fixed term. Indeed many landlords serve the 'section 21 notice' when the tenancy commences so that all the necessary paperwork is signed and delivered at the same time.

22 HA 1988 s21(1) and (5).
23 HA 1988 s21(1)(b).

Notice in respect of a periodic tenancy

6.47 At the end of a fixed-term tenancy agreement, a tenant who remains in occupation becomes a statutory periodic tenant. For such tenants and for those whose tenancies were periodic from the outset, the requirement is different. HA 1988 s21 provides that the notice must:

- be in writing;
- state that possession is required by virtue of section 21;
- after a date specified in the notice, being:
  - the last day of a period of the tenancy;
  - not earlier than two months from the date the notice was given; and
  - not earlier than the date on which the tenancy could be brought to an end by service of a notice to quit.

6.48 The court cannot waive the requirement to serve a section 21 notice or permit amendment to the notice. A notice that does not comply with the requirements of HA 1988 s21 will not be a valid notice.

> In *McDonald v Fernandez*[24] the period of the tenancy was monthly, from the fourth day of each month to the third day of the following month. A section 21 notice was served stating that possession was required 'on 4 January 2003'.
>
> The Court of Appeal upheld the tenant's appeal against the making of a possession order: while a notice to quit would be valid if it expired on the last or first day of a period of the tenancy this did not apply to a section 21 notice. Section 21(4)(a) provides that the notice must require possession 'after a date specified in the notice, being the last day of a period of the tenancy'. The notice should have stated that possession was required *after* 3 January 2003.

6.49 If there is uncertainty about the precise period of the tenancy it is generally sufficient if the notice contains a 'saving phrase' such as:

> Possession is required after [date] or after the last day of a period of your tenancy which will end next after expiration of two months from the service upon you of this notice.

24 [2003] EWCA Civ 1219.

In *Notting Hill Housing Trust v Roomus*[25] the landlords served notice relying on a saving phrase in the following terms:

... possession is required (by virtue of section 21(4) of the Housing Act 1988) of the [property] which you hold as tenant at the end of the period of your tenancy which will end after expiry of two months from the service upon you of this notice.

The tenant argued that the notice was invalid because it contained the phrase '*at the end of* the period of your tenancy' rather than '*after the end of* the period of your tenancy'.

The Court of Appeal dismissed the appeal, holding that the phrase 'at the end of the period of your tenancy' means the same as 'after the end of the period of your tenancy'.

6.50   No higher court cases have examined the requirement in HA 1988 s21 that the notice should state that possession 'is required by virtue of this section' but in the county court case of *Adamson v Mather*[26] a notice that made no reference to section 21 was held to be defective and the possession claim dismissed.

Grounds for possession

6.51   The section 21 notice does not require a landlord to give reasons for seeking possession: the landlord is entitled to possession as of right. However, an assured shorthold tenancy is a form of assured tenancy and all of the statutory grounds relevant to assured tenancies are available. A landlord can seek an order for possession within the first six months if he or she can prove a possession ground is made out. In this case the landlord must serve a notice seeking possession under HA 1988 s8, see above, paras 6.27–6.28 and 6.30.

Section 21 notices and rent deposits

6.52   Since 6 April 2007 landlords who receive deposits are required to deal with them in a certain way: the landlord must protect the deposit and must give prescribed information to the tenant about the way the deposit has been protected (see paras 4.142–4.151).

---

25 [2006] EWCA Civ 407.
26 November 2004 *Legal Action* 26, Harrogate County Court, 24 September 2004.

6.53   The sanctions for non-compliance are described at paras 4.152–4.162 and include a provision that no section 21 notice may be given by a landlord at any time when:[27]

- the deposit is not being held in accordance with an authorised scheme;
- the initial requirements required by the particular scheme being used have not been complied with;
- the prescribed information has not been given to the tenant; or
- a non-monetary deposit has been taken and not returned to the tenant.

6.54   So, it is a defence to a claim for possession brought under HA 1988 s21 that the landlord had not, at the date notice was served, complied with the requirements of the tenancy deposit scheme. In such a case the claim for possession should be dismissed or withdrawn, the tenancy deposit requirements complied with and a new section 21 notice served.

Notices to quit

6.55   A notice to quit is a notice that can be given by either landlord or tenant to bring a periodic tenancy to an end. A periodic tenancy continues automatically from one period to the next unless one party indicates that he or she wants the tenancy to end. A notice to quit is an indication that, at the end of the next complete period of the tenancy, either the tenant intends to leave or the landlord requires the tenant to leave. Landlords' notices to quit have no effect in respect of secure and assured tenancies; the only way a landlord can determine a secure or assured tenancy is by obtaining a possession order.[28] However, any contractual periodic tenancy that is not secure or assured must still be ended by notice to quit before a landlord can make a claim for possession. All periodic tenancies can be ended by a *tenant's* notice to quit (see para 1.62).

6.56   A notice to quit must therefore be served by a landlord to end the following types of tenancy:

- tenancies that have ceased to be secure or assured because the tenant no longer resides in the premises;

---

27 HA 2004 s215.
28 See chapter 2.

- tenancies that are excluded from the secure and assured schemes, for example, tenancies with a resident landlord, tenancies of licensed premises, non-secure tenancies granted to homeless applicants;[29]
- protected and statutory tenancies under Rent Act 1977.

6.57 Furthermore, a contractual licensee is entitled to a notice to quit before a claim for possession can be brought, provided the licence is not an excluded letting (see para 1.101).[30]

Form of notice to quit

6.58 There is no prescribed form for a notice to quit but the Protection from Eviction Act (PEA) 1977 requires that the notice is in writing and includes prescribed information about the tenant's rights.[31]

Time limits

6.59 A notice to quit must give a minimum of 28 days' notice or a complete period of the tenancy, whichever is longer.

6.60 The notice must expire either on the last or first day of a period of the tenancy. Again, a notice may include a saving phrase such as: 'I require you to quit and deliver up possession on [date] or the day on which a complete period of your tenancy expires next after the end of four weeks from the service of this notice.'

6.61 There is no statutory time limit on how long a notice to quit can be relied upon following service. However, the landlord must prove that the contractual tenancy has been ended and usually a notice to quit will be served shortly before the claim is issued. Failure to do this may mean that the tenant can argue that a new tenancy came into being at some point after the expiry of the notice to quit.

6.62 A claim for possession cannot be commenced before a notice to quit has expired.[32]

Errors in a notice to quit

6.63 Minor errors relating to the description of the premises or the name of the tenant will not invalidate the notice provided the tenant is not prejudiced by the error. An error in the date for the giving up of possession will invalidate the notice.

---

29 See paras 3.19 and 3.117.
30 PEA 1977 s3(2B).
31 PEA 1977 s5.
32 *Plaschkes v Jones* (1982) 9 HLR 110.

6.64   If the court holds that the notice is not valid any claim for possession must fail since the contractual tenancy or licence must have ended before a claim for possession is made. The court cannot waive the requirement to serve notice to quit.

Service

6.65   The notice may be served by posting it, hand delivering it to the address of the tenant or by personally serving it on the tenant. The burden is on the landlord to prove that the notice was received by the tenant, so most landlords will deliver or personally serve the notice.

6.66   Problems sometimes arise when a tenant appears to have left the premises and the landlord wishes to end the tenancy before taking possession.[33] A notice to quit left at premises when the tenant is absent will not be effective unless the tenancy agreement specifically refers to the requirement to serve notice to quit. If so, the notice can be served by leaving it at the tenant's last known place of abode or business.[34]

Introductory and demoted tenancies

6.67   An introductory tenancy is a local authority 'probationary' tenancy. A demoted tenancy is a tenancy that was once secure but has been demoted by a court. Both are described at paras 3.149–3.173. A landlord must obtain a possession order before such a tenant can be evicted and notice must be served before the claim can be issued.

Demoted tenancies

6.68   Demoted tenancies are similar to introductory tenancies in that the tenant has limited security for a specified period. However, before a demoted tenancy comes into being, notice must be served and the court must make an order demoting the secure or assured tenancy. Therefore, for demoted tenancies two kinds of notices must be considered:

- the notice served prior to a demotion application (see paras 6.69–6.74); and
- the notice served prior to an application for possession of a demoted tenancy (see paras 6.75–6.76).

---

33 This would be advisable to avoid a potential unlawful eviction. See paras 1.75–1.78.

34 *Wandsworth LBC v Atwell* (1995) 27 HLR 536; Law of Property Act 1925 s196(5).

Notice of intention to apply for a demotion order

6.69 Before applying for a demotion order the landlord must serve notice of intention to apply to demote the tenancy. As for notices seeking possession, the court may dispense with the requirement if it is just and equitable to do so.[35] This applies whether the tenant is secure or assured.

6.70 A landlord may make an application solely for a demotion order but most applications will be in conjunction with an application for possession; the demotion being sought as an alternative to a possession order. In such a case two notices must be served: notice of seeking possession and notice of intention to apply for a demotion order.

Secure tenants

6.71 For secure tenants the notice must be in prescribed form.[36] It is similar to a notice of seeking possession and requires the following information be given:[37]

- particulars of the conduct that has caused the landlord to seek a demotion order;
- the earliest date on which the proceedings may be begun, being no earlier than the date the tenancy could be ended by notice to quit (at least 28 days or a complete period of the tenancy, whichever is longer, ending on the first or last day of a period).

6.72 The notice lapses 12 months after the date specified.

Assured tenants

6.73 A landlord must serve a notice of intention to apply for a demotion of the tenancy before commencing proceedings, but there is no prescribed form of notice. However, HA 1988 s6A(6) provides that the notice must:

- give particulars of the conduct complained of;
- state that proceedings will not begin before the date specified in the notice, being at least two weeks from the date of the notice; and
- state that proceedings will not begin later than 12 months after the notice was served.

35 HA 1985 s83(1)(b); HA 1988 s6A(5)(b).
36 HA 1985 s83(2) and the Secure Tenancies (Notices) (Amendment) (England) Regulations 2004 SI No 1627.
37 HA 1985 s83 as amended by ASBA 2003.

6.74   If the tenancy is demoted a former secure tenant of a local authority will become a demoted tenant. A former assured tenant and a former secure tenant of a registered social landlord (RSL) will become a 'demoted assured shorthold tenant'.

Notice before applying for possession

6.75   Demoted and assured shorthold tenants have limited security of tenure. However, if the landlord wishes to evict a demoted tenant, a possession order must be obtained and before the claim is made further notice must be given to the demoted tenant.

6.76   For both introductory and demoted tenancies the requirements of the notice of intention to seek possession are essentially the same.[38] There is no prescribed form of notice but the notice must:

- state that the court will be asked to make an order for possession;
- set out the reasons for the landlord's decision to apply for possession;
- specify the date after which proceedings for possession may be begun, being no earlier than the date the tenancy could be terminated by notice to quit;
- inform the tenant of the right to request a review of the decision and the time within which the request must be made (14 days); and
- inform the tenant that if he or she needs help or advice about the notice, he or she should take it immediately to a citizens' advice bureau, housing aid centre or a solicitor.

The court has no power to waive the notice requirement or to permit an amendment.

Reviews: introductory and demoted tenants

6.77   Introductory and demoted tenants have the right to seek a review within 14 days of receiving the notice. If a review is requested the authority must conduct the review before issuing the claim for possession.

6.78   The review process for both is governed by regulation and provides:[39]

- the review must be carried out by someone not involved in the decision to apply for a possession order;

---

38   HA 1996 s128(1) and ASBA 2003 s143E.
39   See Introductory Tenants (Review) Regulations 1997 SI No 72 and Demoted Tenancies (Review of Decisions) (England) Regulations 2004 SI No 1679.

- if the review is carried out by an officer, he or she must be senior to the officer who made the decision;
- the tenant may request an oral hearing but must do so within the 14-day period;
- if there is a hearing the tenant may attend and may be accompanied by another person or representative and may call evidence, put questions to other people giving evidence and make written representations;
- the tenant must be given notice of the hearing not less than five days after the request for a hearing is received;
- a hearing may be postponed or adjourned or may proceed in the tenant's absence.

Demoted assured shorthold tenancies

6.79   A demoted assured shorthold tenancy is similar to an ordinary assured shorthold tenancy and a landlord must serve a notice complying with HA 1988 s21.

6.80   An RSL is not required to offer to a tenant a review of the decision although many RSLs have a policy of doing so.

Challenging the review process or the decision to evict

6.81   The statutory framework governing both introductory and demoted tenancies clearly set out to limit the power of the court when considering a claim for possession by providing that the court *must* make a possession order unless the procedural requirements of notice and review had not been complied with by the landlord.[40] However, it is now clear that this does not preclude the county court from considering a defence based on public law grounds (which could include a challenge to the fairness of the review process) or which relies on article 8 of the European Convention on Human Rights (asserting that the decision to evict was not proportionate and therefore unlawful). See paras 7.100–7.144.

---

40 HA1996 ss127(2) and 128 provide that for introductory tenants 'the court shall make an order unless the provisions of s128 apply', and s128 sets out the statutory requirements of the notice. ASBA 2003 Sch 1 (amending the HA 1996) provides that for demoted tenants 'the court must make an order for possession unless it thinks that the [notice and review] procedure ... has not been followed' (HA 1996 s143D).

Issuing a possession claim

6.82 The procedure for issuing possession claims is set out in Part 55 of the Civil Procedure Rules (CPR). A failure to comply with the requirements of Part 55 may be grounds for a claim to be struck out or adjourned. Part 55 and the practice direction to Part 55 can be downloaded from the website of the Ministry of Justice: www.justice.gov. uk/guidance/courts-and-tribunals/courts/procedure-rules/index. htm.

6.83 Chapter 22 provides a general explanation of civil claims in the county court.

6.84 Claims for possession will usually be issued in the county court.[41] Each county court covers a geographical area and the claim must be issued in the county court with jurisdiction for the area where the premises are situated. To find out which court has jurisdiction for a particular address, the court service website has a search facility which can be found at: http://hmctscourtfinder.justice.gov.uk.

6.85 Under CPR Part 55 there are three types of possession claim:

- ordinary claims against tenants, licensees and trespassers and mortgage possession claims, when the claim is dealt with at a hearing (CPR Part 55 Section I);
- claims under the accelerated procedure when a possession order may be made without a hearing. This procedure is only available against assured shorthold tenants (CPR Part 55 Section II);
- claims for interim possession orders against trespassers when the claim is dealt with at a hearing but with very short notice to the occupiers (CPR Part 55 Section III).

Ordinary possession claims – CPR Part 55 Section I

6.86 This section will be used where the claim for possession is against:

- a tenant with substantive security of tenure;
- an occupier with procedural security of tenure;
- an assured shorthold tenant where the landlord also wishes to claim a money judgment for unpaid rent or where there is no written tenancy agreement;
- a borrower (mortgagor) by a lender (mortgagee).

---

41 Only in exceptional circumstances can a possession claim be brought in the High Court, see CPR Part 55 PD 1.1 and 1.3.

6.87   The claim is commenced by the landlord (claimant) sending to the court the following:

- claim form (N5) and copies (one for each defendant);
- particulars of claim and copies;[42]
- written evidence relied on or required by CPR; and
- court fee.

6.88   On receipt the court will:

- give the case a court reference number;
- set a date for the first hearing;
- post to the defendant copies of the following:
  - the claim form, endorsed with the hearing date,
  - particulars of claim,
  - a 'defence form'[43] with guidance notes;
- post to the claimant notice confirming issue and giving notice of the hearing date.

6.89   In some county courts some possession claims can be issued online.[44]

Particulars of claim

6.90   In any civil claim the particulars of claim set out 'a concise statement of the facts on which the claimant relies'.[45] For particular kinds of claim Practice Directions (PDs) specify certain information that must be included in the particulars of claim. The PD to CPR 55 provides that the particulars of claim must:[46]

- identify the land to which the claim relates;
- state whether the claim relates to residential property;
- state the ground on which possession is claimed;
- give full details about any mortgage or tenancy agreement; and
- give details of every person who, to the best of the claimant's knowledge, is in possession of the property.

6.91   If the claim relies on statutory grounds for possession the particulars of claim must specify the ground or grounds relied on.[47]

---

42 The particulars of claim is on form N119 if based on rent arrears and N120 if the claim is a mortgage possession claim.
43 Form N11R if rent arrears and N11M if mortgage possession claim.
44 See PD 55B, which applies to possession claims issued online.
45 CPR 16.4(a).
46 PD 55A.4, para 2.1. The claims forms N5, N11R and N11M, which can be accessed online, are designed to elicit the required information.
47 PD 55A.4, para 2.4B.

Rent arrears cases

6.92   If the claim includes a claim for non-payment of rent the particulars of claim must also set out specific information about the arrears. In particular, a schedule of arrears must be provided. This must cover the two-year period immediately before issue, or, if the first date of default occurred less than two years before the date of issue, from the first date of default. The schedule must give a running total of the arrears.

6.93   If the claimant relies on a history of arrears that is longer than two years, this should be stated in the particulars of claim and a full or longer schedule attached to a witness statement.[48]

6.94   The following information must also be given:

- information about the defendant's circumstances, if known, including whether he or she is in receipt of social security benefits and whether any direct payments are made to the claimants from benefit;
- details of any previous steps taken to recover the arrears, including previous proceedings.[49]

Nuisance and anti-social behaviour cases

6.95   If the claim for possession relates to the conduct of the tenant, details of the conduct alleged must be included in the particulars of claim.[50]

Mortgage arrears cases

6.96   If the claim for possession is brought by a mortgagee (lender of a secured loan) the particulars of claim must state whether certain notices and charges have been registered under the Matrimonial Homes Act 1967, the Matrimonial Homes Act 1983 or the Family Law Act 1996.[51]

6.97   Full details of the mortgage account must be given, including the amount of the advance; any periodic payments; any interest payments required; the amount needed to redeem the mortgage at a stated date not more than 14 days after issue, including any adjustment

---

48 PD 55A.4, para 2.3A.
49 Note also that if the landlord is a social landlord the steps set out in the Pre-Action Protocol should have been followed and should be described in the particulars of claim.
50 PD 55A.4, para 2.4A.
51 PD 55A.4, para 2.5. These refer to the occupation rights of spouses and civil partners, see chapter 11.

for early settlement and specifying the amount of solicitors' costs and administration charges that would be payable. If the claim is brought because of failure to pay the periodic payments when due, detailed information must be given about the arrears, as for rented properties, in schedule form.

6.98   If the claimant wishes to rely on a history of arrears that is longer than two years, this should be stated in the particulars of claim and a full or longer schedule attached to a witness statement.[52]

6.99   If the loan is a regulated consumer credit agreement (see para 7.184), this must be stated.

6.100   The following information must also be given:

- information about the defendant's circumstances, if known, including whether he or she is in receipt of social security benefits and whether any direct payments are made to the claimants from benefit;
- details of any previous steps taken to recover the arrears, including previous proceedings.[53]

Statements of truth

6.101   The claim form, the particulars of claim and defences are 'statements of claim' and must be endorsed with a statement of truth. This should be signed by a person able to verify the truth of the facts stated in the document.[54]

Service of the claim by the court

6.102   The claim form and particulars of claim are served on the defendant by the court usually by first class post. The papers are deemed to be received by the defendant on the second day after posting. At least 21 days' notice of the hearing must be given and the hearing should be within eight weeks of issue.[55] However, the court has the power to shorten the time before the hearing of the claim.[56]

---

52 PD 55A.4, para 2.5A.
53 A pre-action protocol also applies to mortgage possession proceedings.
54 CPR Part 22.
55 CPR 55.5(3).
56 CPR 3.1(2)(a) and (b). PD 55A.5, para 4.2 refers specifically to situations in which the defendant has committed or threatened to commit assault or damage to property but the power is not limited to such situations.

Defendant's response to the claim

6.103   The possession claim forms which are sent by the court to the defendant advise the defendant to complete the defence form and to attend the hearing.

6.104   However, a failure to file a defence form will not prevent the defendant from attending the hearing and contesting the claim; there is no provision for default judgment under CPR Part 55.[57] However, the court could order the defendant to pay any legal costs incurred by the claimant as a result of the defendant's failure to indicate that the claim was contested in advance of the hearing.[58]

6.105   To avoid this, a defendant who intends to defend a claim but cannot file a full defence before the hearing, should tell the claimant as soon as possible before the hearing.

6.106   Where a defence is to be filed it may be possible for the parties to agree what case management directions the court should make (see para 6.111 below). Agreed case management directions should be submitted to the court in advance and the parties may avoid having to attend the first hearing. Even if agreement is not possible, it is important to inform the claimant that the claim is defended so that the claimant is aware that the claim is unlikely to be decided at the first hearing.

The first hearing

6.107   Most courts list a large number of possession claims for hearing during a morning or afternoon session. This means that each claim will be allocated very little court time (sometimes as little as five or ten minutes). This usually means that only very simple cases or undefended claims are decided at the first hearing.

6.108   Possession claims concerning rent arrears, mortgage arrears and applications to suspend possession warrants are held in private, ie members of the public cannot sit in court. Confusingly, however, rent arrears cases are in theory heard in 'open court' rather than 'in chambers', as is the case for mortgage claims and warrant applications. Rights of audience differ according to whether a case is in open court or in chambers. See para 22.85 below.

---

57 Unlike most other civil claims, see chapter 22.
58 CPR 55.7.

Evidence

6.109   Unless the claimant knows that the claim is defended and cannot be finally decided at the first hearing, the claimant should attend court with the necessary evidence to prove the case. This means sufficient evidence to prove any ground for possession and, if necessary, that it is reasonable to make possession order.

6.110   In most cases the claimant will arrange for an appropriate witness to attend court to give evidence orally. A private landlord may present his or her own case *and* give evidence. However, it is possible to rely on written evidence such as the particulars of claim and any witness statements, provided these have been served in advance.[59] Nevertheless, if the defendant challenges the truth of a written statement the hearing will usually be adjourned for the maker of the statement to attend court.[60]

Possible outcome of first hearing

6.111   At the first hearing the possible outcomes are:

- a possession order is made;
- the claim is dismissed or struck out;
- the claim is adjourned generally, or to a date in the future; or
- case management directions are given, setting out the steps the parties must take before the claim comes back before the court.

The accelerated possession procedure – CPR Part 55 Section II

6.112   The accelerated possession procedure is available only in relation to assured shorthold tenancies, including demoted assured shorthold tenancies (see paras 6.79–6.80 above). It can only be used where:

- the original tenancy agreement is a written agreement;
- the only remedy sought is a possession order – rent arrears or any other form of relief cannot be claimed under the accelerated procedure.

6.113   The procedure enables a landlord to obtain a possession order without there being a court hearing. The stages of the procedure are as follows:

59 See CPR 55.8(4): witness statement should be served two clear days before the hearing, unless the claim is against trespasssers when they should be served with the claim form

60 PD 55A.8, paras 6.1–6.4.

- The landlord completes and sends to the court: the claim form (form N5B) which must be endorsed with a statement of truth; copies of the documents relied on (ie, the tenancy agreement, the notice requiring possession, the demotion order in the case of a demoted assured shorthold tenancy, the licence or application in the case of a house in multiple occupation that requires a licence[61]); and the court fee.
- The court then sends to the tenant a copy of the form N5B and the copy documents together with a form of reply (form N11B). The tenant has 14 days to complete and return the form N11B. Even if a tenant does not contest the making of a possession order he or she may use the form of reply to ask the court to postpone the order for up to 42 days on the grounds of 'exceptional hardship'.
- The tenant may also ask for time to pay the court costs (the court fee and the fixed costs which may be claimed if a solicitor is instructed to complete the form N5B). If the tenant files a reply a copy is sent to the landlord and the papers are referred to a judge.
- If the tenant does not file a reply within 14 days the landlord should file a request for a possession order to be made and this will be referred to a judge. On considering the landlord's application and (if filed) the tenant's reply, the judge will do one of three things: make a possession order; fix a hearing for the parties to attend; or dismiss the application.
- Where the tenant requests a postponement the court must fix a hearing unless the landlord has indicated (on the claim form) that he or she is content for the court to decide the issue of postponement without a hearing.
- If a hearing is fixed the parties should be given at least 14 days notice and the judge may direct the parties to take certain steps before the hearing.
- If a possession order is made without a hearing the tenant can apply for the order to be set aside within 14 days. This may be appropriate where the tenant failed to file a reply in time, or in any other case where the tenant contends that the landlord has failed to establish the right to a possession order.

---

61 See paras 7.2 and 11.67–11.76.

Interim possession orders – CPR Part 55 Section III

6.114   A quicker procedure for obtaining an interim possession order against trespassers is available under CPR Part 55 Section III. It does not apply to all claims against trespassers. An application for an interim possession order (IPO) may only be made if:[62]

- the only claim is a possession claim against trespassers;
- the claimant has an immediate right to possession and has had such a right throughout the period of unlawful occupation;
- the occupiers entered the land as trespassers; and
- the claim is made within 28 days of the date the claimant became aware of the defendants' occupation, or the date the claimant ought reasonably to have known of the occupation.

6.115   An application for an IPO cannot be made against someone who entered or remained on premises with the consent of the person who, at the time, had an immediate right to possession. This would include a person allowed into occupation by a tenant where the tenancy is subsequently ended so that the occupier becomes a trespasser.

6.116   Strict time limits apply. The papers must be served on the defendants within 24 hours of issue and a hearing may be listed on as little as three clear days' notice to the defendants. The IPO must be served on the defendant within 48 hours of being sealed by the court. A final hearing should be listed no sooner than seven days after an IPO is made.

6.117   It is a criminal offence to be on premises as a trespasser while the IPO is in force unless the trespasser leaves the premises within 24 hours of service and does not return.

6.118   An IPO will lapse on the date of the final hearing. Either a final possession order will be made, the court will dismiss the claim or the court will give directions for a future hearing.

62   CPR 55.21.

Possession orders

The extended discretion

6.119 When considering a claim for possession on a discretionary ground[63] the court has an 'extended discretion'[64] under which it may:

- adjourn the proceedings for such period or periods as it thinks fit; and

furthermore, when making an order for possession or at any time before the order is executed the court may:

- stay or suspend the execution of the order; or
- postpone the date of possession;

for such period or periods as it thinks fit.

Conditions

6.120 On any such adjournment, stay, suspension or postponement the court must impose conditions regarding the payment of rent arrears and rent (unless to do so would cause exceptional hardship or otherwise be unreasonable) and may impose such other conditions as it thinks fit.

6.121 The court may discharge or rescind the order for possession if it thinks it appropriate to do so, having regard to the conditions imposed and the conduct of the tenant in connection with the conditions.

6.122 If the claim for possession is established on a mandatory ground, or where no grounds are required (for example, claims against assured shorthold tenants or against non-secure tenants) the court does not have the statutory power to adjourn, postpone or suspend orders or execution. It must make an 'outright' order fixing the date for possession, subject to any public law or proportionality defence that the occupier may raise, see paras 7.100–7.144.

6.123 In such a case the court may postpone the effect of the possession order only for a maximum of six weeks if the tenant can show exceptional hardship if an earlier order were made.[65]

---

63 See appendix to chapter 7 for a full list of all of the discretionary grounds for possession.

64 RA 1977 s100, HA 1985 s85 and HA 1988 s9.

65 HA 1980 s89. However, if a tenant's proportionality or public law defence is successful, the court may have the power to postpone possession for a longer period. See paras 7.135–7.136.

6.124   Again, this limit on the court's powers may be challenged if it is argued that an eviction should be deferred for longer to avoid a breach of the occupier's human rights.[66]

Tolerated trespass

6.125   The Housing Act 1980 gave security of tenure to council tenants for the first time by way of the 'secure tenancy'. The provisions were re-enacted in HA 1985 Part IV, which still governs the secure tenancy regime. A secure tenancy can only be ended by the landlord obtaining a possession order and the tenancy ends on the date on which the tenant is to give up possession in pursuance of the order. The extended discretion gives the courts the power to stay or suspend the execution of the order or to postpone the date of possession. The widespread use of 'suspended possession orders'[67] created thousands of occupiers whose secure tenancies had ended but who could not be evicted without an application to the court for a warrant of eviction: 'tolerated trespassers'.[68]

6.126   The courts had decided that if the tenant breached the terms of the suspension the tenancy ended at the moment of the breach. Nevertheless, the former tenant could, and usually would, remain in occupation and could not be evicted unless the landlord applied for a warrant of possession. The court's extended discretion could be exercised at any time up to the execution of the order (the eviction of the former tenant) which meant that warrants could also be suspended. It was also possible for the tenant to make an application to revive the tenancy, which would have retrospective effect.[69] However, even when a tenant cleared all of the arrears this would not necessarily lead to the revival of the tenancy. Indeed, in some cases it was held that having cleared all of the arrears and costs meant that the former tenant could no longer apply for the order to be discharged and the tenancy revived.[70]

---

66 See the judgment of Lord Neuberger at para [103] in *Hounslow v Powell* [2011] UKSC 8, 23 February 2011.

67 There were many variations on the 'suspended possession order' and the precise terms of the order would determine: whether the order brought the tenancy to an end or not; the effect of a breach; and the effect of compliance or non-compliance with the terms of the suspension.

68 See *Thompson v Elmbridge BC* [1987] 1 WLR 1425; *Burrows v Brent LBC* [1996] 4 All ER 577.

69 *Rogers v Lambeth LBC* (2000) 32 HLR 361.

70 *Swindon DC v Aston* [2002] EWCA Civ 1850, 19 December 2002; *London & Quadrant Housing Trust v Ansell* [2007] EWCA Civ 326, 19 April 2007 and *Porter v Shepherds Bush Housing Association* [2008] EWCA Civ 196, 19 March 2008.

6.127   While the tolerated trespasser effectively had the right to continue to occupy the premises indefinitely, he or she lost the rights of the secure tenant, including the right to pass the tenancy to a family member by succession and the right to have repairs carried out or be compensated for a landlord's failure to repair. However, in many cases both the landlord and the tenant proceeded in ignorance of this state of affairs; both behaving as if the tenancy continued.

6.128   For many years it was unclear whether suspended orders made against assured tenants had the same effect, with the House of Lords finally deciding that they did not in December 2008.[71] This was after the Housing and Regeneration Act (H&RA) 2008, which would abolish tolerated trespass, had received Royal Assent.

Postponed possession orders

6.129   To avoid the draconian effect of a suspended possession order a new form of conditional possession order was developed: the postponed possession order.[72] This is a two-stage order under which no date is fixed for the giving of possession. Under the postponed possession order the landlord is given the right to make an application for a date to be fixed but that right is postponed provided the tenant complies with the terms of the order. In the event of an alleged breach, the tenant must be notified by the landlord of the intention to apply for a date to be fixed, with details of the alleged breach. The tenant has a right to reply and both the notice and reply must be sent by the landlord to the court when making the application. Most applications are dealt with without a further hearing. If a date is fixed the landlord may then proceed to obtain a warrant of eviction. If a warrant is not requested, or if the warrant is suspended, the occupier will become a tolerated trespasser after the date fixed for possession. As with other conditional possession orders made on discretionary grounds, the court retains a discretion to vary the order up to the date of eviction.

---

71 *Knowsley Housing Trust v White* [2008] UKHL 70, 10 December 2008.

72 The draconian effect of a certain form of suspended order was highlighted in *Harlow v Hall* [2006] EWCA Civ 156, 28 February 2006, when the Court of Appeal held that the tenancy had ended even though the tenant had complied strictly with the terms of the order. The Court of Appeal confirmed that a possession order could be made under which the date for giving possession was not fixed in *Bristol CC v Hassan* [2006] EWCA Civ 656.

Housing and Regeneration Act 2008: abolition of tolerated trespass

6.130   Housing and Regeneration Act (H&RA) 2008 s299 and Sch 11 largely abolishes tolerated trespass by providing, in relation to secure tenancies, assured tenancies and assured shorthold tenancies:

- The tenancies end when the landlord obtains an order for possession and executes the order. The limbo period between the order taking effect and the eviction is therefore abolished: the tenancy does not end until the tenant is actually evicted.
- The court's power to discharge or rescind a possession order is not limited to situations in which the tenant has complied with the terms of the order. Rather, the court may exercise the power if it is appropriate to do so, having regard to the conditions imposed and the tenant's conduct in relation to those conditions.
- In relation to existing tolerated trespassers a new tenancy (a 'replacement tenancy') automatically arose on 20 May 2009, when this part of the H&RA 2008 came into force, provided the necessary conditions were met (eg, the tenant had continued to occupy the premises as his or her only or principal home throughout).[73]
- Any possession order in force in relation to the premises applies to the replacement tenancy.

Replacement tenancies

6.131   The replacement tenancy will usually be the same kind of tenancy as the original tenancy and will be on the same terms and conditions as applied to the original tenancy immediately before it ended. However, where the original tenancy was a secure tenancy but there has been a stock transfer from a local authority to a registered provider of social housing the tenancy will be an assured tenancy.

6.132   For the following purposes the replacement tenancy and the original tenancy are to be treated as the same tenancy which continued uninterrupted throughout the termination period:

- determining whether an ex-tenant is a successor in relation to the new tenancy;
- calculating the qualifying period for right to buy and discounts.

---

73 There is specific provision for cases in which the tenant ceased to occupy the premises as his or her only or principal home because of an eviction where the warrant of eviction was subsequently set aside: H&RA 2008 Sch 11 para 17(4).

6.133 In addition, when considering claims brought by either the landlord or the tenant for breach of a term or condition of the tenancy and/or claims against the landlord for breach of statutory duty ('relevant claims'), the court may order that the new tenancy and the original tenancy are to be treated as the same tenancy continuing for the purposes of the claim. This means that a former tolerated trespasser bringing a claim for damages for disrepair in respect of any period before 20 May 2009 will have to make an application that the tenancy be treated as a continuing tenancy. It is a matter for the discretion of the court whether or not to do so, see paras 10.93–10.95.

6.134 Similar amendments are made in relation to introductory and demoted tenancies though former introductory and demoted tenants are less likely to have been tolerated trespassers on 20 May 2009 when the replacement tenancy provisions came into force.

6.135 Although tolerated trespassers became tenants again on 20 May 2009, this did not assist where the tolerated trespasser had died before that date. On the date of death there was no secure tenancy and therefore no possibility of a statutory succession.

In *Austin v Southwark LBC*[74] the Supreme Court held that in such a case a person representing the estate of the deceased tenant can make an application under HA 1985 s85(2)(b) to postpone the date for giving possession so as to revive the tenancy.

If granted this will have retrospective effect so as to ensure that, provided the conditions were met at the date of death, a succession can take place. See paras 4.28–4.32.

Enforcing possession orders

6.136 Possession orders of residential premises must be enforced by application for a warrant from the court.[75] The warrant is executed by court bailiffs. There may be a delay of several weeks from the application for a warrant to the date of eviction.

6.137 The landlord may apply for a warrant after the date for the giving of possession. This will usually be the date fixed by the order (if an

---

74 [2010] UKSC 28, 23 June 2010. This overruled the Court of Appeal judgment in *Brent LBC v Knghtley* (1997) 29 HLR 857, which had held that the right to apply for a postponement was not an interest in land capable of being inherited.

75 *Haniff v Robinson* (1994) 26 HLR 386, CA.

outright order) or the date of any breach (if a suspended order). In the case of a postponed order where no date is fixed, see para 6.129 above, the landlord will have to apply for the date of possession to be fixed before applying for the warrant. Applying for a warrant is an administrative act. No further hearing will take place; the completion of a form requesting that a warrant be issued is sufficient. The court will send notice to the occupier that a warrant has been issued, indicating the date and time of the eviction. If the order for possession was made on a discretionary ground the occupier may apply for the warrant to be suspended or stayed. If no such application is made the court bailiffs will attend the premises and can use reasonable force to secure entry.

6.138   So, despite the fact that the H&RA 2008 provides that the tenancy does not end until the order is executed, a postponed possession order will still provide the tenant with significantly more protection than a suspended possession order. Under a postponed order the landlord must make an application to fix a date for possession, the tenant is given notice of the application and an opportunity to respond. Moreover, the application must be considered by a judge, whereas the application for a warrant is an administrative step for which the tenant does not get notice. The first notice the tenant will receive from the court is notice of the date and time set for the eviction.

Challenging the possession order

6.139   Where a possession order is made a defendant may:
- appeal against the order;
- apply to set the order aside; or
- apply to vary the order.

Appeals

6.140   A defendant can appeal against the making of a possession order but will be successful only it can be established that the decision was:
- wrong; or
- unjust because of a serious procedural or other irregularity in the proceedings in the lower court.[76]

6.141   In all cases the permission of the court is required. Permission may be obtained from the judge who made the order or from the judge

---

76 CPR 52.11(3).

or court to which the appeal is made.[77] An appeal against a district judge's order is heard by a circuit judge and an appeal against a circuit judge's order by the Court of Appeal.

6.142 CPR Part 52 sets out the procedure for bringing appeals. The deadline for commencing the appeal (which includes the application for permission to the appeal court) is 21 days from the date of the order.

6.143 It should be noted that lodging an appeal does not mean that the order cannot be enforced.[78] Unless the landlord agrees not to enforce the order until the appeal is heard, a separate application must be made for a stay of execution.

6.144 A party who is unsuccessful in an appeal will usually be ordered to pay any legal costs incurred by the other party, see chapter 22. A landlord who has not instructed solicitors to obtain the possession order may do so if an appeal is lodged. A tenant considering an appeal should be advised of the increased liability for costs and, if possible, public funding should be obtained so that he or she has some protection against being ordered to pay further costs, see para 22.137.

Setting aside an order

6.145 In any case where a party fails to attend the trial of a claim, the court may proceed with the hearing and make an order. In such a case the absent party may apply to set aside the order.

6.146 CPR 39.3 provides that the application must be supported by evidence (a statement endorsed on the application notice will suffice) and that the following conditions must be satisfied:

- the applicant must have acted promptly when he or she found out about the order;
- the applicant must have had a good reason for not attending the hearing; and
- the applicant must have had a reasonable prospect of success at trial.

6.147 Applications to set aside possession orders made in a tenant's absence were, until recently, treated as applications under CPR 39.3.

---

77 Where a party wishes to appeal, permission should be sought orally from the judge immediately after the judge has made his or her order. However, it is often the case that the party is unrepresented or it may not be clear that there are grounds to appeal until after the hearing. If permission is not requested or is refused by the judge who made the order, permission must be sought on the 'Appellant's Notice' (form N161) which is submitted to the appeal court.

78 CPR 52.7.

However, in *Forcelux Ltd v Binnie*[79] the Court of Appeal held that a possession order made at the first hearing was not an order made 'at trial'. Therefore, when the court was considering setting aside the possession order it was not exercising its power under CPR 39.3 but under CPR 3.1(2)(m), which gives to the court very wide case management powers, including a power to 'take any other step or make any other order for the purpose of managing the case and furthering the overriding objective'. The court held that this power was broad enough to include the setting aside of a possession order.

The case was followed by *Hackney v Findlay*[80] in which the Court of Appeal confirmed that when considering an application to set aside a possession order made at the first hearing, it was exercising the wide powers under CPR Part 3, but held that the court should nevertheless apply the CPR 39.3 criteria. However, taking into account the wide powers of the court under the Housing Act 1985 (including the power to vary a possession order) the criteria should be applied less rigorously. So, when considering why the tenant did not attend court the court can take into account the Rent Arrears Pre-Action Protocol and best practice amongst social landlords. Where a landlord has failed to comply with the Protocol and/or follow best practice, the possession order may be set aside even if the conditions under CPR 39.3 are not strictly made out.

6.148   In relation to the CPR 39.3 criteria, in relation to possession orders, it should be noted that a reasonable prospect of success would include having a reasonable prospect of avoiding an outright possession order even if some form of possession order would have been made. Also, in practice, the court may accept as good reasons for not attending the hearing reasons such as attending the wrong court, oversleeping and arriving at court late. What will not usually be accepted is a deliberate decision not to attend, unless this was made in consequence of advice from the landlord that attendance was not necessary, which would be in breach of the Rent Arrears Protocol, see para 6.17.

---

79 [2009] EWCA Civ 854, 21 October 2009.
80 [2010] EWCA Civ 8, 20 January 2011.

6.149 A possession order may be set aside even after it has been exe-cuted, ie after eviction,[81] see below, paras 6.152–6.154.

Variation, stay or suspension

6.150 Where an order has been made on a discretionary ground for posses-sion, the court retains the 'extended discretion' (see para 6.119 above) up to the date of eviction. Under the extended discretion the posses-sion order may be varied if the court thinks it reasonable to do so. In addition the enforcement of the order may be suspended or stayed.

6.151 Where an outright order has been made in the tenant's absence an application may be made to set aside the order and, as an alterna-tive within the same application, to postpone the date of possession or to suspend enforcement on terms.

After eviction

6.152 After eviction the court no longer has a discretion to stay or suspend execution or to vary the possession order. There are, however, two possible ways for the tenant to regain occupation:

- setting aside the possession order, see paras 6.145–6.149 above; or
- setting aside the warrant.

6.153 If the possession order is set aside, the warrant itself 'falls away' and the tenant is entitled to re-occupy. Because of the need to act prompt-ly on finding out about the order it may be difficult to satisfy the criteria of CPR 39.3 (see paras 6.146–6.148 above) in a case in which the order has already been enforced.

6.154 In any case when a person has been evicted it is essential to act quickly in applying to the court. Since it may take some time to pre-pare the application, the landlord should be contacted immediately, informed of the intended application and requested not to re-let the premises until it has been dealt with. If premises are let to someone else before the court considers the application it will be too late to obtain an order allowing the occupier to return.

81 *Peabody Donation Fund Governors v Hay* (1986) 19 HLR 145, CA.

Setting aside a warrant

6.155 A court may set aside a warrant of possession after eviction if satisfied that:

- the warrant was defective;
- the warrant was obtained by fraud; or
- there has been an abuse of process or oppression in the execution of the warrant.[82]

Abuse of process

6.156 A breach of the court rules would usually be an abuse of process.

> In *Hackney LBC v White*[83] the local authority had obtained a possession order in 1986. Subsequently several warrants had been issued and suspended on the tenant's application. In 1995 a further warrant was issued and the tenant evicted. The tenant sought to set aside the warrant because the court rules require that permission to issue a warrant is needed in relation to an order made more than six years before.
>
> The Court of Appeal upheld the tenant's appeal holding that the warrant had been improperly issued and was an abuse of process.

Oppression

6.157 A warrant can be set aside if there has been oppression in the execution of the warrant. Misleading information given by a landlord to a tenant may constitute oppression.

> In *Lambeth LBC v Hughes*[84] a warrant was issued, following which the council wrote to the tenant giving the date for eviction and stating that the only way to stop the eviction was to pay all the arrears in full. The tenant then saw his housing officer who said the same thing but said he could take legal advice. The tenant tried but failed to get advice. He went to the court office but his file could not be found. The court told him to await receipt of a letter from the court bailiff which would contain the eviction date and details of how to stop the eviction. The bailiff's letter was sent on 22 October

---

82 *Hammersmith & Fulham LBC v Hill* (1994) 27 HLR 368, CA.
83 (1995) 28 HLR 219, CA.
84 (2001) 33 HLR 33, CA.

by second class post. It arrived on 28 October as the eviction was taking place.

The Court of Appeal held that:

1) the council's message that only payment in full could prevent eviction was misleading and oppressive, in the absence of any reference to an application to the court;

2) the oppression was not cured by the reference to taking legal advice without indicating what he could seek advice about;

3) the failure of the court office to advise of the procedure was also oppressive; and

4) the failure to post the bailiff's letter in sufficient time for it to be acted upon also made the execution oppressive.

6.158   It is not necessary that the 'oppression' is deliberate and it may not be caused by the landlord.

In *Hammersmith & Fulham LBC v Lemeh*[85] the occupier was aware of the impending eviction and attended court the day before it was scheduled. He was told by the court, mistakenly, that no warrant had been issued and advised to contact the council. The following day he was evicted and applied to have the warrant set aside on the grounds of oppression.

The Court of Appeal held that there is no reason why misleading information given by the court cannot amount to oppression. It is a question of fact and it was clear that if the court had not given the wrong information to Mr Lemeh he would have been able to make his application to stay or suspend execution and have it heard before the eviction took place.

6.159   On receiving notice of eviction, occupiers often contact their landlord to reach agreement. While a landlord is not bound to accept the tenant's proposals the landlord may be guilty of oppression if it is suggested that the only way to stop the eviction is to pay the whole of the arrears. Instead, the landlord may indicate that it is not willing to withdraw the warrant but should make clear that the tenant may apply to the court and that it is for the court to decide whether the eviction can go ahead.

85 (2001) 33 HLR 23, CA.

6.160   To establish oppression it is necessary for the tenant to be misled so that an application is not made to the court before the eviction takes place.

In *Jephson Homes Housing Association v Moisejevs*[86] the occupier took advice from a citizens' advice bureau following receipt of a notice of eviction. The bureau drafted an application to suspend the warrant for the occupier to take to court. However, instead of lodging the application she decided instead to pay to the landlord an amount equal to the shortfall under the terms of the order plus the costs of obtaining the warrant. Despite this, the landlord proceeded with the eviction. The occupier applied to set aside the warrant but her application was dismissed and permission to appeal refused. The court accepted that she was under a genuine misapprehension about what she needed to do to prevent the eviction but held that it did not have a free-standing power to remedy the unfairness of the eviction.

The Court of Appeal held that if the court process has been properly used without fault on the part of the landlord or the court, a warrant will not be set aside.

Effect of setting aside a warrant

6.161   The provisions of the Housing and Regeneration Act 2008 mean that the effect of setting aside a warrant will be automatically to restore the tenancy.

---

86 [2001] 2 All ER 901, CA. See also *Circle 33 Housing Trust Ltd v Ellis* [2006] HLR 106, CA. See however *Southwark LBC v Augustus*, February 2007 *Legal Action* 29, Lambeth County Court, 24 November 2006, in which a warrant was set aside on the basis of oppression where the landlord had failed to follow its stated rent arrears policy requiring it to use eviction only as a last resort.

Defending possession claims

continued

Key points

- There are broadly three types of possession claims for rented property: claims based on discretionary grounds, claims based on mandatory grounds, and claims for which no ground is needed.
- If the ground is discretionary the court must not make a possession order unless it is reasonable to do so.
- The most commonly used grounds are those relying on rent arrears and nuisance/anti-social behaviour.
- Most rent arrears grounds are discretionary: it must be reasonable to make a possession order.
- For assured tenants there is a mandatory rent arrears ground where more than eight weeks' rent is in arrears.
- The nuisance ground for possession is discretionary but outright orders will usually be made for serious breaches of the tenancy or serious anti-social behaviour unless there are exceptional circumstances.
- Social landlords have other powers to deal with anti-social behaviour: they can apply for demotion of tenancies and for anti-social behaviour injunctions to exclude people from their homes or the neighbourhood.
- The county court can also make ASBOs.
- Even where the landlord does not need a ground for possession, in exceptional cases a tenant may defend a claim on public law and/or human rights grounds.
- In mortgage cases, the lender usually has a right of possession under the mortgage so it is rare to have a true 'defence' to the claim.
- The court can postpone or suspend possession in a mortgage case if the borrower can repay mortgage arrears within a reasonable period of time.

Introduction

7.1   Chapter 6 deals with the procedural requirements of possession claims, including notice requirements. This chapter examines the most commonly used grounds for possession, possible human rights and public law defences and considers the impact of the Equality Act 2010 and other provisions affecting vulnerable tenants. Claims for possession of mortgaged property are briefly described. The appendix contains a list of all of the statutory possession grounds for tenants.

Possession claims against assured shorthold tenants

7.2 Since 28 February 1997 almost all tenancies granted by private landlords are assured shorthold tenancies, see para 3.58. An assured shorthold tenant has very limited security of tenure; he or she may be evicted after the first six months unless a longer fixed period is granted. The possible defences to a claim for possession against an assured shorthold tenant are:

- the tenancy is not an assured shorthold tenancy;[1]
- the notice requiring possession is not valid (see paras 6.43–6.50);
- the landlord cannot rely on the notice because of a failure to comply with the mandatory tenancy deposit and/or HMO (houses in multiple occupation) licencing requirements, see paras 4.142–4.151 and 11.67–11.73;
- the requirements of the Civil Procedure Rules (CPR) have not been met.[2]

7.3 Additionally, where the landlord is a public body (which most social landlords are) in exceptional cases it may be possible for an assured shorthold tenant to defend a claim by using public law arguments to challenge the decision to evict (see paras 7.100–7.144 below).

Rent arrears grounds

7.4 The majority of claims for possession are brought because a tenant is in arrears of rent. It should be noted that public sector landlords, including registered social landlords (RSLs), must follow the rent arrears protocol before claiming possession on rent arrears.[3] See para 6.4.

---

1 This may be because the tenancy was granted before 28 February 1997 and the necessary formalities were not complied with or because the tenant is claiming the protection of the anti-avoidance provisions of Housing Act (HA) 1988 s20(3), see paras 3.58 and 3.71–3.79.

2 An example would be where a landlord brings a claim under the accelerated procedure but fails to produce a written tenancy agreement. See para 6.112 and chapter 22.

3 Unless the tenant has no security of tenure.

Discretionary rent arrears grounds

7.5　For regulated, secure and assured tenants there is a discretionary ground for possession where 'rent lawfully due from the tenant' has not been paid.[4]

7.6　In addition, for assured tenants only, there is a further discretionary ground (Ground 11) where the tenant has persistently delayed in paying rent.

Mandatory rent arrears ground

7.7　For assured tenants only, there is a mandatory rent arrears ground. Where at least eight weeks' rent (or, if rent is paid monthly, two months' rent) is in arrears both when the notice seeking possession is served and at the date of the hearing, the mandatory ground is made out.

7.8　All of the rent arrears grounds are set out in full in the appendix to this chapter.

Rent arrears – defending claims for possession

7.9　In all cases the following elements must be established:

- rent;
- lawfully due;
- has not been paid (or there has been persistent delay in payment).

Rent

7.10　Many social landlords collect other charges as part of the rent, including water rates, heating and hot water charges and insurance contributions. Whether such charges can properly be treated as rent for the purpose of a claim for possession is undecided.

> In *Lambeth LBC v Thomas*[5] the Court of Appeal considered a claim for possession brought because of arrears of water rates collected by the council. The court held that it was not necessary to decide whether such sums constituted rent because Ground 1 included

---

4　Rent Act (RA) 1977, Case 1; HA 1985, Ground 1; HA 1988, Ground 10. Under RA 1977 and HA 1985 the full ground is that rent is in arrears or that the tenant is in breach of some other obligation under the tenancy. Under HA 1988 a separate ground exists for other breach: Ground 12.

5　(1998) 30 HLR 89, CA.

other breaches of the tenancy agreement so the ground was made out in any event. However, the court indicated that there was force in the argument that the term 'rent' should be given the meaning adopted in earlier Rent Act cases: all sums payable to the landlord.[6]

7.11   If the tenancy agreement makes provision for the payment of the other charges, failure to pay will constitute a breach of the tenancy agreement and therefore a ground for possession in any event. However, the amount of the total debt made up of non-rent charges will be relevant and advisers should, where possible, ensure that these are distinguished from the arrears of net rent.

7.12   Certainly, in the case of a Ground 8 claim, where the court *must* make an outright order if a certain level of arrears is proved, the narrow definition of rent should be applied and the court should exclude from the arrears figure any sums due to charges other than the net rent.

Lawfully due

7.13   In all cases the landlord must prove that the unpaid rent is 'lawfully due'.

Rent increases

7.14   The ways landlords can lawfully increase rents is described at paras 4.174–4.199. If the landlord has not followed the correct procedure, the tenant may have a defence that the rent claimed was not 'lawfully due'. Advisers must ascertain the correct rent (ie the rent payable before any unlawful increase) and calculate whether there would be arrears in any event. Even if this is the case, the court may nevertheless be prepared to dismiss the claim, depending on the true level of arrears, or, alternatively, to adjourn the claim and order the landlord to prepare an amended rent schedule.

Landlord and Tenant Act 1987 s48

7.15   Under Landlord and Tenant Act (LTA) 1987 s48 rent is not treated as due where a landlord has not given to the tenant an address in

---

6   This was the view taken in the county court case of *Lewisham LBC v Simba-Tola*, June 1993 *Legal Action* 14, Bromley County Court, in which a possession order was made based on arrears entirely attributed to general rates, water rates and other charges, full housing benefit having been paid throughout the tenancy. See also *Rochdale BC v Dixon* [2011] EWCA Civ 1173, 20 October 2011.

England and Wales at which notices may be served. However, it should be noted that as soon as the landlord gives the information, the whole of any rent due becomes payable (see para 4.137).

Has not been paid

7.16 Where the landlord relies on one of the discretionary grounds that some rent is unpaid, the ground is made out if there were arrears both when notice was served and at the date of issue. Clearing the arrears before the date of the hearing does not mean that the ground is not made out. However, it is unlikely that a judge will find it reasonable to make a possession order in such a case. Nevertheless, it is likely that the tenant will be ordered to pay the landlord's legal costs.

7.17 If Ground 11 is used against an assured tenant the allegation is of 'persistent delay'. It is not necessary that there are arrears at the date of the notice or the date of issue, only that there is a history of late payment or the repeated accrual of arrears before payment is made, and that it is reasonable to make an order.

Rent schedules

7.18 The landlord must prove that the rent is unpaid and CPR Part 55 requires that a schedule must be attached to the particulars of claim (see para 6.92). The requirement is mandatory and a failure to comply may lead to a claim being struck out or at least adjourned. An adjournment can be crucial to enable a tenant to resolve outstanding benefit issues and to begin making regular payments before the possession claim is considered by the court.

7.19 The rent schedules must be examined carefully with any evidence the tenant has of payment. Recent payments may not appear on the schedule. Large public sector landlords often operate separate accounts to recover arrears for previous tenancies and payments may be wrongly credited to those accounts.

Offers of rent

7.20 Where rent has been offered and refused by the landlord, this provides the defence of 'tender'. Private landlords sometimes refuse to accept payments of rent, or fail to bank cheques, with the aim of establishing a ground for possession. Although having offered payment gives the tenant a defence, the liability for rent is not extinguished even if the offer of payment has been refused. Tenants must therefore ensure that the rent is set aside so that it is available at the date of any hearing.

7.21   Where a cheque is accepted by the landlord the rent is treated as being paid on the date the cheque is delivered provided the cheque is subsequently honoured (see below at para 7.38).

Housing benefit problems

7.22   Chapter 9 summarises the housing benefit system. Many claims for possession are triggered by problems in relation to housing benefit, particularly in the social rented sector.

7.23   Arrears may accrue entirely as a result of an authority's inefficiency in administering housing benefit claims. However, more often there is a combination of maladministration and some failure on the part of the tenant, for example, failing to comply with requests for information or evidence or to submit claims in time.

7.24   It is important to obtain as much information as possible about any housing benefit problems before a possession hearing. The court will expect detailed information about the outstanding issues, in particular what action is needed to resolve the issues, how long it is likely to take and how much housing benefit is likely to be paid.

7.25   The following housing benefit issues commonly cause or contribute to the accrual of rent arrears.

Issue	Suggested action
Tenant delays or fails to make or renew claim	Consider request to backdate. See paras 9.95–9.99.
Local authority delays processing claim for private tenant	Consider legal action to compel payment on account. See paras 9.92–9.94.
Overpayment recovery	Consider whether decision on recoverability can be challenged; request reduction of rate of recovery. See paras 9.100–9.109.
Non-dependant deductions	Check deduction correctly applied and at correct rate; advise tenant of need to claim contribution from non-dependant/to obtain information on non-dependant's income; advise tenant on right to evict non-dependant who refuses to contribute. See paras 9.81–9.84.

Issue	Suggested action
Local authority claim tenant's failure to provide evidence	Obtain information from authority as to what is required/request copy letters sent to tenant;[7] advise tenant on what to provide and to obtain receipts; consider backdating request if claim closed.
Unexplained delay in processing claim/backlog in HB department	Consider issuing witness summons requiring housing benefit manager to attend court.[8]
Eligible rent or local housing allowance is less than current rent	Consider application for discretionary housing payment. See para 9.85.
For some other reason housing benefit does not meet the full rent	Ascertain reason and consider appeal against assessment of entitlement or advise tenant of amount he or she must pay each week for non-eligible charges and/or because income is too high to receive full housing benefit.

7.26　Where rent arrears have accrued as a result of local authority inefficiency or error, an application may be made for the authority to be joined to the proceedings and ordered to pay the costs.[9] Where the landlord *is* the local authority an application for costs can be made against the authority as claimant.

The relevance of housing benefit problems

7.27　In most cases housing benefit problems are relevant to the issue of whether it is reasonable to make a possession order rather than whether rent lawfully due is unpaid. There is an argument that rent is not 'unpaid' in the case of a local authority tenant who receives a rent rebate which the authority subsequently decides he or she was not entitled to.[10] However, it is rare for the whole of a tenant's arrears

---

7　Local authority landlords sometimes refer to these letters in the particulars of claim as part of the information about previous steps taken to recover the arrears. A party may make a written request for a copy of any document referred to in a statement of case and, provided an undertaking to pay reasonable costs is given, copies must be provided within seven days of the request: see CPR 31.14–31.15.

8　The procedure is set out in CPR Part 34.

9　See *Asra v Coke* June 2001 *Legal Action* 31. See para 22.151 below.

10　See Social Security Administration Act 1992 s134(2).

to be caused by the recovery of an overpayment. Furthermore, this will not assist a tenant of a non-local authority landlord.[11]

7.28　　A tenant awaiting a decision on a housing benefit claim should always be advised to pay the non-rebated charges. If the likely entitlement can be assessed, he or she should also be advised to pay any anticipated shortfall. Where there are bound to be arrears, even after housing benefit has been paid, instalments towards the arrears should also be paid. A failure to do this may mean that there are significant arrears when the housing benefit issues are resolved and a possession order may be made. If adjournments are granted to resolve housing benefit problems, the court may make it a condition of the adjournment that the tenant pays the non-rebated charge plus a sum towards the arrears.

7.29　　It should be noted that in Ground 8 claims it may not assist a tenant that the arrears have accrued as a result of housing benefit problems.[12] Advisers must try to ensure that all outstanding issues are resolved before the hearing of the possession claim and that the arrears are below the mandatory level of eight weeks.

Mandatory rent arrears ground: assured tenants only

7.30　　Ground 8 provides a mandatory ground for possession where at least eight weeks' rent (for a weekly or fortnightly tenancy) or two months' rent (for a monthly tenancy) is in arrears both at the date the notice seeking possession was served and at the date of the hearing. [13]

7.31　　If Ground 8 is proved, the court has no discretion: an outright possession order must be made. This will usually be a 14-day order but if it appears to the court that this would cause exceptional hardship this may be extended to a maximum of six weeks.[14] But, see paras 7.100–7.144 below on the possibility of a public law or proportionality defence where the landlord is a public body.

7.32　　Rent means rent lawfully due from the tenant so advisers should consider the issues referred to above at paras 7.10–7.15. Landlords usually rely on Grounds 8, 10 and 11 at the same time so that if Ground 8 is not made out, the court can still make an order under

---

11　See Housing Benefit Regulations (HB Regs) 2006 SI No 213 reg 95(2).

12　See *North British Housing Association Ltd v Mathews and Others* [2004] EWCA Civ 1736 at para 7.34 below.

13　For yearly or quarterly tenancies, the figure is at least three months' rent or one quarter's rent, in arrears for at least three months. The ground is set out in full in the appendix to this chapter.

14　HA 1980 s89.

one of the discretionary grounds. However, under Grounds 10 and 11 the court may make a conditional order instead of an outright order (see para 6.119).

7.33 The court does not have an 'extended discretion' when Ground 8 is made out. Possession orders cannot be postponed or suspended. A possession order should clearly state whether it has been made on Ground 8. If it does not, the court can, at a later date, exercise its discretion.[15]

Adjournments

7.34 In 2004 the Court of Appeal considered the issue of whether an adjournment could be granted to enable a tenant to resolve housing benefit problems so as to clear the arrears in a Ground 8 claim.

> *North British Housing Association Ltd v Matthews and Others, London & Quadrant Housing Limited v Morgan*[16] concerned four tenants of social landlords against whom possession was claimed on Ground 8. In each case the ground was made out but the arrears had accrued because of maladministration by the local authority housing benefit departments. The judges hearing the claims refused to adjourn to give the tenants time to resolve the housing benefit problems.
>
> The Court of Appeal held that the power to adjourn a hearing to enable a tenant to reduce the arrears to below the Ground 8 threshold may only be exercised in exceptional circumstances and the fact that the arrears are attributable to maladministration on the part of the housing benefit authority was not an exceptional circumstance.
>
> However, the court did refer to circumstances in which the court may properly exercise its discretion to adjourn. One of these was
>
> > ... where the landlord is a public body, and the tenant may have an arguable defence based on abuse of power... A yet further example is where, before or at the hearing date, the landlord accepts a cheque from the tenant for a sufficient sum to bring the arrears below the Ground 8 threshold, but the cheque is conditional payment, it may be a proper exercise of discretion to

---

15 *Diab v Countrywide Rentals 1 plc*, ChD, (2001) *Independent* 5 November.
16 [2004] EWCA Civ 1736.

> adjourn the claim for possession to see whether the cheque will
> be honoured.[17]

7.35   This does not, however, mean that in the absence of such exceptional
circumstances a court can never adjourn such a hearing. The court
has an inherent power to control its own procedure. If a tenant raises
a defence or procedural argument that the court does not have time
to resolve, an adjournment may be granted for the case to be listed
for a longer hearing. Or, where a tenant intends to bring a counterclaim for damages for disrepair, the court may give case management directions. What the court cannot do is adjourn for the express
purpose of giving the tenant an opportunity to reduce the arrears
below the minimum level.

7.36   In fact, given that tenants can now defend possession claims by
public body landlords on grounds of proportionality, the number
of claims based on Ground 8 is expected to diminish. Social landlords are less likely to use Ground 8 and most private tenants will
be assured shorthold tenants and the section 21 procedure is more
likely to be used than Ground 8.

7.37   When seeking an adjournment in such a case it is essential to
make the application before the court has heard evidence. Otherwise,
it may be argued that, the court being satisfied that the ground is
made out, an order for possession must be made.

Payment by cheque

7.38   If, before the hearing, the tenant makes a payment to reduce the
arrears to less than eight weeks the ground will not be made out.

> In *Coltrane v Day*[18] a cheque for the full amount of the arrears was
> sent by the tenant's solicitors to the claimant's solicitors five days
> before the hearing. Had it been paid into the landlady's account
> on the day of receipt it would not have cleared before the hearing.
> In fact, the cheque was given to the claimant by her solicitors on

17 [2004] EWCA Civ 1736, Dyson LJ at [12]. It should be noted that the House of
Lords/Supreme Court has since ruled that such public law and proportionality
defences can be raised in the county court and it is not necessary for a
defendant to seek an adjournment to apply for judicial review. It would not
now be necessary to establish abuse of power – that an eviction would be
disproportionate would be sufficient, see paras 7.100–7.144 below.

18 [2003] EWCA Civ 342, 14 March 2003.

the day of the hearing and subsequently paid into her account. The district judge adjourned the hearing for 56 days. The circuit judge upheld the landlady's appeal holding that at the date of the hearing the rent was unpaid. An order for possession was made.

The Court of Appeal allowed the tenant's appeal. It is an established principle of contract law that if a cheque is delivered and is not returned by the creditor the debt is discharged as at the date of delivery, provided the cheque is met on first presentation. In this case rent had always been paid by cheque, the landlady had accepted the cheque and paid it into her account where it was met on first presentation. However, if in such a case the cheque does not clear on first presentation an order for possession must be made, the date of the hearing being, for the purposes of Ground 8, the earlier and not the adjourned hearing. Furthermore, in the absence of express or implied agreement regarding the payment of rent by cheque a landlord is not bound to accept a last minute cheque from the tenant.

The district judge had been right to adjourn the hearing but the appropriate adjournment would have been seven or 14 days: 56 days was excessive.

7.39 So, unless there is an agreement that rent is paid by cheque, a tenant who wishes to make payment shortly before or at the hearing must do so by paying cash.

Ground 8 and registered social landlords

7.40 In *R on the application of Weaver v London & Quadrant Housing Trust*[19] the tenant sought to judicially review the trust's use of Ground 8 arguing that she had a 'legitimate expectation' that the trust would follow Housing Corporation guidance. The guidance suggested that RSLs should use all reasonable alternatives to recover rent arrears before using Ground 8. The court dismissed the claim, holding that the tenant, having been unaware of the guidance, could not establish any legitimate expectation. Furthermore, on the facts, the trust could not be said to have failed to use reasonable alternatives before pursuing the claim for possession under Ground 8. See para 2.71 for a full summary of the case.

---

19 [2008] EWHC 1377 (Admin), 24 June 2008.

Counterclaims

7.41   The defence of 'set-off' may be available to a claim for possession based on rent arrears. Set-off means that the defendant acknowledges monies owed but claims the right to set off against the debt an amount due from the claimant to the defendant. Commonly the defendant will seek to set off damages for the claimant's breach of the repairing obligation. Even where damages are yet to be assessed the defendant has a right to equitable set-off.[20] However, the defendant's right of action must exist at the date the claim was issued. Chapter 10 describes in detail the repairing obligations of landlords and the way compensation is assessed. Advisers must be aware that a disrepair counterclaim will exist only where:

- there is 'disrepair' as opposed to poor conditions caused, for example, by poor design or overcrowding;
- the repairs are the landlord's responsibility;
- the landlord has had notice of the need for repairs;
- the landlord has failed to carry out the repairs within a reasonable period; and
- the tenant has suffered loss and inconvenience.

7.42   If the assessed damages do not extinguish the arrears the court may make a possession order.[21] A tenant should therefore be advised to pay current rent plus a sum towards the arrears until the proceedings are disposed of.

7.43   The court has the power to order that a counterclaim be heard separately. Provided the court is satisfied that the defendant has a genuine claim this is unlikely but a court may exercise this power if the issue is raised at the first hearing without any evidence of the disrepair (such as photographs or a report) or where the counterclaim is unlikely to result in more than minimal damages and the arrears are substantial.

Nuisance

7.44   Housing Act 1996 Part V introduced several measures to address 'anti-social behaviour' in social housing. These included:

---

20 *British Anzani (Felixstowe) Ltd v International Marine Management (UK) Ltd* [1979] 2 All ER 1063.

21 See *Haringey v Stewart* (1991) 23 HLR 557.

- amending the nuisance ground for secure and assured tenants;
- creating a type of probationary tenancy for local authorities – the 'introductory tenancy'; and
- giving local authorities the power to apply for anti-social behaviour injunctions (ASBIs) against persons who were not tenants of the authority, to which power of arrest could be attached.

7.45 The Anti-social Behaviour Act (ASBA) 2003 strengthened these provisions by making anti-social behaviour injunctions available to other social landlords and by widening the scope of an injunction to include a power to exclude the person from his or her home and from the neighbourhood. ASBA 2003 also gave county courts the power to make anti-social behaviour orders (ASBOs) within existing proceedings.

Nuisance ground for possession

7.46 For secure and assured tenants the possession ground was amended (see italics) to provide that the ground is made out where:[22]

> The tenant or a person residing in *or visiting* the dwelling-house – has been guilty of conduct causing *or likely to cause* a nuisance or annoyance to a person residing, *visiting or otherwise engaging in a lawful activity in the locality,* or has been convicted of using the dwelling-house or allowing it to be used for immoral or illegal purposes, or *an indictable offence*[23] *committed in, or in the locality of, the dwelling-house.*

7.47 The following should be noted:

- It is not necessary to prove that nuisance or annoyance has been caused to another person, only that the conduct was *likely* to cause nuisance or annoyance. This means that it is not necessary for a 'victim' of the behaviour to give evidence.
- The conduct may be that of a visitor to the premises.
- The likely nuisance and annoyance need not be to neighbouring occupiers but may be to someone visiting or engaged in a lawful activity in the locality.
- Any indictable offence committed in the premises or in the locality of the premises is sufficient. The offence need not be such as to be likely to cause nuisance.

22 HA 1985 Sch 2 Ground 2; HA 1988 Sch 2 Ground 14.
23 An indictable offence means any offence other than one that can only be tried in the magistrates' court (known as a summary offence). It includes theft, assault (other than common assault) and all offences relating to the possession of controlled drugs.

- There must be a conviction for such an offence, not merely an allegation or charge.

7.48   However, the nuisance ground is discretionary and such issues as whether the conduct is that of the tenant or a visitor and the seriousness of any offence will be relevant to the reasonableness of making an order.

7.49   The case-law since the ground was amended shows that the courts are now more likely to make outright orders against tenants where there has been serious anti-social behaviour and/or convictions for drug offences.

> *Bristol CC v Mousah*[24] concerned a possession claim against a sole tenant who had recently been granted the tenancy. It was an express term of his tenancy agreement that the tenant must not supply controlled drugs from or in the neighbourhood. Within the first nine months of the tenancy the premises were raided by police several times and it was clear that drugs were being sold from the premises. The tenant's evidence was that he had not been present at the time of the raids and had not been aware of what had been going on. He also gave evidence that he had previously received psychiatric treatment. The county court judge found that the tenant had been aware of the drug dealing but declined to make a possession order taking into account the tenant's medical circumstances and that he would be unlikely to be housed as a homeless person if evicted.
>
> The Court of Appeal allowed the council's appeal. The proper approach was that where there was a very serious breach of the tenancy agreement, it was reasonable to make possession order unless there were exceptional circumstances.

7.50   However, even where there is a serious breach of the tenancy agreement, the circumstances may be such that the court may decline to make an order or may postpone or suspend the order.

---

24 (1998) 30 HLR 32, CA. For other cases where the Court of Appeal has upheld a landlord's appeal against the refusal of a county court judge to make a possession order, see: *Darlington BC v Sterling* (1997) 29 HLR 309, CA; *West Kent Housing Association Ltd v Davies* (1999) 31 HLR 415, CA and *Newcastle upon Tyne CC v Morrison* (2000) 32 HLR 891, CA.

In the county court case of *Tai Cymdogaeth Cyfngedig v Griffiths*[25] the defendant was an assured tenant. Her partner had been convicted four times of possession of Class B drugs and once of possession with intent to supply, between July 2000 and May 2001. In June 2002 an outright possession order was made on Grounds 12 and 14. The tenant appealed to the circuit judge.

The judge held that the court must first consider whether it was reasonable to make an order for possession at all and, then, whether it was reasonable to suspend the order. The judge rejected the council's argument that the Court of Appeal's judgment in *Bristol CC v Mousah* meant that where a serious crime was committed, in the absence of exceptional circumstances, a possession order must be made. While it will be rare to avoid a possession order in such a case, the suggestion that the burden moves to the tenant to establish exceptional circumstances was wrong. Most of the convictions were for possession only, the drugs were restricted to Class B, and there was no evidence of users coming to the premises or causing nuisance; there had been no breach of any terms of the tenancy agreement in the 12 months before the hearing. Furthermore, the following factors were relevant: the tenant herself was not involved save to the extent of allowing the premises to be used; she had not breached any other term and had always paid the rent; she was suffering from depression and had a nine-year-old granddaughter living with her. Also, her partner had left the premises although it was possible that he might return. The order was varied to an order suspended for 12 months on condition that the tenant complied with the terms of the tenancy agreement. The Court of Appeal refused the landlords permission to appeal the order.

Similarly, in *North Devon Homes Ltd v Batchelor*[26] the court refused a possession order in relation to a tenant of sheltered accommodation despite her convictions for possession of Class A drugs and money laundering, which arose due to her son's criminal activities. The Court of Appeal dismissed the landlord's appeal although it was suggested that a one reason for the court having refused to make a possession order was the poor preparation of the case by the landlords.

25 February 2003 *Legal Action* 36, Swansea County Court.
26 [2008] EWCA Civ 840, 22 July 2008.

The court's discretion

7.51   The Anti-social Behaviour Act 2003 imposed on judges a duty to focus on the effect of the nuisance on others when considering whether to make a possession order.[27] This is referred to as the 'structured discretion' under which:

> The court must consider, in particular – the effect that the nuisance or annoyance has had on persons other than the person against whom the order is sought; any continuing effect the nuisance or annoyance is likely to have on such persons; the effect that the nuisance or annoyance would be likely to have on such persons if the conduct is repeated.

Suspending orders

7.52   As the nuisance ground is a discretionary ground, the court may suspend enforcement or postpone a possession order on terms. However, there must be some evidence that the tenant will comply with the terms.

In *Manchester CC v Higgins*[28] a suspended possession order was made against a tenant whose 12-year-old son had been guilty of 'appalling misbehaviour'. The behaviour included abusing and assaulting a neighbour's disabled sons, and smashing the windows of the neighbour's house and car. An injunction was obtained against the tenant with little effect and an ASBO was obtained against her son. His abusive behaviour continued and he was arrested and placed in a bail hostel. By the time of the trial he was subject to a 12-month secure accommodation order. The tenant also had a two-year-old child with serious health problems. The judge found the tenant's evidence was 'inadequate' and that her approach was that if her son told her he had not done something then he had not done it. Nevertheless, the judge indicated that the family needed support and that it would be wrong to give up on any chance that the tenant's son could make some sort of improvement in his behaviour.

The Court of Appeal upheld the council's appeal against the decision to suspend the order. While the discretion on whether to make an order and whether to suspend it was wide, the judge had

27   ASBA 2003 s16(1): the effect was to insert s85A into HA 1985 and s9A into HA 1988.
28   [2005] EWCA Civ 1423, 21 November 2005.

failed to take sufficient account of the effect of the behaviour on the neighbours and there was no evidence to support the view that the nuisance may cease.

Previous unheeded warnings point one way: genuine remorse the other. The level of support available to a parent who is making proper efforts to control an errant child will be relevant. There must, however, always be a sound basis for the hope that the anti-social behaviour will cease.[29]

Other measures

7.53 It may be argued that the availability of other measures to control anti-social behaviour, such as injunctions and ASBOs, means that an outright possession order is not necessary. On the other hand the fact that the behaviour warrants such measures may support the argument that the conduct is so serious that a possession order must be made. It is likely that in the future the availability of steps that could be or have been taken to address anti-social behaviour will be of more significance since the court can review the proportionality of an eviction, ie whether the eviction is a necessary measure under article 8.

7.54 As was pointed out in *Manchester CC v Higgins*:

In one case the facts giving rise to the making of an ASBO may be so serious that both the making a possession order and the refusal to suspend it will be self evident. In another case the making of the ASBO may have served its purpose of restraining future misbehaviour so that although past conduct might make it reasonable to order possession yet suspension might be possible.[30]

7.55 In summary, where there is evidence of conduct causing, or likely to cause, significant nuisance or a conviction for a serious criminal offence, the kinds of exceptional factors that may help avoid an outright order are:

- the person causing the nuisance has left the premises;
- the tenant has shown genuine remorse and a willingness to modify his or her behaviour;
- other measures, such as injunctions or ASBOs, have proved effective.

29 [2005] EWCA Civ 1423, Ward LJ at [37].
30 [2005] EWCA Civ 1423, Ward LJ at [35]. See para 7.52 above.

In *Greenwich v Grogan*[31] it was a term of the defendant's tenancy that he must not 'use the property for any illegal purposes'. At the age of 17 he was convicted of handling stolen goods and sentenced to six months in a young offenders institution. The offence consisted of receiving boilers stolen from council flats in the same block. Possession was sought under HA 1985 Grounds 1 and 2(b). An outright possession order was made. The tenant appealed.

In the Court of Appeal it was conceded that the grounds for possession were made out and that it was reasonable to make a possession order. However, the appeal was allowed on the ground that the judge had given insufficient consideration to the power to suspend the order on terms. The court referred to the possibility that the tenant may be attempting to live a life free of crime and that this was more likely if he was given the opportunity to continue living in the flat. The court suspended the order for 12 months on the condition that there be no further breach of the tenancy agreement.

7.56   It is important that tenants accused of nuisance are advised realistically. If a tenant's defence is that all of the allegations are unfounded it will be very difficult, if the nuisance is proved, to persuade a court that the tenant is willing to change his or her behaviour and that a possession order should be suspended or postponed.

In *Canterbury CC v Lowe*[32] the court heard evidence of serious harassment of neighbours, including threats to kill. The judge suspended an order for possession, taking into account the fact that there had been no incidents since injunctions had been granted eight days before the hearing and that the tenant's partner had belatedly indicated that 'common sense should prevail'. The council appealed, seeking an outright order.

The Court of Appeal allowed the appeal. The judge had treated the compliance with the injunction as decisive rather than one of a number of relevant facts. Given that it had only been in force for eight days, its importance had been overestimated. Also, the statement attributed to the partner had been made in a closing speech by his barrister at a time when he was still denying the harassment. On the evidence of the serious harassment and its

---

31   (2001) 33 HLR 140, CA.
32   (2001) 33 HLR 53, CA.

> impact on the neighbour's family, the only proper conclusion was an outright possession order.

7.57 Contrast *Moat Housing Group South Ltd v Harris and Hartless*[33] at para 7.72 below, which concerned an appeal against the making of an ASBI, an ASBO and an outright possession order. The Court of Appeal replaced the outright order with a suspended order and set aside the ASBO.

Public body landlords and anti-social behaviour policies

7.58 Under ASBA 2003 s12, social landlords are required to publish their policies for dealing with anti-social behaviour (see para 6.3). Whether a landlord has followed its own policies will always be relevant to reasonableness and may even provide a defence when the tenant is non-secure, see *Barber v Croydon*[34] below at para 7.115.

Tenants with mental health problems

7.59 Complaints of nuisance may be made against a tenant with mental health problems. In such a case the tenant's health problems will be relevant to whether or not it is reasonable to make an order for possession,[35] as will the effect on neighbours, the tenant's ability to change his or her behaviour and the steps taken by the landlord to support the tenant, including the consideration that has been given to alternative accommodation. Where a tenant causing nuisance is vulnerable it will be particularly important to consider the landlord's policies for dealing with anti-social behaviour. A failure to follow these policies or a failure to take proper account of the tenant's disability may also amount to disability discrimination. See paras 7.145–7.164 below.

Other anti-social behaviour provisions

7.60 Social landlords have other powers to deal with anti-social behaviour, in addition to, or as an alternative to, claiming possession.

---

33 [2005] EWCA Civ 287.
34 [2010] EWCA Civ 51, 11 February 2010.
35 See *Croydon LBC v Moody* (1999) 31 HLR 738.

Anti-social behaviour injunctions

7.61   Any landlord can apply for an injunction within possession proceedings to restrain a tenant from breaching the tenancy agreement until the final hearing. However, Housing Act 1996, as amended by ASBA 2003, gives social landlords the power to apply for much more wide-ranging injunctions: ASBIs. These are not restricted to tenants of the landlord and the scope of the injunction is wide.

7.62   An ASBI may be obtained by a 'relevant landlord' which means: a housing action trust (HAT), a local authority or an RSL.[36] The following conditions must be satisfied:[37]

- The person against whom the injunction is sought is engaging, has engaged or threatens to engage in conduct capable of causing nuisance or annoyance to:
  - a person with a right to reside in or occupy housing accommodation owned or managed by the relevant landlord or in other housing accommodation in the neighbourhood; or
  - a person engaged in lawful activity in the neighbourhood; or
  - a person employed in connection with the landlord's housing management functions.

7.63   It does not matter where the conduct occurs.[38]

Ouster/exclusion and power of arrest

7.64   Further powers are given to the court where:[39]

- the conduct consists of or includes the use or threatened use of violence; or
- there is a significant risk of harm to the person the order seeks to protect.

7.65   If the court is satisfied that *either* of these conditions is met, the ASBI may include a provision prohibiting the person from entering or being in any premises specified (including premises occupied under a tenancy) or from any area specified in the injunction. Furthermore, a power of arrest may be attached to the ASBI. However, if an ASBI is made without notice to the occupier *both* the conditions must be met

---

36   HA 1996 s153E(7).
37   HA 1996 s153A.
38   HA 1996 s153A(5).
39   HA 1996 s153C.

before the court can exercise the power to make an ouster or exclusion order or to attach a power of arrest.[40]

Anti-social behaviour orders

7.66 The criminal courts have been able to make ASBOs since April 1999.[41] The power is contained in section 1 of the Crime and Disorder Act (CDA) 1998. The ASBA 2003 amended the CDA 1998 to permit applications to be made in the county court by a 'relevant authority'. Relevant authorities are: local authorities, police forces, RSLs and HATs.[42] Before making the application the applicant must consult with at least one other relevant authority.[43]

7.67 A freestanding application for an ASBO cannot be made in the county court; an application may only be made within existing proceedings. A relevant authority may make an application in proceedings in which it is already a party or may apply to be joined in proceedings for the purpose of applying for an ASBO, for example, possession proceedings brought by a private landlord or family proceedings. The application will usually be against a person who is already a party to proceedings. However, an application may be made to join someone not already a party to proceedings in order to be made the subject of an ASBO, for example, a family member of the tenant in a possession claim.

7.68 The procedure for county court ASBOs is set out in the Civil Procedure Rules Part 65.

7.69 To obtain an order it must be proved that:

- the person has acted in an anti-social manner, ie a manner that caused or was likely to cause harassment, alarm or distress to one or more persons not of the same household; and
- the order is necessary to protect other people from further anti-social acts by the person.

7.70 The following features of county court ASBOs should be noted:

- The order may prohibit the person from 'doing anything described in the order'. It cannot compel a person to perform an act.[44]

---

40 See *Moat Housing Group South Ltd v Harris and Hartless* at para 7.72 below.
41 Up to December 2008, 16,999 ASBOs had been made in England and Wales.
42 CDA 1998 s1(1A).
43 CDA 1998 s1E.
44 *Lonergan v Brighton & Hove CC* [2005] EWHC 457 (Admin), 23 March 2005.

- There is no limit to the duration of an ASBO but it must last a minimum of two years.[45] It can only be discharged within two years of being served if the parties agree.
- An ASBO cannot be made by consent.[46]
- A relevant authority must make the application for an ASBO; the court cannot make an order of its own motion.
- The standard of proof in relation to the anti-social behaviour is the criminal standard: beyond reasonable doubt.[47]
- The penalty for breach is not committal but prosecution for the criminal offence of breaching an ASBO without reasonable excuse.[48]

Challenging county court ASBOs

7.71　The decision to apply for an ASBO is the exercise of a discretion and may be challenged by way of judicial review. However, it will usually be more appropriate to challenge the application within the county court proceedings, either by applying to strike out the application or simply defending the application and arguing that the conditions are not made out.

> In *Moat Housing Group-South Ltd v Harris and Hartless*[49] the Court of Appeal considered the making of an ASBI, an ASBO and an outright possession order.
>
> An ASBI with power of arrest had been granted without notice against a tenant with four dependent children. The ASBI required her to vacate her home and excluded her from the neighbourhood. The order was served at 9.00 pm on a Friday evening, three hours after the time specified for compliance with the order. The tenant was able to obtain a stay on the order from the High Court until the matters could be considered at a hearing the following week in the county court.
>
> No previous warnings had been given to the tenant by the landlord about the allegations of anti-social behaviour by herself and two of her children. Most of the evidence of anti-social behaviour in

---

45　CDA 1998 s1(7).

46　*R on the application of T v Manchester Crown Court* [2005] EWHC 1396 (Admin), 7 June 2005.

47　*R on the application of McCann v Manchester Crown Court* [2002] UKHL 39, 17 October 2002.

48　CDA 1998 s1(10).

49　[2005] EWCA Civ 287, 16 March 2005.

the neighbourhood concerned a different family. Notice of seeking possession was subsequently served and at the possession hearing, which took place four weeks after the ASBI had been served, an outright possession order was made together with an ASBO for a period of four years. Much of the evidence presented to the court was hearsay, some from anonymous witnesses.

Considering the granting of the ASBI without notice, the Court of Appeal reiterated the long-standing principle that 'to grant an injunction without notice is to grant an exceptional remedy' and that:

> As a matter of principle no order should be made in civil or family proceedings without notice to the other side unless there is a very good reason for departing from the general rule that notice must be given. Needless to say, the more intrusive the order, the stronger must be the reasons for the departure.[50]

Making an ouster order or an exclusion order without notice was neither proportionate nor necessary to the harm sought to be avoided. The without notice ASBI should have been limited only to that which was necessary, ie an injunction against approaching witnesses. Furthermore, it should not have been made for a period of six months but only until the further hearing. There was no justification for an ASBO for a four-year period and the judge had failed to consider the alternative of an ordinary injunction or undertakings that could be enforced by committal proceedings. In making the outright possession order the judge had failed to have regard to the needs of the tenant and her family.

The Court of Appeal set aside the ASBO, ordering that an injunction or undertakings should be substituted. Furthermore, the outright possession order was set aside and replaced by an order suspended on terms.

Demotion orders

7.72 The nature of the demoted tenancy is dealt with at paras 3.166–3.173 above.

7.73 The court must not make a demotion order unless it is satisfied that the tenant or a person residing in or visiting the dwelling has engaged or threatened to engage in:

---

50 [2005] EWCA Civ 287, Brooke LJ at [71] and [63].

- conduct which is capable of causing nuisance or annoyance to any person and which directly or indirectly relates to or affects the housing management functions of the relevant landlord; or
- conduct which consists of or involves using or threatening to use housing accommodation for an unlawful purpose.[51]

The court must also be satisfied that it is reasonable to make the order.

7.74   In most cases a landlord will apply for a demotion order at the same time as claiming possession on the nuisance ground. A demotion order may be made as an alternative to making a suspended or postponed possession order.

Suitable alternative accommodation

7.75   For protected, statutory and assured tenants the availability of suitable alternative accommodation provides a discretionary ground for possession.[52] For secure tenants there are two classes of grounds under which, in addition to other matters being proved, suitable alternative accommodation must be available to the tenant.

7.76   In all cases where the landlord relies on a suitable alternative accommodation ground, the accommodation must be available at the date the order is made or takes effect. A previous refusal of an offer of suitable accommodation does not give the landlord a ground for possession. So, where a tenant does refuse a suitable offer he or she will not be rendered homeless if a possession order is made on this ground; rather there will be the option of taking up the alternative accommodation. This may be the same accommodation previously offered or different accommodation.

7.77   However, where a tenant has unsuccessfully challenged the decision that the accommodation is suitable but is forced to accept the accommodation after a trial he or she is likely to be ordered to pay the costs of the landlord.

7.78   In most cases the accommodation will be offered by the existing landlord or by arrangement with the existing landlord.

How is suitability assessed?

7.79   Each statute sets out the necessary conditions and relevant matters to be taken into consideration when assessing suitability.[53]

51 See HA 1985 s82A, HA 1988 s6A and HA 1996 ss153A and 153B.
52 RA 1977 s98(1)(a); HA 1988, Ground 9.
53 RA 1977 Sch 15 Pt IV, HA 1985 Sch 2 Pt IV and HA 1988 Sch 2 Pt III.

Private tenants

7.80 A local authority certificate that it will provide suitable alternative accommodation on a specified date is conclusive evidence that suitable alternative accommodation will be available by that date. Such certificates are now rare.

Level of security

7.81 In all cases the alternative accommodation must be let as a separate dwelling. The kind of tenancy offered must be the same kind of tenancy or one with 'equivalent security'.

7.82 For an existing protected or statutory tenant a new protected tenancy may be granted.[54] However, an assured tenancy is capable of offering 'equivalent security' to a protected or statutory tenancy.[55]

7.83 The new protected or assured tenancy cannot be one which would be subject to a mandatory notice ground (see appendix to this chapter) or an assured shorthold tenancy.

Other factors

7.84 The accommodation must be reasonably suitable to the needs of the tenant and the tenant's family in relation to proximity to a work place.

7.85 The accommodation must also be either:

- similar to accommodation let by the local authority to those with similar needs, in terms of the rent and the size of the accommodation; or
- reasonably suitable to the means and needs of the tenant and the tenant's family in terms of the extent and character of the accommodation.

7.86 Accommodation cannot be suitable if it would be statutorily overcrowded.

Secure tenants

7.87 It should be noted that the availability of suitable alternative accommodation is not a 'free standing' ground for possession for secure tenants. It is one element of other grounds, some of which are discretionary. Most of the grounds are to facilitate development or to ensure that special needs or adapted accommodation is occupied by those who need such accommodation. Ground 16, however, provides

54 HA 1988 s34(1)(c).
55 *Laimond Properties Ltd v Al-Sharkarchi* (1998) 30 HLR 1099.

that where a tenancy is obtained by succession, possession may be obtained on the ground of 'under-occupation'. Apart from Ground 16, which is only available for a limited period after the succession, under-occupation is not a ground for possession.

7.88   In all cases the following are factors the court must have regard to:

- the nature of the accommodation which it is the practice of the landlord to allocate to persons with similar needs;
- the distance from the places of work or education of the tenant and the tenant's family;
- the distance from the home of any other family members if proximity is 'essential' to the well-being of the tenant or other family member;
- the needs (as regards the extent of accommodation) and means of the tenant and the tenant's family;
- the terms on which the accommodation is available and the terms of the secure tenancy.

Level of security

7.89   In most cases the authority will offer the tenant another secure tenancy. However, it is possible for a protected or assured tenancy (but not those subject to mandatory grounds or shorthold tenancies) to be deemed suitable alternative accommodation.

Ground 16 (under-occupation by successor tenant)

7.90   Where the landlord is relying on Ground 16, certain additional matters must be taken into account in deciding whether it is reasonable to make an order. These are:

- the tenant's age;
- how long the tenant has occupied the dwelling-house as his or her only or principal home;[56] and
- any financial or other support given by the tenant to the deceased tenant.

7.91   To rely on Ground 16 the authority must serve notice of seeking possession between six and 12 months after the previous tenant's death.[57]

---

56 See *Bracknell Forest v Green* [2009] EWCA Civ 238, 20 March 2009, in which the court refused to order possession of a three-bedroom house occupied by the adult son and daughter of the deceased tenant. The son who succeeded to the tenancy was 50 years old and had lived in the premises his whole life. The Court of Appeal dismissed the landlord's appeal.

57 This applies even in a case where the local authority is not notified of the tenant's death: *Newport City Council v Charles* [2008] EWCA Civ 1541, 11 August 2008.

7.92   It should be noted that the ground is not available if the successor was the spouse or civil partner of the deceased tenant.

7.93   If the tenant accepts suitable alternative accommodation he or she will be treated as a successor in that accommodation, unless the landlord agrees otherwise.

7.94   The date for assessing whether the accommodation is under-occupied is the date of the hearing, not the date of the succession.[58]

Discretionary grounds – reasonableness

7.95   When the landlord is relying on a discretionary ground the burden is on the landlord to prove that:

- the ground is made out; and
- it is reasonable to grant possession.

7.96   The court must always consider whether it is reasonable to grant possession in the particular circumstances. It is for the judge to decide which are the most significant factors:

> The duty of the judge is to take into account all relevant circumstances as they exist at the date of the hearing. That he must do in what I venture to call a broad common-sense way giving weight as he thinks right to the various factors in the situation. Some factors may have little or no weight others may be decisive.[59]

7.97   Although it is open to the court to suspend or postpone an order for possession, the court must first be satisfied that it is reasonable to make a possession order at all, before going on to consider whether it is reasonable to suspend or postpone the order. Because of this requirement, a possession order (whether or not suspended or postponed) cannot be made by consent.[60] If the tenant does not oppose an order he or she must specifically admit all the necessary facts for the court to be satisfied that it is reasonable to grant possession.

7.98   Consideration of an occupier's right to respect for the home under article 8 of the European Convention on Human Rights (ECHR or 'the Convention') should be part of the overall consideration of the question of whether it is reasonable to make an order.

---

58 *Wandsworth LBC v Randall* [2007] EWCA Civ 1126, 7 November 2007.
59 Lord Greene MR in *Cumming v Danson* [1942] 2 All ER 653 at 655.
60 See *Plaschkes v Jones* (1983) 9 HLR 110; *R v Bloomsbury & Marylebone County Court ex p Blackburne* (1985) 14 HLR 56 and *Wandsworth LBC v Fadayomi* (1987) 19 HLR 512.

7.99   Note that when the court is exercising its discretion in relation to the nuisance ground it must take certain specific factors into account (see para 7.51 above).

Public law and article 8 defences

7.100   Two aspects of the Housing Act 1996 led to an increasing number of public sector tenants who had no substantive security of tenure. First, the change to the homelessness duty which became an indefinite duty to provide temporary accommodation, its effect being heightened by the shortage of long-term social housing. Second, the raft of provisions aimed at combating anti-social behaviour. These included the creation of 'probationary' tenancies, by way of the introductory tenancy regime, and later the demoted tenancy. Aside from local authority housing, for the same reasons, the number of tenants of other social landlords occupying under assured shorthold tenancies increased. For all such tenancies (assured shorthold tenants, introductory, demoted and other non-secure tenants) when considering a claim for possession the court does not have to be satisfied that a ground for possession exists, and there is no requirement that the eviction be 'reasonable'.

7.101   The Human Rights Act 1998, which came into force in October 2000, incorporated Convention rights into domestic law (see para 2.41). Since then, the appeal courts have been called upon repeatedly to consider the extent to which an occupier with no security of tenure can defend a claim for possession, relying on either a 'public law' challenge to the landlord's decision to evict or a 'proportionality' ('article 8') defence. The way the law has developed has been described as 'ping pong',[61] with the same issues, and sometimes the same cases, going to and fro between the UK appeal courts and the European Court of Human Rights (ECtHR). To describe the history of these developments would take too much space here and be of little practical use. At last, we appear to have reached a situation in which certain principles are settled.[62] This section summarises those principles and offers some practical tips for advisers assisting occupiers without security of tenure.

7.102   The following principles are now established:

---

61 Nic Madge, 'La Lutta Continua' [2009] JHL 43.

62 The most recent case considered by the Supreme Court was *Hounslow v Powell*, [2011] UKSC 8, 23 February 2011.

- Public law and 'human rights' defences can be raised in the county court.
- This is the case even where statute expressly limits the powers of the county court.
- The county court must, in principle, be able to review the 'proportionality' of an eviction under article 8 but it will only be in exceptional cases that defences based on proportionality will be arguable.
- The personal circumstances of the occupier can be considered by the court when considering proportionality and may be relevant to a public law defence.
- Where an occupier has no security of tenure it will be assumed that, in seeking to evict, the landlord is pursuing a legitimate aim. The burden is on the occupier to show that an eviction would be unlawful on public law grounds and/or a disproportionate interference with the his or her rights under article 8.

Public law and human rights defences: what is the difference?

7.103 It has long been established that a public law defence can be raised in the county court. In *Wandworth v Winder,*[63] as early as 1984, the House of Lords confirmed that a tenant who alleged that the council had acted unlawfully in increasing council rents could defend a claim for possession on that basis and could do so in the county court. The lawfulness of the rent increase was crucial to whether or not the ground for possession was made out. The House of Lords held that it was not an abuse of process to raise a public law argument by way of a defence, rather than by bringing a claim for judicial review.

7.104   A public law defence is one which alleges that the decision to bring and/or pursue the claim for possession is unlawful on established public law principles. These principles are summarised in paras 2.4–2.26 and examples of successful public law arguments in possession claims given below (paras 7.115–7.119). Such a defence focuses on the conduct of the public body rather than the effect of an eviction on the occupier (though the personal circumstances of the occupier may be relevant, provided the public body is made aware of them).

63 *Wandsworth LBC v Winder (No 1)* [1984] UKHL 2. It should be noted that although Mr Winder established the right to raise his defence in the county court , the defence was ultimately unsuccessful: *Wandsworth LBC v Winder (No 2)* (1988) 20 HLR 400.

7.105　　An article 8 or proportionality defence is one in which it is argued that an eviction is not a necessary measure in pursuance of one of the legitimate aims set out in article 8(2), or, in other words, that an eviction would be disproportionate to the aims pursued. Whether or not the eviction is proportionate depends on balancing the aim being pursued by the landlord against the effect of the eviction on the particular occupier; so the occupier's personal circumstances will always be relevant. And, in such a defence, the occupier is asking the court to review the proportionality of the eviction, in other words to carry out that balancing exercise for itself, not just to consider the lawfulness of the landlord's decision-making, as in a public law defence.

Public law defences in the county court

7.106　　While *Wandsworth v Winder* (see para 7.103) confirmed that public law defences *could* be brought in the county courts, the more common practice, where a tenant sought to challenge the decision to evict on public law grounds, was to adjourn the possession claim to enable the tenant to bring a claim for judicial review in the Administrative Court. In *Buscott & Others v Avon County Council*[64] the Court of Appeal held that where the challenge to the decision was that it was 'Wednesbury unreasonable', the correct procedure was to bring the challenge by way of judicial review. *Wandsworth v Winder* was distinguished on the basis that Mr Winder's defence challenged the merits of the claim for possession and related to his private law rights, ie whether or not he was in arrears of rent.

7.107　　In a number of cases, the Court of Appeal considered defences raised by introductory and demoted tenants and held that the proper procedure was for the court to adjourn the possession claim to enable a claim for judicial review to be heard. This was because the statutory regimes for introductory and demoted tenancies sought to limit the county court's powers to a consideration of whether the notice and review procedure had been followed by the authority (see para 6.81).[65] However, the Supreme Court has held that this approach fails to offer the necessary procedural safeguards to ensure that the requirements of article 8 are met. It is essential when article 8 is engaged that there is the *possibility* of an independent and impartial review of the decision to evict, which can encompass not only challenges on points of

---

64　[1988] QB 656.

65　See *Manchester CC v Cochrane* [1999] 1 WLR 809, CA; *McLellan v Bracknell Forest BC* [2001] EWCA Civ 1510 and *R (Gilboy) v Liverpool CC* [2008] EWCA Civ 751.

law but also disputed issues of fact.[66] And, the extent of this review is 'is best left to the good sense and experience of judges sitting in the County Court'.[67]

7.108   So, taking account of the decisions of the ECtHR,[68] the Supreme Court has held that it is no longer necessary to seek an adjournment of a claim for possession to enable judicial review proceedings to be brought. The county court itself must consider a defence founded on public law arguments: there is now a form of judicial review in the county courts. So, in principle, public law defences and article 8 defences can be raised in the county court by demoted and introductory tenants, as well as other non-secure tenants. The same applies for the tenants of other social landlords, who do not have security of tenure (principally assured shorthold tenants), provided their landlord is a public body (see paras 2.68–2.74).

7.109   The principles of public law are described at paras 2.4–2.26. Essentially, a public body landlord must act lawfully, which means:

- in accordance with the law/legally;
- fairly; and
- reasonably.

In accordance with the law/legally

7.110   Public bodies are creatures of statute and must act in accordance with the purpose of the legislation under which they exercise their powers. When exercising their public functions, which include the allocation and management of social housing, they must also act in accordance with statutory guidance and other legislation, such as the Equality Act 2010 (see paras 2.82–2.88 and 7.149–7.164).

7.111   If a public body fails to take account of relevant matters (including its statutory duties as a public body) when making a decision,

---

66 See the House of Lords/Supreme Court decisions in *Kay v Lambeth LBC and Leeds CC v Price* [2006] UKHL 10, 8 March 2006; *Doherty v Birmingham* [2008] UKHL 57, 30 July 2008; *Manchester CC v Pinnock* [2010] UKSC 45, 3 November 2010 and *Hounslow v Powell* [2011] UKSC 8, 23 February 2011. However, how the county court should deal with disputed issues of fact is still not entirely clear: see Lord Hope at [37] contrasted with Lord Phillips at [93] in *Hounslow v Powell* [2011] UKSC 8, 23 February 2011.

67 *Manchester CC v Pinnock* [2010] UKSC 45, Lord Neuberger at 57.

68 See *Connors v UK* App No 66746/01, 27 May 2004; *McCann v UK* App No 19009/04, 13 May 2008 and *Kay v UK* App No 37341/06, 21 September 2010.

this may render that decision unlawful. See, for example, *Pieretti v Enfield*[69] and *Haworth v HMRC*[70] (at paras 2.88 and 7.161).

Fairly

7.112   Procedural fairness will usually mean that a public body must give notice of adverse information it takes into account when making a decision and give the person affected the opportunity to comment. Furthermore, it should follow its own published polices and may be bound to act in accordance with its established practice and, if it proposes to depart from those policies or practices, to consult those affected before doing so.

Reasonably

7.113   It is generally very difficult to challenge a public body decision on the grounds that the decision is 'unreasonable'. Traditional public law defines unreasonableness as 'perversity', or 'irrationality'. The *Wednesbury*[71] test suggests that only a decision that 'no reasonable decision-maker could reach' is capable of being unlawful on this ground.

7.114   One effect of the Human Rights Act 1988, however, has meant that *Wednesbury* unreasonableness is applied in a more flexible way, depending on the nature of the rights at issue. Where fundamental rights are at stake the courts will apply 'anxious scrutiny' of the decisions of public bodies, whereas in the sphere of economic rights the courts will be less willing to intervene. And article 6, which requires an independent and impartial review in the determination of a person's civil rights, means that in some circumstances that review must extend to issues of fact and cannot be restricted to issues of law.[72]

---

69   [2010] EWCA Civ 1104.
70   [2011] EWHC 36 (Ch).
71   *Associated Provincial Picture Houses Ltd v Wednesbury Corporation* [1948] 1 KB 223, CA. See paras 2.15–2.17.
72   See Lord Hope at [110] in *Kay v Lambeth LBC and Leeds CC v Price* [2006] UKHL 10, and later when reviewing the scope of the conventional public law challenge in *Doherty v Birmingham* [2008] UKHL 57 at [55] and again at [7] in *Hounslow v Powell* [2011] UKSC 8.

Examples of successful public law defences

7.115 In *Barber v Croydon LBC*[73] a non-secure tenant accommodated as a homeless person appealed against a possession order. The tenant had learning difficulties and a personality disorder and it was accepted that he was a disabled person within the meaning of the Disability Discrimination Act 1995. It was alleged that he had sworn at, spat at and kicked the caretaker of his block of flats. He denied spitting or assaulting the caretaker though he admitted that there had been an argument and subsequently accepted a police caution for a public order act offence (causing harassment, alarm or distress by the use of threatening and abusive language). The council started possession proceedings. Medical evidence was obtained regarding his disability and the likely effect of an eviction. The council considered the evidence but decided to proceed with the eviction.

The Court of Appeal found that the council had failed to follow its own anti-social behaviour policy which stressed the need to work in partnership with other agencies when dealing with vulnerable persons and seeking alternatives to eviction. The council had also failed to give due weight to the psychiatrist's report and its decision to evict was one that no housing authority, faced with these facts, could reasonably have taken.

7.116 A similar decision was taken in relation to an assured shorthold 'starter' tenant who fell into rent arrears:

In *Eastlands Homes Partnership Ltd v Sandra Whyte*[74] the tenant occupied as an assured shorthold tenant, under a 'starter tenancy'. The agreement provided that after one year the tenancy would convert into an assured tenancy as long as certain events had not happened, including possession proceedings being brought. Because of rent arrears, a further starter tenancy was entered into but the landlords subsequently decided not to offer an assured tenancy and to proceed with an eviction. The landlords operated an appeals process in relation to such decisions.

---

73 [2010] EWCA Civ 51, 11 February 2010. See also the similar case of *McGlynn v Welwyn Hatfield DC* [2009] EWCA Civ 285, 1 April 2009.
74 [2010] EWHC 695 (QB), 31 March 2010.

> The court found that the landlords had not followed their own appeals procedure properly and had acted unfairly in the way the appeal was conducted. Furthermore, they had failed to adhere to their own rent arrears policy which stated that eviction would be treated 'as a last resort when clear and deliberate failure to pay is apparent'. Taking those failings into account, the court concluded that the decision was one that no reasonable authority could have reached and dismissed the claim for possession. Given that the landlords' policy was that assured shorthold tenancies became full assured tenancies after one year, the effect of the court's decision was that Ms Whyte was an assured tenant.

7.117   The failure of a public body to follow its own policies may also be relevant when seeking to avoid eviction *after* the making of a possession order. In *Southwark LBC v Augustus*[75] a warrant was set aside on the basis of oppression where the authority had failed to follow its rent arrears policy which stated that eviction would only be used as a last resort.

7.118   Although these cases focus on the lawfulness of the public body's decision-making, the occupier's personal circumstances are clearly relevant in so far as the court is scrutinising the way the public body has taken those circumstances into account and the extent to which it has applied its own policies.

7.119   When running a public law defence it is essential to ensure that the public body is informed of the occupier's personal circumstances. This is particularly so when the tenant is vulnerable since the basis of the defence will usually be, in some part, that the public body has failed to take those circumstances into account or to abide by a policy or statutory requirement regarding vulnerable tenants.[76]

Article 8 defences

7.120   Article 8 of the ECHR provides:

1) Everyone has the right to respect for his private and family life, his home and his correspondence.
2) There shall be no interference by a public authority with the exercise of this right except such as is in accordance with the law and

75   February 2007 *Legal Action* 29, Lambeth County Court, 24 November 2006.
76   Note that to establish disability discrimination it is necessary that the alleged discriminator is aware that the person is a disabled person, see paras 7.151–7.153 below.

is necessary in a democratic society in the interests of national security, public safety or the economic well-being of the country, for the prevention of disorder or crime, for the protection of health or morals, or for the protection of the rights and freedoms of others.

7.121 To establish that an eviction will breach a person's rights under article 8 the following must be shown:

- the premises are the occupier's 'home';
- the decision to evict is an interference with the occupier's right to respect for his or her home; and
- the interference is either not in accordance with the law or is not necessary in pursuance of one of the interests set out in article 8(2).

The 'home'

7.122 This is a question of fact and does not depend on the person's legal right of occupation. As recently held by the ECtHR: 'Whether or not a particular habitation constitutes a "home" which attracts the protection of article 8(1) will depend on the factual circumstances, namely, the existence of sufficient and continuous links with a specific place.'[77] A man who was technically a trespasser following service of a notice to quit by his ex-wife and joint tenant was held to be occupying as his home.[78] However, where a family had occupied a traveller's site for only two days before proceedings were issued the House of Lords held that it was 'all but unarguable that [the land on which they parked their caravans] was ever their home within the meaning of article 8(1)'.[79] Nevertheless, the Supreme Court has held that 'in most cases it can be taken for granted that a claim by a person who is in lawful occupation to remain in possession will attract the protection of article 8'.[80]

Interference

7.123 Article 8 is a qualified right: interference may be justified if it in accordance with the law and is necessary in a democratic society in pursuance of the legitimate interests set out in article 8(2), see para 7.120 above.

---

77 *Kryvitska v Ukraine* ECtHR Application no 30856/03, 9 November 2010 at [40].
78 *Harrow v Qazi* [2003] UKHL 43, 31 July 2003.
79 *Leeds CC v Price* [2006] UKHL 10, 8 March 2006, Lord Bingham at [48].
80 *Hounslow v Powell* [2011] UKSC 8, 23 February 2011, Lord Hope at [33].

7.124   To evict a person from his or her home will always involve an interference with rights under article 8. 'Loss of one's home is a most extreme form of interference with the right to respect for the home'.[81]

7.125   However, when the court is considering an eviction of an occupier with no security of tenure, the starting point is that the interference is assumed to be lawful and necessary:

> The legislature has excluded [certain] types of tenancy from the statutory scheme which applies to secure tenancies for very good reasons, which are firmly rooted in social policy. In seeking democratic solutions to the problems inherent in the allocation of social housing, Parliament has sought to strike a balance between the rights of the occupier and the property rights and public responsibilities of the public authority.[82]

7.126   If an occupier is arguing that the legislation itself constitutes a breach of his or her article 8 rights and cannot be read in a way that is compatible with those rights, the courts can make a declaration of incompatibility (see para 2.75). However, the following regimes relating to housing rights have been specifically held to be compatible with the Convention:

- the use of non-secure tenancies for homeless applicants accommodated by local authorities;[83]
- the use of assured shorthold tenancies, and the section 21 notice procedure, for homeless applicants accommodated by social landlords;[84]
- the introductory tenancy regime;[85]
- the rules allowing the issuing of warrants without a hearing following a possession order;[86]
- the provisions restricting those members of the family entitled to succeed to a secure tenancy.[87]

---

81 *Kryvitska v Ukraine* ECtHR Application no 30856/03, 9 November 2010 at [41]. See also, *McCann v UK* ECtHR Application No 19009/04 at [50].
82 *Hounslow v Powell* [2011] UKSC 8, 23 February 2011, Lord Hope at [10].
83 *Sheffield CC v Smart & Central Sunderland Housing Co Ltd v Wilson* [2002] EWCA Civ 4.
84 *Poplar Housing v Donaghue* [2001] EWCA Civ 595, see para 2.70.
85 *McLellan v Bracknell Forest* [2001] EWCA Civ 1510 and *Merton LBC v Williams* [2002] EWCA Civ 980.
86 *Sheffield CC v Hopkins* [2001] EWCA Civ 1023.
87 *Michalak v Wandsworth LBC* [2002] EWCA Civ 271.

The margin of appreciation

7.127 These cases illustrate what is called the 'margin of appreciation'. As the ECtHR held in *Kay v UK*:

> In making their initial assessment of the necessity of the measure, the national authorities enjoy a margin of appreciation in recognition of the fact that they are better placed than international courts to evaluate local needs and conditions.[88]

And in *Connors v UK*:

> The margin will tend to be narrower where the right at stake is crucial to the individual's effective enjoyment of intimate or key rights ... On the other hand, in spheres involving the application of social or economic policies, there is authority that the margin of appreciation is wide ...[89]

As Lord Hope said in *Powell*:

> There are clear policy reasons why Parliament has denied security to certain classes of occupier.[90]

Examples of successful article 8 defences

7.128 At the time of writing, there are no examples in the appeal courts of defences that have succeeded purely on the issue of proportionality. It should be noted, however, that in *Croydon v Barber* and *McGlynn v Welwyn Hatfield DC*[91] (see para 7.115 above) the defences succeeded on conventional public law grounds, the court holding that no reasonable authority could have decided to pursue the eviction in the circumstances. These cases were heard before the Supreme Court made clear that the county courts could conduct a proportionality review and would surely have succeeded had they been argued on the ground that the decision was disproportionate under article 8.

Examples of unsuccessful article 8 defences

7.129 It should be noted that on the facts, in the cases of *Manchester v Pinnock* and *Birmingham v Frisby*, the Supreme Court held that the decision to evict had been proportionate. In *Hounslow v Powell* the court held that there might have been grounds to remit the case for consideration by the county court for a review of the proportionality of the decision but this was not necessary as an offer of alternative

88 ECtHR Application no 3734/06, 21 September 2010 at [66].
89 ECtHR Application no 66746/01, 27 May 2004 at [82].
90 *Hounslow v Powell* [2011] UKSC 8, 23 February 2011 at [10].
91 [2009] EWCA Civ 285, 1 April 2009.

accommodation had been made. And in relation to *Leeds CC v Hall* it was held that no grounds had been put before the court to suggest that Mr Hall had a seriously arguable defence, but, as he too had been offered a secure tenancy by Leeds CC, the appeal was upheld and the possession order set aside.

7.130   For a recent case in which an article 8 defence was rejected see *Brighton & Hove CC v Alleyn and Others*[92] in which a claim for possession against a group of travellers was defended on public law and article 8 grounds. The case is an example of the application of a 'structured approach'.[93] However, having balanced the needs of the travellers and the needs of the local community, and taking into account the steps the council had taken to mitigate the effect of an eviction, including previously deferring action against particular occupiers, it was held that the eviction was lawful and proportionate.

Exceptionality

7.131   The courts have repeatedly stressed that it will only be in highly exceptional cases that a proportionality defence will be arguable where the occupier has no domestic law right to remain in occupation. However, this does not mean that that proportionality arguments should be limited to 'very highly exceptional cases'. In *Pinnock* it was held that it would be:

> ... both unsafe and unhelpful to invoke exceptionality as a guide ... exceptionality is an outcome and not a guide. ... The question is always whether the eviction is a proportionate means of achieving a legitimate aim ... in virtually every case where a residential occupier has no contractual or statutory protection, and the local authority is entitled to possession as a matter of domestic law, there will be a very strong case for saying that making an order for possession would be proportionate. However, in some cases there may be factors which would tell the other way.[94]

What this means is that a case does not necessarily have to have highly exceptional features to be arguable but that the cases in which an eviction is disproportionate are likely to be highly exceptional.

---

92 [2011] EW Misc 6 (CC).
93 The judge in the case was Jan Luba QC who had argued, unsuccessfully, for such an approach in *Powell*.
94 *Manchester CC v Pinnock* [2010] UKSC 45, 3 November 2010, Lord Neuberger at [51], [52] and [54].

Relevance of personal circumstances

7.132   In some of the early cases the courts appeared to be saying that the personal circumstances of an occupier with no right to remain in occupation could never be relevant to a public law defence to a claim for possession.[95] The Supreme Court has now confirmed that this is not the case although there is a limit to the extent of the consideration:

> The court need be concerned only with the occupiers' personal circumstances and any factual objection she may raise and, in the light only of what view it takes of them, with the question whether making the order for possession would be lawful and proportionate.[96]

7.133   Clearly, however, if the court is considering whether an eviction is proportionate it is balancing the legitimate aims being pursued by the public body landlord with the effect of the eviction on the occupier, which necessarily involves considering the personal circumstances of the occupier. The harsher the effect of an eviction, the more likely it is to be disproportionate.

7.134   As the Supreme Court held in *Pinnock* (approving the submissions of the Equalities and Human Rights Commission):

> ... proportionality is more likely to be a relevant issue 'in respect of occupants who are vulnerable as a result of mental illness, physical or learning disability, poor health or frailty' and that 'the issue may also require the local authority to explain why they are not securing alternative accommodation in such cases.'[97]

What if the eviction is not proportionate?

7.135   An important consideration is the likely outcome if the proportionality argument succeeds. A non-secure occupier will not generally establish a long-term right of occupation even if he or she successfully defends a claim for possession.[98] Both public law and article 8

---

95   Lord Hope in *Kay v Lambeth LBC* [2006] UKHL 10, 8 March 2006 held that a defence based on the personal circumstances of the occupier should be struck out.

96   *Hounslow v Powell* [2011] UKSC 8, 23 February 2011, Lord Hope at [37].

97   *Manchester CC v Pinnock* [2010] UKSC 45, 3 November 2010, Lord Neuberger at [64].

98   Though in cases where a non-secure or non-assured tenancy automatically becomes secure or assured after a set period of time, this may be the outcome. See *Eastlands Homes Partnership v White*, para 7.116 above. In *Hounslow v Powell* [2011] UKSC 8, 23 February 2011, the fact that the effect of denying a claim for possession against an introductory tenant would be that the tenant would become secure was identified as a factor highly relevant in any assessment of proportionality: Lord Hope at [19].

defences depend on the particular facts and context of the proposed eviction. A successful public law and/or article 8 defence will establish only that a particular decision to evict in the particular circumstances of the case is unlawful or disproportionate.

7.136 So, for example, it may be unlawful for a public body to decide to evict a person without having considered whether alternative accommodation is available. But, having considered the issue, and possibly made offers of alternative accommodation, a decision to evict may be unchallengeable. A decision to evict a person who is undergoing medical treatment may be unlawful if the effect would be to disrupt the treatment but may be lawful if the public body agreed to postpone enforcing the possession order until a later date. A decision to evict an introductory tenant who has rent arrears may be unlawful if the public body operates a blanket policy and refuses to consider any proposal other than the whole of the arrears being cleared. But, if the body properly considers an offer to pay by instalments and decides to proceed with a claim for possession because previous agreements have been breached, the decision to evict may be lawful.

The burden is on the occupier

7.137 The cases have been consistent in holding that the burden is on the occupier to establish that an eviction would be disproportionate:

> The basic rules are now not in doubt. The court will only have to consider whether the making of a possession order is proportionate if the issue has been raised by the occupier and it has crossed the high threshold of being seriously arguable.[99]

7.138 When a landlord is seeking possession against an occupier who has no security of tenure, the presumption is that the landlord is acting lawfully and that the decision to evict is proportionate. In *Pinnock*, Lord Neuberger held that:

> ... in virtually every case where a residential occupier has no contractual or statutory protection, and the local authority is entitled to possession as a matter of domestic law, there will be a very strong case for saying that making an order for possession would be proportionate. However, in some cases there may be factors which would tell the other way.[100]

So, it is for the occupier to prove that such a presumption is wrong, not for the landlord to prove that the eviction is proportionate.

99 *Hounslow v Powell* [2011] UKSC 8, 23 February 2011, Lord Hope at [33].
100 *Manchester CC v Pinnock* [2010] UKSC 45, 3 November 2010.

7.139   However, although the burden is not on the landlord in every case to 'justify its application for a possession order or to plead the reason for seeking this', in most cases when a public body landlord is seeking to evict a tenant with no security of tenure 'the tenant must be informed of the reason for the authority's action so that he can, if so minded, attempt to raise a proportionality challenge'.[101] Of course, under the introductory and demoted tenancy schemes a notice must be served setting out the reasons for the decision to evict but in relation to other non-secure tenancies there is no such requirement.[102] In *Powell* the court declined to indicate whether reasons should be given before the service of a notice to quit but suggested that any procedural requirements were best set out in a practice direction.[103]

7.140   It was suggested by Lord Bingham in *Kay v Lambeth LBC*[104] that the fact that the burden is on the tenant to raise a public law or proportionality defence should be reflected in the procedure. Although this was a dissenting judgment, it has since been approved as the correct approach by the ECtHR in *Kay v UK*, and by the Supreme Court in *Powell*.

In *Kay v Lambeth LBC* Lord Bingham held:

The practical position, in future, in possession proceedings can be briefly summarised as follows.

1) It is not necessary for a local authority to plead or prove in every case that domestic law complies with article 8. Courts should proceed on the assumption that domestic law strikes a fair balance and is compatible with article 8.

2) If the court, following its usual procedures, is satisfied that the domestic law requirements for making a possession order have been met the court should make a possession order unless the occupier shows that, highly exceptionally, he has a seriously arguable case on one of two grounds.

3) The two grounds are:
   a) That the law which requires the court to make a possession order despite the occupier's personal circumstances is Convention-incompatible; and

---

101 *Hounslow v Powell* [2011] UKSC 8, 23 February 2011, Lord Phillips at [116].
102 And for demoted assured shorthold tenancies there is no such requirement. See paras 6.79–6.80.
103 See *Hounslow v Powell* [2011] UKSC 8, 23 February 2011 at [117].
104 *Kay v Lambeth LBC* [2006] UKHL 10, 8 March 2006.

b) That, having regard to the occupier's personal circumstances, the local authority's exercise of its power to seek a possession order is an unlawful act within the meaning of section 6 [of the Human Rights Act 1998].

4) Deciding whether the defendant has a seriously arguable case on one or both of these grounds will not call for a full-blown trial. This question should be decided summarily, on the basis of an affidavit or of the defendant's defence, suitably particularised, or in whatever other summary way the court considers appropriate. The procedural aim of the court must be to decide this question as expeditiously as is consistent with the defendant having a fair opportunity to present his case on this question.

5) If the court considers the defence sought to be raised on one or both of these grounds is not seriously arguable the court should proceed to make a possession order.

6) Where a seriously arguable issue on one of these grounds is raised, the court should itself decide this issue, subject to this: where an issue arises on the application of section 3 [incompatibility] the judge should consider whether it may be appropriate to refer the proceedings to the High Court.[105]

Practical tips

7.141   Be familiar with the public body's policies – particular its equality scheme or policies, its rent arrears policy, any policy for dealing with vulnerable tenants and any homelessness or housing strategy. A failure to follow its own policies may make the public body's decision unlawful.

7.142   Be realistic and put forward information and proposals at an early stage. If it is being argued that the public body should not be evicting someone because of their particular circumstances (for example, a recent bereavement, loss of employment), the public body cannot be criticised if it was not informed of those circumstances. If it is informed early in the proceedings and a realistic proposal put forward, a blunt refusal to consider the information or proposal may make the decision to pursue the eviction unlawful on public law grounds.

105 *Kay v Lambeth LBC* [2006] UKHL 10, 8 March 2006, Lord Bingham at [39].

7.143 Remember that the case will be listed for a very short hearing in the possession list. If possible, make sure that the landlord is aware that the occupier is raising a defence and put the key points of the defence in a witness statement, draft defence, or at the very least a letter.[106]

Conclusion

7.144 To date, the cases in which the courts have considered public law and article 8 defences suggest that a 'public law' defence is more likely to succeed that a proportionality defence, though in many cases these will overlap. However, probably the most likely effect of the recent case-law will not be a large volume of successful public law and proportionality defences but an encouragement to advisers to challenge decisions to evict at an early stage and an improved attitude by public bodies. Knowing that their conduct may be scrutinised by the court should encourage public bodies to adopt a more reasonable response to any reasonable proposals put forward by an occupier to avoid an eviction.

Disability discrimination and vulnerable tenants

7.145 The Disability Discrimination Act (DDA) 1995, which has now been replaced by the Equality (EA) Act 2010, made it unlawful to discriminate against disabled people in a number of spheres of activity, including renting or buying land or property. Under the 1995 Act it was unlawful to discriminate against a person by evicting them. Discrimination was when a person, 'for a reason which relates to the disabled person's disability', treated a disabled person less favourably than he or she would treat others 'to whom that reason did not apply'. An eviction that amounted to discrimination could however be justified on the ground that the eviction was necessary in order not to endanger the health or safety of any person.[107]

7.146 The courts considered the issue in a number of cases when claims for possession were made because of anti-social behaviour and the tenants argued that the behaviour was related to their disability. They

---

106 CPR requires that the occupier file a defence within 14 days. While this may not always be possible every effort should be made to inform the court and the claimant at the earliest opportunity that the claim is defended.
107 See DDA 1995 ss22(3)(c), 24(1) and 24(3).

defended the claims on the ground that the eviction amounted to unlawful discrimination.

7.147 A key issue was whether it was discrimination to evict a tenant because of behaviour related to a disability when a non-disabled tenant would be evicted for the same behaviour. In other words, who is the proper 'comparator'? Was it a non-disabled person who behaved in the same way or a non-disabled person who did not behave in the same way? If it was the latter, then to evict the disabled person behaving in an anti-social way would amount to discrimination. And such discrimination could only be justified on health and safety grounds.

> The issue came before the House of Lords in *Lewisham LBC v Malcolm*[108] in which a tenant with a previous diagnosis of schizophrenia had unlawfully sublet his flat, which led to the loss of the secure tenancy (see para 4.11).
>   The House of Lords held, by a majority of three to two, that in deciding whether an eviction amounted to disability discrimination the proper comparator was a non-disabled person who had sublet his or her flat. As the authority would have sought possession against such a person, Mr Malcolm was not being treated less favourably and the eviction did not constitute disability discrimination. Furthermore, the House also held that an eviction could not be discriminatory if the landlord was not aware of the occupier's disability.

7.148 The problem was that this ruling effectively abolished indirect discrimination, not only in housing cases but in other areas such as employment. The effect of *Lewisham v Malcolm* has now been largely reversed by the Equality Act 2010, which consolidates discrimination legislation into a single Act and extends established protection from discrimination (previously only relevant in relation to race, gender and disability) to other groups with 'protected characteristics'.

The Equality Act 2010

7.149 Most of the Act came into force in October 2010 but some provisions, including the general equality duty[109] (see para 2.84) came into

---

108 [2008] UKHL 43, 25 July 2007.
109 Also referred to as the 'public sector equality duty'.

force in April 2011. The Act extends protection from discrimination to people with protected characteristics. Protected characteristics are: age; disability; gender reassignment; pregnancy and maternity; race; religion or belief; sex; and sexual orientation.

Definition of disability[110]

7.150   A person with a disability is defined as a person with a physical or mental impairment that has a substantial and long-term adverse effect on the person's ability to carry out normal day-to-day activities. 'Long-term' means it has lasted or is likely to last at least 12 months or for the rest of the person's life. Some conditions are specifically defined as disabilities so that it is not necessary to establish evidence of their effect on the ability to carry out normal day-to-day activities. Some conditions, mostly relating to personality disorders or self-inflicted behaviour, are specifically excluded.

Conditions specifically identified as a disability are:

- progressive conditions such as cancer, HIV infection and multiple sclerosis;
- visual impairments certified by a consultant ophthalmologist.

Conditions/impairments specifically excluded are:

- addiction to alcohol, nicotine or other substances (though not if the addiction is the result of initially prescribed medication);
- a tendency to set fires, steal, physically or sexually abuse others, exhibitionism or voyeurism;
- hay fever (but not to the extent it aggravates another condition);
- severe disfigurement which consists of tattoos or piercings.

What is discrimination?

7.151   The Equality Act 2010 provides that a person (A) discriminates against another (B) if because of a protected characteristic A treats B less favourably than A treats or would treat others.[111] This is 'direct discrimination'. However, in relation to disability, it is not discrimination to treat a disabled person *more* favourably than non-disabled

---

110   See EA 2010 s6 and Sch 1, Equality Act 2010 (Disability) Regulations 2010 SI No 2128 and *The Equality Act 2010 Guidance: guidance on matters to be taken into account in determining questions relating to the definition of disability* published by the Office for Disability Issues in May 2011.

111   EA 2010 s13(1). In relation to age however, less favourable treatment is lawful if it is a proportionate means of achieving a legitimate aim: s13(2).

people.[112] There are also certain qualifications that are specific to particular protected characteristics.

7.152   Disability discrimination is more specifically defined in EA 2010 s15(1): a person (A) discriminates against a disabled person (B) if A treats B unfavourably *because of something arising in consequence of* B's disability and A cannot show that the treatment is a proportionate means of achieving a legitimate aim. However, the treatment is not discrimination if A can show that A did not know, and could not reasonably have been expected to know, that B had the disability.[113] So, to establish discrimination the person alleging discrimination must prove that:

- the person is a disabled person as defined in the EA 2010. In most cases medical evidence will be needed;
- he or she was treated unfavourably (note that this is not in comparison with a non-disabled person); and
- the unfavourable treatment was because of something 'arising in consequence of' the disability.

7.153   If this is established, the treatment will amount to discrimination unless the alleged discriminator can show that:

- the treatment is a proportionate means of achieving a legitimate aim; or
- he or she was not aware and could not reasonably be expected to know about the disability.

7.154   By defining disability discrimination as unfavourable treatment because of something 'arising in consequence of' the disability, without reference to a comparision with how someone who is not disabled would be treated, the EA 2010 has removed the problem created by *Lewisham LBC v Malcolm* (see para 7.147). Indirect discrimination, by way of an eviction, is unlawful.[114] However, a person seeking to justify an eviction has an easier test to meet than under the DDA 1995: the eviction will be lawful if it is a proportionate way of achieving a legitimate aim.

7.155   The EA 2010 also makes specific provision for indirect discrimination by way of operating a 'provision, criterion or practice' which places a disabled person at a disadvantage. Furthermore, a breach of the various duties to make 'reasonable adjustments' in relation to

---

112 EA 2010 s13(3).
113 EA 2010 s15(2).
114 EA 2010 s35(1)(b).

disabled persons may also constitute discrimination. Both of these are explained below at paras 7.156–7.163.

Indirect discrimination[115]

7.156   Equality Act 2010 s19 provides that a person (A) discriminates against another (B) if A applies to B a provision, criterion or practice which is discriminatory in relation to a relevant protected characteristic of B's. The provision, criterion or practice will be discriminatory if it puts people who share B's protected characteristic at a particular disadvantage when compared with people who do not share the particular characteristic (and it does or would put B at that disadvantage) and A cannot show that it is a proportionate means of achieving a legitimate aim.

7.157   It should be noted that it is the application of a 'provision, criterion or practice' not the enforcement of legal rights or duties that may be discriminatory. So, to seek to rely on a statutory ground for possession against the disabled person (for example, the rent arrears or nuisance ground) is not discrimination under EA 2010 s19. However, the 'practice' adopted by the landlord in doing so is capable of being discriminatory. An example may be where a landlord communicates about a proposed eviction only in writing to a tenant known to have a learning disability which affects his or her ability to read or understand written communications. Also, if the disabled person's conduct which gives rise to the ground for possession arises in consequence of his or her disability, the eviction itself would be discrimination under EA 2010 s35, and the landlord would have to show that the eviction was a proportionate means of achieving a legitimate aim. A landlord will need to consider alternatives to eviction and a public body landlord will be expected to offer support to the tenant under its policies relating to vulnerable tenants: see, for example, *Barber v Croydon* at para 7.115 above.

7.158   This provision is closely connected to the duty to make reasonable adjustments.

---

115 See EA 2010 s19. Previously indirect discrimination was provided for in relation to race and gender but not disability.

Reasonable adjustments[116]

7.159   In respect of disability there is also a duty to make 'reasonable adjust-ments' and a failure to do so may itself amount to disability dis-crimination. The duty to make reasonable adjustments for disabled persons applies to landlords, to those providing public services and to those exercising public functions.[117] There are three ways the duty may apply:

1) where a provision, criterion or practice puts a disabled person at a substantial disadvantage in comparison with persons who are not disabled;

2) where a physical feature puts a disabled person at a substantial disadvantage in comparison with persons who are not disabled; and

3) where a disabled person would, but for the provision of an auxil-iary aid, be put at a substantial disadvantage.

7.160   In regard to (1) and (2) the duty is to take such steps as it is reason-able to have to take to avoid the disadvantage and in relation to (3) the duty is to take such steps as it is reasonable to have to take to provide the auxiliary aid.

7.161   At the time of writing there are no reported cases in which the courts have considered these provisions in relation to the eviction of an occupier. However, a case about a bankruptcy order obtained against a woman with known mental health problems illustrates how a failure to make reasonable adjustments may amount to disability discrimination.

> In *Haworth v Cartmel and HMRC*[118] HM Revenue & Customs (HMRC) received an anonymous allegation that Ms Haworth was running a profitable business breeding horses. Ms Haworth was a woman with a history of mental health problems and claimed to keep the horses for therapeutic reasons. Following letters sent to her by HMRC requesting her to submit a tax return Ms Haworth's mother contacted HMRC and made them aware of her daughter's mental health problems, indicating that she found it very difficult to deal with correspondence and often failed to open official letters.

116 EA 2010 s20.
117 EA 2010 ss36(1) and 29(7).
118 [2011] EWHC 36 (Ch), 4 February 2011. The case concerned very similar provisions contained in the DDA 1995 as most of the EA 2010 was not then in force.

Ms Haworth also contacted them and indicated the same. As Ms Haworth failed to file a tax return, HMRC then sent to her a statutory demand for payment of the estimated tax due and subsequently served a bankruptcy petition. A bankruptcy order was granted at a hearing which Ms Haworth did not attend. Two years later an application was made to annul the order on the grounds that Ms Haworth had not had capacity under the Mental Capacity Act 2005 to deal with the issues at the time and that HMRC had discriminated against her under the DDA 1995.

The court considered the medical evidence in relation to the relevant period two years earlier and annulled the order on the ground that Ms Haworth had lacked capacity to deal with the notices and court proceedings. But the court went on to consider whether HMRC's actions amounted to disability discrimination. The court held that HMRC had failed to make reasonable adjustments in relation to a 'policy, practice or procedure', namely the way in which they had made the application for a bankruptcy order. In particular, the court found that HMRC should have informed Ms Haworth's mother about when they planned to serve the statutory demand and the petition and should have informed the court about her disability. Her mother could then have made sure that the envelopes were opened and the documents dealt with. Furthermore, the court would have been likely to adjourn for further steps to be taken to ensure that Ms Haworth was aware of the hearing and to investigate the extent of her disability.

7.162   It is easy to see how this may apply in relation to a landlord's conduct in seeking a possession order. What the Equality Act 2010 provides and *Haworth v Cartmel* illustrates is simply that, where a landlord is aware that a tenant is disabled, the landlord must take steps to ensure that he or she is not disadvantaged by the procedures normally followed, that appropriate support is offered or adjustments made and that alternatives to eviction are considered. If not, an eviction may be held to be discriminatory.

7.163   It should be noted that any landlord may be guilty of disability discrimination but where the landlord is a public body the arguments relating to disability discrimination are likely to overlap with defences relying on public law and rights under article 8 of the ECHR (see paras 7.100–7.144 above). Furthermore, a public body is also subject to the public sector equality duties set out in EA 2010 s149 and described in paras 2.84–2.88. These require a public body to have due regard to the need to eliminate discrimination and promote equality of opportunity when exercising its public functions.

7.164   Where disability discrimination is likely to be relevant, the following matters should also be borne in mind:

- *Reasonableness* If a claim for possession is on a discretionary ground the court must be satisfied that it is reasonable to make a possession order. If the tenant has a disability this will be a relevant factor, whether or not the disability is related to the grounds on which possession is sought. If the landlord is a unitary local authority it will be particularly relevant that it also has duties to provide support under community care law (see chapter 18).
- *The rent arrears protocol* Where the tenant is 'vulnerable' and a social landlord is seeking possession on the grounds of rent arrears the landlord must consider at an early stage the issues of capacity, possible disability discrimination and (if the landlord is a local authority) the possible need for a community care assessment (see para 6.7).
- *Public law defences* Where the landlord is a public body, there may be a defence based on public law or proportionality even it is not necessary for the landlord to prove a ground for possession or for a possession order to be reasonable even where there is no requirement that the court is satisfied that an eviction is reasonable. The tenant's circumstances, the landlord's policies for vulnerable tenants, the support offered by the landlord and alternatives to eviction will all be relevant. See paras 7.100–7.144.[119]
- *Capacity* Where a person lacks capacity, the CPR require a 'litigation friend' to be appointed. A landlord bringing a claim must make an application for the appointment if aware of the disability. A failure to inform the court of the person's disability may result in orders being set aside (see *Haworth v HMRC*, para 7.161 above). Capacity is dealt with in more detail in paras 7.165–7.175 below.

Capacity

7.165   The Mental Capacity Act (MCA) 2005 sets out the framework for assessing capacity and for dealing with the affairs of those who lack

---

119 See for example *McGlynn v Welwyn Hatfield DC* [2009] EWCA Civ 285, 1 April 2009 and *Barber v Croydon* [2010] EWCA Civ 51, 11 February 2010, referred to at para 7.115.

capacity. The detailed provisions of the Act are outside the scope of this book. The following, however, are some of the central principles:[120]

- A person is assumed to have capacity unless it is established that he or she lacks capacity.
- A person is not to be treated as unable to make a decision unless all practicable steps to help him or her to do so have been taken without success.
- A person is not to be treated as unable to make a decision merely because he or she makes an unwise decision.

Inability to make decisions

7.166 Capacity is to be assessed not in general terms but in relation to particular decisions[121] and MCA 2005 s3 provides that a person is unable to make a decision if unable:

- to understand the information relevant to the decision;
- to retain that information;
- to use or weigh that information as part of the process of making the decision; or
- to communicate the decision (whether by talking, using sign language or any other means).

7.167 A person is not to be regarded as unable to understand relevant information if he or she can understand an explanation given in an appropriate way, using, for example, simple language, visual aids or other means.

7.168 The fact that a person is able to retain relevant information only for a short period does not prevent a person being regarded as able to make a decision.

7.169 In most cases medical evidence will be needed to establish a lack of capacity to establish the need for a litigation friend. However, CPR Part 21 does not require this and the opinion of a friend or family member who offers to act as a litigation friend may be sufficient. However, it should be noted that MCA 2005 specifically provides that:

> A lack of capacity cannot be established merely by reference to a person's age or appearance, or a ... condition or an aspect of [the person's]

---

120 These are set out in MCA 2005 s1.

121 *Haworth v Cartmel & HMRC* (at para 7.161) illustrates this well. The court examined capacity specifically in relation to three specific steps in the process: the service of the statutory demand, the service of the petition and the court application.

behaviour, which might lead others to make unjustified assumptions about his [or her] capacity.[122]

The Court of Protection

7.170   The Mental Capacity Act 2005 also governs the powers and procedures for the Court of Protection which can make decisions about the property and affairs, healthcare and personal welfare of those without capacity. The Court of Protection has powers equivalent to the High Court and can decide whether someone has the capacity to make a particular decision.

Court proceedings: litigation friends

7.171   Under the Civil Procedure Rules a 'protected party' must have a litigation friend appointed to conduct proceedings on his or her behalf.[123] A protected party means 'a party, or an intended party, who lacks capacity to conduct the proceedings'.[124]

7.172   If proceedings are issued against a protected party, a person may not take any steps in the proceedings until the party has a litigation friend.

7.173   A person appointed by the Court of Protection may conduct proceedings on behalf of the protected party. Otherwise, anyone can put himself or herself forward as a litigation friend by filing and serving on all parties a 'certificate of suitability' (form N235) stating that the necessary conditions are met. The conditions are that the person must be able fairly and competently to conduct proceedings on behalf of the party and has no interest adverse to that of the party.[125] The certificate must also state the grounds of the person's belief that the party lacks capacity and, if based on a medical or other expert opinion, must attach relevant documents.[126]

7.174   An application for the appointment of a litigation friend may be made by the person who wishes to be the litigation friend or by one of the parties to the proceedings.

---

122 MCA 2005 s2(3).

123 CPR Part 21.

124 CPR 21.1(2).

125 CPR 21.4–21.5. If a claim is *brought* by a litigation friend (as opposed to being defended) the person must also undertake to pay any costs the protected party may be ordered to pay, subject to any right to be repaid from the party's assets. If the protected party is entitled to legal aid the litigation friend would enjoy costs protection in the same way, see para 22.137.

126 CPR Part 21, PD para 3.2(c).

7.175   If a claim is made *against* a protected party without a litigation friend the claimant *must* apply for an order appointing a litigation friend.

Mortgage possession claims

7.176   A mortgage operates as the grant of an interest in land giving the right of possession to the lender. It is important to note that, unlike claims for possession against tenants, a lender already has a right of possession and does not depend on the court to grant the right. Rather, the lender applies to the court for an order to *enforce* the right of possession and, in relation to residential premises, the court has statutory powers to postpone the exercise of the right of possession.

7.177   The mortgage agreement will usually provide that the lender's right of possession cannot be *enforced* unless the borrower breaches the terms of the mortgage, and so the lender will have to prove the breach. The Civil Procedure Rules require very specific information to be provided by the lender in the court documents (see paras 6.96–6.100). The Pre-Action Protocol for Possession Claims based on Mortgage Arrears requires that most of the information is given to the borrower before proceedings are commenced so that the parties can reach agreement and, if possible, avoid proceedings.

7.178   This section examines briefly the court's powers to restrict a lender's right of possession and some situations in which a person may apply to set aside a mortgage so as to defeat the claim for possession.

Regulation of mortgages

7.179   Since October 2004, the Financial Services Authority (FSA) has been responsible for regulating the sale of mortgages. The Mortgage Conduct of Business Rules (MCOB) came into effect on 31 October 2004. They replace the Voluntary Mortgage Code which had been in effect since 1997. The MCOB applies to 'regulated mortgage contracts' entered into on or after 31 October 2004.

7.180   The MCOB includes rules for:

- responsible lending, ie giving proper consideration to a borrower's ability to pay;
- the giving of information in prescribed format throughout the life of the loan;

- the giving of prescribed information, including an official FSA leaflet, to borrowers who fall into arrears; and
- the way lenders deal with arrears and possession cases.

7.181   The MCOB rules can be downloaded from the FSA website: www. fsahandbook.info/FSA/html/handbook/MCOB.

7.182   The FSA operates a dispute resolution procedure through the Financial Ombudsman Service (FOS) and awards of compensation can be made.

7.183   A lender's failure to follow the MCOB and/or the Pre-Action Protocol does not prevent a claim for possession being made but may be taken into account by the court when considering whether to exercise its discretion to allow a borrower more time to repay the arrears.

Claims for possession

7.184   There are two separate regimes governing the courts' powers in relation to possession claims of residential property subject to a mortgage:

- The Consumer Credit Act (CCA) 1974[127] governs 'regulated agreements'. Previously, the CCA 1974 only applied to agreements where the credit did not exceed £25,000. However, this limit has been removed by the CCA 2006. Agreements that are exempt from the CCA 1974 are those entered into with banks and building societies and all loans which are regulated mortgage contracts.
- The Administration of Justice Acts (AJA) 1970 and 1973 govern other mortgages of residential premises that are not regulated under the CCA 1974.

Administration of Justice Acts

7.185   Where a lender (mortgagee) seeks a possession order of residential premises against a borrower (mortgagor) the court has powers to adjourn, postpone or suspend an order similar to those under the extended discretion in relation to tenants (see para 6.119). However, the power is dependent on the borrower being able to pay 'the sums due' or remedy the default within a reasonable period.

7.186   The courts powers are contained in the Administration of Justice Acts 1970 and 1973. AJA 1970 s36 of provides that where a mortgagee makes a claim for possession of a dwelling-house:

---

127 As amended by CCA 2006.

(1) ... the court may exercise any of the powers conferred on it by subsection (2) below if it appears to the court that in the event of its exercising the power the mortgagor is likely to be able within a reasonable period to pay any sums due under the mortgage or to remedy a default consisting of a breach of any other obligation arising under or by virtue of the mortgage.

(2) The court–
  (a) may adjourn the proceedings, or
  (b) on giving judgment, or making an order, for delivery of possession of the mortgaged property, or at any time before the execution of such judgment or order, may–
    (i)   stay or suspend execution of the judgment or order, or
    (ii) postpone the date for delivery of possession, for such period or periods as the court thinks reasonable.

(3) Any such adjournment, stay, suspension or postponement as is referred to in subsection (2) above may be made subject to such conditions with regard to payment by the mortgagor of any sum secured by the mortgage or the remedying of any default as the court thinks fit.

(4) The court may from time to time vary or revoke any condition imposed by virtue of this section.

7.187   This power does not apply where the agreement is regulated under the Consumer Credit Act 1974.[128]

7.188   AJA 1973 s8(2) makes it clear that the borrower must be able to pay not only the amount in arrears but the further amounts due, including interest, during the life of the agreement. Effectively, the borrower must be able to show that he or she can maintain payment of the current instalments plus regular payment towards the arrears (or a lump sum payment of the arrears) so that at the end of the reasonable period the arrears will have been cleared.

7.189   Although the Pre-Action Protocol 'does not alter the parties' rights and obligations' the court will take account of a failure to comply when exercising its discretion under the Administration of Justice Acts. The Protocol stresses the need for the exchange of information about the arrears at an early stage, in a way that is 'clear, fair and not misleading' and the consideration of alternatives to court proceedings.

What is a reasonable period?

7.190   This is to be decided having regard to the rights and obligations of both the lender and the borrower. The Court of Appeal considered

128 AJA 1970 s38A.

the issue in *Cheltenham & Gloucester Building Society v Norgan*.[129] The court held that in determining the 'reasonable period' the court 'should take as its starting point the full term of the mortgage and pose at the outset the question: would it be possible for the mortgagor to clear the arrears by instalments over that period?'.[130] The relevant factors in determining the reasonable period were summarised as follows:[131]

- how much the borrower can reasonably afford to pay currently and in the future;
- if the borrower is in temporary difficulty, how long the difficulty is likely to last;
- the reason for the arrears;
- the period of the remaining term;
- the contractual terms, ie the type of mortgage and when the principal sum is due to be repaid;
- whether it is appropriate to disregard any provision in the agreement for the lender to demand early repayment;
- whether it is reasonable to expect the lender to recoup the arrears of interest over the whole term, within a shorter period or even within a longer period;
- whether it is reasonable to expect the lender to capitalise the interest or not;
- any reasons affecting the security which should influence the length of the period for repayment.

7.191 Much will depend on the amount of equity in the property. Where there is substantial equity the court is more likely to be willing to permit a longer period for the borrower to repay the arrears.

7.192 Clearly, where a borrower wants the court to exercises its powers under AJA 1970 it will be necessary to produce evidence of the borrower's ability to pay the amounts due within a reasonable period. Evidence of the value of the property, and therefore the amount of equity, should also be obtained.

Adjourning or suspending to permit a sale by the borrower

7.193 The court can grant an adjournment or suspension to allow the borrower time to sell the property. To do so the court must be satisfied that the proceeds of sale will be sufficient to discharge the whole of

---

129 [1996] 1 All ER 449.
130 Waite LJ at 458.
131 Evans LJ at 463A.

the mortgage debt, including the arrears, within a reasonable period. If the borrower is in negative equity the court cannot suspend possession to permit the borrower to sell unless he or she has other funds to make up the shortfall.[132]

7.194 Where a borrower wants the property to be sold but the lender does not (which may happen where the amount owed exceeds the value of the property and the lender wishes to wait until the value increases) an application can be made by the borrower under the Law of Property Act 1925 s91(2). Under section 91 the court has a wide discretion as to whether to order a sale and, if so, on what terms. However, the court is unlikely to order a sale where the proceeds of sale are likely to be substantially less than the amount owed.

Regulated agreements under the Consumer Credit Act 1974

7.195 The Consumer Credit Act (CCA) 1974 deals with a large range of credit agreements and prescribes the way regulated agreements are entered into. Under the Act the court has more extensive powers than under the Administration of Justice Acts. In particular, a borrower can apply for a 'time order' under which the court can extend the time for repayment of the loan and can reduce the contractual interest rate.

7.196 The Consumer Credit Act 1974 also contains provision for a court to 'reopen the credit agreement so as to do justice between the parties' where there is an 'unfair relationship'.[133]

7.197 Some types of loans are specifically exempt from the Consumer Credit Act. Because of the strict procedural requirements regarding regulated agreements it should be clear from the court documents whether or not an agreement is regulated.

Substantive defences to mortgage possession claims

7.198 A lender has the right to possession by virtue of the mortgage. An application to the court to exercise its discretion is not a 'defence' to a claim for possession. The substantive defences that may be raised are summarised below (paras 7.199–7.205).

---

132 *Cheltenham and Gloucester plc v Krauz* [1997] 1 All ER 21, CA.

133 Under the 1974 Act this applied in relation to an 'extortionate credit bargain' but this has now been amended by the Consumer Credit Act 2006.

Spouse or civil partner in occupation who did not consent to the mortgage

7.199   Where a mortgage is entered into by a sole owner of premises, a spouse or civil partner who is in occupation of the premises has an 'overriding interest' under the Land Registration Act (LRA) 2002.[134] This means that the lender's interest is subject to the right of occupation. Unless the person consented to the mortgage, it will not be binding on him or her.[135] Most lenders will make specific enquiry of such a person and obtain consent before entering into a mortgage.

Forgery

7.200   Where one spouse or civil partner forges the signature of the other the mortgage is ineffective. However, an equitable charge is granted to the lender in relation to the share of the premises owned by the party who entered into the mortgage agreement. In such a case the lender can apply for a money judgment against the borrower and can then apply for a charging order and subsequently an order for sale under section 13 of the Trusts of Land and Appointment of Trustees Act 1996. Section 15 sets out the relevant factors to be considered when the court is considering an order for sale (see para 1.142).

Misrepresentation/undue influence

7.201   It is unusual for a borrower to establish that a lender has misrepresented the effect of the mortgage or placed undue pressure on the borrower to enter into the mortgage. Where a borrower can establish that the lender has been negligent in representing the terms of the mortgage (negligent misstatement) this may give rise to a claim for damages but does not usually mean that the mortgage will be set aside, unless it can be shown that the lender has taken unfair advantage of the borrower.[136]

7.202   Defences based on undue influence are usually raised where a party has acted as surety. The allegation is that the principal debtor has placed undue influence on the person who agreed to act as surety. Most of the cases have involved a husband who has persuaded his wife to enter into an agreement to secure a business debt on the shared home. To establish undue influence as a defence it is necessary to prove not only that there has been misrepresentation, undue influence or other wrong but also that the lender would be affected

---

134 See Sch 3 para 2.
135 Unless inquiry was made and the interest not disclosed.
136 *Cornish v Midland Bank plc* [1985] 3 All ER 513.

by the wrong. For this it must be proved that the lender had actual or constructive notice of the wrong.[137]

7.203   The House of Lords considered the issue in the cases of *Barclays Bank v O'Brien*[138] and *Royal Bank of Scotland v Etridge (No 2)*[139] and gave guidance on the steps a lender should take to satisfy itself that a wife's agreement has been properly obtained. In *O'Brien* the House indicated that a lender should:

- take steps to ensure the wife is aware of the risks she is running; and
- advise her to take independent advice.

7.204   In *Etridge* the court elaborated on the duty to communicate with the wife directly or with her solicitor and on the duty of the solicitor who is advising the wife.

7.205   Although these cases concerned husbands and wives, the same principles apply wherever there is an emotional relationship between the parties, including a same-sex partnership.

Unfair terms

7.206   The Unfair Terms in Consumer Contracts Regulations 1999 apply to mortgage agreements (see paras 4.163–4.173). If a term is deemed unfair by the court it is unenforceable.

Tenants of borrowers

7.207   Where a landlord borrows money on a mortgage, the power to grant a tenancy can only be exercised where no contrary intention is expressed in the mortgage deed.[140] Most mortgage deeds contain a term preventing the borrower from granting a tenancy.

7.208   The position of the tenant of a borrower depends on two factors:

- whether the tenancy commenced before or after the property was mortgaged; and
- whether the lender gave consent.

---

137 Or, unusually, that the wrongdoer was acting as the lender's agent.
138 [1994] 1 AC 180, HL.
139 [2001] 4 All ER 449, HL.
140 Law of Property Act 1925 s99.

Tenancy granted before the mortgage

7.209   A tenancy granted by the landlord/borrower before the mortgage was created is valid as against the lender.

7.210   Even if the mortgage deed prohibits the creation of a tenancy, this does not prevent an existing tenancy from binding the lender: if the lender obtains possession against the landlord/borrower, the tenant becomes the direct tenant of the lender.

7.211   A lender may take advantage of certain of the possession grounds available to landlords.[141] Furthermore, if the tenancy is an assured shorthold tenancy the lender will be able to obtain possession by serving two months' notice and obtaining a possession order against the tenant, provided any fixed term has ended.

Tenancy granted after the mortgage

7.212   If the tenancy is granted with the lender's consent it is binding on the lender.

7.213   If the tenancy is granted without the lender's consent it will not be binding on the lender and when the lender obtains a possession order the tenants can be evicted.[142] However, such 'unauthorised' tenants have the right to seek a postponement of possesion, see paras 7.214–7.216 below.

Notifying occupiers

7.214   The position of 'unauthorised' tenants of borrowers has been strengthened by the Mortgage Repossession (Protection of Tenants etc) Act (MR(PT)A) 2010. The Act applies where there is an 'unauthorised tenancy', ie, an assured, protected or statutory tenancy that does not bind the lender. Any lender who is applying for possession must send a notice to the property (addressed to 'the tenant or the occupier') within five days of receiving notice of the hearing. The notice must state that a possession claim has started, give the name and address of the claimant, the defendant and the court, and details of the hearing.[143] This is to give the occupiers the chance either to apply to be joined, if they assert that their tenancy is binding on the lender,

141 Under RA 1977 if the tenancy is subject to possession under Case 11, Case 12 or Case 20, and under HA 1988, if the tenancy is subject to possession under Ground 1, a lender may obtain possession under Ground 2. See appendix to this chapter.

142 *Dudley and District Building Society v Emerson* [1949] 2 All ER 252, CA.

143 See CPR 55(10)(2). A similar notice must also be served on the local housing department for the area in which the premises are situated.

or to make an application for a postponement under the MR(PT)A 2010. At the hearing the lender must produce copies of the notice and evidence it was sent.

7.215 If an application is made by unauthorised tenants for a postponement, the court has the power to postpone the date for the giving of possession by up to two months. Alternatively, an application can be made to stay or suspend the warrant of execution by up to two months. Note that the court may only stay or suspend the warrant if it did not postpone the possession order and if the unauthorised tenants have first requested the lender to undertake in writing not to enforce the order for two months.

7.216 Where a possession order has been made and the lender is applying for a warrant, the lender must send to the property, at least 14 days before applying to the court, a notice in prescribed form, informing any unauthorised tenants of the right to make such an application.[144] The lender must certify that notice has been given when applying for the warrant.[145]

---

144 Dwelling Houses (Execution of Possession Orders by Mortgagees) Regulations 2010 SI No 1809.
145 See CCR Order 26 rule 17(a)(2A)

APPENDIX

Grounds for possession under Housing Act 1985, Housing Act 1988 and Rent Act 1977

This sets out a summary of the grounds for possession in each Act. In some cases the provisions are condensed and/or paraphrased.

Housing Act 1985 Sch 2

STATUTORY GROUNDS FOR POSSESSION

Part I: discretionary grounds – grounds on which the court may order possession if it considers it reasonable

Ground 1 – rent arrears or breach of tenancy agreement

Rent lawfully due from the tenant has not been paid or an obligation of the tenancy has been broken or not performed.

Ground 2 – nuisance and annoyance

The tenant or a person residing in or visiting the dwelling-house–
- has been guilty of conduct causing or likely to cause a nuisance or annoyance to a person residing, visiting or otherwise engaging in a lawful activity in the locality, or
- has been convicted of using the dwelling-house or allowing it to be used for immoral or illegal purposes, or an indictable offence committed in, or in the locality of, the dwelling-house.

Ground 2A – domestic violence

The dwelling-house was occupied (whether alone or with others) by a married couple or a couple living together as husband and wife and–
- one or both of the partners is a tenant of the dwelling-house,
- one partner has left because of violence or threats of violence by the other towards–
  - that partner, or
  - a member of the family of that partner who was residing with that partner immediately before the partner left, and
- the court is satisfied that the partner who has left is unlikely to return.

Ground 3 – damage to property

The condition of the dwelling-house or common parts has deteriorated due to acts of waste, neglect or default of the tenant or a person residing in the dwelling-house. If the acts are those of a subtenant or lodger, the tenant has not taken such steps as he or she ought reasonably to have taken to remove that person.

Ground 4 – damage to furniture

The condition of furniture provided by the landlord has deteriorated due to acts of waste, neglect or default of the tenant or a person residing in the dwelling-house. If the acts are those of a subtenant or lodger, the tenant has not taken such steps as he or she ought reasonably to have taken to remove that person.

Ground 5 – tenancy granted because of false statement

The tenant is the person, or one of the persons, to whom the tenancy was granted and the landlord was induced to grant the tenancy by a false statement made knowingly or recklessly by–
• the tenant, or
• a person acting at the tenant's instigation.

Ground 6 – mutual exchange for payment

The tenancy was assigned to the tenant by way of mutual exchange and a premium was paid in connection with the assignment.
The ground is also available if the assignment (for which payment was made) was to a member of the tenant's family, who lives with the tenant, and who passed the tenancy to the current tenant.

Ground 7 – employment related accommodation and inappropriate conduct

The dwelling-house is part of or within the grounds of a building held by the landlord mainly for non-housing purposes and consists mainly of accommodation other than housing accommodation, and
• was let to the tenant in consequence of the tenant being employed by the landlord, or a local authority, a new town corporation, a housing action trust, an urban development corporation or the governors of an aided school, and
• the tenant or another person living in the dwelling-house has been guilty of conduct such that, having regard to the purpose for which the building is used, it would not be right for the tenant to continue in occupation.
The ground also applies if a previous tenant, who passed the tenancy to the current tenant was the person to whom the tenancy was granted in consequence of employment.

Ground 8 – temporary accommodation pending works

The tenancy was granted as temporary accommodation pending works to the tenant's home and the works have been completed and the other dwelling-house is available for occupation.

Part II: grounds on which the court may order possession if suitable alternative accommodation is available

Ground 9 – statutory overcrowding

The dwelling-house is statutorily overcrowded, as defined in HA 1985 (see para 11.80).

Ground 10 – demolition or reconstruction

The landlord intends, within a reasonable time, to demolish or reconstruct the building or part of the building comprising the dwelling-house, or to carry out works and cannot do so without obtaining possession.

Ground 10A – redevelopment schemes

The dwelling-house or part of it is in an area which is the subject of a redevelopment scheme and the landlord intends within a reasonable time to dispose of the dwelling-house in accordance with the scheme and for that purpose reasonably requires possession.

Ground 11 – charities

The landlord is a charity and the tenant's continued occupation of the dwelling-house would conflict with the objects of the charity.

Part III: grounds on which the court may order possession if it is reasonable to make a possession order and suitable alternative accommodation is available

Ground 12 – non-housing employment related accommodation

The dwelling-house forms part of, or is within the grounds of, a building held mainly for non-housing purposes and consists mainly of non-housing accommodation, or is in a cemetery, and:
- it was let to the tenant in consequence of employment by the landlord or a local authority, a new town corporation, a housing action trust, an urban development corporation, or the governors of an aided school; and
- that employment has ceased; and
- the landlord reasonably requires the dwelling-house for occupation by a new employee.

The ground also applies if a previous tenant, who passed the tenancy to the current tenant was the person to whom the tenancy was granted in consequence of employment.

Ground 13 – disabled adapted accommodation

The dwelling-house has features which are substantially different from those of ordinary dwelling-houses and which are designed to make it suitable for occupation by a physically disabled person who needs such accommodation and–
- there is no longer such a person residing in the dwelling-house; and
- the landlord needs it for occupation by such a person.

Ground 14 – special needs accommodation – housing associations and trusts

The landlord is a housing association or housing trust which lets dwelling-houses only for occupation by persons whose circumstances make it especially difficult to obtain housing, and:

- either there is no longer such a person residing in the dwelling-house or the tenant has received an offer of a secure tenancy of a separate dwelling; and
- the landlord needs the dwelling-house for another person with such needs.

Ground 15 – special needs accommodation – close to special facilities

The dwelling-house is one of a group of dwelling-houses which it is the practice of the landlord to let for occupation by persons with special needs and–

- a social service or special facility is provided near to the group of dwelling-houses to assist persons with those special needs; and
- there is no longer a person with those special needs residing in the dwelling-house; and
- the landlord needs the dwelling-house for occupation by a person who has those special needs.

Ground 16 – succession and under-occupation

The tenant became the tenant by succession under section 87(b) (ie not as spouse or civil partner but as family member) and

- the accommodation is more extensive than is reasonably required by the tenant; and
- notice of proceedings was served (or if no notice was served, the proceedings were begun) more than six months but less than twelve months after the date of the previous tenant's death.

The matters to be taken into account by the court in deciding whether it is reasonable to make a possession order include:

- the age of the tenant;
- the period during which the tenant has occupied the dwelling-house as his or her only or principal home; and
- any financial or other support given by the tenant to the previous tenant.

Housing Act 1988 Sch 2

MANDATORY GROUNDS

Notice Grounds 1–5

Ground 1 – landlord is previous owner-occupier or needs premises as home

The landlord who is seeking possession, or if there are joint landlords, at least one of them, either:

- occupied the dwelling-house as his or her only or principal home at some time before the beginning of the tenancy; or
- requires the dwelling-house as only or principle home for him or herself or spouse or civil partner and the landlord did not (or if there are joint landlords none of them) purchase the property after the tenancy commenced.

The landlord must have given notice in writing to the tenant, before the beginning of the tenancy, that possession might be recovered under this ground unless the court is satisfied that it is just and equitable to dispense with the notice requirement.

Ground 2 – tenancy subject to Ground 1 and lender taking possession

The dwelling-house is subject to a mortgage granted before the beginning of the tenancy and the lender is entitled to exercise a power of sale under the mortgage and needs possession to dispose of it with vacant possession.

The notice requirement is that the landlord gave notice that possession may be required under Ground 1 unless the court is satisfied that it is just and equitable to dispense with the notice requirement.

Ground 3 – out of season holiday let

The tenancy is a fixed-term tenancy for no longer than eight months and within the 12 months preceding the start of the tenancy it was occupied as a holiday let.

The landlord must have given notice in writing to the tenant, before the beginning of the tenancy, that possession might be recovered under this ground.

Ground 4 – student accommodation let to non-students

The tenancy is a fixed-term tenancy for no longer than 12 months and within the 12 months preceding the start of the tenancy it was occupied as student accommodation under HA 1988 Sch 1 para 8.

The landlord must have given notice in writing to the tenant, before the beginning of the tenancy, that possession might be recovered under this ground.

Ground 5 – minister of religion

The dwelling-house is held for the purpose of being available for occupation by a minister of religion from which to perform the duties of that office and it is required for occupation by a minister of religion as such a residence.

The landlord must have given notice in writing to the tenant, before the beginning of the tenancy, that possession might be recovered under this ground.

Mandatory grounds not requiring advance notice

Ground 6 – demolition or reconstruction

The landlord intends to demolish or reconstruct the whole or a substantial part of the dwelling-house or to carry out substantial works on it or any part of it or the building of which it is a part.

The following conditions must be met:

The intended work cannot reasonably be carried out without the tenant giving up possession because:

- the tenant is not willing to agree to a variation of the tenancy as would enable the work to be carried out, or
- the nature of the work is such that no such variation is practicable, or
- the tenant is not willing to accept an assured tenancy of a 'reduced part' of the dwelling-house to enable the works to be carried out, or
- the nature of the work is such that such a tenancy is not practicable.

The ground is not available if:

- the landlord acquired the interest after the grant of the tenancy; or
- the assured tenancy came into being on succession to a previous Rent Act tenancy.

Where the immediate landlord is an RSL or a charitable housing trust the ground is made out if the demolition or reconstruction is intended by the superior landlord.

Ground 7 – tenant dies and no right of succession

Where a periodic tenancy devolves under the will or intestacy of the previous tenant, provided possession proceedings are commenced no later than 12 months after the death of the former tenant, or, if the court so directs, after the date on which, in the opinion of the court, the landlord became aware of the former tenant's death. Note that the ground will not apply if a spouse, civil partner or co-habitee is entitled to succeed to the tenancy (see para 4.31).

For the purpose of Ground 7, the acceptance of rent from the new tenant will not be regarded as creating a new tenancy unless the landlord agrees in writing to a change in the amount of the rent, the period of the tenancy, the premises that are let or any other term of the tenancy.

Ground 8 – mandatory rent arrears ground

Both at the date of the service of the notice under section 8 of this Act relating to the proceedings for possession and at the date of the hearing:

- if rent is payable weekly or fortnightly, at least eight weeks' rent is unpaid;
- if rent is payable monthly, at least two month's rent is unpaid;
- if rent is payable quarterly, at least one quarter's rent is more than three months in arrears; and
- if rent is payable yearly, at least three months' rent is more than three months in arrears;
- and for the purpose of this ground 'rent' means rent lawfully due from the tenant.

Discretionary grounds – grounds on which the court may order possession if it considers it reasonable

Ground 9 – suitable alternative accommodation

Suitable alternative accommodation is available for the tenant or will be available for him when the possession order takes effect.

Ground 10 – rent arrears or breach of tenancy agreement

Some rent lawfully due from the tenant is unpaid on the date on which the proceedings for possession are begun; and except where [the court considers it just and equitable to dispense with the requirement to serve notice] was in arrears at the date of the service of the notice [seeking possession].

Ground 11 – persistent delay in paying rent

Whether or not any rent is in arrears on the date on which proceedings for possession are begun, the tenant has persistently delayed paying rent which has become lawfully due.

Ground 12 – other breach

Any obligation of the tenancy (other than one related to the payment of rent) has been broken or not performed.

Ground 13 – damage to premises

The condition of the dwelling-house or any of the common parts has deteriorated due to acts of waste, neglect or default of the tenant or a person residing in the dwelling. If the acts are those of a subtenant or lodger, the tenant has not taken such steps as he or she ought reasonably to have taken to remove that person.

Ground 14 – nuisance and annoyance

The tenant or a person residing in or visiting the dwelling-house–
- has been guilty of conduct causing or likely to cause a nuisance or annoyance to a person residing, visiting or otherwise engaging in a lawful activity in the locality, or
- has been convicted of–
  - using the dwelling-house or allowing it to be used for immoral or illegal purposes, or
  - an indictable offence committed in, or in the locality of, the dwelling-house.

Ground 14A – domestic violence

The dwelling-house was occupied (whether alone or with others) by a married couple or a couple living together as husband and wife and–
- one or both of the partners is a tenant of the dwelling-house,
- the landlord who is seeking possession is a registered social landlord or a charitable housing trust,

- one partner has left because of violence or threats of violence by the other towards–
  - that partner, or
  - a member of the family of that partner who was residing with that partner immediately before the partner left, and
- the court is satisfied that the partner who has left is unlikely to return.

Ground 15 – deterioration of furniture

The condition of furniture provided under the tenancy has deteriorated due to ill-treatment by the tenant or other person living in the dwelling-house and, if the ill-treatment is by a lodger or subtenant, the tenant has not taken reasonable steps to remove that person.

Ground 16 – employment related accommodation

The dwelling-house was let to the tenant in consequence of employment by the landlord, or a previous landlord, and the tenant has ceased to be in that employment.

Ground 17 – tenancy granted because of false statement

The tenant is the person, or one of the persons, to whom the tenancy was granted and the landlord was induced to grant the tenancy by a false statement made knowingly or recklessly by–
- the tenant, or
- a person acting at the tenant's instigation.

Rent Act 1977: Sch 15

Suitable alternative accommodation

In addition to the 'cases' set out in Schedule 15, section 98(1)(a) provides that a possession order may be made if suitable alternative accommodation is available to the tenant.

Part I: discretionary grounds – cases in which the court **may** order possession

Case 1 – rent arrears or breach of tenancy agreement

Where any rent lawfully due from the tenant has not been paid, or any obligation of the protected or statutory tenancy has been broken or not performed.

Case 2 – nuisance and annoyance

Where the tenant or any person residing or lodging with him or any subtenant of his has been guilty of conduct which is a nuisance or annoyance to adjoining occupiers, or has been convicted of using the dwelling-house or allowing the dwelling-house to be used for immoral or illegal purposes.

Case 3 – damage to the premises

Where the condition of the dwelling-house has deteriorated owing to acts of waste by, or the neglect or default of, the tenant or any person residing or lodging with him or any subtenant of his and, in the case of any act of waste by, or the neglect or default of, a person lodging with the tenant or a subtenant of his, where the court is satisfied that the tenant has not, before the making of the order in question, taken such steps as he ought reasonably have taken for the removal of the lodger or subtenant, as the case may be.

Case 4 – damage to furniture

Where the condition of any furniture provided for use under the tenancy has deteriorated owing to ill-treatment by the tenant or any person residing or lodging with him or any subtenant of his and, in the case of any ill-treatment by a person lodging with the tenant or a subtenant of his, where the court is satisfied that the tenant has not, before the making of the order in question, taken such steps as he ought reasonably to have taken for the removal of the lodger or subtenant, as the case may be.

Case 5 – tenant's notice to quit

Where the tenant has given notice to quit and, in consequence of that notice, the landlord has contracted to sell or let the dwelling-house or has taken any other steps as the result of which he would, in the opinion of the court, be seriously prejudiced if he could not obtain possession.

Case 6 – subletting or assignment without consent

Where, without the consent of the landlord, the tenant has assigned or sublet the whole of the dwelling-house or sublet part of the dwelling-house, the remainder already being sublet.[146]

Case 7 [repealed]

Case 8 – employment related accommodation, needed for new employee

Where the dwelling-house is reasonably required by the landlord for occupation as a residence for some person engaged in his whole-time employment, or in the whole-time employment of some tenant from him or with whom, conditional on housing being provided, a contract for such employment has been entered into, and the tenant was in the employment of the landlord or a former landlord, and the dwelling-house was let to him in consequence of that employment and he has ceased to be in that employment.[147]

Case 9 – accommodation needed as residence for landlord or family

There are three specific conditions that must be met under Case 9:
- The dwelling-house must be reasonably required by the landlord for occupation as a residence for:
  - the landlord;
  - any adult son or daughter of the landlord;
  - the landlord's father or mother; or
  - the father or mother of the landlord's wife, husband or civil partner.
- The landlord did not become landlord by purchasing the dwelling-house.[148]
- An order may not be made if the court is satisfied that greater hardship would be caused by making the order than by refusing it. The court must have regard to all the circumstances, including the availability of other accommodation to the landlord and to the tenant.

Furthermore, as the ground is discretionary the court must also be satisfied that it is reasonable to make an order.

Case 10 – tenant subletting for excessive rent

Where the tenant is subletting part of the premises and is charging a rent in excess of a registered fair rent.

---

146 For certain kinds of tenancies the subletting or assignment must have taken place after a certain date, the latest of which is 14 August 1974.

147 Note that if an employee is *required* to live in premises for the better performance of the job there will be no tenancy: see para 1.36.

148 This condition applies to purchases after a certain date, the latest of which is 24 May 1974, depending on the particular type of tenancy and how it came to be governed by RA 1977.

Part II: mandatory grounds – cases in which the court **must** order possession

Under RA 1977 for all mandatory cases, other than those relating to farm tenancies (cases 16 to 18), the landlord must have served prior notice on the tenant unless the court dispenses with the requirement. The detailed grounds are complex with different requirements depending on the date the tenancy commenced. These grounds are only briefly summarised here.

Notice grounds – Cases 11 to 16, 19 and 20

In all cases depending on notice the following conditions must be satisfied:
- the landlord gave notice in writing to the tenant that possession might be recovered under the particular ground; or
- the court is satisfied that it is just and equitable to dispense with the notice requirement.

Case 11 – returning owner-occupier + notice

The landlord must have previously occupied the premises as a residence and it must be required as a residence or for sale with vacant possession to enable the landlord to purchase a residence. Alternatively, the owner has died and the person who has inherited wants to sell with vacant possession or a mortgagee is entitled to possession.

Case 12 – accommodation purchased for retirement + notice

The landlord must have intended to occupy the dwelling-house as a residence on retirement and it must be required as a residence or for sale with vacant possession to enable the landlord to purchase a residence. Alternatively, the owner has died and the person who has inherited wants to sell with vacant possession or a mortgagee is entitled to possession.

Case 13 – out of season holiday let + notice

The dwelling-house is let on a fixed-term tenancy not exceeding eight months and has previously been occupied as a holiday let.

Case 14 – out of term student accommodation + notice

The dwelling-house is let on a fixed-term tenancy not exceeding 12 months and has been previously occupied as student accommodation.

Case 15 – letting to minister of religion + notice

The dwelling-house is let to a minister of religion as a residence from which to perform the duties of the office; and is required for occupation by a minister of religion as such a residence.

Case 16 – accommodation used for agricultural employees + notice

The dwelling-house was at any time occupied by a person as an agricultural employee; and the tenant is not so employed, nor ever was and is not the widow of someone who was so employed; and it is required for occupation by an agricultural employee.

Cases 17 and 18

Further grounds applying where the dwelling-house is needed for an agricultural occupier.

Case 19 – protected shorthold tenancy

This ground applies only to protected shorthold tenancies.

In addition to the notice requirements when the tenancy was created, the landlord must have served a possession notice which:

- is in writing and states that proceedings may be commenced under Case 19 after the notice expires;
- must expire no earlier than three months after service; and
- must be served in the three months immediately preceding the anniversary of the last day of the tenancy.

The court can waive the requirements for the creation of the protected shorthold tenancy where it is 'just and equitable' to do so, see para 3.185.

Case 20 – landlord was in armed forces and needs accommodation + notice

The dwelling-house was let after 28 November 1980 by someone who, at the time of acquisition and at the time of the letting, was a member of the regular armed forces; and it must be required as a residence or for sale with vacant possession to enable the landlord to purchase a residence. Alternatively, the owner has died and the person who has inherited wants to sell with vacant possession or a mortgagee is entitled to possession.

CHAPTER 8

Unlawful eviction and harassment by landlords

continued

Key points

- An unlawful eviction means excluding an occupier from his or her home without following the proper procedure. In most cases the proper procedure includes the service of notice, the obtaining of a possession order and the enforcement of the order by the court bailiffs.
- Some occupiers can be evicted without following this procedure but violent eviction is always a criminal offence.
- Harassment means acts likely to interfere with the occupiers' peace and comfort or withdrawing essential services. The acts must be done knowing they are likely to make the occupier leave, or deter the occupier from asserting his or her legal rights.
- Unlawful eviction and harassment are criminal offences. They are usually prosecuted by local authorities. Because of limited resources, prosecutions are rare but the threat of prosecution may persuade a landlord to resolve a dispute, eg let a tenant back into occupation.
- Unlawful eviction and harassment by a landlord also give a tenant the right to take civil action – to seek damages and/or an injunction.
- Substantial damages may be awarded if an unlawfully evicted tenant had security of tenure. These damages are based on the difference in value of the premises with the tenant in occupation and with vacant possession.
- In any case, significant damages may be awarded to tenants who have been harassed and unlawfully evicted. Furthermore, the court can order the landlord to let the occupier back into the premises. In an emergency an order may be obtained very quickly, sometimes on the day of the eviction.

Criminal offences

Unlawful eviction and harassment

8.1   The criminal offences of unlawful eviction and harassment were introduced in 1964 and 1965 respectively and are now contained in the Protection from Eviction Act (PEA) 1977, as amended by the Housing Act (HA) 1988.

8.2 Under Protection from Eviction Act 1977 there are two offences:

- unlawful eviction of a residential occupier; and
- harassment of a residential occupier.

8.3 The first issue then is the definition of a 'residential occupier'.

Residential occupier

8.4 A residential occupier means:

> ... in relation to any premises ... a person occupying the premises as a residence, whether under a contract or by virtue of any enactment or rule of law giving him the right to remain in occupation or restricting the right of any other person to recover possession of the premises.[1]

8.5 There are two aspects to the definition: first, the factual issue of whether the person is occupying as a residence; and, second, whether the person has a right to occupy (see paras 8.6–8.10) or there is some restriction on the right of another person to recover possession (see paras 8.11–8.13).

Occupying premises as a residence

8.6 This is always a question of fact. To be a residential occupier there must be a substantial degree of regular personal occupation.[2] However, it is possible to reside in more than one place.[3]

8.7 A person may be physically absent from premises yet retain the status of residential occupier. In the case of an extended absence it will be necessary for the occupier to prove that he or she had an intention to return to the premises and that there was physical evidence of the continued occupation (for example, belongings, furnishings, or friends or family 'looking after' the premises).[4] See paras 4.5–4.8 for a summary of the cases concerning the extended absence of an occupier.

8.8 As will be seen, however, a landlord has a defence both in criminal and civil proceedings if he or she reasonably believed that the residential occupier had ceased to occupy.

---

1 PEA 1977 s1(1).
2 *Herbert v Byrne* [1964] 1 All ER 882 CA.
3 *Langford Property Co v Athanassoglou* [1948] 2 All ER 722, CA. Note that it is not necessary to occupy as only or principal home to be a residential occupier, as is the case to retain secure or assured status.
4 *Brown v Brash* [1948] 1 All ER 922, CA.

The right to occupy

8.9   In addition to the fact of occupation, the residential occupier must occupy:

- under a contract; or
- by virtue of some enactment or rule of law that either gives the occupier the right to remain in occupation or restricts the right of any other person to recover possession.

8.10   Clearly, tenants are residential occupiers as they occupy under a contract. In addition, for those tenants with security of tenure there is a restriction on the landlord's right to recover possession after the tenancy comes to an end. Those who are married or in a civil partnership have a statutory right to occupy accommodation even if the agreement is in the name of their spouse/civil partner provided the premises have been their shared home.[5] All of these occupiers then are residential occupiers. In addition, the Protection from Eviction Act 1977 itself provides that for other occupiers (other than those specifically excluded – see para 8.13) when an agreement to occupy has been ended an eviction may only be carried out by taking court proceedings. This is a restriction on the right to recover possession and means that the person is a residential occupier.

Restriction on eviction other than by court proceedings

8.11   PEA 1977 s3 applies where 'premises have been let as a dwelling under a tenancy which is neither a statutorily protected tenancy nor an excluded tenancy'. It also applies to licences provided they are not excluded licences. It provides that where the tenancy or licence has come to an end but the occupier continues to reside in the premises, or a part of them, it is not lawful for the owner to enforce the right of possession otherwise than by possession proceedings in the court.

Statutorily protected tenancies

8.12   The term 'statutorily protected tenancy' is defined in PEA 1977 s8 and means the following kinds of tenancies:

- protected and statutory tenancies under the Rent Act (RA) 1977 and the Rent (Agriculture) Act 1976;
- statutory tenancies arising at the end of a long lease;[6]

---

5 See paras 12.35–12.39.
6 These are governed by Landlord and Tenant Act 1954 Pt I and Local Government and Housing Act 1989 Sch 10, see paras 5.48–5.54.

- tenancies which include premises occupied for business purposes, to which Part II of the Landlord and Tenant Act 1954 applies;
- agricultural tenancies;[7] and
- assured and assured shorthold tenancies.

'Excluded occupiers'

8.13   The following are excluded occupiers:[8]

- occupiers who have a resident landlord and who share accommodation with the resident landlord, or with a member of the family of the resident landlord;
- former trespassers granted a temporary licence;
- occupiers granted the right to occupy for a holiday only;
- occupiers granted the right to occupy other than 'for money or money's worth';
- asylum-seekers accommodated under the Immigration and Asylum Act 1999;
- occupiers of hostel accommodation where the landlord is a public sector body and the occupation is under a licence and not a tenancy.

8.14   Excluded occupiers are described in detail at paras 1.101–1.121.

Application of PEA 1977 s3

8.15   Therefore, PEA 1977 s3 provides that, with very limited exceptions described below (paras 8.17–8.21), on the termination of a right to occupy under a licence or tenancy the landlord must use court proceedings to evict the occupier, unless he or she is an excluded occupier. This then is an enactment that restricts the right of another person to recover possession: a person protected by PEA 1977 s3 is a 'residential occupier'.

8.16   It must be noted that PEA 1977 applies only to occupiers who are 'lawfully residing in the premises or part of them at the termination of the former tenancy or licence'.[9]

---

7   Including tenancies of agricultural holdings under the Agricultural Holdings Act 1986, assured agricultural occupancy agreements under the Housing Act 1988 and farm business tenancies within the meaning of the Agricultural Tenancies Act 1995, see para 3.190–3.194.

8   PEA 1977 s3A.

9   PEA 1977 s3(2) and (2B). The fact that the protection is given to those lawfully residing in the premises means that the unlawful tenants of a borrower have no protection against a lender entitled to possession: *Bolton Building Society v Cobb and Others* [1965] 3 All ER 814. The position of unlawful subtenants as against the 'head landlord' is more complex and is dealt with at paras 4.93–4.128.

Eviction without a court order

8.17 Before the occupier can be evicted the occupation agreement must be brought to an end. If the occupation agreement is a tenancy, a notice to quit must be served. If the occupation agreement is a licence, the contractual period of notice must be given. For excluded tenants the requirement that a notice to quit be at least 28 days long does not apply;[10] the only requirement is the common law rule that the notice must be for at least a period of the tenancy (for example, one week or one month, usually depending on the rental period). If there is no tenancy and no express provision about notice, 'reasonable notice' must be given to end the agreement[11] (see para 1.123 for consideration of what constitutes reasonable notice).

8.18 After notice has expired the occupier may be excluded by the owner without obtaining a court order. However, an occupier may not be forcibly evicted as this may constitute a criminal offence under the Criminal Law Act 1977 (see para 8.40 below).

8.19 In *Roma Desnousse v Newham LBC, Paddington Churches HA, Veni Properties Ltd*[12] the Court of Appeal considered the occupation of accommodation provided by a local authority, pending a decision on a homeless application.

Ms Desnousse made a homeless application to the local authority. She and her two children were placed by the local authority in a self-contained flat while her homeless application was investigated. After five months the authority decided that she was intentionally homeless and that no long-term housing duty was owed. Subsequently she was informed that the accommodation booking would be cancelled. She applied to the court for an injunction to prevent the authority or the accommodation providers from evicting her without obtaining a possession order.

The Court of Appeal held that Ms Desnousse was not protected by the PEA 1977 because of the transient nature of her occupation. It was not necessary for court proceedings to be brought by either the authority or the owners of the premises in order for her to be lawfully evicted.[13]

10 PEA 1977 s5.
11 *Smith v Northside Developments Ltd* (1988) 55 P&CR 164.
12 [2006] EWCA Civ 547.
13 The case was argued on the grounds that Ms Desnousse was a licensee not a tenant and the court left open the question of whether PEA 1977 would apply if an occupier were granted a tenancy pending decision.

8.20   It is not therefore necessary to obtain a possession order to evict a licensee occupying accommodation pending a homeless decision. However, the situation will be different if the person remains in the same accommodation after a housing duty has been accepted even though the nature of the occupation agreement and the parties may remain the same.

8.21   So, the following occupiers of residential accommodation may be evicted by a landlord without a court order:

- excluded occupiers listed in PEA 1977 s3A;
- homeless applicants granted a licence pending a homeless decision;
- trespassers who entered as trespassers.

8.22   For all other residential occupiers an eviction without a court order will be unlawful, giving rise to a civil claim for damages and an injunction. It may also be a criminal offence. The criminal offences are summarised below (paras 8.23–8.24).

Unlawful eviction

8.23   The offence is committed if:

Any person unlawfully deprives the residential occupier of any premises of his or her occupation of the premises or any part of the premises, or attempts to do so.[14]

8.24   No offence is committed if the person proves that he or she believed, and had reasonable cause to believe, that the residential occupier had ceased to reside in the premises.

Harassment

8.25   There are two different offences under the Protection from Eviction Act 1977: one committed by a landlord or landlord's agent and one committed by any person.

Harassment by landlord or agent

8.26   The offence is committed if:

- a landlord or landlord's agent does acts likely to interfere with the peace or comfort of the residential occupier or members of the household, or persistently withdraws or withholds services

14   PEA 1977 s1(2).

reasonably required for the occupation of the premises as a residence; and

- he or she knows, or has reasonable cause to believe, that the conduct is likely to cause the residential occupiers to give up occupation of the whole or part of the premises or to refrain from exercising any right or pursuing any remedy in respect of the whole or part of the premises.[15]

8.27   The first part of the definition of the offence describes the two kinds of act that make out the offence. It should be noted that a single act likely to interfere with peace or comfort of the occupier is sufficient. However, if the complaint is about the withdrawal or witholding of services this must be 'persistent', meaning that there must be more than a single act or there must be 'deliberate continuity' (for example, a refusal to reconnect a service).[16]

8.28   In either case there must also be the necessary intention; the act or acts must be done by someone who knows that the likely outcome is that the occupier will leave or refrain from exercising rights in relation to the premises.[17]

8.29   It should be noted that to commit the offence of harassment it is not necessary that the likely outcome is that the occupier leaves the premises. It is sufficient that it is likely to deter an occupier from pursuing a complaint to the council or from taking legal action about disrepair. An intention to force an occupier to give up occupation temporarily while building works are carried out is not sufficient.[18]

Definition of landlord and agent[19]

8.30   The 'landlord' means the immediate landlord and any superior landlord (ie a landlord who granted to the immediate landlord his or her interest). The immediate landlord is the person who would be entitled to possession but for the occupier's right to remain in occupation. This includes a person to whom the original landlord sold or transferred ownership.

8.31   An 'agent of the landlord' is not defined in PEA 1977. An agent is any person who acts on behalf of the landlord. It includes someone who has an express agreement to act on the landlord's behalf,

---

15 PEA 1977 s1(3A).
16 *R v Varol* [1972] Crim LR 318, CA.
17 *R v Burke* (1990) 22 HLR 433, HL, and *R v Yuthiwattana* (1984) 16 HLR 49, CA.
18 *Schon v Camden LBC* (1986) 18 HLR 341, QBD.
19 PEA 1977 s1(3)(c).

whether written or oral. This would include a lettings agent or rent collector. It can also include any person who implicitly acts on behalf of the landlord. This can be difficult to prove but in many cases the evidence makes it clear that the acts have been carried out on behalf of the landlord. However, even if it is the case that the acts are done on behalf of the landlord it is the agent who commits the offence.

Defence

8.32   It is a defence to the offence of harassment if the landlord or agent can prove that he or she had reasonable grounds for doing the acts or withdrawing or withholding the services in question.

Harassment by 'any person'

8.33   An offence of harassment under PEA 1977 may also be committed by any person, not necessarily the landlord or agent. In this case the person must *intend* to cause the occupier to give up occupation of the whole or part or to refrain from exercising any right or remedy in respect of the premises: PEA 1977 s1(3).

Local authority powers

Prosecutions

8.34   Local authorities have the power to prosecute offences committed under the Protection from Eviction Act 1977. However, prosecutions are rare.[20] This is partly because of the limited resources of local authorities, which must carry out all of the investigations and evidence gathering and, to succeed, must prove the case beyond reasonable doubt. Even if a prosecution is successful, the penalties imposed by the courts are usually insufficient to operate as a deterrent. Few local authorities now employ specialist officers (usually known as tenancy relations officers) to deal with such cases. Although the police may prosecute such offences they rarely do so, leaving enforcement of the Act to local authorities.

8.35   Nevertheless, local authorities may use the threat of an eviction to persuade a landlord to resolve a dispute, for example, to allow a ten-

---

20 The number of prosecutions has declined since the early 1990s. In 2008 the total number of prosecutions nationally under PEA 1977 was 34, in 2009, 49 and in 2010, 37: Hansard HC, 7 June 2011, col 164W.

ant back into occupation, to re-connect services or stop committing acts of harassment.

Criminal penalties

8.36 The offences under the PEA 1977 may be tried in a magistrates' court or the Crown Court. If tried in a magistrates' court the maximum penalty is six months in prison and/or a fine of up to £5,000. In the Crown Court the maximum term of imprisonment is two years and/or an unlimited fine. The court also has the usual range of sentencing powers and may grant an absolute or conditional discharge, make a probation or community service order, or make a suspended sentence of imprisonment.

8.37 In addition, the court can order that compensation be paid to the victim 'for personal injury, loss or damage' resulting from the offence.[21] However, awards of compensation by the criminal courts are confined to simple and straightforward cases.[22] Where an offence under the PEA 1977 has been committed, the victim will almost certainly have a strong claim for damages in the county court (see paras 8.117–8.126 below).

8.38 Under the PEA 1977 the criminal courts cannot order that a victim of unlawful eviction be re-instated or restrain future unlawful behaviour by the landlord. In most cases where a landlord is prosecuted, a civil action will be also be brought by the victim to claim damages and an injunction. There is no bar on the two sets of legal proceedings being pursued at the same time.

Re-connecting services

8.39 Local authorities also have the power to make arrangements to secure the restoration or continuance of gas, water or electricity supplies where the supplies have been or are likely to be cut off because of failure by the owner to pay for the services.[23] Many authorities are reluctant to use these powers as it involves expenditure which it may be difficult or impossible to recover from the landlord. Some authorities only use the powers as a last resort if the occupiers include young children or the elderly. Nevertheless, local authorities should be asked to exercise these powers. An authority's unwillingness to do so may assist a person applying as homeless to the same authority as

---

21 Powers of the Criminal Courts (Sentencing) Act 2000 s130.
22 *Herbert v Lambeth LBC* (1991) 24 HLR 299, QBD.
23 Local Government (Miscellaneous Provisions) Act 1976 s33.

he or she may argue that it is not reasonable to continue to occupy accommodation without necessary services.

Offences under the Criminal Law Act 1977

8.40 The offences under the PEA 1977 are committed against 'residential occupiers', see paras 8.4–8.16 above. Even where there is no such right or requirement, it is a criminal offence to use violence in order to secure entry to premises.

8.41 Section 6(1) of the Criminal Law Act (CLA) 1977 provides that it is an offence if:

> ... any person who, without lawful authority, uses or threatens violence for the purpose of securing entry into any premises for himself or for any other person ... provided that:
> (a) there is someone present on those premises at the time who is opposed to the entry which the violence is intended to secure; and
> (b) the person using or threatening the violence knows that is the case.

8.42 The violence may be directed against the person or against property.[24] Forcing open a door or window is therefore an offence, provided there is someone in the premises who is opposed to the entry and this is known to the perpetrator.

8.43 The offence is committed when violence is used to 'secure entry' into the premises. It is immaterial whether it is intended to secure possession or for some other purpose.[25]

Lawful authority

8.44 'Lawful authority' means the authority to use reasonable force to secure entry, not having the legal right to possession.

8.45 The Act specifies situations in which no offence is committed by the use of force to secure entry to premises, ie the situations in which a person does have lawful authority to use reasonable force. These situations are described below in paras 8.46–8.56.

Displaced residential occupiers (DROs)

8.46 Any person who was occupying premises as a residence immediately before being excluded by someone who entered those premises as a

---

24 CLA 1977 s6(4)(a).
25 CLA 1977 s6(4)(b).

trespasser is a DRO. This does not include a person who was occupying as a trespasser or who was let into occupation by a trespasser.[26]

8.47 A person continues to be a DRO so long as he or she continues to be excluded from occupation by the original trespasser or any subsequent trespasser.[27]

8.48 The use of reasonable force by a DRO to gain access is not an offence under the CLA 1977.[28]

Protected intending occupiers (PIOs)

8.49 PIOs are individuals, who require the premises as a residence, and are excluded from occupation by trespassers.

8.50 There are three kinds of PIOs:

- freeholders and long-leaseholders;
- private tenants and licensees;
- tenants and licensees of social landlords, including local authorities.

8.51 In all cases the PIO must require the property for his or her own occupation as a residence. The interest of the PIO must be established by documentary evidence in prescribed form. For freeholders, leaseholders and their tenants or licensees, this means a statement witnessed by a Justice of the Peace. For the tenants and licensees of social landlords a certificate issued by the landlord is sufficient.

8.52 The use of reasonable force by a PIO to gain access is not an offence under the CLA 1977.

8.53 As is indicated below (para 8.56), it is a criminal offence for a trespasser not to leave premises when required to do so by a DRO or PIO. The most common practice will be for the DRO or PIO to attend the premises with police officers. If the person requested to leave refuses to do so he or she can be arrested and removed forcibly by the police thereby enabling the DRO or PIO to take possession.

Court bailiffs

8.54 A court bailiff executing a possession order may use reasonable force to secure entry.

---

26 CLA 1977 s12(4) and (6).
27 CLA 1977 s12(3).
28 CLA 1977 s6(1A).

Police officers

8.55   A police officer exercising a power of arrest or search under the criminal law may use reasonable force to secure entry. There are certain specific criminal offences relating to trespass for which an officer may use these powers thereby effectively removing the trespasser. These include removing:

- a person who is on premises as a trespasser, having entered as a trespasser, who fails to leave premises on being required to do so by a DRO or PIO following the above procedure;[29]
- a person who is on premises as a trespasser, having entered as a trespasser, who has with him or her on the premises an offensive weapon;[30]
- a person who is evicted following the making of an interim possession order who re-enters the premises.[31]

8.56   Note that the Localism Act 2011 will introduce a new criminal offence of squatting in residential property. The offence will be committed where a person is in a residential building as a trespasser, having entered as a trespasser, and knows that he or she is trespassing and is living in the building or intends to live there for any period.

Prosecutions

8.57   Unlike under the Protection from Eviction Act 1977, local authorities have no power to prosecute offences under the Criminal Law Act 1977. Such offences are investigated by the police and prosecuted by the Crown Prosecution Service. The maximum penalties are the same as for PEA 1977 offences described in para 8.36 above.

Civil proceedings

8.58   When a landlord has harassed or unlawfully evicted an occupier there will usually be a number of potential causes of action, based in contract and in tort. See paras 22.8–22.18 for an explanation of causes of action.

---

29   CLA 1977 s7.
30   CLA 1977 s8.
31   Criminal Justice and Public Order Act 1994 s76.

Contract

8.59   A tenancy agreement is a legally binding contract. If one party breaches the contract the other party can bring an action for damages and ask the court to grant an injunction to restrain future breaches of the contract. A tenancy agreement may contain express terms that the landlord will allow the tenant 'quiet enjoyment' of the premises.

Implied terms of the tenancy agreement

8.60   There are two terms implied into all tenancy agreements that are relevant in claims based on harassment or unlawful eviction by landlords:
- the covenant of quiet enjoyment; and
- the covenant not to 'derogate from grant'.

Quiet enjoyment

8.61   It is an implied term of all tenancy agreements, whether written or oral, that the landlord covenants to allow the tenant quiet enjoyment of the premises. However, the term is not implied into licence agreements. This term will always be relied on in a civil claim for unlawful eviction or harassment brought by a tenant.

8.62   Conduct by a landlord that interferes with the right to occupy undisturbed will usually be a breach of the covenant of quiet enjoyment.[32] This can range from minor interference to an actual eviction.

Derogation from grant

8.63   It is also implied into all tenancy agreements that the landlord covenants not to 'derogate' from the grant of the tenancy. This covenant may be relevant if the landlord retains possession of part of the premises, such as the common parts, or of neighbouring premises. A landlord will breach the covenant if he or she does anything in relation to the premises that he or she controls which makes the tenant's premises materially less fit for the purpose of the letting. This could include letting the other premises for a purpose that interferes with peaceful residential use of the tenant's home.

---

32   There may, however, be instances where the landlord's conduct does disturb the tenant's quiet enjoyment but is not a breach of the covenant, eg carrying out necessary repairs provided reasonable steps are taken to minimise the disturbance, see para 10.70.

Common law torts

8.64   A tort is a recognised civil wrong. Some torts exist because of recognition by the courts ('common law torts') and others are created by statute ('statutory torts'). The following common law torts will often be relied on by tenants in civil actions for unlawful eviction and harassment:

- nuisance (see paras 8.65–8.66);
- trespass (see paras 8.67–8.76);
- assault and battery; and
- intimidation (see para 8.77).

For the relevant statutory torts, see paras 8.78–8.100.

Nuisance

8.65   Nuisance is based on interference with the use and enjoyment of land. It may be a state of affairs, condition or activity that interferes with the use of neighbouring land. It includes causing physical damage to premises as well as interference with the use or enjoyment of premises, such as loud noise or obnoxious smells.

8.66   Whether acts complained of amount to a nuisance must be judged according to the standard of a reasonable person[33] and what is judged to be a nuisance depends on the circumstances. Noise caused by home improvements may not constitute a nuisance if carried on for a limited period at a reasonable time. The same level of noise may constitute a nuisance if caused intentionally in order to annoy or if the activities are conducted at unsocial times such as early in the morning or late at night.[34]

Trespass

8.67   There are three kinds of trespass: trespass to land; trespass to goods; and trespass to the person.

Trespass to land

8.68   Trespass means entering premises without the permission of the person entitled to possession, or remaining on premises after permission has been withdrawn.

---

33   *Robinson v Kilvert* (1889) 41 ChD 88, CA.
34   *Christie v Davey* [1893] 1 ChD 316.

8.69   Only a person entitled to possession can sue in trespass. A tenant can make a claim in trespass but a licensee cannot since a licensee does not have a legal right to possession.

8.70   A landlord who enters premises without the tenant's consent commits the tort of trespass.

Trespass to goods

8.71   This means the unlawful interference with goods belonging to another. If the goods are taken and used without permission this is known as 'conversion'.

8.72   Action can be taken by the person who owns the goods and does not depend on rights in relation to the premises.

8.73   A landlord who simply disposes of an occupier's belongings or removes them and leaves them outside the premises may face an action for damages, even if the eviction itself was not unlawful.[35] The occupier can claim damages sufficient to replace the items lost.

Trespass to the person

8.74   This is also known as 'assault and battery'. As well as being a criminal offence, an assault is a tort.

8.75   An assault is an act that puts the victim in immediate and reasonable fear of being physically attacked. Battery is the actual application of physical force to another person.

8.76   Action can be taken by the victim regardless of their rights in relation to the premises.

Intimidation

8.77   The tort of intimidation is committed when a person makes a demand accompanied by an unlawful threat which results in damage to the person threatened or to some other person. The threat may be made verbally or by acts but must be contrary to the criminal or civil law. An example would be a threat to unlawfully evict or assault a person if rent was not paid by a certain date or time.

---

35 Under the law of bailment a person who comes into possession of another person's belongings has a duty to take reasonable care of them for a reasonable period and to give the person a reasonable opportunity to collect them. For local authorities there is statutory provision regarding tenant's belongings, under the Local Government (Miscellaneous Provisions) Act 1982 s41.

Statutory torts

8.78   There are two statutory torts relevant to claims for unlawful eviction and harassment against landlords:

- unlawful eviction under the Housing Act 1988 (see paras 8.80–8.100);
- harassment under the Protection from Harassment Act 1997 (see paras 8.101–8.105).

8.79   In both cases the relevant Act also sets out a particular remedy that is available if the tort is proved.

Housing Act 1988: unlawful eviction

8.80   Section 27 of the Housing Act (HA) 1988 created a specific tort of unlawful eviction. The definition of the tort is based on the criminal offences under the PEA 1977. There are two ways in which the tort can be committed:

- unlawful eviction; or
- attempted eviction or harassment.

Unlawful eviction

8.81   Under HA 1988 s27(1) the tort of unlawful eviction is committed when a landlord or any person acting on behalf of the landlord unlawfully deprives a residential occupier of his or her occupation of the whole or part of the premises.

Attempted eviction or harassment

8.82   The tort under HA 1988 s27(2) is committed where a landlord or any person acting on behalf of the landlord either:

- attempts to unlawfully evict a residential occupier; or
- harasses a residential occupier;

with the result that the occupier gives up occupation.[36]

8.83   An example of the tort under HA 1988 s27(2) would be where a landlord attempts to exclude the tenant by changing the locks but the tenant is able to gain entry. If the tenant subsequently gives up occupation because of the landlord's conduct, the tort under section 27(2) would be committed. If the landlord had successfully excluded the tenant, the tort under section 27(1) would have been committed.

36 HA 1988 s27(2).

8.84   Harassment is defined in the same terms as for the criminal offence. The tort is committed where the landlord or any person acting on behalf of the landlord does acts likely to interfere with the peace or comfort of the residential occupier or members of his or her household, or persistently withdraws or withholds services reasonably required for the occupation of the premises as a residence. Furthermore, he or she must know or have reasonable cause to believe that the conduct is likely to cause the residential occupier to give up occupation of the premises or any part, or to refrain from exercising any right or pursuing any remedy in respect of the premises or any part.

8.85   If the harassment does not result in the occupier giving up occupation, the statutory tort is not committed. However, the tenant can still bring a civil claim relying on the torts described above at paras 8.64–8.77, as well as breach of contract.

8.86   As is the case for the criminal offence of harassment, it is not necessary that the behaviour is intended or likely to make the occupier leave the premises. It is sufficient that the perpetrator knows it is likely to dissuade an occupier from exercising rights, such as taking action about disrepair or complaining to the local authority about the premises or the landlord.

Who to sue

8.87   Although the tort may be committed by someone acting on the landlord's behalf, it is the landlord who is liable to pay damages.[37] This is in contrast to a prosecution of a criminal offence under the PEA 1977 which is brought against the person committing the acts, for example, the landlord's agent.

Defences

8.88   The defences available to a landlord are also the same as for the criminal offences.[38] It is a defence if the landlord can prove the following:

- that he or she believed and had reasonable cause to believe that the person had ceased to reside in the premises; or
- if harassment is alleged, that he or she had reasonable grounds for doing the acts complained of or withdrawing or withholding the services.

---

37 HA 1988 s27(3).
38 HA 1988 s27(8).

8.89   'Reasonable grounds' would include disconnecting services because they were dangerous or where necessary works of repair interfered with the occupier's peace or comfort. It would not extend to harassment by a landlord who had a legitimate claim for possession or rent arrears against an occupier.

8.90   If the tort under HA 1988 s27 is proved the damages will be calculated according to a formula set out in HA 1988 s28.

Section 28 damages

8.91   HA 1988 section 28 damages are assessed on the basis of the difference between:

- the landlord's interest, valued on the basis that the residential occupier continues to have the same right to occupy the premises as before giving up occupation or being evicted; and
- the interest valued on the basis that the residential occupier has ceased to have that right.

8.92   To determine the relevant values expert evidence will be needed.[39]

Reduction of section 28 damages

8.93   The amount of damages may be reduced by the court in the following circumstances:[40]

- where, prior to the acts complained of, the victim was guilty of conduct which makes it reasonable to reduce the amount of damages; or
- where, before the start of the proceedings, the landlord offered to reinstate the victim, who unreasonably refused the offer.[41]

8.94   The offer of re-instatement must be genuine: handing the tenant a key to a lock which did not work and where the room formerly

---

39   The relevant values are assessed as at the time immediately before the person ceased to occupy. Certain assumptions are made for the purposes of the valuation, namely that the landlord is selling on the open market to a willing buyer, that neither the residential occupier nor a member of his or her family wish to buy, and any potential development value of the land is disregarded: HA 1988 s28(3).

40   HA 1988 s27(7).

41   Furthermore, damages may be reduced even if the victim has obtained alternative accommodation before the offer was made, if the court considers that it would have been unreasonable to refuse the offer had he or she not obtained alternative accommodation: HA 1988 s27(7)(b).

occupied had been wrecked was held not to be an offer of re-instatement for these purposes.[42]

8.95 In both cases the court may reduce the damages 'as it thinks appropriate'.

Re-instatement of occupier

8.96 No damages can be awarded under HA 1988 s28 if, before court proceedings are finally disposed of, the victim is re-instated so as to become a residential occupier again. This may be by agreement or by order of the court.[43]

8.97 So, a tenant who is granted an injunction for re-instatement and re-occupies cannot be awarded section 28 damages.

Offers to re-instate

8.98 The consequences of offers to re-instate can be summarised as follows:

- If an offer to re-instate is made *before* the claim for unlawful eviction is *commenced*, an unreasonable refusal may result in a reduction of damages.
- If the offer is made *after* the claim for unlawful eviction is *commenced* the offer may be refused without any consequence in relation to the award of section 28 damages.
- A tenant who *accepts* an offer of re-instatement, before the proceedings are *concluded*, cannot be awarded section 28 damages. Damages for other causes of action, such as breach of contract, nuisance, trespass etc may still be awarded.

Valuing the tenant's interest

8.99 The valuation must be carried out on the basis of the tenant's actual interest and not on a notional basis. This means that the level of HA 1988 section 28 damages in relation to tenants with no long-term security will be limited.

In *King v Jackson*[44] an assured shorthold tenant was unlawfully evicted. In the county court she was awarded £11,000 under section 28.

42 *Tagro v Cafane and Patel* (1991) 23 HLR 250, CA.
43 HA 1988 s27(6).
44 (1997) 30 HLR 541, CA.

> The Court of Appeal upheld the landlord's appeal: where a property was let to a tenant with little security at a market rent the difference in the value of the premises with the tenant in occupation and with vacant possession would be minimal, if anything. An award of £1,500 was substituted.

8.100   In *Wandsworth LBC v Osei-Bonsu*[45] the Court of Appeal considered both the way in which damages should be assessed and the power to reduce damages where the victim is guilty of conduct that justifies a reduction.

> Mr Osei-Bonsu was a joint secure tenant with his wife, who had left the premises as a result of his violence. The authority evicted him following the service by his wife of a defective notice to quit. He succeeded in his claim for unlawful eviction under HA 1988 s27 and was awarded £30,000 on the basis of agreed valuation evidence.
>   The Court of Appeal reduced this by two-thirds to £10,000 on the basis of the husband's violence towards his wife. It was also held that the valuers had failed to have regard to the actual circumstances existing at the time of the eviction, namely that the tenancy was precarious and could be ended by a correct notice to quit. Appropriate damages would have been £2,000. However, the court did not interfere with the valuation evidence as this had been agreed by the parties.

> In *Kalas v Farmer*[46] the landlord took possession during a period when an assured tenant was in prison, and put the property up for sale. On his release from prison the tenant claimed damages for unlawful eviction under HA 1988 s27. He was awarded £49,500 plus £3,200 in special damages. The landlord's defence was that the premises had been abandoned and the tenancy ended or that he believed the premises to have been abandoned. Both arguments were rejected on the evidence. On appeal the landlord also argued that the damages should have been reduced on the basis of the conduct of the tenant, who had been found guilty of theft and storing stolen goods in the premises, which had led to the police breaking down the door following his arrest. This was also rejected as it had not been pleaded or raised at trial.

45   (1998) 31 HLR 515, CA.
46   [2010] EWCA Civ 108, 29 January 2010.

Protection from Harassment Act 1997

8.101 The Protection from Harassment Act (PHA) 1997 provides that harassment is both a criminal offence and a tort. The Act was introduced to address the problem of stalking, where one person's behaviour towards another may not be explicitly threatening or intended to cause fear but nevertheless does cause alarm or distress.

What is harassment?

8.102 The term 'harassment' is not defined in the Act but PHA 1997 s1(1) provides that a person must not pursue a course of conduct which amounts to harassment of another, and which he or she knows or ought to know amounts to harassment of the other.[47] PHA 1997 s7 offers the following definitions:

- a 'course of conduct' must involve conduct on at least two occasions;
- references to harassing a person include alarming the person or causing the person distress;
- 'conduct' includes speech; and
- aiding, abetting, counselling or procuring harassment by another person is also prohibited.

8.103 It is a defence to show that:[48]

- the conduct was pursued to prevent or detect crime; this would include the actions of not only police officers but also tenancy relations officers and private individuals;
- the conduct was pursued under any statute or rule of law or to comply with a statutory condition or requirement; this could include sending a statutory demand for a debt or a notice to quit; or
- the pursuit of the conduct was reasonable in the circumstances.

47 PHA 1977 s1(1). A person 'ought to know that it amounts to harassment of another if a reasonable person in possession of the same information would think the course of conduct amounted to harassment of the other': s1(2).

48 PHA 1997 s1(3). In addition to these defences, certain acts, certified by the Home Secretary, and done on behalf of the Crown, relating to national security, the economic well-being of the UK or to prevent or detect serious crime are excluded from the PHA 1997: s12.

Enforcement

8.104 Since the behaviour prohibited under the Protection from Harassment Act 1997 is both a tort and a criminal offence, the victim has two options: bringing a civil claim against the perpetrator for damages and an injunction or reporting the behaviour to the police to investigate and prosecute the perpetrator.

8.105 Unusually, the civil and criminal remedies overlap in that a breach of a civil injunction is a criminal offence and the criminal courts can make a restraining order to prevent future harassment.

Criminal offences under PHA 1997

Harassment

8.106 Harassment, as defined in para 8.102 above, is a criminal offence punishable by a fine of up to £5,000 and/or up to six months' imprisonment.[49] However, if the offence was 'racially or religiously aggravated' the maximum penalty is two years' imprisonment.[50]

Violent harassment

8.107 The offence of 'violent harassment' is committed where a person pursues a course of conduct which 'causes another to fear, on at least two occasions, that violence will be used against him ... if he know or ought to know that the course of conduct will cause the other so to fear on each of those occasions'.[51]

8.108 The offence is punishable in the magistrates' court by a fine of up to £5,000 and/or imprisonment for up to six months, and in the Crown Court by an unlimited fine and/or imprisonment for up to five years. If the offence was 'racially or religiously aggravated' the maximum penalty is seven years imprisonment.

8.109 The defences available to a charge of violent harassment are the same as the defences to an allegation of harassment (listed above in para 8.103) save that if the person is accused of violent harassment there is no general defence that the conduct was reasonable;

---

49 PHA 1997 s2.

50 Crime and Disorder Act (CDA) 1998 s32. A crime is racially or religiously aggravated if, at the time the offence is committed, there is evidence of a hostility based on the victim's membership or presumed membership of a racial or religious group, or the offence is motivated by such hostility: CDA 1998 s28.

51 PHA 1997 s4(1).

the defendant must show that the conduct was reasonable 'for the protection of himself or another or for the protection of his or another's property'.[52]

Breach of a restraining order

8.110 Following a conviction for either offence the criminal courts can impose restraining orders to protect the victim from further harassment or conduct causing a fear of violence.[53]

8.111 Breach of a restraining order without reasonable excuse is also a criminal offence. The maximum penalty in the magistrates' court is a fine of up to £5,000 and/or imprisonment of up to six months and in the Crown Court an unlimited fine and/or imprisonment of up to five years.

Breach of a civil injunction

8.112 Where a civil injunction has been granted to restrain the defendant from pursuing a course of conduct that amounts to harassment, it is a criminal offence to do anything prohibited by the injunction without reasonable excuse.[54]

8.113 The offence is punishable in the magistrates' court by a fine of up to £5,000 and/or imprisonment for up to six months and in the Crown Court by an unlimited fine and/or imprisonment for up to five years.[55]

8.114 Civil injunctions are enforceable in the civil courts by an application for committal to prison for contempt of court. The Protection from Harassment Act 1997 provides that the civil courts may issue a warrant for the arrest of a person if there is evidence of breach of the injunction[56] and contempt of court may be punished by up to two years' imprisonment. However, a person convicted of the offence of breaching a civil injunction cannot also be punished for contempt of court. Similarly, a person punished for contempt of court cannot also be convicted of the offence.[57]

---

52 PHA 1997 s4(3).
53 PHA 1997 s5.
54 PHA 1997 s3(6).
55 PHA 1997 s3(9).
56 PHA 1997 s3(3)–(5).
57 PHA 1997 s3(7) and (8).

Other remedies in the civil courts

8.115   The above paragraphs (8.91–8.99 and 8.112–8.114) describe the particular remedies available to a claimant who proves the statutory torts of unlawful eviction under the Housing Act 1988 or harassment under the Protection from Harassment Act 1997. However, even if such claims are not made, the usual civil remedies are available to a claimant alleging harassment or unlawful eviction by a landlord.

8.116   A claim may be made for:

- damages; and
- an injunction – to prevent future harassment and/or to force a landlord to re-admit.

Damages

8.117   A claimant may claim the following types of damages:

- special damages,
- general damages,
- aggravated damages,
- exemplary damages.

Special damages

8.118   Special damages are for quantifiable loss or expenditure incurred as a result of the landlord's unlawful actions. They may include amounts for the value of damaged goods, the cost of temporary accommodation and any other loss that can be quantified.

General damages

8.119   General damages are assessed by the court to compensate the claimant for unquantifiable loss or inconvenience.

8.120   General damages may include amounts to compensate a claimant for the anxiety, distress and inconvenience suffered as a result of the landlord's unlawful behaviour, as well as any personal injury suffered. Examples of damages awards are set out below.

In *Addison v Croft*[58] the claimant was an assured shorthold tenant whose landlady was selling the property. When the landlady entered the premises without warning, accompanied by an estate agent and prospective purchaser, there was an argument between the landlady

58   June 2008 *Legal Action* 31, Preston County Court, 17 April 2008.

and the tenant's girlfriend. Later the landlady came to the premises and insisted that the girlfriend leave. Two weeks later the front door was kicked in and four men threw the tenant and his girlfriend out into the street. One of the men was the landlady's former boyfriend. The tenant suffered bruises and scratches. The landlady refused to re-admit the tenant until after he obtained an injunction. He slept in his van for 20 nights.

The tenant was awarded general damages of £3,000 for the actual eviction and the fact that he was deprived of his home and belongings for 20 days. He was also awarded aggravated damages of £1,000 and exemplary damages of £1,000.

8.121 It is common in claims for unlawful eviction and harassment for additional damages to be claimed under the following heads of aggravated damages and exemplary damages.

Aggravated damages

8.122 These may be awarded if the defendant has behaved in a particularly unpleasant or violent way or where he or she has ignored the orders of the court.

In *Youziel v Andrews*[59] the claimant was an assured shorthold tenant of a one-bedroom flat. The defendant was initially his landlord but then transferred his interest to a third party. Notice of this was not given to the tenant and the defendant continued to manage the property. Rent arrears accrued because the defendant was an asylum-seeker not eligible for benefits. Over a six-week period the defendant subjected the claimant to a campaign of harassment. On ten occasions he threatened the claimant, by entering the flat, telephoning and shouting threats, including that the claimant 'would pay with his life'. The claimant and two friends also assaulted the claimant, slapping and kicking him and throwing him to the ground. He sustained an injury to his knee and suffered stress, anxiety and weight loss.

At Lambeth County Court the claimant was awarded general damages of £13,000 for the personal injuries sustained, £4,300 in aggravated damages for the tort of assault and £2,700 in respect of breach of covenant of quiet enjoyment. The total award was £20,000 plus interest of £200.

59 March 2003 *Legal Action* 30, Lambeth County Court, 23 January 2003.

Exemplary damages

8.123   Exemplary damages may be awarded if the defendant intended to profit from the unlawful act. Such damages are in addition to compensatory damages and are intended to punish or set an example in order to deter unlawful behaviour.[60] They are calculated to ensure that any financial gain resulting from the unlawful action is paid in damages to the victim.

> In *Drane v Evangelou*[61] the tenant's rent was reduced following an application to the rent officer. In response, the landlord moved other people into the premises, changed the locks and moved the tenant's belongings into the back yard. An injunction was granted but the tenant was not able to return to the premises for ten weeks. Exemplary damages of £1,000 were awarded for what was described as the landlord's 'monstrous behaviour'.
>
> The Court of Appeal dismissed the landlord's appeal: it was appropriate to award exemplary damages where the defendant's conduct had been calculated to make a profit and those damages may exceed the compensation ordinarily payable. It was said: 'To deprive a man of a roof over his head in my judgment is one of the worst torts which can be committed. It causes stress, worry and anxiety.'[62]

8.124   Aggravated and exemplary damages can only be awarded in respect of a tort and not for breach of contract.[63]

8.125   The statutory damages awarded under HA 1988 s28 are calculated in a similar way and exemplary damages will not be awarded in addition to section 28 damages.[64]

8.126   Although many of the reported cases concern tenants with long-term rights, damages may be substantial even where the occupier occupies under a short-term agreement.

---

60   *Rookes v Barnard* [1964] 1 All ER 367, HL.
61   [1978] 2 All ER 437.
62   Lawton LJ at 461.
63   *Kralj v McGrath* [1986] 1 All ER 54; *Addis v Gramaphone Co Ltd* [1909] AC 488.
64   HA 1988 s27(5).

In *Deelah v Rehman*[65] an assured shorthold tenant had exclusive use of one bedroom with shared use of a kitchen and bathroom. He lived there with his wife and two sons aged nine and 16. They were unlawfully evicted and the landlord swore at and threatened the 16-year-old. They were ineligible for homeless assistance and had to sleep on a sofa and the floor of a friend's house for four nights before obtaining an injunction and resuming possession of the room. After moving back in the locks were tampered with on two occasions meaning the tenant could not get into the room for short periods.

He was awarded damages of £1,000 for the four nights the family were excluded (£250 per night), £1,500 for the harassment before and after the eviction, £1,500 aggravated damages and £2,500 exemplary damages as the eviction had been intended to save the landlord the cost of possession proceedings. The evidence suggested the house was an unlicenced HMO which would have increased the costs for the landlord.

Injunctions

8.127　An injunction is a court order compelling a person to do something or to stop doing something. The terms of an injunction must be clear so that the respondent knows exactly what he or she must do and any time limit. If a person does not comply with an injunction an application may be made to the court for the person to be committed to prison for contempt of court (see para 8.138 below).

8.128　　An injunction is a discretionary remedy. This means that the court may refuse to grant the injunction even if satisfied that the defendant has behaved unlawfully. The court can take account of the claimant's behaviour in deciding whether to grant an injunction.

Interim injunctions

8.129　In cases of unlawful eviction and harassment it is common to seek an interim injunction to ensure that the occupier is re-instated and/ or to restrain further acts of harassment until the claim can be tried by the court. In fact, in cases of unlawful eviction, if an occupier is re-instated in compliance with an injunction, there may be no

65 July 2011 *Legal Action* 19, Clerkenwell & Shoreditch County Court, 10 March 2011.

further hearings; the claim for damages may be settled by agreement between the parties.

8.130   To obtain an interim injunction the applicant must show that:[66]

- damages are not a sufficient remedy;
- there is a serious issue to be tried; and
- the 'balance of convenience' favours the making of an injunction.

8.131   In most cases of unlawful eviction it is clear that the action is unlawful and the court will make an order that the landlord allows the occupier back into the premises. However, this may not be possible if the premises have been re-let (see below, para 8.137).

Cases of urgency

8.132   Normally at least three days' notice must be given of an application for an interim injunction.[67] However, in some circumstances it is possible to obtain an injunction without giving notice to the defendant. A 'without notice' injunction may be applied for where there is 'exceptional urgency'.[68] If the case is too urgent to give three days' notice, the landlord should nevertheless be informed of the application by telephone or fax if possible.

8.133   In addition, if there is a risk of violence to the claimant from the defendant, a without notice application may be made to ensure that the claimant is protected by an injunction before the defendant is given notice of the proceedings.

8.134   Where a without notice order is obtained, the defendant must be served with the order, the application notice, evidence, and notice of any further hearing as soon as possible. Injunctions should always be personally served on the defendant.

8.135   An order made on a without notice application will usually be for a very limited period. The court may list a further on notice hearing within a few days and the injunction will last until that hearing. Alternatively, the defendant may be given the opportunity to apply to discharge the injunction at short notice. In any event the injunction will be reconsidered at any final hearing.

---

66 *American Cynamid Co v Ethicon* [1975] AC 396, HL.
67 Civil Procedure Rules (CPR) Part 23, PD 23A para 4.1.
68 See CPR 3.1(2) and 23.4(2).

Homeless applications

8.136   A person with a right to occupy but who cannot secure entry to premises is homeless.[69] A person who has been unlawfully evicted should be given emergency accommodation by a local authority provided he or she appears to be eligible and in priority need. Usually an authority will provide emergency accommodation only until an injunction can be obtained and enforced. However, if the landlord's conduct is such that it would be unreasonable to continue to occupy the premises, a long-term housing duty may be owed, see para 14.175.

Where premises have been re-let

8.137   Where premises have already been let to innocent third parties the court will not make an injunction against the landlord: for the landlord to comply he or she would have to evict the new tenants unlawfully. Rather, if the unlawfully evicted tenants wish to regain possession they can take possession proceedings against the new tenants on the basis that they are in fact trespassers, the landlord having no lawful authority to let the premises.

> In *Love v Herrity*[70] a landlord changed the locks to premises and re-let them following service of notice to quit because of arrears of rent. A without notice injunction was obtained for re-entry but later discharged on the basis that the balance of convenience favoured waiting until final trial to decide the issues.
>
> The Court of Appeal held that the court had been wrong to find that there was any serious issue to be tried because it was admitted that there was an assured tenancy that could only be determined by a court order; the tenants had clearly been unlawfully evicted. However, as the premises had been re-let it would be pointless to grant an injunction.
>
> A declaration was granted that, as against the landlord, the tenants were entitled to possession and the tenants were given permission to join the new tenant as a defendant to enable them to claim possession against her. It would have been possible for the tenants to apply for a possession order against the new tenant directly using the summary procedure, on the basis that she was a trespasser.

69   HA 1996 s175(2)(a).
70   (1991) 23 HLR 217.

Final injunctions

8.138   An injunction can also be part of the final order made by the court after trial.

> In *Saxby v McKinley*[71] a landlord unlawfully evicted tenants by changing the locks. The tenants' solicitors informed the landlord that he was not entitled to evict the tenants in this way and that he had committed a criminal offence. This was confirmed in writing. The landlord did not re-admit the tenants. The tenants then obtained an injunction without notice. The injunction required the landlord to provide keys and permit them to re-enter. The landlord failed to comply. At a further hearing, of which the landlord was given notice, the landlord did not appear and the injunction was continued. It was not until 21 days later that the landlord allowed the tenants back into the premises. The tenants applied to commit the landlord to prison for contempt of court.
>
> The judge found that there had been a serious contempt and ordered an immediate sentence of imprisonment of 28 days. The landlord appealed but his appeal was dismissed. It was held that there had been a serious contempt of court and the consequence for the tenants was potentially, if not actually, disastrous. The landlord had shown cynical disregard for the order over a substantial period of time.

Public funding

8.139   Subject to the means test, legal aid will usually be available for cases of unlawful eviction and harassment. However, if an occupier is re-admitted and the only claim before the court is for damages it may be difficult to satisfy the costs-benefit test (ie, that the potential benefit to the occupier justifies the likely legal cost of pursuing the claim). Furthermore, the Legal Aid, Sentencing and Punishment of Offenders Bill will remove legal aid from all cases which are for damages only. Legal aid will remain available where an injunction is sought following an unlawful eviction and for claims brought under the Protection from Harassment Act 1998.

8.140   The Civil Procedure Rules provide that cases of unlawful eviction and harassment should not be referred to the small claims track

71 (1996) 29 HLR 569, CA.

whatever the value. This does not necessarily mean that public funding will be granted where the likely damages are not substantial. The parties may, however, agree that the claim should be dealt with as a small claim.

8.141   See paras 22.156–22.169 for a fuller explanation of public funding and civil proceedings.

CHAPTER 9

Housing benefit

continued

Key points

- Housing benefit is paid to help people on low incomes meet rent payments. It does not cover mortgage payments. It can only be paid for accommodation occupied as a home.
- Not all people are eligible for housing benefit, including some people from abroad and some full-time students.
- Some agreements are excluded from the housing benefit scheme, eg some agreements between relatives and other agreements considered not to be commercial.
- For private tenants housing benefit may be less than the contractual rent: for most private tenants the 'maximum housing benefit' is set by a rent officer. For claims made after 7 April 2008, the maximum housing benefit is limited to the local housing allowance – a set amount depending on the size and location of the property and subject to a cap.
- Housing benefit does not cover certain charges such as water rates and heating and hot water charges.
- Claimants on income support, income-based jobseeker's allowance and pension guarantee credit are entitled to the maximum housing benefit. For other claimants the amount of housing benefit entitlement will depend on their income and capital.
- For tenants of landlords other than local authorities, payment should be made within 14 days of a claim that is supported by all relevant information and evidence. If entitlement cannot be assessed within this time a payment on account must be made.
- Housing benefit may be reduced because of other adults living in the claimant's home. These are known as 'non-dependant deductions'.
- Overpayment of housing benefit may be recovered by deduction from future housing benefit so that the claimant has to pay the shortfall to the landlord to avoid falling into rent arrears.
- Most decisions can be appealed. Local authorities may also revise a decision.
- Housing benefit claims can be backdated for up to six months if there is continuous good cause.
- Important changes to the local housing allowance will affect existing claimants over the period from April 2011 to the end of 2012. A cap will apply to the maximum amount of housing benefit that can be paid and will affect people living in expensive areas and in properties with more than four bedrooms.

Introduction

9.1   Housing benefit (HB) is a means-tested benefit available to assist those on a low income to pay for a dwelling occupied as a home. It is administered by local housing authorities. The rules regarding entitlement and the assessment of claims are complex. This chapter contains an overview of the housing benefit system with a focus on the problems commonly experienced by claimants. Housing benefit problems often lead to rent arrears and possession claims and a basic understanding of the housing benefit system is essential for housing advisers.

9.2   The Social Security Contributions and Benefits Act (SSCBA) 1992 provides for the payment of housing benefit. The details of the housing benefit scheme are found in regulations, principally the Housing Benefit Regulations (HB Regs) 2006.[1] For those over the retirement age the relevant regulations are the Housing Benefit (Persons who have attained the qualifying age for state pension credit) Regulations (HB(PC) Regs) 2006[2] which mirror the provisions of the HB Regs 2006. This chapter refers only to the HB Regs 2006.

9.3   Although administered by local authorities, the scheme is a national scheme set out in regulations. The Department for Work and Pensions (DWP) *Housing Benefit Guidance Manual*, though not law, provides a comprehensive summary of the regulations and the way they should be applied by local authorities. The manual can be downloaded from the DWP website at: www.dwp.gov. uk/local-authority-staff/housing-benefit/.

9.4   Housing benefit cannot be paid to cover mortgage payments[3] or other housing costs paid by owner-occupiers, such as service charges and insurance payments.

9.5   Owner-occupiers who receive income support or pension credit may receive, as part of their benefit, sums in respect of these housing costs. Such housing costs can include interest on home loans (but not capital repayments), service charges and insurance. Again, the rules are complex and are outside the scope of this book.

---

1   SI No 213.
2   SI No 214.
3   SSCBA 1992 s130(2).

Entitlement to housing benefit

9.6   Entitlement to housing benefit depends on the following conditions:[4]

- the claimant must be liable to make payments in respect of a dwelling in Great Britain;
- the dwelling must be occupied as a home;
- there is a maximum amount of housing benefit that will be paid;
- the claimant's income and savings must be below a certain level.

9.7   However, some people cannot claim housing benefit because of their immigration status or because they are full-time students. Each of the qualifying conditions is dealt with below.

Liability to make payments

9.8   Mostly housing benefit is paid in respect of a person's liability for rent. However, a liability other than rent may qualify for housing benefit and a person other than the tenant (or person legally liable to make the payment) can be treated as liable.

9.9   Housing benefit can be paid in respect of:[5]

- rent;
- licence payments;
- mesne profits;
- use and occupation charges;
- service charges, where payment is a condition on which the right to occupy depends;[6]
- mooring charges for a houseboat;
- site payments for a caravan or mobile home;
- certain costs charged by housing associations and charities for the maintenance of almshouses and essential services;[7]
- payments under a rental purchase agreement.

4 SSCBA 1992 s130(1).
5 HB Regs 2006 reg 12(1).
6 See para 9.14 below.
7 Because the provision of almshouses is charitable, the occupiers cannot be tenants, see para 1.43. However, the providers may make charges to the occupiers, for which housing benefit is payable.

Mesne profits and charges for use and occupation

9.10   Mesne profits are damages for which a trespasser is liable. They are usually assessed on the basis of rent because this represents the income lost by the landlord/owner as a result of the unlawful occupation. Use and occupation charges are charges made or agreed when an occupier has no legal right to occupy land. The terms 'mesne profits' and 'use and occupation charges' are often used interchangeably. Landlords who are denying that a person has any legal right to occupy may indicate that payments made will be accepted as mesne profits or use and occupation charges only. This is to guard against the occupier arguing that the acceptance of 'rent' is evidence that a tenancy exists. This is common after the expiry of a notice to quit served by a private landlord or when a landlord is disputing a person's right to succeed to a tenancy, see paras 4.28–4.47.

9.11   In some cases the landlord may refuse to accept any payment, either as rent or use and occupation charges, while pursuing a claim for possession. However, the person in occupation remains liable and an application for housing benefit should be made. The authority may suspend actual payment but, provided a timely application has been made, housing benefit may be paid when the dispute has been resolved, either as rent (if the occupier succeeds in establishing a right to occupy) or mesne profits (if the landlord succeeds in establishing unlawful occupation).

9.12   Housing benefit is not paid in respect of:[8]

- payments under a long tenancy[9] except a shared ownership tenancy granted by a housing association or housing authority;
- payments under a co-ownership scheme;
- payments by an owner;
- payments under a hire purchase, credit sale or conditional sale agreement, except to the extent that the agreement is in respect of land;
- payments by a Crown tenant;[10] and
- payments in respect of a dwelling owned by the claimant's partner.

---

8   HB Regs 2006 reg 12(2).

9   A long tenancy is defined as a tenancy for a fixed period of 21 years or more: HB Regs 2006 reg 2.

10   See para 3.33 for the definition of a Crown tenant. Crown tenants on income support or pension credit can claim housing costs. Crown tenants may also claim a rent rebate from the landlord under a voluntary scheme. Inquiries should be made to the landlord.

Non-eligible charges

9.13   Where the weekly amount paid as 'rent' includes sums that are for charges other than the right to occupy the accommodation, the other charges will usually be 'non-eligible charges' and housing benefit will not cover those charges.

9.14   Non-eligible charges include water rates, heating and hot water charges for the premises (as opposed to the common parts) and some service charges. However, service charges that must be paid as a condition of occupation are eligible charges for which housing benefit can be paid. These include charges for such services as general management costs, lifts, entry phones and rubbish removal. Services charges that are not eligible include services that are personal to the occupier. Some service charges in supported accommodation may be paid for by the local authority's social services department, depending on the occupier's means.

Who can claim housing benefit

9.15   Housing benefit will normally be paid to the person who is liable to make the payments, for example, the tenant or licensee.[11] However, the following may be treated as being liable so as to be eligible to receive housing benefit:[12]

- a partner of the person who is liable;
- a person who has to make the payments in order to continue to live in the home because the person liable to make them is not doing so; the person must be a former partner of the liable person or it must be reasonable to treat that person as liable to make the payments;
- a person whose rent liability has been waived by the landlord as compensation for works of repair which are the landlord's responsibility but which were carried out by the tenant, for a maximum period of eight weeks;
- a partner of a student who cannot claim housing benefit (see para 9.18).

11 HB Regs 2006 reg 8(1)(a).
12 HB Regs 2006 reg 8(1)(b)–(e).

Persons ineligible for housing benefit

Persons from abroad

9.16   Housing benefit cannot be paid to certain people because of their immigration status or because they are not habitually resident in the UK.

9.17   There are three categories under which a person may be ineligible for housing benefit:

- those subject to immigration control;
- EEA nationals with no right to reside; and
- persons who are not habitually resident.

These categories are broadly the same as those persons ineligible for homelessness assistance and are explained in detail in paras 14.5–14.140. The main difference between the rules regarding eligibility for housing benefit and for homeless assistance and housing, is that those who come to the UK as jobseekers are entitled to housing benefit for up to six months as long as they register as jobseekers and beyond six months if they can also show that they are actively seeking work and have a genuine chance of being employed. In contrast the jobseeker's right of residence does not qualify the person for homeless assistance or an allocation of housing, see para 14.41.

Students

9.18   The general rule is that full-time students[13] are ineligible for housing benefit.[14] However, the following full-time students *are* eligible for housing benefit:[15]

- a person on income support or income-based jobseeker's allowance;
- a lone parent;
- those who would qualify for the following premiums paid to housing benefit claimants: pensioner premium, higher pensioner premium, disability premium or severe disability premium;
- those who are incapable of work or treated as being incapable of work for a continuous period of not less than 196 days;

13 'Full-time student' is defined as a person attending a full-time course of study including a sandwich course. See HB Regs 2006 reg 53 which provides extensive definition of all terms relevant to students.

14 HB Regs 2006 reg 56(1). As for persons from abroad, they are treated as not being liable to make payments.

15 HB Regs 2006 reg 56(2).

- a person who has a partner who is also a full-time student, if either is responsible for a child or young person;
- a single claimant who is fostering a child placed by the local authority or a voluntary organisation;
- a person aged under 19 whose course of study is not a course of higher education;
- a person who has been awarded a certain kind of educational grant or allowance because of disability by reason of deafness.

Agreements that are excluded from housing benefit

9.19   In addition to individuals being ineligible, certain kinds of agreements are also excluded. A person who is liable to make payment is treated as not being liable in the circumstances set out below.[16]

Non-commercial agreements

- The tenancy or other occupation agreement is not on a commercial basis (see paras 9.23–9.26).

Liability to family members/partners

- The liability under the agreement is to a person also living in the dwelling who is a close relative[17] of the claimant or his or her partner.
- The liability under the agreement is:
  - to the claimant's former partner in respect of a dwelling the couple previously occupied together, or
  - to the claimant's partner's former partner in respect of a dwelling the couple (the partner and his or her former partner) previously occupied together.
- The claimant or his or her partner is responsible for a child of the person to whom the claimant is liable under the agreement.
- Under the agreement the liability is to a trust of which a child of the claimant or the claimant's partner is a beneficiary.

Accommodation previously owned by claimant or partner

- The claimant or the claimant's partner previously owned the dwelling within the last five years (or was a tenant under a long lease). However, this will not apply if the claimant satisfies the

---

16 HB Regs 2006 reg 9.
17 As defined in HB Regs 2006 reg 2(1).

authority that it was necessary to relinquish ownership of the lease in order to continue in occupation.

Employment-related accommodation

- Occupation by the claimant or the claimant's partner is a condition of employment.

Religious orders

- The claimant is a member of a religious order and is wholly maintained by the order.

Care homes

- The claimant is in a care home or independent hospital.

Agreements created to take advantage of the HB scheme

9.20 In addition to the specific exclusions above in para 9.19, an agreement will be excluded if the liability was created to take advantage of the housing benefit scheme.

9.21 The following are excluded unless the claimant can satisfy the authority that the liability was not intended to be a way of taking advantage of the housing benefit scheme:

- An agreement under which the liability is to a company or trust, under which any of the following are directors, employees, trustees or beneficiaries: the claimant, his or her partner, a close relative (of the claimant or his or her partner) who resides with the claimant, or a former partner (of the claimant or the claimant's partner).
- Where, before the liability was created, the claimant was a non-dependant of someone who resided and continues to reside in the dwelling (see paras 9.81–9.84 below for an explanation of non-dependants).

9.22 It should be noted that a liability to a close relative is only automatically excluded where he or she shares the dwelling. However, a tenancy agreement between close relatives may be considered not to be on a commercial basis even where the accommodation is not shared. If the claim does not fall within one of the specific situations listed above in para 9.19, the question of whether an agreement is a commercial agreement is a question of fact in each case.

Non-commercial agreements

9.23 When deciding whether an agreement is on a commercial basis the authority must have regard to whether the agreed terms are legally enforceable.[18]

9.25 Authorities may allege that an agreement is not commercial because the landlord has not taken action to enforce the payment of the full rent where there is a shortfall between the rent and the maximum housing benefit.

> This issue was considered in the Commissioner's case CH 1076/2002. The commissioner overturned the tribunal decision that the agreement was not commercial, holding that the tribunal had failed to give sufficient weight to the evidence that it was common practice for landlords to accept the amount of rent paid by housing benefit. The commissioner found that there was nothing to suggest that this was not a sensible commercial decision for the landlord to make. Furthermore, the tribunal had attached too much weight to the parties' failure to vary the tenancy agreement formally so as to lower the rent to the amount that housing benefit was paying. The issue should have been assessed in the context of parties who knew and could trust each other.

9.25 The DWP Guidance also refers to the following criteria as being relevant to the issue:

- The relationship between the parties – it is important to remember that there is nothing inherently non-commercial about letting to a close friend or relative, but the nature of any personal ties should be considered.
- The living arrangements – where the landlord is resident it is worth considering whether the tenant has exclusive use of any part of the property and how chores and food storage are arranged etc.
- Amount of rent payable – a low rent is not in itself indicative of a non-commercial agreement. Many landlords do not seek to profit from renting out property.
- Evidence of payments made – evidence of non-payment may suggest non-commerciality.

18 HB Regs 2006 reg 9(2).

9.26 It should be noted that a tenancy and a liability to pay rent does not depend on there being a written agreement. An authority should not refuse to pay housing benefit because there is no written agreement provided there is other evidence of the tenancy, for example, letter from the landlord, rent book or other proof of the amount of rent payable. Furthermore, it is not necessary to draw up a new tenancy agreement when a fixed-term agreement expires: a legally binding statutory tenancy automatically comes into existence. See paras 3.45–3.46 above.

Occupying the dwelling as a home

9.27 The general rule is that a person is entitled to housing benefit in respect of a dwelling occupied as his or her home.[19] However, this is subject to express provision for temporary absences and for the payment of housing benefit on two properties.

9.28 As is explained in paras 4.5–4.12, an occupier who is temporarily absent does not necessarily cease to occupy premises as his or her home. Even during an extended absence a person may continue to occupy a dwelling provided:

- he or she intends to return; and
- there is some physical evidence of that intention.

9.29 However, this does not necessarily mean that a person who is absent for an extended period will continue to be entitled to receive housing benefit.

9.30 Specific provision is made in the regulations for:

- periods of absence when housing benefit will continue to be paid; and
- circumstances in which housing benefit will be paid in respect of two dwellings.

Temporary absence

Up to 13 weeks' absence

9.31 Any claimant temporarily absent from home for any reason, for example, holiday, or visiting friends and family, may continue to

---

19 SSCBA 1992 s130(1).

receive housing benefit for a period of up to 13 weeks provided the following conditions are met:[20]

- the claimant intends to return to occupy the dwelling as his or her home;
- it has not been let or sublet during the claimant's absence; and
- the period of absence is unlikely to exceed 13 weeks.

9.32 This does not mean that housing benefit can be paid for the first 13 weeks of an absence which is likely to exceed 13 weeks. If the absence is likely to exceed 13 weeks no housing benefit is payable. Furthermore, if, during the absence, there is a change of circumstance and it becomes likely that the absence will extend beyond 13 weeks, entitlement ends at that point.

Prisoners

9.33 This rule applies to an absence caused by being imprisoned *after* conviction and sentence for a criminal offence. Again, it should be noted that benefit is payable only if the likely absence will not exceed 13 weeks. This means that an assessment must be made of the likely release date. Most prisoners on short-term sentences serve only half the term of imprisonment and may be released earlier under the discretionary home detention curfew schemes ('tagging').

9.34 In contrast, prisoners who are detained on remand pending trial or sentence are entitled to receive housing benefit for up to 52 weeks, see below at para 9.37.

Trial period of residential care

9.35 There is specific provision that housing benefit can be paid for up to 13 weeks in respect of a claimant who goes into residential accommodation on a trial basis.[21]

9.36 In such a case the claimant must intend to return to occupy the dwelling as his or her home only in the event that the residential accommodation proves not to be suitable. As in all cases of housing benefit paid during a temporary absence, the home must not be let or sublet during the absence.

20 HB Regs 2006 reg 7(13).
21 HB Regs 2006 reg 7(11) and (12).

Up to 52 weeks' absence

9.37   Housing benefit may be paid during an absence of up to 52 weeks to the following claimants:[22]

- a prisoner on remand pending trial or sentence;[23]
- a person on bail who is required to live in an approved bail hostel or an address other than the person's usual home;
- a person who is in a hospital or similar institution as a patient;
- a person who is, or whose partner or child is, undergoing medical treatment or medically approved[24] convalescence in the UK or abroad, other than in residential accommodation;[25]
- a person who is receiving medically approved care in the UK or abroad, other than in residential accommodation;
- a person who is providing medically approved care to someone else residing in the UK or elsewhere;
- a person who is caring for a child whose parent or guardian is away from home receiving medically approved care or medical treatment;
- a person undertaking an approved training course in the UK or abroad;[26]
- a person who is a student who would be entitled to housing benefit if not absent from home;
- a person in residential accommodation for respite care; this is different from a person in residential accommodation for a trial period, when the maximum period for which housing benefit can be paid is 13 weeks;
- a person who is away from home because of fear of violence in the home or from a former family member.

22 HB Regs 2006 reg 7(16) and (17).

23 If the prisoner is convicted and sentenced to a term of imprisonment his or her entitlement is then dealt with under the 13-week rule, see para 9.33 above. A prisoner who has already received housing benefit for a period of 13 weeks on remand will be entitled to no further housing benefit.

24 'Medically approved' means certified by a medical practitioner: HB Regs 2006 reg 7(18).

25 Residential accommodation means a care home, an independent hospital or an Abbeyfield Home: HB Regs 2006 reg 7(18).

26 See HB Regs 2006 reg 7(18). An approved training course means a course provided by, or on behalf of, or approved by a government department or the secretary of state, Scottish Enterprise or Highlands and Islands Enterprise. They include courses under various EU initiatives which involve periods abroad and courses for occupational, vocational or social rehabilitation skills offered to disabled persons by the Department for Innovation, Universities and Skills and the Department of Health.

9.38 In all cases it is necessary that the following conditions are met:
- the claimant intends to return to occupy the dwelling as his or her home;
- it has not been let or sublet during the claimant's absence;
- the period of absence is unlikely to exceed 52 weeks or, in exceptional circumstances, is unlikely to substantially exceed that period.

9.39 It should be noted that, although there is provision for benefit to be paid even where the absence is likely to exceed 52 weeks (in exceptional circumstances) the total period for which benefit is paid cannot exceed 52 weeks.

Housing benefit for two homes

9.40 The general rule is that housing benefit can only be paid in respect of one home. However, in certain circumstances housing benefit may be paid on two dwellings, see paras 9.41–9.47.[27]

Unavoidable liability for previous home: up to four weeks

9.41 When a person moves into a new home but remains liable to make payment on his or her previous home, housing benefit can be paid on both homes for up to four weeks, where the dual liability could not reasonably have been avoided.[28] This commonly occurs when a person is allocated a social tenancy under the local authority's allocations scheme (see chapter 17) and the new tenancy is to start before old tenancy can be terminated. See paras 1.62–1.69 regarding the termination of tenancies by tenants.

Delay in moving into new home: up to four weeks

9.42 As housing benefit may only be paid in respect of a home actually occupied, if a person takes on a liability but delays actually moving into a dwelling, housing benefit cannot usually be paid. However, provision is made for a person to be treated as occupying a new home for up to four weeks if the delay is caused by any of the following:[29]
- The delay was necessary to carry out disabled adaptations to the new home.

27 HB Regs 2006 reg 7(6).
28 HB Regs 2006 reg 7(6)(d) and (7).
29 HB Regs 2006 reg 7(6)(e) and (8).

- The move was delayed pending the outcome of an application for a social fund payment necessary to meet needs arising out of the move or in setting up the home. This applies only if:
  - a member of the claimant's family is aged five or under,
  - the claimant is receiving a disability premium, or
  - the claimant is over 60 and neither the claimant nor his or her partner is getting income support or jobseeker's allowance.
- The claimant became liable to make payments in respect of the new dwelling while he or she was a patient or in residential accommodation.

9.43   In all cases the claim for housing benefit must be made before the person moves into the new home. If refused, a new claim must be made within four weeks of moving to qualify. Payment will not actually be made until the claimant moves into the new home.

Fleeing violence: up to 52 weeks

9.44   Where a person remains absent because of a fear of violence in the home or from a former family member, housing benefit may be paid on two homes for up to 52 weeks where it is considered reasonable to do so.[30] This entitlement depends on the victim having a continuing intention to return to occupy the home.

Fleeing violence: up to four weeks

9.45   In addition, benefit may be paid on two homes for up to four weeks even where the victim does not have an intention to return to the home he or she has left.[31]

Accommodation in two dwellings: indefinitely

9.46   Where, because of the number of people in the household, a housing authority has accommodated the household in two separate dwellings, housing benefit will be paid on both dwellings.[32]

Couple including an eligible student: indefinitely

9.47   Where a student who is eligible for housing benefit (see above at para 9.18) is part of a couple benefit may be paid on two homes if it is unavoidable that they should occupy two separate dwellings and it

---

30 HB Regs 2006 reg 7(6)(a).
31 HB Regs 2006 reg 7(10).
32 HB Regs 2006 reg 7(6)(c).

is reasonable to pay housing benefit on both.[33] The same rule applies if he or she is on an approved training course (see above para 9.37).

Maximum housing benefit

9.48 Even where a claimant is entitled to 'full housing benefit', this may not cover the whole of the net rent. The amount of housing benefit paid cannot exceed the 'maximum housing benefit'.[34] For local authority tenants and Rent Act tenants the maximum housing benefit is the contractual rent. For tenants in the unregulated private sector the maximum housing benefit may be less than the contractual rent.

The old system: eligible rents

9.49 From 2 January 1996 housing benefit levels were controlled by a system whereby rent officers would decide on the 'eligible rent' for tenants of private landlords.[35] The eligible rent was the amount the rent officer considered to be a reasonable rent taking into account local rent levels for accommodation of a suitable size for the household.[36] This was calculated on the basis of what was considered to be:

- a reasonable rent for the actual property; or
- (if the actual property was deemed too large) a reasonable rent for a property of a suitable size, in the immediate area (the 'claim related rent'); and
- a reasonable rent for a property of a suitable size in the broader locality (the 'local reference rent').

9.50 The lowest of these was the maximum housing benefit (the eligible rent) that could be paid. The assessment was carried out following a claim for housing benefit being made in respect of a particular agreement for particular premises.

9.51 For most applicants under the age of 25 the maximum rent was calculated on the basis of a reasonable rent for a single room in a shared house: the 'single room rent'.

---

33 HB Regs 2006 reg 7(6)(b).
34 SSCBA 1992 s130(4) and HB Regs 2006 regs 12(3)(a) and 13.
35 The previous scheme is known as 'the Old Scheme' and some claims are still governed by the Old Scheme.
36 See the Rent Officers (Housing Benefit Functions) Order ('Rent Officers Order') 1997 SI No 1984.

9.52 The system of assessing maximum housing benefit changed on 7 April 2008: the 'local housing allowance' was introduced (see paras 9.56–9.73). For claimants who remain in the same accommodation and whose claim continues after that date housing benefit will still be limited by reference to the eligible rent. However, a claimant may withdraw his or her claim and submit a new claim for a local housing allowance.

9.53 One problem with eligible rents as a method of assessing the maximum amount of housing benefit is that claimants often had to sign a tenancy agreement before knowing how much housing benefit would be paid.[37] Many tenants are therefore contractually obliged to pay a rent that is not met in full by housing benefit. Some tenants pay the shortfall from their limited income. In some cases the landlord does not insist on payment of the shortfall but may, after arrears have built up, use the failure to pay as a ground for possession or may seek a money judgment against the tenant.

9.54 Another problem was that the reference to the rent officer added to the delay in assessing and paying housing benefit at the start of the tenancy.

9.55 Local authority rents were not subject to rent officer assessment. For registered social landlord tenancies, referrals to the rent officer were possible but were made only if the rent seemed unreasonably high or the premises were larger than required. Also, private tenancies that started prior to 15 January 1989 (regulated tenancies) were not subject to the scheme; such tenants have the right to a 'fair rent' (see para 4.178).

The new system: local housing allowances

9.56 On 7 April 2008 a new system of 'local housing allowances' (LHAs) came into force nationally. The key principle of the LHA is that the maximum housing benefit is based on a flat rate allowance depending on the size and location of the property rather than a rent officer assessment for an individual claimant. LHAs are set and published locally so that the LHA in a particular area for a certain size of property will be known by tenants and landlords in advance.[38]

---

37 It was possible to obtain a 'pre-tenancy determination' but often, to secure the property, the claimant would have to sign a tenancy agreement before this could be done.

38 Between 1 April 2008 and 1 April 2011 claimants could keep any surplus housing benefit up to a maximum of £15 per week if the actual rent was lower than the LHA. This is no longer the case for new claims made on or after 1 April 2011 and is being phased out for existing claimants.

9.57 LHAs apply to claims made on or after 7 April 2008 and will apply to existing claimants who move to a new property on or after 7 April 2008.

9.58 The LHA scheme applies only to private sector tenancies. It does not apply to:[39]

- tenancies where the landlord is a local authority;[40]
- tenancies where the landlord is a registered provider of social housing;
- exempt accommodation (shelters and supported accommodation);
- excluded tenancies, which includes regulated tenancies (to which the fair rent scheme applies);
- houseboats, caravans, mobile homes, hostels and tenancies where a substantial amount of the rent is attributable to board and attendance.

The LHA cap

9.59 LHAs are based on the area in which the claimant lives and the size of the property. However, from April 2011 a cap applies nationally limiting the maximum housing benefits as follows:[41]

Size of accommodation	Maximum HB
One bedroom (either shared or exclusive use)	£250 pw
Two bedrooms	£290 pw
Three bedrooms	£340 pw
Four bedrooms and above	£400 pw

The area

9.60 The areas for which rents are calculated are based on 'broad market rental areas'. Initially, the amount of housing benefit payable was based on the median rents (ie the middle of the range) but as from

---

39 HB Regs 2006 reg 13C.
40 The scheme applies only to cases in which a rent allowance may be awarded. Local authority tenants receive a rebate and not a rent allowance.
41 Rent Officers (Housing Benefit Functions) Amendment Order 2010 SI No 2836.

1 April 2011 it is based on the rent at the 30th percentile (the highest of rents in the cheapest 30 per cent of all rents in the area).[42]

9.61   The area for which the LHA can be claimed must be an area in which the claimant could reasonably be expected to live, having regard to facilities and for health, education, recreation, banking and shopping, and taking account of public and private transport to and facilities and services.[43]

Size of accommodation

9.62   The size of accommodation deemed appropriate for a particular household is set out in the Rent Officers Order.[44] A household is entitled to one bedroom for:

- every adult couple, whether married or unmarried;
- each other adult aged 16 or over;
- any two children of the same sex aged under 16;
- any two children aged under 10;
- any other child.

A claimant who needs overnight care is allowed one extra bedroom for a carer.[45]

9.63   However, the maximum amount of housing benefit that will be paid for any size of property in any area is £400 per week.

Under 25s – the shared accommodation rate

9.64   For single applicants under the age of 25 the LHA is based on the cost of a shared room: the 'shared accommodation rate', which will vary according to locality but which will usually be much less than the LHA for a one-bedroom property. From January 2012 the shared accommodation rate will also apply to all single applicants under the age of 35.

---

42 Rent Officers (Housing Benefit Functions) (Amendment) Order 2010 SI No 2836.

43 See *R on the application of Heffernan v Rent Service* [2008] UKHL 58, 30 July 2008.

44 1997 SI No 1984. The Order has been amended by the Rent Officers (Housing Benefit Functions) Amendment Orders 2007 SI No 2871, 2008 SI Nos 587 and 3156. 2009 SI No 2459 and 2010 SI No 2836.

45 This provision was introduced in March 2011 by 2010 SI No 2836.

Exceptions

9.65 Care leavers under the age of 22 are entitled to the LHA for a self-contained one-bedroom property. For the definition of 'care leaver' see paras 19.21–19.23.

9.66 Claimants who are severely disabled (in receipt of severe disablement benefit) are also entitled to the LHA for a self-contained one-bedroom property.

Shared accommodation

9.67 For single applicants over 25 and couples with no dependants who live in shared accommodation with exclusive use of only one room, the LHA shared room rate will apply. However, if the claimant or couple occupies more than one room exclusively or has self-contained accommodation the full LHA for a one-bedroom self-contained property will apply.

Payment of the local housing allowance

9.68 Under the previous scheme a claimant could elect for housing benefit to be paid direct to the landlord. Also, payment was made direct to the landlord automatically if the tenant had arrears of rent of at least eight weeks or payment of rent arrears was being made direct from benefits. Under the LHA scheme payment will be made to the claimant unless one of the following applies:

- the authority considers that the claimant is likely to have difficulty in managing his or her financial affairs;
- the authority considers that it is improbable that the claimant will pay his or her rent;
- payment was previously made directly to the landlord because of rent arrears.

9.69 Also, from April 2011, where a landlord agrees to reduce the rent (because of the LHA cap) to enable the tenant to stay in the property housing benefit may be paid direct to the landlord.

9.70 While considering whether to make payment direct to the landlord an authority may pay direct to the landlord for up to eight weeks.

9.71 There is a right of appeal, by either the tenant or the landlord, about a decision on whether to make payments to the landlord.

Information about local housing allowances

9.72   LHAs will be published at the end of each month to apply the following month. They can be checked online through each local authority's website or through 'LHA-direct' which is part of the Rent Service website: https://lha-direct.voa.gov.uk.

9.73   Although LHAs are reviewed each month, the LHA payable to a particular claimant will not be reviewed until 12 months after the claim is made. The new rules under which, in many cases, the LHA will be lower than when the housing benefit claim was initially made, will be applied from the first annual review after 1 April 2011 for most existing claimants.

Transitional arrangements

9.74   When the rules changed in 1996 those claimants who were already receiving housing benefit on 1 January 1996 continued to have their claims assessed under the Old Scheme. Those who have been in receipt of housing benefit continually since 1 January 1996 continue to be dealt with under the Old Scheme. Those whose claims were made on or after 1 January 1996 but before 7 April 2008 will continue to have the maximum rent assessed on the basis of the reference rent as determined by the Rent Service.

Assessment of income and capital

9.75   Subject to the rules regarding the maximum amount of housing benefit described above in paras 9.48–9.74, the amount of housing benefit a claimant receives depends on an assessment of his or her income and capital.

9.76   Claimants who receive income support, income-based jobseeker's allowance or the guarantee credit of pension credit are entitled to maximum housing benefit. However, this may be less than the rent payable if the maximum housing benefit is less than the contractual rent (see paras 9.48–9.74 above), or the benefit is subject to 'non-dependant deductions' (see para 9.81 below).

9.77   For other claimants, an assessment is made which depends on the claimant's 'applicable amount'. The applicable amount for a claimant depends on the age of the claimant, the number and age of any dependants and whether the claimant or a member of the household has any special needs. The claimant's weekly income, less the applicable amount equals 'excess income'. If this is zero or less than zero the person is entitled to full housing benefit (ie the maximum amount). If it is greater than zero, the amount of housing benefit payable will be the maximum housing benefit less 65 per cent of the weekly excess income. Obviously, if the excess income is above a certain level no housing benefit will be payable. Certain income is disregarded: disability living allowance, attendance allowance, mobility allowance, war widows' pension and a proportion of war disablement pension, child benefit.

9.78 If a person has savings (including investments) of £16,000 or more, no housing benefit is payable. Savings below this level may mean that the claimant does not receive full housing benefit, different rules applying for those over the age of 60.

9.79 Many local authorities include on their websites a self-assessment service so that a potential claimant can assess if housing benefit will be payable and at what level.

Shared accommodation – assessment of liability

9.80 Where accommodation is shared, for example, by joint tenants (other than couples), the liability is apportioned between the occupiers.[46] This is the case even though legally each tenant is liable for the whole of the rent (see para 1.52). If only one person is the tenant and liable for the rent, a deduction may be made for other occupiers as 'non-dependant deductions', see below, paras 9.81–9.84.

Non-dependant deductions

9.81 'Non-dependants' are people who normally reside with a claimant, other than dependent children and partners. Because such people are expected to contribute to the rent, a deduction is made from the claimant's housing benefit for each non-dependant in the household. The amount of the deduction depends on the income of the non-dependant. The definition is set out in the HB Regs 2006 reg 3, and includes:

- any member of the claimant's family (apart from one who is part of the claimant's family for benefit purposes, for example, a dependent child);
- a lodger;
- a carer.

46 This is not the case if the LHA scheme applies, see paras 9.59–9.67 above.

9.82   For certain non-dependants no deduction is made. The most common examples are:

- those under the age of 25 who are in receipt of income support or income-based jobseeker's allowance (JSA), or the assessment phase of income-related employment and support allowance (ESA);[47]
- those in receipt of pension credit;[48]
- full-time students;[49]
- any person who resides with a claimant where the claimant is blind or in receipt of attendance allowance or the care component of disability living allowance.[50]

9.83   Where a non-dependant deduction is made, if the non-dependant is in 'remunerative work' this is based on the person's weekly income and is applied on a sliding scale, ranging from £9.40 per week to £60.60 per week, (for the year 2011/12 but this may be increased when benefit rates change). If the non-dependant is not in full-time paid work, the deduction is £9.40 per week regardless of income. Remunerative work means paid employment for not less than 16 hours a week.[51] The lowest deduction (£9.40) is made for each non-dependant aged 25 or over who is in receipt of income support, income-based JSA and 'main phase' ESA.

9.84   It is the claimant's responsibility to submit evidence of the income of a non-dependant. Where no such evidence is submitted, the DWP guidance previously indicated that the authority should make the maximum deduction. However, this approach was successfully challenged in a Commissioner's appeal when it was held that the authority should have made an assessment based on the evidence it did have (ie, the likely income of a 19-year-old shop worker).[52] The guidance now provides that if no, or inadequate, information about the non-dependant's gross income is provided, the highest deduction should only be made after considering all the relevant facts.

47   HB Regs 2006 reg 74(8).
48   HB Regs 2006 reg 74(1).
49   HB Regs 2006 reg 74(7)(c).
50   HB Regs 2006 reg 74(6).
51   HB Regs 2006 reg 6.
52   See CH/48/2006.

Discretionary housing payments

9.85 Discretionary housing payments (DHPs) are not strictly housing benefit.[53] They are, as indicated, discretionary and can be awarded to a person who receives housing benefit where the authority is satisfied that the person needs additional help with housing costs. The budget for DHPs is cash-limited. DHPs can be paid to enable a person to meet a shortfall between the contractual rent and housing benefit but can only be paid for a period when the person is in receipt of housing benefit. Generally, they may be used to cover a shortfall arising because of the difference between the contractual rent and the maximum housing benefit. They can also be made to enable a person to pay rent in advance, a deposit or removal expenses. However, DHPs cannot be awarded to cover any of the following:[54]

- ineligible services charges;
- water rates;
- reductions in social security benefits;
- repayment of rent arrears;
- shortfalls arising because of the recovery of previous over-payments.

9.86 The DWP publishes useful guidance on DHPs which is also available on the DWP website: www.dwp.gov.uk/docs/dhpguide.pdf.

Housing benefit applications and payments

9.87 Although the housing benefit scheme is a national scheme each local authority has its own application forms on which housing benefit is claimed. An application form should be completed and given to the local authority as soon as possible so that no benefit is lost. Claims may also be made at the same time as a claim is made for income support, jobseeker's allowance, pension credit or employment and support allowance.

9.88 In addition to completing an application form, the claimant must provide further information and evidence, as indicated by the form or as the authority subsequently decides is reasonably required to determine entitlement. This will usually include, as a minimum, proof of

---

53 See Discretionary Financial Assistance Regulations 2001 SI No 1167, as amended by the Discretionary Financial Assistance (Amendment) Regulations 2008 SI No 637.
54 2001 SI No 1167 reg 3 sets out the full list of excluded payments.

identity, rental liability, residence and income, plus any documents necessary to establish immigration status, if relevant.

9.89   The authority is only obliged to process the claim when all this information and evidence has been submitted.

9.90   Authorities often request further information and evidence following receipt of a claim. The general rule is that this must be provided within one month of the request, or a longer period if the authority considers this reasonable. If the information is not provided within the specified time period the claim may be assessed as being made at a date later than the date the application form was delivered to the authority. This will mean a loss of benefit and the accrual of rent arrears. In such a case, a person may make an application for back-dated housing benefit (see para 9.95 below).

9.91   Disputes as to whether information and evidence has been provided are common and claimants should always obtain and keep receipts for information delivered to local authority offices.

Delays

9.92   Following receipt of the written application form together with all supporting evidence, the local authority must make a decision within 14 days or as soon as reasonably practicable thereafter.[55] The authority should notify the claimant of its determination within 14 days or as soon as reasonably practicable.

Payments on account

9.93   Where the landlord is not the local authority, if it is impracticable for a decision to be made within 14 days, the authority *must* make a payment on account of entitlement.[56] This duty arises only if the delay in making a decision is not caused by the claimant's failure, without reasonable excuse, to provide information or evidence. The amount of the payment will be the amount the authority considers reasonable having regard to the information that is available. Usually, authorities will pay a percentage of the anticipated entitlement.

9.94   Authorities routinely ignore this provision, often resulting in substantial arrears of rent arising at the start of the tenancy. Legal action may be taken in the county court to enforce the duty to make interim payments on account. In practice, the threat of a claim based

---

55   HB Regs 2006 reg 89(2).
56   HB Regs 2006 reg 93(1).

on breach of the statutory duty often results either in a payment on account being made or the claimant's entitlement being assessed.

Backdating housing benefit

9.95 Claims for housing benefit can be backdated for up to six months if there is good cause for the late claim.

9.96 If a claimant is aged 60 or over and is not (and his or her partner is not) on income support or income-based jobseeker's allowance, benefit can be backdated for up to three months without good cause provided there was continuous entitlement to housing benefit during the relevant period.[57]

9.97 For other claimants there must be continuous good cause for the failure to claim.[58]

9.98 In deciding whether a claimant has shown good cause for not claiming earlier the authority must be satisfied that the reason for not claiming earlier is such that any reasonable person of that age, health and experience would probably not have claimed earlier in the same way as the claimant. The burden of proving good cause rests on the claimant but the authority must examine all the relevant facts in each case.

9.99 Annex A to the Adjudication Officers' Guide (AOG) contains a useful summary of the situations in which good cause should be accepted, based on Commissioners' decisions. Although the AOG is no longer current the annex is still referred to in the DWP Guidance Manual (see para 9.3 above).

Overpayments of housing benefit

9.100 Where a person receives housing benefit that he or she was not entitled to, this is an overpayment and will be recoverable unless:

- it was the result of an official error; and
- the claimant did not materially contribute to the error; and
- he or she could not reasonably have realised that he or she was being overpaid.

9.101 This definition of a recoverable overpayment means that most overpayments are recoverable. However, decisions regarding overpayment of housing benefit are contentious and the DWP website

---

57 HB(PC) Regs 2006 reg 64(1).
58 HB Regs 2006 reg 83(12).

contains guidance (HB/CTB Overpayments Guide) which runs to more than 280 pages.

Notification

9.102　The authority must notify a claimant that he or she has been overpaid and that the overpayment is recoverable. The notification should also inform the claimant of the right of appeal and must:[59]

- state that there is a recoverable overpayment;
- give the reason why there is a recoverable overpayment;
- state the amount of the recoverable overpayment;
- explain how the amount has been calculated;
- indicate the benefit weeks to which the recoverable overpayment relates.

In addition:

- if recovery is to be made by deduction from future housing benefit this must be stated and, if so, the amount of the deduction;
- if recovery is to be made from the landlord, the notice must identify the person on whose behalf the recoverable overpayment was made and the person (ie another tenant) from whose benefit deduction will be made.

Underlying entitlement

9.103　An overpayment may occur when a person's situation changes, for example, when he or she moves from one type of benefit to another, or commences employment. If the authority is not notified at the time, an overpayment will occur. However, it may be the case that the claimant would have continued to be entitled to housing benefit. In all such cases the local authority should calculate the claimant's 'underlying entitlement' and deduct from the overpayment any housing benefit that he or she was entitled to.[60]

9.104　　If the authority needs more information or evidence to calculate the underlying entitlement it must request this of the claimant. The claimant need not make an application for underlying entitlement to be assessed. However, if the claimant fails to respond to a request for information within one month, the full amount of the overpayment will be recoverable and the claimant should receive notification of this.

59　HB Regs 2006 Sch 9 para 15.
60　HB Regs 2006 reg 104.

Recovery of overpayments

By deduction from future benefit

9.105 An authority can recover a previous overpayment by making deductions from a claimant's future benefit.[61] The maximum weekly deduction, calculated as a percentage of a claimant's personal allowance, is, for the year 2011/12, £10.20 per week (£13.60 if the overpayment is due to fraud) plus 50 per cent of any income disregarded for benefit purposes. However, authorities may reduce the weekly deductions where this is causing hardship.

9.106 Advisers should always request a deduction in the rate of recovery when a claimant on means-tested benefit is in arrears of rent. If the maximum deduction continues, the claimant will be expected (by the landlord or by the court) to pay at least £3.40 per week towards the arrears as well as to make up the shortfall of housing benefit, resulting in a weekly payment of £13.60 (on 20011/12 rates) in addition to water rates and any service charges. Most claimants will be unable to maintain the payments resulting in breaches of any agreement or conditions imposed by the court.

As a 'lump sum' from the tenant

9.107 An authority cannot suspend the payment of housing benefit until the whole overpayment is recovered. Nor can a housing authority which is also the tenant's landlord recover an overpayment by entering the sum as arrears on the rent account. However, where there is a delay in assessing a claim, an authority may recover any outstanding overpayment from a lump sum that is due to a claimant for a past period. This will place a claimant in arrears. For example, a claimant may have an outstanding overpayment in the sum of £2,000. Following a delay in assessing a renewed claim, the authority may decide that a credit of £1,000 is due in respect of the period between the making of the claim and the assessment. The authority may set off the £1,000 against the amount outstanding so that although weekly housing benefit payments commence, the lump sum of £1,000 is not paid. The result is that the tenant is in rent arrears of £1,000 and the balance of the outstanding overpayment is reduced to £1,000.

9.108 The authority can make a claim to a county court for a money judgment, see chapter 22.

---

61 HB Regs 2006 reg 102.

From the landlord

9.109   Where payment was made to the landlord the authority may recover the overpayment from the landlord.[62] If the authority does this the landlord is entitled to treat the rent as unpaid.[63]

Challenging decisions

Decisions

9.110   A claimant is entitled to notification of a decision in writing[64] and the notification must include certain information, including:[65]

- the right to request a written statement of reasons; and
- the right to apply for a revision and the right to appeal against the decision, and the time limits and way to do so.

9.111   Particular kinds of decision (for example, where a decision is made that a recoverable overpayment has been made – see para 9.102 above) require particular information to be given.

Time limits

9.112   The time limit for appealing against a decision is one calendar month. However, if a claimant requests written reasons for a decision, the time stops running until the reasons are given. This means that if a request for reasons is made ten days before the deadline for appealing, on receipt of the reasons, the claimant still has ten days in which to bring an appeal.

Revisions

9.113   In response to a request for reasons or an indication that the claimant wishes to appeal, an authority may reconsider its decision. If the authority accepts that the decision was wrong it can revise the decision. A revised decision takes effect from the date the decision was first made. An example would be an error in the calculation of the claimant's income.

---

62 HB Regs 2006 reg 101.
63 HB Regs 2006 reg 95(2), see para 7.27 above.
64 HB Regs 2006 reg 90.
65 HB Regs 2006 Sch 9.

9.114　　A claimant who believes the authority has made an error may request a reconsideration. However, a claimant should also indicate an intention to appeal as a request for a reconsideration does not extend or suspend the time limit for appealing.

Supersession

9.115　Where the claimant's representations indicate a change of circumstances, a decision may be superseded. An example would be a change in income or a change or the make-up of the household. Supersession takes effect from the date of the change of circumstance (or, in fact, the first Monday following notification of the change of circumstance).

9.116　　If an authority supersedes a decision, the claimant can still appeal against the original decision on the basis that it was wrong at the time.

Appeals

9.117　Some decisions may not be appealed. These include decisions by the rent officer about the eligible rent or the level of the local housing allowance and decisions to suspend the payment of housing benefit.

9.118　　Where there is a right of appeal, any person affected by the decision may appeal, including the landlord. If the authority is not willing to revise the decision the appeal will be referred to the First-tier Tribunal (Social Security and Child Support)

9.119　Appeals are usually dealt with at a hearing but may be determined without a hearing if both parties agree. Public funding is not available for representation at an appeal but currently assistance may be given to prepare for a hearing under the Legal Help scheme, see chapter 22. However, at the time of writing, it is proposed that all welfare benefit advice will be out of the scope of legal aid when the Legal Aid, Sentencing and Punishment of Offenders Bill takes effect (see paras 22.156–22.158).

9.120　　An appeal against a decision of the First-tier Tribunal is made to the Upper Tribunal (Administrative Appeals Chamber).

CHAPTER 10

Disrepair and housing conditions – action by occupiers

Key points

- An occupier can take two sorts of legal action to address disrepair and poor housing conditions: a civil action in the county court and a criminal action in the magistrates' court. Legal aid is available for representation in civil actions but not for criminal actions.
- Most civil actions rely on contractual rights under a tenancy agreement.
- In all short-term tenancies a landlord has a legal obligation to keep in repair the structure and exterior and the installations for gas, electricity, sanitation and heating. This applies whether or not the tenancy agreement is in writing. The landlord cannot avoid this obligation.
- Usually a landlord will not be in breach of the obligation until the tenant has given notice of the necessary repairs and a reasonable time has elapsed.
- If a landlord is in breach of the repairing obligation a county court can award compensation and order the landlord to carry out the necessary works of repair.
- In most tenancies there is no legal requirement on a landlord that premises let as dwellings are fit for human habitation. A tenant cannot therefore take civil legal action against a landlord because premises are unfit unless this is caused by disrepair.
- The general rule is that a tenant can only take civil action against a landlord if there is 'disrepair' as opposed to poor housing conditions caused by bad design or insufficient amenities.
- Where poor housing conditions are caused by bad design and/or lack of amenities, an occupier may be able to bring a criminal prosecution.
- An occupier with a social landlord may also make a formal complaint about a landlord's failure to carry out repairs and refer to an Ombudsman if the landlord does not resolve the problem.
- Although it is inadvisable for a tenant to withhold rent because of disrepair, damages for disrepair may be set off against arrears of rent and may provide a defence to a claim for possession.

Introduction

10.1   Many people who live in rented accommodation are unhappy about their living conditions. They may want more suitable and healthy accommodation provided by a social landlord. Unfortunately, the shortage of affordable accommodation is such that even those in great need may wait for many years to be offered more appropriate accommodation.[1] Advisers will need to be familiar with the transfer and allocation policies of local authorities and other social landlords to advise realistically about the prospects of obtaining better accommodation. Chapter 17 explains the law relating to local authorities' duties to operate fair allocations and transfer systems.

10.2   This chapter examines the action occupiers may take to obtain repairs or improvements to their homes. The following options are available to an occupier:

- a civil claim in the county court for compensation and an order for works of repair;
- a criminal action in the magistrates' court for an abatement order and compensation;
- a formal complaint to a social landlord;
- using the rent to pay for repairs.

Occupier's status

10.3   Before advising anyone about the best course of action consideration must be given to the occupier's status. Most private tenants are assured shorthold tenants with no more than six months' security. A private landlord may respond to a complaint or threat of legal action by serving notice requiring possession and applying to the court for a possession order to which there is no defence.

10.4   In addition, many local authority tenants may have previously been subject to a suspended possession order which had the effect of terminating their tenancies. They should now have a 'replacement tenancy' under the Housing and Regeneration Act 2008. In such cases an application will need to be made to the court to enable the tenant to claim compensation for any period during which they were not tenants (see para 10.93 below). Therefore, advisers must always check to see whether a possession order has previously been made against a local authority tenant.

---

1   1.75 million households were registered on council waiting lists in England as at the end of 2010: www.communities.gov.uk/housing/housingresearch.

Action in the county court

10.5 A county court claim will usually be based on two 'causes of action':[2]

- breach of contract (see paras 10.6–10.96); and
- tort (see paras 10.97–10.146).

Breach of contract

The repairing covenant

10.6 A claim for breach of contract relies on the landlord's repairing covenant. This means the landlord's legal obligation to repair the premises, which is set out in the tenancy agreement, or implied by statute or by common law.

Express terms of the tenancy agreement

10.7 A tenancy agreement is a legal contract and the obligations on the landlord and tenant are legally binding. A written tenancy agreement may contain express terms setting out the landlord's and the tenant's respective obligations for repairs. There is a minimum obligation on the landlord that cannot be overridden by the express terms (see below, paras 10.9–10.25). However, the tenancy agreement may set out more extensive obligations on the landlord, and advisers should always obtain a copy of the tenancy agreement. Tenancy agreements used by private landlords often say little or nothing about the landlord's repairing obligations while those issued by social landlords usually set out the landlord's obligations. In more recent standard tenancy agreements the express repairing obligation tends to mirror the minimum legal standard but older tenancy agreements, particularly local authority agreements, often contain more generous repairing covenants.

> In *Welsh v Greenwich LBC*[3] the landlord's obligation was to keep the premises 'in good condition and repair' which was held to include liability for severe condensation. This would not normally fall within the landlord's repairing obligations.

2 See para 22.10.
3 (2001) 33 HLR 438, CA.

In *Long v Southwark LBC*[4] the landlords covenanted 'to take reasonable steps to keep the estate and common parts clean and tidy'. The tenant brought a claim against the landlords because of inadequate arrangements for collecting rubbish on the estate.

The Court of Appeal held that a failure to supervise the performance of outside contractors engaged to collect rubbish amounted to a failure to take reasonable steps and the landlords were in breach of the tenancy agreement.

Variation of tenancy agreement

10.8   Local authorities are able to vary the terms of a tenancy agreement provided they follow the proper procedure (see para 3.147). Advisers should therefore check to see whether the original tenancy agreement has been varied.

Section 11: landlord's implied repairing obligation

10.9   Section 11 of the Landlord and Tenant Act (LTA) 1985 implies into every tenancy agreement granted for a period of seven years or less an obligation on the landlord to carry out certain repairs. In this chapter this is referred to as 'section 11'. Disrepair claims in the county court are often referred to as 'section 11 claims'.

Section 11 – the dwelling-house

10.10   In relation to the premises let to the tenant, section 11 provides that there is an implied covenant on the landlord:

(a) to keep in repair the structure and exterior of the dwelling-house (including drains, gutters and external pipes);

(b) to keep in repair and proper working order the installations in the dwelling-house for the supply of water, gas and electricity and for sanitation (including basins, sinks, baths and sanitary conveniences but not other fixtures, fittings and appliances for making use of the supply of water, gas or electricity); and

(c) to keep in repair and proper working order the installations in the dwelling-house for space heating and heating water.

4 [2002] EWCA Civ 403.

Section 11 – the building

10.11 For tenancies that began on or after 15 January 1989 the covenant extends to other parts of the building in which the dwelling-house is situated, provided that the building is also owned by the landlord. In such a case LTA 1985 s11(1A) provides that the landlord must also keep in repair the structure and exterior of the building. Furthermore, he or she must keep in repair and proper working order any installation that serves the dwelling, directly or indirectly, provided that it is part of the building that the landlord owns or it is in the landlord's control.

10.12 The wider duty applies only if the disrepair affects the tenant's enjoyment of his or her own dwelling or of the common parts.[5]

When section 11 doesn't apply

10.13 LTA 1985 s11 is implied into almost all tenancy agreements.[6] It is implied into a weekly or monthly periodic agreement, even if the tenant has lived in the accommodation for seven years or more.

10.14 Section 11 is not implied if:[7]

- the tenancy began before 24 October 1961; or
- the tenancy is for a fixed term of seven years or more.

Section 11 is unavoidable

10.15 Landlords cannot avoid LTA 1985 s11 by providing in the tenancy agreement that the repairing obligations fall on the tenant or by seeking to exclude section 11. Any attempt to contract out of the section 11 duty is void.[8] A term in the tenancy agreement that limits or restricts the landlord's obligation under section 11 is valid only if authorised by a county court. The court can do this only if the parties agree and the court considers that it is reasonable.[9]

10.16 Furthermore, terms that seek to make the landlord's repairing obligation dependent on the tenant complying with the tenancy agreement or to prevent a tenant from setting off damages for disrepair against rent arrears may be held to be unfair and unenforceable.[10]

---

5 LTA 1985 s11(1B).
6 This includes tenancy agreements that are not in writing.
7 LTA 1985 s13(1).
8 LTA 1985 s12(1).
9 LTA 1985 s12(1)(b).
10 See para 3.158, the Unfair Terms in Consumer Contracts Regulations 1999 SI No 2083; *Cody v Philps*, January 2005 *Legal Action* 28, 4 November 2004, see para 4.171.

What does section 11 cover?

Keep in repair the structure and exterior

10.17   'Keep in repair' has been interpreted by the courts to mean 'put and keep in repair'.[11] It is no defence for a landlord to argue that the item was in disrepair when the tenancy started.

10.18   The 'structure and exterior of the dwelling-house' does not mean 'the entire dwelling-house, or the entire constructed building' but 'consists of those elements of the overall dwelling-house which give it its essential appearance, stability and shape'. This is to be contrasted with 'the many and various ways in which the dwelling-house will be fitted out, equipped, decorated and generally made to be habitable'. It is not limited to:

> ... those aspects of the dwelling-house which are load bearing ... but ... to be part of the structure of the dwelling-house a particular element must be a material or significant element in the overall construction.[12]

10.19   It includes:

- drains, gutters and external pipes (section 11 expressly states this);
- all outside parts of the dwelling;[13]
- the external walls;[14]
- partition walls between the dwelling and another house or flat;[15]
- partition walls within the flat;[16]
- internal plaster applied to walls and ceilings;[17]
- the roof (including skylights); however, if the dwelling is a flat, only if it is a top floor flat and the ceiling and roof are part of the same unit;[18]
- external joinery;
- external doors.

11   *Saner v Bilton* (1878) 7 Ch D 815.
12   *Irvine v Moran* (1990) 24 HLR 1, QB.
13   *Campden Hill Towers Ltd v Gardner* (1976) 13 HLR 64, CA.
14   *Campden Hill Towers Ltd v Gardner* (1976) 13 HLR 64, CA.
15   *Green v Eales* (1841) 2 QB 225.
16   *Campden Hill Towers Ltd v Gardner* (1976) 13 HLR 64, CA.
17   *Grand v Gill* [2011] EWCA Civ 554, 19 May 2011.
18   *Douglas-Scott v Scorgie* (1984) 13 HLR 97, CA. If disrepair to the roof of a building is causing damage to a flat within the building the tenant could rely on section 11(1A) which places on the landlord an obligation to keep in repair the structure and exterior of the building. This is only possible if the landlord owns the building and the tenancy started on or after 15 January 1989. If the tenancy commenced before this date an action in nuisance may be possible, see below, paras 10.117–10.129.

- windows, including glass, sashes and necessary window furniture;[19]
- paths and steps that are part of the immediate access to the dwelling.[20]

10.20 The following are not part of the structure and exterior:

- internal doors;
- internal glazing;
- internal joinery such as skirting boards and architraves;[21]
- floor coverings.

The installations

10.21 The landlord's obligation is to keep the installations 'in repair and proper working order'. If there is a defective installation in the dwelling when the tenancy commences the landlord must put it in a state of repair and proper working order. Furthermore, it is no defence if an installation is not in working order because of a design defect.[22]

10.22 'Installations' include:

- basins, sinks, baths and toilets;
- radiators;
- gas fires;
- fitted electric fires or heaters (including storage heaters) but not moveable plug-in electric heaters;
- boilers within the premises;
- water tanks within the premises;
- water and gas pipes and electrical wiring;
- under-floor heating vents.

10.23 It does not include fixtures and fittings for sanitation apart from basins, sinks, baths and toilets. This means that installations such as showers or bidets will not be the landlord's responsibility unless specified in the tenancy agreement.

10.24 However, if there is no installation (for example, no central heating system or hot water boiler) there is no obligation on the landlord to provide one. Tenants may be able to persuade the local authority to take action against a landlord to improve the premises by installing some facility if it is necessary to make the accommodation free from hazards (see paras 11.17–11.53).

---

19 *Irvine v Moran* (1990) 24 HLR 1.
20 *Brown v Liverpool Corporation* [1969] 3 All ER 1345, CA.
21 *Irvine v Moran* (1990) 24 HLR 1.
22 *Liverpool CC v Irwin* (1976) 13 HLR 38, HL.

10.25   In addition a landlord must comply with the Gas Safety (Installation and Use) Regulations 1998 (see para 11.87).

Landlord's right of access

10.26   Landlord and Tenant Act 1985 s11(6) provides that there is an implied covenant on a tenant to allow the landlord (or someone authorised in writing by the landlord) to enter to inspect the premises. The right is to enter at reasonable times of the day and on giving 24 hours' notice in writing.

10.27   In addition to section 11 the landlord can rely on the following provisions to gain access:

- At common law a landlord who has a duty to keep premises in repair has a right to enter premises to carry out the works.[23]
- Rent Act 1977 ss3(2) and 148 place a duty on statutory tenants and protected tenants to give access to a landlord to carry out repairs.
- Under Housing Act 1988 s16 it is an implied term of every assured tenancy that the tenant shall give access to a landlord to carry out repairs.

10.28   Almost all written tenancy agreements also contain an express obligation on the tenant to give access to the landlord to inspect or carry out works.

When is the landlord in breach of section 11?

10.29   Before action can be taken in the county court the landlord must be in breach of his or her contractual repairing obligations. The tenant must therefore prove:

- that there is disrepair that falls within the landlord's repairing covenant;
- that the landlord knows about the disrepair (the position is different if the disrepair is outside the dwelling, see below, para 10.58);
- that the landlord has failed to carry out repairs within a reasonable time;
- if damages are claimed, that the tenant has suffered some inconvenience or loss.

10.30   Each of these aspects of a claim is considered below.

---

23 *Saner v Bilton* (1878) 7 Ch D 815.

Disrepair

10.31 There must be 'disrepair'. This means that part of the dwelling is in a worse condition than it was at some earlier time as opposed to lacking some amenity or being of defective design.[24]

10.32 The disrepair must be because of a failure by the landlord to carry out repairs for which he or she is responsible under the tenancy agreement.

Defective installations or absent installations

10.33 As indicated above at para 10.24, the fact that the accommodation is in poor condition because of the absence of an installation does not mean that the property is in disrepair. Under the terms of the tenancy agreement a landlord can be forced to repair a defective installation but not to install something that is not present in the dwelling when the tenancy started.

Disrepair or design defect?

10.34 Poor housing conditions such as damp and cold may be caused by disrepair or by the design of the dwelling, or sometimes a combination of both. In some local authority accommodation condensation dampness is common. This is frequently caused by poor design in the form of inadequate insulation, poor ventilation and insufficient heating. This is not disrepair.

In *Quick v Taff Ely Borough Council*[25] the tenant occupied a house on an estate constructed in the 1970s. It was agreed that there was severe condensation such that the house was virtually unfit for habitation in winter. The cause of the condensation was a combination of the following factors: cold bridging due to lack of insulation, sweating from the windows and inadequate heating. The condensation had caused extensive damage to the tenant's belongings. The county court judge awarded damages and, in accordance with the tenant's expert evidence, ordered the landlords to replace the windows and install insulation to alleviate the high levels of condensation. The Court of Appeal upheld the local authority's appeal, holding that the damage to property was not caused by a breach of the repairing obligation because the dampness was caused by a design defect not disrepair.

24 *Post Office v Aquarius Properties* [1987] 1 All ER 1055; *Quick v Taff Ely BC* [1986] QB 809.
25 (1985) 18 HLR 66.

10.35 The question of whether a problem is caused by a design defect or by disrepair is closely related to the issue of whether the landlord's repairing obligation can extend to remedying a design defect.

Repair or improvement?

10.36 A tenant cannot bring a civil action to force a landlord to remedy a design defect. However, if the tenant can show that there is disrepair, the landlord's repairing obligation may extend to remedying the design defect that has caused the disrepair. Whether a landlord's repairing obligation will extend to taking action to remedy a design defect will depend upon the following factors:

- whether the works are to the whole or substantially the whole of the structure or only a subsidiary part;
- whether the effect of the works will be to produce a building of a wholly different character than that which had been let; and
- the cost of the work in relation to the previous value of the building and the effect of the works on the value and lifespan of the building.

These criteria were set out in *McDougal v Easington DC*.[26] The premises were stripped back to the original framework with new front and rear elevations, windows, doors and roof installed. The cost of the works exceeded £10,000, increased the value of the premises from £10,000 to £18,000 and extended the expected life of the premises by about 30 per cent. The works were held not to constitute works of repair.

10.37 Below are some examples of cases where the courts have found that the landlord's repairing obligation extended to remedying a design defect.

In *Ravenseft Properties Ltd v Davstone Holdings Ltd*[27] a block of flats was clad in stone on a concrete frame. Because of a design fault the construction lacked any expansion joints which caused the stone cladding to fall away from time to time. Without the inclusion of expansion joints this would continue to happen so that the only way to reinstate the cladding would be by also providing expansion joints. It was argued that this amounted to remedying an inherent defect and was outside the repairing covenant.

---

26 (1989) 21 HLR 310, CA.
27 [1980] QB 12.

The court rejected this, holding that it is always a question of fact and degree whether works constitute works of repair or improvement. The works fell within the repairing covenant.

Elmcroft Developments Ltd v Tankersley-Sawyer[28] concerned premises that suffered from rising damp caused by the fact that the slate damp-proof course (DPC) was ineffective as it was below ground level. The county court judge found that the necessary remedial work included the installation of a horizontal DPC by silicone injection, the formation by silicone injection of vertical barriers where the front and external walls met the dividing walls, plus re-plastering and redecoration.

The Court of Appeal rejected the landlord's appeal. Following *Ravenseft*, it was a question of fact and degree whether the remedial works fell within a repairing covenant. The works were works of repair.

In *Stent v Monmouth District Council*[29] there was a design defect in the premises: the concrete step outside was same level as the floor inside the entrance hall. This caused water ingress beneath the door which, in turn, caused the door to warp and eventually to rot. After carrying out patchwork repairs several times a new door was fitted by the council but this did not remedy the design defect. Several years later a self-sealing aluminium door was fitted in accordance with the recommendations of the tenant's surveyor.

The Court of Appeal decided that the tenant was entitled to damages because of the council's failure to carry out appropriate remedial works sooner. It was held that where there was no disrepair (as in *Quick*, see para 10.34) there was no obligation on the landlord to remedy design defects. However, where there was a defect that the landlord was obliged to repair, 'on a true construction of the covenant to repair there is required to be done, not only the making [good] of the immediate occasion of disrepair, but also, if this is what a sensible, practical man would do, the elimination of the cause of that disrepair through the making good of an inherent design defect at least where the making good of that defect does not involve a substantial rebuilding of the whole'.[30]

28 (1984) 15 HLR 63.
29 (1987) 19 HLR 269, CA.
30 The President, Sir John Arnold, at 285.

10.38   These cases can be contrasted with *Quick v Taff Ely* (see para 10.34): the landlords had an obligation to repair and the issue was the extent of works necessary to comply with that obligation. In *Quick* the tenant had not argued that the works were necessary to remedy disrepair but rather to alleviate the effects of the condensation and it was held that 'there must be disrepair before any question arises as to whether it would be reasonable to remedy a design fault when doing the repair'.[31]

Dampness

10.39   The fact that premises are damp does not necessarily mean that a landlord is in breach of the repairing obligation. It is for the tenant to identify the cause of the dampness. Unless it is obvious (for example, a leaking roof or rotten windows) expert evidence will be needed. As is clear from the cases referred to above (paras 10.34–10.37), if the cause of the dampness is a design defect this is not disrepair and the landlord has no obligation under the tenancy agreement to prevent the premises being damp. This has been held to be the case where the dampness was caused by condensation due to inadequate heating and thermal insulation (see *Quick* above at para 10.34).

> In *Post Office v Aquarius Properties*[32] the basement of the premises was ankle deep in water whenever the water table rose because of a design defect. However, this caused no damage to the structure.
> The Court of Appeal held that there was no obligation under the covenant to repair to remedy the defect.

10.40   If dampness caused by a design defect results in damage to the structure of the premises (which includes damage to wall and ceiling plaster) there will be an obligation to carry out repairs. This obligation may include remedying the design defect depending on the nature of the defect and the cost of remedial works (see the cases discussed at para 10.37).

10.41   Clearly, if dampness is caused by disrepair (such as defective windows or leaking roof) then the landlord will be liable if he or she has failed to carry out repairs within a reasonable period of time.

10.42   As in any civil claim it is for the claimant to prove the case on the balance of probabilities.

31   (1985) 18 HLR 66, Lawton LJ at 77.
32   [1987] 1 All ER 1055.

In *Southwark LBC v McIntosh*[33] an award of general damages of £7,500 was made to the tenant whose flat was damp and whose claim against the council alleged a breach of the repairing covenant.

The council's appeal succeeded: the tenant had failed to establish that the dampness was caused by a breach of the covenant or that the dampness had caused damage to the structure and exterior. All that the tenant had pleaded was the existence of dampness which was insufficient to establish that the landlords were in breach.

10.43   This does not mean that there is nothing a tenant can do about damp conditions where there is no actual disrepair. The premises may be prejudicial to health so that a prosecution under the Environmental Protection Act 1990 can be brought against the landlord. Also, the dampness may constitute a 'hazard' under the Housing Health and Safety Rating System (HHSRS). This would give the local authority the right to serve an improvement notice on the landlord. These options are discussed below in paras 10.217–10.242 and also in paras 11.17–11.61.

Common disputes

Kitchen units

10.44   Kitchen units and work surfaces are not covered by section 11 – they are neither part of the structure and exterior nor installations. It is therefore the tenant's responsibility to repair or replace broken or worn out parts, unless the tenancy agreement provides otherwise.

10.45   It should be noted, however, that in the social rented sector works have been or are being carried out in many homes to improve properties in order to bring them up to the 'Decent Homes' standard (see para 11.84). In most cases this includes installing new kitchens and bathrooms. If a new kitchen is fitted by the landlord the work must be carried out to a reasonable standard and any problems caused by poor workmanship or defective fittings will be the landlord's responsibility. However, future repairs needed because of 'fair wear and tear' will not be the landlord's responsibility unless the tenancy agreement expressly states that the landlord will be responsible.

33 [2002] 08 EG 164.

Broken windows and other 'accidental' damage

10.46 Window panes are covered by LTA 1985 s11. However, many social landlords will not agree to repair window panes without evidence that the damage was not caused by the tenant or his or her family or visitors. Alternatively, the landlord may agree to replace the pane but re-charge the repairs to the tenant (see para 10.50 below).

10.47 A landlord is not legally responsible for repairing damage caused by the tenant: LTA 1985 s11(2)(a) provides that a landlord is not required to carry out works or repairs for which the tenant is liable by virtue of the duty to use the premises in a 'tenant-like manner'. The duty to use the premises in a tenant-like manner includes a duty not to cause damage to the premises deliberately or carelessly, see below, para 10.91.

10.48 Some landlords have a policy that they will repair broken window panes provided the tenant can provide a crime reference number as evidence that the damage was caused by someone outside the premises and was reported to the police as a crime.

10.49 Sometimes there may be a dispute about the evidence available regarding the cause of the damage. If unexplained damage has been caused within the premises it is reasonable for the landlord to hold that the tenant is responsible.

10.50 A landlord may carry out repairs for which the tenant is legally responsible and then charge the cost of the repairs to the tenant. Most public sector tenancy agreements include a term permitting the landlord to do this. It is common for a landlord to enter the charge as arrears of rent on the rent account. If the landlord then seeks possession on the basis of rent arrears, this can be challenged. The correct way for the landlord to recover the cost of repairs is by sending to the tenant an invoice and seeking a money judgment in the county court if the invoice is not paid.

Tenant's improvements and tenant's fixtures

10.51 Tenants may carry out works of improvement or install fittings that become 'fixtures'. A fixture is something that becomes part of the premises. This would include laminate flooring, shower fittings, fitted cupboards and fitted shelving. Most tenancy agreements require the tenant to obtain the landlord's consent to carry out such works. A tenant who fails to obtain consent is in breach of the tenancy agreement and this can provide a ground for possession. However, the ground is a discretionary one and a possession order will be made only if it is reasonable to do so. A tenant who has carried out improvements without the landlord's consent can seek consent retrospectively and consent must not be unreasonably withheld.

10.52 Installations and improvements made by the tenant without consent will not fall within the landlord's repairing obligation. Furthermore, most public sector tenancy agreements provide expressly that the landlord is not responsible for repairs and improvements carried out by the tenant.

10.53 Under landlord and tenant law, tenant's fixtures become part of the premises and should be left in the premises when the tenant leaves. However, many tenancy agreements in the social housing sector provide that a tenant should remove fixtures and fittings and ensure that the premises are in their original state before leaving. This will override the usual rule.

Knowledge/notice of disrepair

Disrepair within the dwelling

10.54 A landlord is only in breach of section 11 if he or she has had notice of the disrepair and has failed to carry out effective repairs within a reasonable time.[34]

10.55 There is no requirement that the tenant gives notice in a particular way and the landlord may be placed on notice by events other than a direct complaint by the tenant. For example:

- a local authority inspection that is communicated to the landlord;[35]
- a visit by an agent or employee of the landlord such as a rent collector, environmental health officer or housing officer, provided the disrepair is visible;[36]
- a report prepared by a rent officer that is sent to the landlord;
- a valuer's report prepared in respect of a right-to-buy application sent to the chief executive's office.[37]

10.56 A tenancy agreement may provide that notice of disrepair must be given in a particular form or within a particular period. However, this does not mean that the tenant cannot prove that the landlord is in breach of the tenancy agreement if notice is given in a different

---

34 *O'Brien & Another v Robinson* [1973] 1 All ER 583; *McGreal v Wake* (1984) 13 HLR 107

35 *McGreal v Wake* (1984) 13 HLR 107.

36 *Dinefwr BC v Jones* (1987) 19 HLR 445.

37 *Dinefwr BC v Jones* (1987) 19 HLR 445.

way.[38] Oral notice is sufficient although obviously more difficult to prove than written notice.

10.57   It is not necessary for the tenant to identify the cause of any problem or specify each defect. It is sufficient that the landlord is made aware that something may need to be investigated.[39]

Disrepair in the building in which the dwelling is situated

10.58   Where the disrepair is in the building rather than within the dwelling itself the landlord is liable as soon as the disrepair occurs regardless of notice.

In *British Telecommunications plc v Sun Life Assurance Society plc*[40] the landlords argued that any liability for damages could only start after a reasonable period had elapsed from the date the defect became apparent.

The Court of Appeal rejected this holding that the general rule where a landlord had to keep premises in repair was that the landlord was liable as soon as the premises fell into disrepair. It was an exception to this general rule that in relation to disrepair inside the premises let, liability only arose after notice had been given and the landlords had had a reasonable opportunity to carry out the repairs.

So, in *Passley v Wandsworth LBC*[41] the council was held liable when pipes in the roof of a block of flats burst causing damage to the belongings of the tenant in the top flat. This was despite the fact that neither the tenant nor the landlord had been aware that the pipes were in disrepair prior to the flood.

10.59   The reason for this distinction is that a landlord can inspect the exterior and common parts of the building at any time but, because a tenant has exclusive possession of the premises let, the landlord must be given notice of disrepair within the premises.

---

38   *Dinefwr BC v Jones* (1987) 19 HLR 445. Furthermore, such a term may contravene the Unfair Terms in Consumer Contracts Regulations 1999 SI No 2083 and be unenforceable, see para 4.163.

39   *Griffin v Pillet* [1926] 1 KB 17.

40   [1995] 4 All ER 44, CA.

41   (1986) 30 HLR 165, CA.

10.60   This does not mean that a tenant need not report defects in the building to the landlord. A tenant who knows about disrepair to the building and fails to inform the landlord may have any damages reduced on the basis that he or she failed to 'mitigate' loss (see para 10.67 below).

Long leases

10.61   The situation is different if the tenant is a long-leaseholder because the landlord may have a duty to consult all of the long-leaseholders before carrying out works. In such a case the duty to repair will be set out in the lease and LTA 1985 s11 will not apply as the lease will be for more than seven years.[42]

> In *Earle v Charalambous*[43] the disrepair was in a building let to various long-leaseholders. In a claim for damages for breach of the landlord's repairing obligation the parties had proceeded on the basis that the starting point for liability was the date of notice.
>
> The Court of Appeal held that, following notice by the tenant, the landlord was entitled to a further reasonable period to carry out the works and commented that the *British Telecommunications* case (see para 10.58) was about a commercial lease and was not decided in the context of the modern statutory and contractual framework concerning residential leases. A landlord's repairing obligation in respect of a long residential lease was linked to the leaseholder's obligations to pay service charges and subject to a duty to consult the leaseholders about major works. The court suggested that the rule set out in *British Telecommunications v Sun Life* case may have to be modified to take account of modern residential long leases.

Failure to carry out repairs within a reasonable time

10.62   What is a reasonable time will depend on the effect of the disrepair and the nature of the repairs needed. A landlord may be in breach if he or she fails to repair a leaking pipe within a number of hours but a timescale of several months may be reasonable if the works are extensive, for example, fitting a new roof. Where extensive works will take a long time to complete, a landlord may be expected to carry

---

42 LTA 1987. See chapter 5.
43 [2006] EWCA Civ 1090.

out patchwork repairs to ensure minimum inconvenience in the interim.

10.63   Social landlords sometimes publish expected response times for certain kinds of repairs and these may provide a good starting point in deciding what would be a reasonable time. However, these response times are set by the landlords and the court may find that a landlord is liable even when the repairs have been carried out within the target time. A surveyor will be able to comment on what is a reasonable time to repair a particular defect.

10.64   There may be a dispute about whether a landlord has carried out repairs within a reasonable time when ineffective works have been done and the problem has recurred. This is common when the defects concern central heating systems. Tenants often complain that the system keeps breaking down and that the landlord carries out works so that the system functions only for a short time before breaking down again. Whether and at what point a landlord must accept that the whole system or boiler needs to be replaced will normally be a matter for expert evidence. If this is in dispute it may be necessary to obtain expert evidence from a heating engineer rather than a general surveyor.

Tenant's inconvenience or loss

10.65   If a tenant is claiming damages for the landlord's breach, it must be established that he or she has, as a result, suffered some inconvenience or loss.

10.66   Damages are not limited to quantifiable loss, such as damage to furniture or belongings or the cost of alternative accommodation. Damages may also be awarded to compensate for the tenant's loss of the enjoyment of the accommodation and for such things as injury to health. See below, paras 10.153–10.163 for a description of the way in which such damages are assessed.

Mitigating loss

10.67   A tenant has a duty to 'mitigate' (or minimise) his or her losses. For example if water is leaking into the premises the tenant would be expected to place a bucket to catch the falling water rather than to allow it to damage carpets.

Giving access to the landlord and workmen

10.68   Landlords sometimes argue that they are not in breach of the repairing obligation because the tenant has not given access. If it is proved that access has been unreasonably refused it may be held that the landlord is not in breach or damages may be reduced on the basis that the tenant has delayed the completion of the works (and thereby failed to mitigate his or her loss). Disputes often arise in relation to access. Advisers should ensure that the tenant is aware of the obligation to give access. The tenant should also be advised to keep records of the dates and times access is requested and whether the tenant was at home when it is alleged that access has not been given. Sometimes landlords allege a failure to give access when an unscheduled attendance was made and the tenant was not at home. The duty to give access under section 11 is conditional upon the landlord giving written notice 24 hours in advance. However, once works have been agreed, a tenant will be expected to act reasonably in giving access to the landlord's workmen and contractors. If a court takes the view that the tenant has failed to act reasonably damages could be reduced on the basis of the tenant's failure to mitigate his or her loss.

10.69   If reasonable access *is* being refused a landlord can seek an injunction to obtain access and any legal costs incurred will be set off against any damages subsequently awarded to the tenant.

Disturbance during works

10.70   In every tenancy agreement it is implied that a landlord will allow the tenant 'quiet enjoyment' of the premises. The covenant is breached if a landlord 'does anything which substantially interferes with the tenant's title to or possession of the ... premises or with his ordinary and lawful enjoyment of the demised premises. The interference need not be direct or physical'.[44] The carrying out of works of repair may cause some unavoidable interference with the tenant's enjoyment of his or her home but the landlord has a duty to minimise the interference: a landlord should take 'all reasonable precautions' to avoid disturbing the tenant but need not take 'all possible' precautions.[45] Where a landlord fails to take all reasonable precautions, the tenant may be awarded additional damages for breach of the covenant of quiet enjoyment. Alternatively, the damages recovered in the disrepair claim may be higher to reflect the additional distress and inconvenience.

---

44   *Southwark LBC v Tanner* [2001] 1 AC 1, Lord Millett at 23.
45   *Goldmile Properties v Lechouritis* [2003] EWCA Civ 49.

Alternative accommodation during works

10.71   One issue that often arises when extensive works of repair are to be carried out is whether it is necessary for the tenant to vacate the premises and, if so, who will arrange for alternative accommodation to be provided.

10.72   Whether it is necessary for the tenant to vacate will depend on the nature and extent of the works and whether it is possible to carry out the works so as to minimise inconvenience without disproportionately increasing the cost of the work. Experts should be asked to comment on whether works can reasonably be expected to be carried out with the tenant in occupation.

10.73   If it is necessary for the tenant to give vacant possession to enable the works to be completed, the court can make an order to this effect.[46] In practice, it is often the tenant who maintains that it will be necessary to move into alternative accommodation while the landlord proposes to carry out extensive work with the tenant in occupation. The dispute often occurs because of the expense to the landlord of providing alternative accommodation.

10.74   In fact, there is no legal obligation on a landlord to arrange alternative accommodation for a tenant even if it is clearly necessary for the tenant to vacate to enable the works to be completed. However, if the landlord is in breach of the repairing obligation and vacant possession is necessary for the works to be completed, the tenant can include in the claim for damages the cost of the alternative accommodation. In practice, social landlords will usually arrange alternative accommodation if satisfied it is necessary.

> In *McGreal v Wake*[47] the court held that, although it would have been possible to remain in occupation during the works, it was reasonable for the tenant to choose to move into temporary accommodation as this meant that the works could be carried out more quickly and more cheaply. On that basis the cost of the temporary accommodation could be recovered by the tenant as part of her damages for the landlord's breach of covenant.

10.75   If a landlord is refusing to provide alternative accommodation and the tenant cannot afford to obtain it and claim reimbursement later from the landlord, the tenant may make an application to the court

---

46 See *English Churches Housing Group v Shine* [2004] EWCA Civ 434.
47 (1984) 13 HLR 107.

for interim payment of damages. To obtain an interim payment, a claim has to be commenced in the county court and the court must be satisfied that if the claim went to trial the tenant would obtain judgment for a substantial amount of money from the landlord.[48]

10.76 Where works are being carried out by a private landlord in compliance with a local authority notice (see chapter 11), the local authority may agree to provide alternative accommodation for which the landlord must pay.

Redecorating following works

10.77 A landlord is responsible for 'making good' decorations following repair works. Disputes often arise about the extent of this duty.

> In *Vukelic v Hammersmith & Fulham LBC*[49] damage was caused to the tenant's restaurant due to the landlord's nuisance. The landlord argued that, following repair works, the obligation was to redecorate only the immediate areas in which repairs had been carried out.
> The court held that:
>
> ... the decoration should be undertaken utilising good quality materials and a good standard of workmanship. It is not ... demonstrating a good standard of workmanship to hang a couple of strips of non-matching wallpaper on a wall where the other paper would not otherwise need replacement, or to patch a hole in wallpaper caused by removal of a light switch by sticking a random piece of non-matching wallpaper over the hole. It makes no difference ... that the non-matching wallpaper and the original wallpaper is then painted the same colour if the non-matching wallpaper remains ... obtrusive.[50]

Other implied contractual terms

Fitness for habitation

10.78 There is no general term implied into tenancy agreements that a property let as a dwelling is fit for habitation.[51] If a property is unfit

---

48 CPR 25.7, see chapter 22.
49 [2003] EWHC 188 (TCC).
50 HHJ Richard Seymour QC at 102.
51 The Law Commission recommended that a fitness term should be implied into tenancy agreements in its report *Landlord and Tenant: Responsibility for the State and Condition of a Property*, report no 238, published in 1996. This report has not yet been implemented.

for habitation the local authority has the power, or in some cases a duty, to take action against the landlord (see chapter 11). However, the fact that there is no contractual term as to fitness means that a tenant cannot bring legal proceedings against his or her landlord on the ground that the premises let are unfit for human habitation.

10.79   There are, in fact, two situations in which a term as to fitness for habitation is implied but both are extremely limited. These are furnished dwellings (para 10.80) and premises let at a low rent (paras 10.81–10.82).

Furnished dwellings

10.80   In relation to lettings of furnished houses and flats, common law implies a contractual term that they are fit for habitation at the date of letting. The term relates to initial fitness only.[52]

Premises let at low rent

10.81   Section 8 of the Landlord and Tenant Act 1985 implies into lettings at a low rent a contractual term that the premises are fit for habitation at the date of the letting and that they will be kept fit for habitation by the landlord throughout the tenancy.

10.82   The current limit was set in 1957 and has remained unchanged: for lettings starting on or after 1 April 1965, the term is implied only where the rent is less than £80 per annum (£1.54 per week!) in Greater London and £52 per annum elsewhere. It would be surprising if there were a single tenancy to which this implied term applies. Moreover, any tenancy at such a low rent would fall outside all the schemes of statutory protection and the tenant would have no long-term rights.[53]

Unfit premises and human rights

10.83   In *Lee v Leeds City Council and Ratcliffe and Others v Sandwell MBC*[54] the tenant argued that the effect of the Human Rights Act 1998 was that a local authority landlord had a duty to ensure that her home was fit for habitation. The argument was rejected by the Court of Appeal but the court did accept that there may be cases in which the state of the premises is such as to establish a breach of human rights.

---

52 *Smith v Marrable* (1843) 11 M&W 5; *Wilson v Finch Hatton* (1877) 2 Ex D 336.
53 See chapter 3.
54 [2002] EWCA Civ 6.

Maintaining common parts and facilities

10.84   Where a landlord retains control of facilities that are essential or necessary to the tenant, the landlord is under a contractual obligation to maintain those facilities so that they remain available for the use of the tenant. This will include communal stairs, lifts and door entry systems.[55]

10.85   A repairing obligation may also be implied into the tenancy agreement if necessary to give the agreement 'business efficacy', ie to make it workable. Such a term will only be implied when 'necessary', not because it appears fair or desirable.

> In *Barrett v Lounova*[56] the tenancy was granted in 1941 so section 11 did not apply. The only term relating to repairs provided that the tenant was responsible for internal repairs. The exterior of the premises fell into substantial disrepair causing water penetration and damage to the internal plaster and timbers.
>
> The Court of Appeal held that the only way to make the tenancy agreement 'workable' was to imply a repairing obligation on the landlord in respect of the exterior of the premises.

Landlord's covenant of quiet enjoyment

10.86   This has been referred to above at para 10.70 in relation to the way in which repair works are carried out. It is also discussed below at para 10.143 in relation to inadequate sound insulation.

10.87   A landlord's breach of a repairing obligation may also constitute a breach of the covenant of quiet enjoyment. This was held to be the case in *Gordon v Selico Ltd*[57] where the failure to observe a covenant regarding the building in which the flat was situated caused water penetration and extensive dry rot in the leased flat. However, the covenant cannot create an obligation to repair where none exists by virtue of the express or implied terms of the tenancy agreement.

---

55 *Liverpool Corporation v Irwin* [1977] AC 239. This is in addition to LTA 1985 s11(1A) which applies only to tenancies commencing on or after 15 January 1989, see para 10.11 above.

56 (1988) 20 HLR 584.

57 (1986) 18 HLR 219.

Non-derogation from grant

10.88　It is also implied into every tenancy agreement that a landlord shall not 'derogate from the grant' of the tenancy. This is an obligation on the landlord not to do anything in relation to premises he or she retains control of that will interfere with the tenancy. This obligation is closely related to the covenant of quiet enjoyment.

10.89　As is the case with the covenant for quiet enjoyment the covenant does not create new repairing obligations.

10.90　It is more likely that a landlord will be found to be in breach of the covenant of quiet enjoyment and/or non-derogation from grant by virtue of the way in which works are carried out than by virtue of an omission to carry out works.

Using the premises in a tenant-like manner

10.91　A tenant has an obligation to use the premises in a 'tenant-like manner' which means 'taking proper care of the place'. This includes mending lights and fuses, clearing minor blockages in the sink, and doing 'the little jobs about the place which a reasonable tenant would do'. It also means that a tenant must not damage the premises wilfully or negligently. However, it does not extend to carrying out works where premises fall into disrepair through fair wear and tear or carrying out the necessary regular maintenance to ensure the premises do not fall into disrepair.[58]

10.92　See above (paras 10.46–10.50) in relation to broken windows.

The limits of contractual claims

Tolerated trespassers and replacement tenancies

10.93　Prior to the Housing and Regeneration Act (H&RA) 2008, a secure tenancy ended when a possession order took effect, including when the terms of a suspended order were breached. The H&RA 2008 amended the Housing Acts 1985 and 1988 to provide that secure and assured tenancies do not end until the order is executed and the tenant evicted. For those former tenants whose tenancies had ended under a possession order but who remained in occupation, the H&RA 2008 provided that they automatically became tenants again under a 'replacement tenancy'. The replacement tenancy will usually be the same kind of tenancy as the one that ended under the court

---

58　*Warren v Keen* [1954] 1 QB 15.

order (see paras 6.131–6.134) but is one which commenced on 20 May 2009 when that part of the Act came into force. For some purposes the tenancy is automatically treated as if it had been continuing but not for the purpose of a claim for disrepair (see para 6.132). There will therefore be a 'gap' in the tenancy from the date the possession order took effect (usually the date the tenant breached the terms of suspension). During this gap the tenancy was not in existence so a tenant cannot claim compensation for the landlord's 'breach' during that period unless the court makes an order that the tenancy is to be treated as a continuing tenancy.[59]

10.94   Such an application will be made within the disrepair claim and should be dealt with as a preliminary issue. For examples of county court cases concerning such applications see: *Lewisham v Litchmore*[60] in Bromley County Court and *Chase v Islington LBC*[61] in Clerkenwell and Shoreditch County Court. Relevant to the court's exercise of the discretion will be the conduct of both parties (including the tenant's compliance with the terms of the suspended order), the extent of the disrepair, the length of the period at issue and what is fair as between the parties. It should be noted that the court can impose conditions on the grant of relief, including limiting the amount of damages that can be recovered. In *Chase v Islington LBC* the judge limited the amount of damages to the amount of arrears outstanding as at 20 May 2009.

10.95   Alternatively, a tenant could apply to discharge the original possession order. This will have the effect of reviving the tenancy retrospectively (see para 6.121). Where the purpose of such an application is to enable a tenant to claim damages for disrepair the court is likely to apply similar principles to those that are developing in relation to applications for the replacement tenancy to be treated as a continuing tenancy.

Only parties to the contract can sue

10.96   The general rule is that only a party to a contract can take action to enforce the contract or claim damages for a breach of the contract. This rule is called 'privity of contract'. This means that a civil claim for breach of the repairing obligation can only be brought by the tenant or tenants. However, a tenant can include a claim for damages

---

59 See H&RA 2008 Sch 11 para 2(3)–(5).
60 December 2009 *Legal Action* 21.
61 January 2011 *Legal Action* 17.

for the inconvenience and loss suffered by his or her family because the benefit of the contract is for the whole family.[62]

Tort

10.97 A tort is a civil wrong which does not depend on a contractual relationship. The law recognises that certain situations create a 'duty of care': one party owes the other a duty to take reasonable care to ensure that he or she does not suffer injury or damage by reason of some act or omission. A breach of the duty gives the injured party the right to seek damages in the civil courts. The relationship of landlord and tenant does not, of itself, create a duty of care. What this means is that, at common law, a landlord may let to a tenant a property that is unsafe, unfit for habitation or in a poor state of repair. The landlord does not commit a tort by doing so. The tenant's rights relating to the state of the premises are contractual: they are found in the express terms of the tenancy agreement or implied by LTA 1985 s11. Nevertheless, there are some situations in which a duty of care *is* placed on a landlord.

10.98 Some torts have developed through case-law and are called 'common law' torts, others are set out in legislation and are called 'statutory' torts. In a disrepair claim the common law torts of nuisance and negligence may be relevant. Also, the Defective Premises Act (DPA) 1972 and the Occupiers' Liability Act 1957 set out statutory duties of care that may be owed in relation to residential premises. Some of the statutory duties set out in those Acts reflect common law duties previously recognised by the courts.

10.99 An action in tort is usually only possible *after* a person has suffered some injury or damage to belongings. In a disrepair claim it is usually the case that the tenant is relying on both breach of the contract *and* a breach of a duty of care, sometimes arising out of the same facts.

The builder's duty: DPA 1972 s1 and common law

10.100 Section 1 of the Defective Premises Act 1972 places a duty on those who carry out work in connection with the provision of a dwelling. This includes building or converting premises. The duty is to do the work in a workmanlike or professional manner; to use proper materials; and to ensure that the dwelling is fit for human habitation when completed. The duty is owed to the person for whom the dwelling was provided and to anybody who later acquires an interest,

---

62 *Jackson v Horizon Holidays* [1975] 3 All ER 92, CA.

including future tenants. It applies to all work commenced after 1 January 1974.[63]

10.101　Dwellings covered by the National House Building Council (NHBC) warranty scheme are excluded from DPA 1972.[64] Most new dwellings in the private sector are covered by the NHBC scheme.

10.102　A social landlord that builds or converts a building for letting therefore owes a duty of care to the initial tenant and subsequent tenants. Any injury or damage suffered as a result of any breach of the duty under DPA 1972 s1 will create a liability.

10.103　In addition to DPA 1972, there is a common law duty on a person who builds or designs a dwelling to use reasonable skill and care and a landlord also has a common law duty to exercise a reasonable degree of care and skill when undertaking works of repair or improvement.[65]

In *Rimmer v Liverpool CC*[66] the tenant injured himself on a glass pane in an internal wall. It was held that, although landlords of unfurnished dwellings did not owe any general duty of care to tenants, a landlord who also designed and built the dwelling owed a duty of care to anyone who might reasonably be expected to be affected by faults in the design or construction of the premises. The authority was held to have been negligent and liable to pay damages.

Duty to maintain or repair: DPA 1972 s4

10.104　Section 4(1) of the Defective Premises Act 1972 provides that where premises are let on a tenancy under which the landlord has an obligation to repair or maintain the premises:

> ... the landlord owes to all persons who might reasonably be expected to be affected by defects in the state of the premises a duty to take such care as is reasonable in all the circumstances to see that they are reasonably safe from personal injury or from damage to their property caused by a relevant defect.

63　For an example of a successful claim under DPA 1972 s1, see *Bole v Huntsbuild Ltd* [2009] EWCA Civ 1146, 20 October 2009. The Court of Appeal upheld the finding that the premises were unfit for habitation by reason of inadequate foundations causing widespread cracking due to 'heave'.

64　DPA 1972 s2.

65　*Ball v London CC* [1949] 2 KB 159 and *Billings (AC) & Sons v Riden* [1957] 3 All ER 1.

66　[1984] 1 All ER 930. The premises were built before 1974 so DPA 1972 was not relevant.

10.105 A landlord who has a *right* to enter to carry out any kind of mainte-nance or repair is treated as if he or she were under an *obligation* to maintain or repair.[67]

10.106 The duty is owed 'if the landlord knows ... or if he ought in all the circumstances to have known of the relevant defect'.[68] The duty there-fore exists independently of actual notice being given to the landlord.

10.107 The landlord cannot restrict or exclude liability. Any provision in the tenancy agreement attempting to do so, will be void.[69]

Relevant defects

10.108 The 'section 4 duty' under DPA 1972 depends on there being a 'rel-evant defect'. A relevant defect is one that arises or continues because of the landlord's failure to carry out repairs or maintenance (whether there is a duty or only a right to repair or maintain). It covers items of repair or maintenance even where notice has not been given.[70]

10.109 The definition of 'relevant defect is therefore tied to the definition of disrepair – it does not extend to a defect that arises from something other than the landlord's obligation or right to carry out 'repairs'. It does not include design defects or defects that arise because of the tenant's failure to carry out any obligation under the tenancy.[71] However, the duty under DPA 1972 s4 is wider than the contractual repairing obligation in the following ways:

- the landlord may be liable for defects that affect not only the ten-ant but also other occupiers and visitors to the property;
- the landlord may be liable for a defect that has not been reported if the landlord 'ought' to have known of the defect; and
- the defect may arise from disrepair that the landlord is not obliged to remedy but that he or she has a right to remedy.

10.110 The following cases illustrate the way in which liability under DPA 1972 s4 is more extensive than the landlord's contractual repairing obligation.

---

67 DPA 1972 s4(4).
68 DPA 1972 s4(2).
69 DPA 1972 s6(3).
70 DPA 1972 s4(3).
71 DPA 1972 s4(4).

In *Clarke v Taff Ely BC*[72] the sister of one of the joint tenants was helping them to decorate. She suffered an injury when the leg of a table on which she was standing went through the floorboards. No complaint had been made to the council about the floorboards but it was known that the area was damp and that there was no ventilation under the floorboards.

It was held that the council was liable for the injury suffered: arrangements should have been made for regular inspections and the tenant's sister was someone who 'might reasonably be expected to be affected by defects' in the premises.

In *Smith v Bradford MDC*[73] a tenant had built a patio outside the dwelling. A subsequent tenant complained to the council that it was dangerous and later suffered an injury when he fell from the patio onto a grassed area several feet below.

The Court of Appeal held that the council was liable: the patio was part of the 'premises' and the council had a right to enter and repair it and were therefore liable.

10.111   However, DPA 1972 s4 does not extend to an obligation to make safe; the duty arises only in relation to defects, ie disrepair.

In *Alker v Collingwood Housing Association*[74] the tenant injured her hand on a glass panel to the entrance door of her home. The panel was not constructed of safety glass but ordinary annealed glass. It was likely that, at the time of construction, the door complied with the relevant building regulations but it has been accepted since at least 1963 that the use of annealed glass in doors presents a safety hazard. The tenancy agreement set out the landlord's repairing obligations, including the term: 'We must keep your home in good condition'.

The Court of Appeal held that the landlords were not liable because the unsafe glass panel was not a 'relevant defect': it was not in need of repair or maintenance. Even the duty to keep the premises in good condition did not encompass a duty to put them in safe condition.

72   (1984) 10 HLR 44.
73   (1982) 4 HLR 86.
74   [2007] EWCA Civ 343, 7 February 2007.

Duty to visitors: Occupiers' Liability Act 1957 and common law

10.112 The Occupiers' Liability Act 1957 provides that the occupier of premises owes a common duty of care to visitors. A landlord who lets premises but retains control of the common parts, such as stairs, paths and other means of access, is the occupier for the purposes of the Act. The landlord therefore owes a duty to all visitors 'to take such care as in all the circumstances of the case is reasonable to see that the visitor will be reasonably safe in using the premises'.

10.113   There is also a common law duty of care owed by the occupier of premises to visitors. Again, this duty rests on a landlord in relation to the common parts that remain in his or her control.[75]

Common law negligence

10.114 In addition to the specific duties of care set out above in paras 10.100–10.112, the common law also recognises a general duty not to cause injury or damage because of careless or negligent behaviour.

10.115   The tort of negligence is committed when a person fails to do something which a reasonable person in similar circumstances would have done, or does something which a reasonable person in similar circumstances would not have done. If, as a result of the act or omission, a person suffers damage or injury that was reasonably foreseeable the courts can award compensation.

10.116   When letting premises, a landlord does not owe to the tenant a duty of care and the premises may be unfit or dangerous when let without the landlord being liable. However, this does not mean that a landlord is immune from liability for acts or omissions during the course of the letting. An example would be where the landlord fits a dangerous installation[76] or carries out repair works in a negligent way.

Common law nuisance

10.117 Nuisance is some act or state of affairs in one set of premises which amounts to unlawful interference with another person's use or enjoyment of neighbouring premises.[77] Where the condition of common parts retained by the landlord is affecting the tenant's enjoyment of the premises let an action may be brought in nuisance. This would cover, for example, a leaking pipe from a communal boiler which is

---

75 *Dunster v Hollis* [1918] 2 KB 795; *Cockburn v Smith* [1924] 2 KB 119.
76 See *Ball v London CC*, referred to above at para 10.103.
77 *Read v Lyons & Co Ltd* [1945] KB 216.

causing dampness in the tenant's premises. For a tenancy granted on or after 15 January 1989 the tenant can rely on the extension of LTA 1985 s11 to the common parts. For other tenancies, the tenant could rely on the law of nuisance.

10.118   It should be noted that the definition of 'statutory nuisance' is different. This is explained at paras 10.219–10.224 below.

Infestations

10.119 Tenants may complain of infestations of vermin. Cockroach and ant infestations frequently occur in local authority estates of a certain design. Infestation in itself is not disrepair and the landlord's repairing obligation will not usually extend to preventing or abating infestation within a dwelling. Although infested premises will usually be unfit for human habitation, there is no implied term in most tenancy agreements that the premises are fit for habitation.

10.120   There are two situations in which the landlord may be held liable for an infestation under the repairing covenant:

- if the tenancy agreement contains an express term such as that the landlord will keep the premises 'in good or habitable state', this may be interpreted as including an obligation to prevent infestations; and
- if there is disrepair that is causing or contributing to the infestation, such as holes in the floors or skirting boards.

10.121 In some circumstances it may be possible to use the law of nuisance and/or negligence to take action to force a landlord to take action to prevent infestations and to claim damages for a failure to do so.

> In *Sharpe v Manchester MDC*[78] the tenant of a local authority flat suffered from a cockroach infestation. It was likely that the cockroaches came through the service ducts which remained in the control of the authority, although other flats were unaffected. The authority carried out ineffective works to eliminate the infestation over a two-year period.
>
> The Court of Appeal held that the council was liable in nuisance and was also negligent as it had failed to treat the service ducts and the other spaces in the walls and floors and had used a discredited insecticide.

---

78 (1977) 5 HLR 71.

However, in *Habinteg Housing Association v James*[79] there was no
liability on the landlord for an infestation of cockroaches even
where several tenants on the estate suffered from similar problems.
There was no evidence that the infestation emanated from property
occupied by the landlord. Although, following service of a statutory
notice by the local authority, an effective block treatment had been
carried out to abate the nuisance, there had been no negligence in
failing to carry out a block treatment earlier; the association did not
have the power to carry out a block treatment in the absence of the
local authority notice.

10.122   Where premises are suffering from an infestation and the landlord
cannot be held responsible, complaint may be made to the local
authority. Local housing authorities have powers and duties in relation to premises that are prejudicial to health or contain health hazards (see chapter 11). If the landlord is the local authority, while it
may not be responsible as a landlord, most authorities have pest control departments which will carry out treatments to eradicate infestations. Most charge for such services although in some cases tenants
of the authority are not charged. Alternatively, private companies
offer pest control services.

In the county court case of *Dolan v Sefton MBC*[80] the tenant brought
a claim in nuisance and negligence for three years of severe
cockroach infestation following which she abandoned the premises.
After two days of evidence the council agreed to pay £16,000
in damages and to abandon a claim for rent arrears of £2,500.
Personal injury claims in respect of the claimant's two children were
also settled. Each had suffered insect bites that became infected and
developed a disease causing rashes, swollen joints and abdominal
pains for a year. The court approved awards of £2,000 per child.

Water penetration from neighbouring properties

10.123   Tenants of flats may suffer from water penetration from neighbouring flats, usually those above. Landlords often deny responsibility,
maintaining that the tenant must take up the issue with the tenant
above. Liability depends on whether the water penetration causes

79   (1994) 27 HLR 299.
80   July 2001 *Legal Action* 27.

'disrepair' to the tenant's premises and the reason for the water penetration.

Disrepair caused by flooding

10.124 Where a flood from a neighbouring property causes damage to the structure of the tenant's premises (for example, collapsed ceiling) the tenant's landlord has an obligation to repair, regardless of the cause of the water penetration.

10.125 However, unless the landlord is responsible for the flood, there will be no liability for any damage caused to the tenant's belongings or to compensate for any inconvenience caused by the flood. The landlord is only responsible for damage and inconvenience which results from the landlord's breach, ie failing to carry out repairs within a reasonable period of being notified.[81]

10.126 If the flood was caused by the neighbour's misconduct or carelessness (for example, badly fitted washing machine, or bath left to overflow) action could be taken against the neighbour in nuisance or negligence. The landlord could claim damages from the neighbour for the cost of the repairs and the tenant could also make a claim against the neighbour for compensation for inconvenience and damage to belongings.

Sustained water penetration

10.127 Where there is a problem of less severe but enduring water penetration, liability for repairs also depends on whether the water penetration causes damage to the structure.

10.128 Where there is damage to the ceiling or wall plaster, the landlord will be responsible for repairing the damage.

> In *Grand v Gill*[82] the Court of Appeal held that the judgment in *Irvine v Moran*[83] had been correct in describing the structure and exterior as consisting of 'those elements of the overall dwelling-house which give it its essential appearance, stability and shape', but was wrong to hold that internal plasterwork was not part of the structure but more in the nature of a decorative finish. Rather,
>
>> In the days when lath and plaster ceiling and internal partition walls were more common than now, the plaster was ... an

---

81 See *Hyde Southbank Homes v Oronsay and Obadiara*, December 2005 *Legal Action* 28, 18 February 2005.

82 [2011] EWCA Civ 554, 19 May 2011.

83 (1990) 24 HLR 1, QB, see para 10.18.

> essential part of the creation and shaping of the ceiling or partition wall, which serve to give a dwelling-house its essential appearance and shape ... plasterwork generally, including that applied to external walls, [is] ordinarily in the nature of a smooth constructional finish to walls and ceilings, to which the decoration can then be applied, rather than a decorative finish in itself.[84]

However, if the only damage is to the tenant's belongings, the landlord will not be liable unless the water penetration is caused by disrepair (eg leaking service pipes).

10.129   If sustained water penetration is caused by the neighbour's conduct, although the landlord will have an obligation to repair any consequent damage to the structure, the tenant will have to take direct action against the neighbour to prevent ongoing problems. A tenant may bring a county court action in nuisance and/or negligence to obtain an injunction against the neighbour. Alternatively, he or she may bring a criminal prosecution against the neighbour based on statutory nuisance, described below at paras 10.217–10.240.

Neigbouring tenants with same landlord

10.130   A tenant may want the landlord to take action against another tenant where there is sustained water penetration or repeated floods. If the problem is caused by the other tenant's misconduct or carelessness the landlord can take possession proceedings against him or her under the nuisance ground. However, one tenant cannot take legal action to force the landlord to take action against another tenant guilty of nuisance.[85] Furthermore, the landlord cannot be held liable for nuisance committed by tenants because nuisance is based on the occupation of land and where there is a tenancy, the tenants and not the landlords are the occupiers.

10.131   The situation is different if the nuisance is coming from land occupied by the landlord (such as the common parts) and the nuisance is not being caused by other tenants but by trespassers.

---

84 Rimer LJ at [25].
85 *O'Leary v Islington LBC* (1983) 9 HLR 83, CA. The situation may be different if the tenancy agreement contains a term stating that the landlord will take action to prevent nuisance by other tenants.

In *Octavia Hill Housing Trust v Brumby*[86] the tenant complained of nuisance caused by people sitting directly outside her living room on a paved area that was part of the common parts. The landlords applied to strike out the claim relying on cases which held that a landlord could not be held liable for nuisance caused by its tenants, including *Southwark v Mills*.[87]

The court dismissed the landlord's application to strike out the claim. The House of Lords has previously held that an occupier of land can be liable for nuisance committed by someone else if they have 'continued or adopted' the nuisance. This requires that they know of the nuisance and have failed to take reasonable steps to bring it to an end (*Sedleigh-Denfield v O'Callaghan*[88]). The cases relied on by the landlord were about nuisance caused by tenants who were the occupiers. In this case the landlords were the occupiers of the common parts so could be liable if the evidence supported them having continued or adopted the nuisance.

10.132   If the tenants share a social landlord, a complaint may be made if the landlord declines to take action against the neighbour. Social landlords must have a published policy on nuisance and anti-social behaviour, see para 10.138 below.[89]

Disrepair in the neighbour's flat

10.133   It may be that the cause of the water penetration is disrepair in the neighbour's flat. If this is the case and the landlord is notified of the need for repair, or asked to inspect but takes no effective action, the landlord may be liable not only for the repairs to the affected flat but also for loss, inconvenience and damage to the tenant's belongings. It is no defence for the landlord to argue that access cannot be obtained to the premises above. If access is refused, the landlord can apply for an injunction to force the tenant to give access.

10.134   As disputes about access often delay matters being resolved, tenants should try to maintain an amicable relationship with the neighbour where possible. If the neighbour agrees to allow the tenant access to inspect, the cause of the water penetration will be identified more quickly.

---

86   [2010] EWHC 1793 (QB), 15 July 2010.
87   [1999] 4 All ER 449, see para 10.144 below.
88   [1940] AC 880.
89   HA 1996 s218A, as amended by Anti-social Behaviour Act (ASBA) 2003 s12.

Noise nuisance/sound insulation problems

10.135   The intrusion of noise from other tenants is also a common problem in flats. The cause may be particularly noisy neighbours or inadequate sound insulation between the flats. Sometimes this is difficult to determine or the problem may be a combination of both. Sensitivity to noise varies from one person to another and tenants who have suffered from noise penetration for some time may become hyper-aware of the sound of their neighbours.

10.136   There are two types of sound transmission: airborne sound and impact sound. Inadequate sound insulation between properties can mean that ordinary footsteps sound like stamping and that the bass notes of amplified music are heard in another property. This can lead tenants to believe, incorrectly, that the problem is excessively noisy neighbours. If other household sounds, such as telephones ringing, toilets flushing, light switches etc, are also heard, this suggests a sound insulation problem.

10.137   It may be necessary to obtain an expert report on the cause of the problem. This will require the co-operation of the neighbour so it is important to avoid bad feeling if possible.

Noisy neighbours

10.138   If the problem is caused by the behaviour of neighbours who are also tenants of the same landlord complaint may be made to the landlord. Local authorities and other registered providers must publish their policies on 'anti-social behaviour'. This should set out the steps a landlord will take on receipt of a complaint, including the timescale for action.[90] The landlord may serve notice of seeking possession and take steps to evict the tenant. Sometimes the service of notice will be sufficient to stop the behaviour. In most cases, it is advisable for tenants first to make the neighbours aware of the way their behaviour is disturbing them to see if the problem can be resolved amicably.

10.139   Tenants who complain in the hope that their neighbours will be evicted should be aware that the landlords may decide not pursue a possession claim. The complaining tenant cannot force the landlord to do so (see para 10.129 above). If possession proceedings *are* issued, the complaining tenant will usually be required to give evidence by way of a statement and/or in person at a possession hearing.

10.140   Alternatively, or in addition, complaint can be made to the local authority's environmental health team. Some authorities operate

90   HA 1996 s218A, as amended by ASBA 2003 s12.

mobile noise patrols and may visit the neighbouring property to measure the noise and to advise the occupier about reducing the noise. The authority can also serve a notice requiring the occupier to 'abate' the nuisance and can prosecute if the notice is not complied with.[91]

Action against the neighbour

10.141　An occupier may bring a civil claim against a neighbour relying on the common law tort of nuisance. The court can award damages and an injunction to restrain future nuisance.

10.142　　In addition, an occupier could bring a private prosecution in the magistrates' court under the Environmental Protection Act 1990, seeking an order that the neighbour abate the nuisance (see para 10.229 below).

Action against the landlord for inadequate sound insulation

10.143　Current building regulations require minimum levels of sound insulation in newly built dwellings or conversions. However, the regulations do not have retrospective effect and, before 1976 for new dwelling and 1985 for conversions, there were no specific requirements for builders to meet designated standards for sound insulation.[92] Many dwellings and conversions therefore have little or no sound insulation.

10.144　　As noted above (paras 10.78–10.83), in respect of most tenancies there is no implied term that premises are fit for habitation. A landlord therefore has no contractual obligation to ensure that premises are properly insulated against sound transmission from outside.

> In *Southwark LBC v Mills and Camden LBC v Baxter*[93] the tenants relied on the covenant of quiet enjoyment[94] and the tort of nuisance in claims brought against their respective landlords. Both tenants occupied local authority flats, one in a purpose-built block and the other in a converted house. They complained that the absence of sound insulation meant that they were disturbed by the ordinary household noise made by their neighbours. Both wanted their landlords to carry out works to remedy the situation.

91　Under the Environmental Protection Act 1990, discussed below at paras 10.217–10.244 and 11.5–11.10.

92　The minimum standards for the construction of buildings are set out in the Building Acts and Regulations. Local authorities are responsible for ensuring that the minimum standards are met.

93　[1999] 4 All ER 449.

94　Despite the term, the covenant is not specifically about noise but about the tenant's right to use the premises without interference by the landlord.

> The House of Lords held that the landlords had no obligation to install sound insulation. There was no breach of the covenant of quiet enjoyment: the covenant can only be breached by the landlord doing something to interfere substantially with the tenant's quiet enjoyment *after* the grant of the lease, not by reason of the state of the premises at the commencement of the tenancy and thereafter. With regard to nuisance, it is possible for a landlord to be liable for nuisance caused by his or her tenant if the landlord authorises or permits the nuisance. However, the nuisance complained of was caused by the other tenants using their premises in the ordinary way. Such use is not capable of being an actionable nuisance.

10.145 There is therefore no way for a tenant to bring a civil action against a landlord to compel the landlord to install sound insulation.

10.146 Furthermore, the Environmental Protection Act 1990 cannot be used to achieve the same end.[95]

Remedies in county court proceedings

10.147 The above paragraphs (10.6–10.146) describe the possible 'causes of action' in a civil claim for disrepair. In practice, in most disrepair claims the same set of facts may establish several different causes of action.

10.148 The cause of action is the legal basis for the tenant's claim. The remedy is what the tenant is asking the court to order.

10.149 In most disrepair claims the tenant will be seeking:

- damages (compensation); and
- an order for works.

10.150 The vast majority of claims are settled before a final hearing; the parties agree what works will be carried out and how much compensation will be paid. The Disrepair Protocol, described at para 10.185 below, means that works will often be started soon after the landlord receives the initial protocol letter. This may mean that when the claim is issued the tenant is seeking damages only because all of the works have been completed. If damages are agreed there will be no need for litigation.

---

95 See *R on the application of Vella v Lambeth LBC* [2005] EWHC 2473 (Admin) at para 10.228 below.

10.151   Even though most claims are settled without a final hearing advisers must be familiar with the powers of the court and the level of damages a court would be likely to award.

10.152   In disrepair claims there are usually two kinds of damages awarded:

- *general damages*: these are quantified by the court to compensate the tenant for the inconvenience and loss of enjoyment caused by the disrepair; and
- *special damages*: these are damages capable of precise quantification by the claimant.

General damages

10.153 Where a landlord has breached the contract and/or a duty of care towards a tenant the purpose of damages is to place the tenant in the position he or she would have been in had the landlord not breached those legal obligations, as far as it is possible for a financial award to do so.

Assessing by loss of value

10.154 In many of the early cases a tenant's damages were assessed on the basis of 'loss of value' or 'diminution of value' to the tenant. These cases mostly concerned tenancies that had a commercial value to the tenant: the tenant had a long lease and was entitled to sublet or assign the lease. In such cases the assessment of damages is straightforward: the difference between the value of the lease with the property in its present condition and its value had the property been kept in repair. This may be assessed by obtaining expert valuation evidence. Such an approach is not appropriate when assessing damages for a tenant who remains in occupation while the property is in disrepair. Furthermore, for most periodic tenants, as opposed to long-leaseholders, the tenancy does not have a commercial value – it cannot be sublet or sold.

In *Calabar Properties Ltd v Stitcher*[96] the Court of Appeal considered the way in which damages should be assessed when a tenant remains in occupation of a property in disrepair.

96 (1983) 11 HLR 20, CA.

> The court held:
>
> 1) 'The object of awarding damages against a landlord for breach of his covenant to repair is not to punish the landlord but, so far as money can, to restore the tenant to the position he would have been in had there been no breach'.
> 2) Where a tenant remains in occupation it is 'wholly artificial' to award damages on the basis of the loss in market value.
> 3) In such a case valuation evidence is unnecessary.
> 4) When a tenant remains in occupation the damages should 'include the cost of the redecoration, a sum to compensate for the discomfort, loss of enjoyment and health involved in living in the damp and deteriorating flat and any reasonable sum spent on providing alternative accommodation after the flat became uninhabitable'.[97]

Global awards and assessing by reference to rent

10.155   Although 'diminution of value' is not an appropriate way to assess damages for a tenant in occupation, one approach adopted by the courts has been to assess damages by reference to the rent paid by the tenant. For example, if one third of a property has been affected by disrepair it may be appropriate to assess damages on the basis of a rebate of one-third of the rent for the relevant period. However, this approach sometimes leads to an award that is inadequate to compensate a particular tenant for the 'discomfort, loss of enjoyment and health' caused by the landlord's breach. Courts may therefore adopt an alternative approach of making a 'global' award of damages to cover such loss.

> In *Wallace v Manchester CC*[98] the tenant argued that the court was bound to assess damages on both bases: diminution of value/rent rebate *plus* an award for discomfort and inconvenience.
>
> The Court of Appeal rejected this argument holding that 'diminution of value' and 'discomfort' were alternative ways of expressing the same concept for a tenant who remains in occupation: damages for the 'loss of comfort and convenience which results from living in a property which was not in the state of repair it ought to have been if the landlord had performed his

---

97   Griffiths LJ at 34 and 36.
98   (1998) 30 HLR 1111, CA.

obligation'. A court may assess damages on one basis or the other, or by a combination of the two. The Court of Appeal recommended that where damages are assessed on a global basis it is advisable to cross-check the assessment by reference to the rent payable for the period of disrepair. This will avoid over- or under-assessment 'through failure to give proper consideration to the period of the landlord's breach of obligation or the nature of the property'.[99] The court also held that when assessing damages by reference to the rent payable the fact that most or all of the rent is actually paid by housing benefit is irrelevant.

In *English Churches Housing Group v Shine*[100] the Court of Appeal overturned a global award of £19,000 for a seven-year period and substituted an award of £8,000. The original award exceeded the total amount of rent payable over the relevant period. The judge had failed to cross-refer the global award with the rent payable and had failed to give reasons for the award. It was held that 'the basic rule of thumb [is] that – all other things being equal – the maximum award for damages in the case such as the present should be the rental value of the premises'.[101] The court, however, recognised that there will be cases in which an award in excess of the rent payable will be justified but held that in such a case clear reasons need to be given.

Amount of general damages

10.156   In *Wallace* (para 10.155) the appeal was argued on the basis that there was an 'informal tariff' for damages for discomfort and inconvenience. The Court of Appeal did not decide the issue but did consider the damages awarded on the assumption that there was such a 'tariff' ranging from £1,000 per year at the bottom of the tariff to £2,750 per year at the top. Given inflation this would translate, in 2010, as a range of between approximately £1,320 and £3,600 per year. For information about the levels of damages awarded by county courts (or agreed between the parties to litigation) advisers should refer to the 'Disrepair roundup' published in *Legal Action* on a regular basis.

---

99 (1998) 30 HLR 1111, CA, Morritt LJ at 1121.
100 [2004] EWCA Civ 434.
101 [2004] EWCA Civ 434, Wall LJ at [109].

Special damages

10.157　Special damages are those that can be precisely calculated by the claimant. If possible, the parties should agree the amounts. A defendant may agree the quantification of special damages while maintaining that he or she is not liable for the loss. In a disrepair claim special damages may include for example, the value of damaged belongings, the cost of alternative accommodation, the cost of extra heating to dry out damp premises or while central heating systems were not functioning, and any other item of expenditure caused by the landlord's breach.

10.158　The calculation of special damages should be included as a schedule in the particulars of claim if possible. Sometimes special damages are ongoing and it will be necessary to serve a schedule of special damages at a later date.

Damaged belongings

10.159　Where disrepair causes damp conditions damage is often caused to items of furniture, carpets and clothing. Details of the damage caused and the amount claimed must be included in the special damages schedule. Appendix 1 to this chapter gives an example of a schedule giving the relevant details. It is important that the amounts claimed are realistic and not exaggerated. Landlords will sometimes indicate that they will only offer compensation for items where there is proof of purchase such as receipts or bank statements. Tenants on low incomes often do not have such documentation as many goods are purchased with cash at markets or second-hand shops. There is no reason why the courts will not award compensation on the basis of the tenant's oral evidence or witness statement provided the amounts claimed are reasonable.

10.160　If an item can be repaired or professionally cleaned then the tenant will only recover the cost of this and not replacement value.

10.161　There is often a dispute about whether items were so badly damaged that they needed to be disposed of. Tenants should be advised to keep damaged belongings for a reasonable period to allow the landlord to inspect. Furthermore, photographs should be taken before damaged goods are disposed of.

Valuing damaged belongings

10.162　When something has been damaged beyond repair the damages awarded should enable the tenant to replace the item. If a tenant chooses to replace the damaged item with something better the damages awarded will not be for the full amount of the replacement item but will be discounted to take account of the fact that the tenant is getting something better than that which was damaged. This is referred to as 'betterment'. However, if the tenant has no choice but to purchase something that, incidentally, is better than the original item there should be no discount. Furthermore, if the landlord is maintaining that there should be a discount for betterment, the landlord must establish this.

> In *Lagden v O'Connor*[102] the House of Lords held:
> It is for the defendant who seeks a deduction from expenditure in mitigation on the ground of betterment to make out his case for doing so. It is not enough that an element of betterment can be identified. It has to be shown that the claimant had a choice, and that he would have been able to mitigate his loss at less cost. The wrongdoer is not entitled to demand of the injured party that he incur a loss, bear a burden or make unreasonable sacrifices in the mitigation of his damages.[103]

10.163 In terms of damages for disrepair, this may mean, for example, that there would be no discount for replacing a fitted carpet with a new fitted carpet even though the existing carpet was a few years old. However, where it is possible and reasonable to purchase second-hand items, only the second-hand cost would be awarded.[104]

Orders for works

Interim injunction

10.164 A tenant may apply for an injunction to compel a landlord to carry out urgent repairs before the final hearing. However, interim injunctions (unlike final orders for works) are discretionary remedies. They are to be granted only in exceptional circumstances.

---

102 [2003] UKHL 64, 4 December 2003.
103 [2003] UKHL 64, Lord Hope at 34.
104 It may be argued that it is reasonable to purchase a second-hand table but not more personal items such as a beds, bedding or clothing.

In *Parker v Camden*[105] a number of tenants took action against the local authority because they were without heating and hot water as a result of a strike of boiler workers employed by the council. They sought a mandatory injunction on an urgent basis to compel the council to restore the heating and hot water systems. The council admitted the breach but offered to provide electric heaters and undertake to reduce heating charges at a future date. It argued that to bring in external contractors would risk escalating the industrial dispute.

The Court of Appeal held that mandatory interlocutory injunctions should be granted only in 'the most exceptional circumstances' but that this was such a case in that there was 'an undoubted breach of covenant giving rise to actual and immediate major discomfort and inconvenience and to a real risk of damage to health flowing from the admitted breach'.[106]

10.165 To succeed in obtaining an interlocutory injunction, a tenant will need to have an expert report identifying those repairs that require urgent attention and the remedial works necessary. The application must be supported by evidence in the form of a witness statement from the tenant and a copy of the expert report. Three clear days' notice must be given to the landlord (this does not include the date notice is given or the date of the hearing).[107] In a case of exceptional urgency an application may be heard without three clear days' notice but in all cases the landlord should be notified and invited to put forward proposals to deal with the urgent issues.

Final order for works

10.166 Unless all outstanding works have been completed when the claim is heard, part of the final order will be that the landlord carries out specified works within a specified time. If they are works the landlord is contractually obliged to carry out the order is an order of specific performance. Otherwise the order will be a mandatory injunction. An injunction is a discretionary remedy which means that it may be refused because of the tenant's conduct. An order for specific performance is not discretionary: Landlord and Tenant Act 1985 s17.

---

105 (1985) 17 HLR 380, CA.
106 Browne Willkinson LJ at 389.
107 CPR 23.7(1)(b).

10.167   The terms of the order must be sufficiently clear for the defendant to know exactly what must be done and by what time.[108]

10.168   It is usual for a schedule of works to be drawn up by the expert or experts with a deadline for completion and some mechanism for ensuring that the works are completed satisfactorily (for example, confirmation by the tenant's surveyor). This agreed schedule will be attached to a consent order. Such an order is known as a 'Tomlin Order': see appendix to chapter 22 for a precedent. A consent order must be signed by the parties or their representatives and sent to the court for approval. Once approved and sealed by the court it is sent to the parties. Alternatively, at a hearing the landlord may give to the court an undertaking to carry out works set out in an agreed schedule by an agreed time.

Enforcement of orders

10.169   A court order is legally binding. However, the court does not take action to enforce the orders it makes unless the claimant makes further application. Social landlords usually comply with orders although there may be some delay before they do so. For tenants of private landlords it is often necessary to make further application to the court after the order has been made.

Money judgments

10.170   The various methods of enforcing money judgments are set out in CPR Parts 70–73, summarised at para 22.113 below.

10.171   It is essential *before* starting a claim for damages against a private landlord to know whether it is going to be possible to enforce the order. A Land Registry search may be carried out to establish who owns the premises let and/or the landlord's home address, if known.[109] Such a search will reveal whether the premises are mortgaged.

Orders for works

10.172   An injunction or order of specific performance will require that the landlord carry out certain works by a specified time. If the order is not complied with it may be enforced by an application to commit the landlord to prison for contempt of court.[110]

108 *Morris v Redland Bricks Ltd* [1970] AC 652.
109 See para 4.139 above.
110 The procedure is set out in CCR Order 29.

10.173   An application can be made for committal only if the order contains a penal notice. This is a notice addressed to the respondent warning him or her that disobedience with the order is a contempt of court punishable by imprisonment. A penal notice can be attached when the order is made or approved by the court. If the order does not contain a penal notice, a further application must be made for a penal notice to be attached to the order.

10.174   In all cases the order must be personally served on the respondent. In the case of a local authority landlord the order will usually be served on the director of housing or the chief executive and in the case of a registered provider on a director or other senior officer.

10.175   An application for committal will be listed for a hearing before a circuit judge. The respondent must be personally served with the application notice and notice of the hearing date. Unsurprisingly, when an application for a penal notice or committal is made, the landlord will usually ensure that the works are completed. The court may make a suspended order for committal providing that, if the works are not completed by a certain time, the landlord, or the named officer employed by the landlord, will be liable to imprisonment.

10.176   An undertaking given by a landlord may also be enforced by committal proceedings, provided again that a penal notice has been attached.[111]

10.177   If the works and the timescale have been agreed between the parties and set out in a schedule to a consent order (a Tomlin Order) the proceedings must be restored and the court asked to make an order against the defendant with penal notice attached.

Appointment of receivers

10.178 The court also has the power to appoint a receiver who can receive rents and arrange for works to be completed in compliance with any order.[112]

Time limits for county court claims

10.179 The ordinary time limits for bringing civil claims are set out in the Limitation Act 1980. The general rule for claims in contract and tort is that they must be brought within six years. In a disrepair claim where the breach is ongoing this means that any damages can only

---

111 CCR Order 29 rule 1A.
112 CPR 69, see para 22.126. In addition, under the Commonhold and Leasehold Reform Act 2002, leaseholders have a right to manage, see para 5.62.

be awarded for a period starting six years before the claim was issued. However, the time limit is 12 years if the agreement is a deed, which includes long leases.

10.180 In respect of a contractual claim, the time limit begins at the date of the breach (not necessarily the date the premises first fell into disrepair, see para 10.54 above). In respect of a claim in tort, the time limit runs from the date of the damage or injury, even though the negligence or unlawful act may have occurred years earlier.

10.181 Personal injury claims must be brought within three years. Where a disrepair claim includes a claim for personal injury (for example, a claim that ill health has been caused by the housing conditions) the three-year time limit applies to the whole claim. Before issuing a disrepair claim including a claim for personal injury both the personal injury and the disrepair protocols should be followed. In practice, disrepair claims often make reference to the effect of the disrepair on the claimant's health without being treated by the courts as personal injury claims. Advisers should, however, be aware that including a claim for personal injury may result in the period for which damages are awarded being limited to three years rather than the usual six years.[113]

10.182 Where a claim is for injury to the health of a child a separate action should be brought in the name of the child. A litigation friend must be appointed to represent the child (see para 7.171). As time limits do not begin to run until a child reaches adulthood, a claim can be brought up to the child's 21st birthday.

10.183 The limitation of actions is a defence that must be pleaded by the defendant. If the defence fails to refer to the limitation period there will be no limit to the period for which damages can be awarded. However, the courts will usually be willing to allow a late amendment to permit the defendant to rely on the limitation defence.

10.184 The Limitation Act 1980 permits the usual time limits to be extended by the court in certain situations, for example where the claimant was under a disability, or where there has been fraud or concealment.

---

113 For example in *Vukelic v Hammersmith & Fulham LBC* (see para 10.77 above) the claimant included a claim for injury to health, namely depression and anxiety. The conditions complained of had existed for many years. The court limited the period for which any damages could be claimed to three years prior to issue even though ultimately the claimant was not awarded damages for personal injury. Had the claimant omitted the reference to injury to health she would have been entitled to claim for a six-year period.

Procedural issues

10.185   Advisers must be aware of the way claims are dealt with under the Civil Procedure Rules before advising a person about the most appropriate course of action. Most importantly, in most cases the Pre-Action Protocol must be followed before proceedings are issued. Furthermore, the value of the claim will determine how the court will deal with it and whether public funding will be available.

The Disrepair Protocol

10.186   The Pre-Action Protocol for Housing Disrepair ('Disrepair Protocol') applies to all civil claims arising from the condition of residential premises. The protocol can be found on the Ministry of Justice website at www.justice.gov.uk and includes precedent letters for use by advisers or litigants in person. If a claim proceeds to litigation, the court will expect all parties to have complied with the protocol as far as possible. The court has the power to order parties who have unreasonably failed to comply with the protocol to pay costs or be subject to other sanctions.

10.187   The protocol does not apply to Environmental Protection Act 1990 prosecutions (see para 10.217 below) or to disrepair claims brought under CPR Part 20 (counterclaims).

10.188   The protocol is intended to encourage the exchange of information between parties at an early stage and to encourage the settlement of claims prior to issue.

10.189   The specific aims of the protocol are:

- to avoid unnecessary litigation;
- to promote the speedy and appropriate carrying out of any repairs which are the landlord's responsibility;
- to ensure that tenants receive any compensation to which they are entitled as speedily as possible;
- to promote good pre-litigation practice, including the early exchange of information and to give guidance about the instruction of experts; and
- to keep the costs of resolving disputes down.

10.190   The steps set out in the protocol include the following (paras 10.191–10.200).

Letter to landlords

10.191   The tenant must send to the landlord a letter setting out the nature of the potential claim. If the claim needs further investigation this letter will be an 'early notification letter'. If not, it will be a 'letter of claim'. Precedents for both are included in the protocol. Certain information must be included in the initial letter (whether an early notification letter or a letter of claim), including:

- the tenant's name, address and telephone number;
- details of the defects;
- details of previous notice given to the landlord;
- proposed single joint expert;
- proposed letter of instruction to expert;
- disclosure of relevant documents in the tenant's possession.

10.192 The letter should request disclosure from the landlord of relevant documents including the tenancy agreement and records of complaints and works carried out.

10.193   If the initial letter is a letter of claim it should also include the following information:

- the effect of the defects on the tenant; and
- details of special damages.

Landlord's response

10.194 The landlord should respond within 20 working days and should:

- give the disclosure requested; and
- respond to the tenant's proposal for an expert indicating whether the single joint expert is agreed or, if not agreed, whether the landlord agrees to a joint inspection.

10.195 If the letter is a letter of claim the landlord's response should also indicate:

- whether liability is admitted;
- any points of dispute;
- a full schedule of intended works with timescale for completion;
- any offer of compensation; and
- any offer of costs.

10.196 This may be done either 20 days after receipt of the letter of claim or 20 days after receipt of an expert report or schedule of works.

Failure to respond

10.197 If no response is received to an early notification letter, a letter of claim should be sent. If no response is received to a letter of claim, proceedings may be issued.

Cases of urgency/preserving evidence

10.198   It is specifically stated that the protocol does not prevent a tenant from instructing an expert at an earlier stage if it is considered necessary because of urgency or to preserve evidence.

Alternative dispute resolution

10.199   The protocol provides that the parties should consider whether some form of alternative dispute resolution (ADR) procedure would be more suitable than litigation and, if so, should endeavour to agree the form of ADR.

Experts

10.200   Expert evidence is essential in most disrepair claims. The written evidence of a surveyor,[114] in the form of an inspection report, will usually be necessary to:

- specify the outstanding works;
- express an opinion on which works are the landlord's responsibility under the tenancy agreement;
- comment on the severity of each defect;
- specify the works necessary to remedy the defect;
- give an estimate of the cost of the necessary works; and
- express an opinion on the likely timescale for the completion of the works.

10.201   Before the Disrepair Protocol was introduced the parties would usually instruct separate experts, with social landlords often using in-house surveyors. The protocol recommends the use of a single joint expert (SJE). If the parties can agree on which SJE to use they will jointly instruct the SJE, whose duty is to the court rather than to the parties. In disrepair claims against social landlords it is common for the landlord to refuse to agree the proposed SJEs put forward by the tenant's advisers and either to maintain that it is not necessary to instruct an expert at all or to put forward one of their own employed surveyors as the proposed SJE. As landlords must usually prepare a schedule of works anyway they often send their own surveyors to inspect and continue to use them as their expert. Despite the protocol, therefore, it is common in disrepair cases for each party to instruct their own expert witness. In all cases attempts should be made to ensure that there is a joint inspection by the experts and that the experts clarify precisely what is agreed. The courts will sometimes order the experts

---

114   Depending on the nature of the defect(s), reports may also be needed by other experts, such as heating engineers or damp-proof specialists.

to provide a statement of issues specifying precisely what is agreed and what is disputed. If fundamental issues, such as the cause of dampness, cannot be agreed it will be necessary for the parties to seek the court's permission to call the experts to give oral evidence. It must be remembered that the burden to prove the case is on the claimant.

> In *McIntosh v Southwark LBC*[115] and *Ball and Ball v Plymouth City Council*[116] the claimants and the defendants each relied on written expert evidence which was in conflict. In both cases the tenants failed to satisfy the court, on balance of probabilities, that the dampness was caused by the landlord's failure to carry out repairs and the claims were dismissed.

10.202 As is the general rule in county court litigation, if the tenant is successful in bringing a claim, the court should order that the landlord pays the tenant's legal costs. Commonly under the protocol landlords carry out works following receipt of the protocol letter, leaving only the amount of damages to be resolved. In such a case, even if the damages are less than £5,000, the landlord should pay the tenant's pre-allocation costs.[117]

Track allocation

10.203 A defended claim will be allocated to one of the three tracks which are:[118]

- the small claims track;
- the fast track; and
- the multi-track.

10.204 The main criteria in determining track allocation is the financial value of the claim. In respect of money claims, the small claims track is for claims of less than £5,000, the fast track for claims of between £5,000 and £25,000 and the multi-track for claims of more than £25,000. For the purpose of track allocation the claimant must, when completing the claim form, estimate the amount of damages he or she expects to recover. However, factors other than the value of the claim are also taken into account and a claim will not generally be allocated to the

---

115 [2001] All ER (D) 133 (Nov) and see para 10.42 above.
116 [2004] EWHC 134 (QB).
117 See *Birmingham CC v Lee* [2008] EWCA Civ 891, 30 July 2008.
118 See CPR Parts 27, 28 and 29.

fast track if it is likely to take more than one day to resolve and there is disputed expert evidence.

10.205   For disrepair claims where the only claim is for damages the small claims limit of £5,000 applies: claims for less than this amount will be allocated to the small claims track on receipt of the defence. However, if a claim includes an application for an order for works it will be allocated to the small claims track only if *both:*

- the estimated damages are less than £1,000; and
- the estimated cost of the works is less than £1,000.

10.206   So if either is expected to exceed £1,000 the claim should be allocated to the fast track or the multi-track.

10.207   An expert should always be asked to give an opinion on the estimated cost of the works so that the claim can be allocated appropriately.

10.208   The other factors that should be taken into account in allocating claims are:

- the complexity of fact, law or evidence;
- the number of parties or the importance of the case to people who are not parties;
- the amount of oral evidence that will be required; and
- the views and circumstances of the parties.

10.209   In practice, the allocation is usually done on the basis of the estimated damages and/or cost of works and any more subtle arguments may have to be made on an application to re-allocate to a different track.

10.210   The court can make an order for works in a claim allocated to the small claims track: *Joyce v Liverpool City Council.*[119]

Public funding

10.211   At the time of writing public funding is available for disrepair claims though it will only be granted if the usual merits tests is satisfied: for a damages claim this involves the application of the cost benefit test, which compares the likely legal costs with the likely level of damages. If the claim is not principally about damages but about getting the works done, legal aid will usually be granted unless the outstanding works are trivial.

10.212   The Legal Aid, Sentencing and Punishment Bill will remove legal aid from many areas of law including disrepair claims other than

119 (1995) 27 HLR 548, CA.

where there is a 'serious risk of harm to the health or safety' of the individual or a member of his or her family because of a deficiency in the rented home. Many cases where premises are in substantial disrepair will satisfy this test: it is well established that damp conditions cause and excacerbate such conditions as asthma and other respiratory conditions, particularly in children. However, it may be that expert evidence will be needed from a doctor or environmental health officer before legal aid will be granted.

Other funding

10.213   Clients should always be asked to provide a copy of their home insurance policies, which sometimes cover legal advice and representation. Indeed, it will always be necessary to check such policies for the purposes of a legal aid application.

10.214   Conditional fee agreements (CFAs) can be used to fund disrepair claims. CFAs provide that if the claim is successful the claimant's legal fees will be paid by the defendant; if the claim fails the claimant's lawyers will not be paid for their services. It has to date been possible for solicitors acting under a CFA to also recover a 'success fee' – a percentage increase on the solicitors' basic rates to represent the risk that the solicitor is taking or, to put it another way, to compensate for the fact that in some cases the solicitors will recover no fees. The Legal Aid, Sentencing and Punishment Bill will provide that any success fee will not be recoverable from the opponent. The CFA may still provide for a success fee but this will have to be paid by the claimant out of his or her damages. To compensate claimants, the Bill proposes that general damages be increased by 10 per cent. It remains to be seen whether many solicitors will be willing to undertake disrepair claims on this basis.

10.215   A further consideration for claimants is the risk of being unsuccessful and being ordered to pay the defendant's legal costs (see paras 22.119–22.139). To guard against this risk it is possible to obtain insurance which covers the payment of fees such as court fees and expert reports and that also will meet the defendant's costs if the claim fails. Obviously, the availability and cost of such insurance polices will depend on the strength of the case.

10.216   A solicitor may indeminify the client against the risk of a costs order, effectively agreeing to be liable for the opponent's costs if the claim is unsuccessful.

> In *Sibthorpe and Danri Morris v Southwark LBC*,[120] the local authority sought to challenge the lawfulness of such an agreement on the basis that is was 'champerty' (an arrangement under which the legal representatives have a financial interest in the outcome of litigation, which is unlawful).
>
> The court rejected this: while the lawyers would lose out if the claim failed they would not gain anything other than the payment of their fees if the claim succeeded.

Action in the magistrates' court

Environmental Protection Act 1990

10.217   The Environmental Protection Act (EPA) 1990 concerns dwellings and public nuisances that may affect health. The EPA 1990 replaced the Public Health Act 1936, which had itself replaced earlier legislation first introduced to address concern about outbreaks of cholera and typhus. The temporary Act of 1846 provided 'For the speedy removal of certain nuisances'. Prosecution could follow a certificate of two doctors 'of the filthy and unwholesome condition of any dwelling-house or other building, or of the accumulation of any offensive or noxious matter, refuse, dung, or offal, or of the existence of any foul or offensive drain, privy, or cesspool' and that 'the same is likely to be prejudicial to the health' of the occupiers or neighbours. The concept of dwellings that are 'prejudicial to health' remains central under the 1990 Act.

10.218   Under EPA 1990 local authorities have the power to take action to ensure that nuisances are 'abated' to prevent prejudice to health. This is done by the local authority serving an abatement notice on the person responsible and, if the notice is not complied with, the authority may then prosecute the person. However, sometimes the buildings that constitute a nuisance are owned or controlled by local authorities. To enable action to be taken against local authorities, the Act provides a procedure for a private individual to bring a prosecution in order to abate a nuisance. The procedure is set out in EPA 1990 s82. Although it has mainly been used against local authority landlords by their tenants a 'section 82 prosecution' may be brought against any landlord. In recent years the number of these private prosecutions has diminished, mainly because legal aid is not

120 [2011] EWCA Civ 25, 25 January 2011.

available and alternative funding is problematic. This is explained in more detail below in paras 10.245–10.246.

Statutory nuisance

10.219 A prosecution under Environmental Protection Act 1990 depends on there being a statutory nuisance as defined in section 79. This includes 'any premises in such a state as to be prejudicial to health or a nuisance'.[121] Section 79 lists a number of 'matters' that may constitute a statutory nuisance. The definition is not confined to dwellings and may include such things as smoke, fumes and noise.

Prejudicial to health

10.220 Prejudicial to health means 'injurious, or likely to cause injury, to health'.[122] Premises are prejudicial to health if they are in such a state as would cause a well person to become ill or the health of a sick person to deteriorate further. 'Health' has been interpreted broadly to include physical and mental health and well-being.[123]

10.221 To succeed in a prosecution based on prejudice to health the burden is on the tenant to prove beyond reasonable doubt that the state of the premises is likely to cause ill health. It is not necessary to prove that the state of the premises has actually caused ill health, only that it is likely to do so. Usually medical evidence of the effect of the premises on the health of the occupants will be needed. However, in some cases it may be sufficient to rely on the expert evidence of an environmental health officer (EHO).

10.222 Some housing conditions are such that prejudice to health is well established, such as premises severely affected by dampness and mould growth. In most cases an EHO report will be essential anyway to prove the case beyond reasonable doubt and because the court will need expert opinion on the works necessary to abate the nuisance.

Or a nuisance

10.223 The term 'nuisance' in EPA 1990 s79 has been interpreted restrictively to mean either:[124]

- a public nuisance at common law: this requires that the comfort or quality of life of the general public, or of a class of persons, is adversely affected; or

121 EPA 1990 s79(1)(a).
122 EPA 1990 s79(7).
123 *Malton Board of Health v Malton Manure Company Ltd* (1879) 4 Ex D 302.
124 *National Coal Board v Thorne* [1976] 1 WLR 543.

- a private nuisance at common law: this means something that causes substantial interference with the use and enjoyment of neighbouring property.

10.224 If it is the conditions *within* the property that are affecting the occupiers of the property there will not be such a nuisance. In most cases therefore when an occupier is bringing action against a landlord it is the 'prejudice to health' limb of the condition that is relied upon.

When are premises prejudicial to health?

Dampness and mould growth

10.225 Many successful prosecutions have been brought in relation to buildings that are badly designed and prone to condensation and mould growth, the kind of property described in *Quick v Taff Ely*.[125] There is considerable evidence that such conditions may cause injury to health by exacerbating asthma and other respiratory conditions.

Likelihood of accident and unhygienic layout

10.226 In *R v Bristol ex p Everett*[126] the Court of Appeal held that an offence under EPA 1990 is not committed where the design of the premises is dangerous and likely to cause accidental injury. 'Prejudicial to health' means a risk of disease or illness and does not extend to the danger of accidental physical injury.

Similarly, in *Oakley v Birmingham City Council*[127] the House of Lords held that the 'unhygienic layout of premises' is not a statutory nuisance. In *Oakley* the only WC was located next to the kitchen. There was no hand basin or room to install one. The court accepted that there was a risk of cross-infection because it was necessary, after using the WC, for the tenant and her family to either wash their hands in the kitchen sink or to cross the kitchen to get to the bathroom. However, by a majority of 3:2 it was decided that the implications of holding that a landlord must carry out works to re-arrange the layout were such, in terms of the expenditure of public funds, that this was a decision for Parliament and not the courts.

125 (1985) 18 HLR 66, see para 10.34 above.
126 (1999) HLR 1102, CA.
127 (2000) 33 HLR 283, HL.

10.227 In fact the kind of 'hazards' that were the cause of complaint in both *Everett* and *Oakley* may now be dealt with by a local authority under the Housing Act 2004, see chapter 11.

Lack of sound insulation

10.228 Premises that lack sound insulation so that the occupant is disturbed by the noise of his or her neighbours are not in such a state as to be prejudicial to health or a nuisance.

> In *R on the application of Vella v London Borough of Lambeth*[128] a tenant of an RSL was disturbed by noise from the flat above and the communal stairs caused by a lack of sound insulation. He requested that the local authority serve an abatement notice on his landlords to force them to carry out works of sound insulation. There was evidence that the tenant suffered from depression and that the 'noise pollution' he suffered was a 'significant perpetuating factor' in his depressive illness. The local authority refused to serve an abatement notice and the tenant sought judicial review of that decision.
>
> The court, following *Everett* and *Oakley* (above, para 10.226), held that EPA 1990 and the previous legislation are 'sanitary statutes' and that 'there can be no room for holding that a lack of sound insulation sufficient to comply with current standards renders premises in such a state as to be prejudicial to health'.[129] The earlier cases of *Southwark LBC v Ince*[130] and *Network HA v Westminster*,[131] were held to have been wrongly decided in light of the judgments in *Everett* and *Oakley*.

Noisy neighbours

10.229 EPA 1990 s79(1)(g) specifically provides that 'noise emitted from premises so as to be prejudicial to health or a nuisance' is a statutory nuisance. This, however, is distinct from noise pollution caused by the state of the premises. Section 79(1)(g) can be used against a person who is making excessive noise. As this is a private nuisance at common law (see para 10.223 above) it is not necessary to prove

128 [2005] EWHC 2473 (Admin), 14 November 2005.
129 [2005] EWHC 2473 (Admin), Poole J at [69].
130 (1989) 21 HLR 505.
131 (1995) 27 HLR 189.

prejudice to health. This is one option for a person who is suffering from disturbance by a noisy neighbour. The prosecution is brought against the neighbour and the court can make an abatement order requiring the neighbour to stop making the noise. Alternatively, the local authority can be asked to prosecute (see chapter 11).

Parties to the proceedings

The complainant

10.230   Proceedings can be brought by 'any person aggrieved by the statutory nuisance'.[132] This will usually be the occupier of the premises if the complaint is about the state of premises.

The defendant

10.231   Where the statutory nuisance arises from any defect of a structural character, proceedings must be brought against the owner of the premises.[133]

10.232   If the statutory nuisance is noise caused by a neighbour, he or she will be the defendant.

Procedure

Notice of intended prosecution

10.233   Before proceedings under EPA 1990 s82 can be started, the tenant must give written notice of the intended prosecution to the intended defendant.[134] There is no prescribed form for such notice but it must state the nature of the statutory nuisance and its effect on the occupants. It is not necessary to specify the works required to remedy the nuisance.[135] If an expert report has been obtained it should be attached to the notice. If the complaint is about the state of the premises, the notice must give the defendant at least 21 days to respond; if it is about excessive noise, at least three days' notice must be given.

10.234   If the action is against a local authority, notice must be served on the chief clerk or chief executive and, if posted, must be sent to the registered or principal office, unless the authority have specified a different address at which notices must be served.[136] In *Leeds v*

---

132 EPA 1990 s82(1).
133 EPA 1990 s82(4)(b).
134 EPA 1990 s82(6).
135 *East Staffs BC v Fairless* [1998] EGCS 140.
136 EPA 1990 s160(4)–(5).

Islington LBC[137] notice was served on the senior estate manager of the local housing office. The proceedings were dismissed on the basis that notice had not properly been given.

Starting the prosecution

10.235   The action is a criminal prosecution, initiated by 'laying a complaint or information' in the local magistrates' court. There is no prescribed form but the complainant must describe the offence in ordinary language and give the necessary particulars to provide reasonable information about the nature of the charge.[138] Following the complaint being sent to the court, the court will issue a summons with a hearing date and send this to the defendant. It is good practice for the claimant to send a further copy to the defendant in case of any dispute about receipt.

Hearings

10.236   At the first hearing the defendant will usually be asked to enter a plea of guilty or not guilty to the charge of failing to abate a statutory nuisance. Sometimes the defendant may seek an adjournment with the intention of carrying out the necessary works to abate the nuisance. If works are completed before the final hearing there will be no conviction. It is the court's decision whether to grant an adjournment but the wishes of the parties will be relevant. The complainant may be willing to adjourn if this means that the works will be carried out quickly. However, if the nuisance is abated before a guilty plea is entered or before a trial, the court will have no power to award compensation.

10.237   If a plea of not guilty is entered, the court will list the case for a trial to take place at a later date. At the trial the court will hear evidence from both parties and decide whether the complainant has proved the case beyond reasonable doubt. Any expert witness must be available to give oral evidence.

10.238   If the defendant pleads guilty it will not be necessary to call evidence to prove the offence. In practice a schedule of works with timetable will usually be agreed between the parties for the court to endorse. Evidence may be given to enable the court to assess the appropriate fine or compensation.

---

137 [1998] Env LR 655; [1998] EGCS 15.
138 See Magistrates' Courts Act 1980 s1 and the Criminal Procedure Rules 2005 Part 7.

Court's powers

Order for works

10.239   If the court is satisfied that a statutory nuisance exists at the date of the hearing it must make an order requiring the defendant to abate the nuisance. The abatement order must set out in detail the works to be carried out and the time limit. The court will usually adopt a schedule prepared by the environmental health officer acting on the complainant's behalf or agreed between the parties. If, at the date of the hearing, the nuisance has abated but the court is satisfied that recurrence is likely it can make an order requiring works within a specified time to prevent recurrence. In either case, a conviction will be entered against the defendant.

10.240   The court may order the defendant to do whatever is necessary to abate the nuisance.

> In *Birmingham DC v Kelly*[139] the order required the authority to install central heating. The council's appeal was dismissed: the order was made not because the absence of central heating was prejudicial to health but because mould growth was present and was likely to cause health problems and food poisoning. The installation of central heating was a way to remove the threat to health created by the mould growth. The court was entitled to make such an order even though the effect was to require the landlord to improve the premises.

Fines and compensation

10.241   The court can impose a fine and can also order the defendant to pay compensation to the complainant. The compensation is for 'any personal injury, loss or damage' resulting from the offence.[140] The action is a summary prosecution which means that it must be brought within six months of the offence. A failure to abate a statutory nuisance will usually be a continuing failure so this does not prevent someone bringing a prosecution even if the problem started more than six months ago. However, the court cannot award compensation for losses occurring earlier than six months before the complaint was laid. Furthermore, the offence is only committed if a nuisance is not abated within 21 days of notice being given. Therefore compensation

139 (1985) 17 HLR 572.
140 Powers of the Criminal Courts (Sentencing) Act 2000 s130(1).

can only be for the period starting 21 days after the notice was served.[141] This will usually be a period of weeks or months (up to a maximum of six months before the proceedings commenced), so the level of compensation will be limited. The maximum amount the courts can award is £5,000. The maximum fine is also £5,000.

10.242　The court can only award compensation or impose a fine if there is a conviction. If the nuisance is abated, and not likely to recur, before the final hearing (or guilty plea) there will be no conviction.

Costs

10.243　Where a court is satisfied that the statutory nuisance existed when the information was laid then, even if it has been abated by the time of the hearing, the court *must* order the defendant to pay the complainant's fair and reasonable legal costs.

Enforcement

10.244　If there is a failure, without reasonable excuse, to comply with any requirement of a nuisance order within the time limit specified, the defendant commits a further offence.[142] A further prosecution may be brought for the non-compliance. On conviction, a further fine may be imposed and, if the nuisance remains unabated, the court can impose, in addition, a daily fine continuing until such time as the order is fully complied with.

Funding an EPA 1990 action

10.245　Public funding is not available for representation in private prosecutions. To date the Legal Help scheme has been available for advice and assistance to prepare for the issue of proceedings. This could include obtaining an expert report and drafting the complaint but will not cover representation at any hearings. The Legal Aid, Sentencing and Punishment Bill proposes that in future Legal Help will be available in relation to disrepair claims only where there is a 'serious risk of harm to the health or safety' of the individual or a member of their family because of a deficiency in the rented home (see para 10.212 above). Arguably, this will include most cases where the conditions are such as to be prejudicial to health.

141　*R v Liverpool Crown Court ex p Cooke* (1997) 29 HLR 249.
142　EPA 1990 s82(8).

10.246   It is possible for a solicitor to represent a client in an EPA 1990 prosecution under a conditional fee agreement (CFA) (see para 10.214 above).[143] However, it may be difficult to find solicitors willing to do so. Also, expert evidence is almost always needed to succeed in a prosecution and the client must be able to pay the fees for any expert required to attend at court.

Costs orders against the complainant

10.247 Unlike civil proceedings, when the usual order is that the unsuccessful party must pay the legal costs of the successful party, a complainant can be ordered to pay the costs of the defendant only if he or she required proceedings to be issued or continued improperly.[144]

Formal complaint/landlords' internal procedures

10.248 This section examines the ways a tenant may use a landlord's internal procedures to ensure that repairs are completed and compensation paid. This is generally possible only if the landlord is a social landlord.

Voluntary compensation schemes

10.249 Many local authorities and registered providers operate internal procedures for compensating their tenants for disrepair, particularly the loss of heating and hot water caused by the failure of block systems. Such a scheme will usually be for the payment of compensation on a daily or weekly basis after a minimum period during which the tenant has been without services. The levels of compensation tend to be low, some schemes only reimbursing charges actually paid by the tenant to the landlord as part of an inclusive rent.

Statutory 'right to repair' scheme

10.250 In addition, for secure tenants there is a statutory 'right to repair' scheme.[145]

---

143 Courts and Legal Services Act 1990 s58(a), as amended by Access to Justice Act 1999 s27(1).
144 See Prosecution of Offences Act 1985 ss16–19.
145 Secure Tenants of Local Housing Authorities (Right to Repair) Regulations 1994 SI No 133; also DoE Circular 2/94.

10.251 The scheme is convoluted and of limited application. It applies only to 'qualifying repairs' which are specified in a schedule. Each type of repair has a prescribed period during which the repair should be completed. These are essentially minor repairs that will not, in the opinion of the landlord, cost more than £250 to carry out. The process is triggered by the tenant giving notice of the necessary repair, following which the landlord must, if satisfied that the repair is a qualifying repair, issue a repair notice to a contractor.

10.252 If the work is not then carried out within the prescribed period, the tenant may require the landlord to appoint a different contractor. If still not completed within the prescribed period, the tenant is entitled to compensation of £10 plus £2 per day, up to a maximum of £50 for any one repair.

10.253 The disadvantages of the scheme are:

- the onus is on the tenant to serve the appropriate notices on the landlord;
- the scheme depends on the landlord accepting that the repair is a qualifying repair;
- the prescribed period may be suspended by the landlord if there are exceptional circumstances beyond the landlord's control;
- only relatively minor repairs are covered;
- the level of compensation is extremely low.

Formal complaint and Ombudsman complaint

10.254 The complaints procedure and the Local Government and Housing Ombudsman schemes are described in paras 2.89–2.96.

10.255 Complaints about repairs make up a significant proportion of all Ombudsman complaints. The Housing Ombudsman's annual report for the year 2009/10 indicates that disrepair was the single most common problem referred to the Ombudsman service, making up 38 per cent of all complaints. The Local Government Ombudsman's annual report for the same year shows a similar proportion: of all housing complaints just over 39 per cent are about repairs.

10.256 Most complaints are resolved or abandoned prior to an investigation by the Ombudsman. In a disrepair claim resolution may mean that outstanding works are carried out but no compensation offered. If compensation is offered or recommended by the Ombudsman it will usually be much less than the amount that a court would award.

10.257 The Ombudsman can recommend that the authority or association make a contribution to any legal costs incurred by the complainant but has expressed the view that legal representation is unnecessary in pursuing complaints to the Ombudsman and such recommendations are rare.

Rent and disrepair

10.258   There are three different situations to consider regarding unpaid rent:

- a tenant may withhold rent and use the money to pay for repairs;
- a tenant may withhold rent in protest to try to force a landlord to carry out repairs; and
- a tenant whose landlord is in breach of the repairing obligation may be in arrears of rent for reasons unconnected with the disrepair.

Applying rent to pay for repairs

10.259   There is a common law right to use money due as rent to pay for repairs.[146] However, a tenant must follow the following steps:

- Give the landlord notice of the need for repair in writing.
- If, after a reasonable period has elapsed, the repairs have still not been done, write again telling the landlord of the intention to arrange the repairs and to deduct the cost from the rent.
- Obtain estimates for the cost of the work from at least two reputable contractors and write again enclosing copies of the estimates, and giving the landlord a deadline to carry out the work, failing which the tenant will arrange for the works to be done and deduct the cost from the rent.
- If there is no response from the landlord, arrange for the work to be done by the contractor who submitted the lowest estimate, obtaining receipts showing the extent of the work.
- Send to the landlord a copy of the receipts and explain exactly how the rent deductions will be made, or have been made, so as to cover the cost of the work.

10.260   This remedy depends on the tenant being able to pay the contractor at the time of carrying out the work and recouping the money from future rent payments or from rent previously withheld. It is therefore unlikely to be available to a tenant with a limited income where the repair works are extensive. Furthermore, a tenant in receipt of

146   *Lee-Parker v Izzett* [1971] 1 WLR 1688.

housing benefit may not be in control of the payment of rent as benefit may be paid direct to the landlord. Housing benefit for local authority tenants is made by way of a rent rebate.

Withholding rent/'rent strike'

10.261 A tenant may simply withhold rent to try to force the landlord to carry out works or as a protest for the landlord's breach. While it is true that landlords who are receiving rent regularly may have little incentive to carry out expensive works of repair, this is a dangerous tactic. Tenants on a low income who withhold rent often find it difficult not to use the money for ordinary household expenses. A tenant in rent arrears risks the landlord issuing possession proceedings. If the tenant is an assured tenant the mandatory ground (HA 1988 Ground 8) is made out if there is at least eight weeks' arrears, see appendix to chapter 7. Although the tenant can bring a counterclaim in the possession proceedings, the court has a discretion to order that the disrepair claim be heard separately (see para 7.43).

10.262 If the tenant is an assured shorthold tenant the landlord is entitled to possession as of right and any counterclaim in disrepair will be irrelevant.

Set off against rent

10.263 A tenant sued for arrears of rent may have a defence of 'set off': a tenant is entitled to set off any damages awarded against the arrears of rent. The defence exists even when the damages have yet to be assessed. See paras 7.41–7.43.

10.264 It is often the case that advisers are consulted only after rent arrears have built up, at the point when the tenant receives a notice of possession or a possession summons. Even if there appears to be a strong claim for damages for disrepair the tenant should be advised to pay current rent plus a regular payment towards the arrears, pending a final hearing. This is to guard against the risk of the arrears exceeding the damages awarded. If the ground for possession is a discretionary one a tenant who has been making regular payments towards arrears will be more likely to succeed in establishing that it is not reasonable to make a possession order even if the arrears do exceed damages.

APPENDIX

Example of schedule of damaged belongings

Item	Age/date of purchase	Purchase price/value	Place of purchase	Nature/ cause of damage	Repaired/ replaced	[Estimated] cost of repair/ replacement
Two seater sofa	2006	£350	Argos	Damaged by damp and mould growth. Stained and foul smelling. Beyond repair and disposed of.	No	£400
Fitted carpet in living room	2004	£800	Carpet World	Stained by flood of foul water.	Professionally cleaned	£70
School uniform blazers x 2	6 months old	£40 each	Bloggins	Stained by flood of foul water.	Dry cleaned	£7 per item x 2=£14
Midi hi-fi system	Dec 2008	£80	Secondhand at market	Blew up because of water penetration. Beyond repair.	No	£80
						Total: £564

CHAPTER 11

Disrepair and housing conditions – action by local authorities

Key points

- Local authorities have a power and in some cases a duty to take action against landlords of premises that pose a risk to the health and safety of the occupants. However, such action cannot be taken against a local authority landlord.
- Local authorities can prosecute landlords for failing to abate a statutory nuisance, which may include the state of premises.
- Local authorities can force landlords to carry out improvements to premises that contain 'hazards' – risks to the health and safety of the occupants.
- Local authorities can also prohibit landlords from letting certain buildings for residential use and can make orders that buildings are demolished or that whole areas are cleared.
- The 'Decent Homes' programme aimed to ensure that all social housing met the 'Decent Homes' standard by 2010. This target was not met and the 'backlog' programme is now managed by the Homes and Communities Agency.
- If a local authority fails to take action against a private landlord following a tenant's complaint, the authority's internal complaints scheme may be used and complaint may be made to the Ombudsman.
- In some circumstances a person may judicially review a local authority's decision or failure to take action.

Introduction

11.1   A local housing authority has a range of powers and duties with regard to the condition of dwellings in its area. They are set out in different statutes:

- the Environmental Protection Act (EPA) 1990 – power to deal with 'statutory nuisances';
- the Building Act (BA) 1984 – emergency procedure for dealing with 'statutory nuisances' in dangerous buildings; and
- the Housing Act (HA) 1985 and the Housing Act 2004 – power to deal with 'hazards' in dwellings and houses in multiple occupation (HMOs).

11.2   Although an authority may act on its own initiative, most action will be prompted by a complaint to the authority. People making a complaint need not identify the powers they wish the authority to exercise but must draw attention to the conditions about which they are concerned. Since local authorities are sometimes slow to respond to complaints, it is best to put the complaint in writing with sufficient information to enable the authority to prioritise the complaint. Alternatively, if made by telephone, a note should be kept of the date of the call and the name of the officer who recorded the complaint.

11.3   Complaint will usually be made to the authority's Environmental Health Department but some authorities have other teams such as Housing Standards and specific teams dealing with HMOs.

11.4   The Acts and the powers given to local authorities are described below.

Environmental Protection Act 1990

11.5   The Environmental Protection Act 1990 is described at para 10.217 in relation to private prosecutions. Under the Act it is the duty of every local authority to inspect its area from time to time to detect any statutory nuisances which ought to be dealt with. However, local authority action under EPA 1990 will usually be instigated by a complaint made by an occupier to the local authority. Where a complaint of a statutory nuisance is made to an authority by someone living within its area, the authority is under a duty 'to take such steps as are reasonably practicable to investigate the complaint'.[1]

11.6   The procedure is different from action taken by a tenant under EPA 1990 s82 and is set out in section 80. If the authority is satisfied that a statutory nuisance exists or is likely to recur, the authority must serve an abatement notice on the person responsible for the nuisance.[2] The notice must do the following:[3]

- require that the nuisance be abated or prevented from recurring;
- if works are required to abate the nuisance, specify the works;[4]
- specify the time limit for compliance; and
- indicate the time limit for appealing against the order (21 days).

11.7   A person served with an abatement notice must carry out the works specified or appeal to the magistrates' court within 21 days of service of the notice.

---

1 EPA 1990 s79(1).
2 EPA 1990 s80(1).
3 EPA 1990 s80.
4 *Kirklees MBC v Field* (1997) 30 HLR 869.

11.8   If the person does not appeal and does not comply with the notice without reasonable excuse, he or she is guilty of an offence. A landlord convicted of the offence is liable to a fine of up to £5,000, plus a further fine of £500 for each further day of non-compliance.

11.9   Whether or not the authority prosecutes the owner, the authority can itself do the work necessary to abate the nuisance and seek reimbursement from the owner or from the person served with the abatement notice. In practice, local authorities are very reluctant to carry out works because obtaining reimbursement is difficult.

11.10   It should be noted that the authority has a duty to take reasonable steps to investigate and, if satisfied that a statutory nuisance exists, a duty to serve a notice.[5] Where an authority fails or refuses to act on a complaint or, having inspected, declines to serve a notice, an application may be made for judicial review to obtain a mandatory order against the authority. Alternatively, a formal complaint may be made and, if not resolved satisfactorily, the complaint may be referred to the Local Government Ombudsman (see paras 2.89–2.96).

Building Act 1984: emergency procedure

11.11   A speedier procedure which local authorities can use in urgent cases is found in BA 1984 s76. This provides that, where a local authority is satisfied that a statutory nuisance exists and that following the standard procedure under the Environmental Protection Act 1990 would cause unnecessary delay, it may serve notice on the landlord stating its intention to do the remedial works and specifying the defects which it proposes to remedy.

11.12   Nine days after service, the authority may carry out the work and recover its expenses from the person on whom the notice was served. However, this cannot be done if, within seven days of the notice, the landlord serves a counter-notice on the authority stating that he or she intends to remedy the defects. The authority can then take no further action unless:[6]

- the landlord fails to start remedial works within a reasonable time; or
- having started them, the landlord proceeds unreasonably slowly or makes no progress at all.

---

5 EPA 1990 s80(1).
6 BA 1984 s76(3).

Housing Acts 1985 and 2004

11.13   Since the middle of the 19th century local authorities have been able to enforce improvements to dwellings and to demolish slums and build new dwellings. These powers are now contained in the Housing Acts 1985 and 2004. Under these Acts local authorities have a range of options when dealing with dwellings in poor condition. These include serving notice on an owner to improve a dwelling, carrying out works in default, prohibiting the use of a building as a dwelling, demolishing individual buildings or providing that whole areas be cleared of dwellings.

11.14   The Housing Act 1985 was, until April 2006, the statute which set out these powers. The key concept was 'fitness for habitation'. If premises were unfit by reason of specific matters[7] the local authority could serve notice on the landlord to carry out the necessary works to make the dwelling fit for habitation. The fitness standard has now been replaced by the Housing Health and Safety Rating System (HHSRS)[8] introduced by the Housing Act 2004. The new system is based on identifying 'hazards' in dwellings and is described below at paras 11.17–11.62.

11.15   In addition to the powers relating to unfit premises, Housing Act 1985 also gave local authorities special powers in relation to houses in multiple occupation (HMOs) and overcrowded premises. The Housing Act 2004 has replaced the provisions of HA 1985 in relation to HMOs but the powers relating to overcrowding are still found in the 1985 Act.

11.16   Although the assessment process and enforcement action to improve dwellings is now governed by the Housing Act 2004, the local authority powers to make demolition orders and declare clearance areas are still to be found in the Housing Act 1985, as amended by the 2004 Act.

---

7   These matters were set out in HA 1985 s604 and concerned: structural stability, serious disrepair, damp that is prejudicial to health, adequacy of lighting, heating and ventilation, adequacy of supply of 'wholesome' water and facilities for the preparation and cooking of food (including a sink with hot and cold water), suitably located WC, baths, showers and wash-hand basins with hot and cold water, and effective drainage.

8   HA 2004 Part 1 and the Housing Health and Safety Rating System (England) Regulations 2005 SI No 3208 and Housing Health and Safety Rating System (Wales) Regulations 2006 SI No 1702 (HHSRS Regs).

Housing Act 2004 – hazardous dwellings

11.17   The fitness standard, as the trigger for local authority action, has been replaced by the concept of hazards in residential premises. A hazard is a risk of harm to the health or safety of an actual or potential occupier of a dwelling or HMO that arises from a deficiency in the dwelling or HMO or any building or land in the vicinity. The deficiency may arise because of the construction of the building, or because of a failure to maintain or repair.[9]

11.18   A prescriptive system of assessment is set out in the Housing Act 2004, the HHSRS Regulations 2005 and Guidance. The assessment should result in a determination as to whether there are in the premises serious hazards ('Category 1' hazards) and/or less serious hazards ('Category 2' hazards). Authorities have a duty to take enforcement action in relation to Category 1 hazards and a power to do so in relation to Category 2 hazards.

Triggering an assessment

11.19   Local authorities are required to keep housing conditions in their area under review.[10] However, in practice it will usually be necessary for the occupier to request that the local authority carry out an inspection. Local authorities are sometimes slow to respond to such requests or give them low priority so that there may be a considerable delay before an inspection is arranged.

Official complaints

11.20   If an authority receives an 'official complaint' which indicates that a Category 1 or 2 hazard may exist, an inspection must be made by a 'proper officer'.[11] An official complaint means one made by a Justice of the Peace with local jurisdiction or by the parish or community council.[12] An occupier whose request for a local authority inspection is ignored should therefore arrange for an official complaint to be submitted on his or her behalf. This will place the authority under a duty to inspect.

---

9   HA 2004 s2(1).
10   HA 2004 s3.
11   HA 2004 s4.
12   Parish and community councils are the first tier of local government in England and Wales. In Wales the community councils are the equivalent of parish councils in England (although there are some DEFRA (Department for Environment, Food and Rural Affairs) funded rural community councils in England).

11.21   If, following an official complaint, an authority refuses or fails to inspect, a claim for judicial review can be brought for a mandatory order forcing the authority to inspect and comply with its duties under the Housing Act 2004.

11.22   Alternatively, a complaint may be made under the authority's complaints procedure. Ultimately, complaint may be made to the Ombudsman if the authority does not resolve the complaint satisfactorily (see paras 2.89–2.96).

Assessing hazards

11.23   The inspection must be carried out in accordance with the HHSRS Regulations and Guidance[13] and, if the officer is of the opinion that a Category 1 or 2 hazard exists, a report in writing must be made to the authority. Authorities must consider any report made to them as soon as possible and take the most appropriate action in relation to the hazard. See below, paras 11.30–11.36.

11.24   The HHSRS Regulations set out the assessment process. There are two stages: first, an assessment of the likelihood of an occupier suffering any harm as a result of the hazard; then, an assessment of the range of probable harmful outcomes. The two factors are combined using a standard method and expressed as a numerical score. There are prescribed bands applicable to the range of numerical scores: where a hazard falls within bands A, B or C the hazard is a Category 1 hazard. Where it falls within any other band it is a Category 2 hazard.

11.25   The assessment must record the presence of all hazards. Whether they are classed as Category 1 or Category 2 will determine the action the local authority must or may take. A record of the inspection must be prepared and kept either in written or electronic form.[14]

11.26   The HHSRS Regulations list the 'matters and circumstances' that may give rise to a hazard and set out the classes of harm that may occur. The classes of harm are set out in four bands: Classes I to IV.

11.27   By way of example, the first two matters and circumstances listed are:

- damp and mould growth – exposure to house dust mites, damp, mould or fungal growths; and
- excess cold – exposure to low temperatures.

13 The *Housing Health and Safety Ratings System – Operating Guidance* was published in February 2006, runs to 188 pages and is available on the website of the Communities and Local Government Department (formerly ODPM): www. communities.gov.uk.

14 HHSRS Regs 2005 reg 5.

11.28   In the list of classes of harm, regular severe pneumonia is included under Class I, with cardio-respiratory disease, asthma and non-malignant respiratory diseases under Class II and occasional mild pneumonia and regular serious coughs or colds under Class IV.

11.29   The likelihood of the class of harm arising as a result of the matter described, combined with the severity of the class of harm will result in a numerical assessment of the hazard such that it can be classified as Category 1 or Category 2.

Action following the assessment

11.30   If a local authority discovers a Category 1 hazard it has a duty to take the most appropriate enforcement action. Where a Category 2 hazard exists the authority has a power to take enforcement action.

11.31   The action available to local authorities is:

- serving an improvement notice (see paras 11.37–11.40);
- making a prohibition order (see paras 11.41–11.47);
- serving a hazard awareness notice (see paras 11.56–11.57);
- making a demolition order (see paras 11.58–11.60); or
- declaring the area to be a clearance area (see paras 11.61–11.62).

11.32   In addition, in cases of imminent risk from a Category 1 hazard, an authority may:

- take emergency remedial action; or
- make an emergency prohibition order.

11.33   In deciding which course of action to take, authorities must have regard to the Enforcement Guidance issued in February 2006.[15]

11.34   If only one course of action is possible, the authority must take that action. If more than one course of action is possible, it must decide which is the most appropriate. More than one form of action cannot be taken at the same time but if the chosen action does not prove satisfactory the authority may take another course of action in the list.[16]

11.35   Although the authority may have a duty to act it is for the authority to decide which course of action to take. If the chosen course is to serve a hazard awareness notice, this merely warns the occupier of the existence of the hazard.

11.36   When the authority has decided on one of the above courses of action it must prepare a statement of the reasons for its decision. The

15   The Enforcement Guidance is available at www.communities.gov.uk.
16   HA 2004 s5(3)–(5).

statement of reasons must be served on every person on whom the relevant notice or order is served.

Improvement notices

11.37 An improvement notice requires the person on whom it is served to take specified remedial action in respect of the hazard or hazards concerned.[17] Where a Category 1 hazard exists, the remedial action must, as a minimum, be sufficient to ensure that the hazard ceases to be a Category 1 hazard but may extend beyond such action.[18] The notice must give certain information about the hazard, specify the remedial action required and give a date when the action must start and be completed. It must also inform the recipient of the right of appeal and the time limit for bringing an appeal, which is 21 days.

11.38 As is clear from the name, the works that a landlord can be forced to carry out may be works to improve as well as works to repair the premises. An example might be the installation of central heating or the fitting of a handrail on a steep stair.

11.39 The notice may provide for its operation to be suspended until a time or event specified in the notice.[19] This could be the time when certain kinds of occupier move in or out of the premises.

11.40 If the notice is complied with the local authority must revoke it. If the notice specifies more than one hazard, the authority must revoke the part of the notice that concerns the hazard or hazards that have been remedied. The authority may vary the remainder of the notice.[20]

Prohibition orders

11.41 A prohibition order prohibits the use of premises for specified purposes, for example, use as a dwelling or HMO.[21]

11.42 A prohibition order must also specify the hazard concerned and the action the authority considers would result in revocation of the order.[22] The order must also inform the recipient of the time limit for appealing, which is 28 days.

---

17 HA 2004 s11(2).
18 HA 2004 s11(5).
19 HA 2004 s14(1) and (2).
20 HA 2004 s16.
21 HA 2004 s20(3).
22 HA 2004 s22(2)(e).

11.43   Prohibition orders may also be suspended until a time or event specified in the order. For example, if the order prohibits the use of the building as a dwelling, its operation may be suspended until the current occupiers have vacated. The effect of such an order would be to then prohibit future use of the premises as a dwelling until works had been carried out to remove the hazard or hazards.

11.44   The prohibition order must be revoked when the hazard specified in the notice has been removed.

Tenants' loss of security

11.45   If a prohibition order is made, and its operation is not suspended, any tenants and/or licensees may be evicted by the landlord. The security of tenure enjoyed by statutory and assured tenants is effectively removed by the making of such an order.[23]

11.46   The Enforcement Guidance requires the authority to 'consider the availability of local accommodation for re-housing any displaced occupants' when considering the making of a prohibition order[24] and states that 'the authority may consider offering temporary or permanent alternative accommodation to the tenant to assist in progressing remedial works'.[25] If the tenant loses his or her home because of the order there is a limited re-housing duty on the authority, see para 11.66 below.

11.47   It is likely that authorities will avoid making outright prohibition orders whenever possible and, in a case where remedial works cannot be carried out with the tenants in occupation, may opt to serve a suspended prohibition order or a hazard awareness notice.

Access

11.48   It may be that the works can be carried out with the tenants in occupation. In such a case, if access is not given, the magistrates' court has the power to order an occupier to permit the owner or manager of the premises to carry out any action necessary and expedient for the purpose of complying with an improvement notice or a prohibition order.[26]

---

23 Section 33 provides that nothing in the Rent Act 1977, Housing Act 1988 and the Rent (Agriculture) Act 1976 prevents a landlord from obtaining possession if necessary to comply with the order.
24 Enforcement Guidance para 6.23.
25 Enforcement Guidance para 6.21.
26 HA 2004 s5(2).

Emergency cases

11.49 If a local authority is satisfied that a Category 1 hazard exists on any residential premises and that 'the hazard involves an imminent risk of serious harm to the health or safety of any of the occupiers' it can take emergency remedial action or make an emergency prohibition order.

11.50 Emergency remedial action means 'such remedial action in respect of the hazard concerned as the authority consider immediately necessary in order to remove the imminent risk of serious harm'.[27]

11.51 If emergency remedial action is decided on as the most appropriate course of action, the local authority has an immediate right of access and the notice regarding the remedial action must be served on the occupiers. Notice may be served by being fixed to a conspicuous part of the premises or building.[28] Notice must also be served on the owner or manager within seven days of starting emergency remedial action. This notice must identify the hazard, the works that are to be carried out and must give information about the right of appeal.

11.52 The local authority may recoup the cost of taking emergency remedial action from the owner or manager.

11.53 An emergency prohibition order is an alternative to carrying out emergency remedial action. An emergency prohibition order also has immediate effect.[29] The order must be served on the day it is made.

Appeals

11.54 The person on whom a notice of improvement or a prohibition order is served has a right to appeal. The time limit for appealing is 21 days in the case of an improvement notice and 28 days in the case of a prohibition order. Appeals against emergency remedial action or an emergency prohibition order must be brought within 28 days. Appeals are to the Residential Property Tribunal.

Sanctions

11.55 Failure to comply with an improvement notice or prohibition order is an offence punishable by a fine of up to £5,000.[30] In respect of a prohibition order, a further fine of £20 per day can be imposed for

27 HA 2004 s40.
28 HA 2004 s40(6).
29 HA 2004 s43.
30 HA 2004 ss30 and 33.

each day following the conviction that the defendant uses or permits the premises to be used in contravention of the order.

Hazard awareness notices

11.56　A hazard awareness notice is a notice advising the person on whom it is served of the existence of a Category 1 or Category 2 hazard.[31] It must specify the nature of the hazard and give details of any remedial action the authority consider would be practicable and appropriate. However, the notice does not require that such action is taken.

11.57　There is no appeal against a hazard awareness notice.

Demolition orders

11.58　A demolition order may be made only if there is a Category 1 hazard and the building is not a listed building. In deciding whether to make a demolition order, the authority must take into account the availability of local accommodation for re-housing the displaced occupants, the demand for and the sustainabiity of the accommodation if the hazard was remedied, the prospective use of the cleared site, and the impact on the local environment.[32]

11.59　A demolition order may be substituted by a prohibition order if proposals are submitted to use the premises other than for human habitation.

11.60　An appeal lies to the Residential Property Tribunal and must be exercised by 'an aggrieved person' within 21 days.

Clearance areas

11.61　An authority can declare an area a clearance area if it is satisfied that each of the residential buildings in the area contains a Category 1 hazard or that the buildings are dangerous or harmful to the health and safety of inhabitants because of the arrangement of the buildings.[33] The declaration of a clearance area means that all of the buildings in the area will be demolished. It will be part of the authority's proposals for the wider neighbourhood of which the area forms part. Such a declaration will only be made after extensive consultation with all owners and occupiers and the authority must be satisfied that alternative accommodation can be provided for the displaced occupiers.

31　HA 2004 ss28 and 29.
32　HA 1985 s265, as amended by HA 2004, and Enforcement Guidance para 6.44.
33　HA 1985 s289, as amended by HA 2004, and Enforcement Guidance para 6.48.

11.62   Such action may be taken in conjunction with the declaration of a renewal area under the Local Government and Housing Act 1989.

Compensation and re-housing

11.63   Whenever a house is demolished as a result of a demolition order or slum clearance, displaced occupiers are entitled to compensation. Displaced owner-occupiers are entitled to a 'home loss' payment depending on the value of the property. Currently the maximum payment is £47,000.[34]

11.64   Tenants who are permanently displaced are entitled to a home loss payment currently set at £4,700. To qualify, the tenants must have occupied the property as their only or principal home for at least 12 months prior to eviction.

11.65   Although local authorities will not make prohibition orders or demolition orders in relation to their own properties, they may decide to demolish properties or redevelop areas. In such cases possession can be gained under Grounds 10 or 10A (see appendix to chapter 7) which require the landlord to make suitable alternative accommodation available for the tenant.

11.66   For tenants of other landlords who lose their homes as a result of a prohibition order, demolition order or clearance order, the local authority has a duty to ensure that some form of alternative accommodation is available. The Land Compensation Act 1973 provides that wherever

> ... suitable alternative residential accommodation on reasonable terms is not otherwise available to that person, then ... it shall be the duty of the relevant authority to secure that he will be provided with such other accommodation.

However, this duty has been interpreted by the courts as requiring the authority to do no more than to act reasonably and to do its best, as soon as practicable, to provide the person with other accommodation. The authority is not required to give the person priority over other people on the waiting list.[35] Temporary accommodation will be sufficient pending permanent accommodation becoming available.[36] Many local authorities award a certain level of priority under their

---

34 Land Compensation Act 1973 s30; Home Loss Payments (Prescribed Amounts) (England) Regulations 2008 SI No 1598. The prescribed amounts are usually increased on a regular basis.

35 *R v Bristol Corporation ex p Hendy* [1974] 1 All ER 1047.

36 *R v East Hertfordshire DC ex p Smith* (1990) 23 HLR 26, CA.

allocation schemes to those forced to move because of demolition and redevelopment schemes (see chapter 17).

Houses in multiple occupation

11.67   HMOs are buildings in which more than one household lives, sharing facilities. The Housing Act 2004 has introduced a new system of regulation in relation to HMOs.

11.68   The following are now defined as HMOs:[37]

- a house or flat which is let to three or more tenants who form two or more households and who share a kitchen, bathroom or toilet;
- a house converted into bed-sits or other forms of non-self-contained accommodation which is let to three or more tenants who form two or more households;
- a house converted into one or more flats which are not wholly self-contained (ie, do not contain within the flat a kitchen, bathroom and toilet) and which is occupied by three or more tenants who form two or more households;
- a building converted entirely into self-contained flats if the conversion did not meet the standards of the Building Regulations 1991[38] and more than one-third of the flats are let on short-term tenancies.

11.69   In order to be an HMO the property must be used by the occupiers as their only or main residence[39] and must be used solely or mainly as residential accommodation.

11.70   A single household means members of the same family, which includes spouses, unmarried couples (including same-sex couples) and blood relatives.[40]

Mandatory licensing

11.71   Larger HMOs are subject to mandatory licensing operated by the local authority. These are HMOs which:

- have five or more occupants;
- comprise two or more households; and
- are situated in a dwelling that has three or more habitable storeys.

---

37   HA 2004 ss254–260. The Localism Act 2011 will exempt fully mutual co-operatives from the HMO requirements.
38   Building Regulations 1991 SI No 2768.
39   This includes students occupying while undertaking a full-time course of education and those occupying a building as a refuge: HA 2004 s259(2).
40   HA 2004 s258.

11.72   Application must be made to the local authority for a licence and before granting a licence the authority must be satisfied that:

- the HMO is reasonably suitable for occupation for the number of people allowed under the licence;
- the proposed licence holder is a fit and proper person and the most appropriate person to hold the licence;
- the proposed manager, if there is one, is a fit and proper person;
- the proposed management arrangements are satisfactory and the manager(s) competent;
- the financial structures for the management are suitable.

11.73   An appeal against the refusal of a licence is to a residential property tribunal and should be made within 28 days.

Penalties for failing to apply for a licence

Fines

11.74   If a landlord fails to apply for a licence he or she commits an offence and can be fined up to £20,000.[41]

Rent repayment orders

11.75   Furthermore, a tenant living in a property that should have been licensed but was not can apply to a Residential Property Tribunal to re-claim rent paid during the unlicensed period, for a maximum period of 12 months and the local authority can reclaim the total amount of housing benefit paid during the unlicensed period.[42]

Restriction on possession proceedings

11.76   No section 21 notice may be given in relation to a shorthold tenancy of the whole or part of an unlicenced house so long as it remains unlicenced. An assured shorthold tenant would therefore have a defence against a claim for possession (see para 7.2).[43]

Selective registration

11.77   In addition to the mandatory scheme, Housing Act 2004 provides for local authorities to operate local registration and licensing schemes for HMOs that do not fall within the mandatory scheme.

---

41   HA 2004 s95.
42   HA 2004 s73.
43   HA 2004 s98.

Overcrowding

11.78   The mandatory licensing provisions for HMOs give local authorities the power to specify the number of people permitted to live in a property. It is an offence to permit more people than the maximum specified and the offence carries a fine of up to £20,000.

11.79   Overcrowding is also relevant to the hazard rating process. One of the 'matters and circumstances' that may give rise to a potential hazard is 'a lack of adequate space for living and sleeping'. Depending on the number of occupants and the likely consequences in relation to the health and safety of the occupants overcrowding may therefore create a Category 1 or Category 2 hazard in any dwelling.

Statutory overcrowding

11.80   The Housing Act 1985 still sets out the statutory test for over-crowding.[44] The provision is often misunderstood. The statutory overcrowding test is the basis for local authority powers to prevent overcrowding in private sector dwellings. Overcrowding was first recognised in legislation in the Nuisance Removal Act of 1855. The concern was about the moral as well as the health consequences of overcrowding, hence a statutory definition that focuses on preventing people of opposite sex (other than couples) being required to share a sleeping room.

11.81   There are two alternative tests to determine whether a dwelling is statutorily overcrowded: the room standard and the space standard.[45] Under the room standard, a household is overcrowded whenever two persons of the opposite sex must share a sleeping room. However, in applying the room standard, children under the age of ten are not considered at all. Under the space standard the number of people in the household is compared with either the number of sleeping rooms or the floor area of those rooms. In applying the space standard, children under the age of ten count as half a person and children under the age of one are not considered at all. Whichever standard is applied, living rooms are considered to be rooms in which people can sleep.

11.82   An occupier or landlord may be prosecuted for causing premises to be statutorily overcrowded but no offence is committed if the overcrowding is caused by children in the household reaching the age of ten. In practice, many overcrowded households are living in dwellings owned by local authorities and registered social landlords

---

44   HA 2004 makes provision for this test to be amended by regulations but there are no firm plans to do this at present.

45   HA 1985 ss325 and 326.

(RSLs) and have become overcrowded because of the natural growth of their families.[46]

11.83 Many occupiers who live in overcrowded accommodation believe that if they are statutorily overcrowded they must be entitled to be transferred or allocated social housing. Unfortunately, this is not the case. Most allocation and transfer schemes give some priority to overcrowded households but this will not guarantee an offer of more suitable accommodation. Furthermore, statutory overcrowding does not mean that the occupiers will qualify as homeless although it is one factor an authority must take into account when deciding whether it is reasonable for the occupier to remain in occupation. See *Harouki v Kensington & Chelsea RLBC*[47] at para 14.186.

Decent Homes Standard

11.84 In the green paper *Quality and Choice: A Decent Home for All*, published in July 2000, the government set out targets in relation to the quality of social housing. The green paper defined a 'decent home' as 'one which is wind and weather tight, warm and has modern facilities'. The two targets set by the government were:

- to reduce by one-third the number of dwellings in the social rented sector which fall below the standard by 2004; and
- to have all social rented homes meet the standard by 2010.

11.85 The Decent Homes Standard is based around four components. To comply with the Standard a dwelling should:

- be free from Category 1 hazards;
- be in a reasonable state of repair;
- have reasonably modern facilities (in particular kitchens and bathrooms); and
- offer a reasonable degree of thermal comfort, which means having efficient heating, insulation and ventilation.

11.86 Both targets were missed. The Homes and Communities Agency is now responsible for the backlog Decent Homes programme and estimates that 92 per cent of homes in the social sector satisfied the Decent Homes Standard by the end of 2010. It is now intended that the target of all social rented homes meeting the standard will be achieved by 2015.

---

46 The offence can also be committed by a local authority but the consent of the Attorney-General is needed for an authority to be prosecuted.

47 [2007] EWCA Civ 1000.

Gas Safety Regulations

11.87   Under the Gas Safety (Installation and Use) Regulations 1998[48] landlords are legally responsible for making sure that any gas appliances,
gas piping and flues are well maintained and safe.[49] The landlord
must ensure that an annual gas safety check is carried out by a registered gas engineer.[50] A landlord who fails to do so commits a criminal offence.

11.88   The regulations are enforced by the Health and Safety Executive
(HSE) whose website is www.hse.gov.uk. This gives information
about the local HSE offices to whom complaint may be made. Alternatively, the matter can be reported to the local authority who may
take action under the HA 2004, see above, paras 11.17–11.36.

11.89   The duty is owed by any landlord of a short-term tenancy, for
example, a tenancy for a period of seven years or less, and to residential licences. It does not apply to long leases.

---

48 SI No 2451.
49 Reg 36.
50 Reg 36(3). The register is now kept by Gas Safe who replaced CORGI. Gas Safe
    is the national watchdog for gas safety. All registered gas engineers must carry
    photo ID bearing their registration number. This can be checked on the Gas
    Safe website at www.gassaferegister.co.uk.

CHAPTER 12

Relationship breakdown

Key points

- Being married or in a civil partnership with someone gives a person the right to occupy the shared home and to pay the rent or mortgage. These are known as 'home rights'.
- Additionally, where accommodation is shared the court can make orders to regulate rights of occupation. An 'occupation order' may give a person a right to occupy and/or prevent a person otherwise entitled to occupy accommodation from exercising a right to occupy.
- To protect a person from violence or harassment a 'non-molestation order' may be made against any 'associated person'. Associated persons are not confined to those who are or have been a 'couple'. It includes relatives and other people who share accommodation.
- It is a criminal offence to breach a non-molestation order without reasonable excuse.
- Non-molestation orders and occupation orders are for limited duration to protect a person or child until a long-term housing solution is achieved.
- If the shared home is rented and the parties are married, civil partners or cohabitants the court can transfer the tenancy from one party to the other.
- Where property is owned by one or both parties the court may transfer ownership or order a sale only if the parties are married or in a civil partnership.
- A person who is not a legal owner may be able to establish a beneficial interest by having contributed to the purchase of a property.
- Where the parties have children the court can transfer a tenancy or ownership for the benefit of the children.

Introduction

12.1   This chapter deals with some of the housing issues that arise when a relationship breaks down. Where the parties are in dispute about finance, property and/or children it will be necessary to consult a specialist family lawyer. This chapter, therefore, provides only an overview of the following issues:

Immediate/short-term issues:
- protection from domestic violence;
- establishing rights of occupation;
- homeless applications.

Long-term solutions – property adjustment:
- transfer of tenancies;
- owner-occupied accommodation.

Immediate/short-term issues

Protection from domestic violence

12.2 Where someone is facing violence within or around the home he or she may do one or more of the following:
- apply to the local authority as a homeless person (see paras 12.3–12.4);
- obtain emergency shelter in a refuge or with friends or family (see paras 12.5–12.7);
- apply to the court for an injunction (a non-molestation order) and/or for an order excluding the prepetrator from the home (an occupation order), see paras 12.8–12.68.

Homeless applications

12.3 A person is homeless if it is probable that continuing to occupy accommodation will lead to violence against him or her. Violence is defined as 'violence from another person; or threats of violence from another person which are likely to be carried out',[1] it need not be physical violence, see paras 14.177–14.181. A local authority only has a duty to house applicants who have priority need. This includes pregnant women, those with dependent children and those considered vulnerable as a result of having become homeless because of violence, see paras 14.195–14.199.

12.4 Some applicants will want temporary accommodation only until they can take other steps, such as applying for an injunction, an occupation order and/or a property adjustment order. Some applicants, however, may wish to be permanently accommodated away from the home in which they suffered domestic violence. An authority cannot

---

1 Housing Act (HA) 1996 s177, see para 14.152.

find that a person is intentionally homeless because the person does not wish to seek an injunction and return home, see para 14.178.

Women's refuges

12.5   A local authority may discharge its immediate duty to secure emergency accommodation by securing a place in a refuge. It is also possible to contact the National Domestic Violence Helpline directly to find a place in a refuge.[2]

12.6   Refuge places are generally available only to people who have the funds to pay for the accommodation or who can claim housing benefit. Victims of violence who are subject to immigration control may not be entitled to claim benefits or apply as homeless, see paras 9.16 and 14.1. Their only option may be to seek help from social services if they have children or have community care needs, see chapters 18 and 19.

12.7   Women's Aid and Refuge offer refuge only to female victims of domestic violence. Information about support available to male victims of domestic violence may be obtained by contacting Supportline at www.supportline.org.uk and Respect at www.respect.uk.net, which focuses on the causes of domestic violence and offers a telephone advice service to male victims of domestic violence: www.mensadviceline.org.uk.

Non-molestation orders

12.8   The courts' powers to make injunctions to protect the victims of domestic violence are found in the Family Law Act (FLA) 1996 Part IV. The injunction is known as a non-molestation order, which means an order that:[3]

- prohibits a person from molesting an 'associated person'; and/or
- prohibits a person from molesting a 'relevant child'.

What is molestation?

12.9   The term is not defined in legislation. It covers actual or threatened violence but also includes behaviour that may be considered to be

---

2   Womens' Aid and Refuge jointly operate the National Domestic Violence Helpline: Tel 0808 200 0247. The Respect telephone advice line for male victims is 0808 801 0327.
3   FLA 1996 s42.

'pestering'.[4] It has been held to include 'any conduct which can properly be regarded as such a degree of harassment as to call for the intervention of the court'.[5] The following are examples of behaviour that amounts to molestation:

- a man, who had previously been violent, repeatedly calling on his ex-wife at her home and workplace, making a 'perfect nuisance of himself', knowing that his behaviour was frightening to his ex-wife;[6]
- a man giving his wife notes that were upsetting and intercepting her journey to the railway station;[7]
- a man rifling through a woman's handbag.[8]

12.10 It has been held that an order cannot be granted to an applicant who is living with and intends to continue living with the respondent.[9] The decision was not a decision of a higher court and is not therefore binding. However, where a couple are still living together and intend to continue to do so the courts are likely to take a different view of what behaviour amounts to molestation than where the relationship has ended and one is still 'pestering' the other.

Associated person

12.11 A person is associated with another person if:[10]

- they are or have been married to each other;
- they are or have been civil partners;
- they are cohabitants or former cohabitants ie a couple who live together as husband and wife or (if of the same sex) in an equivalent relationship;
- they live or have lived in the same household, otherwise than merely by reason of one of them being the other's employee, tenant, lodger or boarder;
- they are relatives;[11]
- they have agreed to marry each other;

---

4 *Vaughan v Vaughan* [1973] 3 All ER 449.
5 *Horner v Horner* [1982] Fam 90, Ormrod LJ at 93.
6 *Vaughan v Vaughan* [1973] 3 All ER 449.
7 *Horner v Horner* [1982] Fam 90.
8 *Spencer v Camacho* (1983) 4 FLR 662.
9 *F v F* [1989] 2 FLR 451, Nigel Fricker, QC.
10 FLA 1996 s62(3).
11 Relatives are defined in FLA 1996 s63(1).

- they have entered into a civil partnership agreement, ie an agreement to become civil partners;[12]
- they 'have or have had an intimate personal relationship with each other which is or was of significant duration';[13]
- in relation to any child, they are both parents of the child or have or have had parental responsibility for the child;
- in relation to an adopted child, one person is the natural parent or grandparent and the other is either the child or any adoptive parent or prospective adoptive parent;
- they are parties to the same family proceedings (not under FLA 1996 Part IV).[14]

Relevant child

12.12   In addition, the court has a general power to make an order in relation to 'any relevant child'. A 'relevant child' means:

- any child who is living with either party;
- any child in relation to whom an order is in question in the proceedings;[15] and
- any other child whose interests the court considers relevant.[16]

12.13   A relevant child therefore includes any child the court considers needs protection.

12.14   A child may apply for an order but the leave of the court is required if the child is under the age of 16. The court will grant leave only if satisfied that the child has sufficient understanding to make the proposed application.[17]

When will the court make an order?

12.15   In deciding whether to make an order the court must have regard to 'all the circumstances including the need to secure the health, safety and well-being' of the applicant and any relevant child.[18]

---

12   This is defined in the Civil Partnership Act 2004 s73. Orders in relation to those who have agreed to marry or agreed to be civil partners can only be made within three years of the termination of the agreement: s42(4)–(4ZA).

13   FLA 1996 s62(3)(ea).

14   This would include a party to adoption proceedings, such as the natural father.

15   The proceedings may be under the Adoption Act 1976, Adoption and Children Act 2002 or Children Act 1989.

16   FLA 1996 s62(2).

17   FLA 1996 s43.

18   FLA 1996 s42(5).

12.16   As a general rule, the courts are reluctant to grant civil injunctions against anyone who is mentally ill because the person may not be capable of complying with the order and the order may not be enforceable by way of committal.[19]

12.17   It is common practice where the respondent attends the hearing for the court to accept an undertaking instead of making an injunction. An undertaking should not be accepted in a case where the respondent has used or threatened violence against the applicant or a child. In such a case the court should make a non-molestation order, breach of which is a criminal offence, see para 12.21 below.[20]

Urgent cases – orders without notice

12.18   Under FLA 1996 s5 the court may make an order before the respondent has been given notice of the proceedings. In deciding whether to do so, the court must consider all of the circumstances including:

- a risk of significant harm[21] to the applicant or a relevant child if the order is not made immediately;
- whether it is likely that the applicant will be deterred or prevented from pursuing the application if an order is not made immediately; and
- whether there is reason to believe that the respondent is aware of the proceedings but deliberately evading service and that the applicant or a relevant child will be seriously prejudiced by any delay in arranging service of the papers.

12.19   If an order is made without notice to the respondent, he or she must be given an opportunity to make representations at a full hearing. The practice of the courts when making a without notice order is either to list the application for a full hearing at a later date, or to give the respondent the right to apply for a full hearing, the order remaining in force until any further hearing.

---

19   *Wookey v Wookey* [1991] 3 WLR 135.
20   FLA 1996 s46(3A).
21   'Harm' is defined in FLA 1996 s63. In relation to an adult it means ill treatment or the impairment of physical or mental health and, in relation to a child it means ill treatment or the impairment of physical or mental health or development.

Scope of a non-molestation order

12.20   The order may prohibit molestation in general, prohibit particular acts of molestation, or both. It may be for a specified period or until further order.[22]

Sanctions for breach of non-molestation order

12.21   Since 1 July 2007 it has been a criminal offence to breach a non-molestation order without reasonable excuse.[23] The offence can only be committed at a time when the respondent is aware of the existence of the order. The maximum punishment is up to five years' imprisonment and/or a fine, if dealt with by a Crown Court. If the magistrates' court deals with the case, the maximum punishment is up to 12 months' imprisonment and/or a fine not exceeding £5,000.

12.22   In consequence of the new criminal offence, the court can no longer attach a power of arrest to a non-molestation order. This is in contrast to occupation orders in respect of which the court can still attach power of arrest, see para 12.67 below.

12.23   It is still possible for a person who breaches a non-molestation order to be committed to prison for contempt of court, see paras 10.172 and 22.116. However, a person cannot be convicted of the criminal offence of breaching a non-molestation order *and* punished for contempt of court.[24]

Protection from Harassment Act 1997

12.24   A victim may also apply for an injunction under the Protection from Harassment Act (PHA) 1997 or make a complaint to the police who can prosecute a person guilty of harassment. See paras 8.101–8.114 for a summary of the provisions of the Act.

Occupation orders

12.25   In addition to or instead of a non-molestation order an application may be made for an occupation order under the Family Law Act 1996. An occupation order may grant a person a right to occupy and may prevent another person from interfering with such a right. It may also suspend another person's rights of occupation or even exclude

---

22   FLA 1996 s42(6)–(7).
23   FLA 1996 s42A was inserted by the Domestic Violence, Crime and Victims Act 2004 s1.
24   FLA 1996 s42A(3) and (4).

the person from the area where the home is. The purpose of an occupation order is to provide short-term protection where there has been violence or where one of the parties, or children living in the home, are likely to suffer harm without the court's intervention.

12.26   Occupation orders are always for a temporary period pending a more long-term arrangement being agreed or ordered by a court.

12.27   The courts' powers under the Family Law Act 1996 depend on the parties' existing rights of occupation. A person may have a right to occupy under the general law, for example, because he or she is a tenant or owner or under FLA 1996 by virtue of marriage to or civil partnership with the tenant or owner. These rights of occupation are summarised below, paras 12.28–12.64.

Rights to occupy under the general law

Joint tenancy/jointly owned property

12.28   Where accommodation is let to two joint tenants or is jointly owned both are entitled to occupy the whole of the accommodation, see paras 1.50–1.53. Other than by applying for an order under the Family Law Act 1996, one joint tenant or owner cannot exclude the other.

12.29   However, one joint tenant can terminate a joint tenancy without the consent of the other (see para 1.65). This may be done in order to frustrate a future application for a transfer into the sole name of one of the joint tenants (see below para 12.88). It is also sometimes encouraged by local authority landlords that also have a duty to accommodate the victim of domestic violence. The notice to quit determines the tenancy and the authority can then seek a possession order.

12.30   If seeking to procure a notice to quit, an authority must consider the remaining occupier's right to respect for his or her home under the European Convention on Human Rights and whether such a course of action is necessary and proportionate.[25]

Sole tenancy/sole ownership

12.31   Where one party is the sole tenant or sole owner of a property and the parties are not married or in a civil partnership that person's cohabitant does not have a right to occupy. He or she has a licence (permission) to occupy given by the sole tenant or owner. Because they share the accommodation the tenant or owner may give the other

---

25 See *McCann v UK*, App No 19009/04, 13 May 2008, ECtHR. See paras 7.100–7.144.

reasonable notice to leave (see para 1.122). What is reasonable notice depends on the circumstances. If there has been violence or unreasonable behaviour, very short or immediate notice may be considered reasonable. The notice need not be in writing.

12.32   After the period of notice has expired, the tenant or owner can exclude the cohabitant by changing the locks. However, the use of force to evict a person who is inside the home is a criminal offence under the Criminal Law Act 1977 (see para 8.41).

12.33   Where a cohabitant refuses to leave, a sole tenant or owner may apply for a possession order and use the court bailiffs to evict, even though under landlord and tenant law this is not necessary. See chapter 6 for an explanation of the procedure for possession claims and chapter 22 for a general description of civil proceedings.

12.34   In theory, a person who has been excluded and believes that he or she was not given reasonable notice can apply to a court for an injunction ordering the other party to allow him or her to continue to occupy until reasonable notice has expired. In practice, a court is unlikely to make an order that forces two people to live together, even for a short period, after relationship has broken down.

Rights to occupy under FLA 1996 – home rights

12.35   The right of a spouse to occupy the 'matrimonial home' is well established and such rights were prevously referred to as 'matrimonial home rights'. Since the Civil Partnership Act 2004 these rights have been renamed 'home rights': a person has a legal right to occupy accommodation that is solely owned or rented by his or her spouse or civil partner, provided it is or has been their shared home during the marriage or civil partnership.[26]

12.36   Home rights are set out in FLA 1996 s30. The following points should be noted:

- Home rights only exist in relation to accommodation which is, has in the past been, or was intended to be, a matrimonial home or a civil partnership home.[27]
- Home rights can exist in relation to a dwelling-house, which includes a building or part of a building, a caravan, house-boat or any structure occupied as a dwelling.[28]

---

26 FLA 1996 s30. The provisions are not limited to rights of occupation under tenancies. Section 30(1)(b) also refers to 'any enactment giving ... the right to remain in occupation'.

27 FLA 1996 s30(7).

28 FLA 1996 s63(1).

- If the spouse or civil partner claiming home rights is in actual occupation, the right exists independently of the court. However, if the person is not in actual occupation, he or she must apply for the permission of the court to gain the right to enter and occupy.[29]
- The right of occupation ends when the marriage or civil partnership ends, unless extended by court order.[30]

12.37 In relation to tenancies, the occupation of a spouse or civil partner satisfies any residence condition necessary for the tenant to have long-term security.[31]

12.38 A spouse or civil partner exercising a home right is entitled to pay rent or mortgage payments, and any payment or offer of payment is as good as if made by the tenant or borrower.[32] Housing benefit can be awarded if necessary to enable the person to continue living in the home (see para 9.15).

12.39 Where accommodation is owner-occupied, home rights can be registered as a charge with the Land Registry.[33] This would protect the right in the event that the sole owner tried to sell the property.

Applying for an occupation order

12.40 Different provisions apply depending on the status of the applicant and whether he or she has a right to occupy.

FLA 1996 s33: applicant entitled to occupy

12.41 Most applications are made under FLA 1996 s33, which applies when the applicant has a right to occupy, whether under the general law or by virtue of a home right under FLA 1996, see para 12.35 above.

The court's powers under FLA 1996 s33

12.42 The court may make an order to:[34]

- enforce the right of occupation against the other person (the respondent);

29 FLA 1996 s30(2).
30 FLA 1996 s30(8)(a).
31 FLA 1996 s30(4). See paras 4.2–4.12 for an explanation of the issues arising in relation to tenants' residence conditions.
32 FLA 1996 s30(3). This means, for example, that if a landlord refuses a payment from the spouse or civil partner, there would be a defence to a possession claim based on rent arrears.
33 FLA 1996 s31.
34 FLA 1996 s33(3).

- require the respondent to permit the applicant to enter and remain in the home;
- regulate the occupation of the home by either or both parties;
- prohibit, suspend or restrict the rights of a respondent who is ordinarily entitled to occupy under landlord and tenant law;
- restrict or terminate a right of occupation the respondent has under FLA 1996 s30 (home rights);
- require the respondent to leave the home or part of it;
- exclude the respondent from a defined area where the home is.

In practice the courts will usually make orders to restrict a right of occupation where there has been violence.

12.43   The court may also make orders declaring that a person has a right of occupation by virtue of the general law or under FLA 1996 s30, where this is in dispute. Such orders simply state the entitlement and do not restrict the exercise of any right of occupation.

Criteria for making orders under FLA 1996 s33

12.44   When deciding whether to make an order and in what terms the court must have regard to all of the circumstances, including:[35]

- the housing needs and housing resources of each of the parties and any relevant child;
- the financial resources of each of the parties;
- the likely effect of any order, or refusal to make an order, on the health, safety or well-being of the parties and any relevant child; and
- the conduct of the parties in relation to each other and otherwise.

12.45   See para 12.12 above for the definition of 'relevant child'.

The balance of harm test

12.46   The court must make an order if it appears that the applicant or any relevant child is likely to suffer significant harm if an order is not made which is greater than the harm the respondent or any child is likely to suffer if an order *is* made.[36] There is a presumption therefore in favour of making an order.[37]

---

35   FLA 1996 s30(6).
36   FLA 1996 s33(7).
37   See para 12.18, note 21 for definition of harm.

12.47 When considering an occupation order and applying the balance of harm test the court will take account of whether an applicant or respondent is likely to be owed a homeless duty.

> In *B v B*[38] a woman left her husband because of his violence. She took their 2-year-old daughter leaving him and his 6-year-old son from a previous relationship in occupation of their home. She was placed in temporary accommodation by the local authority and applied for an occupation order. An order was made ordering the husband to vacate with his son.
> The Court of Appeal allowed his appeal. The authority was likely to find that he was intentionally homeless and that no housing duty was owed. The likely harm to the son would therefore be greater to that caused to the wife and daughter who would be housed by the local authority.

12.48 When considering an occupation order a central issue will be which party is likely to have primary responsibility for any children in the future. An application for an occupation order can be made at the same time as an application for a residence order under the Children Act 1989.[39]

12.49 Where the court is making a declaratory order relating to entitlement rather than restricting the exercise of a right of occupation, the balance of harm test need not be applied.

How long does the order last?

12.50 Occupation orders are for limited duration. An order must be for a specified period, until a specified event or until further order.[40]

12.51 The court may make an order that home rights extend beyond the death of the spouse or civil partner or the end of the marriage or civil partnership.[41]

FLA 1996 s35: applicant (former spouse or civil partner) not entitled to occupy

12.52 An application for an occupation order may be made by a former spouse or former civil partner who has no existing right of occupation.[42] This

---

38 [1999] 1 FLR 715, CA.
39 FLA 1996 s39(2).
40 FLA 1996 s33(10).
41 FLA 1996 s30(5).
42 FLA 1996 s35.

would be the case when a marriage or civil partnership has ended, thereby terminating any home rights previously enjoyed (under FLA 1996 s30). An order may only be made in respect of a dwelling which was or was intended to be the matrimonial or civil partnership home. The application will be against the former spouse or civil partner.

12.53　If an order is made it must:

- if the applicant is in occupation, give the applicant the right not to be evicted or excluded from the home and prohibit the respondent from doing so;
- if the applicant is not in occupation, give the applicant the right to enter into and occupy the home and require the respondent to permit the exercise of the right.

12.54　An order may also restrict the respondent's rights of occupation, as under FLA 1996 s33 (see para 12.42 above).

12.55　When considering an application for occupation rights under FLA 1996 s35 the court must apply the criteria set out at para 12.44 above but in addition the court must consider the following:

- the length of time that has elapsed since the parties ceased to live together;
- the length of time that has elapsed since the marriage or civil partnership ended;[43] and
- the existence of any pending proceedings for property transfer or relating to the legal or beneficial ownership of the home, see para 12.96 below.[44]

12.56　If the court is considering an order that restricts the respondent's occupation rights, the court need not take account of the additional considerations set out above (para 12.55), save for the time since the parties lived together. However, the balance of harm test must be applied, see para 12.46 above.

12.57　An order under FLA 1996 s35 may not be made for a period longer than six months, but one application to extend the period for a further six months may be made.

FLA 1996 s36: applicant (cohabitant or former cohabitant) not entitled to occupy

12.58　A cohabitant who has no right of occupation may apply under FLA 1996 s36 for an occupation order. An order may only be made in

---

43　FLA 1996 s35(6)(f).
44　FLA 1996 s35(6)(g). Such applications may be pending under the Matrimonial Causes Act 1973, Civil Partnership Act 2004 or Children Act 1989.

respect of a dwelling in which the parties cohabit or at any time cohabited or intended to cohabit. The application will be against the other cohabitant or former cohabitant.

12.59 If an order is made it must:

- if the applicant is in occupation, give the applicant the right not to be evicted or excluded from the home and prohibit the respondent from doing so;
- if the applicant is not in occupation, give the applicant the right to enter into and occupy the home and require the respondent to permit the exercise of the right.

12.60 An order may also restrict the respondent's rights of occupation.

12.61 When considering an application for occupation rights under FLA 1996 s36 the court must apply the criteria set out at para 12.44 above but in addition the court must consider the following:

- the nature of the parties' relationship and in particular the level of commitment involved in it;
- the length of time during which they cohabited;
- whether there are or have been any children of the relationship, or children for whom both parties have or have had parental responsibility;
- the length of time that has elapsed since the parties ceased to live together; and
- the existence of any pending proceedings for financial provision under the Children Act 1989 or relating to the legal or beneficial ownership of the property, see para 12.96 below.

12.62 If the court is considering an order that restricts the respondent's occupation rights, the court need not take account of the additional considerations set out above (para 12.61) but the balance of harm test must be applied (see para 12.46 above). However, under FLA 1996 s36 there is no presumption that an order should be made, as there is when the court is considering making an order under FLA 1996 ss33 or 35.

12.63 An order under section 36 may not be made for a period longer than six months, but one application to extend the period for a further six months may be made.

Occupation orders under other circumstances

12.64 Under FLA 1996 s34 an occupation order can be made in relation to premises where the respondent's interest has passed to someone else. Under FLA 1996 s37 an order may be made where neither party is entitled to occupy the premises where the parties have been married or civil partners. Under FLA 1996 s38 an order may be made in respect of cohabitants where neither has a right to occupy.

Ancillary provisions

12.65 When making an occupation order the court may also make orders that:[45]

- either party is responsible for repairs and maintenance, the payment of rent, mortgage payments or other outgoings;
- a party occupying the home makes payments to the other;
- either party has possession or use of furniture or other contents; and
- either party takes reasonable steps to keep the home and any furniture or contents safe.

Cases of urgency

12.66 An occupation order may also be made at a hearing of which the respondent has not been given notice if the court considers it just and convenient to do so. The same criteria apply when considering making such an order as when considering a non-molestation order, see para 12.18. However, the court should only make an occupation order without notice in an exceptional case. In *Moat Housing Group-South Ltd v Harris and Hartless*,[46] which concerned anti-social behaviour injunctions, the Court of Appeal commented that 'as a matter of principle no order should be made in civil or family proceedings without notice to the other side unless there is a very good reason for departing from the general rule that notice must be given'.

Enforcement

12.67 The court can attach a power of arrest to an occupation order and must do so unless satisfied that the applicant or any child will be adequately protected without one. However, if the order is made without notice the court may attach a power of arrest only if it appears that the respondent has used or threatened violence against the applicant or a relevant child and there is a risk of significant harm to the applicant or child attributable to the respondent if a power of arrest is not attached immediately.

---

45 FLA 1996 s40(1).
46 [2005] EWCA Civ 287, 16 March 2005. See para 7.71 above.

12.68   Where a power of arrest is attached this means that the police can arrest the perpetrator and bring him or her before the civil courts to be punished for contempt of court. Otherwise, the applicant must make an application for committal, see paras 10.172 and 22.116. Breach of an occupation order, unlike breach of a non-molestation order, is not a criminal offence.

Long-term solutions

Property adjustment: courts' powers

12.69 Under Family Law Act 1996 when a marriage, civil partnership or cohabiting relationship breaks down the court can make an order transferring a tenancy from one party to another, or from joint names into sole names.

12.70   In addition, under the Matrimonial Causes Act (MCA) 1973[47] and the Civil Partnership Act (CPA) 2004[48] a court can transfer ownership of property from one party to the other on divorce or termination of a civil partnership.[49] Alternatively the court can order that a property is sold and the proceeds of sale divided between the parties.

12.71   Under the Children Act (CA) 1989 the court can order one party to transfer property to a child or to another adult for the benefit of the child.[50]

12.72   In addition, where a property is legally owned by one person, a party who made a contribution to the purchase may have a 'beneficial interest'. If this cannot be agreed between the parties an application may be made to a court. This is not the same as property adjustment; it is asking the court to make a declaration about the ownership of the property in accordance with the principles of the law of trusts. In the same proceedings the court can be asked to make an order for the sale of the property and the division of the proceeds of sale. A brief summary of the relevant principles is set out at paras 12.96–12.104 below.

47 MCA 1973 s24.
48 CPA 2004 Sch 5.
49 Such orders can also be made on judicial separation (married partners) or when a separation order is made (civil partners). This is where the partners are formally separated but the marriage or civil partnership has not ended.
50 CA 1989 Sch 1 para 1.

Transfer of tenancies

12.73   Under the Family Law Act 1996, on divorce, termination of a civil partnership[51] or if cohabitants cease to cohabit, the following tenancies may be transferred from one party to the other or from joint names into sole names:

- a secure tenancy;
- an introductory tenancy;
- an assured tenancy;
- an assured agricultural occupancy;
- a protected tenancy;
- a statutory tenancy;
- a statutory tenancy under the Rent (Agriculture) Act 1976.

12.74   The following are not capable of being transferred:

- any licence;
- a demoted tenancy;
- a family intervention tenancy.

12.75   See chapter 3 for an explanation of the types of tenancy listed above.

12.76   The court can only make an order in relation to a dwelling-house which was a home shared by the parties.[52]

12.77   A landlord must be notified of a pending application.[53]

How does the transfer happen?

12.78   Under the Family Law Act 1996 the court order has the effect of transferring the interest. The tenancy vests in the party at the date specified in the order.

12.79   Under the Matrimonial Causes Act 1973, Children Act 1989 and Civil Partnership Act (CPA) 2004 the court can order one party to assign the tenancy to the other. If such an order is made, the tenancy is only transferred when the actual assignment takes effect. This must be done by a properly executed deed entered into by both parties, see paras 4.56–4.57.[54]

12.80   If the tenancy agreement prohibits assignment, the fact that the court has ordered the assignment does not mean that it is not in breach of the tenancy agreement. An assignment in breach of the

---

51   Again, such orders may also be made when a decree of judicial separation or a separation order is made.

52   FLA 1996 Sch 7 para 4.

53   FLA 1996 Sch 7 para 14(1).

54   FLA 1996 Sch 7 para 5.

tenancy agreement will give the landlord a ground for possession but the ground is discretionary and the circumstances in which the transfer took place will be relevant.

When will the court transfer a tenancy?

12.81 The court must apply certain criteria when deciding whether to transfer a tenancy. These are set out in the relevant Acts.

12.82 Under the Family Law Act 1996, where the transfer is on the termination of a marriage or civil partnership, the criteria are:[55]

- the circumstances in which the tenancy was granted;
- the housing needs and housing resources of each of the parties and of any relevant child;
- the financial resources of each of the parties;
- the likely effect of any order, or refusal to make an order, on the health, safety or well-being of the parties and any relevant child;
- the suitability of the parties as tenants.

12.83 If parties are cohabitants the court must also have regard to:

- the nature of the parties' relationship and in particular the level of commitment involved in it;
- the length of time during which they cohabited;
- whether there are or have been any children of the relationship, or children for whom both parties have or have had parental responsibility;
- the length of time that has elapsed since the parties ceased to live together.

Effect of a transfer

12.84 When a tenancy is transferred, whether by a court order or by assignment, the new tenant takes the tenancy subject to any limits or restrictions on the tenancy. If the tenancy was a tenancy by succession, the new tenant will be treated as if he or she is a tenant by succession.[56]

12.85 The court can order that one party pays compensation to the other for the loss of the tenancy[57] and can also make orders setting out the respective liabilities of the parties, for example, ordering one party to pay rent arrears pre-dating the transfer.[58]

55 FLA 1996 Sch 7 paras 8(2)–(4), 9 and 10. See para 4.31 above for a description of the different rights of succession.
56 FLA 1996 Sch 7 para 10.
57 FLA 1996 Sch 7 para 11.
58 MCA 1973 s37(2) and CPA 2004 Sch 5 para 74.

Protecting home rights and/or safeguarding future transfer

Tenants' residence conditions

12.86   Where the tenant is out of occupation but his or her spouse or civil partner remains in occupation this fulfils any residence condition under the tenancy agreement, see above at para 12.37. However, this applies only as long as the marriage or civil partnership subsists. It is essential therefore that the tenancy is transferred before the divorce is made absolute or the civil partnership terminated. Otherwise the landlord may terminate the tenancy and evict the occupier on the basis that the tenancy has ceased to be statutorily protected.

Preventing dispositions that would frustrate a transfer

12.87   As indicated above (para 12.39), a spouse or civil partner can protect home rights in relation to owner-occupied accommodation by registering a charge at the Land Registry. Furthermore, the court can prevent a party from making a 'disposition' intended to defeat an application for a property adjustment order. If the disposition has already been made it can be set aside.[59]

12.88   A home right in relation to a tenancy cannot be registered. In most cases it will not be possible to 'sell' or transfer the tenancy to another person to avoid an application for a transfer to an ex-partner. However, the tenant can terminate the tenancy in order to defeat such an application. A sole tenant can do this by either surrendering the tenancy or by serving notice to quit.[60] A joint tenant can serve notice to quit to end a periodic joint tenancy, regardless of the wishes of the other joint tenant, see para 1.65.

12.89   A surrender is a disposition of property and could be prevented by the court or set aside where the parties are or have been married or in a civil partnership. However, a notice to quit is not a disposition and where a joint tenant serves notice to quit in order to prevent a future application for a transfer of the tenancy into the other tenant's sole name the court does not have the power to set the notice aside.[61]

12.90   A joint tenant can apply for an injunction to prevent the other party from serving notice to quit. This was suggested by the Court of Appeal in *Bater v Greenwich LBC*.[62] However, it is unclear whether an order prohibiting service of a notice to quit would render a notice

59   *Sanctuary Housing Association v Campbell* (2000) 32 HLR 100, CA.
60   See paras 1.62–1.78.
61   *Newlon Housing Association v Al-Sulamain* (1998) 30 HLR 1132, HL.
62   [1999] 4 All ER 944.

served in breach of the order ineffective. The point is undecided but it may be that while serving notice would be contempt of court the notice would nevertheless determine the joint tenancy.[63]

Assignment by agreement

12.91 Where the parties are in agreement that the tenancy should be transferred into the sole name of one person the tenancy may be assigned. However, in most cases assignment will be prohibited and an assignment in breach of the tenancy agreement will give the landlord a ground for possession. The landlord's consent should always be sought. If the landlord does not object to the proposed transfer, the landlord may, instead of consenting to an assignment, agree to a surrender and then grant a new tenancy to the party remaining in the home. Some social landlords have policies under which an offer of alternative accommodation will be made to the departing tenant on relationship breakdown. However, such policies are increasingly rare; more commonly a tenant who voluntarily leaves the home following the breakdown of a relationship will be left with the possibility of a homeless application and/or an application for an allocation. See paras 14.205–14.216 below for an explanation of the homeless duty when the care of children is to be shared by two parents living in different places.

12.92 If the landlord will not agree to an assignment, an application may be made for an order under the Family Law Act 1996 transferring the tenancy. The landlord will have an opportunity to make representations as to why the tenancy should not be transferred.

12.93 Under the Housing Act 1985 a secure tenant can assign to a person who would be qualified to succeed to the tenancy, see para 4.64. This would include a spouse or civil partner or a cohabitant who has lived with the tenant for at least one year and still does so immediately before the date of the assignment. However, such an assignment would prevent a future succession so a transfer under FLA 1996 may be preferred.

Owner-occupied accommodation

12.94 Under the Matrimonial Causes Act 1973 and Civil Partnership Act 2004 the court may transfer the ownership of property from one party to the other or may order the sale of property and the division of the proceeds of sale. An order for sale may be postponed until a future

63 *Harrow LBC v Johnstone* (1997) 29 HLR 475, HL.

date, for example when children reach a certain age. Such orders will usually be made as part of a package of financial provision and the assistance of a specialist family lawyer should be sought to negotiate and make the necessary applications.[64]

12.95   The court has no power to make such orders in relation to cohabitants unless there are children of the family, in which case an application can be made under the Children Act 1989 for the benefit of the children.

Beneficial ownership

12.96   Where property is held in the sole name of one party, another party may nevertheless have a 'beneficial' interest. This arises under the law of trust, see para 1.139.

12.97   An express trust may be created by deed setting out the terms of the trust.

12.98   In addition, a person who has contributed to the purchase of a property may be able to establish that an implied trust has arisen even though the parties did not expressly agree that the property was to be held on trust.

12.99   Where the parties intended that the interest would be shared this is known as a 'constructive trust' and indirect as well as direct contributions may be taken into account, such as payment of household expenses.

12.100   Where there is no shared intention that the interest would be shared this is known as a 'resulting trust'. In such a case only direct contributions to the purchase will be taken into account. This would include paying part of the deposit or the mortgage payments.

12.101   The extent of the beneficial interest will correspond to the contributions made. If the parties made equal contributions to the deposit and the mortgage payments the property will usually be held in equal shares.

12.102   If the parties are in dispute about whether there is a trust or the extent of the respective shares it will be necessary to apply to the court for a declaration. The court can also order that the property be sold and the proceeds of sale (the 'equity') divided between the parties in the proportions determined by the court. See para 1.142.

---

64   It should be noted that the Legal Aid, Sentencing and Punishment of Offenders Bill will remove legal aid for family cases involving disputes between separating couples about children and financial provision, unless one party has been the victim of domestic violence from the other party.

12.103   Where a party is seeking to establish a beneficial interest, specialist advice should be sought. If the parties are able to reach agreement about the existence of a trust and their respective interests the costs of legal proceedings will be avoided. If not, the costs incurred will reduce the value of one or both parties' interests. This is the case even if one party is legally aided because the statutory charge will usually apply, see para 22.168.[65]

12.104   It should be noted that a spouse or civil partner who is a beneficial owner but not a legal owner is treated as having a right of occupation by virtue of FLA 1996 (as opposed to by virtue of the beneficial interest). Such a home right can be registered as a charge to prevent sale until resolution of any dispute about the beneficial ownership.[66]

65 Though in future legal aid will rarely be available for such proceedings, see para 12.94 and note 64 above.
66 FLA 1996 s30(9).

CHAPTER 13

Homelessness applications, inquiries and miscellaneous duties

continued

Key points

- A local authority should accept a homeless application and make formal inquiries if it has *reason to believe* a person *may be* homeless and eligible (an immigration test).
- If the authority also has *reason to believe* the person *may be* in priority need, interim accommodation must be provided until inquiries are complete and a decision made.
- 'Homeless Prevention' strategies often result in people being discouraged from making homeless applications and encouraged to find privately rented accommodation. A homeless person is entitled to pursue a homeless application and to insist on a formal written decision from the authority as to what housing duty, if any, is owed to him or her.
- The interim accommodation provided pending inquiry must be suitable but, because it is for a very temporary period, what is deemed suitable may be of a low standard.
- A failure or refusal to accept a homeless application or to provide suitable interim accommodation pending a decision can be challenged by an application for judicial review.
- An applicant who has had a negative decision may apply again to the same authority but the authority need not investigate an application based on the same facts. It is for the applicant to demonstrate that the application is not on the same facts.

Introduction

13.1   This chapter provides an overview of the law on homelessness, and examines the following issues:

- applications;
- interim accommodation pending decision;
- the local authority duty to make inquiries;
- repeat applications;
- miscellaneous duties.

13.2   Some homeless people are entitled to be provided with accommodation by a local housing authority. The duties of local authorities in relation to homeless people are set out in statute, with some of the detail being found in statutory instruments. Additionally, when dealing with homeless applications, local authorities must have regard to the *Homelessness Code of Guidance for Local Authorities* ('Homelessness Code'). Since 1997 there has been a clear distinction between a local authority's duty to accommodate homeless applicants and the way permanent accommodation is allocated by authorities. Part VII of the Housing Act (HA) 1996 sets out the homeless duties and Part VI deals with the way permanent accommodation is allocated.

Reference materials

13.3   The main reference materials when dealing with homeless applications are:

Housing Act 1996 Part VII	Sets out: the legal tests applied to decide whether a housing duty is owed; the nature of the housing duties; and the way decisions are challenged.
Homelessness Act 2002	Amended the HA 1996 and added some general duties to prepare and review homelessness strategies.
Homelessness Code of Guidance	A summary of the law and good practice. Local authorities must 'have regard' to the code. It is regularly updated. The current version is dated 6 July 2006 and came into force on 4 September 2006.[1]
Supplementary Guidance on Intentional Homelessness	Supplements the Code of Guidance – deals with how authorities should treat homeless applications from those who apply following mortgage difficulties (5 August 2009).
Statutory Guidance on the provision of accommodation for 16- and 17-year-olds	Sets out the arrangements local authority housing and social services departments should make for 16- and 17-year-olds (1 April 2010).
Homelessness (Priority Need for Accommodation) (England) Order 2002[2]	Sets out some additional categories of people with priority need.

1 All of the Codes and Guidance can be downloaded from the website of the Department for Communities and Local Government at: www.communities.gov.uk.

2 SI No 2051. This applies in England. A similar order applies in Wales, see para 14.197.

Allocation of Housing and Homelessness (Eligibility) (England) Regulations 2006[3]	Sets out the classes of people from abroad who are and are not eligible for homeless assistance.
Case-law	The courts are frequently asked to decide disputes between applicants and local authorities. The decisions of the Court of Appeal and above are binding. County courts generally follow the decisions of the Administrative Court. Previous decisions will be reflected in the Code of Guidance. Many challenges succeed because of a failure in the process of decision-making rather than on the merits of the decision itself.

13.4   A duty to provide accommodation specifically for homeless people was first introduced by the Housing (Homeless Persons) Act 1977. Previously, local authorities had various powers and duties to provide temporary accommodation only in emergencies.

13.5   The way a duty to accommodate homeless persons is established has changed little since 1977: the authority must investigate an application to satisfy itself of certain matters relating to the applicant's circumstances and the way in which he or she became homeless. The outcome of the authority's investigations will determine what duty is owed. This may range from simply providing advice and assistance to securing suitable accommodation for the applicant and his or her family. In some cases the authority's duty will be limited to providing a written decision giving reasons why no substantive duty is owed.

The 'full housing duty'

13.6   What has changed most significantly since the Housing (Homeless Persons) Act 1977 is the nature of the 'full housing duty'. Before the Housing Act (HA) 1996, a successful homeless applicant would usually be offered a long-term tenancy by the authority or other social landlord. HA 1996 was introduced because of concern that most permanent tenancies of social housing were being allocated to homeless applicants who had priority over those on local authority housing waiting lists. HA 1996 provides that the full housing duty to homeless

---

3 SI No 1294. For issues of eligibility other regulations relating to European nationals are also relevant: see para 14.40.

applicants is a duty to provide temporary accommodation only; the person's need for permanent accommodation is assessed in the same way as waiting list applicants. Everyone in need of housing, including those housed temporarily as homeless people, are allocated permanent accommodation through the particular authority's allocation scheme. All such schemes must comply with the provisions of HA 1996 Part VI, which specifies the groups to whom 'reasonable preference' must be given. Homeless people are a group that must be given reasonable preference, but local authorities have considerable discretion regarding how much priority to give each group. Given the shortage of social housing, this means that many successful homeless applicants may reside in 'temporary' accommodation under HA 1996 Part VII for many years before they obtain permanent accommodation under Part VI. The way permanent accommodation is allocated is dealt with in chapter 17.

13.7   The Localism Act 2011 will amend the housing duty further so that the authority's duty will be discharged by the making of a 'private accommodation offer'. At present local authorities can use private sector accommodation when discharging their duty to accommodate homeless applicants but if the applicant is forced to leave the private sector accommodation the authority still has an ongoing duty to provide suitable accommodation. Under the Localism Act, the authority's duty will end when it secures the private accommodation. However, provision is made for a person to be exempt from the priority need test on a further application. The current and proposed future housing duties are described in more detail in chapter 16.

Homelessness prevention

13.8   The number of people applying and being accepted as homeless and owed a housing duty (acceptances) increased year on year between 1997 and 2001. At the same time, families accommodated by authorities were spending longer periods in temporary accommodation before securing a permanent home. The government began to promote 'homelessness prevention' strategies following the publication of its report: *More than a roof – a report into tackling homelessness* in March 2003. Some local authorities have adopted measures to encourage homeless or potentially homeless applicants to find accommodation in the private sector by offering rent guarantee schemes and by liaising with private landlords to encourage lettings. However, many local authorities have also adopted procedures to discourage or even prevent people from pursuing homeless applications – such practices are commonly known as 'gatekeeping'. The recent homelessness statistics[4] show that the numbers of both homeless applications and homeless acceptances have fallen to the lowest levels since the early 1980s. Although 2010/11 saw a significant increase in homeless applications from an all time low in 2009/10, the total number of applications is still less than half those recorded in the years between 1998 and 2005. These figures, however, are based on local authority returns, which indicate only those applications recorded by the authority. What is not recorded is the number of homeless people who approach an authority, but whose approach is not recorded as a formal application. Ways of assisting those faced with 'gatekeeping' are discussed below at paras 13.29–13.33.

Summary of the homelessness tests and duties

13.9   A housing authority must be satisfied of certain matters (referred to here as the 'homelessness tests') before deciding whether a housing duty is owed. Each test is dealt with in chapter 14. They are summarised here because they are essential to an understanding of the process of homeless applications and the nature of the duty that may be owed.

13.10   The full housing duty will be owed if, after inquiry, the authority is satisfied of the following matters:

- the applicant is *homeless;*
- the applicant is *eligible for assistance* – an immigration test;
- the applicant has a *priority need;*
- the applicant is not *intentionally homeless.*

13.11   Although the full housing duty will be owed, it may be that the duty is not owed by the authority which investigated the application. At this point the authority *may* consider:

- whether the applicant can be referred to another authority to be housed by the other authority.

13.12   It is important that these tests are applied in the correct order because the duties of the authority depend on the outcome of each test. If an applicant 'fails' one test, it may be unnecessary to go on to determine other matters. A summary of the tests and the duties owed is as follows overleaf.

---

4   Available from the website of the Department for Communities and Local Government: www.communities.gov.uk.

The test	The duty
Is the applicant eligible?[5] Yes: Apply the next test	No: Decision letter only.
Is the applicant homeless? Yes: Apply the next test	No: Decision letter only.[6]
Is the applicant in priority need? Yes: Apply the next test	No: Decision letter and housing advice and assistance addressing the applicant's needs.[7]
Is the applicant intentionally homeless? No: Apply the next test	Yes: Decision letter and housing advice and assistance addressing the applicant's needs plus accommodation for a 'reasonable' period.
Can the applicant be referred elsewhere?	No: Full housing duty owed. Yes: Full housing duty owed by the other authority. Duty to accommodate temporarily continues until referral is accepted or any dispute resolved.

Making an application

13.13   It should be easy to apply as homeless to a local authority: no particular form of application is prescribed and an authority has a duty to make formal inquiries under HA 1996 Part VII if they 'have reason to believe' a person 'may be' homeless and eligible. Often, however, the opposite is true and the most difficult part of the process is persuading the authority to accept an application in the first place. Those who approach an authority for help may be told:

- 'you can't apply here as you have no local connection';
- 'you aren't homeless if you had somewhere to sleep last night';
- 'you have no priority need, so we can't help you';

---

5   An authority may inquire first into homelessness or eligibility. In either case, if the answer is no, the authority's duty is limited to issuing a decision letter giving reasons.

6   An applicant who is found not eligible or not homeless is entitled to use the advice and information services that authorities are bound to provide or fund locally but there is no specific duty to advise and assist the particular applicant.

7   An authority has the power to accommodate non-priority need applicants, but only if they are found not intentionally homeless.

- 'you were previously evicted for rent arrears or anti-social behaviour, so you will be found intentionally homeless';
- 'here is an application form for the housing waiting list';
- 'we can't see you until next week';
- 'we will make an appointment with the private sector team who can help you to find somewhere to live'.

13.14 In many cases the approach is not recorded or is recorded as a simple housing inquiry. It is unlawful and amounts to maladministration for an authority to refuse to accept a homeless application for such reasons.[8] However, it is often difficult to prove that the authority had evidence sufficient to trigger the duty to commence inquiries under HA 1996 Part VII. Advisers may therefore find it useful to ensure that a letter is sent or taken by the applicant summarising the situation and making clear that the person wishes to make an application under Part VII. See the appendix to this chapter for an example of such a letter.

The law on applications and the duty to make inquiries

13.15 HA 1996 ss183 and 184 provide that:

> ... where a person applies to a local housing authority for accommodation, or for assistance in obtaining accommodation, and the authority have reason to believe that he is or may be homeless or threatened with homelessness ... they shall make such enquiries as are necessary to satisfy themselves – whether he is eligible for assistance, and if so, whether any duty, and if so, what duty, is owed to him under [HA 1996 Part VII].

13.16 The duty to make inquiries under HA 1996 Part VII should therefore be triggered not only when a person specifically indicates a wish to make a homeless application, but whenever a person seeks help with housing, provided the authority has *reason to believe* that the applicant *may be* homeless or threatened with homelessness.[9]

---

8 See the Ombudsman report into a complaint against Thurrock Council: 05/A/09461. Three approaches had been made by a woman who was clearly homeless and in priority need. However, none resulted in a proper inquiry or any decision letter being issued. The Ombudsman found that there had been injustice caused by maladministration and recommended compensation of £2,250. See also the report into a complaint against Hammersmith & Fulham LBC, 09001262, published in January 2010.

9 See Code of Guidance, paras 6.2 and 6.6 and *Bury MBC v Gibbons* [2010] EWCA Civ 327, 26 March 2010.

13.17   Authorities must also ensure that emergency assistance is available to applicants out of office hours. This may be by arrangement with social services or sometimes the local police, who may arrange emergency accommodation until a formal application can be taken.[10]

13.18   A refusal to accept an application may be challenged by judicial review. See paras 2.4–2.40.

Restrictions on who can apply

13.19   HA 1996 Part VII imposes no restriction on who can make an application. However, the courts have considered arguments by local authorities that they are not bound to accept applications from the following:

- people in the UK unlawfully;
- dependent children; and
- people lacking mental capacity.

13.20   In *R on the application of Westminster v Castelli and Tristan-Garcia*[11] the Court of Appeal held that an authority was not bound to accept an application from a person who was present in the UK unlawfully. Since 1997 the eligibility test has excluded such people from assistance, along with those whose leave to remain in the UK is limited. An authority would now determine that an applicant was not eligible rather than refuse to accept an application. However, an applicant found to be ineligible has the right to a decision letter giving reasons and can challenge the decision by seeking a review and, if appropriate, by county court appeal.

13.21   Applications by children aged four years were considered by the House of Lords in *R v Oldham ex p Garlick* and *R v Bexley LBC ex p Bentum*.[12] The applications had been submitted on behalf of the children because the parents had been found intentionally homeless. The House of Lords held that the authorities owed no duty. This was not because an applicant must be an adult but because dependent children had no priority need: it was presumed that they were cared for by adults and it was the adults with whom they lived who had priority need.

13.22   While the House of Lords in *R v Oldham ex p Garlick* and *R v Bexley LBC ex p Bentum* held that the homeless duty was intended for

10 Code of Guidance, para 7.8.
11 (1996) 28 HLR 607, CA.
12 [1993] AC 509; (1993) 25 HLR 319, HL.

those who could decide whether or not to accept an offer of accommodation, and not for dependent children, it was acknowledged that the situation would be different where the children had left home and ceased to be dependent. Since the case was decided the Priority Need Order has been made, which specifically identifies homeless 16- and 17-year olds as having priority need. See paras 14.195–14.199 and chapter 19.

13.23   In *R v Tower Hamlets ex p Begum*[13] an application was submitted on behalf of a profoundly disabled adult whose parents had been found intentionally homeless.

The House of Lords held that an authority was entitled to refuse an application from someone who lacked the capacity to make an application herself, to instruct an agent to do so or to respond to an offer and understand the responsibilities of being a tenant.

Again, if such a person was in need of accommodation, social services would owe a duty, but this may not extend to the whole family.[14]

Multiple applications

13.24   It is possible for a person to apply to more than one authority at the same time. The Homelessness Code, at para 7.7, suggests that where this happens the authorities should agree which authority will take responsibility for making inquiries. In reality, many authorities will instead indicate that only one application can be pursued and that an application will be closed unless the other is withdrawn. This approach may be challenged, although it is difficult to see any benefit to pursuing more than one application simultaneously.

13.25   The issues that arise when a person makes a further application, having previously received a negative decision, or where an authority has discharged its duty are dealt with below at paras 13.59–13.76.

13 [1993] AC 509; (1993) 25 HLR 319, HL.
14 National Assistance Act 1948 s21. See paras 18.14–18.15.

Accommodation pending inquiries

13.26   An authority should accept an application if it has 'reason to believe' that a person may be homeless. However, it must still go on to make full inquiries to 'satisfy' itself of the necessary matters to decide what duty, if any, is owed. In most cases, the necessary inquiries will take several days at least, more often weeks or months. The Homelessness Code recommends that inquiries be completed within 33 working days,[15] but where the authority is seeking information from third parties they may take longer. In most cases authorities will have a duty to provide 'interim accommodation' until they have completed their inquiries. This duty is referred to as the 'section 188 duty'.

Accommodation duty: HA 1996 s188

13.27   Housing Act 1996 s188(1) provides:

> If the local housing authority have reason to believe that an applicant may be homeless, eligible for assistance and have a priority need, they shall secure that accommodation is available for his occupation pending a decision on the duty (if any) owed to him under [Part VII].

13.28   The key features of the duty under HA 1996 s188 are:

- the duty to provide interim accommodation is triggered by a low level of 'evidence': whenever the authority have reason to believe the applicant may be homeless, eligible and in priority need: s188(1);
- the duty arises immediately and there is no 'reasonable period' for a local authority to find accommodation;
- the duty arises irrespective of any possible referral to another local authority: s188(2);
- the duty ends when the applicant is notified of a decision: s188(3);
- the authority have a discretion to provide interim accommodation after a negative decision, pending a review: s188(3);
- the accommodation must be provided for the applicant and the family members he or she normally lives with, and for anyone who might reasonably be expected to live with the applicant: s176;
- the accommodation must be suitable: s206.

---

15   Homelessness Code of Guidance, para 6.16.

Common issues in relation to interim accommodation

Avoiding the section 188 duty

13.29　The Act is clear – applicants with apparent priority need who present as homeless to local authorities should not remain without accommodation until a final decision is made. However, the cost of providing interim accommodation is such that many authorities seek to avoid doing so. This is usually done in one of two ways, see paras 13.30 and 13.31.

Refusing to admit that a homeless application was made

13.30　This can be challenged by ensuring that the local authority has sufficient evidence such that the duty to inquire and to provide interim accommodation arises, for example, reason to believe that the person may be homeless, eligible and in priority need. A letter summarising the person's situation should be sufficient (see appendix to this chapter).

Arguing that there is no evidence that the person is homeless or in priority need

13.31　If the authority is saying that it has satisfied itself of these issues, a decision letter should be requested. If the authority is unable to provide a decision letter, or indicates that its inquiries are not complete, this itself indicates that the interim duty to accommodate is owed.

13.32　　An example of a letter to a local authority regarding the section 188 duty is in the appendix to this chapter.

13.33　　In both cases, if the authority maintains its refusal to provide interim accommodation, a claim for judicial review can be made.

Suitability of interim accommodation

13.34　The accommodation provided on an interim basis must be suitable. It is expressly provided that to be suitable, accommodation must be affordable.[16] Furthermore, in deciding what is suitable, the authority must have regard to the law on slum clearance, overcrowding and houses in multiple occupation: HA 1996 s210. The accommodation must be suitable for the particular needs of the applicant.[17]

16　Homelessness (Suitability of Accommodation) Order 1996 SI No 3204.
17　*R v Brent LBC ex p Omar* (1991) 23 HLR 446, QBD.

13.35   It is for the local authority to decide what is suitable and the temporary nature of the accommodation will be relevant: accommodation that is suitable for short-term occupation may not be suitable in the longer term. The limited resources of an authority may mean that accommodation secured for short-term occupation may not be of a high standard. However, there is a 'bottom line' for the standard, below which the accommodation could not be said to be suitable, however constrained resources are: see *R on the application of Sacupima v Newham LBC*.[18]

13.36   Any challenge to the suitability of interim accommodation must be brought by way of judicial review.

13.37   Because of the very temporary nature of the accommodation and the pressure on authorities' resources, the courts are reluctant to interfere with local authority decisions as to the suitability of section 188 accommodation. Set out below are a number of cases in which the issue has been considered.

> **Location**
>
> In *R on the application of Sacupima v Newham LBC*[19] a decision to provide section 188 accommodation in the Great Yarmouth area to a family settled in Newham was quashed. The authority had failed to have regard to the effect on the children's schooling and the employment of other family members.
>
> In *R on the application of Yumsak v Enfield LBC*[20] the court upheld the challenge to an offer of accommodation under section 188. The applicant was a single parent who had lived as an asylum-seeker in Enfield for seven years with her three children. The accommodation had been provided by social services. After being granted leave to remain in the UK, she applied as homeless and was provided with bed & breakfast accommodation in Birmingham. She contended that the accommodation was unsuitable as she suffered from epilepsy, she had no friends or family in Birmingham and her children's schooling would be disrupted. Furthermore, the children's father was based in London and was keen to maintain contact with the children. The court held that there was an interference with the applicant's rights under ECHR article 8 and that the authority had not provided any evidence to demonstrate that no other accommodation had been available or to justify the interference.

18   (2000) 33 HLR 1, CA, see para 13.37.
19   (2000) 33 HLR 1, CA.
20   [2002] EWHC 280 (Admin).

Split accommodation

In *R v Ealing LBC ex p Surdonja*[21] the authority made an offer of section 188 accommodation to a family comprising a couple and their three young children. The accommodation was at two separate addresses less than a mile apart. The court held that the accommodation was not suitable: section 176 requires that accommodation must be available for the applicant and those family members who normally live with the applicant.

Size

In *R on the application of Flash v Southwark LBC*[22] the applicant challenged the suitability of a one-bedroom flat provided for her and her grandson on the ground that it was too small. The court held that the offer was suitable: the grandson could sleep in the living room.

Bed & breakfast accommodation

13.38   Bed & breakfast (B&B) accommodation is commonly used as interim accommodation. The Homelessness Code provides that authorities should avoid using B&B accommodation wherever possible and, where it is used in an emergency situation applicants should be moved to more suitable accommodation as soon as possible (see para 7.6).

13.39   However, there may be specific reasons why B&B may not be suitable for particular applicants, such as those with disabilities or mental health problems.

13.40   In relation to families and pregnant women, B&B accommodation is not to be regarded as suitable unless there is no other accommodation available and then only for a period of up to six weeks.[23]

13.41   The Homelessness Code provides that B&B accommodation is unlikely to be suitable for 16- and 17-year-olds who are in need of support and that where it is used for this group it ought to be as a last

21 (1998) 31 HLR 686.
22 [2004] EWHC 717 (Admin).
23 Homelessness (Suitability of Accommodation) (England) Order 2003 SI No 3204. In Wales, the Homelessness (Suitability of Accommodation) (Wales) Order 2006 SI No 650 is more prescriptive in relation to the matters to be taken into account in relation to suitability, and more restrictive in relation to the use of B&B accommodation for any applicant.

resort for the shortest time possible. Furthermore, housing authorities should ensure that appropriate support is provided where necessary (see para 12.14). Statutory guidance issued by the Department for Children, Schools and Families in April 2010 also states that bed and breakfast accommodation is not appropriate for homeless 16- and 17-year olds, see para 19.41.

Refusal of offers made under section 188

13.42   The nature of the interim duty means that an applicant rarely has the opportunity to view accommodation or take advice if he or she believes it to be unsuitable. An applicant may be sent to the accommodation late in the evening, it may be a considerable distance away and may be in a hostel or B&B establishment. An applicant may fail to go to the accommodation or may decline to accept the offer. Alternatively, an applicant may move into the accommodation but be evicted because of his or her conduct.

13.43   In such a situation two issues arise:

- whether the authority has any further duty to make interim accommodation available; and
- the authority's duty to continue with its inquiries into the homeless application.

Continuation of the section 188 duty

13.44   If an applicant has refused an offer of interim accommodation, a decision must be made as to whether the authority's decision on suitability can be challenged. As indicated, accommodation may be deemed suitable for very short-term occupation that would not be suitable in the longer term. Because of this, successful challenges to the suitability of interim accommodation are rare. Applicants may be well advised to indicate to the authority that, having taken advice, they now wish to accept the accommodation. The HA 1996 section 188 duty is not like the full housing duty: there is no express provision that the duty ends because of a failure to accept an offer of interim accommodation. It may be argued that the applicant misunderstood the nature of the offer or did not intend to refuse it. An authority that adopts a rigid approach, maintaining that the duty has ended because of the failure to take up the offer may be challenged by way of judicial review.

13.45   Where an applicant is evicted from interim accommodation because of his or her behaviour, an authority may indicate that it has no further section 188 duty. There is no authoritative case-law on this issue but the Court of Appeal has considered it in relation to accommodation offered under National Assistance Act (NAA) 1948 s21.[24]

In *R v Kensington and Chelsea RLBC ex p Kujtim*[25] an asylum-seeker was provided with hotel accommodation by the authority under NAA 1948. He was evicted from two hotels because of his behaviour.

The Court of Appeal held that the duty under NAA 1948 s21 was a continuing duty: once a person had been assessed as needing accommodation, the authority was under a duty to provide it. However:

... if an applicant assessed as in need of ... accommodation [under section 21] either unreasonably refuses to accept the accommodation provided, or if, following its provision, by his conduct he manifests a persistent and unequivocal refusal to observe the reasonable requirements of the local authority in relation to the occupation of such accommodation then the local authority is entitled to treat its duty as discharged and to refuse to provide further accommodation. That will remain the position unless or until, upon some subsequent application, the applicant can satisfy the local authority that his needs remain such as to justify provision of ... accommodation and that there is no longer reason to think that he will persist in his refusal to observe the reasonable requirements of the local authority in respect of the provision of such accommodation.[26]

13.46   It should be noted that the court held that the section 21 duty was discharged by a 'persistent and unequivocal refusal to observe reasonable requirements' but that the duty may be revived if the applicant is able to satisfy the authority that he or she will no longer persist in the behaviour complained of.

Continuation of the duty to inquire into homeless application

13.47   Even if an applicant refuses section 188 accommodation unequivocally, this does not mean that the authority can treat the homeless application as withdrawn or closed. The authority is still under a duty to complete its inquiries and issue a decision. However, a refusal of

24   See para 18.13 for an explanation of the duties under NAA 1948.
25   (1999) 32 HLR 579.
26   Potter LJ at 593.

section 188 accommodation may have an adverse effect on the outcome of the inquiries. This may be the case if an applicant chooses to remain in accommodation which he or she was previously told to leave or which it is argued is unreasonable for continued occupation.

13.48   However, some authorities encourage applicants to remain in their current accommodation by accepting a 'homeless at home' application. In such cases advisers must ensure that the authority proceeds to make a decision on the housing duty and, if a duty is owed, makes an offer of suitable accommodation without delay.[27]

Homeless inquiries

13.49   The triggering of the duty to inquire is dealt with above (paras 13.13–13.18). To decide what, if any, housing duty is owed, the authority must satisfy itself that the relevant tests are met: homelessness, eligibility, priority need and unintentional homelessness. As a general rule, it is the local authority that must make the decision and it cannot be delegated to another person or body. An authority can, however, ask for assistance from another body in the discharge of its functions.[28] Furthermore, it is now possible for an authority to contract out almost all of its functions under HA 1996 Parts VI and VII.[29]

Extent of the inquiries

13.50   The burden is on the authority to make appropriate inquiries to obtain the relevant information. An applicant is not required to prove his or her case, but must co-operate with the authority's inquiries.[30] This will mean agreeing to the authority contacting third parties for information and providing information when required.

13.51   The inquiries should be rigorous, but an authority need not conduct 'CID type' inquiries.[31]

13.52   An authority is not under an obligation to make all necessary inquiries to determine the truth, but can be challenged if it fails to make an inquiry that no reasonable authority could fail to regard as necessary.

---

27 See, however, *Birmingham CC v Ali* [2009] UKHL 36, see para 16.25 below.
28 See HA 1996 s213; *R v West Dorset HA ex p Gerrard* (1994) 27 HLR 150, QBD and *R v Hertsmere BC ex p Woolgar* (1995) 27 HLR 703, QBD.
29 Local Authorities (Contracting Out of Allocation of Housing and Homelessness Functions) Order 1996 SI No 3205.
30 See Code of Guidance, para 6.15, and *R v Woodspring DC ex p Walters* (1984) 16 HLR 73, QBD.
31 *Lally v Kensington and Chelsea RLBC* (1980) *Times* 27 March, QBD.

In *R v Nottingham CC ex p Costello*[32] the applicants had left accommodation that was adapted for their disabled son, alleging that it was unsuitable because they were dissatisfied with the modifications. Also, Mr Costello alleged that the property was troubled by a poltergeist. Social services had indicated that Mr Costello blamed his wife for the visitations and believed that they would occur wherever she was present. He denied having said this. The applicants challenged the decision that they were intentionally homeless on the ground that the authority had failed to make adequate inquiries of Mr Costello regarding his beliefs about the poltergeist.

This was rejected, the court holding that:

> The duty to make necessary enquiries is not a duty to make all enquiries in fact necessary before the truth is ascertained. A council which makes numerous enquiries can, in my judgment, only be attacked for failing to make one more, if it fails to make an enquiry which no reasonable council could have failed to regard as necessary.[33]

13.53   Nevertheless, if it is found that an authority has carried out inadequate inquiries, its decision will be unlawful (see para 2.11).

13.54   An alleged failure to inquire into relevant matters may be corrected during the review process. The general rule is that any complaint about inadequacy of inquiries must be raised at the review stage and an applicant may be prevented from arguing at an appeal matters which were not put to the authority on review.

In *Cramp v Hastings BC* and *Phillips v Camden LBC*[34] the applicants challenged decisions that they were not in priority need. At the county court appeals they argued that the decisions were flawed because of failures to make sufficient inquiries. However, this point had not been made in the representations submitted as part of the reviews and the Court of Appeal held that it was not appropriate to interfere with the local authorities' decisions that the applicants were not in priority need:

> Given the full-scale nature of the review, a court whose powers are limited to considering points of law should now be even more

---

32 (1989) 21 HLR 301, QBD.
33 Schiemann J at 309.
34 [2005] EWCA Civ 1005, 29 July 2005.

> hesitant [than before the right of review was introduced] if
> the applicant's ground of appeal relates to a matter which the
> reviewing officer was never invited to consider, and which was
> not an obvious matter he should have considered.[35]

13.55   However, there are exceptions to this general rule. For example, in *R (Pieretti) v Enfield LBC*[36] the Court of Appeal held that where an authority had breached its disability equality duty when making inquiries, the fact that this argument was not raised in the review did not prevent it being a ground of appeal in the county court. See para 2.88 for details of the case. Similarly, an authority has a clear, freestanding duty to take into account the issue of affordability when assessing the suitability of accommodation. And the county court may still take account of a failure to do so, even if the issue was not raised in the review representations.

Fairness

13.56   The inquiries must be carried out fairly and interviews conducted in a sympathetic way, but this does not preclude asking searching questions in appropriate cases.[37]

13.57   Where an authority intends to take account of information adverse to the applicant, it should give the applicant the opportunity to comment on the information.[38] An authority cannot take account of information obtained in confidence if it is not able to disclose it to the applicant and obtain the applicant's comments.[39]

13.58   If, following inquiries, the authority is undecided, the issue should be resolved in favour of the applicant.[40]

---

35 [2005] EWCA Civ 1005, Brooke LJ at [14].
36 [2010] EWCA Civ 1104, 12 October 2010.
37 *R v Tower Hamlets LBC ex p Khatun* (1994) 27 HLR 465, CA.
38 *R v Tower Hamlets LBC ex p Rouf* (1989) 21 HLR 294.
39 *R v Poole BC ex p Cooper* (1994) 27 HLR 605, QBD.
40 *R v North Devon DC ex p Lewis* [1981] 1 WLR 328, QBD and *R v Thurrock BC ex p Williams* (1981) 1 HLR 129, QBD.

Repeat applications

13.59 Many of those who receive a negative decision, or to whom a housing duty has ended, remain homeless. Several issues arise: the circumstances in which an applicant can apply again to the same authority; whether another member of the household can make an application; and whether an application can be made to a different authority.

Same applicant applying to same authority

13.60 If the reason an applicant was refused assistance is that the person was found to be not homeless, not eligible or not in priority need, it may be that there is a change of circumstances which means that a fresh application may be made. For example, a person may be evicted from accommodation, having previously argued that it was not reasonable to occupy the accommodation; a woman found not to be in priority need on health grounds may become pregnant; a previously ineligible person may be granted leave to remain in the UK.

13.61 The issue will be less clear where the basis of the claim is the same, but the issue is one of degree: a person found not to be in priority need may claim that a medical condition has worsened or that he or she has obtained a new medical report. A person found not to be homeless on the basis of the condition of accommodation may claim that the conditions have deteriorated. An example of such a case is *Gardner v Haringey LBC*,[41] at para 13.66 below.

13.62 The issue also arises when the authority has found that an applicant is intentionally homeless or decided that the HA 1996 section 193 duty has come to an end because an offer of suitable accommodation has been refused.

13.63 The combined effect of HA 1996 ss183 and 184 and s193(9) suggest that there is nothing to prevent such a person from making a further application to the authority, which will be bound to carry out full inquiries and offer interim accommodation pending a decision. Not surprisingly, the issue has been considered by the courts on a number of occasions.

13.64 The question is whether the authority is required, in every case, to go through the whole statutory inquiry process. Alternatively, is there a 'threshold test' which the authority can apply before deciding whether it is under a duty to undertake the full inquiry process? If so, what is the threshold test?

41 [2009] EWHC 2699 (Admin), 30 October 2009.

In *R v Harrow LBC ex p Fahia*[42] the court considered a second application made by a woman previously found to be intentionally homeless by the same authority. Since the first decision, she had remained in the accommodation previously provided as interim accommodation, successfully applying for housing benefit to be paid. After 12 months she was evicted and made a fresh application to the authority. The authority declined to accept the application on the basis that she had not had settled accommodation since the decision. Following a number of previously decided cases, it maintained that a fresh application would only be considered if there had been a 'material change of circumstances' or some new relevant fact had come to light.

The House of Lords held that this was the wrong approach. Where a person has been found intentionally homeless, he or she cannot make a further application 'based on exactly the same facts as [the] earlier application' but such cases are 'very special cases' where it can be said that there is no application before the authority.[43] Harrow LBC had argued that it was entitled to make 'non-statutory inquires' before deciding whether it was under a duty to take a fresh application. This was rejected: there was no such short-cut available to the authority. Unless the application was based on exactly the same facts, the authority was bound to make inquiries under HA 1996 s184 and to provide interim accommodation under section 188 until a decision was made.

13.65 *Fahia* suggested that there *was* a threshold test: whether the application was based on exactly the same facts as the previous application. Having specifically excluded the possibility of 'non-statutory' inquiries, however, this left open the question of how an authority could decide whether the application was based on the same facts without making some inquiry.

13.66   This issue was considered by the Court of Appeal in *Rikha Begum v Tower Hamlets LBC*.[44]

In *Rikha Begum* the applicant had rejected a suitable offer of accommodation made under Part VII. She returned to live with her parents. Subsequently, two of her brothers, one a heroin addict,

---

42 [1998] 1 WLR 1396; (1998) 30 HLR 1124, HL.
43 Lord Browne-Wilkinson at 1402D–E.
44 [2005] EWCA Civ 340.

also moved in. After almost two years she applied to the authority again. The authority declined to accept her application on the basis that there was no material change in her circumstances since the authority had discharged its duty on the previous application.

Following *Fahia*, the court held that the authority had applied the wrong test: there was no requirement that the applicant demonstrate a material change of circumstances. Rather, an authority may only treat a fresh application as 'no application at all' if it is based on exactly the same facts as the previous application. The court went on to consider how an authority should determine the issue, setting out the following principles:

- in deciding whether an application is based on the same facts, the authority must compare the facts at the date of the subsequent application with the facts known at the date of the previous determination (ie the section 184 decision or decision on review, not at the date of application);
- it is the applicant's responsibility to identify which facts make the application different from those at the date of the previous determination;
- if no new facts are revealed or if the facts are, to the authority's knowledge, not new or are fanciful or trivial, the authority should reject the application;
- if the new facts are not within the authority's knowledge and are not, in light of the information known to them, fanciful or trivial, the authority must accept a new application;
- it is not open to the authority to investigate the accuracy of the new facts before deciding whether to accept a new application.

This test was applied in *Gardiner v Haringey LBC*.[45] The applicant, who was a British national, had been found not to be homeless because she had accommodation in Colombia. She contended that it was not reasonable for her to occupy the accommodation in Colombia because her daughter was severely disabled and needed special educational provision available in the UK but not in Colombia. While the council accepted that the provision in the UK was better than that in Colombia it did not accept that this meant it was not reasonable for the family to live in the accommodation

45 [2009] EWHC 2699 (Admin), 30 October 2009.

in Colombia. The applicant was unsuccessful in the review and county court appeal and had applied for permission to appeal further to the Court of Appeal. Having obtained new medical reports on the progress the girl had made since receiving the special educational provision in the UK, a fresh application was made. The council refused to investigate the fresh application, claiming it was based on the same facts as the previous application.

The applicant's judicial review of the decision was successful. The court held that it was not enough that the council had already made a decision that the provision in Colombia was inferior to that in the UK,

> ... the extent of the difference and the impact of that difference upon [the child] would be important factual matters in determining the question of reasonableness [to occupy the Colombia property] ... I am unable to accept the Council's submission that they did not need to look beyond whether Colombian facilities were better or worse than those available here.[46]

13.67   It should be noted that whether an application is accepted and investigated is an issue distinct from the question of whether any duty will be owed. In *Rikha Begum* it was specifically suggested that the likely outcome of the application would be a decision that no housing duty was owed.

Applications by other household members

13.68   Where a decision has been made that no duty is owed to an applicant, can another member of the household make an application in his or her name? This will depend on the reason for the decision that no duty is owed.

13.69   If the issue is intentional homelessness, another member of the household may apply to the authority. The authority cannot refuse to accept the application on the basis of the previous decision: each individual is entitled to individual consideration. The authority may, however, decide that the applicant is also intentionally homeless, having acquiesced in the decision or behaviour that caused the homelessness, see para 14.286.

46   [2009] EWHC 2699 (Admin), at [22].

13.70   The Court of Appeal held in *R v Camden LBC ex p Hersi*[47] that an adult daughter who had been unaware of her mother's refusal of an offer could not re-apply on behalf of the household. At best she could apply for housing as a single person. However, in that case the daughter had no priority need because the children in the household were not dependent on her. Had she had a priority need in her own right the outcome is likely to have been different.

Applying to another authority

13.71 There is nothing to prevent a person refused assistance by one authority from applying to a different authority. The outcome will depend on two things:

- whether the applicant can be referred, under the local connection provisions, back to the first authority; and
- the reason why no duty is owed by the first authority.

No local connection referral possible

13.72 If the applicant has been refused because he or she failed one of the substantive tests, the second authority cannot simply adopt the findings of the first authority.[48] It must make its own decision. Usually, however, the second authority will obtain information from the first authority and is likely to make the same decision. While carrying out the inquiries, interim accommodation must be provided if there is reason to believe the applicant is homeless, eligible and has priority need.

13.73   If the applicant is homeless because the HA 1996 section 193 duty owed by the first authority has ended, the second authority must consider the application, but, given the circumstances in which the duty ends, it is likely that the second authority will not have a duty to accommodate. If the person has refused an offer of accommodation or has been evicted from the section 193 accommodation he or she is likely to be found to be intentionally homeless by the second authority.

13.74   If the authority makes a different decision from the first authority on a substantive issue (for example, priority need or intentional homelessness), the second authority may owe the full housing duty.

---

47 (2001) 33 HLR 52, QBD.
48 *R v Newham LBC ex p Khan and Hussain* (2000) 33 HLR 29, QBD.

Local connection referral possible

13.75   Again, if the applicant was refused assistance by the first authority because of failing one of the substantive tests, the second authority must consider the application and make its own decision. An authority which knows that the full housing duty will be owed by another authority may be less rigorous in its inquiries. The second authority may find that the person is in priority need or not intentionally homeless even though the first authority had decided those issues negatively. Unless the first authority can challenge the decision by way of judicial review, it will be under a duty to accept a referral and will owe the full housing duty.[49]

13.76   However, if a HA 1996 section 193 duty owed by the first authority has ended (for example, because of the refusal of an offer) the first authority can refuse to accept the full housing duty following a local connection referral on the basis that it has already discharged its duty to the applicant. In that instance, a duty will be owed by neither authority.

Miscellaneous duties

Duties to particular applicants

Threatened homelessness

13.77   Local authorities also have duties to those who are 'threatened with homelessness'. A person is threatened with homelessness if he or she is likely to become homeless within 28 days.[50]

13.78   If the authority is satisfied that a person is eligible, has a priority need and is not threatened with homelessness intentionally, the duty is to 'take reasonable steps to secure that accommodation does not cease to be available for [the applicant's] occupation'.[51]

13.79   If the authority is not satisfied that the applicant has a priority need, or is satisfied that the applicant is threatened with homelessness intentionally, the duty is to provide the applicant with advice and assistance in any attempts he or she makes to secure that the accommodation does not cease to be available. Alternatively, it may refer the applicant to another agency for such advice and assistance.[52]

49 See *R v Newham LBC ex p Tower Hamlets LBC* [1992] 2 All ER 767, see para 14.328.
50 HA 1996 s175(4).
51 HA 1996 s195(2).
52 HA 1996 s195(5).

13.80   In practice, local authorities rarely make full inquiries or issue decision letters at the stage when a person is threatened with homelessness. Assistance will usually be given by the authority's housing advisory services or by voluntary agencies acting in cooperation with the authority. Strictly, the duty does not arise unless homelessness is likely within 28 days. However, where there is a chance of avoiding homelessness, for example by negotiating with a landlord or helping to resolve housing benefit problems, any effective homeless prevention service will offer assistance at an early stage.

13.81   The duty is most relevant when a person is certain to become homeless, but the date of actual eviction is not imminent. In such cases most authorities will advise a person to return nearer to or on the date of eviction. The specific duty to begin the inquiry process in relation to a particular applicant does not arise until the date of expected homelessness is within 28 days. However, within the 28-day period, steps should be taken by the authority to identify suitable accommodation.[53]

13.82   Local authorities also have general duties regarding the provision of advice and assistance (see para 13.89) and in relation to the prevention of homelessness and those services will be available to an applicant even if a specific duty has not yet arisen.

Protection of property

13.83   A local authority has a duty in relation to the property of a homeless applicant, where the authority:

> ... have reason to believe that –
> (a) there is a danger of loss of, or damage to, any personal property of an applicant by reason of his inability to protect it or deal with it, and
> (b) no other suitable arrangements have been or are being made.[54]

13.84   The duty is to 'take reasonable steps to prevent the loss of the property or mitigate damage to it'.[55] The authority may make 'reasonable charges' and may specify conditions regarding the disposal of the property, for example if charges are not paid or the belongings are not collected.[56] In most cases when an applicant is in receipt of means-tested benefit, no charge or minimal charges will be made.

---

53 *R v Newham LBC ex p Khan and Hussain* (2000) 33 HLR 29, QBD.
54 HA 1996 s211(1).
55 HA 1996 s211(2).
56 HA 1996 s211(4).

However, the full cost of the storage of belongings may be charged to an applicant with sufficient means to pay.

Liaison with social services – children

13.85 Where a local authority has reason to believe that an eligible applicant whose household includes a dependent child may be intentionally homeless, or threatened with homelessness intentionally, it must ask the applicant for consent to refer his or her case to the relevant social services department. If consent is given, the case must be referred to the social services department to consider exercising its powers and duties under the Children Act (CA) 1989.[57]

13.86 Local authorities may give financial assistance to such a family under CA 1989 s17 to assist them to secure private sector accommodation. However, such assistance is discretionary and many authorities will instead offer assistance by way of taking the children into care. See chapter 19 and particularly paras 19.9–19.11 for an explanation of social services' duties under CA 1989.

Advice and assistance

13.87 Local authorities have a duty to provide advice and assistance to applicants who are found not to be in priority need and to those found intentionally homeless. In both cases the advice and assistance must be tailored to the needs of the applicant:[58]

- the authority must provide the applicant with advice and assistance in any attempts he or she makes to find accommodation (or must ensure that others do so);
- the applicant's housing needs must be addressed before advice and assistance is given; and
- the advice and assistance must include information about the likely availability of types of accommodation appropriate to the person's housing needs (including in particular, the location and sources of such types of accommodation).

13.88 It should be noted that under HA 1996 s192(3) an authority has a power to secure accommodation for a person found not to have a priority need. For someone found to be intentionally homeless there is a duty to provide temporary accommodation for a reasonable period (see para 16.14).

---

57 HA 1996 s213A.
58 HA 1996 ss190 and 192.

General duties

Advice and information

13.89   Every local authority must ensure that advice and information about homelessness and the prevention of homelessness is available free of charge in their district.[59] An authority may also fund voluntary organisations to provide services to prevent or alleviate homelessness.

Homelessness strategies

13.90   The Homelessness Act 2002 placed on all local housing authorities a duty to formulate and publish a 'homelessness strategy' at least every five years. However, this obligation does not apply to local authorities rated excellent or three or four star authorities under the best value auditing regime established under the Local Government Act 2003.[60]

13.91   The published document must set out the authority's strategy for:[61]

- preventing homelessness;
- ensuring that sufficient accommodation is available for the homeless in the district; and
- securing the satisfactory provision of support for the homeless in the district.

13.92   In exercising its functions (including those under HA 1996 Part VII) the authority must take its homelessness strategy into account.[62]

13.93   Often, an authority's strategy may be expressed in expansive terms, in contrast to the restrictive application of HA 1996 Part VII by the authority's homeless persons' department. Being familiar with the authority's strategy may assist in challenging a decision made in relation to an individual application.

In *R on the application of Omatoyo v City of Westminster*[63] the applicant was a man with a history of homelessness, drug and substance abuse, offending and prison. He was found not to be in priority need and refused interim accommodation pending review.

59   HA 1996 s179(1).
60   See Local Authorities' Plans and Strategies (Disapplication) (England) (Amendment) Orders 2005 SI No 157 and 2009 SI No 714.
61   Homelessness Act 2002 s3.
62   Homelessness Act 2002 s1(5).
63   [2006] EWHC 2572 (Admin), 21 September 2006.

The council's homelessness strategy indicated that it aimed to reduce the numbers of rough sleepers in the district and that it had a target of ensuring that all offenders released on licence were assisted to access appropriate accommodation. Mr Omatoyo applied for permission to bring judicial review proceedings to challenge the decision not to provide interim accommodation.

At the hearing, the court was required to consider the merits of the decision subject to review. One of the factors the judge considered relevant to the lawfulness of the decision was that the authority had failed to take account of its own homelessness strategy. Permission to bring the claim was granted.

13.94   Failing to follow its own policies without good reason will usually make a public body's decision unlawful. Advisers should be aware of other policies and strategies that local authorities are bound to publish which may impact upon the homelessness duties. For example, authorities must also publish their strategies on tackling anti-social behaviour,[64] on implementing the various equality duties[65] and will be required under the Localism Act 2011 to publish local housing strategies. In addition, they may have adopted policies for dealing with rent arrears and for supporting vulnerable people, see paras 7.115–7.119.

64 Anti-social Behaviour Act 2003 s12.
65 Equality Act 2010 s153 and the Equalities Act (Specific Duties) Regulations 2011 SI No 2260.

APPENDIX

Homeless applications letter

Letter to local authority – homeless applications and interim accommodation

Dear Sir/Madam, Re: Mrs A

We are advising the above named who has made a homeless application to your authority.

[Set out some details about application/dealings with the council]

Mrs A is a British national who has lived in the UK all her life. She is therefore eligible for assistance.

Mrs A is homeless, having been told to leave her sister's accommodation.

Mrs A is pregnant and has a dependent child, aged two years. She is clearly in priority need.

Mrs A first approached your authority on [date] and informed you that she had been asked to leave her sister's accommodation as it is overcrowded. She was advised by an officer at reception that her sister was required to give her written notice. Her sister then gave her seven days' written notice and she returned to your offices on expiry of the notice. She was then advised that she could not be seen until the following week. She was forced to return to her sister's home and her sister reluctantly agreed that she could stay until her appointment with the homeless persons unit.

At the appointment a homeless application form was completed but Mrs A was told that she must remain at her sister's home until a decision had been made. Our client's sister indicated that our client could stay for only two further days.

When our client returned to your offices two days later she was told that the authority did not accept that she was homeless. When we telephoned your office we were told that your authority was of the view that our client could continue to reside with her sister but that any decision must be approved by the manager, who was currently on leave.

[Set out the law]

As your authority is aware, under section 188 of the Housing Act 1996 if you have *reason to believe* that an applicant *may be* homeless you have a duty to carry out inquiries under Part VII of the Act. Further, if you have *reason to believe* that an applicant *may be* eligible and in priority need you have a duty to provide interim accommodation until a decision is notified to our client.

If you are still carrying out inquiries then the duty is to provide interim accommodation until our client is notified of your decision.

If you have concluded your inquiries then our client is entitled to be notified in writing of the decision.

[What you want them to do and by when]

Can you please confirm by close of business today that interim accommodation will be provided to Mrs A until you notify her of your decision on her application. Alternatively, please can you forward to us the decision letter made pursuant to section 184. We enclose our client's signed authority for you to send this to us.

If we do not hear from you by [time and date] we can only assume that you are refusing either to provide interim accommodation or to issue a decision letter.

We will then advise our client to commence judicial review proceedings/refer our client to our legal team/a solicitor with a view to a claim for judicial review.

Yours faithfully

Adviser

Advice Agency

[If this letter is being sent by solicitors or an agency able to to provide legal representation the letter should be in the form of a judicial review protocol letter – see chapter 18, appendix 2 for the template. This means that proceedings can be issued immediately if the issue is not resolved within the deadline.]

CHAPTER 14

The homelessness tests

continued

Key points

- A local authority has to provide accommodation for homeless people only if it is satisfied of the matters set out below.

The person is homeless

- A person can be homeless if he or she has accommodation but it is not reasonable to continue to live in it.
- It is not reasonable to live in accommodation if violence is probable.

The person is eligible

- Certain people from abroad are 'ineligible'. This includes people who do not have leave to be in the UK or who have leave that is limited. It also includes European nationals who do not have a 'right to reside' in the UK and some people, including British nationals, who are not habitually resident in the UK. If a person is ineligible no housing duty will be owed.

The person has priority need

- There are several categories of priority need. If a homeless person does not have priority need the only duty an authority has is to give advice and assistance to find accommodation. Some categories of priority need depend on the local authority finding that a person is 'vulnerable'. Such decisions usually depend on the strength of expert evidence about a person's physical or mental health.

The person is not intentionally homeless

- If a person has caused his or her homelessness by something done or not done deliberately, he or she will usually be intentionally homeless. There are several elements to the test and each element must be addressed. An authority must identify the deliberate act or omission that caused the homelessness.

The person may be referred to another authority

- If a person applies to a local authority where he or she has no local connection, that authority may refer the person to another authority to be housed. This should only be done after all the inquiries have been completed and it has been decided that a housing duty is owed.

Eligibility

14.1   In homelessness law 'eligibility' has a specific meaning: it is a test that excludes certain people from abroad from homeless assistance.[1]

14.2   The test of eligibility is relevant to three classes of people:

- people from outside Europe who need leave to enter or remain in the UK ('persons subject to immigration control');
- European nationals and their families;
- people who are not 'habitually resident'.

14.3   The basic provisions are set out in section 185 of the Housing Act (HA) 1996, with the detail found in the regulations. The most important regulations are:

- Allocation of Housing and Homelessness (Eligibility) (England) Regulations 2006 (Eligibility Regs 2006), as amended;[2]
- Immigration (European Economic Area) Regulations 2006 (EEA Regs 2006).[3]

14.4   A person who is not eligible cannot be provided with homeless assistance: HA 1996 s185(1). In addition, special rules may apply if there is an ineligible person in the applicant's household (see paras 14.141–14.148 below).

Persons subject to immigration control

14.5   People 'subject to immigration control' are not eligible unless they are in one of the classes of exceptions set out in the Eligibility Regs 2006: HA 1996 s185(2).

14.6   To apply the test therefore the first question is whether the person is subject to immigration control. If so, the next question is whether he or she is on the list of exceptions.

1   Similar tests are applied to exclude access to social security benefits and community care services.
2   SI No 1294. These regulations apply to all applications made on or after 1 June 2006. For applications made before that date the regulations in force at the time apply. Between 1996 and 2006 the regulations were amended and replaced several times. The 2006 Regulations were amended by the Allocation of Housing and Homelessness (Miscellaneous Provisions) (England) Regulations 2006 SI No 2527.
3   SI No 1003.

Who is subject to immigration control?

14.7   Anyone who needs leave (permission) to enter or remain in the UK, whether or not such leave has been granted, is a person subject to immigration control.[4] It is simplest to list those persons who do not need leave to enter or remain. They are:[5]

- British citizens;
- Commonwealth citizens with 'right of abode';[6]
- nationals of certain European countries who have a right to reside (see below, paras 14.30–14.132);
- Irish nationals.[7]

14.8   Anyone not listed above will be subject to immigration control. To be eligible such a person must be in a class listed in regulation 5 of the Eligibility Regs 2006. These are set out below, paras 14.9–14.21.

People subject to immigration control and eligible

Class A: refugees

14.9   This means someone recognised as a refugee in the UK who has been granted leave on that basis.

14.10   The current practice of the UK Border Agency[8] (UKBA) is to grant five years' 'limited' leave to refugees. Prior to 30 August 2005 the practice was to grant indefinite leave to remain (ILR).

---

4 See HA 1996 s185(2); Asylum and Immigration Act 1996 s13(2); Immigration Act (IA) 1971 s1, and IA 1988 s7(1).

5 In addition, certain diplomatic and military personnel do not require leave to enter or remain in the UK.

6 Right of abode is enjoyed by Commonwealth citizens born before 1 January 1983 who had a parent born in the UK, and women who were Commonwealth citizens before 1 January 1983 and who were married before that date to a man who was born, registered or naturalised in the UK, or who is a Commonwealth citizen with a parent born in the UK. Whether or not a person has a right of abode may be endorsed in the passport. It is also possible to obtain a 'certificate of entitlement' from the UK Borders Agency (UKBA). In the absence of such evidence or if there is any uncertainty, a person who believes they may have a right of abode should be referred to a specialist in immigration and nationality law. In immigration law a person claiming a right of abode has the burden of proving the right.

7 See IA 1971 s1(3).

8 UKBA was formed on 1 April 2008 by a merger of several government departments. It is part of the Home Office.

Class B: exceptional leave – no condition as to public funds

14.11 A person with exceptional leave to remain[9] (ELR) is eligible provided the leave is not subject to a condition that he or she cannot have 'recourse to public funds'.

14.12 ELR means any leave granted outside the Immigration Rules. Before 2003 ELR was given to asylum-seekers who were not granted full refugee status but who nevertheless needed protection. Since April 2003 this type of ELR has been replaced by 'humanitarian protection' and 'discretionary leave'. Humanitarian protection is granted under the Immigration Rules and is dealt with below at para 14.17. Discretionary leave remains a form of exceptional leave granted outside the Immigration Rules. It is granted to child asylum-seekers whose asylum claims have been refused and is now granted until the child is 17.5 years old. It is also used when a person is disqualified from a grant of humanitarian protection but nevertheless cannot be removed. Where discretionary leave is granted to an asylum-seeker it will not be subject to the 'no recourse to public funds' rule.

14.13 Leave may also be granted outside the Immigration Rules for compassionate reasons, for example to allow an elderly relative to join family members in the UK. In such cases, the leave will usually be subject to the 'no recourse to public funds' condition which should be stamped on the passport. Such people are not eligible for homeless assistance.

Class C: leave to enter or remain without limit or condition

14.14 The grant of leave to enter or remain in the UK that is not subject to any limitation or condition is often referred to as indefinite leave to remain (ILR). It is also referred to as 'settlement' or 'settled status'. ILR used to be granted to refugees prior to 30 August 2005. ILR is granted to certain people who have previously enjoyed more limited leave, for example, spouses of British nationals. Since April 2007 most applicants for ILR must pass a test in English and demonstrate knowledge of life in the UK.

Sponsored immigrants – not usually eligible

14.15 'Sponsored immigrants' are an exception to the general rule that a person with ILR is eligible. Sponsorship exists when a person is given leave to enter the UK on the basis of an undertaking given by someone else in the UK that he or she will be responsible for that

---

9 In April 2003 the Home Office abandoned the term 'exceptional leave to remain' and instead adopted the term 'leave outside the rules' (LOTR).

person's accommodation and maintenance. A sponsored immigrant is not eligible unless more than five years have passed (since entry or the undertaking was given, whichever is later) or the sponsor has died.

14.16   In all cases a person who is eligible because of having ILR must also be habitually resident in the UK, the Channel Islands, the Isle of Man or the Republic of Ireland (see below, paras 14.133–14.140).

Class D: humanitarian protection

14.17   A person who has been granted humanitarian protection (HP) under the Immigration Rules is eligible. HP is granted to people who are not recognised as refugees but who would, if returned, face a real risk of suffering serious harm. Serious harm consists of: the death penalty or execution, unlawful killing, torture or inhuman or degrading treatment or punishment, or serious and individual threat to life by reason of indiscriminate violence in situations of international or internal armed conflict.[10] In some cases a person may be excluded from humanitarian protection, for example, because of war crimes or other serious crimes, or being deemed a threat to national security. Such people will usually be granted discretionary leave.

Class E: pre-April 2000 asylum-seekers

14.18   Before 1996 all asylum-seekers were entitled to homeless assistance. Between 1996 and 2000 only asylum-seekers who claimed asylum at the point of entry to the UK were entitled to homeless assistance. However, eligible asylum-seekers became ineligible if the asylum claim was refused, despite having the right to appeal against the decision. There remains some transitional protection for those who claimed asylum before the law changed in 1996 and 2000. The following asylum-seekers are still eligible for homeless assistance:

- an asylum-seeker who claimed asylum before 3 April 2000 on arrival in the UK;
- an asylum-seeker who was in Great Britain when a 'declaration of upheaval' was made and who claimed asylum within three months – this applies only to nationals of Sierra Leone or Democratic Republic of Congo (DRC, formerly Zaire) who made their claims in 1997;[11] and

---

10 Immigration Rules paras 339C–339D.
11 The only relevant declarations were made on the following dates: DRC – 16 May 1997, Sierra Leone – 1 July 1997. The person must also have been in Great Britain on the day the declaration was made.

- an asylum-seeker who claimed asylum on or before 4 February 1996 and who was, on that date, entitled to housing benefit.

14.19   Note that in all of the above cases UKBA must have recorded the claim for asylum at the relevant date. The provisions apply only to those whose claim for asylum is still outstanding. There is a very small number of cases in which a claim for asylum was made many years ago and no decision has yet been made by UKBA. If the claim is refused the person immediately becomes ineligible. If some kind of leave is granted, the person will be eligible under Class A, B, C or D (above, paras 14.9–14.17).

14.20   Advisers should take care when assisting someone whose claim for asylum was made several years ago. Some asylum-seekers may be unaware that a negative decision has been made. For those whose claims were made before 2000 it is advisable to contact the UKBA general enquiry number to find out what its records indicate. The Home Office/UKBA reference number will be needed.

14.21   No other asylum-seekers are eligible: asylum-seekers need leave to enter the UK and do not have it. The temporary admission granted to asylum-seekers is not leave.

Common problems for persons subject to immigration control

Spouses and domestic violence

14.22   A person who marries a British national or someone settled in the UK will be granted leave to remain for an initial period of two years and this will be subject to the 'no recourse to public funds' condition. This is because, before granting leave, UKBA must be satisfied that the couple will have adequate accommodation and resources without relying on state benefits. If, during this two-year period, the foreign spouse is the victim of domestic violence and leaves the matrimonial home, he or she will be ineligible for homeless assistance or any social security benefits. The only possible assistance will be from social services under the Children Act 1989 or, if the person has community care needs, under the National Assistance Act 1948: see chapters 18, 19 and 20.

14.23   UKBA has a policy to grant ILR to such victims of domestic violence provided the necessary evidence of the domestic violence exists.[12] However, until a decision is made by the UKBA the person remains ineligible for homeless assistance.

---

12   Immigration Rules, para 289A.

Long-standing residents without documentation

14.24 Some people, particularly from Commonwealth countries, have been in the UK since childhood but have never been granted any form of leave to enter or remain in the UK. Often such people will have a National Insurance number and will have been living and working in the UK for many years. However, unless they have a right of abode (see para 14.7 above) they are subject to immigration control and are therefore ineligible for homeless assistance (and social security benefits).

14.25 Such a person may apply for ILR and, depending on the circumstances, this may be granted under the Immigration Rules, under certain policy concessions, or because the refusal of leave would involve a breach of human rights. However, there is often a long delay before a decision is made on an application and during this period the person will be ineligible for homeless assistance.

Leave that expires

14.26 A person with leave to enter or remain in the UK may apply to extend the period of leave, or to vary the conditions of leave. Provided an application is made before the leave expires the person is treated as continuing to have the same leave subject to the same conditions until UKBA make a decision.[13] If refused, an appeal can be made from within the UK and the person continues to be treated as having the same leave until the appeal is determined.

14.27 However, if leave expires before an application is submitted to UKBA the person becomes an 'over-stayer' and does not have any form of leave pending a UKBA decision. Such a person is ineligible for homeless assistance until UKBA grants further leave.

Home Office delays

14.28 In all of the above examples (paras 14.22–14.27), great hardship may be caused by the long delays that are common when UKBA is considering applications.[14] Until UKBA grants leave to remain the applicant may face destitution: the person will be prevented from receiving social security benefits such as income support and housing benefit and, in most cases, will also be prohibited from working.

---

13 Immigration Act 1971 s3C.

14 In July 2006 the Home Secretary announced a five-year plan to clear a backlog of applications then estimated at up to 450,000. Although there is evidence of an increased number of decisions to remove or grants of permission to stay, made in the first half of 2011, at the time of writing, it appears that UKBA failed to meet its self-imposed deadline.

14.29   It is possible to make a claim for judicial review of a failure by UKBA to make a decision. The person's immigration solicitor or adviser should be asked to advise on this course of action: sometimes a person's right to remain in the UK will be stronger if a decision is made after a longer period of residence.

Rights under European law

Introduction

14.30   The European Union (EU)[15] is a group of countries that have entered into treaties whereby certain rights are enjoyed by nationals of each member state in other member states. The most significant of these rights is the right to work and to seek work in another member state. Member nationals who are exercising EU rights in another European country generally enjoy the same rights as nationals of that country. The UK therefore has an obligation under the EU treaties to allow EU nationals, exercising treaty rights, access to the UK's social welfare provisions. These rights also extend to family members of EU nationals, even if the family members are not themselves EU nationals. In some cases the rights of non-EU nationals under European law may conflict with the domestic laws regarding immigration control and many of the cases in which EU rights are at issue concern the rights of nationals from outside the EU.

14.31   One confusing factor in relation to EU nationals is that law and practice diverge. In theory, an EU national who is not exercising rights under the EU treaties is a person subject to immigration control.[16] However, under EU law the UK has an obligation to admit all European nationals to the UK on production of a national identity card or passport.[17] Most EU nationals are not bound to obtain documentary evidence or passport stamps to confirm their right to reside in the UK as EU citizens. Decisions about eligibility therefore often depend on consideration of a person's current or past activity and residence in the UK.

14.32   In 1996, as part of a raft of legislation restricting the access of persons from abroad to various kinds of social assistance, the 'habitual

---

15   The European Community was established in 1957 and renamed the European Union in 1993 by the Maastricht Treaty. The terms EC and EU are generally used interchangeably.

16   Immigration Act 1988 s7(1).

17   Directive 2004/38/EC ('Citizenship Directive') and EEA Regs 2006 reg 11.

residence test' (HRT) was introduced in housing and benefit law. The test was directed at so-called 'benefit tourism' and provided that certain European and British nationals who were not habitually resident in the UK were ineligible for homeless assistance. However, the test could not exclude from assistance EU nationals exercising EU rights in the UK: such people were exempt from the test.

14.33 In 2004 the EU was enlarged when ten new countries became members. Concern that nationals from the poorer of the new member states would become eligible for homeless assistance and social security benefits led to a further condition being introduced: only those with a 'right to reside' would be eligible. Most EU nationals exercising European treaty rights, principally the right to work in another member state, have a right to reside in that state. However, for an initial period after the accession of the new member states, it was necessary for nationals from eight of those states ('A8 nationals') not only to be working but to be registered to work in order to be eligible. This provision does not apply to A8 nationals after 30 April 2011 (see below, para 14.61).[18]

Rights to reside: the Citizenship Directive and the EU Treaty

14.34 The Citizenship Directive (2004/38/EC),[19] passed on 29 April 2004, sets out the rights of EU citizens to move and reside freely throughout the EU. This directive was brought into UK law by the EEA Regs 2006.[20] However, the directive is not the only source of such rights and in some cases, discussed below at paras 14.126–14.132, rights of residence have been established by relying on the main EU Treaty. However, most of the rights that establish eligibility to housing and homeless assistance are found in the Citizenship Directive and the EEA Regs 2006, which reflect the directive. Local authorities will generally refer to the regulations but it must be remembered that the Citizenship Directive is binding on the UK and the regulations are intended to incorporate the directive into UK law. Reference to the relevant provisions of both the Citizenship Directive and the EEA Regs are given in this chapter.

---

18 It does, however, still apply to A2 nationals, see para 14.38 below.
19 The Citizenship Directive amended and repealed certain previous directives that concerned the rights of free movement and residence throughout the EU. The repealed directives are: 64/221/EEC, 68/360/EEC, 72/194/EEC, 73/148/EEC, 75/34/EEC, 75/35/EEC, 90/364/EEC, 90/365/EEC and 93/96/EEC. EU Regulation No 1612/68 was amended and partly repealed. The Citizenship Directive is also sometimes referred to as the Residence Directive.
20 SI No 1003.

14.35   The Citizenship Directive applies 'to all Union citizens who move to or reside in a Member State other than that of which they are a national, and to their family members [as defined in the Directive] who accompany or join them'.[21] So, the Directive is about the rights of those who move to another state within the EU and not about the rights of EU nationals in their own EU state. However, certain rights to reside have been established by reference to the fundamental rights enjoyed by EU citizens under the EU Treaty.[22] The current EU Treaty is the Consolidated Version of the Treaty on the Functioning of the European Union (TFEU), which can be downloaded from www.consilium.europa.eu/uedocs/cmsUpload/st06655.

14.36   Where an issue arises between an EU national and an EU state about rights under EU law this may be referred for determination by the national courts to the European Court of Justice (ECJ), whose decisions are binding on all member states.

14.37   The Citizenship Directive lays down:

- the conditions governing the exercise of the right of free movement and residence within the EU by EU citizens and their family members;
- the right of permanent residence; and
- the limits placed on those rights on the grounds of public policy, public security or public health.

The European Economic Area

14.38   The European Economic Area (EEA) comprises the countries that are members of the EU plus four countries that are members of the European Free Trade Association (EFTA), which have free trade agreements with the EU. All the EEA countries are listed in the table overleaf, with a distinction made between some of the more recent member states whose nationals' rights have been limited for an initial period (known as the 'accession states') and 'full member' states.

---

21 Citizenship Directive article 3(1).
22 See *McCarthy v UK* and *Ruiz Zambrano*, discussed at paras 14.130–4.131 below.

Full member states	A8 states – joined 1 May 2004	A2 states – joined 1 January 2007
EU members Austria Belgium Cyprus* Denmark Finland France Germany Greece Ireland Italy Luxembourg Malta* Netherlands Portugal Spain Sweden * Malta and Cyprus also joined the EU in 2004 but enjoyed 'full member' rights in the UK on joining. **Plus** Iceland Liechtenstein Norway Switzerland	EU members – limited rights – until 1 April 2011 Czech Republic Estonia Latvia Lithuania Hungary Poland Slovakia Slovenia	EU members – limited rights Bulgaria Romania
Workers' rights		
Right to reside if working.	Right to reside if working but must be registered for first 12 months. If work starts after 30 April 2011 no need to register – rights as for full member states.	Right to reside if working but must be registered for first 12 months. Must obtain registration before taking up employment in UK.

Europeans and eligibility

14.39 Only European nationals with a 'right to reside' in the UK can be eligible for homeless assistance. However, two types of right to reside do not confer eligibility for homeless assistance:

- a jobseeker's right to reside; and
- an initial right to reside for three months.

If a person's only right to reside is one or both of these rights, he or she is not eligible for homeless assistance.[23]

14.40　The relevant regulations in relation to European nationals and eligibility are:

Regulations	Provisions	Short Name
Immigration (European Economic Area) Regulations 2006 SI No 1003	Sets out the way rights of residence are established.	EEA Regs 2006
Accession (Immigration and Worker Registration) Regulations 2004 SI No 1219	Sets out the registration requirements for accession state nationals.	Accession Regs 2004
Accession (Immigration and Worker Authorisation) Regulations 2006 SI No 3317	Sets out the particular registration requirements for A2 nationals. Makes some amendments to the Accession Regulations 2004, to include reference to A2 nationals.	Accession Regs 2006
Accession (Immigration and Worker Registration) (Revocation, Savings and Consequential Provisions) Regulations 2011 SI No 544	Revokes the registration requirements for A8 nationals. Applies to those whose employment commences on or after 1 May 2011.	Accession Regs 2011

23 Eligibility Regs 2006 reg 6(b).

The right to reside

14.41   An EU national without a right to reside under EU law cannot be eligible for homeless assistance. However, two types of right to reside do not confer eligibility: a jobseeker's right to reside and an initial right to reside for three months. If the person's only right to reside is one or both of these rights, he or she is not eligible for homeless assistance.[24]

14.42   The EEA Regs 2006 define the right to reside by way of the 'qualified person'. Qualified persons and their family members are entitled to reside in the UK while the relevant person remains a qualified person.[25] In addition, provision is made for certain family members to enjoy extended rights of residence in certain circumstances and permanent rights of residence may be acquired after specified periods of residence and/or activity.

Qualified persons and family members

14.43   A qualified person is an EEA national who is in the UK as one of the following (see paras 14.44–14.85):[26]

- a jobseeker;
- a worker;
- a self-employed person;
- a self-sufficient person;
- a student.

14.44   Workers and self-employed people may retain their status during temporary periods of incapacity in certain circumstances.

14.45   In addition, close family members of qualified persons also have a right to reside. Extended family members may have a right to reside if they satisfy certain conditions. This is dealt with below at paras 14.103–14.112.

Jobseekers

14.46   Jobseekers have a right to reside but neither they nor their family members are eligible for homeless assistance if this is their only right to reside.

24 See Eligibility Regs 2006 reg 6(b).
25 EEA Regs 2006 reg 14(1) and (2).
26 EEA Regs 2006 reg 6. This reflects articles 6 and 7 of the Citizenship Directive.

14.47   A 'jobseeker' means a person who entered the UK to seek employment and who can provide evidence that he or she is seeking employment *and* has a genuine chance of being engaged.[27]

14.48   However, A2 nationals do not have any rights of residence by virtue of being jobseekers.[28]

Unemployed former workers who are jobseekers

14.49   A former worker who is unemployed and registered as a jobseeker may continue to be classed as a worker and therefore continue to have a right to reside and to be eligible for homeless assistance. See below at para 14.55.

Workers

14.50   Qualified persons include:

- full member nationals (including A8 nationals) who are working;
- A2 nationals who are working and are registered workers.

Rights of residence by working – full member nationals

14.51   For full member nationals (which includes A8 nationals after 1 May 2011), simply working in the UK gives a right to reside. Such a person becomes eligible as soon as he or she commences employment.

14.52   Furthermore, the status of 'worker' may be retained even during extended periods of unemployment, provided certain conditions are met, see below, paras 14.55–14.56.

Registered working – A8 and A2 nationals

14.53   Between 1 May 2004 and 30 April 2011, all A10 nationals (ie, A8 nationals and A2 nationals) had a right to reside initially only if they were registered as workers. From 1 May this no longer applies to A8 nationals. A2 nationals are still required to register as workers. See paras 14.64–14.66 below.

Meaning of 'worker'

14.54   The decisions of the European Court of Justice (ECJ) on the question of what it is to be a worker indicate the following:

- being a worker means being employed, in the sense of being obliged to provide services for another person in return for money

---

27   EEA Regs 2006 reg 6(4). Citizenship Directive article 14(4)(b).
28   Accession Regs 2004 (as amended) reg 4(2).

and being subject to the control of the other person as regards the
way the work is done;

• there is no minimum period for which the person must have
been employed and the employment need not be permanent or
full-time;

• the employment must be 'effective and genuine economic activity' and not activity that could be regarded as 'purely marginal and
ancillary';

• the fact that the remuneration may be below the minimum wage
or insufficient to support the person without the person claiming
benefits in addition is irrelevant.[29]

Sickness and unemployment

14.55   The status of 'worker' may be retained during periods of sickness and
unemployment. A person is still treated as a worker if he or she:[30]

• is temporarily unable to work as a result of an illness or accident;
or

• having been employed in the UK, is unemployed involuntarily,
provided he or she has registered as a jobseeker; and

   – was previously employed for at least one year before becoming
   unemployed; or

   – has been unemployed for no more than six months; or

   – can provide evidence that he or she is seeking employment in
   the UK and has a genuine chance of being engaged; or

• is unemployed involuntarily and has embarked on vocational
training; or

• has voluntarily stopped working and has embarked on vocational
training related to the previous employment.

14.56   When relying on a period of employment of less than 12 months, a
relatively short period of work may be sufficient.

> In *Barry v Southwark*[31] a period of temporary work for two weeks as a
> security guard at Wimbledon was sufficient to ensure that Mr Barry
> continued to be classed as a worker for the following six months
> when unemployed. Mr Barry had previously been employed as a
> security guard for nine months was then unemployed for a period

---

29 See Homelessness Code of Guidance (see para 13.8), Annex 12.
30 EEA Regs 2006 reg 6(2) and Citizenship Directive article 7(3).
31 [2008] EWCA Civ 1440, 19 December 2008.

of weeks before taking up the job at Wimbledon, during which he continued to receive jobseeker's allowance.

The Court of Appeal held that the work at Wimbledon could not be regarded as marginal and ancillary; it was real and genuine and of economic value and meant that for the following six months he continued to be classed as a worker.

Pregnancy

14.57 A woman who takes maternity leave while she is employed remains a worker during the maternity leave, even if it is unpaid.[32] Similarly, a self-employed woman who takes a period of maternity leave continues to be classed as self-employed.[33] And time spent on maternity leave counts towards meeting the continuous employment requirement for A8 and A2 nationals.[34]

14.58 The significant feature of maternity leave is that the woman still has a contract of employment and retains her continuity of employment for all purposes. However, a woman who stops working or cannot take up work because of pregnancy or child-care responsibilities after the baby is born, does not retain the status of worker. In several Social Security Commissioner decisions regarding eligibility for income support, it has been held that worker status is not retained since pregnancy is not an illness and temporary incapacity for work in the late stages of pregnancy can be anticipated unlike illness or accident.[35]

14.59 This does not preclude a woman from retaining the status of worker if she has a pregnancy-related illness which means that she is temporarily incapable of work.[36]

14.60 A further issue arises when a pregnant woman is an eligible jobseeker. To retain worker status it is necessary for the woman to be registered as a jobseeker (see above, para 14.55) but women in the later stages of pregnancy are often advised by the Department for Work and Pensions (DWP) to switch from a claim for jobseeker's allowance to income support. The woman has the right to continue to

---

32 CIS/4237/2007 (CIS refers to Commissioners' decisions relating to income support).
33 CIS/1042/2008.
34 CIS/4237/2007.
35 CIS/4010/2006.
36 CIS/731/2007.

claim jobseeker's allowance although she must be able to satisfy the test of being available for work, which is a decision for the DWP.

Worker registration scheme: A8 nationals[37]

14.61   Although A8 nationals are no longer required to register for work, knowledge of the way the scheme operated prior to 1 May 2011 is still important since this may affect whether a person has a permanent right to reside (see below, paras 14.86–14.99).

14.62   Prior to 1 May 2011, all accession state nationals were required to register with the Home Office/UKBA as an 'accession state worker' for the first 12 months of being employed in the UK. A8 nationals could commence employment and apply for registration within the first month. The employer was known as an 'authorised employer' and the registration was specific to that employer.

14.63   If the A8 national stopped working for the authorised employer but found employment with another employer, a new application for registration was required, again within the first month of the new employment.

Worker registration scheme: A2 nationals

14.64   For A2 nationals (Romanians and Bulgarians) the restrictions were more onerous and these remain in place: registration documents must be obtained from UKBA before commencing employment. The proposed employment must be within an authorised category of employment.[38] These include 'sector based schemes' (mainly temporary contracts in agriculture and food processing), au pair placements, domestic workers in private households, postgraduate doctors, dentists and trainee GPs. The aim of these schemes is to limit the number of unskilled workers entering the UK.

14.65   In addition, registration documents will be issued to A2 nationals who qualify for work permits under the Home Office work permit scheme and to 'highly skilled' persons seeking employment in the UK. A highly skilled person means someone with a degree with 2nd class honours or above, a master's degree or doctorate awarded by an institution in England, Wales or Northern Ireland or a higher national diploma or degree awarded by an institution in Scotland.

14.66   In all cases, to have a right to reside in the UK and to be eligible for homeless assistance the A2 worker must have the necessary

---

37   See Accession Regs 2004 and Accession Regs 2006.
38   These are set out in the Accession Regs 2006 Sch 1.

documentation from UKBA authorising him or her to work for a particular employer, unless authorised to seek work as a highly skilled person.

After 12 months' continuous employment

14.67 After 12 months' continuous registered employment the accession state worker became entitled to the same rights as a full member national. A cumulative period of up to 30 days' unemployment in the first 12 months was permitted and did not break the required 12-month period. However, if the period of unemployment exceeded 30 days in the first 12 months, this meant that the worker had to build up a further 12 months' continuous employment.

14.68 For an A2 national, the same rules applied, and theoretically still apply. However, it is more difficult for an A2 national to satisfy the condition if not employed continuously by the same employer. An A2 worker cannot legally commence employment without registration in advance. To ensure continuity, an A2 national would have to find new employment and obtain the necessary documents from UKBA before commencing that employment, all within 30 days.

Self-employed people

14.69 Article 43 of the EU Treaty[39] specifically provides that European nationals have a right to 'establish' themselves in another member state for the purpose of being self-employed or running a business. The EEA Regs 2006 do not define 'self-employment' but simply state that a self-employed person means a person who establishes him or herself to pursue activity as a self-employed person in accordance with article 43.[40]

14.70 To establish eligibility a person will have to provide evidence of economic activity as a self-employed person, such as invoices, bank statements and tax returns.

14.71 It is not necessary for a self-employed person also to be 'self-sufficient'. Those who are self-employed but whose income is limited may be eligible for working tax credit and child tax credit as well as housing benefit and council tax benefit.

14.72 Arguably, self-employment must, like employment, be 'genuine and effective' and more than a 'marginal and ancillary' activity (see para 14.54 above).

---

39 Treaty of Nice. Now TFEU article 49.
40 EEA Regs 2006 reg 4(1)(b).

14.73   A2 nationals are not required to register in order to be self-employed in the UK. But, being self-employed for 12 months does not give accession state nationals the rights enjoyed by full member nationals.[41]

14.74   A person temporarily unable to pursue activity as a self-employed person as the result of an illness or accident is still treated as self-employed.[42] Furthermore, a person who is temporarily unable to find work as a self-employed person may continue to be a self-employed person and therefore eligible.[43] For how long a person may retain the status of a self-employed person without having remunerative work is a question of degree.

Self-sufficient people

14.75   A self-sufficient person is someone who has:

- sufficient resources not to become a burden on the social assistance system of the UK during the period of residence; and
- comprehensive sickness insurance in the UK.[44]

14.76   Self-sufficient people have a right to reside and are therefore eligible but the very fact of applying for homeless assistance may be evidence that the conditions are not met and that the person is no longer a qualified person. However, the circumstances of the person's homelessness will be relevant. If the difficulty is temporary or caused by an emergency such as a flood or fire, it may be argued that the emergency assistance required does not necessarily mean that the person has become a burden on the social assistance system.

14.77   It should be noted, however, that, in contrast to workers and the self-employed, there is no specific provision that a person in temporary difficulty should continue to be regarded as self-sufficient.

14.78   The Homelessness Code of Guidance ('Homelessness Code')[45] suggests that where an applicant was previously self-sufficient, guidance should be sought from UKBA.

---

41 This was also the case for A8 nationals prior to 1 May 2011. Also, see *R (Tilianu) v Secretary of State for Work and Pensions* [2010] EWCA Civ 1397, 8 December 2010: an A2 national who had been self-employed but was incapacitated could not benefit from the provisions of EEA Regs 2006 reg 6(2) (see para 14.55) which apply only to workers.

42 EEA Regs 2006 reg 6(3).

43 CIS/340/2010.

44 EEA Regs 2006 reg 4(1)(c). The requirement to have comprehensive sickness insurance is not a formality but an essential condition: *FK (Kenya) v Secretary of State for the Home Department* [2010] EWCA Civ 1302.

45 Annex 12 para 34.

14.79   A2 nationals are not required to register as self-sufficient persons, nor were A8 nationals prior to 1 May 2011. However, as is the case for the self-employed, being self-sufficient for 12 months does not qualify accession state nationals for the rights enjoyed by full member nationals.

Students

14.80   An EEA national who is a student in the UK has a right to reside. However, the term 'student' is strictly defined. A student is someone who:[46]

- is enrolled to follow a course of study at a private or public establishment listed on the Department of Education and Science Register, or an establishment financed from public funds (this may include vocational training); and
- has comprehensive sickness insurance; and
- assures UKBA, by means of a declaration or something similar, that he or she has sufficient resources not to become a burden on the social assistance system of the UK during the period of residence.

14.81   There is no distinction between full member state nationals and accession state nationals who are students. All enjoy the same rights.

14.82   If the student has family members who will live with him or her in the UK, the assurance given to UKBA must cover the whole family, who must also be covered by comprehensive sickness insurance.[47] The family members of students who enjoy rights of residence are defined more restrictively than for other qualifying persons (see para 14.104).

14.83   In contrast to those who are self-sufficient, a student would not cease to be a qualified person by virtue of making an application for social assistance, for example, making a homeless application. However, such an application would suggest that the assurance given to UKBA initially has not been honoured.

Working while studying

14.84   Other than for A2 nationals, there is no limit on the number of hours a student may work while studying. An EEA student who is working as well as studying will also have a right of residence as a worker provided the work is not marginal and ancillary.

46   EEA Regs 2006 reg 4(1)(d) and Citizenship Directive article 7.1(c).
47   EEA Regs 2006 reg 4(3) and Citizenship Directive article 7.1(c).

14.85   A2 national students are permitted to work for up to 20 hours a week and as part of vocational training and during vacations. They must have registration certificates confirming this. Before 30 April 2011, A8 students were also only permitted to work for up to 20 hours per week but were not required to have registration certificates or to obtain worker authorisation under the worker registration scheme. However, unregistered working as a student did not lead to full member rights after 12 months.

Permanent rights of residence

14.86   Those who have a right of residence by virtue of working, being self-employed, self-sufficient or a student retain the right of residence while they are pursuing the relevant activity and may continue to be qualified persons during temporary periods of inactivity. The Citizenship Directive and the EEA Regs 2006 also provide for the acquisition of rights of permanent residence.

14.87   The following people may gain a right of permanent residence:

- those who have resided legally in the UK for a continuous period of five years (see paras 14.88–14.92);
- those who have previously worked in the UK but are now retired or permanently incapacitated (see paras 14.94–14.98);
- the family members of the above (see para 14.103);
- the family members of a deceased worker who was a qualifying person (see para 14.99).

Five years' continuous residence

14.88   Article 16 of the Citizenship Directive provides that:

> Union citizens who have resided legally for a continuous period of five years in the host Member State shall have the right of permanent residence there.

This must be read in conjunction with recital (17) of the preamble to the directive which provides that:

> A right of permanent residence should ... be laid down for all Union citizens and their family members who have resided in the host Member State in compliance with the conditions laid down in this Directive during a continuous period of five years without becoming subject to an expulsion measure.

14.89   The EEA Regulations 2006 provide that an EEA national who has resided in the UK 'in accordance with these Regulations' for a continuous period of five years acquires the right to reside in the UK permanently[48] as does a non-EEA national who has resided in the UK as a family member of an EEA national for the same period 'in accordance with these Regulations'.[49]

14.90 The meaning of 'residing legally' in the directive and whether the regulations are correct in defining this as residence 'in accordance with these Regulations' has been considered in a number of recent cases by the UK courts and by the ECJ.

In *Lekpo-Bozua v Hackney LBC and Secretary of State for Communities and Local Government*[50] the claimant was a British citizen whose niece was a French national and had lived with her since the age of nine and was 16 at the date of the homeless application. Hackney decided that the niece was a 'restricted person' under the amended section 184(7) so that the duty to the family was only to provide a private sector tenancy (see paras 14.141–14.148). The decision was challenged on the basis that the niece had a permanent right to reside in the UK by virtue of five years' lawful residence.

The Court of Appeal held that, although the niece had been lawfully resident since arriving in the UK, under article 16, residing 'legally' meant 'in compliance with the conditions laid down in this Directive ... The lawful residence contemplated by Article 16 of the Directive is residence which complies with Community law requirements specified in the Directive'.[51]

The Court of Appeal reached the same conclusion in *Okafor v Secretary of State for the Home Department*[52] which concerned the rights of non-EEA family members following the death of the EEA national. The conditions under articles 7 and 12 were not met (see paras 14.114–14.115 and 14.118–14.119). The family argued that, as they had resided in the UK for a continuous period of five years, they had acquired permanent rights of residence.

The Court of Appeal rejected this, holding that the right of permanent residence under article 16 was a right acquired by virtue

48 EEA Regs 2006 reg 15(1)(a).
49 The condition expressly includes any period during which a person carried out an activity or was resident in accordance with the EEA Regs 2000 SI No 2326, which preceded the EEA Regs 2006 Sch 4 para 2.
50 [2010] EWCA Civ 909, 29 July 2010.
51 Sir Anthony May, President of the QBD, at [18].
52 [2011] EWCA Civ 499, 20 April 2011.

of establishing rights of residence under the directive, not merely by 'residence that is not unlawful for a period of five years'.[53]

14.91 The following periods of residence have been held not to be residence that can count towards the five-year period for the purpose of establishing a permanent right to reside:

- periods spent in prison;[54]
- residence by a person with dual Irish and British nationality: this was because the right to reside was not pursuant to rights under the EU treaty but was by virtue of being British.[55]

However, the argument that periods of lawful residence prior to the directive coming into force cannot count has been dismissed by the ECJ. In *Lassal*[56] and *Dias*,[57] the ECJ held that periods spent as a worker prior to April 2006, when the directive came into force, could count towards the requisite five-year period of residence.

14.92 In addition to qualifying persons and their family members, family members who have 'retained' rights of residence (see paras 14.113–14.117 below) also gain a permanent right to reside after five years' continuous residence.[43] Note, however, that the retained rights of residence depend on the person working, being self-employed or being self-sufficient.

Retirement or permanent incapacity

14.93 A worker or self-employed person who has ceased activity, because of retirement or permanent incapacity, will gain a permanent right to reside if the conditions set out below at paras 14.94–14.98 are met.

14.94 If retired, the person must have been employed or self-employed for at least 12 months and have lived in the UK continuously for more than three years. If previously employed, the person must either have reached the age to qualify for a state pension or have

---

53 [2011] EWCA Civ 499, Thomas LJ at [33].

54 *HR (Portugal) v Secretary of State for the Home Department* [2009] EWCA Civ 371, 5 May 2009; *Carvalho v Secretary of State for the Home Department and Secretary of State for the Home Department v Omar* [2010] EWCA Civ 1406, 14 December 2010.

55 *McCarthy v Secretary of State for the Home Department* [2008] EWCA Civ 641, 11 June 2008. This was confirmed as correct in the judgment of the ECJ dated 5 May 2011, see para 14.130 below.

56 *Secretary of State for Work and Pensions v Lassal* C-192/09, 25 May 2010, ECJ.

57 *Secretary of State for Work and Pensions v Dias* C-325/09, 21 July 2011, ECJ.

taken early retirement. If previously self-employed, the person must have reached the age to qualify for a state pension.[58]

14.95 If permanently incapacitated, either:

- the person must have lived in the UK continuously for more than two years before the termination; or
- the incapacity must have been caused by an accident at work or an occupational disease that entitles him or her to an occupational pension paid in full or part by a UK institution.[59]

14.96 In both cases, the necessary period of residence or activity must have been immediately before termination of employment or self-employment.

14.97 The requirement for a minimum period of residence or activity does not apply to an EEA national who is married to or in a civil partnership with a UK national.[60]

14.98 During periods of inactivity a person may still be treated as being employed or self-employed provided it is for reasons not of the person's own making or it is due to illness or accident. Similarly, a worker who is registered as a jobseeker during a period of involuntary unemployment is classed as continuously working for these purposes.[61]

Family members on death of worker or self-employed person

14.99 Where the worker or self-employed person has died before gaining a permanent resident status, a family member gains a right to reside in the UK permanently if the following conditions are met:[62]

- the family member resided with the person immediately before the death; and, either
  - the deceased had resided continuously in the UK for at least the two years immediately before the death; or
  - the death was the result of an accident at work or an occupational disease.

58 EEA Regs 2006 reg 5(2) and article 17.1(a) of the Citizenship Directive.
59 EEA Regs 2006 reg 5(3) and article 17.1(b) of the Citizenship Directive.
60 EEA Regs 2006 reg 5(6) and article 7.2 of the Citizenship Directive.
61 EEA Regs 2006 reg 5(7) and article 17.1 of the Citizenship Directive.
62 EEA Regs 2006 reg 15(1)(e) and article 17.4 of the Citizenship Directive.

Meaning of 'continuous residence'

14.100   In calculating any period of 'continuous residence' referred to in the Citizenship Directive and the regulations, the following are disregarded:[63]

- any periods of absence from the UK that do not exceed six months in total in any year;
- periods of absence for military service; and
- any one absence from the UK not exceeding 12 months for an important reason such as pregnancy and childbirth, serious illness, study or vocational training or an overseas posting.

Losing the permanent right of residence

14.101   Once acquired, the right of permanent residence is only lost through absence from the UK for a period exceeding two consecutive years.[64]

14.102   However, all of the permanent rights of residence are subject to the Home Office powers to remove or exclude EEA nationals in specified circumstances. See para 14.121 below.

Family members of qualifying persons

Close family members

14.103   The close family members of qualified EEA nationals (other than students) and EEA nationals with a permanent right of residence also enjoy a right to reside. Close family members are defined as:[65]

- a spouse or civil partner;
- children and grandchildren, including those of the spouse or civil partner, provided they are under 21 or dependent on the qualified person or his or her spouse or civil partner; and
- dependent parents and grandparents, including those of the spouse or civil partner.

Students

14.104   In the case of those who are qualified as students, the only family members who have a right to reside for longer than for an initial three months are:

---

63   EEA Regs 2006 reg 3 and article 16.3 of the Citizenship Directive.
64   EEA Regs 2006 reg 15(2) and article 16.4 of the Citizenship Directive.
65   EEA Regs 2006 reg 7 and article 2.2 of the Citizenship Directive.

- a spouse or civil partner;
- dependent children under the age of 18.[66]

Family resources – self-sufficient persons and students

14.105 If the EEA national is a qualified person by virtue of being self-sufficient, the resources of the whole family must be sufficient to ensure that none become a burden on the social assistance scheme and the necessary comprehensive sickness insurance must cover all of the family members.[67]

14.106   If the qualified person is a student, the assurance given by the student to the Home Office regarding sufficient resources is satisfied only if the resources are sufficient to avoid the student and his or her family members becoming a burden on the social assistance system.[68]

14.107   When calculating whether a family has sufficient resources the resources will be deemed sufficient if they are more than the maximum level to qualify for social assistance (ie above the income limit for eligibility for receipt of income support).[69]

Extended family members

14.108 The following relatives and members of the household may gain a right to reside as 'extended family members' if they satisfy certain conditions.[70]

14.109   *Dependent member of household* This means a relative of an EEA national, his or her spouse or civil partner who is dependent on him or her and is a member of the household.

14.110   *Relatives requiring personal care* This means a relative of an EEA national, his or her spouse or civil partner who 'on serious health grounds' strictly requires the personal care of the EEA national, his or her spouse or civil partner.

14.111   *Relatives who would qualify for ILR* This means a person who is a relative of an EEA national and who, if he or she were applying to join

---

66 In all cases the children and grandchildren must be the direct descendants of the qualified person or his or her spouse or civil partner. This, however, includes adopted children and stepchildren.

67 EEA Regs 2006 reg 4(2). However, if the family members are themselves EEA nationals they may be qualified persons in their own right.

68 EEA Regs 2006 reg 4(3) and article 7.1(c) of the Citizenship Directive.

69 EEA Regs 2006 reg 4(4) and article 8.4 of the Citizenship Directive.

70 EEA Regs 2006 regs 7(1)(d) and 8(2)–(5) and article 3.2 of the Citizenship Directive.

a non-EEA national who was present and settled in the UK, would qualify for indefinite leave to remain on that basis.

14.112   *Co-habitees* This means the same or opposite sex partner of an EEA national who is not a civil partner or spouse and who can prove he or she is in a durable relationship with the EEA national.

Family members – retaining the right of residence

14.113   The general rule is that family members enjoy a right of residence in the UK only so long as the EEA national remains a qualified person and they remain family members.[71] However, there is provision for the family members' rights of residence to continue in the following circumstances:

- on the death of the qualified person (see paras 14.114–14.115);
- on divorce or termination of a civil partnership (see paras 14.116–14.117);
- where children are in education (see 14.118–14.120).

Death of qualified person[72]

14.114   If the qualified person dies, a non-EEA family member retains the right of residence provided he or she had lived in the UK for at least the year immediately before the death and is a worker, self-employed or self-sufficient person or the family member of such a person.

14.115   Note that, in addition, in certain circumstances a family member of a qualified person who dies may gain a permanent right of residence, see para 14.99 above.

Termination of marriage or civil partnership[73]

14.116   Where a non-EEA national ceases to be a family member of a qualified person because of the termination of the marriage or civil partnership the right of residence will be retained provided the following conditions are satisfied:

- the person was residing in the UK at the date of termination; and
- he or she is a worker, self-employed or self-sufficient person or the family member of such a person; and
- one of the following conditions is satisfied:

---

71   EEA Regs 2006 reg 14(2).
72   EEA Regs 2006 reg 10(2) and articles 12 and 7 of the Citizenship Directive.
73   EEA Regs 2006 reg 10(5) and articles 13 and 7 of the Citizenship Directive.

- the marriage or civil partnership had lasted for at least three years and the parties had resided in the UK for at least one year of its duration;
- the former spouse or civil partner has custody of a child of the qualified person;
- the former spouse or civil partner has the right of access to a child (under the age of 18) of the qualified person and a court has ordered that it must take place in the UK; or
- the continued right of residence in the UK is warranted by particularly difficult circumstances, such as the person or another family member having been a victim of domestic violence during the marriage or civil partnership.

14.117 In all the above cases the right to reside is retained only if the family members are themselves working, self-employed or self-sufficient. Family members who are EEA nationals already have such rights by virtue of their nationality. This provision therefore only benefits non-EEA family members.

Children in education

14.118 Where a qualifying member dies or ceases to be a qualified person on ceasing to reside in the UK, any children or grandchildren attending educational courses in the UK retain a right of residence as long as they continue to attend such a course.[74] They must have been attending an educational course immediately before the qualified person died or ceased to be a qualified person.

14.119 In addition, if the person in education is a child, any parent with actual custody also retains a right of residence in the same circumstances.[75]

14.120 Moreover, the ECJ has decided that a primary carer of a child in full-time education may have a right to reside in a member state by reference to EU law outside of the Citizenship Directive, see para 14.128 below.

Exclusion and removal

14.121 The Citizenship Directive and the EEA Regulations 2006 provide for removal if justified on the grounds of public policy, public security or public health. The decision-making framework in relation to the powers of removal gives enhanced protection depending on the

74 EEA Regs 2006 reg 10(3) and articles 12 and 7 of the Citizenship Directive.
75 EEA Regs 2006 reg 10(4) and articles 12 and 7 of the Citizenship Directive.

length of residence enjoyed by the person concerned. So, a person with a permanent right to reside can be removed only if there are 'serious grounds of public policy or public security' and a person who has resided in the UK for a continuous period of at least 10 years can only be removed if there are 'imperative grounds of public security'.[76] Given that most decisions to remove will be taken in relation to those who have served prison sentences in the UK, it must be borne in mind that long periods in prison will not usually count towards the relevant residence period. This does not, however, mean that someone who has enjoyed long residence before serving a prison sentence must start again in establishing a period of continuous residence to establish a permanent right to reside under the Citizenship Directive.[77]

Documents and evidence of status

14.122   EEA nationals must be admitted freely to the UK[78] and they are not required to have any form of documentation, such as a residence permit or passport stamp confirming a right to enter or to reside in the UK.

14.123   The only people with a right to reside that derives from EU law who are required to have documentation to confirm their status are as follows:

Person	Documents issued by Home Office
Accession state workers and their family members in first 12 months of working (applies to A8 nationals prior to 30 April 2011 only).	Workers registration certificate and workers registration card.
Non-EEA nationals with a right to reside by virtue of being the family member of an EEA national.	Family permit, residence card or permanent residence card. The permit will usually be endorsed by UKBA in the person's passport.

76 See EEA Regs 2006 reg 21 and article 28 of the Citizenship Directive.
77 See EEA Regs 2006 regs 19 and 20 and *HR (Portugal) v Secretary of State for the Home Department* [2009] EWCA Civ 371, 5 May 2009 and *Carvalho v Secretary of State for the Home Department and Secretary of State for the Home Department v Omar* [2010] EWCA Civ 1406, 14 December 2010.
78 EEA Regs 2006 reg 11(1).

14.124 Any other EEA national or family member who has a right to reside *may* apply for registration or a residence card from the Home Office but need not do so in order to establish a right to reside. Such documents will be issued free of charge. A local authority is not entitled to insist that a person obtain such documentation.

14.125   In all cases the local authority must assess for itself whether the person has a right to reside in the UK. A local authority will usually need to seek documentary evidence of status, for example, contracts of employment, wage slips, tax returns, bank statements, marriage or civil partnership certificates etc. However, as in all cases, obtaining documentary evidence is part of the inquiry process and not a prerequisite before the inquiry process can begin or before interim accommodation can be provided.

Rights of residence outside the Citizenship Directive

14.126 The conditions set out in the EEA Regs 2006 and the Citizenship Directive are described above. However, these do not set out exhaustively the rights of EU nationals and their family members. The main EU Treaty, now the Consolidated Version of the Treaty on the Functioning of the European Union (TFEU), has been relied on in a number of cases considered by both the domestic courts and the ECJ.

14.127   In *Abdirahman v Leicester City Council & Secretary of State for Work and Pensions, Ullusow v Secretary of State for Work and Pensions*[79] the Court of Appeal considered the cases of two EEA nationals who had been refused benefits. Both appellants were in the UK to be near to family members but did not have a right to reside by virtue of either their own economic activity or as family members of a qualified person. They argued that they had each entered the UK lawfully; they had remained in the UK without any breach of immigration law; and they were entitled to remain unless and until action was taken to remove them. They submitted that they must be regarded as having a right to do what they were doing lawfully, that is, residing in the UK and relied on what is now article 21 of TFEU which provides that:

Every citizen of the Union shall have the right to move and reside freely within the territory of the Member States, subject to the limitations and conditions laid down in this Treaty and by the measures adopted to give it effect.

79 [2007] EWCA Civ 657, 5 July 2007.

> The Court of Appeal dismissed the appeals, holding that this did not establish a right of residence so as to entitle the appellants to benefits because the relevant directive provided that:
>
> > ... beneficiaries of the right of residence must not become an unreasonable burden on the public finances of the host Member State.
>
> Any rights of residence were subject to the limitations imposed by the directive which were proportionate to the legitimate objective of protecting the public finances of the host member state.[80]

Parents gaining a 'derivative' right to reside through dependent children

Children in education

14.128   In *Ibrahim v Harrow* and *Teixeira v Lambeth LBC*[81] the applicants applied for homeless assistance from the local authorities. Both had dependent children who were in full-time education. Ms Ibrahim was a Somali national married to a Dutch national. She could not rely on the EEA Regs 2006 reg 10(3) (see para 14.118 above) because her husband had ceased to work (and therefore ceased to be a qualifying person) before leaving the UK. Ms Teixeira was Portugese and had worked in the UK intermittently but was not working when her daughter started school. Both argued that the Citizenship Directive was not the sole source of rights of residence and relied on article 12 of Directive 1612/68 which provides that:

> The children of the national of a Member State who is or has been employed in the territory of another Member State shall be admitted to that State's general educational, apprenticeship and vocational training courses under the same conditions as the nationals of that State, if such children are residing in its territory. Member States shall encourage all efforts to enable such children to attend these courses under the best possible conditions.

The ECJ found in favour of Ms Ibrahim and Ms Teixeira: the children of an EEA national who works, or has worked, in another

---

80 This approach was also adopted by the Court of Appeal in *Lekpo-Bozua v Hackney LBC* [2010] EWCA Civ 909, 29 July 2010 and *Okafor v Secretary of State for the Home Department* [EWCA] Civ 499, 20 April 2011, see para 14.89 above.

81 C-480/08 and C-310/08.

> member state and the parent who is their primary carer have a right of residence by virtue of article 12 of Directive 1612/68 and that right is not conditional on their having sufficient resources and comprehensive sickness insurance in that member state.

14.129 This means that an EEA national who has worked in the UK has an unconditional right to reside in the UK if he or she is the parent and primary carer of a child in education, so long as the child remains in education. A non-EEA national enjoys the same rights if he or she is married to an EEA national who has worked in the UK.

Children with British nationality

14.130 The general rule is that British people have a right to reside in the UK by virtue of their nationality. Their right to reside in the UK does not arise from EU law and therefore they cannot benefit from some of rights under EU law that are more generous than the rights in domestic law (for example, the right to have non-EU family members live with them in the UK). Furthermore, the rights under EU law are about moving and residing freely within the territory of the EU and are generally established only when the person is exercising the right of free movement, rather than simply remaining in their country of nationality.

> This is illustrated by *McCarthy v UK*[82] which concerned a woman with joint British and Irish nationality. She sought to rely on her rights under EU law to obtain a residence permit for her Jamaican husband. Mrs McCarthy had lived in the UK her whole life. She argued that she was entitled to the residence permit because she had a permanent right to reside under article 16 of the Citizenship Directive and reg 15 of the EEA Regs 2006.
>
> The ECJ held that the Citizenship Directive has no application where a person has never exercised the right of free movement but has always resided in a member state of which he or she is a national. The fact that Mrs McCarthy was also a national of another member state did not mean that she had made use of the right of freedom of movement. The court also considered articles 20 and 21 of TFEU (establishing EU citizenship and providing that all citizens of the EU shall enjoy the rights provided for in the Treaties, including the right to move and reside freely within the territory of

82 Case C-434/09, 5 May 2011.

the member states (subject to the limitations and conditions laid down in the Treaty)). Although these rights can be relied on to challenge a national law or provision which has the effect of depriving a person of their rights as an EU citizen, or preventing the exercise of the right to move and reside freely within the EU, the national measure at issue here was the UK's failure to grant to Mrs McCarthy's husband permission to remain in the UK. This did not have the effect of depriving Mrs McCarthy of the enjoyment of her rights as an EU citizen. This was in contrast with *Ruiz Zambrano* (see below, para 14.131). Mrs McCarthy enjoyed an unconditional right of residence in the UK because she was a national of the UK and not by virtue of her EU citizenship.

14.131   However, the situation is different in the case of children who are EU citizens when the provision complained of would force the parents, and therefore the children, to leave the EU, thereby depriving them of their rights as EU citizens.

Ruiz Zambrano v ONEM[83] concerned a challenge by a Colombian national living in Belgium to the refusal of a work permit and/or unemployment benefit. Mr Zambrano had resided in Belgium with his wife since 1999. They had been refused asylum though it was accepted that they could not be sent back to Colombia because of the civil war. They had three children, the second and third being Belgian citizens.

The ECJ held that the Citizenship Directive did not apply because it applied only to EU citizens who move to or reside in a member state other than that of which they are a national. The children, who were EU nationals, had never left Belgium. The ECJ held that article 20 of TFEU prevents national measures that have the effect of depriving EU citizens of the genuine enjoyment of the substance of their rights as EU citizens. In this case:

A refusal to grant a right of residence to a third country national with dependent minor children in the Member State where those children are national and reside, and also a refusal to grant such a person a work permit, has such an effect. ... This is because it must be assumed that [a refusal to grant a right of residence]

83   ECJ, Case C-34/09, 8 March 2011 (ONEM is the Belgian National Employment Office).

> would lead to a situation where those children, citizens of the Union, would have to leave the territory of the Union in order to accompany their parents. Similarly, if a work permit were not granted to such a person, he would risk not having sufficient resources to provide for himself and his family, which would also result in the children, citizens of the Union, having to leave the territory of the Union.[84]

14.132 So, where the children of non-EEA nationals are British and the effect of a refusal to grant a right to reside or to work would be that the parents would be forced to leave the UK the parents have a right to reside in order to ensure that their children are not deprived of their rights as EU citizens, even though the children are not exercising rights of free movement within the EU.

The habitual residence test

14.133 When first introduced in 1996, the test was designed to exclude European nationals who were not ordinarily resident in the UK and who would otherwise have been eligible for homeless assistance immediately on arrival in the UK. The test had to be applied equally to British and European nationals otherwise it would have breached EU law. Between 1996 and 2004 any EEA national who was habitually resident in the UK was eligible for homeless assistance. Furthermore, any European exercising a Treaty right, such as working, did not have to satisfy the test at all. The test is less important now since only those EEA nationals with a right to reside can be eligible and most of those with a right to reside are exempt from the habitual residence test.

Who must satisfy the habitual residence test?

14.134 The following homeless applicants must be habitually resident in order to be eligible:

- persons who are subject to immigration control but who have indefinite leave to remain in the UK;
- British nationals;
- EEA nationals whose right to reside is by virtue of being self-sufficient (see paras 14.75–14.79 above);

84 ECJ, Case C-34/09, at [43] and [44].

- EEA nationals, and their family members, who have a permanent right to reside by virtue of five years' residence (see paras 14.88–14.92).

Who is exempt from the habitual residence test?

14.135 None of those persons who are subject to immigration control but eligible, except those with ILR, are required to be habitually resident.[85]

14.136 Furthermore, the Eligibility Regs 2006 provide that the following people shall not be treated as ineligible by virtue of not being habitually resident:[86]

- EEA nationals who are workers, self-employed or registered accession state workers, and their family members;
- EEA nationals who have a right to reside permanently in the UK under EEA Regs 2006 reg 15(1)(c), (d) or (e) (workers and self-employed people who are retired or permanently incapacitated and their family members, plus the family members of a deceased worker or self-employed person: see paras 14.93–14.99 for the conditions as to gaining a permanent right of residence under these provisions);
- people who are in the UK as a result of deportation, expulsion or other removal by compulsion of law from another country to the UK;
- people who left Monserrat after 1 November 1995 because of the volcanic eruptions; and
- people who left Zimbabwe to settle in Great Britain between 26 February 2009 and 18 March 2011 having accepted an offer of settlement from the government.[87]

What is the habitual residence test?

14.137 To satisfy the test a person must be habitually resident in the UK, the Channel Islands, the Isle of Man or the Republic of Ireland: all of which comprise the 'common travel area' (CTA).

14.138 Legislation provides no definition of the term 'habitual residence' but it has been considered by the courts in a number of cases. Usually, a person must show that he or she has taken up residence and lived

---

85 These classes of eligible persons are those who may not have been in the UK for a long period and may not necessarily wish to settle in the UK: refugees, those with unconditional ELR or humanitarian protection.

86 Eligibility Regs 2006 reg 6(2).

87 Allocation of Housing and Homelessness (Eligibility) (England) (Amendment) Regulations 2009 SI No 358.

for a period in the CTA.[88] However, the situation is different for a person who has previously been habitually resident and is returning to resume an habitual residence previously established. He or she should not fail the habitual residence test solely on the ground that he or she has not lived in the CTA long enough.[89]

14.139   There is no minimum period that will establish habitual residence. The central question is where a person's 'centre of interest' is. This will involve considering the person's home, family ties, social connections and employment. Someone who has lived in the UK for only a few months may nevertheless be found to have established his or her centre of interest in the UK. Another person may have been in the UK for longer but his or her centre of interest may be elsewhere, for example someone who retains a home elsewhere and whose family is in another country. The test is not simply about how long a person has been present in the UK but about whether he or she is resident for a settled purpose.

14.140   Annex 10 of the Homelessness Code of Guidance sets out a useful summary of the application of the test.

Ineligible members of the household/restricted cases

14.141   When originally enacted, HA 1996 s185(4) provided that a person who is not eligible must be disregarded for the purpose of deciding whether another person is homeless or in priority need. In *R on the application of Morris v Westminster City Council*[90] the Court of Appeal made a declaration that HA 1996 s185(4) was incompatible with the European Convention on Human Rights. Mrs Morris was a British citizen but her infant daughter was subject to immigration control. Section 185(4) compelled the authority to disregard the daughter with the effect that Mrs Morris did not have a priority need. The Court of Appeal held that the section discriminated on the grounds of nationality and could not be justified.

14.142   In response the government amended HA 1996 s185 as set out in paras 14.143–14.148.[91] In *Bah v UK*,[92] the ECtHR rejected a claim that the new provisions breached articles 8 and 14, the court finding that the 'discrimination was justified'.

---

88 *Nessa v The Chief Adjudication Officer* [1999] 1 WLR 1937, HL.
89 *Swaddling v Adjudication Officer* (ECJ) [1999] ECR I-1090, EC.
90 [2005] EWCA Civ 1184, 14 October 2005, see paras 2.75–2.77.
91 See Housing and Regeneration Act 2008 s314 and Sch 15.
92 App no 56328/07, 27 September 2011, ECtHR.

Restricted persons

14.143   A new class of eligible person was created: a 'restricted person'. The provisions regarding restricted persons affect only British nationals and EEA nationals who have a right to reside in the UK, but who are homeless or have priority need only by virtue of a person who is ineligible. The ineligible person is a restricted person and the case is a 'restricted case'.

Restricted cases

14.144   The housing duty in relation to restricted cases is limited to providing a suitable private sector assured shorthold tenancy for a period of 12 months.

14.145   The new provisions do not change the position of an applicant who is eligible but is a person subject to immigration control. If such an applicant is only homeless or in priority need by virtue of an ineligible person that person continues to be disregarded.

14.146   So, for example, if a British national with an ineligible disabled wife applies as homeless and the only reason for the couple having a priority need is because of her disability, she is now treated as a restricted person. As a restricted case the authority's housing duty would be limited to providing a 12-month assured shorthold tenancy.

14.147   If an eligible person who was subject to immigration control (for example, a person with indefinite leave to remain) was in the same situation, the spouse would be ignored with the effect that the couple would not be held to have a priority need.

14.148   Note, however, that both rules apply only in relation to homelessness and priority need: if the applicant is homeless and in priority need for other reasons, and the full housing duty is owed, account must be taken of the ineligible members of the household when deciding what accommodation is suitable for the household.[93]

93   But the fact that some members of the household are ineligible will be relevant when deciding on the size of the accommodation that is offered, see *Ariemuguvbe v Islington LBC* [2009] EWCA Civ 1308, 21 October 2009.

Homelessness

14.149 The homelessness test, like the eligibility test, can be described as a 'threshold' test: if the authority is not satisfied that a person is homeless, no duty is owed under HA 1996 Part VII.

14.150 To be homeless does not necessarily mean to be without any form of accommodation. A person is also homeless under Part VII if he or she has accommodation but living in it puts the person at risk of violence, or if the nature of the accommodation is such that it is not reasonable to continue to live there.

Definition of homelessness

14.151 Housing Act 1996 s175 defines homelessness as follows:

(1) A person is homeless if he has no accommodation available for his occupation, in the United Kingdom or elsewhere, which:

(a) he is entitled to occupy by virtue of an interest in it or by virtue of an order of a court,

(b) he has an express or implied licence to occupy, or

(c) he occupies as a residence by virtue of any enactment or rule of law giving him the right to remain in occupation or restricting the right of another person to recover possession.

(2) A person is also homeless if he has accommodation but:

(a) he cannot secure entry to it, or

(a) it consists of a moveable structure, vehicle or vessel designed or adapted for human habitation and there is no place where he is entitled or permitted both to place it and to reside in it.

(3) A person shall not be treated as having accommodation unless it is accommodation which it would be reasonable for him to continue to occupy.

14.152 Housing Act 1996 s177 refers to the risk of violence. It provides:

(1) It is not reasonable for a person to continue to occupy accommodation if it is probable that this will lead to domestic violence or other violence against him, or against:

(a) a person who normally resides with him as a member of his family, or

(b) any other person who might reasonably be expected to reside with him.

For this purpose 'violence', means violence from another person; or threats of violence from another person which are likely to be carried out; and violence is 'domestic violence' if it is from a person who is associated with the victim.

14.153 Broadly therefore there are three possible ways in which a person may be homeless:

- *No accommodation* The person has no accommodation in which he or she is permitted or has a legal right to reside. See paras 14.160–14.174.
- *Accommodation but not reasonable to occupy* The person may have accommodation but it is not reasonable to occupy it.[94] This may be because of the risk of violence or for other reasons. See paras 14.175–14.189.
- *Accommodation but excluded from occupation* The person may have a legal right to occupy accommodation but be physically excluded from it; or the accommodation may be a mobile home and the person has no pitch or mooring for it. See paras 14.190–14.191.

14.154 The legislation and case-law in respect of each of these categories is examined below.

Meaning of 'available' accommodation

14.155 In every case, accommodation must be available for a person to occupy together with his or her family or household. A central aim of the homelessness legislation has always been to keep families together. HA 1996 s176 applies in relation to any reference in Part VII to 'accommodation' and provides:

> Accommodation shall be regarded as available for a person's occupation only if it is available for occupation by him together with:
> (a) any other person who normally resides with him as a member of his family, or
> (b) any other person who might reasonably be expected to reside with him.

14.156 Section 176 applies not only to the definition of homelessness but also to the definition of intentional homelessness and to the accommodation provided by an authority when discharging its housing duties.

14.157 Family members are not defined, but the Homelessness Code of Guidance provides that 'the phrase "member of the family" will include those with close blood or marital relationships and cohabiting partners (including same sex partners)'.[95]

---

94 Although the term used is 'continue to occupy', it is not necessary that the person has previously occupied: *Waltham Forest LBC v Maloba* [2007] EWCA Civ 1281, 4 December 2007. See para 14.172 below.
95 Homelessness Code para 8.5.

Who might reasonably be expected to live with the applicant?

14.158 Family members who normally live with a person must be regarded as part of that person's household. However, it is for the authority to decide in respect of other people whether it is reasonable to expect them to reside with the person. This could include partners who have not previously lived together or other family members who do not normally live together but wish to do so. In addition it may include people who are not family members and the Homelessness Code suggests that this group 'might include a companion for an elderly or disabled person, or children who are being fostered by the applicant or a member of his or her family'.[96]

14.159 The family members who normally live with a person and anyone else who might reasonably be expected to live with a person are referred to in this chapter as 'the household'.

Having no accommodation

What constitutes 'accommodation'?

14.160 The mere fact that a person's right to occupy accommodation is only temporary does not mean that the person is homeless. However, he or she must occupy 'a place which can fairly be described as accommodation'.[97] The following has been held not to be 'accommodation':

- a night shelter where a bed was provided on a nightly basis and the occupant was not allowed to remain indoors during the day;[98]
- a prison cell occupied by someone eligible for release on licence.[99]

14.161 This issue overlaps with the question of whether it is reasonable to occupy accommodation which is dealt with below, paras 14.182–14.189.

What is a right or permission to occupy accommodation?

14.162 Housing Act 1996 s175 refers to entitlement to occupy by virtue of an interest or by virtue of a court order. A tenant or owner-occupier has an interest in a property. A person may occupy by virtue of a court order where a family court has made an order that he or she may occupy a former matrimonial home despite not being the tenant or owner.

---

96 Homelessness Code para 8.5.
97 *R v Brent LBC ex p Awua* (1996) 27 HLR 453 at 459.
98 *R v Waveney DC ex p Bowers* (1983) 4 HLR 118, CA.
99 *R on the application of B v Southwark LBC* [2004] HLR 3, QBD.

14.163   Section 175 also refers to having an express or implied licence to occupy. This would include a person granted permission to share premises as a lodger or family members who live in the family home.

14.164   A person may also occupy a home because of 'any enactment or rule of law' that gives the person the right to remain in occupation or that restricts 'the right of another person to take possession'.[100] This would include a statutory tenant who no longer has a contractual tenancy (see para 3.84) and also a person against whom a possession order has been made but who has not yet been evicted.

Practical issues

Possession proceedings – when does the occupier become homeless?

14.165   As is described in paras 6.119–6.121 the court can make possession orders that allow occupiers to remain in occupation provided they comply with certain conditions. Some orders end the tenancy and others give the landlord the right to apply to end the tenancy if the conditions are breached. Even where the order ends a tenancy, a person who remains in occupation is not homeless if, as in most cases, there is a restriction on the right of the landlord to take possession (see paras 8.11–8.16). So, even where the court has no power to suspend or postpone possession, in most cases the occupier does not actually lose the right to occupy until the date of the eviction.

> In *R v Newham LBC ex p Sacupima*[101] the Court of Appeal considered the issue of exactly when someone subject to a possession order becomes homeless. The applicant had an assured shorthold tenancy and occupied the accommodation with her five children. Her landlord obtained a possession order and she approached the local authority for help. She was advised to await the bailiff's warrant and to return on the day of the eviction with her children and belongings. Ms Sacupima brought the claim to challenge the suitability of the interim accommodation. She also argued that the authority's duty to provide interim accommodation under HA 1996 s188 had arisen as soon as the possession order was made, as this ended her legal right to occupy the accommodation.
> The Court of Appeal held that this was not the case: she became homeless only when evicted by the bailiffs. Until that date there was a restriction on the landlord's right to take possession.

100 HA 1996 s175(1)(c), see para 14.151 above.
101 (2001) 33 HLR 1, CA.

14.166   It is the practice of many local authorities to advise people against whom a possession order has been made to return on the day of the eviction or shortly before. However, an authority should always consider whether it is reasonable for an occupier to remain in occupation until the eviction. Indeed this issue may need to be addressed at an earlier point – when the occupier receives notice of intended possession proceedings, particularly where the occupier has no defence to a possession claim.

14.167   The Homelessness Code of Guidance sets out the approach an authority should take to applicants who have received notice of possession proceedings:

> Para 8.32: Each case must be decided on its facts, so **housing authorities should not adopt a general policy of accepting – or refusing to accept – applicants as homeless or threatened with homelessness when they are threatened with eviction but a court has not yet made an order for possession or issued awarrant of execution.** In any case where a housing authority decides that it would be reasonable for an applicant to continue to occupy their accommodation after a valid notice has expired – and therefore decides that he or she is not yet homeless or threatened with homelessness – that decision will need to be based on sound reasons which should be made clear to the applicant in writing ...
>
> **The Secretary of State considers that where a person applies for accommodation or assistance in obtaining accommodation, and:**
> **(a) the person is an assured shorthold tenant who has received proper notice in accordance with section 21 of the Housing Act 1988;**
> **(b) the housing authority is satisfied that the landlord intends to seek possession;**
> **and**
> **(c) there would be no defence to an application for a possession order;**
> **then it is unlikely to be reasonable for the applicant to continue to occupy the accommodation beyond the date given in the section 21 notice, unless the housing authority is taking steps to persuade the landlord to withdraw the notice or allow the tenant to continue to occupy the accommodation for a reasonable period to provide an opportunity for alternative accommodation to be found.**

14.168   In practice authorities rarely issue a formal decision at this stage, but the Homelessness Code is clear: an authority should consider whether it is reasonable for such a person to remain in occupation pending eviction and, if it decides that it is, a reasoned decision should be given in writing. This will be a decision that the person is not homeless and carries a right of review.

14.169   An authority may lawfully depart from the Homelessness Code if there is reason to do so. Many authorities will justify their decision on the grounds of the expense of interim accommodation and the fact that the time people spend in interim accommodation can be reduced by remaining in their own home as long as possible. However, this will only be a valid justification if the authority is actively dealing with the application prior to eviction rather than just advising people not to approach until the day of eviction. Advisers may wish to press an authority for a written determination at an early stage, addressing the issue of whether it is reasonable for the occupier to remain in occupation. When forced to explain the decision in writing, the authority may concede the issue and offer interim accommodation prior to the actual eviction.

The cost of possession proceedings

14.170   When a possession order is made by the county court, the usual rule is that the occupier will be ordered to pay the landlord's legal costs. It is possible for any party to civil proceedings to make an application to join another party (a third party) to the proceedings and to seek an order that the third party pays the costs of the claimant, the defendant or both (see para 22.151). It is possible therefore, in possession proceedings, to ask the court to join the local authority and order it to pay the costs of the landlord. However, if such an application is made and is unsuccessful, this will increase the total costs of the proceedings and the occupier will usually be ordered to pay both the costs of the landlord and the local authority.

14.171   An alternative course of action is to make a formal complaint to the authority and seek reimbursement of the costs of the possession claim. If not resolved satisfactorily, further complaint may be made to the Local Government Ombudsman. However, the Ombudsman would have to find that there was maladministration in order to uphold the complaint and recommend compensation.[102]

Accommodation available anywhere in the world

14.172   If an applicant has accommodation anywhere in the world, he or she may not be homeless. The accommodation must, however, be available to the applicant and his or her household, and it must be reasonable to live in the accommodation.

---

102 See para 2.93 above.

In *Nipa Begum v Tower Hamlets LBC*[103] the Court of Appeal considered a decision that the applicant was not homeless because accommodation was available to her in Bangladesh. Ms Begum was a 21-year-old British national, born in Bangladesh. She had lived in the UK from the age of 13 or 14, but at the age of 17 had married in Bangladesh before returning to the UK. Later she stayed in Bangladesh with her husband at his father's home for 12 months. Shortly after returning to the UK, she gave birth to a son and then travelled to Bangladesh with her son, again staying in her husband's father's house. After a short while her son became ill and she returned to the UK. Her husband remained in Bangladesh awaiting entry clearance to join her in the UK. After a short stay with relatives she was asked to leave and applied to the authority as homeless. The authority decided that she was not homeless because her father-in-law's accommodation in Bangladesh was available to her and was reasonable to occupy. She requested a review, arguing that she could not afford to live in Bangladesh permanently, but acknowledging that it was Bengali tradition for a married couple to live with the husband's family, that she could continue to live in the house and that her husband's family were supporting him financially. The review decision confirmed the original decision. A county court appeal was lodged and the court quashed the decision holding, amongst other things, that the authority had failed to consider the issue of whether Ms Begum could afford to travel to the accommodation. The authority appealed.

The Court of Appeal upheld the authority's appeal, holding that:

Financial inability to travel is only one of many possible reasons why it may not be reasonable for an applicant to return to occupy overseas accommodation. In addition to factors concerning the legal availability, suitability and affordability of the accommodation, others may be, for example, connected with family or other personal problems, ill health, immigration restrictions, physical security and many others. In the absence of an indication of a particular difficulty or difficulties of that sort it is not, in my view, an authority's duty to take an applicant through a check list to negative all possible obstacles to his or her return to the overseas property.[104]

---

103 (1999) 32 HLR 445, CA.
104 (1999) 32 HLR 445, CA, Auld LJ at 458.

In *Waltham Forest LBC v Maloba*[105] the applicant was from Uganda but had lived in the UK for many years and become a British citizen. He met his wife on a visit to Uganda and they married and lived for two years in an annex to the family home. After his father's death other family members moved into the house and Mr Maloba and his wife and child returned to the UK and applied as homeless. The local authority found that he was not homeless, arguing that it was not required to consider whether it was reasonable for Mr Maloba and his family to live in the accommodation in Uganda; it was sufficient that it was available. The court quashed the decision and the authority appealed.

The Court of Appeal held that 'continue to occupy' did not mean that reasonableness was only relevant if the person was still in occupation. To find that a person was not homeless an authority must be satisfied not only that accommodation was available, but also that it was reasonable for the person to reside in it. The authority's alternative argument was that, when considering reasonableness, it was required only to consider the size, structural quality and amenities of the accommodation. The Court of Appeal rejected this: the authority had erred in failing to consider whether it was reasonable for Mr Maloba to relocate to Uganda, having lived in the UK for many years and becoming a British citizen.

14.173   As is clear from the judgment in *Nipa Begum,* it is essential to put forward to the authority any reasons why it would not be reasonable to occupy accommodation. However, the authority must consider, in all cases, the affordability of the accommodation (see para 14.185 below).

Matrimonial/civil partnership home

14.174   A person who is married or in a civil partnership has a right to occupy accommodation owned by or rented by the spouse or civil partner, provided that it has been the matrimonial or civil partnership home. This right lasts until the marriage or civil partnership comes to an end. Where the relationship has broken down, the authority will consider whether it is reasonable for the person to continue to occupy the shared accommodation. An authority may decide that it is, in spite of the fact that the couple no longer wish to be in partnership. Relevant factors will be the size of the accommodation and the

105 [2007] EWCA Civ 1281, 4 December 2007.

nature of the relationship. However, if continued occupation means that a person would be at risk of domestic violence, he or she should be accepted as homeless (see below, paras 14.176–14.181).

Not reasonable to continue to occupy

14.175 There are two distinct parts to this category: (1) where it is not reasonable to occupy because of the risk of violence; and (2) where it is not reasonable to occupy for other reasons. If violence is probable, an authority must find the applicant to be homeless. If considering reasons other than the risk of violence, the authority has a wide discretion and can take account of housing needs in its own area.

Probability of violence

14.176 Housing Act 1996 s177 provides that 'it is not reasonable for a person to continue to occupy accommodation if it is probable that this will lead to violence against him or her, or a member of the household'. Violence is defined as 'violence from another person; or threats of violence from another person which are likely to be carried out'.

What is violence?

14.177 Violence is not restricted to physical violence or the threat of physical violence.

> In *Yemshaw v Hounslow LBC*[106] the Supreme Court overturned the decision of the Court of Appeal and held that that violence 'includes physical violence, threatening or intimidating behaviour and any other form of abuse which, directly or indirectly, may give rise to the risk of harm'.[107]

14.178 A local authority must make a finding of fact: whether violence is probable if the person remains in occupation. The authority cannot refuse assistance or find a person not homeless because there are other remedies available for his or her protection. If the authority concludes that violence is probable, it must find the person to be homeless.

---

106 [2011] UKSC 3, 26 January 2011.
107 Lady Hale at [28]. See also the Homelessness Code of Guidance at para 8.21.

In *Bond v Leicester CC*[108] the applicant had fled two properties
because of domestic violence from the father of her two young
children. She was re-housed by a housing association, but again
suffered violence from the same man. He began to visit her at the
premises and would refuse to leave when asked. On one occasion
he assaulted her and she began to refuse to allow him into the
property, but he continued to visit, shouting and throwing stones
at the windows. Ms Bond left and fled to London. After staying
in a refuge, she returned to Leicester and alternated between her
mother's address and a friend's. She then applied to the council.
At that stage the housing association property was still available
and the authority decided that it was reasonable for her to return
there and that she was not homeless. The authority noted that,
although she had a long history of fleeing harassment from the
perpetrator, she had 'never taken any preventative measures to
address this matter', referring to the possibilities of contacting the
police or other bodies in relation to the 'alleged harassment'. She
was advised to 'take action to address the alleged harassment'. A
request for a review was made. The housing association property
was then repossessed and the review decision found that Ms Bond
was, by then, homeless, but homeless intentionally. The reason was
that she had deliberately ceased to occupy accommodation that
was available for her occupation and reasonable for her to continue
to occupy. The review letter accepted that Ms Bond had been the
subject of domestic violence for some considerable time, but stated
that in the opinion of the reviewing officer she 'should have taken
action under the criminal/civil law to prevent [the perpetrator] from
coming near her' or her property. The letter went on to detail the
various actions Ms Bond could or should have taken and stated
that 'she became homeless intentionally as she failed to take these
measures and as a consequence of her failure, she ceased to occupy
accommodation which was available for her occupation and would
have been reasonable for her to continue to occupy'.

The Court of Appeal held that when considering whether a
person is homeless or intentionally homeless: 'The only test is
what is probable. This ... is a pure question of fact, devoid of value
judgments about what an applicant should or should not do'.[109]
The decision was varied to the effect that Ms Bond was not
intentionally homeless.

---

108 [2002] HLR 6, CA.
109 [2002] HLR 6, CA, Hale LJ at 25–26.

14.179 The Homelessness Code reflects the decision in *Bond v Leicester CC*: 'An assessment must be based on the facts of the case and devoid of any value judgments about what an applicant should or should not do, or should or should not have done, to mitigate the risk of any violence (for example, seek police help or apply for an injunction against the perpetrator)'.[110]

14.180 Nevertheless, an authority may legitimately advise the applicant of the measures that may be taken to provide protection or increase security in the home. The Code recommends that authorities should consider the option of improving the security of the applicant's home, which may enable him or her to continue to live there safely and thereby prevent homelessness. However, it is a matter for the applicant whether to accept such assistance or to pursue the application for homeless assistance.

Evidence of violence

14.181 It is not necessary to show a history of violence. The question is whether it is probable that continued occupation would lead to violence, which includes the threat of violence from someone likely to carry out the threat. Local authorities sometimes suggest that certain kinds of evidence are necessary before they can accept a homeless application from someone alleging violence: police reports, doctor's letters or court orders are often requested. While it is lawful for the authority to request supporting evidence to complete its enquiries, it is unlawful to refuse assistance on the basis that an applicant cannot provide the evidence requested. The availability of evidence is relevant to the determination of whether violence is probable. An authority is entitled to conclude that, on the available evidence, violence is not probable, but if it is rejecting the applicant's account this must be made clear to the applicant and reasons given.

Unreasonable to occupy for other reasons

14.182 If the issue is whether someone is homeless because it is not reasonable to occupy accommodation for reasons other than the risk of violence, an authority has a wide discretion. There is no restriction on the nature of the factors that may make it unreasonable to occupy accommodation, but paras 8.29–8.34 of the Code of Guidance draw attention to the following factors:

- affordability;
- physical characteristics;

110 Homelessness Code para 8.22.

- type of accommodation;
- people fleeing harassment;
- the fact that a person has been given notice to leave (see para 14.167 above).

14.183   When considering the issue, an authority may take account of the general housing circumstances in its area. HA 1996 s177(2) provides:

> In determining whether it would be, or would have been, reasonable for a person to continue to occupy accommodation, regard may be had to the general circumstances prevailing in relation to housing in the district of the local housing authority to whom he has applied for accommodation or for assistance in obtaining accommodation.

14.184   This means that in an area of great need, where many people are living in dwellings that are overcrowded and/or in substantial disrepair, it will be difficult to satisfy the authority that it is not reasonable to continue to occupy on the basis of the condition of the accommodation.

Affordability

14.185   Affordability must be considered in all cases. The Homelessness (Suitability of Accommodation) Order 1996[111] specifies that an authority must take into account the financial resources available to the applicant, the cost of the accommodation, any maintenance payments made in respect of a former spouse or children, and the applicant's reasonable living expenses. If a property is not affordable, an authority must find the applicant to be homeless. However, it is for the authority to decide what are reasonable living expenses.[112] Most authorities will consider a property to be affordable if, after discharging all necessary outgoings, including rent or mortgage payments, a person is left with a disposable income equivalent to the level of income support. If arguing that a property is unaffordable, it will usually be necessary to prepare a detailed financial statement.

Overcrowding

14.186   Overcrowding is a factor that may mean that it is not reasonable to remain in occupation of accommodation. Paragraph 11.78 above explains 'statutory overcrowding' – a legal measure of overcrowding that can lead to prosecution of owners or occupiers. The threshold for statutory overcrowding is very high, but even a household that is statutorily overcrowded is not necessarily homeless.

---

111   SI No 3204.
112   See *R v Brent ex p Baruwa* (1997) 29 HLR 915, CA.

In *Harouki v Kensington and Chelsea RLBC*[113] the Court of Appeal upheld a decision by the authority that the applicant was not homeless. The family of six occupied a small three-bedroom flat in contravention of the 'space standard' set out in HA 1985. Despite the fact that this meant that the occupation constituted a criminal offence, the authority was entitled to find that it was reasonable for the family to remain in occupation and await an allocation under HA 1996 Part VI.[114]

Challenging decisions

14.187 It is very difficult to challenge decisions under this provision successfully. If it is argued that conditions are such that it is unreasonable for the person to remain in occupation, strong evidence will be needed, such as medical reports, environmental health reports and recommendations from social services. Even then, the final decision is one for the housing authority. If an authority has considered all the relevant issues and decided that it is reasonable to continue to occupy, the only possible challenge will be that the decision is irrational or perverse, ie a decision no reasonable authority could reach (see para 2.15).

14.188 However, local authorities have certain powers and duties in relation to the condition of private sector accommodation. These are described in chapter 11. Even where a person wants to pursue a homeless application rather than remain in occupation, it may assist to report the premises to the appropriate department of the authority. This may result in enforcement action that compels a private landlord to carry out works. Alternatively, it may result in the landlord terminating the tenancy and claiming possession.

14.189 Whether it is better to pursue a homeless application rather than await an allocation or bidding under a choice-based lettings scheme depends on the level of priority given to those in unsatisfactory housing conditions in the particular authority's allocations scheme. A successful homeless application may result in more suitable accommodation being provided temporarily, but may also mean that the applicant will wait longer for suitable permanent accommodation.

---

113 [2007] EWCA Civ 1000, 4 July 2007.
114 However, in *Elrify v Westminster CC* [2007] EWCA Civ 632, the local authority's decision that the family were not homeless was held to be flawed as it had applied the overcrowding standard incorrectly. The authority was ordered to reconsider its decision.

Excluded from occupation

Illegal eviction

14.190   A person who has been unlawfully evicted retains a legal right to occupy, but is homeless under HA 1996 s175(2)(a). Such a person will usually be entitled to a court order to gain re-entry. In such a case, if the person is in priority need, a local authority should provide temporary accommodation for as long as it takes to obtain and enforce an injunction. However, there may be reasons why a person does not wish to seek re-entry, for example, fear of the landlord, having limited rights of occupation, being unable to obtain legal aid or find a solicitor to assist. Authorities often indicate that a person who does not enforce his or her rights through the courts will be found intentionally homeless. In making such a decision an authority must consider whether it would have been reasonable for the person to take the necessary steps to be able to resume occupation, taking account of the reasons for not doing so.

Mobile homes

14.191   A caravan or houseboat is capable of being 'accommodation' so that an occupant may not be homeless. However, this is the case only if there is somewhere the person can keep the mobile home and live in it. The fact that a site or mooring is only temporary will not of itself mean that the person is homeless.[115]

Being threatened with homelessness

14.192   A person is threatened with homelessness if it is likely that he or she will become homeless within 28 days: HA 1996 s175(4). A specific duty may arise under HA 1996 s195 in relation to a person threatened with homelessness. The duty is described at paras 13.77–13.81.

Priority need

14.193   No housing duty will be owed to a person who does not have a 'priority need'. A person who is homeless, eligible but does not have priority need is entitled to advice and assistance only. Authorities do, however, have a power to provide accommodation to those who do not have a priority need, see HA 1996 s192(3).

115 Homelessness Code of Guidance para 8.17.

Categories of priority need

14.194 There are several categories of priority need. Some are easily established on the facts, others depend on a judgment by an authority as to whether something is 'reasonable' or whether a person is 'vulnerable'.

Priority need categories under HA 1996 s189(1)

14.195 Housing Act 1996 s189(1) provides:

The following have a priority need for accommodation:
(a) a pregnant woman or a person with whom she resides or might reasonably be expected to reside;
(b) a person with whom dependent children reside or might reasonably be expected to reside;
(c) a person who is vulnerable as a result of old age, mental illness or handicap or physical disability or other special reason, or with whom such a person resides or might reasonably be expected to reside;
(d) a person who is homeless or threatened with homelessness as a result of an emergency such as flood, fire or other disaster.

14.196 Housing Act 1996 s189(2) provides that further categories may be added by the secretary of state and by the Welsh National Assembly. In both cases regulations have been made, adding further classes of priority need: 16- and 17-year-olds, care leavers under the age of 21, and additional classes of vulnerability. The substance of the English and Welsh regulations is different.

The Welsh regulations

14.197 The Welsh regulations came into force on 1 March 2001[116] and added the following further categories of priority need:

- 18- to 20-year-olds who are 'care leavers' or who are at 'particular risk of sexual or financial exploitation';
- children aged 16 or 17;
- a person without dependent children who has been subject to domestic violence, is at risk of such violence or, if he or she returns home, is at risk of domestic violence;
- former armed service personnel who have been homeless since leaving the armed forces;

116 Homeless Persons (Priority Need) (Wales) Order 2001 SI No 607.

- former prisoners who have been homeless since leaving custody and who have a local connection with the area of the local housing authority.

14.198   None of the Welsh categories of additional priority need require that the person is vulnerable. However, 18- to 20-year-olds who are not care leavers are only in priority need if judged to be at 'particular risk of sexual or financial exploitation'.

The English regulations

14.199   In England the following further categories were added by regulations as from 31 July 2002:[117]

- children aged 16 or 17 (provided they are not owed certain accommodation duties by social services under the Children Act 1989);
- 18- to 20-year-old 'care leavers' (provided they are not students to whom social services owe a duty to provide out-of-term accommodation);
- a person who is vulnerable as a result of:
  - being a care leaver who is 21 or older,
  - having been in the armed forces,
  - having been in custody, or
  - having become homeless because of violence.

14.200   Each category of priority need is examined below in paras 14.201–14.255.

Pregnancy

14.201   This should be a relatively straightforward category. There is no minimum period of pregnancy required. However, disputes often arise at the point of application about the evidence of pregnancy.

Interim duty to accommodate

14.202   This arises if the authority 'has reason to believe' that a woman 'may' be pregnant (as well as homeless and eligible).[118] If a woman approaches an authority in an emergency late in the day or out of hours, she may have no evidence of her pregnancy. In such a situation, her explanation of why she believes she is pregnant should

---

117 Homeless Persons (Priority Need for Accommodation) (England) Order 2002 SI No 2051.
118 HA 1996 s188, see paras 13.26–13.28.

be sufficient until she can obtain a doctor's letter. However, it is common for authorities to refuse interim accommodation until supporting evidence is produced. This is unlawful, but in practice it is often simpler to obtain a doctor's letter than to challenge the authority by way of judicial review.

Inquiries/full decision

14.203 As in all cases, the burden is on an authority to satisfy itself of the relevant matters. An applicant will usually be requested to provide documentary evidence in the form of doctor's letters, pre-natal appointment cards, copies of scans or letters stating the expected date of delivery. If an applicant fails to provide such evidence, an authority may decide that it is 'not satisfied' that she is pregnant.

14.204　It is unlawful for an authority to delay making a decision in case the pregnancy does not go to full term.[119] Furthermore, once a decision has been made that a housing duty is owed, the duty does not end if the applicant is no longer in priority need (see para 16.46).

Dependent children

14.205 There are three possible issues the authority must decide:

- is the child dependent on the applicant?
- does the child reside with the applicant?
- if not, is the applicant someone with whom the children 'might reasonably be expected to reside'?

Dependence

14.206 The term 'dependent children' is not defined. The courts have held that a 16-year-old who was in receipt of a training allowance was not dependent on his father, but indicated that the concept of dependence was not confined to financial dependence: *R v Kensington and Chelsea RLBC ex p Amarfio*.[120]

14.207　The Homelessness Code para 10.7 states that authorities:

> ... may wish to treat as dependent all children under 16, and all children aged 16–18 who are in, or are about to begin, full-time education

---

119　*R v Ealing LBC ex p Sidhu* (1982) 2 HLR 45, QBD: it is unlawful for an authority to defer a decision in case there is a change of circumstance in the future. This is discussed below at para 14.248 in relation to priority need based on age.

120　(1995) 27 HLR 543, CA.

or training or who for other reasons are unable to support themselves and who live at home.

14.208   The children need not be the natural children of the applicant, but there must be 'some form of parent/child relationship'.[121] Where an application was made by a man married to a person under the age of 18 on the basis that she was a dependent child, the court upheld the authority's decision that he was not in priority need: *Hackney LBC v Ekinci*.[122]

14.209   The child must be dependent in some way on the applicant, but need not be 'wholly and exclusively' dependent on the applicant.[123]

> In *R v Westminster CC ex p Bishop*[124] the applicant had two children. When he and their mother separated it was agreed that the children would live with him for part of each week and that during holidays they would divide their time equally. The mother received child benefit for both children. He applied for homeless assistance from the council. The authority decided that he was not in priority need, as it was not satisfied that the children were dependent children who resided with him. The reasons were that the children were adequately housed with their mother and they were not dependent on him because the mother received child benefit for them and the applicant did not have the financial means to support them.
>
> His application for judicial review was dismissed: it was necessary that a child should be dependent at least in part on an applicant, and it was for the authority to decide the issue. The authority had taken account of relevant facts and was entitled to reach that conclusion.

Residing with the applicant

14.210   There must be some degree of permanence or regularity in the residence, as opposed to a temporary or limited arrangement.

14.211   Where parents are separated, it is possible for children to reside with both parents, but an authority may find, as a matter of fact, that children do not reside with the parent with whom they spend less time.

121 Homelessness Code para 10.8.
122 [2001] EWCA Civ 776, 24 May 2001.
123 *R v Lambeth LBC ex p Vagliviello* (1990) 22 HLR 392, CA.
124 (1997) 29 HLR 546, QBD.

> In *R v Port Talbot BC ex p McCarthy*[125] the parents were separating. They agreed that their child would stay with Mrs McCarthy for four nights each week and with Mr McCarthy for three. The authority decided that he was not in priority need and that the arrangement was one of 'staying access' rather than residence. The court upheld the decision.

14.212 In the following case, the decision was quashed because the authority had failed to apply the correct test.

> In *R v Leeds ex p Collier*[126] the parents had separated and the father applied for housing, indicating that the children stayed with him for part of each week. The authority found that he had no priority need on the basis that the children's mother had 'greater residency responsibility for the children'. The court held that the council's decision was 'fatally flawed' as it had applied an incorrect test.

14.213 Residence of children with an applicant in interim accommodation provided under HA 1996 s188 is not to be ignored in applying the test.

> In *Oxford CC v Bull*[127] the applicant's three children stayed with their mother in the three-bedroom council property when the couple separated. Mr Bull left the family home and rented a single room in a shared house. Subsequently, the children, unhappy about their mother's new relationship, decided they wanted to live with their father and moved in with him which caused his landlord to serve notice to quit. He applied as homeless and was accommodated on an interim basis with the children pending inquiries. During this period the children lived with Mr Bull but also spent time staying with their mother. He was found not to be in priority need on the basis that the children did not live with him; the period in interim accommodation was not taken into account. He was also found to be intentionally homeless because his decision to take the children into his home led to his eviction. The decisions were upheld on review but Mr Bull succeeded in his county court appeal.

125 (1990) 23 HLR 207, CA.
126 June 1998 *Legal Action* 14, QBD.
127 [2011] EWCA Civ 609, 18 May 2011.

The authority appealed to the Court of Appeal which held that it was wrong to disregard the time spent in interim accommodation. In accordance with the House of Lords' decision in *R (M) v Hammersmith & Fulham LBC*[128] the relevant time for deciding the issue was the date of the review and at that date the children clearly resided with the applicant. However, the Court of Appeal upheld the appeal in relation to intentional homelessness. By inviting the children to live with him Mr Bull had deliberately done something that led to the loss of his accommodation.

Reasonable to reside with the applicant

14.214   Where a separated parent does not have accommodation and is therefore unable to have the children residing with him or her, the authority must be satisfied of two things: first, that the children are dependent in some way on the non-resident parent and, second, that the person is someone with whom they might reasonably be expected to reside. The courts have considered this in the following cases.

In *R v Kingswood BC ex p Smith-Morse*[129] the applicant's son lived with him for part of the week following his divorce. The authority found that he had no priority need as the child's 'main residence' was with the mother. The decision was quashed: the authority should have gone on to consider whether the child might reasonably be expected to reside with the applicant in the future.

However, in *R v Westminster CC ex p Bishop* (para 14.209 above), the fact that the children were adequately housed with the mother and that the father could not support them financially was held to justify a decision that they were not dependent on him.

14.215   Where the family court has made an order that separating parents should have joint residence, whether by consent, or after a contested hearing, this does not determine the issue of whether it is reasonable to expect the children to reside with both parents for the purpose of priority need.

---

128 [2001] UKHL 57, see para 14.324 below.
129 (1994) *Times* 8 December.

In *Holmes-Moorhouse v Richmond upon Thames LBC*[130] the House of Lords considered a case in which a joint residence order had been made by the family court in respect of the couple's three children. The court held (1) a joint residence order made by the family court does not determine the issue of whether it is reasonable for the children to live with both parents, in separate accommodation; (2) it was not unlawful for the housing authority to consider the scarcity of accommodation when deciding whether it would be reasonable for the children to live with the both parents; (3) the family courts should not make joint residence orders unless it appears reasonably likely that both parties will have accommodation in which the children can reside and should not make such orders to place pressure on the housing authority to allocate accommodation in a particular way.

Children in the care of the local authority

14.216 The local authority's duty to consider whether it is reasonable to expect children to reside with an applicant is to avoid a 'Catch-22 situation': applicants who cannot live with their children for lack of accommodation being refused housing because they do not live with their children. Although the decision about reasonableness is a judgment for the housing authority, where social services wish the children to return to their parents, this should determine the issue. The Homelessness Code states that in such a case 'liaison with the social services authority will be essential'.[131]

Vulnerability

14.217 Several categories of priority need depend on the local authority being satisfied that a person is vulnerable because of some personal characteristic or circumstance. The term 'vulnerable' is not defined in HA 1996, but it has been considered by the courts on many occasions.

14.218 In *R v Waveney DC ex p Bowers*[132] it was held that the term means 'less able to fend for oneself so that injury or detriment will result when a less vulnerable man will be able to cope without harmful effects'. Subsequent cases suggested that a person would be

---

130 [2009] UKHL 7, 4 February 2009.
131 Homelessness Code para 10.11.
132 (1983) 4 HLR 118, CA, Waller LJ at 122.

vulnerable only if two tests were satisfied: first, being less able to obtain suitable accommodation than the ordinary person and, second, if suitable accommodation is not found, that the person will suffer more than most. However, the Court of Appeal in *R v Camden LBC ex p Pereira*[133] held that this approach was wrong.

In *Pereira* the applicant was a former drug addict. He was accommodated on an interim basis while the authority investigated his application. There was psychiatric evidence that if he became homeless he would be under immense psychological stress that would adversely affect his efforts at rehabilitation. The authority applied the two-part test suggested by previous case-law and found Mr Pereira not to be vulnerable; the council's medical officer found that he had an ability to find accommodation and was therefore no less able to fend for himself than other people.

The Court of Appeal held that this was the wrong approach. The authority should have asked whether the applicant was, when homeless, less able to fend for himself than an ordinary homeless person so that injury or detriment to him would have resulted when a less vulnerable man would be able to cope without harmful effect. There is a single composite test that is about the applicant's ability to cope with being homeless. A particular inability of a person to obtain housing for himself may be an aspect of his inability as a homeless person to fend for himself.

14.219   The Homelessness Code of Guidance reflects the *Pereira* test in setting out the approach an authority should take in deciding whether a person is vulnerable:[134]

> 10.13 It is a matter of judgement whether the applicant's circumstances make him or her vulnerable. When determining whether an applicant in any of the [relevant] categories ... is vulnerable, the local authority should consider whether, when homeless, the applicant would be less able to fend for him/herself than an ordinary homeless person so that he or she would suffer injury or detriment, in circumstances where a less vulnerable person would be able to cope without harmful effects.
>
> 10.14 ... The assessment of an applicant's ability to cope is a composite one taking into account all of the circumstances. The applicant's vulnerability must be assessed on the basis that he or she is or will

133 (1999) 31 HLR 317.
134 Homelessness Code paras 10.13–10.14.

become homeless, and not on his or her ability to fend for him or herself while still housed.

14.220 It is for the authority to weigh up all of the relevant factors in deciding whether a person is vulnerable and, if all relevant issues have been taken into account, the decision can only be challenged on the grounds that it is irrational or perverse (see paras 2.15–2.17). Some common errors in decisions on vulnerability are:

- Considering the person's physical or mental health at a time when interim accommodation is being provided. What the authority must do is to assess whether the person would suffer injury or detriment *when homeless.*
- Considering several potential categories of vulnerability, including 'other special reason', in isolation. An authority must consider whether, as a result of a combination of all of the relevant factors, the person is vulnerable.
- Delegating decision-making to a medical expert. The decision as to whether a person is vulnerable must be taken by the housing authority, not by a medical adviser. An authority should take account of the opinion of a medical adviser, but it is not for the medical adviser to decide whether an applicant is in priority need.[135]

The non-vulnerable homeless person

14.221 The applicant's ability to cope with homelessness is compared with that of the non-vulnerable homeless person. It was recently observed that this is 'a legal test which itself makes the dubious assumption that homelessness is something fit people can always cope with'.[136] However, any person is likely to suffer injury or detriment if homeless. The issue is whether, because of one or more of the specified reasons, the applicant would suffer more than the non-vulnerable homeless person. In relation to depression, it has been held that any homeless person is likely to suffer depression and that continued homelessness is likely to exacerbate the depression.[137] To establish vulnerability, evidence will be needed that, in the applicant's case, homelessness will cause or exacerbate his or her depression to a significant extent.

---

135 *R v Lambeth LBC ex p Carroll* (1987) 20 HLR 142, QBD.

136 *Shala v Birmingham CC* [2007] EWCA Civ 624, 27 June 2007, Sedley LJ at [24].

137 See *R on the application of Yeter v Enfield LBC* [2002] EWHC (Admin) 2185 at [16].

Extent of necessary inquiries

14.222   In cases of vulnerability it is often argued that the authority has made insufficient inquiry. In such a case it is not enough to show that the authority could have made more inquiries; it must be established that the inquiries the authority failed to make are those that no reasonable authority could have failed to regard as necessary.

14.223   In *Cramp v Hastings BC* and *Phillips v Camden LBC*[138] (see para 13.54) the Court of Appeal held that the county court had been wrong to quash decisions on the basis of insufficient inquiry into potential vulnerability. At the review stage no representations had been made that further inquiry was necessary and:

> The duty to decide what inquiries are necessary rests on [the review officer], and her decision will be a lawful decision unless no reasonable council could have reached the same decision on the available material.[139]

14.224   However, it has also been observed by the courts that in certain cases, what is at stake for the applicant is such that the authority's duty to inquire may be set at a high level.

In *Khelassi v Brent LBC*[140] the authority was considering an application by a man suffering from depression. A psychiatrist had expressed concern about the risk of suicide. The authority, without offering reasons, preferred the opinion of a general practitioner whose opinion was that the man was not vulnerable. At the applicant's appeal the county court judge stated:

> I agree ... that the local authority's duty is to make such inquiries as are necessary ... I further agree ... that the decision as to what inquiries are necessary is primarily a question for the decision-maker, not for the court. What is necessary will depend on what is at stake. Where a significant risk of suicide is in issue a great deal is at stake.

The decision was quashed and the Court of Appeal endorsed the county court decision when refusing the authority permission to appeal.

---

138   [2005] EWCA Civ 1005, 29 July 2005.
139   [2005] EWCA Civ 1005, Brooke LJ at [68].
140   [2006] EWCA Civ 1825.

Decisions to be made by local authority not court

14.225 In all cases involving local authority decision-making, the starting point is that local authorities, not the courts, have the decision-making responsibility. This has been emphasised in relation to decisions about priority need.

> In *Osmani v Camden LBC*[141] the applicant's doctor confirmed that he was suffering from depression and post-traumatic stress disorder, that this made it difficult for him to find secure accommodation and that leaving him without secure accommodation would put his mental health at risk. However, the authority found that he was not vulnerable.
>
> The Court of Appeal dismissed the applicant's appeal: the council had applied the correct test and reached a decision that was not perverse; the issue of vulnerability is not exclusively or even necessarily a medical question:
>
> > Given that each authority is charged with local application of a national scheme of priorities but against its own burden of homeless persons and finite resources, such decisions are often likely to be highly judgmental. In the context of balancing the priorities of such persons a local housing authority is likely to be better placed in most instances for making such a judgment.[142]

14.226 The fact that, in relation to priority need, the local authority is best placed to make judgments about competing demands and entitled to take account of scarce resources was also stressed by the House of Lords in *Holmes-Moorhouse*, above, para 14.215.

Role of medical evidence

14.227 The long-established categories of priority need include those who are vulnerable as a result of mental illness, disability and 'other special reason'. Medical evidence of the extent of a person's mental illness or disability will usually be needed. If it is the opinion of the authority that medical evidence is necessary, it is the authority's responsibility to obtain it. Most authorities will require an applicant to complete a medical questionnaire, which may then be referred to a medical adviser employed by the authority. Alternatively, the authority may

141 [2004] EWCA Civ 1706, 16 December 2004.
142 [2004] EWCA Civ 1706, Auld LJ at [38].

send a questionnaire to the applicant's GP. The decision on vulnerability will be taken on the basis of the contents of the questionnaire indicating the nature of any illness or disability and the treatment received.

14.228   The Homelessness Code para 10.16 provides that, where there is doubt about the extent of vulnerability, authorities 'may' consider seeking a clinical opinion, but stresses that the final decision is for the authority to make.

14.229   In practice, authorities are reluctant to seek an independent clinical opinion because of the cost. Those representing applicants under the Legal Help scheme may be able to obtain an independent report paid for by the Legal Services Commission provided the 'sufficient benefit test' is met (see para 22.160 below).

14.230   If an expert is asked to offer an opinion it is essential that he or she is asked to give relevant information, namely:

- a description of the person's health problems/disability;
- an opinion as to how the person would be able to cope if homeless, in light of the health problems/disability; and
- an opinion as to the likely effect on the person of being homeless; in particular, whether the person would suffer greater 'injury or detriment' when homeless, than the average person, by reason of his or her health problems/disability.

Contested medical reports

14.231   Several reported cases have concerned applicants who have obtained medical reports suggesting vulnerability, while the authority's medical adviser offers the opinion that the person's condition is not severe enough to establish vulnerability.[143] Some of the principles established in those cases are as follows:

- Where the potential vulnerability arises from a mental health problem, it may be necessary to obtain an opinion that is more expert than that of a GP.
- The opinion of a medical adviser who merely considers another expert's report and advises the authority on its content does not have the same weight as the opinion of an expert who has actually examined the patient. It is a valid role, but must be distinguished

---

143 See: *Hall v Wandsworth LBC; Carter v Wandsworth LBC* [2004] EWCA Civ 1740, 17 December 2002; *Bellouti v Wandsworth LBC* [2005] EWCA Civ 602, 20 May 2005; *Khelassi v Brent LBC* [2006] EWCA Civ 1825 and *Shala v Birmingham CC* [2007] EWCA Civ 624, 27 June 2007.

from the role of an expert who has examined the patient or who has personal knowledge of the patient.

- Where the authority relies on the advice of a medical adviser on the content of a report, it should make this clear in the decision letter. Where the opinion of the medical adviser differs from that of the other expert, the authority should indicate why it prefers the view of one over the other.

- Where the authority obtains an opinion that raises new issues or contentious points, the applicant should normally be given a chance to comment on the opinion, in the interests of fairness. However, if the advice is merely directed to helping the authority assess the weight of evidence on matters already fully in play, there is no automatic obligation to disclose it. There is no 'absolute rule of natural justice that an applicant must have the last word in every case'.[144]

- If there is a difference of opinion between the medical adviser and the applicant's expert, the medical adviser could be asked to examine the patient or to contact the applicant's expert to resolve the difference of opinion.

Vulnerability because of old age

14.232 Authorities must not apply a rigid age criteria, either by accepting all applicants over a certain age or by rejecting those below a certain age; an applicant is only in priority need if vulnerable.[145]

Other special reasons

14.233 There is no restriction on the nature of the 'other reasons' that may make a person vulnerable.

14.234 The Homelessness Code provides:[146]

The legislation envisages that vulnerability can arise because of factors that are not expressly provided for in statute. Each application must be considered in the light of the facts and circumstances of the case. Moreover, other special reasons giving rise to vulnerabiity are not restricted to the physical or mental characteristics of a person. Where applicants have a need for support but have no family or friends on whom they can depend they may be vulnerable as a result of an other special reason.

---

144 *Bellouti v Wandsworth LBC* [2005] EWCA Civ 602, Jonathon Parker at [62].
145 Homelessness Code para 10.15.
146 Homelessness Code para 10.30.

14.235   In practice, it is difficult to establish vulnerability in cases where a combination of factors is relied on, particularly when drug and alcohol addiction are amongst those factors.

> The Court of Appeal dismissed the applicants' appeals in *Simms v Islington LBC*[147] and *Mangion v Lewisham LBC*.[148] Mr Simms had a history of crack cocaine and cannabis addiction, had suffered family bereavements, had asthma, depression and anxiety and suffered panic attacks. Ms Mangion had an alcohol addiction and suffered back problems and moderate depression. In both cases the authority had correctly applied the *Periera* test and the court held that the detailed letters, read as a whole, did not give grounds for the decisions to be quashed.

The new categories: institutional history and fleeing violence

14.236   The Welsh regulations provide that those fleeing violence and those who have been homeless since leaving the armed forces or custody are automatically in priority need. There is no requirement that they are also vulnerable. The English regulations require that those with an institutional background are also vulnerable. In the English regulations care leavers aged 21 or over who are vulnerable are in priority need. There is no equivalent in the Welsh regulations.

Institutional background

14.237   The following paragraphs (14.238–14.239) on vulnerability refer only to the English regulations. The Homelessness Code of Guidance sets out the relevant factors in assessing potential vulnerability amongst these groups. Common to all those with an institutional background are the following relevant factors:

- the length of time a person was in care, in prison or in the armed forces;
- the length of time since the person was in care, in prison or in the armed forces and whether the applicant has been able to obtain and/or maintain accommodation during that period; and

---

147 [2008] EWCA Civ 1083, 16 August 2008.
148 [2008] EWCA Civ 1642, 11 December 2008.

- whether the person has existing support networks, particularly by way of family, friends or mentor.

Fleeing violence

14.238 In relation to those who have left accommodation because of violence, the Homelessness Code also provides that the authority may wish to take account of:[149]

(i) the nature of the violence or threats of violence (there may have been a single but significant incident or a number of incidents over an extended period of time which have had a cumulative effect);

(ii) the impact and likely effects of the violence or threats of violence on the applicant's current and future well being;

(iii) whether the applicant has any existing support networks, particularly by way of family or friends.

14.239 The Homelessness Code also provides:[150]

In cases involving violence, the safety of the applicant and ensuring confidentiality must be of paramount concern. It is not only domestic violence that is relevant, but all forms of violence, including racially motivated violence or threats of violence likely to be carried out. Inquiries of the perpetrators of violence should not be made. In assessing whether it is likely that threats of violence are likely to be carried out, a housing authority should only take into account the probability of violence, and not actions which the applicant could take (such as injunctions against the perpetrators).

Children and care leavers

14.240 In addition to the new classes of vulnerability, two other categories of priority need were added in both England and Wales by regulation: children aged 16 or 17 and young people aged 18 to 20 who are 'care leavers'. In both cases there is some overlap between the duties that a local housing authority may owe under HA 1996 and the duties a local social services authority may owe under the Children Act (CA) 1989.

14.241 See paras 19.6–19.32 for an explanation of the Children Act 1989, in particular the accommodation duties arising under CA 1989 ss17 and 20 and the duties under the 'leaving care' provisions.

---

149 Homelessness Code para 10.29.
150 Homelessness Code para 10.28.

Children aged 16 and 17

14.242   Under the English regulations any child aged 16 or 17 is in priority need unless a duty to accommodate is owed by social services. In Wales there is no such exception: all homeless 16- and 17-year-olds have priority need.

14.243   In the following circumstances in England, the young person will not be in priority need:

- where social services owe a duty to accommodate him or her as a 'child in need' under CA 1989 s20; or
- where he or she is a 'relevant child' under the Children (Leaving Care) Act 2000; this will be the case if the child has previously been in the care of the authority for at least 13 weeks, ending after the age of 16 (see para 19.32).

14.244   In *R (G) v Southwark LBC*[151] the House of Lords made it clear that the primary duty for homeless 16- and 17-year-olds is the duty under CA 1989 s20. This case and the way CA 1989 s20 operates is discussed in detail in paras 19.35–19.36.

14.245   It should be noted, however, that the homelessness duty may still be relevant where the child is not a child in need or does not require accommodation but only help with accommodation. However, the circumstances in which this is likely to be the case will be exceptional. In *R (G) v Southwark LBC* the court referred to examples such as a 16 or 17 year old who has accommodation but is temporarily unable to occupy and has the resources to pay for hotel accommodation or who simply needs help in getting to the accommodation. In almost all cases, a homeless 16- or 17-year-old will be a child in need by virtue of being homeless and will require accommodation, and so the authority will owe a duty under CA 1989 s20. However, the section 20 duty cannot be forced on an unwilling child and a child may make an informed decision that he or she does not wish to be provided with accommodation by social services. In such a case it is essential that the child is advised of the services that will be available if he or she is accommodated under section 20. This includes help with education and training and ongoing support up to the age of 21, or possibly 24 if in full-time education.

14.246   Social services and housing departments must operate joint working practices or protocols. Statutory guidance was issued in April 2010 by the Department for Children, Schools and Families

---

151 [2009] UKHL 26, 26 May 2009. See para 19.35.

and the Department for Communities and Local Government.[152] This provides that, if the homeless child approaches housing services, interim accommodation should be provided but that 'housing services should make an immediate referral to children's services for an assessment.'[153]

14.247 The guidance states (reflecting the previous judgments of the House of Lords) that:

> It is essential that services for homeless 16- and 17-year-olds are underpinned by written joint protocols which set out clear, practical arrangements for providing services that are centered on young people and their families and prevent young people from being passed from pillar to post.[154]

Despite this it would appear that at the date of writing only a small minority of local authorities have developed any such protocols, see para 19.42.

Delays in decision-making

14.248 Clearly, since both automatic priority need and Children Act 1989 duties depend on the child's age, it is essential to apply in sufficient time so that a decision is made before the child reaches the age of 18. In most homeless applications a final decision is not made immediately on presentation. The general rule is that a decision under HA 1996 Part VII is made on the basis of the circumstances at the date of the decision, whether this is an initial decision or a decision on review.[155] However, a local authority cannot take advantage of this general rule to refuse assistance to an applicant who was in priority need by virtue of age when he or she applied to the authority.

In *Akilah Robinson v Hammersmith and Fulham LBC*[156] the court held that an authority had acted unlawfully in postponing a decision on priority need, with the effect that the young person had turned 18 when the decision was taken. The applicant applied to the authority, having been asked to leave the family home by her mother.
Initially she was told that it would take 28 days for her case to be investigated and that, as she would be 18 within 28 days, there was

---

152 *Provision of accommodation for 16 and 17 year old young people who may be homeless and/or require accommodation*, available from www.communities.gov. uk/publications/housing/homelesssixteenseventeen.
153 Guidance (see note 152) para 2.11.
154 Guidance (see note 152) para 5.2.
155 *Mohamed v Hammersmith & Fullham LBC* [2001] UKHL 57, see para 14.324.
156 [2006] EWCA Civ 1122.

no point in continuing with the application. However, having taken advice, she approached the authority again the following day. She was placed in interim accommodation and the authority referred her case for mediation, in accordance with the Homelessness Code. It postponed making a decision until after mediation. The mediation failed and the authority then made its decision that, having become 18, the applicant was not in priority need. The decision was upheld on review on the basis that the decision-maker had been correct to refer the case to mediation.

The Court of Appeal held that the authority had acted unlawfully in postponing a decision. It was clear when Ms Robinson first applied that she was homeless unintentionally and, as she was under the age of 18, was in priority need. The fact that inquiries normally take a certain time does not mean that a person who will become 18 within that time is not priority need.

Furthermore, if, on review, the decision had been found to be unlawful, the review officer should have ensured that Ms Robinson had the rights she would have had if the decision had been lawful.

Nevertheless, there are cases in which it may take a reasonable period of time for the necessary inquiries to be made and the applicant may reach the age of 18 before the inquiries are complete. In such a case the authority is entitled to take the decision by reference to the facts as they exist at the date of the decision.

14.249   It is now clear that in such a case the applicant should be referred to social services for an assessment under the Children Act 1989. Again, it is important to ensure that there is no delay in carrying out an assessment and particularly in providing accommodation. A child who is accommodated under CA 1989 s20 for any period of time between the ages of 16 and 18 will be in automatic priority need as a care-leaver after the age of 18 and before the age of 21. And, if the child is accommodated for at least 13 weeks before his or her 18th birthday, he or she will be entitled to ongoing support under the Children (Leaving Care) Act 2000, see para 19.32.

Care leavers aged 18–20

14.250   A care leaver under the age of 21 is in priority need, regardless of vulnerability. The English and Welsh regulations differ slightly. In England the person must have been in care after reaching the age of 16 but while under the age of 18. In Wales the period in care is 'at any time while still a child'. In both cases this means having been 'looked after, accommodated or fostered'.[157] In England 'relevant students' are excluded. These are students to whom social services owe a duty under the Children (Leaving Care) Act 2000, which includes a duty to provide out-of-term accommodation, see para 19.32.

14.251   An authority may deny that a child was accommodated under s20 and assert that instead assistance was given under CA 1989 s17, see paras 19.37–19.39. The label given by the authority is not determinative and advisers should seek further information. The young person may request a copy of his or her social services file under the Data Protection Act 1998 (see para 2.98). Even if the assistance has been described throughout as 'section 17' it may be possible to establish that, in reality, the authority was acting under a section 20 duty.

Emergency or disaster

14.252 Someone made homeless because of an emergency such as a flood, fire or other disaster is treated as having a priority need regardless of personal circumstances.[158]

14.253   The event that makes the person homeless must be both an emergency and a disaster. Homelessness resulting from an unlawful eviction does not come within this category.[159] The sudden disappearance of a mobile home, however, was accepted as an emergency akin to flood or fire as: 'It involved the sudden and wholly unexpected loss of [his] home in circumstances wholly outside his control by the loss of the structure in which he made his home'.[160]

Household members

14.254 It should be noted that most of the 'old' priority need categories provide that anyone with whom such a person resides or might reasonably be expected to reside also has a priority need. The exception is a person made homeless as a result of flood, fire or other disaster. However, none of the new categories of priority need extend to household members.

14.255   But, if a duty is accepted, accommodation must be made available for the person to whom the duty is owed:

157 This is defined in CA 1989 s24.
158 This is a category of priority need that reflects the original provisions of the National Assistance Act 1948 – local authorities owed a duty to provide emergency accommodation to people made homeless in such circumstances.
159 *R v Bristol CC ex p Bradic* (1995) 27 HLR 584, CA.
160 *Higgs v Brighton & Hove CC* [2004] HLR 9, Kay LJ at [20].

... together with:

(a) any other person who normally resides with him as a member of his family, or

(b) any other person who might reasonably be expected to reside with him.[161]

> In *R (Ogbeni) v Tower Hamlets LBC*[162] permission was granted for a claim for judicial review to challenge the authority's decision that this did not apply in relation to a 17-year-old who had priority need by virtue of his age. He had been living with his aunt but both became homeless when she lost her tenancy. Had she applied, she would have been found intentionally homeless. The court rejected the council's argument that it was implicit that this category of priority need related only to single applicants.

Intentional homelessness

14.256 Being 'intentionally homeless' does not mean intending to become homeless. Rather, it means that a person's homelessness was caused by something he or she did (or did not do) deliberately. Where a person is found to be intentionally homeless the local authority's duty will be limited; it must provide advice and assistance and accommodation for a 'reasonable period' to give the person an opportunity to find his or her own accommodation.

14.257 The definition of intentional homelessness is set out in HA 1996 s191:

(1) A person becomes homeless intentionally if he deliberately does or fails to do anything in consequence of which he ceases to occupy accommodation which is available for his occupation and which it would have been reasonable for him to continue to occupy.

(2) ... an act or omission in good faith on the part of a person who was unaware of any relevant fact shall not be treated as deliberate.

14.258 In addition, since 1996 there has been an additional limb to the test of intentional homelessness: 'contrived homelessness'. This is dealt with below at paras 14.306–14.307.

14.259 There are several elements to the definition. In all cases, the following questions must be asked:

---

161 HA 1996 s176.
162 [2008] EWHC 2444 (Admin), 8 August 2008.

- Which accommodation did the person cease to occupy, thereby causing the homelessness?
- Was that accommodation available to the applicant, ie available for the occupation of the applicant *and* his or her household?
- Would it have been reasonable for the applicant to continue to occupy the accommodation?
- What was the act or omission in consequence of which he or she ceased to occupy?
- Was the act or omission deliberate?
- If apparently deliberate, was it an act or omission made in good faith in ignorance of a relevant fact?

14.260 It is useful to examine each of these questions separately, see paras 14.261–14.305.

Which accommodation did the person cease to occupy, thereby becoming homeless?

Ceasing to occupy

14.261 First, it must be noted that to be intentionally homeless a person must cease to occupy accommodation.[163] A failure to take up accommodation does not, in most cases, make a person intentionally homeless. An apparent exception to this is when an offer of suitable accommodation is refused (whether under HA 1996 Part VI or Part VII). In such a case, the person can be said to have ceased to occupy interim or temporary accommodation provided by the authority in consequence of refusing the offer.[164]

14.262 This situation must be distinguished from that of a person who, when homeless, declines to take up accommodation that is made available to him or her.

14.263 Under homeless prevention strategies (see para 13.8 above) many authorities offer to those who present as homeless help to obtain private sector accommodation. Applicants may prefer to take a tenancy in the private sector rather than pursue a homeless application. However, an authority should not advise the person that to refuse an offer of accommodation from a private landlord will render them intentionally homeless. A person can only be intentionally homeless if he or she ceases to occupy accommodation *as a result of* his or her act or omission. A person who is already homeless or threatened with

163 *R v Westminster CC ex p De Souza* (1997) 29 HLR 649, QBD.
164 *R v East Hertfordshire DC ex p Hunt* (1986) 28 HLR 51, QBD.

homelessness cannot be found intentionally homeless for refusing to accept assistance to take up a private sector tenancy. Note, however, that under the Localism Act 2011 the housing duty under HA 1996 Part VII will be discharged by an offer of private sector accommodation, see paras 16.73–16.75.

14.264   However, this must be distinguished from a situation in which an authority accepts a homeless duty and discharges its housing duty by arranging a private sector tenancy. In such a case, the housing duty *will* end if a suitable offer is refused. If the offer is being made pursuant to a housing duty, the authority must write to the applicant clearly stating the effect of a refusal and informing the applicant of the right to seek a review of the suitability of the accommodation. See below at paras 16.64–16.73 for an explanation of the different situations in which private sector accommodation is used in discharging the homeless duty.

Which accommodation?

14.265   It may be that the loss of the most recent accommodation is not the cause of the person's homelessness.

> In *Dyson v Kerrier*[165] the applicant voluntarily gave up a council tenancy and took an unprotected 'out of season' holiday let. When she was required to leave the unprotected tenancy she applied to the local authority as homeless. The authority found that she was intentionally homeless; her homelessness had been caused by the deliberate act of giving up her council tenancy.
>
> The court upheld the council's decision. The cause of the applicant's homelessness was not the loss of the unprotected tenancy but the previous deliberate act of giving up the council tenancy.

14.266   *Dyson v Kerrier* was decided in 1980 and subsequently the courts developed the concept of 'settled accommodation'[166] and applied it in the following ways:

- when considering intentional homelessness an authority was to ignore any non-settled accommodation;
- a person who did not have settled accommodation was by definition homeless; and

165 [1980] 3 All ER 313, CA.
166 *Din v Wandsworth LBC* (1982) 1 HLR 73, HL.

- it was necessary that the accommodation provided by an authority under the homeless duty was settled.

14.267 In 1995 the House of Lords held that this was the wrong approach. In *R v Brent LBC ex p Awua*[167] it was held that the concept of settled accommodation was only applicable in relation to intentional homelessness. Moreover, it was only relevant to the *Dyson v Kerrier* type of situation: to ensure that a person who is intentionally homeless, following the loss of permanent accommodation, does not cease to be intentionally homeless by obtaining non-settled accommodation which later ceases to be available. What this means is:

- A person who has non-settled accommodation is not homeless provided it is reasonable to continue to occupy the accommodation.
- The duty to secure accommodation does not necessarily mean securing accommodation that is settled.
- In relation to intentional homelessness, non-settled accommodation is ignored only if the person has lost that accommodation unintentionally. Then the authority can look back to the accommodation previously occupied. However, a person may be intentionally homeless from non-settled accommodation.

14.268 Given the development of the case-law advisers must be cautious of reported cases regarding settled accommodation decided before *Awua* in 1995.

What is settled accommodation?

14.269 The term 'settled' means something more than merely temporary: 'What amounts to a "settled residence", is a question of fact and degree depending on the circumstances of each individual case'.[168] An assured shorthold tenancy is capable of being settled accommodation but is not necessarily so, depending on the circumstances.

> In *Knight v Vale Royal BC*[169] the applicant had been found intentionally homeless by the authority. She then obtained an assured shorthold tenancy for a six-month term. She was informed by the landlord at the outset that he would require the property back after six months. After she was evicted the authority again found her to be intentionally homeless on the basis that there was still a

---

167 (1995) 27 HLR 453, HL.
168 Ackner LJ in *Din v Wandsworth LBC*, CA, 23 June 1981 (unreported).
166 [2003] EWCA Civ 1258, 31 July 2003.

causal link between her previous loss of accommodation and her homelessness. She argued that she had had settled accommodation which had broken the chain of causation. In the Court of Appeal it was submitted that because the assured shorthold tenancy was the most commonly available form of tenure in the private sector such a tenancy must necessarily be settled accommodation.

The court rejected this, holding:

> In our judgment the occupation by a tenant of accommodation let on a six months' assured shorthold tenancy is capable of constituting settled accommodation for the purposes of breaking a chain of causation from past intentional homelessness ... What we cannot accept is that the occupation by a tenant of accommodation let on a six months' assured shorthold tenancy is, as a matter of law, always sufficient to constitute settled accommodation. The question remains one of fact and degree to be determined by the local authority in the circumstances of a particular case.[170]

Ms Knight's appeal was dismissed.

But, see *Moran v Manchester CC*,[171] para 14.276 below, in which it was held that a woman evicted from a refuge was not intentionally homeless on the ground that it was not reasonable to occupy such accommodation indefinitely.

14.270   While the parties' intentions are relevant in deciding whether accommodation is settled, the test is not entirely subjective; an authority may find that accommodation was not settled even if the applicant states that the intention was to remain in the accommodation permanently.[172] Other factors, such as the level of security and the suitability of the accommodation, will also be taken into account.

Examining the accommodation history

14.271   What all this means is that, in deciding the cause of homelessness, a local authority can look back through an applicant's history of previous accommodation until it finds either settled accommodation which was not lost intentionally or accommodation, settled or not, from which the applicant was intentionally homeless. The finding in

---

170 [2003] EWCA Civ 1258, Sir Martin Nourse at [24]–[25].

171 [2009] UKHL 36, 1 July 2009.

172 *R v Purbeck DC ex p Cadney* (1985) 17 HLR 534, QBD.

the first case would be that the person is not intentionally homeless and in the second case that he or she is intentionally homeless.

14.272　This is also referred to as 'breaking the chain of causation': in most cases a person who is intentionally homeless will only cease to be intentionally homeless (break the chain of causation) by obtaining settled accommodation. If this is later lost unintentionally, so that the person becomes homeless again, this homelessness will no longer be 'intentional'. However, there may be other events which can break the chain or be the true cause of present homelessness, such as suffering domestic violence or relationship breakdown. See para 14.281.

Was the accommodation available for the applicant and his or her household?

14.273　The authority must be satisfied that the accommodation was available for the applicant to occupy together with any other person who normally resides with the applicant as a member of his or her family, or any other person who might reasonably be expected to reside with him or her.[173]

14.274　Which family members normally live with the applicant is a question of fact. However, in relation to other people, it is for the authority to decide whether it is reasonable to expect a person to live with the applicant.[174] It is not necessary that the person has previously lived with the applicant. See paras 14.158–14.159 above.

Would it have been reasonable for the applicant to continue to occupy that accommodation?

14.275　The test is the same as when considering whether a person is homeless. If the authority is satisfied that violence would have been probable if the person had remained it cannot find the person to be intentionally homeless. The fact that the person could have taken other steps to protect him or herself is irrelevant: *Bond v Leicester CC*, para 14.178 above.

14.276　While it is possible to be intentionally homeless when the cause of the homelessness was the loss of non-settled accommodation, a place in a women's refuge is not accommodation that it would be reasonable to continue to occupy indefinitely. A woman in a refuge

173　HA 1996 s176. See *R v Hillingdon LBC ex p Islam* (1981) 1 HLR 107, HL.
174　See *R v Barking & Dagenham LBC ex p Okuneye* (1995) 22 HLR 174, QBD.

was therefore still homeless and could not found to be intentionally homeless by virtue of eviction from the refuge.[175]

14.277　If the applicant contends that it would not have been reasonable to remain for a reason other than the likelihood of violence, the issue is one for the authority to decide. In making the decision, it may take account of housing conditions in the local area.[176]

14.278　The question is not whether it was reasonable to leave but whether it would have been reasonable to remain.[177] This is judged on the basis of the facts at the time the accommodation ceased to be available, not at the date of the application. So, the fact that accommodation would inevitably have been lost does not prevent a person from being found intentionally homeless if he or she decided to leave at a time when it would have been reasonable to remain.[178] Furthermore, it will not assist an applicant who left accommodation when it would have been reasonable to remain that a subsequent change in circumstances (for example, having children) would have made it unreasonable for continued occupation.[179]

14.279　It may be that a person was acting reasonably in giving up accommodation but if it would also have been reasonable to remain in occupation, he or she may be intentionally homeless. The reasons why a person left accommodation will, however, be relevant if considering whether a person was acting in good faith, in ignorance of a relevant fact (see para 14.300).

What was the act or omission in consequence of which he or she ceased to occupy?

14.280　The authority must identify what the applicant is alleged to have done or failed to do and be satisfied that this act or omission caused the homelessness. Where the act or omission was not that of the applicant, he or she may nevertheless be intentionally homeless if there was 'acquiescence' in the act or omission.

175　*Moran v Manchester CC* [2009] UKHL 36, 1 July 2009.
176　HA 1996 s177(2), see paras 14.182–14.186 above.
177　*R v Hammersmith and Fulham LBC ex p Duro-Rama* (1983) 9 HLR 71.
178　*Din v Wandsworth LBC* (1981) 1 HLR 73, HL.
179　See *R v Hackney LBC ex p Ajayi*, June 1997 *Legal Action* 23, CA, and *R v Brent LBC ex p Yusuf* (1997) 29 HLR 48, QBD.

Causation/foreseeability

14.281 Where the law provides that one act must cause another, or that an outcome must be a consequence of an act, this is referred to as 'causation'. Related to this is the notion of 'foreseeability': for a person to be deemed to have caused a certain event by his or her action, the consequence of the action must be, to a certain degree, foreseeable.

14.282 For an act or omission to be the cause of a person's homelessness this must be a reasonably foreseeable consequence of the act or omission. The courts have considered this issue in the following cases.

Tenant's imprisonment

14.283 In *R v Hounslow LBC ex p R*[180] the applicant was convicted of several offences of indecent assault and sentenced to seven years' imprisonment. He surrendered his tenancy while in prison as he could not maintain the rent payments. On his release he applied as homeless, but was found to be intentionally homeless on the basis that the offences were deliberate acts and that the surrender of the tenancy was the 'direct and reasonable' result of the acts. His judicial review of the decision was dismissed. The court held that:

> ... the question to be asked is whether his ceasing to occupy the accommodation would reasonably have been regarded at the time as the likely consequence of the deliberate conduct. It is an objective, not a subjective test.[181]

The same test was approved and applied by the Court of Appeal in *Stewart v Lambeth LBC*.[182] Mr Stewart was a tenant of the authority, but a suspended possession order had been made on the basis of rent arrears. He was sentenced to five years' imprisonment for drugs offences and made an arrangement that, while he was in prison, his sister would maintain his tenancy and pay the rent. No rent was received and a warrant was executed. He found this out after the event. When he applied as homeless following his release on licence, he was found to be intentionally homeless. It was argued

---

180 (1997) 29 HLR 939, QBD.
181 (1997) 29 HLR 939, Stephen Richards J at 947.
182 [2002] EWCA Civ 753, 26 April 2002.

that the cause of his homelessness was not his imprisonment, but the failure by the sister to make rent payments.

The Court of Appeal held that 'the chain of events that ultimately led to Mr Stewart's eviction began with the supply of heroin in respect of which he was duly convicted'.[183] The fact that arrangements could have been, or were, made to avoid the eviction were irrelevant, especially as the arrangements made were ineffectual. The authority's decision that he was intentionally homeless was upheld.

Rent/mortgage arrears

14.284   Where rent or mortgage payments are unaffordable, the failure to pay will not be deliberate.[184] However, a person may be intentionally homeless because of a decision to enter into an unaffordable arrangement.

In *R v Barnet ex p Rughooputh*[185] an applicant was evicted following mortgage possession proceedings, having entered into a mortgage that she could not afford. She had represented that she earned £18,000 a year, but was in fact unemployed. The council decided that she was intentionally homeless. The deliberate act causing the homelessness was not the failure to make the mortgage payments, but the taking out of the mortgage. The Court of Appeal upheld the council's decision.

14.285   The same principles may apply where a person agrees to a tenancy at a clearly unaffordable rent, although where an applicant moves from one rented property to another, other issues may arise: for example, whether the subsequent accommodation was settled and whether the applicant was acting in good faith, in ignorance of something relevant. See para 14.300 below.

---

183 [2002] EWCA Civ 753, Longmore LJ at [20].

184 This is stressed in the Supplementary Guidance on Intentional Homelessness issued in August 2009 which concerns 'Applicants who face homelessness following difficulties in meeting mortgage commitments'.

185 (1993) 25 HLR 607.

Acquiescence

14.286 The act or omission must be that of the applicant. Although authorities often treat applications by couples or families as 'joint' applications, there is no provision under the Act for doing so. An authority may be required to consider each applicant individually where it is the act or omission of one person that is alleged to have caused the homelessness. However, a party who acquiesced in (ie, passively accepted) the act or omission of another may also be found homeless intentionally.

14.287 An authority is entitled to assume that members of a family were party to the conduct of one member, unless there is evidence to the contrary.[186]

> In *R v North Devon DC ex p Lewis*[187] a man who gave up his employment and lost his tied accommodation was found to be intentionally homeless. His wife then applied and the authority found her also to be intentionally homeless on the basis that she had acquiesced in her husband's decision to give up his job. Her application for judicial review was dismissed, Woolf J holding:
>
> ... the fact that the Act requires consideration of the family unit as a whole indicates that it would be perfectly proper in the ordinary case for the housing authority to look at the family as a whole and assume, in the absence of material which indicates to the contrary, where the conduct of one member of the family was such that he should be regarded as having become homeless intentionally, that was conduct to which the other members of the family were a party.
>
> So, for example, where the husband is a tenant and gives notice in circumstances where he is properly to be regarded as having become homeless intentionally, the wife, even though she was not the tenant and she did not give the notice, can be regarded in the same way. In normal circumstances this would be treated as a joint decision. If, however, at the end of the day because of material put before the housing authority by the wife, the housing authority is not satisfied that she was a party to the decision, it would have to regard her as not having become homeless intentionally.

---

186 *R v Tower Hamlets LBC ex p Khatun* (1993) 27 HLR 344, CA, see para 14.294.
187 [1981] 1 WLR 328, QBD.

14.288 The reasoning in *Lewis* has been approved in a number of subsequent cases.

14.289 The correct approach therefore is that:

- each family member is entitled to individual consideration;
- an authority may assume that the members of a family agree to the decision of one family member;
- however, there may be evidence that this is not the case.

14.290 Effectively, this means that, where a person says that they did not acquiesce in another's decision, the burden of proof is reversed and the person must provide evidence of this.

14.291 The courts have upheld decisions that a family member has acquiesced in the act or omission causing the homelessness in the following cases:

In *R v Swansea CC ex p John*[188] the applicant was the sole tenant of a council property. A possession order was made because of nuisance and annoyance caused by the tenant's long-term partner, who was her lodger. The court found that the tenant had acquiesced, in as much as she could have terminated his right to occupy, but failed to do so.

R v East Hertfordshire DC ex p Bannon[189] concerned an application made by the ex-partner of a man whose anti-social behaviour had led to both being evicted. The decision that she was intentionally homeless, having either been a party to his behaviour or done nothing to prevent it, was upheld.

14.292 The same approach is appropriate when a family is evicted because of a failure to pay rent:

In *R v Ealing LBC ex p Salmons*[190] a couple were evicted for rent arrears of some £12,000. Both maintained that the husband had been unaware of the arrears and that he had provided his wife with the money to pay the rent but she had not done so. The authority held that it was inconceivable that he was unaware of the arrears or

188 (1982) 9 HLR, 58, QBD.
189 (1986) 18 HLR 515, QBD.
190 (1990) 23 HLR 272, QBD.

> the threat of eviction and that he had acquiesced in the non-payment of the rent.
>
> The court dismissed the claim for judicial review of the decision: the authority had made sufficient enquiries and was entitled to conclude that the applicant had known about or at least turned a blind eye to the arrears.

14.293 However, simply being aware of arrears may not be sufficient to establish that there was acquiescence.

> In *R v East Northamptonshire DC ex p Spruce*[191] a couple were evicted because of substantial rent arrears. The evidence was that Mrs Spruce had become aware of the arrears only at a late stage.
>
> The court quashed the decision that she was intentionally homeless: it was not sufficient that she was aware of the arrears; the authority had failed to make sufficient inquiries into whether or not she had acquiesced in the failure to pay the rent.

14.294 Even where an applicant has had no part in a decision leading to the loss of accommodation, if he or she is content to leave such decisions to someone else, an authority may find there has been acquiescence.

> In *R v Tower Hamlets ex p Khatun LBC*[192] a man gave up accommodation with his brother when his wife was about to give birth to their third child. They subsequently applied as homeless and his wife argued that her husband had not consulted her about the decision and that she had not wanted to leave, but that her husband had told her that if she wanted them to remain together she must follow him. She was nevertheless found to be intentionally homeless.
>
> Her claim for judicial review was refused and her appeal dismissed by the Court of Appeal: if a wife is content to leave decisions about where the family lives to her husband, then a decision in which she co-operates may be regarded as a decision in which she had joined, unless there is some reason for holding that she did not do so.

191 (1988) 20 HLR 508, QBD.
192 (1993) 27 HLR 344, CA.

Breaking the chain of causation

14.295 If a person found to be intentionally homeless, when, in the future, might he or she no longer be homeless intentionally? In other words, when might the chain of causation be broken?

14.296   It will usually be necessary for a person who is intentionally homeless to obtain settled accommodation in order to break the chain. However, it is possible that some other event may break the chain: for example, a person who subsequently becomes homeless as the result of domestic violence or a relationship breakdown.[193]

14.297   This issue is discussed at para 13.59.

Was the act or omission deliberate?

14.298 It is not the case that the person must have deliberately become homeless: only that the act or omission was deliberate in the ordinary sense of the word.

14.299   A person who is suffering from a mental health problem may act in a way that cannot be said to be deliberate. This will depend on the nature of the mental illness and an opinion of a psychiatrist will usually be needed. However, a person may be found to be in priority need by reason of mental illness but be capable of deliberate acts or omissions.[194]

Was the act or omission made in good faith in ignorance of a relevant fact?

14.300 This provision is to ensure that a person who gives up accommodation, honestly but mistakenly believing that circumstances are such that he or she will have accommodation elsewhere, is not found intentionally homeless. The fact of which the person is ignorant must, of course, be relevant to the person's housing.

14.301   A person may give up accommodation to move to another area or country in order to work there. In such a case the courts have distinguished between 'mere aspiration' and belief in specific employment or housing opportunities.

---

193 See for example: *R v Camden LBC ex p Aranda* (1998) 30 HLR 76, CA and *R v Basingstoke and Deane BC ex p Bassett* (1983) 10 HLR 125, QBD.
194 See *R v Wirral MBC ex p Bell* (1995) 27 HLR 234, QBD.

In *Aw-Aden v Birmingham CC*[195] the applicant, a well-qualified scientist, came from Belgium to the UK to seek work. He was unable to find work and when his family joined him in Birmingham the accommodation he was staying in became overcrowded and he applied as homeless to the authority. He was found intentionally homeless for giving up his accommodation in Belgium. He submitted that he had not acted deliberately, having been ignorant of his true prospects of finding employment and therefore his ability to afford to pay for accommodation privately.

The Court of Appeal dismissed his appeal, approving the approach of the court in *Obeid*[196] in which it was said:

> ... an applicant's appreciation of the prospects of future housing or future employment can be treated as 'awareness of a relevant fact' for the purposes of this subsection, provided it is sufficiently specific (that is related to specific employment or specific housing opportunities) and provided it is based on some genuine investigation and not mere 'aspiration'.

14.302 In all cases, to benefit from the provision, the person must have acted in good faith. The question is not whether the person acted reasonably, although this may be relevant to whether or not the person was acting in good faith. It is possible to be guilty of 'honest blundering and carelessness' but still be acting in good faith.[197] As is made clear in the Supplementary Guidance on Intentional Homelessness issued in relation to mortgage arrears:

> Intentionality does not depend on whether applicants have behaved wisely or prudently or reasonably. Where an applicant's failure to seek help may have been foolish, imprudent or even unreasonable, this would not necessarily mean his or her conduct was not in good faith.[198]

14.303 Ignorance of the law or the legal consequences of an act or omission should be disregarded when considering whether an act or omission is deliberate.[199] So, for example, the provision will not assist a person who claims that he or she did not know that abandoning premises

195 [2005] EWCA Civ 1834, 7 December 2005.
196 *R v Westminster CC ex p Obeid* (1996) 29 HLR 389, QBD, Carnwath J at 398.
197 *R v Hammersmith & Fulham LBC ex p Lusi* (1991) 23 HLR 260, QBD.
198 Supplementary Guidance para 9.
199 See *R v Eastleigh BC ex p Beattie (No 2)* (1984) 17 HLR 168, QBD and *R v Croydon LBC ex p Toth* (1988) 20 HLR 576, CA.

would lead to the loss of a tenancy. However, a belief that premises were still available, despite having been out of the UK for a long period, has been held to constitute ignorance of a relevant fact.[200]

14.304   It is not always easy to draw a distinction between ignorance of the law and ignorance of fact: ignorance about a person's entitlement to housing benefit has been held to constitute ignorance of a fact, as has ignorance of the fact that a tenant did not have to leave accommodation until a court order was obtained.[201]

> In *Ugiagbe v Southwark LBC*[202] the applicant had a one-year assured shorthold tenancy agreement expiring on 27 May 2007. On 16 April 2007 the landlord wrote to her stating that he could not extend the agreement and asking her to leave by 31 May 2007. She sought advice from the council's One Stop Shop where she was told that she should go to the Homeless Persons Unit (HPU), that they would place her in temporary accommodation and that, if she had friends or relations who could store her belongings, they could be left with them. Not wanting to be treated as homeless, she did not go to the HPU but instead hoped to secure accommodation by bidding through the allocations scheme and by asking her landlord for more time. The landlord agreed for a short period but in November 2007 he told her that he needed the property back and asked her to leave. Believing that she had to go, she left the premises. It was common ground that had she followed the advice and attended the HPU she would have been advised that she did not have to leave until ordered by the court to do so.
>
> The Court of Appeal held that her ignorance of the fact that she could not be made to leave without a court order meant that she was unaware of a relevant fact. On the issue of whether she was acting in good faith, the council found that this was wilful ignorance as she had deliberately chosen not to seek advice. The court rejected this:
>
> > Her failure to go to the HPU for help could be said to have been foolish or imprudent. But neither of those would be sufficient to put her conduct into the category of not being in good faith, nor would it even if she were regarded as having been unreasonable ... She was not turning a blind eye to that which she knew she

200 *R v Tower Hamlets LBC ex p Rouf* (1991) 23 HLR 460, QBD.
201 *R v Westminster ex p Moozary-Oraky* (1994) 26 HLR 213, QBD.
202 [2009] EWCA Civ 31, 10 February 2009.

> would be told, and did not want to know. On the contrary, she had been led to think that she would be treated as within the scope of the homeless duty, and wanted to avoid that if she possibly could. Foolish or not, her subjective motivation seems to me to be the opposite of bad faith. [203]

14.305 When considering intentionality in a case when there is evidence that the applicant may have a disability, the authority may be under a duty to be proactive in investigating the extent of any disability and whether it may be relevant to the issue of any 'deliberate' act or omission: *Pieretti v Enfield LBC*.[204]

Contrived homelessness

14.306 An additional definition of intentional homeless was introduced by the Housing Act 1996. Section 191(3) provides that:

A person shall be treated as becoming homeless intentionally if:
(a) he enters into an arrangement under which he is required to cease to occupy accommodation which it would have been reasonable for him to continue to occupy, and
(b) the purpose of the arrangement is to enable him to become entitled to assistance under this Part, and there is no other good reason why he is homeless.

14.307 The provision is to prevent collusion in order to take advantage of the homeless duty. The Homelessness Code refers to the possibility of parents and children taking advantage of the automatic priority need given to homeless 16- and 17-year-olds, where a parent and child agree that the child is given notice to leave to enable the child to make a homeless application. This may make the child intentionally homeless. However, it is likely that authorities will find it difficult to obtain evidence of such an agreement and the Code stresses that the authority must 'be satisfied that collusion exists, and must not rely on hearsay or unfounded suspicions'.[205] Furthermore, for a person to be intentionally homeless 'there should be no other good reason for the person's homelessness'. Examples of good reasons are identified as overcrowding or an obvious relationship breakdown.

---

203 [2009] EWCA Civ 31, Lloyd LJ at [26] and [28].
204 [2010] EWCA Civ 1104, 12 October 2010. See para 2.88 for a summary of the case.
205 See para 11.28.

Decision letters

14.308 If a decision is made that a person is intentionally homeless, the authority must ensure that all of the elements of the test are addressed. In cases where a complex accommodation history is at issue this is particularly important.

14.309   In *City of Gloucester v Miles*[206] the Court of Appeal held that the decision letter must state:

- that the authority is satisfied that the applicant became homeless intentionally;
- when the applicant is considered to have become homeless;
- what the deliberate act or omission was that caused the homelessness; and
- that it would have been reasonable for the applicant to have continued to occupy the accommodation.

14.310 Furthermore, if an issue is raised which suggests that the act or omission should not be treated as deliberate, the authority must explain why it has found otherwise.

In *O'Connor v Kensington and Chelsea RLBC*[207] a couple were assured tenants of a housing trust. They went to Ireland to attend to an ailing relative, who subsequently died. They had intended to be absent for a short period only and left a friend looking after the property who was expected to pay rent. The rent was not paid and a suspended possession order was made in their absence. After 16 months they returned to the UK and discovered the arrears and possession order and that the friend had allowed others into occupation of their home. They were able to pay off most of the arrears, but the trust nevertheless executed a warrant of possession. The authority found that they were intentionally homeless, but failed to state the date at which it considered them to have become homeless. The authority had therefore failed to consider whether the act or omission at that time had been in good faith. The Court of Appeal quashed the authority's decision.

206 (1985) 17 HLR 292, CA.
207 [2004] EWCA Civ 394, 30 March 2004.

Referral to another authority

14.311 A homeless person may apply for assistance to any local authority, regardless of whether he or she has ever lived in that authority's area. The duty to make inquiries falls on the authority to which the application is made. However, after this authority has decided whether a housing duty is owed, it may consider whether the person can be referred to another authority for the actual provision of housing. HA 1996 is clear that referral should be considered only if and when the authority is satisfied that the applicant is eligible, homeless, in priority need and not intentionally homelessness.[208] Unfortunately, it is common for authorities to consider the issue on first presentation. While an authority may legitimately advise a person that the duty to provide housing will probably rest with a different authority, it is unlawful to refuse to accept an application while informing the person that they must apply to a different authority. Such an approach can be challenged by way of judicial review.

Local referral conditions

14.312 The conditions for a referral are set out in HA 1996 s198. A referral can be made in two situations:[209]

- where the person has no local connection with the authority making the referral;
- where the person was accommodated in the area within the last five years by another authority, acting under a homeless duty;

14.313 The most common reason for a referral is under the local connection provisions.

Local connection referral

14.314 An authority can refer a case to another authority if it considers that the relevant conditions are satisfied. The conditions are:[210]

- neither the applicant nor any person who might reasonably be expected to live with the applicant has a local connection with the district of the authority to which the application was made; and

---

208 HA 1996 ss184(1)–(2) and 198(1).
209 There is also provision applicable only to asylum-seekers but asylum-seekers have been ineligible for homeless assistance since 2000, and so this is no longer relevant.
210 HA 1996 s198(1)(a)–(c).

- the applicant or any person who might reasonably be expected to live with the applicant has a local connection with the other district; and
- neither of the following applies:
  (1) the applicant or any person who might reasonably be expected to live with the applicant would run the risk of domestic violence in the other district, or
  (2) the applicant or any person who might reasonably be expected to live with the applicant has suffered violence (other than domestic violence) in the other district and it is probable that the return to that district will lead to further violence of a similar kind.[211]

14.315   A referral cannot be made because an applicant has a stronger connection with another authority. Only if there is *no* local connection with the referring authority can a referral be made.

What is a local connection?

14.316   HA 1996 s199(1) provides that:

> A person has a local connection with the district of a local housing authority if he has a connection with it:
> (a) because he is, or in the past was, normally resident there, and that residence is or was of his own choice,
> (b) because he is employed there,
> (c) because of family associations, or
> (d) because of special circumstances.

Residence of choice

14.317   Residence must be residence of choice. This is not the case if the residence is because of service in the armed forces or while in prison or some other form of detention.[212] Similarly, service in the regular armed forces does not count as employment in the district.[213]

Former asylum-seekers

14.318   Former asylum-seekers who have previously been provided with accommodation by the UK Border Agency in a dispersal area do gain a local connection in the dispersal area, despite this not being residence of choice: HA 1996 s199(6). If a person was accommodated

---

211 Violence is defined in the same way as under HA 1996 s177, see above para 14.177.
212 HA 1996 s199(3).
213 HA 1996 s199(2).

in more than one dispersal area, the local connection is with the area in which he or she was most recently accommodated: HA 1996 s199(7)(a). However, being accommodated in an 'accommodation centre'[214] does not create a local connection: HA 1996 s199(7)(b).

14.319 The situation is different for asylum-seekers who were dispersed in Scotland (where the Housing Act 1996 does not apply). Where a former asylum-seeker who was previously accommodated in dispersal accommodation in Scotland has no local connection with any authority in Scotland, England or Wales, no duty under HA 1996 s193 arises. An authority has power to provide accommodation for a reasonable period to enable the applicant to find accommodation in the private sector and to provide advice and assistance.[215] The intention is that the person should either find accommodation privately or return to apply as homeless to the Scottish authority in whose area he or she was dispersed.

14.320 It should be noted however that an asylum-seeker or family member may gain a local connection by obtaining employment in the relevant area or may have a local connection by virtue of family association. In such a case referral to the dispersal area will not be possible. Similarly, after a period of residence in the area a local connection will be established. As in all cases, no referral can be made unless there is *no* local connection with the authority to which the application is made.

The local authority agreement

14.321 To avoid disputes between authorities about local connection, there is an agreement between local authorities. This is the Local Authority Association Joint Local Connection Agreement.[216] It sets out a working definition of the way in which local connection is established. The Agreement provides:[217]

- 'Normal residence' should be accepted if the person has lived in the area for six months during the previous 12 months or no less than three of the previous five years.
- 'Family associations' normally arise where an applicant or a member of the household has parents, adult children or brothers or

214 Section 22 of the Nationality, Immigration and Asylum Act 2002 provides for accommodation centres to be set up for asylum-seekers but none have yet been established.
215 Asylum and Immigration (Treatment of Claimants) Act 2004 s11 (2)–3).
216 See A Arden, E Orme and T Vanhegan, *Homelessness and allocations*, 8th edition, LAG, 2010.
217 Paragraph 3.5.

sisters currently living in the area who have been resident for at least five years, and the applicant indicates a wish to be near them.
- A referral should not be made on the basis of family association if the person objects.
- Employment should not be of a casual nature.

14.322 The Agreement is not law, and where an applicant challenges a referral it may be possible to establish a local connection even if the Local Connection Agreement tests are not met.

> In *R v Southwark ex p Hughes*[218] a woman moved to Southwark to set up a permanent home with a man by whom she became pregnant. The relationship ended because of domestic violence and she applied as homeless. The authority's decision to refer her to another authority on the basis that she had resided in Southwark for less than six months was quashed: the authority had failed to make proper inquiry into whether she had gained a local connection by virtue of ordinary residence or other special reason.

14.323 However, it is for the local authority to decide, on the evidence, whether a person has a local connection. While the Local Connection Agreement must not be applied rigidly, an authority is entitled to take it into account as a guideline.

> In *Betts v Eastleigh BC*[219] an applicant and his family had moved to the district of Eastleigh to take up employment. The employment ended and he was forced to leave his private sector accommodation. The family had lived in the area for less than six months but it was their intention to settle in the area. Eastleigh found that the full housing duty was owed, but referred him to the local authority where the family had previously resided. Both authorities agreed that the referral was properly made, but the applicant sought judicial review, arguing that the family was normally resident in the area of Eastleigh and that the authority had erred in applying the criteria contained in the Local Connection Agreement too rigidly.
>
> Although the challenge was successful in the Court of Appeal, the House of Lords upheld the local authority's appeal. It is for the local authority to decide whether an applicant has a local connection because of normal residence. The decision must be made by

218 (1998) 30 HLR 1082, QBD.
219 *Re Betts* [1983] 2 AC 613, HL.

reference to the facts of each individual case, but an authority may operate a policy or establish guidelines, provided it does not close its mind to the particular facts of the individual case. On the facts of the case the authority had made a lawful decision.

Relevant date for establishing local connection

14.324 The general rule in relation to homeless decisions is that the person's circumstances are assessed as at the date of the decision, not the date of the application. In relation to local connection, this means that an applicant may not have local connection by way of normal residence when the application is made, but may have established such a connection by the time of the decision.

In *Mohamed v Hammersmith and Fulham LBC*[220] the applicant applied to the authority after living in the borough for about three months. He and his family were placed in interim accommodation and a decision was made that they would be referred to another authority. He argued that he had acquired a local connection because of the time the family had spent in interim accommodation awaiting a decision.

The House of Lords held that the relevant time for deciding on local connection was the date of the decision, whether the original decision or the decision on review. Furthermore, time spent in interim accommodation could, in appropriate circumstances, amount to 'normal residence' for the purpose of establishing a local connection.

Disputes between authorities

14.325 The authority proposing to refer the applicant must notify the applicant and the other authority at the same time, giving reasons why it is considered that the local referral conditions are met.[221] The applicant may challenge the decision by requesting a review and, if unsuccessful, appealing to the county court. As between the two authorities, any issue about whether the local referral conditions are

---

220 [2001] UKHL 57, 1 November 2001.
221 HA 1996 s184(4).

met should be decided by agreement or, in the absence of agreement, by arbitration.

14.326   The procedure is set out in the Homelessness (Decisions on Referrals) Order 1998.[222] The Local Government Association operates an independent panel to resolve such disputes.

14.327   If the authorities are in dispute about the referral, the applicant should be kept in temporary accommodation by the referring authority until the dispute is resolved. It is unlawful for the referring authority simply to terminate interim accommodation on the basis that it believes the referral conditions are met. The applicant must continue to be accommodated until either the referral is accepted or the dispute resolved. If the referral is ultimately accepted, the referring authority may claim reimbursement from the receiving authority for the cost of interim accommodation pending the resolution of the dispute.

Challenging the decision that a housing duty is owed

14.328   A referral can only be considered after it has been decided that a housing duty is owed. A local authority, aware it will be referring an applicant to another authority, may be tempted to apply the relevant tests less rigorously than usual. In such a case, the authority to whom the referral is made may challenge the decision by way of judicial review if the decision is flawed on recognised public law grounds.

> In *R v Newham LBC ex p Tower Hamlets LBC*[223] Newham found that a housing duty was owed to the applicant. It then referred the case to Tower Hamlets, where the applicant had a local connection. He had previously been found to be intentionally homeless by Tower Hamlets while Newham had found him not intentionally homeless. In reaching that decision, Newham had taken account of housing conditions in the area of Newham. Tower Hamlets challenged the decision, arguing that Newham had erred in law in considering housing conditions in its own area rather than in the area of Tower Hamlets.
>
> The Court of Appeal agreed and quashed Newham's decision that a housing duty was owed.

222 SI No 1578.
223 (1991) 23 HLR 62, CA.

14.329 It should be noted that in such a case the receiving authority must have the decision quashed by a court on public law grounds. A dispute about whether the housing duty is owed cannot be resolved through the arbitration procedure.[224] Unless the decision is quashed by a court, the receiving authority is bound to accept the referral if the referral conditions are met.

Challenging a decision not to refer

14.330 The decision to refer an applicant to another authority is discretionary: there is no right to be referred or to review a decision not to refer.

In *Hackney LBC v Sareen*[225] a homeless application was made to Hackney with an indication that the family would like to be housed in another part of London because of family and friends who lived there. Hackney made inquiries and decided that a housing duty was owed. The decision letter made no reference to referral, but stated that the applicant had a right to a review of the decision. The applicant requested a review of the decision not to refer the case to the area where he wished to be housed, stating that he had no local connection with Hackney, but did have connections with the other local authority. Hackney responded that he had no right to a statutory review of the decision, but agreed to reconsider the issue. It then confirmed the decision not to refer. A county court appeal was lodged and was successful.

However, the Court of Appeal upheld Hackney's appeal, holding that the decision to refer was discretionary and that: (1) there was no duty to investigate local connection, only a power to do so; (2) there was no right to a statutory review of a decision not to refer; (3) there was therefore no county court appeal in relation to such a decision; and (4) although an 'extra statutory' reconsideration could be challenged if there were grounds, this would not be by way of county court appeal, but by judicial review. Put simply: 'If an applicant wants to be housed in another local authority housing area, he should apply there'.[226]

---

224 *R v Slough ex p Ealing LBC* [1981] 1 All ER 601.
225 [2003] EWCA Civ 351, 19 March 2003.
226 Auld LJ at [28].

Out of borough placements

14.331   The provision under HA 1996 s198(4), which permits a referral where a person has been accommodated out of borough within the last five years, is to ensure that an authority cannot avoid future responsibility by placing homeless applicants outside its own area. The provision operates regardless of any local connection and also takes no account of any risk of violence in the area to which the referral is made. As the HA 1996 s193 duty lasts indefinitely unless one of the events specified in section 193 occurs, this provision is rarely relevant. If the section 193 accommodation ceases to be available, the placing authority will be bound to provide alternative accommodation under its continuing section 193 duty.

CHAPTER 15

Homeless decisions, reviews and appeals

Key points

- A local authority must give written notification of its decision to a homeless applicant.
- The notification must give reasons for any adverse finding.
- An applicant can request a review of the decision but must do so within 21 days of notification.
- An authority may agree to conduct a review even if the request is made outside the 21-day time limit.
- The review should be completed by the authority within eight weeks of the request.
- The review must be conducted by someone who was not involved in the original decision and, if an officer, must be someone senior to the decision-maker.
- The parties can agree in writing to extend the time limit for completion of the review.
- An authority has a power but not a duty to provide interim accommodation pending a review.
- The review decision must be notified in writing, with reasons, to the applicant.
- An applicant may appeal to a county court against a negative review decision on a point of law. This covers all of the matters that can be challenged by judicial review.
- The appeal must be lodged within 21 days of notification of the review decision.
- The court may allow an out of time appeal in certain circumstances.
- An authority has a power but not a duty to provide interim accommodation pending the appeal.
- If interim accommodation pending review is refused the applicant may judicially review the decision.
- If interim accommodation pending appeal is refused the applicant may appeal to the county court.

Notification of the decision

15.1   When its inquiries are complete, a local authority must notify the applicant of its decision.[1] The decision letter is often referred to as a 'section 184 decision'. The section 184 decision must:

---

1 Housing Act (HA) 1996 s184(3).

- be given in writing;
- inform the applicant of the decision and give reasons for any issue decided against the applicant's interests;
- inform the applicant of the right to request a review of the decision; and
- inform the applicant of the time within which the request must be made, which is 21 days from the date of notification.

Reasons

15.2   The reasons given by the authority must explain why the decision has been reached. It is not sufficient simply to recite the relevant legal test, list all of the matters taken into consideration and state the conclusion. The Court of Appeal has held that:[2]

> ... where ... an authority is required to give reasons for its decision, it is required to give reasons which are proper, adequate and intelligible and enable the person affected to know why they have won or lost. That said, the law gives decision-makers a certain latitude in how they express themselves and will recognise that not all those taking decisions will find it easy to express themselves with judicial exactitude.

15.3   A decision may be found to be flawed solely because of a failure to give reasons or sufficient reasons for the decision. However, the review process enables local authorities to correct such a deficiency. In such a case, the applicant must be given the opportunity to make further representations before the final review decision. See below, paras 15.33–15.34.

Matters arising after the decision

15.4   After the decision has been made, in the absence of fraud or a mistake of fact, an authority has no power to make further inquiries or re-open the decision unless the applicant seeks a review or makes a fresh application.

> In *R v Lambeth LBC ex p Miah*[3] following acceptance of a housing duty the applicant was granted a non-secure tenancy. The authority, having evidence that the applicant was not living in the accommodation but was subletting it, issued a second decision letter stating that the applicant was not homeless.

2   *R v Brent LBC ex p Baruwa* (1987) 29 HLR 915, Schiemann LJ at 920.
3   (1994) 27 HLR 21, QBD.

> The court held that the authority had no power to make further inquiries following the decision: there was no application to be investigated. In such a situation, however, a local authority may consider itself discharged from its obligation to continue to provide accommodation. If the authority believed the applicant was abusing the temporary accommodation, the correct course of action would have been to determine the licence to occupy.

15.5   This decision pre-dates the Housing Act 1996 and the position is now clearer: HA 1996 s193 sets out the specific circumstances in which the duty to accommodate ends. This includes becoming homeless intentionally from the accommodation provided or ceasing to occupy it.

Fraud/false information

15.6   The situation is different where there has been fraud or the information given to the authority is untrue.

> In *R v Dacorum BC ex p Walsh*[4] an applicant was found to be homeless and not intentionally homeless, having reported a threat of an eviction by her landlord. Subsequently the authority conducted further inquiries and concluded that she had pretended to be locked out of her home and her claim to be threatened with eviction was false. A second decision was made stating that she was intentionally homeless.
>   The applicant's claim for judicial review was dismissed: it was absurd to suggest that the Housing Act made it impossible to do what the authority had done.

Re-opening an application wrongly decided

15.7   Where an application was decided against the applicant, an authority may re-open the application after receiving new information.[5] However, where the applicant wishes the authority to consider new information, the proper course of action is to seek a review and to submit the new information in support of the review.[6]

4 (1991) 24 HLR 401.
5 *R v Hambleton DC ex p Geoghan* [1985] JPL 394, QBD.
6 *Demetri v Westminster CC* (2000) 32 HLR 470, CA.

15.8   An authority is also entitled to re-open an application where its decision was based on a fundamental mistake of fact.

> In *Porteous v West Dorset DC*[7] the applicant had a secure tenancy of a local authority property in London. She moved to Germany in 2002, believing that the tenancy had been transferred into her sister's name. In fact the tenancy had not been transferred and remained in the applicant's sole name. On her return from Germany she applied to the authority as homeless. The authority's inquiries did not reveal that the tenancy remained in her sole name and a decision was made that she was eligible, homeless, in priority need and not intentionally homeless and was therefore owed a housing duty. A few weeks after the decision was made, the London authority contacted West Dorset DC and informed them that Ms Porteous was still the tenant of the property and that it remained available for her occupation. A second decision was then made stating that she was not homeless because she had a right to reside in the London property and it was reasonable for her to do so. Ms Porteous applied for a review. Although a notice to quit was served in respect of the London property, the landlord authority indicated that it would await the outcome of the review before commencing possession proceedings. The review decision confirmed the later decision that Ms Porteous was not homeless. She appealed to the county court. At the hearing of the appeal, evidence was submitted that the London property remained available for her occupation. Her appeal was dismissed, the judge holding that the authority had been entitled to re-consider its original decision and that the London property was available to Ms Porteous.
>
> The Court of Appeal dismissed her appeal, holding that an authority was entitled to revisit and change a decision if the decision resulted from a fundamental mistake of fact, even where there was no bad faith on the part of either party.

The statutory review

15.9   Before 1997 the only way to challenge a homeless decision was by way of judicial review. The Housing Act 1996 introduced a statutory right to an internal review and a county court appeal on a point of law

7   [2004] HLR 30, 4 March 2004.

in respect of most substantive homeless decisions. Judicial review remains available in respect of decisions that do not carry the right of review.

15.10   The way reviews must be conducted is set out in regulations, currently the Allocation of Housing and Homelessness (Review Procedures) Regulations 1999 ('the Review Regs 1999').[8]

Decisions with a right of review

15.11   Under HA 1996 s202 an applicant has a right to a review of a decision that he or she:[9]

- is not eligible;
- is not homeless or threatened with homelessness;
- is not in priority need;
- is intentionally homelessness;
- is to be referred to another authority.

15.12   There is also a right to a review of any decision on:

- the suitability of accommodation offered following the acceptance of a housing duty – the temporary accommodation duty;
- the suitability of accommodation offered under HA 1996 Part VI (the refusal of which may end the duty to provide temporary accommodation);
- whether it is reasonable for the applicant to accept the accommodation offered under Part VI; and
- whether the duty to accommodate has come to an end.

Decisions with no right of review

15.13   There is no right of review in relation to:

- a refusal to accept a homeless application;
- a refusal to provide interim accommodation pending a decision;
- the suitability of interim accommodation pending decision;
- a decision not to provide interim accommodation pending a statutory review and/or appeal to the county court;
- decisions about the protection of an applicant's belongings;

---

8   SI No 71.
9   HA 1996 s202 refers specifically to decisions about eligibility, local referral and suitability. In relation to the other matters it refers to any decision as to what duty (if any) is owed under ss190–193, 195 and 196. The duties owed under these sections depend on the decisions regarding the substantive issues of homelessness, priority need and intentional homelessness.

- a refusal to review a decision which has already been reviewed;
- a refusal to extend the time limits within which a review should have been requested.

15.14   Decisions about these issues may be challenged by judicial review, with the exception of decisions about interim accommodation pending a county court appeal: such decisions are challenged by way of a second county court appeal (see para 15.59 below).

Time limits

Requesting the review

15.15   The request for the review must be made within 21 days of the 'day on which [the applicant] is notified'.[10] The time limit runs from the receipt of the letter, not the date of the letter. If the letter is not received by the applicant, or there is no address where it can be sent, it can be treated as having been given to him or her if it is made available at the authority's office for a reasonable period for collection.[11]

15.16   It is only the request for the review that must be made within 21 days. Representations and any new evidence can be submitted later. In most cases, the way the decision was made will be relevant and advisers should always request a copy of the homeless file at the same time as requesting a review, indicating that further representations may follow. A standard letter requesting a review is included in the appendix to this chapter. At the same time it may be necessary to request an extension of interim accommodation pending review. This is dealt with in chapter 16 and a model letter is included in the appendix to chapter 16.

Completing the review

15.17   Following a request for a review, the authority should complete the review in accordance with the procedure set out in regulations and within a specified time, currently eight weeks from the day the request is made. This time limit may be extended by written agreement between the parties.[12]

---

10   HA 1996 s202(3).
11   HA 1996 s184(6).
12   Review Regs 1999 reg 9(1)–(2). The time limits are different if the review concerns a disputed local referral. In such a case the time limit may be ten or 12 weeks, depending on the nature of the decision: reg 9(1)(b)–(c).

Out of time reviews

15.18   An authority has a discretion to extend the time for requesting a review and must exercise this discretion in a lawful way. This means that the decision must not be made in bad faith or capriciously for improper motives. Furthermore, it must not be limited to rigidly defined situations because that would involve an unlawful fetter on the discretionary power given by the Housing Act 1996[13] (see para 2.14).

15.19   In most cases the authority will consider both the reasons for the delay in requesting a review and the potential merits of the review when exercising its discretion. However, the discretion is very wide and it is not necessary in all cases to consider the merits of the review.[14] Notwithstanding this, there may be some cases where a failure to consider the merits of a review would be 'obvious perversity' if, on the face of it, the review was bound to succeed.[15]

Conduct of the review

15.20   The following rules are laid down in the Review Regs 1999:

- after receiving a review request the authority must notify the applicant:
  - of the right to make written representations, and
  - what the authority's review procedure is;
- the authority must then carry out the review, considering any representations made;
- if the person conducting the review is an officer (as opposed to a member or person independent of the authority) he or she must be someone who was not involved in the original decision and who is senior to the officer who made the original decision;
- if the reviewer considers that there is a deficiency or irregularity in the decision or the way it was made, but is still minded to make an adverse decision, the reviewer must notify the applicant:
  - that the reviewer is so minded and the reasons why, and
  - that the applicant has the right to make oral and/or written representations (in person or by a representative).

---

13   *R on the application of C v Lewisham LBC* [2003] EWCA Civ 927, 4 July 2003.

14   *R on the application of C v Lewisham LBC* [2003] EWCA Civ 927, 4 July 2003.

15   *R on the application of Radhia Slaiman v Richmond upon Thames LBC* [2006] EWHC 329 (Admin), 9 February 2006.

Scope of the review

15.21 The review is not limited to a consideration of whether the original decision was correct. The reviewer must take account of any representations made in support of the review and must make a decision based on all of the information and evidence available at the date of the review.[16]

Submissions

15.22 When making submissions in support of a review, it is important that the alleged flaws in the original decision are identified. If they are not, it may not be possible to rely on these flaws in any subsequent county court appeal.

15.23 In *Nipa Begum*[17] (see para 14.172 above) the court refused to quash a decision even though the authority had failed to consider whether the applicant could afford to travel to Bangladesh to occupy accommodation there, because the issue had not been raised during the review process.

15.24 Similarly, in *Cramp v Hastings BC*[18] (see para 13.54 above) the court upheld the council's appeal against the quashing of a decision for failure to make adequate inquiries. The inquiries the applicants alleged should have been made had not been mentioned in the review submissions.

15.25 There are, however, certain issues that an authority must address, regardless of the review submissions. An example is the affordability of accommodation when the issue is whether it is reasonable to occupy.[19] Furthermore, a failure to comply with the disability equality duty when making a decision may make the decision unlawful even if the issue was not raised in the review.[20]

New information/evidence

15.26 Where vulnerability is the issue, it is common for advisers to seek further medical evidence to submit as part of the review. While this

16 The previous regulations (Allocation of Housing and Homelessness (Review Procedures and Amendment) Regulations 1996) stated: 'The authority shall – ... carry out the review on the basis of the facts known to them at the date of the review.' The Review Regs 1999 do not state this, only that the reviewer should consider any representations made.

17 (1999) 32 HLR 445, CA.

18 [2005] EWCA Civ 1005.

19 Homelessness (Suitability of Accommodation) Order 1996 SI No 3204.

20 See *Pieretti v Enfield LBC* [2010] EWCA Civ 1104, 12 October 2010, at para 2.88.

is often the most effective way to challenge a decision, the agency advising the applicant may not be in a position to pay for expert evidence.[21] In such a case, the submission should nevertheless be made that further medical evidence is necessary. If the authority declines to obtain such evidence the county court may uphold a challenge based on inadequate inquiry.

15.27   Where a local authority does obtain new medical evidence or advice it will usually be necessary, in the interests of fairness, to disclose it to the applicant and invite his or her comments. However, if the advice relates to issues of which the applicant is fully aware this may not be necessary.[22]

Relevant date for decision

15.28   The requirement to consider the information and evidence at the date of the review means that the review decision must take account of any change of circumstances since the original decision.

15.29   This was held to be the case even where an applicant had no local connection when he applied as homeless, but had established one by the time of the final decision: *Mohamed v Hammersmith and Fulham LBC*[23] (see para 14.324).

> The same principle was applied in *Sahardid v Camden LBC*.[24] The review was about the suitability of an offer of accommodation. The offer had been made in accordance with the council's policy to offer a single parent with a child under the age of five years a one-bedroom dwelling. The review decision was taken three days after the child's fifth birthday and the Court of Appeal held that the decision was flawed because it had failed to take account of the fact that the applicant was entitled, under the council's policy, to accommodation with two bedrooms.

15.30   An exception to this rule may apply when the decision is about the priority need of an applicant aged 16 or 17. This priority need is

---

21 The fee for further expert evidence may be covered by the Legal Help scheme, see para 22.160.

22 See *Hall v Wandsworth LBC; Carter v Wandsworth LBC* [2004] EWCA Civ 1740, 17 December 2002 and *Bellouti v Wandsworth LBC* [2005] EWCA Civ 602, 20 May 2005.

23 [2001] UKHL 57.

24 [2004] EWCA Civ 1485, 26 October 2004.

automatically lost when the young person reaches the age of 18. An authority cannot take advantage of an unlawful decision made at a time when the applicant was under 18 by finding, at the date of the review, that the young person is no longer in priority need, because of turning 18: *Akilah Robinson v Hammersmith & Fulham LBC.*[25]

Independence of reviewing officer

15.31   The review may be conducted by a panel of members or may be contracted out to an independent person.[26] If the review is carried out by an officer, he or she must be senior to the original decision-maker and must not have been involved in the original decision. However, a reviewing officer may be assisted in making inquiries by the junior officer who made the original decision.[27]

15.32   In some cases there will be more than one review. An authority may accept that a review decision was flawed and agree to carry out a further review. Also, in most successful county court appeals the review decision will be quashed, with the result that the authority must carry out a further review. It is not unlawful for a subsequent review to be carried out by the same officer who carried out the first review.[28] However, as in all local authority decision-making, actual bias would make the decision unlawful (see paras 2.20–2.21).

Irregular decision – further representations

15.33   Regulation 8(2) of the Review Regs 1999 applies where the reviewer has decided that there was a 'deficiency or irregularity' in the original decision or the manner in which it was made, but is nevertheless minded to make a decision which is against the interests of the applicant on one or more issues. Under regulation 8(2) the applicant must be notified that the reviewer is so minded and that the applicant, or someone acting on the applicant's behalf, 'may make representations to the reviewer orally or in writing or both orally and in writing'.

---

25 [2006] EWCA Civ 1122, see para 14.248.
26 Local Authorities (Contracting Out of Allocation of Housing and Homelessness Functions) Order 1996 SI No 3205; *De-Winter Heald, Al-Jarah, Ahmad & Kidane v Brent LBC* [2009] EWCA Civ 930, 20 August 2009.
27 *Butler v Fareham BC,* May 2001 *Legal Action* 24, CA.
28 *Feld v Barnet LBC; Ali Pour v Westminster CC* [2004] EWCA Civ 1307, 18 October 2004.

In *Hall v Wandsworth LBC*[29] the Court of Appeal held that the word 'deficiency' does not have any particular legal connotation. It simply means 'something lacking' which is 'of sufficient importance to the fairness of the procedure to justify an extra procedural safeguard'. Therefore

... the reviewing officer should treat reg 8(2) as applicable, not merely when he finds some significant legal or procedural error in the decision, but whenever (looking at the matter broadly and untechnically) he considers that an important aspect of the case was either not addressed, or not addressed adequately, by the original decision-maker, he must give notice of the grounds on which he intends to do so, and provide an opportunity for written and (if requested) oral representations.[30]

In *Makisi v Birmingham CC*[31] the Court of Appeal held that the right to an 'oral hearing', means having the opportunity to make 'face-to-face' representations and that an authority cannot limit the right to making representations by telephone. It does not, however, mean having a 'hearing' with witnesses or conducting cross-examination.

15.34   So, once the reviewing officer has identified a deficiency or irregularity he or she must send a 'minded to' letter to the applicant, explaining the reasons for the provisional view and giving the applicant the opportunity to make further representations. The reviewing officer does not have a discretion as to whether to offer the right of review on the basis that further representations will make no difference as that would mean that 'the reviewing officer has the power to decide, in effect, that nothing the applicant can say will cause him to change his mind on the issue which he has found against the applicant'.[32]

---

29 [2004] EWCA Civ 1740, 17 December 2002.
30 Carnwath LJ at [29] and [3].
31 *Makisi v Birmingham CC, Yosief v Birmingham CC, Nagi v Birmingham CC* [2011] EWCA Civ 355, 31 March 2011.
32 *Mitu v Camden LBC* [2011] EWCA Civ 1249, 1 November 2011, Lewison LJ at [28].

In *Lambeth LBC v Johnston*[33] the Court of Appeal held that the applicant's right under regulation 8(2) is 'a valuable procedural right' in all such cases. It 'is not a discretionary option that the reviewing officer can apply or disapply depending on whether he or she considered that giving a "minded to find" notice would be of material benefit to the applicant' or where it was considered the applicant had already made representations on the relevant issues.

Notification and reasons

15.35   Notification of the review decision must be given in writing. If it is not received, it is treated as having been given if it is made available at the authority's office for a reasonable period for collection.[34]

15.36   If the original decision is confirmed, reasons must be given.[35] Furthermore, the applicant must be informed of the right to appeal to the county court on a point of law and of the time limit for bringing such an appeal, which is 21 days from the date of notification.[36] If reasons are not given or if the applicant is not informed of the right to appeal to the county court, the notice of the decision is treated as not having been given.[37] This means that any deadline for appealing to the county court does not apply until proper notice is given.

15.37   As is the case for the HA 1996 s184 decision, the period for appealing runs from the date of notification (ie receipt of the letter), not the date endorsed on the letter or the date it was posted. Notice can be given to the applicant's representatives where they have made representations on the applicant's behalf and the applicant has authorised the local authority to deal with them.

In *Dharmaraj v Hounslow LBC*[38] the review decision had been faxed to the applicant's solicitors and stated that: 'Any application for appeal must be made within 21 days of the date of the letter.'

The Court of Appeal rejected the argument that the review decision must be sent personally to the applicant because his

---

33 *Lambeth LBC v Johnston* [2008] EWCA Civ 690, 19 June 2008.

34 HA 1996 s203(8).

35 HA 1996 s203(4). There is no right to be given reasons where the review succeeds and the decision is withdrawn: *Akhtar v Birmingham* [2011] EWCA, Civ 383, 12 April 2011.

36 HA 1996 s203(5).

37 HA 1996 s203(6).

38 [2011] EWCA Civ 312, 24 January 2011.

solicitors had made representations in support of the review and the applicant had signed an authorization to correspond with them about it. Furthermore, the letter was not defective for failing to state that the 21-day period runs from the date of notification: in this case, since the letter was sent by fax, that was the same as the date of notification. However, the court went on to suggest that even where such a letter was received a few days later so that the review letter had misinformed the applicant about the deadline for the appeal by 'a couple of days', this would not necessarily make the review letter defective. Clearly, however, if this contributed to the applicant missing the 21-day deadline, the court would almost certainly entertain a late appeal.

Outcome of the review

15.38   The best outcome for the applicant will be an acceptance of the full housing duty. Often, however, the review decision is that the HA 1996 s184 decision should be withdrawn and further inquiry carried out. If this is the outcome, then the authority will automatically have a duty to provide interim accommodation pending further decision (provided there is reason to believe the applicant is in priority need).

15.39   If the review decision confirms the adverse conclusion of the section 184 decision, the applicant may bring an appeal in the county court.

Appeals to the county court

15.40   Section 204 of the HA 1996 provides that:

> ... if an applicant who has requested a review under section 202:
> (1) is dissatisfied with the decision on the review, or
> (2) is not notified of the decision on the review within the time prescribed ...
> he may appeal to the county court on any point of law arising from the decision or, as the case may be, the original decision.

Time limits

15.41   An appeal must be brought within 21 days of the applicant being notified of the review decision. If the appeal is being brought to challenge the original decision, following a failure to carry out a review within the statutory period, it must be brought within 21 days of the date on which the applicant should have received notification (in most cases this means 11 weeks from the original notification under s184).[39]

15.42   Where the 21 days ends on a day on which the court is closed, an appeal is brought in time if lodged on the next working day.[40]

Out of time appeals

15.43   The court may give permission for an appeal to be brought out of time only if satisfied that there was a good reason for the failure to bring the appeal in time and for any delay in applying for permission.[41] It is also possible to apply, *within* the 21-day period, for permission to lodge the appeal out of time. If a person is in a position to make such an application, it is probably better simply to draft and lodge the appeal notice itself, since the detailed grounds can be lodged by way of a skeleton argument later.

15.44   When considering permission for a late appeal, the court must be satisfied that there is a good reason for the delay. If not, permission must be refused and the court should not consider the merits of the appeal.[42]

Procedure on appeals

15.45   Although there is no requirement to be legally represented, in most cases the applicant will need to instruct solicitors to advise whether there is a point of law arising from the decision and to draft the notice of appeal or to instruct a barrister to do so. Legal aid will be available, depending on the applicant's means and the likelihood of success. It is important that someone seeking to challenge a review decision is referred to solicitors without delay. It will usually be necessary for the solicitor to send a letter before claim to the authority and consider the response before legal aid will be granted. Most solicitors will then instruct a barrister to draft the appeal notice.

15.46   The procedure is set out in Part 52 of the Civil Procedure Rules (CPR) and the appeal notice is form N161. Part 52 and form N161 are available online, along with guidance notes. Chapter 22 contains a general explanation of county court procedure. In most cases the

---

39 HA 1996 s204(2).
40 *Adan v Brent LBC* (1999) 32 HLR 848, CA.
41 HA 1996 s204(2A).
42 *Short v Birmingham CC* [2004] EWHC 2112 (QB), 10 September 2004.

form N161 will be drafted by a solicitor or barrister, as it is necessary to set out the legal grounds on which it is argued the decision is unlawful. A skeleton argument setting out the legal principles and case-law relied on should be either included in the appeal notice or filed within 14 days. The forms and procedure are confusing because they are designed primarily for appeals against court decisions rather than local authority decisions.

15.47　　The hearing of an appeal will usually consist of purely legal argument about the lawfulness of the decision. Oral evidence is not given and it is unusual even for witness statements to be used. If the appellant (the homeless applicant) is legally represented, he or she is not strictly required to attend the hearing. However, it is good practice to do so because proposals may be put forward to resolve the appeal on which his or her instructions will be needed.

Reconsidering a review decision

15.48　There is nothing to prevent an authority reconsidering a decision made on review.[43] Indeed it is common for an authority to respond to a letter indicating an intention to appeal by offering to reconsider the decision. However, if this is agreed between the parties, the authority must be asked to confirm that it is withdrawing its previous review decision and that the reconsidered decision will be the review decision for the purposes of any appeal. If the authority does not agree, any appeal must be lodged within 21 days of the notification of the initial review decision.

> In *Demetri v Westminster CC*[44] the authority's decision on review was notified in the correct form to the applicant, including information about the right to appeal to the county court within 21 days. The applicant's advisers discovered that certain documents had not been sent to the review officer and the council agreed to consider its review decision further in light of these documents. Two months later the council indicated that it had considered the documents, but would not change its review decision. An appeal was lodged in the county court but was struck out on the grounds that it had been lodged out of time. The applicant's appeal to the Court of Appeal was dismissed.

43　*R v Westminster CC ex p Ellioua* (1998) 31 HLR 440, CA.
44　(2000) 32 HLR 470, CA.

15.49 It should be noted that *Demetri* was decided at a time when the county court had no power to extend the time for an appeal. However, advisers should always ensure that the authority confirms that the first review decision is withdrawn pending reconsideration. In *Demetri* the court indicated that where an applicant is unrepresented the authority must make it clear if the time for a county court appeal is not being extended.

Appealing the original section 184 decision

15.50 Where a review is requested but the authority fails to carry out the review, the applicant has two choices: a county court appeal against the original decision or judicial review to force the authority to carry out the review. Often it will be sufficient to invite the authority to agree an extension of time to complete the review. This must be confirmed in writing. If agreed, the deadline for any county court appeal is 21 days after the agreed deadline. Where the applicant wishes to submit new information or make submissions to the authority, it is better for a review to be conducted than to appeal against the original decision. Any such appeal will be limited to a consideration of the lawfulness of the decision at the time it was made. If the appeal is successful the likely outcome is the quashing of the decision so that the authority must make a fresh HA 1996 s184 decision. Furthermore, there is nothing to prevent an authority from notifying the applicant of the decision on review after a county court appeal has been commenced. The appellant would then need to amend the appeal grounds or (if the review decision is positive or unchallengeable) to withdraw the appeal. In such a case the local authority should be ordered to pay the costs of the appeal.

What is a point of law?

15.51 A 'point of law' is not limited to matters of legal interpretation, but embraces all of the matters usually challenged by way of judicial review, including irrationality and inadequacy of reasons.[45]

15.52 Broadly, the main types of judicial review challenge have been categorised under the following heads:[46]

- illegality;
- irrationality; and
- procedural impropriety.

45 *Nipa Begum v Tower Hamlets LBC* (1999) 32 HLR 445, CA.
46 *CCSU v Minister for Civil Service* [1985] AC 374, HL.

15.53   In addition, a failure to give reasons, or adequate reasons, may in itself make a decision unlawful.

15.54   The grounds for judicial review are examined in more detail in paras 2.8–2.26. All of the grounds that may be used in judicial review proceedings may be argued as a point of law in a homeless appeal.

The powers of the county court

15.55   It is not for the court to reach its own decision on the facts. The court is exercising a supervisory function, as in judicial review, and is limited to considering the lawfulness of the authority's decision. The court may:[47]

- confirm a decision;
- quash a decision; or
- vary a decision.

15.56   If an appeal is successful, the most common order is the quashing of the review decision. This means that the authority must conduct a fresh review. This may, of course, mean that even after a successful appeal the authority then makes another negative review decision. Indeed, it is sometimes the case that an authority makes several review decisions in relation to the same applicant.

15.57   When a court is asked to vary a decision, the question is whether there is any real prospect that the authority, acting rationally and with the benefit of further inquiry, might be satisfied that the issue could be decided in an adverse way.[48] If so, the decision should be quashed, rather than varied.

> In *Ekwuru v Westminster*[49] the Court of Appeal considered an appeal against a county court decision not to vary a decision that the appellant was intentionally homeless. In this case the authority had already agreed on two occasions to its decision being quashed, following successful appeals by Mr Ekwuru. On the third occasion it again indicated that it would submit to the decision being quashed and carry out what would be a fourth review. Mr Ekwuru argued that the court should vary the decision. The county court declined to do so on the basis that such a decision would involve a hearing of the original facts. Mr Ekwuru appealed to the Court of Appeal, which

---

47 HA 1996 s204(3).
48 *R on the application of Deugi v Tower Hamlets LBC* [2006] EWCA Civ 159, 7 March 2006.
49 [2003] EWCA Civ 1293, 31 July 2003.

considered his appeal almost four years after he had applied as homeless.

It was held that there was no realistic possibility that the further inquiries the authority proposed would produce more information than was available at the date of the third review. On the basis of the material before the authority at that time, it could not lawfully have come to the conclusion that Mr Ekwuru was intentionally homeless and the court varied the decision to one that he was not intentionally homeless.

Time limit for further review

15.58 There is no specific provision for a time limit for a further review, following the quashing or withdrawal of a previous review decision. If the review is to be carried out following a county court appeal, the court may be asked to set a time limit for the further review decision. If the review is withdrawn by agreement, a time limit should also be agreed.

15.59 In all cases advisers will wish to stipulate that the applicant is provided with interim accommodation pending any further review decision.

Accommodation pending appeal

15.60 An authority has a discretion to provide interim accommodation pending an appeal. If this is refused, an applicant may bring a second appeal in the county court, under HA 1996 s204A, to challenge the refusal. Interim accommodation pending review or appeal is discussed in paras 16.4–16.13.

APPENDIX

Request for review

Dear Sir/Madam,

Re: Mrs A – section 184 decision dated

We are advising Mrs A with regard to her homeless application. Mrs A requests a review of the above decision.

Please provide to us a copy of the complete homelessness file under the Data Protection Act 1998. We enclose a cheque in the sum of £10 together with our client's signed authority.

We intend to make representations in support of the review following receipt of the file. We would therefore be grateful if this could be provided as a matter of urgency.

Yours faithfully,

Adviser

Advice Agency

CHAPTER 16

Homelessness: accommodation duties

Key points

- Whenever an authority is under a duty to provide accommodation it must be available to the applicant and the family members he or she normally lives with and any other person who might reasonably be expected to live with the applicant.
- An authority *must* provide interim accommodation pending a decision if it has reason to believe the applicant may be in priority need.
- An authority *may* provide interim accommodation pending review or appeal.
- Interim accommodation must be suitable but the temporary nature of the accommodation means that the standard may be low.
- If the 'full housing duty' is owed, the authority must make available suitable accommodation. The applicant can challenge the suitability of accommodation offered by way of review and county court appeal.
- If an applicant refuses the accommodation and fails, through a review or appeal, to change the decision about suitability the authority will owe no housing duty.
- An applicant can accept the accommodation and still challenge the suitability by way of review and county court appeal.
- The duty to provide suitable accommodation under the full housing duty is indefinite: it only ends in specified circumstances set out in HA 1996 s193.
- The accommodation provided under the full housing duty will not give long-term security to the applicant.
- Accommodation with long-term security will only be made available through the authority's allocations scheme.
- The Localism Act 2011 will change the section 193 duty so that it is a duty to provide a private sector tenancy only.

Introduction

16.1   At various stages throughout the homeless application process an authority may have a duty or a power to provide accommodation for the applicant. The different stages at which an accommodation duty may arise are as follows:

Temporary accommodation:
- interim accommodation pending decision;
- interim accommodation pending review;
- interim accommodation pending appeal;
- temporary accommodation for a person found intentionally homeless.

The 'full housing duty':
- indefinite accommodation under Housing Act (HA) 1996 s193.[1]

Permanent accommodation:
- the allocation of permanent social housing.

16.2   The principles involved at each stage vary, as do the ways of challenging decisions. Chapter 13 deals with the interim accommodation duty pending decision. This chapter deals with the power to provide interim accommodation pending review and appeal, the accommodation duty owed to those found intentionally homeless and the 'full housing duty' under HA 1996 s193. It also outlines the proposed changes in the Localism Act. The allocation of permanent accommodation is dealt with in chapter 17.

Temporary accommodation duties

Accommodation pending decision

16.3   This is dealt with in detail in paras 13.26–13.46. The principal features of the duty to provide interim accommodation pending a decision are:

- the duty is triggered when the authority has reason to believe the applicant may be eligible, homeless and in priority need;
- the accommodation must be suitable and it must be made available for the applicant and his or her household;
- the duty ends when a decision is made on the homeless application;
- challenging a failure to provide accommodation or the suitability of the accommodation is by way of judicial review.

---

1 The Localism Act 2011 will change this to a duty to provide a private sector tenancy for a minimum term of 12 months with provision for further accommodation to be provided if the person becomes unintentionally homeless again within two years.

Accommodation pending review

16.4 The *duty* to provide interim accommodation ends if a negative decision is made. If the applicant seeks a review, the authority has a *power* to continue to provide interim accommodation pending the review decision.

16.5   The authority does not have to consider whether to provide or extend interim accommodation pending review unless requested to do so.[2]

16.6   A refusal to provide interim accommodation pending review is challenged by way of judicial review.

16.7   The principles to be applied by an authority in deciding whether or not to provide interim accommodation were set out by the Court of Appeal in *R v Camden LBC ex p Mohammed*.[3]

> In *Mohammed* the authority operated a policy of exercising its discretion to provide interim accommodation only in exceptional circumstances. The evidence was that the proportion of successful reviews was small.
>
> The Court of Appeal held that it is not unlawful to operate such a policy and that an authority must balance the objective of maintaining fairness between homeless persons to whom they have decided no duty is owed, with proper consideration of the possibility that the applicant may be right and may therefore be deprived of an entitlement. In carrying out the balancing exercise certain matters will always require consideration:
>
> - the merits of the case – that is, the merits of the case that the decision is flawed, not the merits of the case on the facts, once all necessary inquiries have been made;[4]
> - whether there is new material, information or argument which should be considered and which could have a real effect on the decision under review; and
> - the personal circumstances of the applicant and the consequences of a refusal to provide interim accommodation.

2   *R v Newham LBC ex p Lumley* (2003) 33 HLR 111, 28 January 2000.

3   (1997) 30 HLR 315, CA.

4   See the comments of Brooke LJ in *Lumley* (2003) 33 HLR 111, CA (see para 16.9 below) at [52] and [54]. This is an important distinction because in many cases the quality of the initial decision-making is poor, with cursory inquiries being made and letters issued in a pro forma manner. The conclusion may be the same following full inquiries, but the applicant is entitled to a lawful decision made in accordance with HA 1996 and properly explained.

In *Mohammed* the applicant claimed to have left her home because of domestic violence from her husband. The authority had taken account of inconsistencies in her account of his conduct. The authority did not give her the opportunity to explain the inconsistencies, but decided that accommodation was available to her and that therefore she was not homeless.

The court decided that the merits of the challenge to the initial decision were such that the original decision was tainted with unfairness; the authority had been wrong to refuse to provide interim accommodation pending review.

16.8   These criteria should be addressed when requesting interim accommodation. Because such requests usually have to be made on an urgent basis, it is useful to use a template when submitting such a request. An example of such a letter is contained in the appendix to this chapter.

16.9   Local authorities often cite *R v Brighton and Hove Council ex p Nacion*[5] in arguing that, where an authority has considered all material factors, successful judicial review applications will be exceptional. *Nacion* concerned a refusal to provide interim accommodation *after* a review decision and pending a county court appeal.[6] In *Nacion* the court did refer to the fact that the provision of accommodation pending appeal *and review* was entirely within the discretion of the local authority. However, it is more likely that there will be merit in the argument that the original decision is flawed than that the review decision is flawed. On the other hand, a local authority that has extended acommodation pending review will usually agree a further extension until appeal.

In *R v Newham LBC ex p Lumley*,[7] the applicant was a man suffering from depression who had been homeless for some time. The authority was provided with a medical report referring to the risk of suicide if he remained homeless. The authority's medical officer considered the doctor's report and indicated, without giving reasons, that he did not consider the applicant to be vulnerable. The decision letter, it was conceded, simply recited the terms of

5   (1999) 31 HLR 1095.
6   This was at a time when judicial review was the only way to challenge a refusal to accommodate pending appeal.
7   (2003) 33 HLR 111, CA.

> HA 1996 s189 (the priority need categories) 'parrot-fashion' and
> gave no substantive explanation for its decision that the applicant
> was not in priority need. It was held that the authority had failed in
> its duty to carry out proper inquiries into the applicant's psychiatric
> history. In relation to the provision of interim accommodation
> pending review, the court held that the authority
>
> > ... had clearly not yet made a lawful decision, because of
> > the shortcomings which [were conceded]. Justice therefore
> > demanded that it should continue to provide him with temporary
> > accommodation until it did.[8]

Accommodation pending appeal

16.10   An authority also has a power to provide interim accommodation
pending a county court appeal: HA 1996 s204(4). Prior to the Homelessness Act 2002 the only way to challenge a refusal to do so was by
way of judicial review (as in *Nacion*, see para 16.9 above). Now such
challenges are brought by way of a county court appeal.

16.11   Housing Act 1996 s204A(2) provides that, where an applicant
has a right to a county court appeal against a homeless decision, the
applicant may also appeal against a decision not to provide accommodation up to the date of appeal.

16.12   The court may order the authority to secure that accommodation
is available until the determination of the main appeal, or an earlier
time, as specified, and must confirm or quash the decision not to provide interim accommodation. The court cannot order the authority to
provide interim accommodation beyond the final determination of
the homeless appeal.[9]

16.13   The court may only order an authority to provide interim accommodation if the court is satisfied that a failure to exercise the power
would 'substantially prejudice the applicant's ability to pursue the
main appeal'.[10] The most compelling argument will be where, without interim accommodation, the appellant will be 'street homeless'
pending the appeal, so that his or her solicitors may find it impossible to obtain instructions to pursue the appeal.

---

8   (2003) 33 HLR 111, CA, Brooke LJ at [55].
9   HA 1996 s204A(6)(b).
10   HA 1996 s204A(6)(a).

Temporary accommodation for the intentionally homeless

16.14 If an applicant is found to be eligible, homeless and in priority need, but intentionally homeless, HA 1996 s190(2) provides that an authority must:

(a) secure that accommodation is made available for his occupation for such period as they consider will give him a reasonable opportunity of securing accommodation for his occupation; and

(b) provide him with advice and such assistance as they consider appropriate in the circumstances in any attempts he may make to secure that accommodation becomes available for his occupation.

16.15 In determining what is a reasonable period the authority must consider an applicant's individual circumstances and should not operate a blanket policy as to the period of temporary accommodation offered in all cases.[11]

> The Court of Appeal considered the nature of the HA 1996 s190 duty in *R on the application of Conville v Richmond upon Thames LBC*.[12] The decision that the applicant was intentionally homeless was made in February 2005 and she was told she could remain in the interim accommodation for a further 28 days. She was subsequently granted a number of extensions until 8 June 2005. She made genuine but unsuccessful attempts to find her own accommodation. Her efforts were hampered by the fact that she could not afford the deposit and advance rent required by most private landlords. She could not borrow the money and was ineligible for the council's rent deposit scheme. In deciding on the period that was reasonable, the authority had taken into account the applicant's circumstances, the authority's limited resources and the needs of other homeless applicants.
>
> The Court of Appeal held that the authority should not have taken account of its resources, but should have assessed what was a reasonable period
>
> > ... by reference to the particular needs and circumstances of the applicant. It should have regard to the possibilities open to the applicant ... If the applicant is not making reasonable efforts

11 *Lally v RLBC Kensington and Chelsea* (1980) *Times* 27 March.
12 [2006] EWCA Civ 718, 8 June 2006.

> to pursue the possibilities open to him, that will be a strong indication that he should not be given more time.[13]
>
> However, giving a person a reasonable opportunity to find accommodation does not mean a period sufficient to ensure that the person will necessarily succeed.
>
> What amounts to a reasonable opportunity will depend on the particular circumstances but it is an assessment the authority are capable of making without converting it into a duty to meet the appellant's needs. In this statutory context, a distinction is maintainable between giving a reasonable opportunity and giving such opportunity as will succeed in obtaining accommodation.[14]

Advice and assistance

16.16   In addition to providing accommodation for a reasonable period, the authority must also provide, or ensure the applicant is provided with, advice and assistance in any attempt made to secure accommodation: HA 1996 s190(2)(b). Before providing the advice and assistance the applicant's housing needs must be assessed: s190(4). Furthermore, the advice and assistance provided must include information about the likely availability in the district of the types of accommodation appropriate to his or her housing needs (including, in particular, the location and sources of such types of accommodation): s190(5).

The full housing duty – HA 1996 s193

16.17   If, following inquiry, the authority is satisfied that the applicant is eligible, homeless, in priority need and not intentionally homeless, the 'full housing duty' is owed. The duty is owed by the authority to which the application was made, unless the local referral conditions are met, in which case it is owed by the authority to which the case is referred.

---

13 [2006] EWCA Civ 718, Pill LJ at [38].
14 [2006] EWCA Civ 718, Pill LJ at [40].

How the s193 duty can be discharged – the current position[15]

16.18 Housing Act 1996 s193(2) provides that the full housing duty is to 'secure that accommodation is available for occupation by the applicant'. HA 1996 s206 provides that this can be done in the following ways:

(a) by securing that suitable accommodation provided by them is available;

(b) by securing that he obtains suitable accommodation from some other person; or

(c) by giving him such advice and assistance as will secure that he obtains suitable accommodation from some other person.

Note, however, that if the application is a 'restricted case', the duty is limited to arranging a suitable private sector tenancy for 12 months. See paras 14.43–14.148 and 14.90.

16.19 Most commonly, an authority will provide the accommodation itself, or arrange for some other person or agency to provide it. However, in some circumstances it could simply give advice and assistance such that accommodation will be obtained from someone else. This could cover, for example, advising and assisting a person with sufficient means to purchase accommodation. It could also include mediation to ensure that accommodation provided by family members was made available.[16]

16.20 If the authority offers a tenancy, it will be a non-secure tenancy. If an arrangement is made with a private landlord or a registered social landlord, any tenancy will be an assured shorthold tenancy. Tenancies with social landlords can become secure or fully assured only if the person subsequently qualifies for an allocation under HA 1996 Part VI. The accommodation does not have to be under a tenancy and could, for example, be a licence in a hostel, provided the accommodation was suitable.

16.21 Although the tenancy or licence will not give the occupier long-term rights in the particular property, the duty of the authority to provide accommodation under HA 1996 s193 is indefinite. It ends only in the circumstances set out in section 193, listed at para 16.49

---

15 The way the section 193 duty is discharged will be fundamentally changed when the Localism Act 2011 comes into force. The changes are explained at paras 16.73–16.75 below.

16 Though usually mediation would be offered as part of a homeless prevention strategy. See *Akilah Robinson v Hammersmith & Fulham LBC* [2006] EWCA Civ 1122 (para 14.248 above).

below. This means that a person who is provided with an assured shorthold tenancy under section 193 must be provided with alternative accommodation if the landlord subsequently seeks possession. The section 193 duty is a continuing one and the person need not make a fresh homeless application. This should be made clear to the applicant when the offer of accommodation is made.[17]

When does the duty arise?

16.22　Usually, when a decision is made that the full housing duty is accepted, the applicant will be residing in interim accommodation. It is possible for the authority to propose that the applicant remain in the same accommodation pursuant to the HA 1996 s193 duty. If so, it must make it clear that the accommodation currently occupied is considered suitable and that the applicant has the right to seek a review of its suitability, and state the time limit for requesting a review. This information may be included in the section 184 letter stating that a duty is accepted. If the applicant does not agree that the accommodation is suitable for occupation for the immediate future, he or she must request a review within 21 days.

16.23　　More commonly, the interim accommodation will be unsuitable for long-term occupation. Clearly, in most cases, some time will elapse before the authority can identify and make available accommodation suitable for longer-term occupation. However, disputes may arise where there is significant delay in providing suitable accommodation.

16.24　　In some cases an authority may acknowledge that the accommodation being provided is not suitable, but maintain that no suitable accommodation is currently available.

Delays in providing suitable accommodation

16.25　The following cases illustrate the courts' approach to the issue of delay.

> In *R v Southwark ex p Anderson*[18] the HA 1996 s193 duty was accepted in May 1997. The authority agreed to discharge its duty by providing four-bed accommodation. However, to speed the process the applicants agreed to take three-bed accommodation, in or out of the borough. Three offers were made, but withdrawn because they were unsuitable. A fourth offer was the subject of an internal review.

17　*Griffiths v St Helens Council* [2006] EWCA Civ 160, 7 March 2006.
18　(1998) 32 HLR 96, QBD.

The applicants sought judicial review of the council's failure to secure accommodation between May 1997 and February 1999.

The application was dismissed. It was held that 'there is no time limit within which the housing authority is obliged under the statute to comply with a duty to secure available accommodation for those who fall within s193'. On the evidence the council was trying to secure suitable accommodation but was hampered by the lack of available stock; it was in the process of complying with its duty and was not in breach of its obligations.

In *R v Merton LBC ex p Sembi*[19] the council accepted a section 193 duty towards a disabled applicant. It decided that her needs would be best met by specially adapted long-term accommodation. In the meantime, she was provided with a place in a home for the elderly and terminally ill. The applicant sought judicial review of the delay in securing more appropriate accommodation.

Her application was dismissed. The suitability of the current accommodation could be challenged by way of a review and county court appeal. With regard to the delay, the reasoning of *Anderson* was followed. The authority was not in breach of the duty, but was in the process of complying.

In *R v Newham LBC ex p Begum and Ali*[20] it was held that any suggestion in *Anderson* and *Sembi* that an authority had a 'reasonable period' to comply with the HA 1996 s193 duty was incorrect. The applicants comprised a family including six children, another young relative and an elderly disabled relative who was a wheelchair-user. On their application they were provided with bed & breakfast accommodation outside the borough. This was conceded to be unsuitable. Following acceptance of the full duty, the family was placed in a four-bedroom privately leased house which was also unsuitable as it was not adapted for wheelchair use. The applicants sought judicial review to require the council to discharge its duty by providing suitable accommodation. The council argued that, following *Anderson* and *Sembi*, there was no time limit for the provision of s193 accommodation and that provided it was using its best endeavours it could not be criticised. Alternatively, the HA 1996

19 (1999) 32 HLR 439, QBD.
20 (1999) 32 HLR 808, QBD.

was to be read as giving a reasonable period for a council to find suitable accommodation, and the authority could not be required to achieve the impossible – the provision of suitable accommodation if none was available.

The application for judicial review was allowed. It was held that HA 1996 s193 (and ss188, 190 and 200) required that the council secure suitable accommodation as soon as the duty to accommodate arose. The performance of those duties could not be deferred and any suggestion in *Anderson* and *Sembi* that that was the case was based on an erroneous approach to HA 1996 Part VII.

However, the 'safeguards' for a council faced with a housing duty under Part VII were threefold: (1) the test of suitability was flexible – what could be provided might not be ideal, but might be suitable if intended for the very short-term; (2) a premature application to the court would be refused; and (3) if the court was satisfied that performance was really impossible, relief might be refused.

In this case the council had not considered using its own stock, but had confined itself to considering 'temporary' accommodation such as privately leased premises and bed and breakfast hotels. An order was made, compelling the council to provide suitable accommodation within 28 days.

In *Birmingham CC v Ali*[21] the House of Lords considered the issue of the suitability of accommodation under HA 1996 s193 and the duty to applicants who had been found to be homeless because it was not reasonable for them to continue to occupy grossly overcrowded accommodation. Having accepted the applicants as homeless, the authority then indicated that they should remain in that accommodation until suitable permanent accommodation became available.

The House of Lords held that when considering homelessness under HA 1996 s175(3) and intentional homelessness under s191(1) it was necessary to look to the future as well as to the present: it may not be reasonable for a person to occupy accommodation indefinitely but it may be reasonable for them to continue to do so in the short term. Thus it was not unlawful for Birmingham to accept that a family was homeless because it was not reasonable for them to occupy severely overcrowded

---

21 [2009] UKHL 36. In the Court of Appeal the case was known as *R on the application of Aweys v Birmingham CC*.

accommodation yet at the same time discharge their duty to provide accommodation under section 193(2) by virtue of the family remaining in the same accommodation in the short term. Despite it being unreasonable for the family to occupy the accommodation indefinitely, the accommodation could be suitable for the purposes of the section 193(2) duty. However, it would not be lawful for an authority to leave a family in the accommodation indefinitely and there would be bound to come a time when the accommodation could no longer be described as suitable.

16.26   So, what may be held to be suitable for short-term occupation may become unsuitable if the applicant remains in the accommodation for an extended period (even if the applicant's circumstances do not change). Although the issue was not made clear in *Birmingham v Ali,* it seems that any challenge to suitability on the basis that the time has come so as to render the accommodation unsuitable should be brought by way of a request for a review of suitability and county court appeal rather than judicial review. However, some caution must be exercised since the HA 1996 s193 duty will end where alternative suitable accommodation is offered and refused.

In *Muse v Brent LBC*[22] a housing duty was accepted and Mrs Muse was placed in social housing, under an assured shortold tenancy. At the time she had one child. After the birth of her third child her landlords wrote to the local authority stating that she was overcrowded and her solicitors wrote to the authority asking that she be reallocated to a higher band within the allocations policy, and also to be transferred to more suitable housing or (confusingly) to be accommodated as a homeless person, whichever would be sooner.

The housing authority made an offer of alternative temporary accommodation but Mrs Muse declined to move on the basis that it was unsuitable, preferring to stay in her overcrowded accommodation. The property was re-offered and the offer letter stated that if she failed to take the accommodation the authority would conclude that it had discharged its duty to her. The letter stated: 'This means that any temporary accommodation that you are currently occupying will be terminated and your homeless application will be closed. If you are already in temporary

22 [2008] EWCA Civ 1447, 19 December 2008.

accommodation managed by a housing association, the council will instruct the association to obtain a court order for possession.' Her solicitors responded that their client was already bidding for properties and that: 'She is not obliged to accept an alternative temporary accommodation if she does not wish to do so.' The authority responded by sending a further letter to Mrs Muse extending the deadline for accepting the accommodation and warning her that, if she did not accept it, the authority would conclude that it had discharged its statutory duty towards her. After the deadline expired the authority wrote to Mrs Muse stating that it considered that the housing duty was now discharged and that it would instruct her housing association landlords to commence eviction proceedings. A review of the decision was then requested on the grounds that the s193(2) duty did not apply to Mrs Muse and that the property was unsuitable. The review officer rejected both arguments and upheld the decision that the offer was suitable and the s193 duty had ended. The county court upheld Mrs Muse's appeal and the authority appealed to the Court of Appeal.

The appeal was allowed. The Court of Appeal held that the authority was obliged to, and did, offer alternative suitable accommodation. It complied with that duty and, pursuant to s193(5), the offer was on terms that its duty would be discharged if Mrs Muse declined to accept the alternative accommodation.

16.27   Where an authority is maintaining that accommodation is suitable then a review should be requested. However, if the authority accepts that the current accommodation is not suitable but is not using its best endeavours to find suitable accommodation, or is limiting the type of accommodation that may be used (for example only considering private sector accommodation), a claim for judicial review may be appropriate. In such a case, a request should be made for the authority to disclose the steps it is taking to find suitable accommodation. Often, such pressure results in more suitable accommodation being located. If, however, the authority is making all reasonable endeavours but is hampered by the lack of suitable accommodation, a court may refuse to make an order. This is more likely to be the case where only accommodation of an unusual size or type will be suitable.

16.28   Most authorities use private landlords to discharge their HA 1996 s193 duties. Complaints about the standard of accommodation and disrepair are common. If a tenancy has been granted, the occupier will have the right to have certain repairs carried out by the landlord: see chapter 10.[23] However, in many cases the occupier communicates not with the landlord directly, but with a local authority's temporary accommodation section or with a social landlord who is managing the property. He or she may be more concerned to be allocated alternative accommodation than to have repairs carried out. In such a case the making of a formal complaint and, ultimately, an Ombudsman complaint may be effective.

An Ombudsman complaint was made against Hackney LBC[24] about a seven-year delay in making accommodation available to a homeless applicant. A duty to house under the HA 1985 was accepted in 1992 and a succession of private sector leased properties were made available until 1999, when the applicant was nominated to a housing trust for permanent accommodation. A complaint was made of maladministration for (1) the delay in securing permanent accommodation, and (2) the poor quality of the temporary accommodation.

The Ombudsman found that in 1993 an offer of permanent accommodation had been made, but had been sent to an old address and had not come to the applicant's attention. This had resulted in the applicant remaining in temporary accommodation for six years longer than necessary. Furthermore, because of mistakes by the council's agents (a housing association), the quality of the temporary accommodation had been unsatisfactory and for three years the family had lived in accommodation deemed 'prejudicial to health' by the council's environmental health department. The Ombudsman recommended compensation of £6,000.

23 If the tenancy agreement is between the private landlord and the applicant, the applicant's rights will be against the private landlord. However, the private landlord may have leased the property to the local authority, which will then be the applicant's landlord.

24 98/A/1857, reported in November 1999 *Legal Action* 17.

Suitability

16.29   It is for the authority to decide what is suitable. In doing so it must have regard to:

- the legislation on slum clearance, overcrowding and houses in multiple occupation (HMOs);[25]
- the particular circumstances of the applicant and his or her family, including any medical and physical needs or social considerations such as the risk of racial harassment or domestic violence, access to and stability in schools, and access to other facilities;[26]
- the affordability of the accommodation, in particular, the financial resources available to that person, the cost of the accommodation and his or her other reasonable living expenses.[27]

Housing standards

16.30   It should be noted that HA 1996 s210 requires that an authority 'have regard to' the legislation on slum clearance, overcrowding and HMOs. The legislation is found in the Housing Acts 1985 and 2004 (see paras 11.13–11.83) and gives enforcement powers to local authorities where properties in the private sector fall below certain standards. The 'fitness standards' previously set out in the HA 1985 have been replaced by a system of hazard assessment, which is described at paras 11.17–11.29. The Homelessness Code provides:

> **The Secretary of State recommends that when determining the suitability of accommodation secured under the homelessness legislation, local authorities should, as a minimum, ensure that all accommodation is free of Category 1 hazards.** In the case of an out-of-district placement it is the responsibility of the placing authority to ensure that accommodation is free of Category 1 hazards.[28]

Particular circumstances of the applicant

16.31   Generally, a homeless applicant has little choice over the type or location of accommodation offered under HA 1996 s193. While an authority must take account of the needs of the applicant's household, it is difficult to challenge decisions as to suitability unless the applicant has particular needs that have been ignored.

---

25 HA 1996 s210.
26 Homelessness Code of Guidance paras 17.5–17.6.
27 Homelessness (Suitability of Accommodation) Order 1996 SI No 3204.
28 Homelessness Code of Guidance para 17.5.

In *R v Brent LBC ex p Omar*[29] the applicant was offered accommodation in a basement flat on an estate. She had been granted refugee status, following imprisonment and abuse in Somalia. She rejected the offer, indicating that the premises were reminiscent of the conditions of her imprisonment and that she would rather commit suicide than live there. The authority maintained that the offer was suitable because there were no pure medical grounds or other social grounds why it should not be accepted.

The applicant's judicial review claim was upheld. In addition to the matters the Housing Act referred to, an authority must also have regard to the particular circumstances of the applicant and her family. This was an exceptional case in which no reasonable housing authority, properly directing itself, could conclude that the property was suitable for the applicant.

Location

16.32   The location of accommodation is relevant to suitability, and the Homelessness Code para 17.41 refers to the need to take account of family members in paid employment and to minimise disruption to the education of young people, particularly at critical points, such as when they are close to taking GCSE examinations. Many applicants wish to be accommodated in the locality where they are settled, and where their family and friends live. However, given the shortage of available accommodation, very strong reasons will be needed to challenge suitability on the grounds of location.

In *Abdullah v Westminster CC*[30] an applicant rejected accommodation on the grounds that it was too far from her family and friends who provided her with support to care for her children. The county court upheld her first appeal: the review officer had failed to take sufficient account of her need to be near family and friends. A reconsideration was undertaken, but the review officer again found that the property was suitable. On a second county court appeal the decision was upheld.

The Court of Appeal dismissed the applicant's appeal. The review officer had relied on advice and information received from social services to the effect that the property was suitable. The medical

29 (1991) 23 HLR 446, QBD.
30 [2007] EWCA Civ 1566, 21 June 2007.

officer had indicated that it would be advantageous for the applicant
to be near family and friends, but not that she would be unable to
cope without it. There was sufficient material for the review officer
to reach the decision and no grounds to appeal against the county
court's refusal to interfere.

Out of area placements

16.33   Housing Act 1996 s208 provides that:

> So far as reasonably practicable a local housing authority shall in dis-
> charging their housing functions under this Part secure that accom-
> modation is available for the occupation of the applicant in their
> district.

16.34   An authority's starting point must be to locate accommodation
within its own area. However, it is not unlawful to operate a policy
under which some out of borough accommodation is used, providing
it is suitable for the particular applicant. In deciding whether it is
reasonably practicable to secure accommodation within the borough, the authority may take into account the cost of providing the
accommodation.

In *R on the application of Calgin v Enfield LBC*[31] the court held that
the authority's policy of using accommodation in Birmingham
and Luton to house a small proportion of homeless applicants
was lawful. Furthermore, when deciding what was 'reasonably
practicable' the issue of the authority's resources and the
comparative cost of providing accommodation within and outside
the borough were relevant. In the circumstances the offer of
accommodation in Birmingham was suitable, having regard to the
needs of the family and their links in the borough of Enfield.

16.35   However, as in all cases, the accommodation must be suitable for
the particular applicant. A challenge to the same authority was successful in *R on the application of Yumsak v Enfield LBC*,[32] see para
13.37. The applicant had a number of good reasons to remain in the
area where she had lived for seven years and the authority had failed
to justify the breach of her rights under article 8 of the European

---

31   [2005] EWHC 1716 (Admin), 29 July 2005.
32   [2002] EWHC 280 (Admin), 5 February 2002.

Convention on Human Rights that would be involved in her being accommodated in Birmingham.

Affordability

16.36   An authority must in all cases consider whether accommodation is affordable for the applicant. The Homelessness (Suitability of Accommodation) Order 1996[33] requires a local authority to take account of the income and necessary outgoings as well as the reasonable living expenses of a household when deciding if it is affordable to the particular applicant.[34] The Homelessness Code suggests that if, after taking these into account, the 'residual income' would be less than that of a household reliant on income support or income-based jobseeker's allowance, a property is unaffordable.[35]

16.37   It is common in the private sector for the amount of housing benefit awarded to a tenant to be less than the full amount of the rent. Where an authority discharges its duty by arranging for the offer of a private tenancy, it may use its powers to top up payments of housing benefit so that the landlord receives the full rent.[36] It may be argued that, where an applicant is in receipt of income support, any shortfall that he or she is expected to meet makes the property unaffordable and therefore unsuitable. On the other hand, where the shortfall is small, an authority may argue that other tenants in the same situation must make such payments in order to maintain private tenancies.

Reviews of suitability

16.38   An applicant can accept an offer and still seek a review of the offer's suitability.[37]

16.39   Conversely, where an applicant refuses accommodation and seeks a review of its suitability, the authority is not obliged to keep the accommodation available pending the outcome of the review.[38]

16.40   Challenges to the suitability of accommodation offered under HA 1996 s193 rarely succeed. It is therefore always safer for an applicant to accept an offer while challenging the suitability. A person who refuses an offer and is unsuccessful in challenging the suitability will

---

33   SI No 3204.
34   The Order prescribes the income and outgoings that must be taken into account.
35   Homelessnes Code of Guidance para 17.40.
36   See Homelessness Code of Guidance para 16.20.
37   HA 1996 s202(1A).
38   *Osseily v Westminster CC* [2007] EWCA Civ 1108, 5 October 2007.

be entitled to no further housing assistance. The section 193 duty will have ended and the person will also lose any priority given under the allocations policy to those owed a homeless duty by the authority.

16.41   When advising on the merits of a challenge to suitability, it must be remembered that it is for the local authority to decide whether the offer is suitable. If it has taken account of all relevant information, an authority will only be acting unlawfully if no reasonable authority could have decided that the particular accommodation was suitable for the particular applicant.

16.42   The Allocations Code[39] provides that, in relation to HA 1996 Part VI offers, an applicant should be given a reasonable time to consider the offer. However, the Homelessness Code makes no similar provision. In practice, most authorities will allow an applicant a short time to decide whether to accept an offer. Nevertheless, the Court of Appeal has held[40] that an authority is not obliged to allow an applicant to view accommodation offered under HA 1996 s193 before being required to sign a tenancy agreement. It is for the authority to decide whether the accommodation is suitable and, if the applicant disagrees, he or she may request a review of its suitability.

16.43   It may happen that an applicant indicates to the authority, before having taken advice, that he or she will not accept the accommodation. If, following advice, the person agrees to accept the offer while seeking a review of its suitability, urgent steps need to be taken to contact the authority to see if the property is still available. Provided the property has not been let to someone else, an authority will usually allow the person to accept the offer. An authority that rigidly applies an arbitrary deadline for acceptance may be subject to challenge by way of judicial review. However, if the applicant was properly advised of his or her rights by the authority and nevertheless refused the accommodation, the authority need not keep the accommodation vacant until the dispute about suitability is resolved.[41]

16.44   HA 1996 s193 prescribes the information that must be given to an applicant in relation to offers made under s193 or under Part VI, and is detailed below at paras 16.53–16.55.

39 *The Code of Guidance on the Allocation of Accommodation in England*, 2002. Note that the code has been amended and some parts replaced by later codes, see para 17.8.

40 *Newham LBC v Khatun, Zeb, Iqbal & the OFT* [2004] EWCA Civ 55, 24 February 2004.

41 See *Osseily* above para 16.39.

Change of circumstances

16.45 Section 193 accommodation may be occupied for many years. During that time the composition of the applicant's household may change or the applicant's health may deteriorate. If the applicant argues that, because of a change of circumstance, the accommodation has become unsuitable, a request for a review of the suitability should be made. The duty to provide suitable accommodation is an ongoing duty and it may be argued that the accommodation provided has become unsuitable, whether because of a change of circumstance or because of the length of time the applicant has remained in the accommodation (see paras 16.25–16.26 above). If so, a local authority has a duty to conduct a statutory review on request.[42] If the review decision is unfavourable, a county court appeal may be brought. If the authority fails to respond to the request for a review, a county court appeal may be brought to challenge the decision that the accommodation is suitable. The deadline for such an appeal is 21 days from the date the review should have been completed (ie 11 weeks from the date of the request). Note however that a refusal of an offer of alternative suitable accommodation will bring the section 193 duty to an end, see: *Muse v Brent* at para 16.26 above.

When does the section 193 duty come to an end?

16.46 The accommodation provided under HA 1996 s193 is not permanent accommodation and the occupier will not have long-term security of tenure. However, although an applicant may be evicted from particular accommodation, the section 193 duty will continue until ended by a specific event.

16.47 This key feature of the section 193 duty will be changed by the Localism Act 2011. Instead of the duty continuing indefinitely while the applicant is in temporary accommodation, the section 193 duty will end where an applicant accepts or refuses a private sector offer of accommodation that is for a fixed period of at least 12 months.

16.48 This is already the situation for an applicant whose case is a 'restricted case' (see paras 14.141–14.148).

16.49 Currently the circumstances which bring the section 193 duty to an end are where the applicant:

---

42 *R on the application of Zaher v City of Westminster* [2003] EWHC 101 (Admin), 28 January 2003.

- refuses an offer of suitable accommodation, made under section 193, provided he or she was informed of the possible consequences of refusal or acceptance and the right to request a review of suitability: s193(5);
- ceases to be eligible for assistance: s193(6)(a);
- becomes homeless intentionally from the accommodation made available by the authority ('the section 193 accommodation'): s193(6)(b);
- accepts an offer of accommodation under HA 1996 Part VI: s193(6) (c);
- accepts an offer of an assured tenancy (other than an assured shorthold tenancy) from a private landlord: s193(6)(cc);
- voluntarily ceases to occupy the section 193 accommodation as his or her only or principal home: s193(6)(d);
- refuses a final offer made under HA 1996 Part VI, having been informed of the possible consequences of refusal or acceptance and of the right to a review of suitability: s193(7);
- accepts a 'qualifying offer' of an assured tenancy from a private landlord: s193(7B).[43]

Decision that section 193 duty has ended

16.50   An applicant has a right to seek a review of the decision that the HA 1996 s193 duty has ended.[44] Despite this, there is no express duty under section 193 to inform the applicant of the decision or to give reasons.

16.51   The way an applicant is informed that the section 193 duty has ended will depend on the reason for the duty ending. Broadly, the reasons fall into three categories:

- refusing an offer of accommodation (under HA 1996 Part VII or Part VI);
- accepting an offer of accommodation (under Part VI or from a private landlord);
- a change of circumstance, such as ceasing to be eligible, becoming homeless intentionally from the section 193 accommodation or ceasing to occupy it.

---

43 Qualifying offers are extremely rare and will be abolished by the Localism Act 2011.

44 See HA 1996 s202(1)(b) and *Warsame v Hounslow LBC* (1999) 32 HLR 335, CA.

Refusing an offer

16.52   The duty ends if an applicant refuses an offer of temporary accommodation under HA 1996 s193 or an offer of permanent accommodation under the allocations scheme (HA 1996 Part VI). In both cases certain conditions must be met and certain information given to the applicant.

Refusal of Part VII offer

16.53   For the section 193 duty to end following an offer of temporary accommodation, the following conditions must be met:

- the authority must be satisfied that the accommodation is suitable;
- the applicant must be informed of the possible consequences of refusing the offer and of the right to request a review of the suitability of the accommodation;
- the applicant must refuse the offer;
- the authority must notify the applicant that it regards itself as having discharged its section 193 duty.

16.54   As indicated above (paras 16.38–16.43), an applicant may accept the offer and request a review of suitability. There is no express duty to inform the applicant of this, but it would be unreasonable not to do so. If an authority was seeking to pressurise an applicant to accept the accommodation by indicating a deadline, it may be argued that, where an applicant indicates that he or she wishes to take advice, the accommodation was not refused.

Refusal of final Part VI offer

16.55   For the section 193 duty to end because of the refusal of a final offer made under the allocation scheme, the following conditions must be met:

- the authority must be satisfied that the accommodation is suitable;
- the authority must be satisfied that it is reasonable for the applicant to accept the offer;[45]
- the offer must be made in writing and must state that it is a final offer;

---

45   This is distinct from the issue of suitability. An authority must be satisfied that it is reasonable for a particular applicant to accept the particular accommodation: *Ravichandran v Lewisham LBC* [2001] EWCA Civ 755, 2 July 2010.

- the applicant must be informed of the possible consequences of refusing the offer and of the right to request a review both as to the suitability of the accommodation and whether it is reasonable to accept it;
- the applicant must refuse the offer;
- the authority must notify the applicant that it regards itself as having discharged its section 193 duty; the applicant also has a right to a review of the decision that the duty has been discharged.

16.56   Whether the accommodation is suitable and whether it is reasonable for the applicant to accept the offer are not the same issues, though there is some overlap. When making the offer the authority must be satisfied that it is a suitable offer *and* that it is reasonable for the applicant to accept the offer and if the applicant challenges the offer must conduct a review of both issues. Where an authority had reviwed only the suitability of the accommodation it was held to have erred in law and the applicant's appeal against the decision was successful: *Ravichandran v Lewisham LBC.*[46] Section 193(8) specifically provides that an applicant may reasonably be expected to accept an offer even though he or she may have obligations in respect of existing accommodation, provided it is possible to bring those obligations to an end before taking up the offer.

16.57   As is the case for offers of HA 1996 Part VII accommodation, the applicant may accept the offer and request a review of its suitability. If the offer is not accepted, an authority has no obligation to keep the offer open until the review process is complete. If the offer is a Part VI offer, however, the applicant has a right to a review of the suitability of the accommodation, whether it is reasonable to accept it, and the decision that the section 193 duty has ended. It is desirable (though not essential) that the three issues are reviewed at the same time and if this is to be the case the applicant should be informed of this.[47]

Accepting an offer

16.58   Unsurprisingly, the duty ends if a person *accepts* an offer under HA 1996 Part VI. The duty also ends if a person accepts an offer of an assured tenancy by a private landlord. Since it is rare for private landlords to offer assured, as opposed to assured shorthold, tenancies, this is unlikely.

46   [2010] EWCA Civ 755.
47   See *Ravichandran v Lewisham LBC* [2010] EWCA Civ 755, 2 July 2010.

Change of circumstances

Ceasing to be eligible

16.59 A person whose immigration status changes may cease to be eligible after a duty has been accepted. If this happens, the section 193 duty will end.

16.60   Examples of when this may happen are:

- A person's leave to remain in the UK may expire without an application having been made to extend or vary the leave.
- In rare cases the Home Office may revoke a person's leave.
- The eligibility of a European national depends on the person having a right to reside and this right may end, for example, if a person who was working is no longer working. The law relating to the gaining or loss of a right or residence is complex and is explained in paras 14.30–14.132.

Becoming homeless intentionally

16.61 If a person is evicted from the accommodation provided under HA 1996 s193(2) because of a failure to pay rent or anti-social behaviour, he or she is likely to be found to be intentionally homeless. If so, the duty ends. The definition of intentional homelessness is found in HA 1996 s191 (see paras 14.256–14.305). For the section 193 duty to end, all of the elements of the intentional homelessness test must be met; a policy that the duty will end in relation to any person evicted because of rent arrears or complaints of nuisance will be unlawful.

Ceasing to occupy as only or principal home

16.62 Again, this has a specific meaning and an authority cannot conclude that the duty has ended simply because a person has been absent from accommodation for a period. Where a person is occupying hostel accommodation, the accommodation provider may simply terminate the licence on the basis of a short absence, or a failure to sign a register. This is not sufficient to end the section 193 duty unless the test for intentional homelessness is met or there is evidence that the person no longer occupies as his or her only or principal home. See paras 4.4–4.7 for an explanation of the law on 'only or principal home'.

Notifying the applicant of the decision

16.63 Where the duty ends because of a refusal of an offer, the applicant will usually be informed that the HA 1996 section 193 duty has ended and of the right to seek a review following the refusal. Where the duty ends because an applicant accepts an offer, it is common that no notification is given and rare that there will be any dispute about the ending of the section 193 duty. However, disputes will commonly arise where it is alleged that the duty has ended because of a person being evicted from the section 193 accommodation or ceasing to occupy it.

16.64   Although there is no express duty to give a written explanation of a decision that the section 193 duty has ended, the applicant has a right to request a review of the decision and to bring a county court appeal. Arguably, the authority must give written notice, indicating the grounds on which the duty has ended, and giving sufficient reasons to enable the applicant to know if the decision can be challenged.

16.65   Furthermore, the Supreme Court has held that reasons should be given by an authority seeking to evict a non-secure tenant, to enable the tenant to know if he or she might defend any claim for possession on public law or proportionality grounds (see para 7.139).

Use of the private sector under HA 1996 Parts VI and VII – a summary

16.66   Most local authorities use private landlords to assist in the discharge of their various housing duties under HA 1996 Part VII. The standard form of occupation agreement in the private sector is the assured shorthold tenancy and there are many different situations in which a homeless applicant may be offered an assured shorthold tenancy by a private landlord. Below is a summary of the different ways in which such tenancies may be used and the implications for the applicant.

Homeless prevention/gate-keeping

16.67   Some authorities offer to those approaching them as homeless, or threatened with homelessness, assistance to obtain an assured shorthold tenancy from a private landlord. If an assured shorthold tenancy is accepted, no homeless application is recorded and no ongoing duty is owed by the authority.[48] If the offer is refused, the applicant may pursue the homeless application.

---

48 See *Hanton-Rhouila v Westminster Council* [2010] EWCA Civ 1334, 24 November 2010.

Discharge of section 193 duty

16.68   Where an authority accepts the full housing duty, it may discharge this duty by making an arrangement with another person to secure that accommodation becomes available. This may be done by arranging that a private landlord enters into an assured shorthold tenancy with the applicant. The accommodation must be suitable for the applicant.

16.69   An authority must inform the applicant that:

- the accommodation is offered in discharge of the section 193 duty;
- the applicant has a right to seek a review of its suitability; and
- the applicant can accept the offer and seek a review.

16.70   In addition, the Court of Appeal has indicated that the authority should make clear to the applicant that if, in the future, the accommodation ceases to be available, the HA 1996 s193 duty will nevertheless continue.[49]

16.71   Accepting the offer means that the applicant continues to be owed the section 193 duty and retains priority under the allocations scheme. Refusing the offer means that the authority's duty under HA 1996 s193 ends. Furthermore, any priority under the allocations scheme given to those to whom a homeless duty is owed will be lost.

16.72   In theory, another way of using the private sector which brings the section 193 duty to an end is by way of the qualifying offer. A qualifying offer is the offer of an assured shorthold tenancy by a private landlord arranged and approved by the local authority. The authority must be satisfied that the accommodation is suitable, it must be offered for a fixed period and the offer must be accompanied by a written statement explaining that there is no obligation to accept the offer but that if it is accepted the authority will no longer be under a duty under section 193. The applicant must sign a statement indicating that he or she has read and understood the statement. Few local authorities use 'qualifying offers' and they will be abolished when the Localism Act 2011 comes into force.

Changes to section 193 – the Localism Act 2011

16.73   Under the Localism Act 2011 the HA 1996 s193 duty to provide suitable accommodation will not last indefinitely until one of the events in section 193 occurs. Rather, the duty will be satisfied, *and will end,*

---

49 *Griffiths v St Helens Council* [2006] EWCA Civ 160, 7 March 2006.

where the authority makes an offer of suitable accommodation in the private sector. The accommodation must be for a fixed period of at least 12 months.

16.74   While it is currently possible to use private sector accommodation under section 193 (as described in paras 16.68–16.71), the difference is that the duty continues even if the particular private sector tenancy is terminated (through no fault of the tenant). Under the Localism Act 2011 the authority's duty will end.

16.75   However, if the applicant becomes homeless again within two years (provided it is not the applicant's fault) the section 193 housing duty will 'recur'. For this to happen, it will not be necessary for the applicant still to have priority need but it will be necessary that he or she is still eligible.

Fresh applications

16.76   Housing Act 1996 s193(9) provides:

> A person who ceases to be owed the [section 193] duty ... may make a fresh application to the authority for accommodation or assistance in obtaining accommodation.

16.77   An authority may decide that no duty is owed, but cannot simply refuse to accept an application on the basis that the section 193 duty has ended following a previous application. See paras 13.59–13.76.

APPENDIX

Request for review and interim accommodation

Dear Sir/Madam,

Re: Mrs A – section 184 Decision dated

We are advising Mrs A with regard to her homeless application.

[Request for review]

Mrs A requests a review of the above decision.

[Request for interim accommodation to be extended]

We ask you to confirm that our client will continue to be provided with interim accommodation pending the outcome of the review. It is our view that our client satisfies the test set out in the case of *R v Camden LBC ex p Mohammed* (30 HLR 315, CA):

The merits of the case

[what is wrong with the decision]

New information or argument

[anything likely to change the decision, including medical evidence not yet obtained]

The applicant's personal circumstances

[whether any alternative accommodation, likely effect of being homeless on applicant, children etc]

[Deadline for reply]

Our client has been informed that she must leave the accommodation currently provided on ... In order that we may advise our client about possible judicial review proceedings we would ask you to communicate your decision regarding interim accommodation no later than 4 pm on ... If the decision is that interim accommodation will not be provided pending review please give reasons.

[Data Protection request]

Please provide to us a copy of the complete homelessness file under the Data Protection Act 1998. We enclose a cheque in the sum of £10 together with our client's signed authority.

We intend to make further representations in support of the review following receipt of the file. We would therefore be grateful if this could be provided as a matter of urgency.

Yours faithfully,

Adviser

Advice Agency

CHAPTER 17

Allocation of social housing

                                                               continued

Key points

- All new allocations of social housing must be made through the local housing authority's 'allocations scheme'.
- Authorities must publish their allocations scheme and a summary must be available free of charge.
- Certain assistance must be given free of charge to people in the district who wish to apply and may have difficulties, eg language and literacy.
- Certain people from abroad cannot be allocated social housing – they are 'ineligible'.
- An authority can also treat as 'ineligible' a person guilty of unacceptable behaviour, eg behaviour that makes him or her unsuitable to be a tenant.
- Although an authority may decide that a person is ineligible for an allocation or that little or no priority will be given, all applications must be considered.
- Authorities have a wide discretion as to the kind of allocation scheme they operate but must give 'reasonable preference' to certain people.
- 'Reasonable preference' does not mean absolute preference.
- There is a right of review for decisions about eligibility and unsuitability to be a tenant. There is also a right of review about the facts taken into consideration in making an allocation decision. There is no county court appeal but decisions may be challenged by judicial review.
- A scheme itself may be unlawful if it is not in accordance with the principles set out in the Housing Act 1996 Part VI. This can only be established by judicial review. Choice-based lettings schemes are encouraged. Such schemes usually place applicants within 'bands' reflecting the level of priority. Within the bands, it is lawful to give priority to those who have waited longest.
- The House of Lords has stressed that local authorities have a wide discretion in how they devise their allocation schemes. The Localism Act 2011 will give local authorities more power to decide who is qualified to apply for an allocation.

Introduction

17.1   In most areas of the UK there is a severe shortage of affordable rented accommodation. Since 1989 private tenancies have been at market rents and usually offer no more than six months' security. This means that for many households the only way to obtain a secure home at an affordable rent is to be allocated social housing, ie accommodation let by local authorities and other social landlords (registered providers of social housing – formerly registered social landlords (RSLs)).[1] However, the supply of social housing has decreased significantly in recent years. The Barker report, published in March 2004, estimated that the supply of social and affordable houses would need to increase by 17,000 units per year for the next ten years to meet the anticipated need for social housing.[2] This has not happened and over the 13 years to 2008 there was a 72 per cent increase in the number of people on council waiting lists in England. In 2010 there were almost 1.8 million households (estimated at approximately 5 million people) on the waiting lists.[3]

17.2   It is clear that in many areas only a small proportion of those who apply for social housing have a realistic chance of ever being offered a tenancy.

17.3   Not surprisingly, therefore, many people seek advice about the fact that they are in housing need and have been on the council's waiting list for a considerable time without receiving any offers of accommodation. In most cases there is little that can be done: there is no right to an allocation of social housing. Part VI of the Housing Act (HA) 1996 requires all local housing authorities to have an allocations scheme and sets out the principles on which such schemes must operate. A person who seeks social housing has a right, with some exceptions, to make an application, to have the application recorded and to be given the appropriate level of priority, in accordance with the particular authority's allocation scheme. However, there is no guarantee that the person will ever be offered social housing.

17.4   The common issues that arise are in relation to:

---

1   Under the Housing and Regeneration Act 2008, registered social landlords became 'registered providers of social housing', see para 2.91.

2   Kate Barker, *Review of housing supply, delivering stability: securing our future housing needs*, March 2004. The report can be downloaded from: www.hm-treasury.gov.uk.

3   See Table 600 Rents, lettings and tenancies: numbers: England 1997–2010, www.communities.gov.uk/housing/housing research.

- decisions that a person is not eligible for an allocation, or to defer or suspend an application;
- decisions that no priority should be given because the person is unsuitable to be a tenant (see para 17.51 below);
- decisions about whether the correct level of priority has been given under the authority's policy;
- a particular allocations policy and whether it is lawful, ie whether it complies with HA 1996 Part VI and is in accordance with recognised principles of good administrative decision-making.

17.5 Before examining these issues, this chapter sets out the way in which HA 1996 Part VI governs allocation schemes.

Allocation of housing: Housing Act 1996 Part VI

17.6 Since 1980 the stock of social housing has decreased, primarily because of the introduction of the right to buy for secure tenants. At the same time, the number of homeless applicants, to whom authorities have a statutory housing duty, has increased. This meant that, in some areas, by the mid-1990s almost all social housing was allocated to those owed a homeless duty. This was seen as unfair to those in housing need who were not statutorily homeless. To address this problem, the aim of Part VI is to create 'a single route into social housing'.[4] Part VII sets out the homeless duty: instead of granting long-term social tenancies to homeless applicants, the duty is to provide only temporary accommodation. Homeless applicants temporarily accommodated by housing authorities are considered for an allocation in the same way as others in housing need. The fact that a homeless duty is owed will give the person some priority on the allocation scheme – such people must be given 'reasonable preference' (as must people falling into other reasonable preference categories).

17.7 Whenever a local housing authority is allocating accommodation it must comply with HA 1996 Part VI.[5] Local authorities have a broad discretion as to how they frame their allocation policies; subject to the provisions of Part VI 'a local housing authority may allocate housing accommodation in such manner as they consider appropriate'.[6] However, once it has devised an allocation scheme, an authority can

4 Hansard (HC), Standing Committee G, 16th Sitting, col 614, 12 March 1996, Minister for Local Government, Housing and Urban Regeneration.
5 HA 1996 s159(1).
6 HA 1996 s159(7).

only allocate in accordance with the scheme. Part VI sets out the principles that must be followed when framing the policy.

17.8   Authorities must have regard to the relevant codes of guidance.[7] The *Code of Guidance on the Allocation of Accommodation in England* ('Allocation Code 2002') was published in November 2002. However, this code is supplemented by the further code of guidance, published on 28 August 2008: *Allocation of Accommodation: Choice Based Lettings* ('Choice Based Lettings Code 2008') and the most recent guidance: *Fair and Flexible: statutory guidance on social housing allocations for local authorities in England* ('Fair and Flexible Code 2009'), published in December 2009, which replaces parts of the two previous codes. All of the codes can be downloaded at www.communities.gov. uk. Unfortunately, at the present time it is essential to refer to all three codes. Further guidance will be issued when the provisions of the Localism Act 2011 relating to allocations come into force.

Allocations governed by Part VI

17.9   An allocation is defined as:[8]

- Selecting someone to be a secure or introductory tenant of accommodation held by the local authority. This includes notifying an existing (non-secure) tenant or licensee that he or she is to become a secure tenant of the same premises. It also includes a new tenancy offered by way of a 'transfer', at the tenant's request.[9]
- Nominating someone to be a secure or introductory tenant of accommodation held by a different authority.
- Nominating someone to be an assured tenant of accommodation held by a registered social landlord.

Allocations not governed by Part VI

17.10   Housing Act 1996 Part VI does not apply to:

- the provision of alternative accommodation to an existing secure or introductory tenant where this is instigated by the authority (usually as a decant for major works).[10]

---

7   HA 1996 s169.

8   HA 1996 s159(2).

9   Prior to the Homelessness Act 2002 all transfers were excluded from the requirements of HA 1996 Part VI but transfers instigated by the tenant are now governed by Part VI: s159(5).

10   HA 1996 s159(2).

17.11 In addition, the following are not 'allocations' for the purpose of HA 1996 Part VI:[11]

- a succession to a secure or introductory tenancy;[12]
- an assignment of a secure or introductory tenancy by mutual exchange;
- an assignment of a secure or introductory tenancy to someone who would have been entitled to succeed to the tenancy;
- a transfer of a secure or introductory tenancy pursuant to a court order made in matrimonial proceedings or on relationship breakdown;[13]
- an introductory tenancy becoming secure.

Dealing with applications

17.12 A housing authority must ensure that:[14]

- advice and information is available free of charge to people in the district who wish to apply for an allocation;
- any necessary assistance in making such an application is available free of charge to those people in the district likely to have difficulty making an application without assistance;
- the fact that a person is an applicant is not divulged to any other member of the public without his or her consent; and
- any applicant is informed of his or her right to request information about the application, how it is likely to be treated, whether appropriate housing is likely to be made available and when that is likely to happen.

Most importantly, every application for an allocation must be considered by the authority.[15]

17.13 An authority cannot refuse to make a decision on an application or simply advise a person that he or she cannot make an application. A formal decision must be made, informing the applicant of the outcome of the application (ie, whether the person is eligible and what priority has been given) and of the right to seek a review of

11 HA 1996 s160.
12 See para 4.28 above.
13 This includes orders made under Matrimonial Causes Act 1973 s24, Matrimonial and Family Proceedings Act 1984 s17(1), Children Act 1989 Sch 1 and Civil Partnership Act 2004 Schs 5 and 7. See chapter 12.
14 HA 1996 s166.
15 HA 1996 s166(3).

certain decisions made in relation to the application (see para 17.59 below).

An applicant's duty

17.14   An applicant for an allocation must give correct information to the authority in support of the application and may commit an offence if false information is given or if information is withheld.

17.15   Housing Act 1996 s171 provides that an offence is committed if, in connection with an application under Part VI, a person:

- knowingly or recklessly makes a statement which is false in a material particular; or
- knowingly withholds information which the authority has reasonably required.

17.16   The offence can be committed by any person, not just the applicant, and is punishable by a fine of up to £5,000.

17.17   In addition, if an assured or secure tenancy is granted because of a false statement made by the tenant or someone acting on his or her behalf, the landlord has a ground for possession and may seek possession of the tenancy if this comes to light after the tenancy has been granted, see appendix to chapter 7.

Eligibility for allocations

17.18   A local authority cannot allocate housing accommodation to a person who is not 'eligible'.[16] This includes certain people from abroad, together with people who the authority has decided will be treated as ineligible because of 'unacceptable behaviour'.

People from abroad

17.19   As is the case under HA 1996 Part VII, certain people from abroad are not eligible for an allocation of accommodation. The rules regarding eligibility are applied in the same way as for homeless assistance. The provisions are set out briefly below at paras 17.20–17.27. More detail is found in chapter 14.

---

16   HA 1996 s160A.

Persons subject to immigration control

17.20 A person who is subject to immigration control[17] is not eligible for an allocation unless he or she is prescribed by the regulations as being eligible. The classes of eligible people are the same as for homelessness, save for asylum-seekers (see para 17.21 below) and are set out in the same regulations: Allocation of Housing and Homelessness (Eligibility) (England) Regulations 2006 (Eligibility Regs 2006).[18] Those who are eligible are set out in regulation 3:

- Class A – a refugee;
- Class B – a person with exceptional leave to remain in the UK that is not subject to the condition that he or she cannot have recourse to public funds;
- Class C – a person who has leave that is not subject to any limitation or control and who is habitually resident in the UK, Channel Islands, the Isle of Man or the Republic of Ireland (this is generally known as 'indefinite leave to remain' or 'settled status'). This does not include sponsored immigrants unless more than five years has passed (since entry or the undertaking was given, whichever is later) or the sponsor has died.
- Class D – a person who has been granted humanitarian protection under the Immigration Rules.

17.21 It should be noted that no asylum-seekers are eligible for an allocation, whereas a small number of asylum-seekers who applied for asylum before April 2000 are eligible for homeless assistance. Former asylum-seekers granted some form of leave to remain in the UK will usually be eligible for an allocation under one of the categories listed above.

Persons not subject to immigration control

17.22 As is the case in relation to homeless assistance, a person may be treated as ineligible because of not being habitually resident or having no 'right to reside' in the UK.

17.23 The following are treated as ineligible:[19]

- people who are not habitually resident in the UK, Channel Islands, Isle of Man or Republic of Ireland (unless they are exempt from this requirement: see para 17.24 below);

---

17 As defined in the Asylum and Immigration Act 1996.
18 SI No 1294.
19 Eligibility Regs 2006 reg 4(1).

- people whose only right to reside in the UK is derived from being a jobseeker, or is an initial three months' right of residence under the EEA Regs 2006;[20]
- people whose only right to reside in the Channel Islands, the Isle of Man or the Republic of Ireland is equivalent to one that is derived from being a jobseeker, or is an initial three months' right of residence under the EEA Regs 2006.

17.24   The following EEA nationals are not to be treated as being ineligible by virtue of not being habitually resident:[21]

- a worker;
- a self-employed person;
- an accession state worker[22] who is registered as a worker for an initial period;
- a family member of any of the above;
- certain people with a permanent right of residence in the UK under the EEA Regs 2006 which is derived from: (1) being former workers or self-employed people who are now retired or permanently incapacitated; (2) being the family members of such people; and (3) being the family members of deceased workers or self-employed EEA nationals;[23]
- a person who left Montserrat after 1 November 1995 because of the volcanic eruptions;
- a person in the UK as a result of deportation, expulsion or other compulsory removal from another country to the UK; and
- a person who left Zimbabwe to settle in Great Britain between 26 February 2009 and 18 March 2011 having accepted an offer of settlement from the government.[24]

---

20 The 'EEA Regs 2006' are the Immigration (European Economic Area) Regulations 2006 SI No 1003. The regulations are summarised in paras 14.30–14.136. The countries that make up the EEA are set out at para 14.38.

21 Eligibility Regs 2006 reg 4(2).

22 The term 'Accession States' refers to ten states that joined the EU in 2004 and 2007 for which special rules apply, see paras 14.53 and 14.64–14.66.

23 A person who has a permanent right of residence for another reason, such as by virtue of five years' previous residence, must be habitually resident to qualify for an allocation.

24 Allocation of Housing and Homelessness (Eligibility) (England) (Amendment) Regulations 2009 SI No 358.

Summary: main categories of ineligible people from abroad

17.25 The main categories of people who are ineligible for an allocation are the following:

- A person whose leave to enter or remain in the UK is subject to a condition that he or she can have no recourse to public funds.
- A person who requires leave to enter or remain and does not have it. This will include 'overstayers', asylum-seekers and failed asylum-seekers. This is the case even if the person has an application for leave outstanding with the Home Office. However, a person who previously had leave to enter or remain in the UK and has made an 'in-time'[25] application to extend or vary that leave is treated as continuing to have the same leave until a decision is made by the Home Office.
- European nationals who are not working, self-employed or self-sufficient (with some exceptions for those who have established a right to reside in the UK under the EEA Regs 2006).
- Anyone subject to the habitual residence test who has recently come to the UK, or returned to the UK and not yet established habitual residence. Note, however, that most Europeans with a right to reside are exempt from the habitual residence test, including workers, self-employed people, self-sufficient people and members of their families.

17.26 The rules regarding the right to reside under European law are complex and are described in more detail in paras 14.41–14.136.

Existing tenants

17.27 These provisions do not affect the eligibility of anyone who is already a secure or introductory tenant or an assured tenant of a registered provider.[26] Unlike the provision of temporary accommodation to a homeless applicant, such a tenancy cannot be terminated because of a change in the tenant's immigration status which means that he or she ceases to be eligible. Furthermore, there is no restriction on an existing tenant applying for and being granted a transfer regardless of his or her immigration status.

---

25 This means an application submitted before the leave expires. A person whose leave expires before submitting an application is an 'overstayer'.
26 HA 1996 s160A(6).

Unacceptable behaviour

17.28   In addition, an authority may decide to treat a person as ineligible because of 'unacceptable behaviour'.[27] Unacceptable behaviour is behaviour serious enough to make the applicant unsuitable to be a tenant of the authority[28] and is limited to behaviour by the applicant or a member of his or her household that would entitle the authority to a possession order if the applicant were a secure tenant.[29]

17.29   This provision is described in more detail below at para 17.51.

Future applications

17.30   A person treated as ineligible because of unacceptable behaviour may make a fresh application on the basis that he or she should no longer be treated as ineligible.[30] An example would be where a person previously evicted for rent arrears has subsequently established a good record of payment or where there has been anti-social behaviour in the past but the tenant has established a period of untroubled occupation of accommodation, or the perpetrators have left the household.

17.31   Clearly a person who was ineligible because of being a person from abroad can also re-apply if his or her status changes, for example, leave to remain is granted or a European national obtains employment.

Decisions about eligibility

17.32   If an authority decides that an applicant is ineligible for an allocation, it must notify the applicant in writing of the decision and the grounds for the decision.[31] The applicant has the right to request a review of the decision.[32]

27 HA 1996 s160A(1)(b).
28 HA 1996 s160A(7)(a).
29 HA 1996 s160A(8).
30 HA 1996 s160A(11).
31 HA 1996 s160A(9).
32 HA 1996 s167(4A)(d).

Allocation schemes

17.33   HA 1996 s167(1) provides that:

> Every local authority shall have a scheme (their 'allocation scheme') for determining priorities, and as to the procedure to be followed, in allocating housing accommodation.
>
> For this purpose 'procedure' includes all aspects of the allocation process, including the persons or descriptions of persons by whom decisions are to be taken.

17.34   The authority can only allocate accommodation in accordance with its allocation scheme.[33]

17.35   The scheme must include a statement of the authority's policy on offering applicants a choice of accommodation, or an opportunity to express preferences.[34] Note that this does not mean that the scheme must offer choice or the opportunity to express a preference: only that the scheme must state what the authority's policy is.

The reasonable preference categories

17.36   The scheme *must* be framed so as to secure that reasonable preference is given to the following classes:[35]

a) people who are homeless within the meaning of HA 1996 Part VII – this includes non-priority need applicants to whom no duty is owed;

b) people who are owed a duty by an authority under HA 1996 s190(2) (intentionally homeless but in priority need), s193(2) (the full housing duty) or s195(2) (duty to those threatened with homelessness) or those accommodated under s192(3) (discretion to accommodate non-priority need homeless applicants);[36]

c) people occupying insanitary or overcrowded housing or otherwise living in unsatisfactory housing conditions;

d) people who need to move on medical or welfare grounds, including grounds relating to a disability; and

---

33   HA 1996 s167(8).
34   HA 1996 s167(1A).
35   HA 1996 s167(2).
36   This provision covers those actually accommodated by an authority as homeless applicants. Also included are those who applied as homeless prior to the coming into force of the Housing Act 1996 and who are owed a duty under HA 1985 s65(2) or s68(2).

e) people who need to move to a particular locality in the district where a failure to meet that need would cause hardship to themselves or others.

17.37 In addition, the scheme *may* be framed so as to give additional preference to people with urgent housing needs.[37]

17.38 In deciding on the relative priority of people to whom reasonable preference must be given (groups (a) to (e) above), the scheme *may* allow the following factors to be taken into account:

- the financial resources available to the applicant to meet his or her housing costs;
- any behaviour affecting the suitability of the applicant or a member of his or her household to be a tenant (see para 17.57 below);
- any local connection (as defined under HA 1996 Part VII) existing between the applicant and the authority.

What is 'reasonable preference'?

17.39 Reasonable preference does not mean absolute preference; it has been defined giving an applicant a 'reasonable head start'.[38] Authorities do not have to give equal priority to each category but must give reasonable preference and ensure that the scheme does not result in a situation where one of the categories is effectively given no priority at all. As the Fair and Flexible Code 2009 puts it:

> While local authorities must demonstrate that, overall, reasonable preference is given to applicants in all the reasonable preference categories, this does not mean that they must give equal weight to each of the reasonable preference categories.[39]

17.40 'Preference' should not be confused with the prospect of being successful in obtaining accommodation: it is possible that a person with reasonable preference may never be allocated accommodation under HA 1996 Part VI.

> In *R on the application of Mei Ling Lin v Barnet LBC*[40] the authority's scheme gave extra points to homeless applicants in temporary accommodation, but these were insufficient to enable them to bid successfully for an allocation. It was only when the temporary

---

37 HA 1996 s167(2A).
38 *R v Wolverhampton MBC ex p Watters* (1997) 29 HLR 931, Leggatt LJ at 936.
39 Fair and Flexible Code 2009, para 18.
40 [2007] EWCA Civ 132, 22 February 2007.

accommodation was coming to an end (often as long as ten years after the applicant was given the accommodation) that sufficient points were given to enable an applicant to bid successfully. One of the grounds of challenge was that the policy failed to give adequate priority to homeless applicants.

The Court of Appeal rejected the argument, stating that:

Preference should not be confused with prospects of success. Prospects of success depend on many factors, of which the most material is the fact that the demand for accommodation greatly exceeds the supply. It is quite possible for a lawful scheme to give reasonable preference to a person within section 167(2) and for that person never to be allocated Part VI housing. Such a person is entitled to no more than a reasonable preference.[41]

Points schemes

17.41   Prior to the year 2000, most housing authorities operated 'points based' systems. These generally operate by giving a certain number of points to an applicant, based on an assessment of the level of need, and which reflect the reasonable preference categories: a person with a serious medical condition affected by his or her housing will be awarded more points than a person with a less serious condition. Furthermore, to reflect 'cumulative' need, a household with more than one member with particular needs may be awarded more points than a household with only one member in need, and applicants who qualify under several reasonable preference categories may be awarded more points than those who qualify under only one category. Those with the highest number of points when a suitable property becomes available will be offered that property.

17.42   One of the problems with such schemes is that new applicants coming on to the scheme may be awarded more points, so that a person who was top of the list is then pushed down the list. And, as needs change, frequent re-assessment may be needed. Furthermore, although such schemes usually allow an applicant to express some preference as to area and type of accommodation, the decision on whether to offer particular accommodation is made by the authority. This sometimes leads to a significant proportion of offers being refused, often with the consequence that further offers will not be made for a period of time, if at all.

41 [2007] EWCA Civ 132, Dyson LJ at [25].

Choice-based lettings

17.43   The Housing Green Paper, *Quality and Choice: A Decent Home For All*, published in April 2000, recommended that authorities adopt choice-based lettings schemes. It was suggested that such a scheme could operate at its simplest level on the basis of three 'bands' of applicants:

- those with an urgent need for social housing;
- those in non-urgent need of social housing; and
- those with no particular need for social housing.

17.44   Within the bands, priority could be determined on the basis of waiting time. However, it was recognised

> ... that in areas of high demand the number of households within the urgent category will be significant and that authorities in such areas may introduce additional bands to differentiate between demand priorities. However, the principle of giving priority according to the time spent in housing need remains valid.[42]

17.45   One of the amendments introduced by the Homelessness Act 2002 to facilitate choice-based lettings schemes was the addition to the Housing Act 1996 of section 167(2E), which provides that, subject to the requirement to give reasonable preference to certain categories of people (see para 17.36 above):

> ... the scheme may contain provision about the allocation of particular housing accommodation ... to a person who makes a specific application for that accommodation.[43]

17.46   On 28 August 2008 the Department for Communities and Local Government issued the Choice Based Lettings Code 2008 (see para 17.8 above), which supplemented the Allocation Code 2002.

Giving most priority to those in greatest need

17.47   In a series of cases, both before and after local authorities began to adopt choice-based lettings, allocations policies were challenged for failing to assess cumulative need or to operate a system of allocations

---

42   *Quality and Choice: A Decent Home For All* para 9.23.

43   Furthermore, HA 1996 s167(2E) also permits an authority to determine that particular accommodation may be allocated to persons 'of a particular description' whether or not they are in the reasonable preference categories. This enables authorities to allocate accommodation to essential workers or in order to effect a change in the ratio of adults to children on a particular estate. See para 5.26 of the Allocation Code 2002.

that gave greatest priority to those in greatest housing need.[44] A number of choice-based lettings policies that operated on the basis of the broad bands recommended in the green paper were held to be unlawful for failing to give priority *within* the bands to those in greatest need.

17.48   However, these cases were overruled by the House of Lords in *R (Ahmad) v Newham LBC*[45] following which, in December 2009, a new supplementary code: Fair and Flexible Code 2009 (see para 17.8 above) was issued, replacing those parts of the Allocation Code 2002 and the Choice Based Lettings Code 2008 which stated that authorities must ensure that those in greatest housing need are given the highest priority.

> In *Ahmad* the challenge was to an allocations policy that operated a choice-based lettings scheme in which applicants were placed in one of three categories: 'Priority Homeseekers', which were households containing at least one person who satisfied one or more of the reasonable preference criteria in HA 1996 s167(2); 'Tenants Seeking a Transfer', which were council tenants not within the Priority Homeseekers category who wanted to move; and 'Homeseekers' who fell into neither of the other two categories. 75 per cent of properties were let through the choice-based lettings scheme with the other 25 per cent being let as 'Direct Offers'. The Direct Offers lettings were to applicants who would be Priority Homeseekers but who had especially pressing needs for re-housing. The criteria for this group were very stringent. For example, under the Direct Offers scheme was a category for 'multiple needs' which depended on three family members having a certain level of need.
>
> Mr Ahmad's family of six, who lived in very overcrowded accommodation, had one daughter who was very severely disabled. Mr Ahmad also suffered from depression and one of the other children had behavioural problems. Under the Direct Offers scheme, they did not pass the threshold and no additional priority was given. This meant that they were in the Priority Homeseekers band of the choice-based lettings scheme. Within that band priority was given to those who had been on the waiting list the longest.

---

44 See: *R v Islington LBC ex p Reilly and Mannix* (1998) 31 HLR, 651; *R v Tower Hamlets LBC v Uddin* (1999) 32 HLR, 391; *Lambeth LBC v A and Lambeth LBC v Lindsay* [2002] EWCA Civ 1084, 23 July 2002; and *R (Cali, Abdi and Hassan) v Waltham Forest LBC* [2006] EWHC 302 (Admin), 24 February 2006.

45 [2009] UKHL 14, 4 March 2009.

The Court of Appeal held that the scheme was unlawful for failing to give preference to those with cumulative need over others in the same band. It also held that the authority's policy of allocating 5 per cent of choice-based lettings to ordinary transfer applicants in the same band was unlawful for failing to give reasonable preference to those in housing need, as required under HA 1996 s167.

The House of Lords, however, upheld the council's appeal:

> Identifying the individual households in greatest need could only be done though some sort of points based system and experience has shown that these too may be open to attack, either on the ground that they are too rigid and therefore unduly fetter the council's discretion or on the ground that the particular distribution of points is for some reason irrational ... Furthermore, relative needs may change over time, so that if the council were really to be assessing the relative needs of individual households, it would have to hold regular reviews of every household on the waiting list in order to identify those in greatest need as vacancies arose ... the question is how broad the brush can be ... it is not irrational to have a policy which gives priority to some tightly defined groups in really urgent need and ranks the rest of the 'reasonable preference' groups by how long they have been waiting ... Section 167(6) makes it clear that, subject to the express provisions, it is for the council to decide on what principles the scheme is to be framed.[46]

Furthermore, a 5 per cent 'quota' for transfer applicants was not unlawful:

> ... section 167(2) only requires that these groups be given a 'reasonable preference'. Still less does it require that an individual household in one of those groups should be given absolute priority over an individual household which wishes to transfer.[47]

17.49   The Fair and Flexible Code 2009 promotes the use of the simple banding systems considered in *Ahmad* which 'are clear, relatively simple to administer and highly transparent'.[48] As for determining priority for those with a similar level of need, it is suggested that

46 [2009] UKHL 14, Baroness Hale at [15] and [16].
47 [2009] UKHL 14, Baroness Hale at [18].
48 Fair and Flexible Code 2009, para 71.

'waiting time' is the simplest, most transparent and easiest to understand. However, it is also suggested that higher priority may be given to those demonstrating 'good behaviour' such as being model tenants or whose actions have directly benefited other residents on their estate of the community generally. It is also suggested that more priority may be given to 'those who live or work in the district or who have close family connections'.[49]

In *R (Van Boolen) v Barking & Dagenham LBC*,[50] the court considered a policy which provided that where two applicants were in the same needs band, priority would be given to those with a local connection over those without. It held that it was not 'remotely arguable' that such a policy was irrational. The court also rejected the argument that the policy was unlawful for failing to state in the published policy that the authority had a discretion where a person had a need to move that was sufficiently compelling as to require an exception to be made to the general policy on local connection.

17.50   However, the Fair and Flexible Code 2009 reminds authorities that they must ensure that their allocation scheme is compatible with the requirements of equality legislation.[51]

In a case about the setting of eligibility criteria for adult social care,[52] Birmingham CC argued that *Ahmad* supported its argument that when considering how to decide priorities for the allocation of resources the courts should be reluctant to intervene because an authority's long-term strategy considerations, expertise, political and social awareness, and local knowledge all had a part to play.

However, the court rejected this argument, holding that the council's decision was unlawful because it had failed to have due regard to its general disability equality duty under the Disability Discrimination Act 1995 s49A (now Equality Act 2010 s149), see para 2.84.

49 See Fair and Flexible Code 2009, paras to 63 to 69.
50 [2009] EWHC 2196 (Admin), 31 July 2009.
51 Para 21.
52 *R (W, M, G and H) v Birmingham CC* [2011] EWHC 1147 (Admin), 19 May 2011.

Unacceptable behaviour – suitability to be a tenant

17.51   An authority may decide that a person is guilty of 'unacceptable behaviour' such that he or she should be given no priority despite being a person who ordinarily would have priority under the authority's scheme.[53] The definition of unacceptable behaviour is the same as when determining eligibility (see para 17.28 above). An authority therefore has a choice: it may have a policy that those guilty of unacceptable behaviour are not eligible or that they are eligible but will be given no or limited priority.

17.52   In either case, an authority must be satisfied that, at the time of the application, the person is unsuitable to be a tenant by reason of the behaviour. The behaviour must be such that it would, if the person were a secure tenant, entitle the authority to a possession order on one of the tenant's fault grounds.[54] In respect of all these grounds the court must be satisfied not only that the ground is made out but also that it is reasonable to make a possession order. In all cases the court has the power to postpone a possession order or suspend its execution.

17.53   An authority must consider whether it is likely that an order would be postponed or suspended when deciding if the behaviour is sufficient to make the person unsuitable to be a tenant. The Allocation Code 2002 provides:

> Having concluded that there would be entitlement to an order, the housing authority will need to satisfy itself that the behaviour is serious enough to make the person unsuitable to be a tenant of the housing authority. For example, the housing authority would need to be satisfied that, if a possession order were granted, it would not be suspended by the court.[55]

---

53   HA 1996 s167(2B).
54   The relevant grounds are those in HA 1985 Part 1 Sch 2: (1) rent arrears or other breach of the tenancy agreement; (2) nuisance and annoyance; (2A) domestic violence; (3) neglect causing deterioration of premises; (4) neglect causing deterioration of furniture; (5) obtaining the tenancy by deception; (6) mutual exchange with illegal payment; and (7) inappropriate conduct in non-housing accommodation. For further details about the statutory grounds for possession, see appendix to chapter 6.
55   Paragraph 4.22(ii).

In *Dixon v Wandsworth LBC*[56] the claimant sought to challenge a decision that he was ineligible on the grounds of unsuitability to be a tenant. He had previously been a tenant of the authority, and following the determination of that tenancy by his joint tenant, it was agreed that he would receive a discretionary offer of alternative accommodation under the authority's allocation policy. A few months before the decision was made, he had pleaded guilty to a charge of possession of cocaine at his home. Shortly afterwards he had also been cautioned for possession of a small quantity of cannabis at the premises. His precise criminal history was disputed, but he had received a caution for the possession of cannabis ten years previously and admitted that he had also used cocaine at that time. The authority decided that he was unsuitable to be a tenant, finding that his behaviour was unacceptable and behaviour against which the county court would be able and willing to grant an outright possession order. The authority also referred to his problems with substance misuse being 'very long standing and therefore ... likely to be more difficult to overcome'.

The court held that, where an authority has reason to believe that a person may be ineligible for this reason, the following approach should be adopted:

1) The authority must satisfy itself that there has been unacceptable behaviour such as to found a claim for possession.
2) Having concluded that there would be entitlement to an order, it must satisfy itself that the behaviour is serious enough that an outright order should be made.
3) It must satisfy itself that the behaviour is serious enough, at the time the application is made, that an outright order should be made.
4) Only if satisfied on all those matters, can the authority consider exercising its discretion to treat the applicant as ineligible for an allocation. In reaching such a decision, the authority must act reasonably and consider all relevant matters before it.

In this case the court held that the authority had adopted this approach and was entitled to make the decision to treat the applicant as ineligible.

---

56 [2007] EWHC 3075 (Admin), 20 December 2007.

Right to information and reviews

General information

17.54   Authorities must publish a summary of their allocation scheme and provide a copy free of charge to any member of the public on request.[57]

17.55   The scheme itself must be available for inspection at the principal office of the authority and a copy provided on request to any member of the public, on payment of a reasonable fee.[58] Most authorities now publish a summary and/or the full allocation policy on their websites.

17.56   Any alterations to the scheme reflecting major changes of policy should be brought to the attention of those likely to be affected within a reasonable time.[59]

Particular information

17.57   An authority's allocation scheme must also ensure that an applicant has the right to the following information, on request:[60]

• general information so as to be able to assess how his or her application is likely to be treated;
• whether he or she is likely to be given preference under the scheme;
• whether it is likely that accommodation will be made available; and, if so, the timescale; and
• the facts that have been taken into account (or are likely to be taken into account) in considering whether to allocate accommodation to him or her.

17.58   Furthermore, an applicant has the right to be notified in writing of a decision that he or she is to be given no priority by virtue of being guilty of unacceptable behaviour, and of the grounds for the decision.

57   HA 1996 s168(1).
58   HA 1996 s168(2).
59   HA 1996 s168(3).
60   HA 1996 s167(4A).

Reviews

17.59 There is a right to request a review of any of the following:[61]

- a decision that, because of unacceptable behaviour, an applicant is ineligible or is to be given no priority;
- a decision that an applicant is ineligible by virtue of being a person from abroad;
- a decision about the facts of an applicant's case which have been taken into account in considering the application for an allocation.

17.60 It should be noted that these are the only decisions which carry the right of review. If an applicant believes that he or she has been given insufficient priority, unless this concerns a decision about the facts taken into consideration, there is no right of review. Furthermore, there is no right of review where the applicant is seeking to challenge the lawfulness of the policy itself.

17.61 Unlike homeless decisions, there is no right of appeal to the county court following the internal review. Judicial review will therefore be the only way to challenge a decision confirmed on review, as well as any decision that does not carry the right of review. However, as with all public decision-making, an authority may reconsider a decision and advisers will usually invite an authority to do so before beginning a claim for judicial review.[62]

Common issues for advisers

17.62 In practice, the most common complaint is simply that an applicant has been waiting for a long time but no offers have been made. Under the choice-based lettings schemes the complaint is likely to be that numerous unsuccessful bids have been made. In most cases this will be because the number of applicants greatly exceeds the number of available properties and only a small minority of applicants will obtain accommodation. In some cases, however, it may be possible to challenge the way in which the applicant's priority has been assessed or the lawfulness of the decision-making or the policy itself.

---

61 HA 1996 s167(4A)(d).
62 Initially regulations provided for the procedure to be followed in conducting both homeless and allocation reviews. However, the power to make such regulations was contained in HA 1996 165, which was repealed in 2003, and no similar provision is contained in section 167(4A). An authority should nevertheless follow a fair procedure and this should be described in the published scheme.

Has the applicant been given the correct number of points or placed in the correct band?

17.63   To advise a person about whether their needs have been properly assessed, it may be necessary to obtain further information from the authority. Note that in addition to the right to information under the Data Protection Act 1998 an applicant has a right to specific information pursuant to section 167(4A) (see para 17.57 above).

17.64   An example of a pro forma letter requesting relevant information is contained in the appendix to this chapter.

17.65   If the facts taken into account are correct and the level of priority awarded is in accordance with the policy, there will be no action that can be taken on a client's behalf unless the policy itself is unlawful. Advisers must also make clients aware that, even if a policy is declared to be unlawful or a re-assessment ordered, this will not necessarily result in an offer of accommodation to a particular applicant. The court cannot order an authority to make an offer, only to operate a lawful scheme and to allocate in accordance with such a scheme.

17.66   Where medical assessment is at issue, an applicant may find it useful to obtain his or her own medical report and to request a re-assessment of any medical priority. As is the case for priority need, any request for a medical report should set out clearly the relevant criteria under the allocation scheme and ask the expert to express an opinion directed to the relevant issues.

Challenging the lawfulness of the policy itself

17.67   Judicial review is available to challenge not only a specific decision, but also the authority's adoption of a particular scheme. Paragraphs 2.8–2.26 explain the general principles of administrative decision-making. This chapter highlights some of the principles established by case-law regarding the lawfulness of allocation policies.

Allocations must be in accordance with the policy

17.68   Section 167(8) provides that an authority can only allocate accommodation in accordance with its published policy. There are two aspects to this:

- an authority cannot make decisions in accordance with policies or practices that are not clearly indicated in the allocation scheme; and

- an authority cannot 'earmark' a vacant property for a particular applicant prior to allocation through the scheme.

17.69　The following case illustrates the first point:

> In *Gallacher v Stirling Council*[63] the authority operated a policy of only considering homeless applicants for low-demand, high-turnover housing, but this policy did not appear in the published housing allocations scheme.
> 　An application for judicial review by a person offered accommodation following a homeless application was successful. It was held that the policy was invalid in so far as it rendered inapplicable to homeless applicants the provisions of its allocations policy and applied special rules to such applicants. Furthermore, any decision made in accordance with a policy that was unpublished would be invalid. To treat as valid an unpublished rule or a decision made on the basis of such a rule would destroy the value of requiring the publication of allocations schemes.

17.70　With regard to the second point in para 17.68, it is very common for applicants to become aware of a vacant property which they believe would be suitable and which they wish to be allocated to them. Authorities will rarely accede to such a request and, under HA 1996 Part VI, such an allocation may be unlawful.

> In *Amirun Begum and Nashima Begum v Tower Hamlets LBC*[64] the claimants had applied as homeless and were placed in temporary accommodation, consisting of two neighbouring houses sublet by the authority to an RSL. The household comprised 14 individuals, several of whom had special needs. Wheelchair-adapted accommodation was required. The authority conceded that the accommodation provided was unsuitable. There was a proposal that the two houses should be adapted to comprise a single home. A judicial review claim was commenced, seeking, among other things, an order that the authority nominate the family for the allocation of specific accommodation, ie the same two houses, following refurbishment and adaptation.

63　May 2001 *Legal Action* 22. See also *R on the application of Faraah v Southwark LBC* [2008] EWCA Civ 807, 11 July 2008.

64　[2002] EWHC 633 (Admin), 30 April 2002.

> It was conceded at the hearing that the court could not make such an order, the judge stating:
>
> I am satisfied that only in exceptional circumstances, if at all, may a local authority lawfully earmark a property for a particular applicant on its waiting list before that property is allocated. It must apply its policy, and exercise any residual discretion, when it allocates the accommodation in question, not before. There is otherwise a risk that when the accommodation is allocated, there will be someone who has priority according to the allocation scheme over the person for whom the property has been earmarked.[65]

17.71　Similarly, those in unlawful occupation of council accommodation may argue that the authority would owe a homeless duty if they were evicted and that they should therefore be allowed to remain in occupation and be granted a secure tenancy. This may arise, for example, where a tenant dies and a family member is not entitled to succeed to the tenancy. Unless the authority has a policy to grant 'non-statutory succession' (see para 4.48) an authority would be acting unlawfully if it sought to grant a secure tenancy to such a person outside of its allocation scheme.

The scheme must sufficiently explain the way accommodation is allocated

17.72　This is closely related to the above principle. Allocations must be in accordance with the published policy and the published policy must describe, in sufficient detail, how the policy operates. This includes the criteria on which priority is assessed.

> In *R on the application of Mei Ling Lin v Barnet LBC* (see para 17.40), although the applicant failed to establish that the policy did not give reasonable preference to homeless applicants, it was nevertheless held to be unlawful in failing to make sufficiently clear the way in which extra points were awarded to homeless applicants when their temporary accommodation was coming to an end.

17.73　However, provided a decision is properly explained, it is not necessary, in the allocation scheme, to set out in prescriptive detail how priority is awarded. In *R (Van Boolen) v Barking & Dagenham LBC*,[66]

---

65 [2002] EWHC 633 (Admin), Stanley Burnton at [29].
66 [2009] EWHC 2196 (Admin), 31 July 2009.

(para 17.49 above) the court held that the council's policy was not unlawful for failing to state in the allocation scheme that the council had a discretion to make exceptions to a policy which gave greater priority to applicants with local connection.

Deferrals and suspensions

17.74 Long before HA 1996 Part VI came into force, the courts had considered the lawfulness of the deferring or suspending of applications by local authorities. Many authorities operate a policy of suspending active consideration of applications because of such factors as rent arrears owed to the authority or a previous refusal of an offer of accommodation. The courts have held that such policies are not unlawful, provided they are not so rigidly applied as to fetter the discretion of the authority.

> *R on the application of Wolverhampton MBC ex p Watters*[67] concerned an authority's policy regarding applications by those in rent arrears to go on the council's waiting list. The applicant had been a council tenant, but had been evicted because of rent arrears in excess of £2,300. The council's policy was that applicants with more than two weeks' rent arrears would not be eligible for council accommodation unless (a) they had a social or medical need award of 60 points in one single category; (b) they had made substantial efforts to reduce the arrears; or (c) there were other exceptional circumstances. The applicant brought judicial review proceedings to challenge the policy. She fell into three of the statutory groups to whom reasonable preference was to be given and argued that the council's policy was unlawful because its effect was that she was accorded no preference at all.
>
> The court dismissed her application: the policy was not so inflexible as to be a fetter on the council's discretion. Furthermore, the council was required only to give reasonable and not absolute preference to certain groups and this meant that the authority was entitled 'to consider any other relevant fact including the extent to and circumstances in which the applicants have failed to pay due rent or have otherwise been in breach of the obligations of the existing or earlier tenancies. Such considerations are not excluded from the selection process.'[68]

67 (1997) 29 HLR 931, QBD.
68 (1997) 29 HLR 931, Judge LJ at 938.

17.75   The issue has also been considered in relation to allocations governed by HA 1996 Part VI.

> In *R v Westminster CC ex p Nadhum Hussain*[69] the authority's policy was to suspend applicants from the waiting list for two years if they unreasonably refused an offer. The authority's social services department had carried out an assessment and referred to the need for an additional room to enable a carer to stay from time to time. The assessment also stated that 'Mr Hussain needs separate sleeping and living rooms to be able to store specialist equipment for that room'. An offer was made of a ground floor bed-sit and the authority made no reference to the social services assessment. When the applicant refused the offer, he was suspended from the waiting list.
>
> The court held that, as the policy to suspend applicants did not, in most cases, allow for exceptions, it was therefore an unreasonable fetter on the discretion of the authority. The decision was also flawed as no mention had been made of the social services assessment (see para 17.86 below).

17.76   The change in the courts' approach following *Ahmad* is illustrated by a more recent consideration of this issue:

> In *R (O) v Newham LBC Lettings Agency*[70] the applicant was the victim of domestic violence and therefore qualified for the council's additional preference group as being in need of emergency rehousing. However, the council's policy also provided that those with 'any property related debt' would be given less priority than other applicants. The applicant owed more than £3,000 from temporary accommodation occupied as a homeless applicant. In one of the letters to the applicant it was stated that 'Newham operates a "no debt" policy' and that until the matter was resolved satisfactorily she would receive no offers of accommodation. The council maintained that it always considered exercising discretion in exceptional circumstances but that because the applicant had made no attempts to reduce the debt or even enter into an agreement to do so, it was not minded to exercise that discretion.

69   (1998) 31 HLR 645.
70   [2010] EWHC 368 (Admin), 27 January 2010.

The court held that, despite the fact that some of the council's letters suggested the restriction of the exercise of discretion by a rule, taken as a whole, the council's correspondence and its stated position, 'describe a rational exercise of the discretion vested in the council with reference, as the decision letter also makes clear, to the whole file'.[71] The council's decision was not unlawful.

Exercising discretion

17.77   Where a local authority is by statute given a discretion to make certain decisions, a policy that is rigidly applied may be unlawful on the basis that it fetters the discretion of the authority.

17.78   As is illustrated in *Nadhum Hussain* (see para 17.75 above), a policy that suspends or defers applications in certain circumstances may be unlawful if it fails to provide for exceptions to be made.

17.79   Similarly, a policy that any tenant who had previously been evicted because of rent arrears would be ineligible for an allocation would be unlawful. A decision about eligibility based on unsuitability to be a tenant must be made in accordance with HA 1996 Part VI (see *Dixon v Wandsworth LBC,* para 17.53 above) and must be the lawful exercise of the authority's discretion, not a 'foregone conclusion'. However, see *R (O) v Newham LBC Lettings Agency* (para 17.76 above), in which the court held that the authority was not operating a rigid rule in refusing to give priority to an applicant in rent arrears.

Fairness

17.80   As in all administrative decision-making, the process of decision-making must be 'fair' and comply with the rules of 'natural justice'. As is explained in chapter 2 the rules of natural justice are embodied in a duty to act fairly and the extent of that duty varies according to the circumstances.

17.81   It is a fundamental principle of fair decision-making that a person should be given notice of adverse information and the opportunity to comment on any such information.

17.82   In many allocation cases an applicant will submit medical reports and the authority may take its own medical advice on reports sent by the applicant or obtain medical information directly from those treating the applicant. In such cases, where significant information

71 [2010] EWHC 368 (Admin), Lord Carlile of Berriew QC at [30].

is obtained by the authority, there will be a duty to disclose this to the applicant and invite him or her to comment on the information. However, there is no duty to give the applicant the last word in every case.[72]

> In *Amirun Begum and Nashima Begum v Tower Hamlets LBC*[73] (see para 17.70 above) information sent to the authority by the applicant's GP was inconsistent with that provided by the applicant. It had been taken into account by the authority without offering the applicant the opportunity to comment.
>
> It was held that: 'The information provided by the claimants' general practitioner is significant, and has materially affected [the defendant's] conclusions. It follows that the defendant may not lawfully finally decide whether any particular accommodation is suitable for the claimants without taking into account their responses, now in evidence, to their general practitioner's letters'.[74]

17.83   Part of the duty of fairness also requires that a decision is taken by a person who is impartial. Most allocations decisions will be taken by officers who are employed to do so and whose impartiality will not be questioned.[75] However, some authorities may use elected members as part of an appeal or review process. Previous regulations provided that no elected member may take part in any decision-making in relation to allocations if either the accommodation is in his or her ward or the person concerned lives in that ward.[76]

Giving reasons

17.84   There is no general duty on local authorities to give reasons for all decisions made. However, HA 1996 Part VI requires that reasons are given when a decision is made:

72 *Bellouti v London Borough of Wandsworth* [2005] EWCA Civ 602, 20 May 2005, Jonathan Parker LJ at [62]. This case concerned the assessment of priority need under HA 1996 Part VII but similar principles apply when medical evidence is at issue in relation to an assessment of an application for an allocation. See paras 14.227–14.231.

73 [2002] EWHC 633 (Admin), 30 April 2002.

74 [2002] EWHC 633 (Admin), Stanley Burnton J at [35].

75 Applicants may complain that an officer they have dealt with is 'biased'. However, it is extremely difficult to establish bias in such cases, see para 2.21.

76 Allocation of Housing (Procedure) Regulations 1997 SI No 483 reg 3. However, those regulations were made under HA 1996 s165 which has since been repealed.

- that a person is ineligible (on the grounds of being a person from abroad or because of unacceptable behaviour); or
- that a person will be given no priority because of unacceptable behaviour.

17.85 Where an authority is required to give reasons for a decision, the reasons must be 'proper, adequate and intelligible and enable the person affected to know why they have won or lost'.[77]

17.86 In addition to these statutory requirements, in respect of specific decisions, there may be situations in which the circumstances demand that reasons be given, even when there is no express duty to give reasons.

> In *R v Westminster CC ex p Nadhum Hussain*[78] (see para 17.75 above) it was held that the authority could lawfully have decided not to follow the recommendation of the social services department if it had identified reasons for declining to do so. However, the decision letters had ignored the assessment altogether and the authority had therefore failed to provide adequate reasons for the offer of a bed-sitting room rather than a flat with a bedroom and separate living room, as recommended by social services. This was a further reason for holding the decision unlawful.

The future for allocations challenges

17.87 It is likely that challenges both to the lawfulness of allocations schemes and individual decisions will be less common in the future. The House of Lords clearly indicated in *Ahmad* that:

> ... it is for the local authority to provide an allocation scheme according to its Part VI duty, and the merits as to who, how and when priority should be afforded is a matter for the local authority subject to its special duties. Judges must be particularly slow in entering the politically sensitive area of allocations policy by over-broad use of the doctrine of irrationality. A particular scheme cannot be castigated as irrational simply because it is not a familiar one to the court or is not considered to be the perfect solution to a difficult, if not impossible, question to resolve.[79]

---

77 *R v Brent ex p Baruwa* (1997) 29 HLR 915 at 929.

78 (1998) 31 HLR 645.

79 [2009] UKHL 14, 4 March 2009, Baroness Hale, endorsing the words of the first instance judge, at [22].

Localism Act 2011

17.88   The Localism Act 2011 will amend Part VI of the Housing Act 1996 as it applies in England only. The existing provisions will continue to apply in Wales.

17.89   The principal change is that local authorities will be able to decide what classes of persons are 'qualifying persons'. The second limb of the test of 'eligibility' for an allocation, which currently excludes those who are considered unsuitable to be a tenant, will be abolished. But local authorities can themselves determine in their allocation scheme who is a qualifying person. This will be subject to regulations which will prohibit certain criteria being used to decide who is or is not a qualified person. Essentially, therefore, local authorities will have more power to decide who can be considered for an allocation and will not be bound to accept any person who makes an application.

17.90   In addition, Part VI will not apply to existing assured tenants of registered providers/RSLs (in addition to existing secure and introductory tenants) unless it is the tenant who applies for a transfer and the tenant is in a reasonable preference category.

17.91   To bring the allocations provisions into line with the limited homeless duty in relation to 'restricted cases', see paras 14.41–14.48, provision is made for a situation in which a person is homeless and/or provided with accommodation as a homeless person but only because of a restricted person. In such cases it is provided that the person is to be disregarded when deciding if the application is to be given reasonable preference under the scheme. Otherwise, the reasonable preference categories remain the same but the category of those needing to move on medical or welfare grounds is expanded to add '(including any grounds relating to a disability)'.

Legal aid

17.92   A further development that will affect the number of challenges is that cases involving allocations and transfers are to be taken out of the scope of legal aid by the Legal Aid, Sentencing and Punishment of Offenders Bill. This means that advice and assistance about allocations will no longer be funded by legal aid. However, legal aid will remain available for cases of judicial review.

APPENDIX

Letter requesting information about allocation decision

Dear Sir/Madam,

Re: *[name of client/DOB/current address]*

We are advising [client] who has applied to your authority for an allocation of accommodation.

In order that we may advise him/her as to the way in which the application is being dealt with can you please provide the following information:

- A copy of our client's application form, any relevant documents submitted in support and a summary of the relevant facts that have been taken into account in considering his/her application.
- A breakdown of the number of points/the priority category into which our client has been placed.
- Whether any medical priority has been awarded to our client and, if so, a breakdown of the way in which the points have been awarded/explanation of the way in which the priority has been assessed.
- How likely it is that accommodation will be made available to our client, and when this is likely to happen.

This request is made pursuant to our client's right to information under section 167(4A) of the Housing Act 1996. Our client's signed authority is enclosed and we look forward to receiving the information requested.

[Please treat this request as also being made pursuant to the Data Protection Act 1998. A cheque in the sum of £10 is enclosed.]

Yours faithfully,

[Adviser]

Notes
1) Advisers may prefer to give to clients a draft letter addressed to the authority from the client.
2) The letter will need to be adapted depending on whether the authority has a system of points or banding and how medical priority is assessed.
3) The advantage of also making reference to the Data Protection Act is that there is a statutory time limit for the provision of the information and an applicant is entitled to all relevant data held, not just the information

specified in section 167. An authority may decline to provide some documents under section 167 because the section refers only to information about the facts that have been taken into account. If the request is made under the Data Protection Act a fee of £10 is usually required by the authority before it will comply with such requests – see para 2.98.

CHAPTER 18

Community care: accommodation duties to adults

Key points

- For adults, the main accommodation duty under community care law is the duty under the National Assistance Act 1948 s21. This is a duty to provide residential accommodation to adults in need of care and attention and falls on social services.
- For section 21 to apply there must be a need for care and attention because of age, illness, disability or any other circumstance.
- Ordinary accommodation and financial support may be provided under section 21 if this is necessary to ensure that the need for care and attention is met.
- If, following an assessment, an authority decides that a person needs accommodation, then this may become an enforceable duty.
- For some patients discharged from detention under the Mental Health Act 1983 there is a duty to provide aftercare services which may include accommodation and financial support. This is a joint social services and health authority duty.
- Before any community care service will be provided the person's needs must be assessed by the local authority. A refusal or failure to assess may be challenged by an application for judicial review.
- In cases of urgent need an authority may have a duty to provide emergency services, including accommodation, until the assessment is completed. A refusal to provide emergency services may also be challenged by judicial review.
- Local authority social services departments must operate a formal complaints procedure for both adults and children.

Introduction

18.1   The main ways of obtaining accommodation from a local authority are by applying under the Housing Act (HA) 1996 for an allocation of accommodation under the authority's allocation scheme or by making a homeless application. These housing duties are described in detail in chapters 13 to 17. In addition, a local authority may have a duty to provide accommodation to a person in need of community care services. In practice, it is usually those who are unable to obtain accommodation under the Housing Act 1996 who seek accommodation under community care law.

18.2   This chapter deals with the main accommodation duties for adults under community care law. Chapter 19 deals with the possible accommodation duties to children and chapter 20 with the immigration restrictions on access to community care services. Chapter 21 deals with other kinds of community care services that may be provided to improve or adapt existing accommodation.

18.3   This chapter covers the following:

- the definition of community care services;
- possible accommodation duties to adults;
- the duty to assess adults' needs;
- judicial review and complaints.

Sources of community care law

18.4   In May 2011 the Law Commission published its *Adult Social Care Report* (LC 326). The summary of the report describes the current position in this way: 'The legal framework for the provision of adult social care services dates back to 1948, and consists of a complex and confusing patchwork of legislation.' The report recommends the simplification of the system for assessment, eligibility and provision of all adult social care services. However, for now there remains the 'confusing patchwork of legislation'. This chapter seeks to summarise that legislation focusing on the duties to provide accommodation for adults.

Legislation

18.5   There are a number of statutes that set out the powers and duties of local authorities to provide what are referred to as 'community care services'. The NHS and Community Care Act (NHSCCA) 1990 places the responsibility for arranging community care services on local authorities. The Act:

- defines community care services; and
- provides the legal framework for assessing a person's needs for community care services and for the provision of such services.

18.6   The primary legislation listed below at paras 18.10–18.12 sets out the kinds of services that a local authority social services department *may* or, in some cases, *must* provide. Social services departments must follow statutory guidance and directions issued by the Secretary of State for Health.[1]

---

1 Local Authority Social Services Act (LASSA) 1970 s7.

Directions

18.7   Directions are mandatory and authorities must act in accordance with them. An example is the *Secretary of State's Approvals and Directions under section 21(1) of the National Assistance Act 1948* (LAC(93)10) referred to below at para 18.14. Directions and Guidance are usually referred by the year of issue and the number. LAC stands for 'Local Authority Circular' and this was the tenth circular issued in 1993.

Guidance

18.8   Formal guidance issued under LASSA 1970 s7 is usually referred to as 'policy guidance' or 'statutory guidance' and will state that it is issued under section 7. Such guidance should be followed by local authorities but an authority has 'liberty to deviate from it where the local authority judges on admissible grounds that there is good reason to do so, but without freedom to take a substantially different course'.[2]

18.9   Additionally, general or practice guidance is issued by the Department of Health. Local authorities should have regard to such guidance but are not bound to follow it. A decision may be challenged where an authority has failed to have regard to relevant guidance. However, an authority will not be acting unlawfully if it can show that it has taken the guidance into consideration but decided, for a legitimate reason, not to follow it.

What are community care services?

18.10   NHSCCA 1990 defines 'community care services' as services that a local authority may provide or arrange to be provided under any of the following provisions:

National Assistance Act (NAA) 1948 Part III
NAA 1948 places on local authorities a duty to provide residential accommodation to adults in need of care and attention not otherwise available. This is the duty most often relied on to obtain accommodation for adults excluded from access to housing and/or homeless assistance under HA 1996.

---

2   *R v Islington LBC ex p Rixon* (1997–98) 1 CCLR 119, 15 March 1996, Sedley J at 123.

Health Services and Public Health Act (HSPHA) 1968 s45

Under section 45 local authorities may make arrangements 'for promoting the welfare of old people'. This may include assisting a person to find lodgings but there is no direct duty to provide accommodation under this Act.

National Health Service Act (NHSA) 1977 s21 and Sch 8

This Act sets out the government's general duty to provide a comprehensive health service designed to secure improvement in the population's physical and mental health and to prevent, diagnose and treat illness. Section 21 and Schedule 8 empower local authorities to provide services in the home, day centres and training facilities but there is no power or duty to provide accommodation.

Mental Health Act (MHA) 1983 s117

Section 117 provides that, when certain patients are released from detention under MHA 1983, the local social services authority and the health authority jointly owe a duty to provide aftercare services which may include accommodation. This is dealt with below at paras 18.26–18.31.

18.11　The main community care provisions that may be used to obtain accommodation are therefore NAA 1948 s21 and MHA 1983 s117.

18.12　In addition to the Acts specifically referred to, a local authority may provide community care services under the Chronically Sick and Disabled Persons Act (CSDPA) 1970 s2. This Act mainly concerns the provision of adaptations and services in the home and is dealt with in paras 21.39–21.46.

National Assistance Act 1948

18.13　NAA 1948 was part of the post-war package of social welfare legislation. When introduced, it made provision for both adults and children in need of care and attention and included a system for the payment of social security benefits (national assistance). Part III of the Act dealt with accommodation and included a duty to provide temporary accommodation for people made homeless in unforeseen circumstances. The provisions for children are now contained in the Children Act 1989 and social security benefits are governed by different statutes and regulations. The duty to provide accommodation to homeless people was removed from Part III when the Housing (Homeless Persons) Act 1977 came into force. Part III, however, still contains the main accommodation duty to adults in need of care and attention and remains the 'safety net' for those unable to gain access to mainstream accommodation. It has been described as 'the last refuge for the destitute'.[3]

Section 21 accommodation duty

18.14   Local authorities have a duty to provide: 'residential accommodation for persons who are aged 18 or over who by reason of age, illness, disability or any other circumstances are in need of care and attention which is not otherwise available to them.'[4]

18.15   Also, local authorities *may* 'make arrangements to provide residential accommodation for expectant and nursing mothers who are in need of care and attention which is not otherwise available to them'.[5] This means that local authorities have a power but not a duty to provide accommodation. This power is not limited to those who are over the age of 18.

Nature of the section 21 duty

18.16   Since 1996 the courts have considered the duty under NAA 1948 s21 in a number of cases. This has mainly been in consequence of the legislation restricting the rights of people from abroad to work, claim benefits or gain access to mainstream housing. This legislation created a large group of destitute adults who were prevented from providing for themselves and therefore sought the help of local authorities. Other people unable to obtain appropriate housing under HA 1996, have also sought to use NAA 1948 to obtain accommodation. This has created a significant volume of case-law about the nature of the section 21 duty, which is summarised below at paras 18.17–18.25.

Provision of ordinary housing

18.17   There is no requirement that the residential accommodation provided by the authority must be institutional accommodation in which other services are also provided. Under NAA 1948 s21 ordinary accommodation may be provided along with food or vouchers for food.

---

3   See *R v Wandsworth LBC ex p O* and *R v Leicester CC ex p Bhikha*, (2000) 3 CCLR 237, CA, 26 February 2000. See also para 20.13.
4   NAA 1948 s21(1)(a) and *Secretary of State's Approvals and Directions under section 21(1) of the National Assistance Act 1948* (LAC(93)10).
5   NAA 1948 s21(1)(aa).

In *R v Newham LBC ex p Medical Foundation for the Care of Victims of Torture*[6] the local authority accepted a duty under NAA 1948 s21 to provide accommodation to the applicants but argued that the duty was to provide residential accommodation together with board and other services as part of a package. The authority offered accommodation in a hotel in Eastbourne on the grounds that this would enable it to provide the package of services required under NAA 1948.

The court rejected the authority's argument, holding that the services additional to accommodation need not be provided 'in' the accommodation. Furthermore, statutory guidance required an authority, as far as possible, to preserve or restore normal living. It is therefore lawful for an authority to provide ordinary accommodation, which is suitable to the needs of the applicants. Other services may be provided from outside the accommodation.

Need for care and attention

18.18 While the need may be met by providing ordinary accommodation rather than a package of care, a section 21 duty will arise only if there is an unmet need for care and attention, as opposed to a need for housing or for more appropriate housing.

In *R on the application of Wahid v Tower Hamlets LBC*[7] the applicant suffered from schizophrenia. He and his wife lived with their eight children, aged between 28 and 9, in a two-bedroom flat. The applicant's wife was his carer and wished to continue to be his carer but the family contended that his mental health was likely to deteriorate because of the stress of the overcrowded home. Social services decided that he was not in need of care and attention that was 'not otherwise available'; his needs were being met.

The Court of Appeal dismissed the family's appeal: Tower Hamlets was entitled to conclude that the overcrowding did not create the need for care and attention within NAA 1948 s21. The need for care and attention is a pre-condition to the duty to accommodate under section 21. The fact that a person is in need of ordinary accommodation does not mean that he needs care and

6 (1998) 30 HLR 955. The case concerned destitute asylum-seekers before NAA 1948 was amended to exclude those whose need arose solely because of destitution, see para 20.11.
7 (2001) 4 CCLR 455, 7 March 2002.

attention. The provision of ordinary accommodation is merely one way in which a need for care and attention can be met.

18.19   The situation will be different, however, where the person is excluded from mainstream housing and benefits because of immigration status. In such a case the provision of accommodation may be essential even if family or friends are able to provide the care and attention. See for example *R on the application of Mani v Lambeth LBC*[8] at para 20.16 below. In *R (SL) v Westminster CC*[9] the Court of Appeal held that in the case of a destitute asylum-seeker, 'care and attention is not otherwise available unless it would be reasonably practicable and efficacious to supply it without the provision of accommodation'.[10] This case is discussed in more detail at para 20.18.

The duty is enforceable

18.20   If an authority assesses a person's needs and finds that appropriate accommodation is a need that should be met, this may create an enforceable duty.

18.21   In *R v Kensington and Chelsea ex p Kujtim*[11] the Court of Appeal described the section 21 duty as follows:

> Once a local authority has assessed an applicant's needs as satisfying the criteria laid down in section 21(1)(a), the local authority is under a duty to provide accommodation on a continuing basis so long as the need of the applicant remains as originally assessed.[12]

In *R on the application of Batantu v Islington LBC*[13] the local authority's social services department carried out an assessment of a man with mental health and mobility problems. He lived with his wife and four children in a two-bedroom flat on the twelfth floor of a high rise block. The authority's assessment was that he needed a ground floor property with enough space to house the rest of the family. Proceedings were issued to force the authority to provide the accommodation and, nine months after the assessment, the court

---

8   [2003] EWCA Civ 836, 9 July 2003.
9   [2011] EWCA Civ 954, 10 August 2011.
10   [2011] EWCA Civ 954, Laws LJ at [39].
11   (1999) 2 CCLR 340, 9 July 1999.
12   (1999) 2 CCLR 340, Potter LJ at 354C.
13   (2001) 4 CCLR 445, QBD.

made an order that the authority provide accommodation in accordance with its statement of need. The authority was given three months to identify suitable accommodation, in consultation with the family, and a further three months to make the accommodation available to the family.

18.22 It should be noted that in *Batantu* the social services department prepared a care plan stating that the applicant needed a safe, secure, easily accessible and spacious environment. Having assessed this as a need, the social services department could not just leave the issue to be resolved by the housing department. In contrast, in *Wahid,* the authority determined that the applicant did not have any unmet need for care and attention.

18.23 Whether an enforceable duty to accommodate arises will depend on the precise terms of the needs assessment. In light of cases such as *Batantu,* local authorities will usually ensure that housing needs are addressed in terms of a need for help to obtain housing and will avoid simply stating that a person has a need for housing or more appropriate housing.

In *R on the application of Mooney v Southwark LBC*[14] the claimant was a disabled single parent with three children, including twins, both of whom had special needs. A community care assessment was carried out, as were Children Act 1989 assessments and a carer's assessment on the claimant's eldest child. A number of recommendations were made, including that the twins should have separate bedrooms and that the family should have new accommodation in which the claimant could gain access to all rooms. Following this, and in accordance with the council's allocations scheme, the social services department made a nomination to the housing department. The nomination was accepted and she was placed in the highest priority band for rehousing under the authority's choice-based lettings scheme. After 11 months the claimant had not obtained a suitable property. This was because of a combination of factors: others in the same band took precedence having being registered before the applicant; not every four-bedroom property was capable of being fitted with a lift; and, the claimant was not willing to accept any area in the borough because she wanted to be near her extended family, who provided

14 [2006] EWHC Admin 1912, 6 July 2007.

support and assistance. It was also held that, even within those constraints, the claimant had been 'overly selective' in the properties she had bid for. In the claim for judicial review it was alleged that there was a continuing failure to make provision for the family's need. A mandatory order was sought, requiring the authority to identify and make available an appropriate property.

The claim was dismissed. Although the assessments undoubtedly identified a need for more suitable accommodation, this did not trigger a duty under NAA 1948 s21. As in *Wahid*, the court held that the assessments did not identify any need for care and attention that was not available other than by the provision of accommodation under section 21. Rather, the assessment concluded that the proper course was for social services to provide additional support and to make a priority nomination under the allocations policy. Furthermore, NAA 1948 s21(8) provides that section 21 cannot authorise or require a local authority to make any provision that was authorised or required to be made by another statute. The fact that suitable accommodation can be provided under HA 1996 prevented an obligation arising under section 21.

18.24   Nevertheless, it is still the case that if social services assess a person as having an unmet need for care and attention which requires the provision of accommodation, social services may then have the duty to provide that accommodation and judicial review proceedings can be brought to enforce the duty. In addition, where there is a delay in providing for the assessed need, damages may be awarded on the ground that the authority's failure has led to a breach of the person's human rights.

In *R on the application of Bernard v Enfield LBC*[15] the applicant was a wheelchair-user, living in unadapted accommodation, having previously been found intentionally homeless by the housing department. An assessment prepared by the authority concluded that the family needed assistance to move to suitably adapted property but no steps were taken to make such accommodation available for 20 months. In judicial review proceedings damages were claimed on the grounds that the applicant's rights under article 3 (inhuman and degrading treatment) and article 8 (the right to respect for private and family life) of the European Convention on

15   [2002] EWHC Admin 2282, 25 October 2002.

Human Rights had been breached. For the period in question Mrs Bernard had been unable to access the toilet or keep herself clean without great difficulty. She soiled herself several times each day, was unable to go out of the house or upstairs and relied on her husband to assist her to move about downstairs. She had no privacy because she shared a room with her husband and two youngest children, and the older children had to pass through the room to go upstairs. Her husband's back problem was exacerbated by having to carry her to the bathroom.

The court dismissed the claim under article 3 on the basis that the authority had failed to deliver a service rather than subjecting the family to 'treatment'. However, it found that there had been a breach of the claimant's rights under article 8. Damages of £10,000 were agreed.

Immigration status

18.25 Where the person in need of community care services is a 'person subject to immigration control' the duty under NAA 1948 s21 arises only if the person's need for care and attention is not caused solely by destitution. This issue is explained in detail in paras 20.11–20.18.

Mental Health Act 1983

18.26 Mental Health Act 1983 s117(2) provides that:

It shall be the duty of the Primary Care Trust or Health Authority and of the local social services authority to provide, in co-operation with relevant voluntary agencies, aftercare services for any person to whom this section applies until such time as the Primary Care Trust or Health Authority and the local social services authority are satisfied that the person concerned is no longer in need of such services ...

18.27 The duty applies to patients who have been detained in hospital under one of the following sections of MHA 1983:

- *section 3*: detention for treatment (as opposed to detention for assessment under section 2);
- *section 37*: a 'hospital order' made by order of a criminal court after conviction of an offence committed when the offender was suffering from a 'mental disorder';[16]

---

16 Mental disorder means mental illness, psychopathic disorder, severe mental impairment or mental impairment.

- *section 45A*: detention following a direction by the Crown Court that a person suffering from a psychopathic disorder should be detained in a specified hospital (this power is available when sentencing such a person to a term of imprisonment);
- *section 47*: detention of a prisoner serving a sentence who is suffering from a mental disorder;
- *section 48*: detention of a prisoner, imprisoned on remand, a civil prisoner or someone detained under the Immigration Act 1971, who is suffering from a mental disorder.

18.28   Section 117 does not define 'aftercare services' and there is limited guidance on the nature of the duty. However, the *Code of Practice to the MHA 1983*[17] deals with the assessment of aftercare needs and makes clear that this includes consideration of appropriate accommodation. The guidance on the Mental Health (Patients in the Community) Act 1995 also refers to MHA 1983 s117 services including 'appropriate daytime activities, accommodation, treatment, personal and practical support, 24-hour emergency cover and assistance in welfare rights and financial advice'.[18] In most cases accommodation will be provided by the appropriate housing authority, which, if accommodation is an issue, should be involved in the assessment. However, some people from abroad may be unable to access housing in this way and may be able to rely on section 117 to obtain accommodation arranged by social services and/or the health authority. The duty under section 117 is one of the few community care duties for which there is no restriction based on immigration status.

> However, in *R (Mwanza) v Greenwich LBC and Bromley LBC*[19] the court refused permission for a judicial review to challenge the refusal to provide accommodation under MHA 1983 s117. The man and his family had no access to housing or benefits because of their immigration status.
>   The court held that 'an aftercare service must ... be a service that is necessary to meet a need arising from a person's mental disorder' and that although it was not the case that ordinary accommodation could never be provided under section 117, 'it is difficult readily to

17   The current Code of Practice came into force on 3 November 2008 and is available on the Department of Health website: www.dh.gov.uk.
18   *Mental Health (Patients in the Community) Act 1995 guidance on supervised discharge (after-care under supervision) and related provisions*, published by the Department of Health, 1 January 1996.
19   [2010] EWHC 1462 (Admin), 15 June 2010.

envisage circumstances in which a mere roof over the head would, on the facts of a particular case, be necessary to meet a need arising from a person's mental disorder'.[20]

18.29 The duty arises on discharge and continues until the authorities 'are satisfied that the person concerned is no longer in need of such services'.[21] A person who has been discharged from one of the relevant sections some time ago should receive aftercare services until he or she is assessed as no longer needing such services.

18.30 The section 117 duty applies to only a small proportion of patients who receive in-patient psychiatric care. However, other people with mental health problems are entitled to receive services under NAA 1948 providing they have an unmet need for care and attention.

18.31 Local authorities can make charges for the provision of most community care services, including under NAA 1948, subject to an assessment of means. However, no charge can be made in respect of services provided under section 117.[22]

How to obtain community care services

18.32 The two main community care duties that may result in accommodation being provided are NAA 1948 s21 and MHA 1983 s117. However, the duty to provide accommodation will arise only when a person has been assessed as needing accommodation. Under the Mental Health Act 1983, the assessment of needs must be carried out before discharge but for other community care services it is often very difficult to persuade an authority to carry out an assessment.

Community care assessments

18.33 Section 47 of the NHSCCA 1990 sets out the circumstances in which local authorities have a duty to carry out an assessment of a person's need for community care services. Section 47(1) provides:

> ... where it appears to a local authority that any person for whom they may provide or arrange for the provision of community care services may be in need of such services, the authority –
> (a) shall carry out an assessment of his needs for those services; and

20 [2010] EWHC 1462 (Admin) at [64] and [67].
21 MHA 1983 s117(2), see para 18.26.
22 *R v Manchester CC ex p Stennett and Others* [2002] UKHL 34.

(b) having regard to the results of that assessment, shall then decide whether his needs call for the provision by them of any such services.

18.34   The duty to assess a person's needs should therefore be easily triggered. The authority should not refuse to assess because it anticipates that the person may not actually be eligible to *receive* a service. The duty arises if it *appears* that a person for whom the authority *may* provide a service *may* be in need of services. This is a 'very low threshold test'.[23] In practice many authorities are reluctant to carry out assessments and only do so on threat of complaint or legal action. Additionally, the pressure on staff resources in social services authorities means that there is often significant delay before an assessment is commenced.

18.35   It is usually necessary to make the request for an assessment in writing and a precedent letter for such a request is contained in appendix 1 to this chapter.

Assessment procedure

18.36   Section 47 of NHSCCA 1990 requires an authority to carry out a two-stage procedure:

- to assess the apparent needs of the person ('presenting needs'), and
- to decide which of them call for the provision of services ('eligible needs').

18.37   The authority must have regard to the results of the assessment of need in deciding what services to provide. There is no obligation to meet all presenting needs.

Relevance of resources

18.38   In *R v Gloucestershire CC ex p Barry*[24] the House of Lords considered services provided under NAA 1948 s29 and the Chronically Sick and Disabled Persons Act (CSDPA) 1970.

   The court held that an authority could not assess a person as needing a service but decline to provide it because resources were limited. However, in determining which needs called for the provision of a service, an authority was entitled to take account of

---

23   See *R v Bristol CC ex p Penfold* (1997–98) 1 CCLR 315 and *Fair Access to Care Services 2002 Policy Guidance* LAC(2002)13, para 30.

24   [1997] 2 All ER 1, 20 March 1997.

> the availability of resources: 'needs for services cannot sensibly be assessed without having some regard to the cost of providing them.'[25]

18.39 Since 2003 local authorities have been obliged to set 'eligibility criteria' in accordance with the *Fair Access to Care Services 2002 Policy Guidance in England*[26] ('FACS guidance'). The criteria are set with a view to preserving or facilitating independence and are contained in bands based on risk factors. The four bands are graded according to a risk assessment of the likely consequences of failing to provide a service as follows:

- critical;
- substantial;
- moderate; and
- low.

18.40 The FACS guidance means that authorities must estimate the likely need for services and the costs of meeting the needs falling into each band. If the authority's resources are sufficient only to meet critical need then its eligibility criteria would mean that only critical needs would be met. If the resources were sufficient to meet critical and substantial, then needs assessed as falling into those bands would be met.[27] So, although each authority is obliged to follow the same process in setting its eligibility criteria, different authorities will operate different criteria and some will provide services that others will not.

18.41 Local authorities frame their community care assessments in accordance with the FACS guidance. If an authority assesses a person's need as moderate or low it may conclude that the person does not 'meet the authority's eligibility criteria' and is therefore not eligible for a service, including accommodation under NAA 1948 s21.

18.42 There is some doubt as to whether the decision in *Barry* covers all possible community care services, including accommodation under NAA 1948 s21. The subsequent cases of *R v Sefton MBC ex p Help the*

---

25 [1997] AC 584, Lord Nicholls at 604C.
26 LAC(2002)13. This has been superseded by new guidance issued in February 2010 but the new guidance adopts the FACS eligibility bands.
27 According to evidence given to the Joint Committee on Human Rights' *Inquiry Into the Implementation of the Rights of Disabled People to Independent Living*, as at 12 July 2011, 78 per cent of local authorities meet only critical and substantial needs and 4 per cent only critical needs.

Aged and others[28] and *R v East Sussex County Council ex p Tandy*[29] suggested that the decision in *Barry* was confined to services provided under CSDPA 1970.

18.43   It should also be noted that the FACS criteria do not apply when a duty to accommodate destitute asylum-seekers and failed asylum-seekers is at issue. See paras 20.11–20.18.

Form of assessment

18.44   Although there is no statutory requirement that the assessment is in writing, local authorities usually complete pro forma documentation and practice guidance recommends that a 'copy of the assessment of needs should normally be shared with the potential service user ... Except where no intervention is deemed necessary, this record will normally be combined with a written care plan'.[30] The FACS policy guidance states that the person should receive a copy of the care plan.[31]

Cases of emergency

18.45   NHSCCA 1990 s47(5) provides that a local authority may temporarily provide a service without carrying out a prior assessment of needs 'if, in the opinion of the authority, the condition of that person is such that he requires those services as a matter of urgency'. Where services are provided in an emergency, the duty to assess still remains and an assessment should be done as soon as reasonably practicable. Although this is a power rather than a duty, an authority must consider whether or not to exercise the power and, in clear cases of urgent need, the courts will order an authority to make provision pending an assessment.

Ordinary residence

18.46   Under the National Assistance Act 1948, the responsibility for providing accommodation under section 21 is that of the authority in whose area the person is 'ordinarily resident'. Ordinary residence means 'abode in a particular place or country which [a person] has adopted voluntarily and for settled purposes as part of the regular

---

28 (1997–98) 1 CCLR 57, CA, 26 March 1997.
29 (1997–98) 1 CCLR 352, HL, 20 May 1998.
30 *Care Management and Assessment: A Practitioner's Guide*, 1991, Department of Health, para 4.54.
31 FACS guidance LAC(2002)13, para 49.

order of his life for the time being, whether of short or long duration'.[32] Any dispute between authorities as to who owes the accommodation duty can be determined by reference to the secretary of state. However, pending the determination of such a dispute, one or other of the authorities must provide accommodation. Unless it is clear which authority owes the accommodation duty, where two authorities are in dispute and both are refusing to provide accommodation, proceedings could be issued against both, seeking an order that either one provide emergency accommodation pending resolution of the dispute. See *S v Lewisham LBC, Lambeth LBC and Hackney LBC* at para 18.47 below.

Urgent cases and people with no settled residence

18.47 When a person has no settled residence or is of no fixed abode, the authority to which they present should accept responsibility. Asylum-seekers who have lived in different areas for short periods may have no ordinary residence.

> In *R on the application of S v Lewisham LBC, Lambeth LBC and Hackney LBC*[33] the claimant had come to the UK from Jamaica in 1999. Between 2000 and 2003 she lived in Lambeth but was imprisoned in May 2003, being released in May 2004. From 12 May 2004 she stayed with a friend in Hackney and presented to the social services office in Lewisham on 26 May. It was accepted that as at 26 May 2004 the she had no settled residence.
>
> The court held that the applicant's physical presence in Lewisham was sufficient to entitle her to seek assistance under NAA 1948 s21.

18.48 Furthermore, whenever there is urgent need, the authority to which the person presents should assist on an emergency basis. The resposibility may later be transferred to the authority where the person is ordinarily resident.[34]

---

32 *Shah v Barnet LBC* [1983] 1 All ER 226, 16 December 1982.
33 [2008] EWHC 1290 (Admin), 15 May 2008.
34 NAA 1948 s24 and LAC(93)7 and 10.

Resolving disputes: judicial review or complaint?

18.49   Social services authorities must operate complaints procedures in accordance with specific regulations. Social services decision-making can also be challenged by way of judicial review. Judicial review is described in more detail in paras 2.8–2.40. This section highlights some of the issues that arise in relation to social services decision-making and explains when decisions should be challenged by judicial review and when the complaints procedure will be appropriate.

18.50   The sources of community care law are complex. Several different statutes set out community care powers and duties, and these must be discharged in accordance with a range of directions and guidance. Nevertheless, local authorities are subject to the following clear duties:

- a duty to assess an adult who is potentially in need of services;
- as part of the assessment process, a duty to set out the person's needs and to state what services are to be provided, by whom and by when;
- a duty to provide accommodation to adults assessed to be in need of care and attention not otherwise available.

18.51   It is the *enforcement* of these duties that has generated a large volume of litigation. In most cases the reason for this is, as Lord Nicholls pointed out in *G, W and A* (see para 19.9), 'the seemingly intractable problem of local authorities' lack of resources'.[35]

Judicial review

18.52   In judicial review, the role of the court is 'supervisory'; a claim for judicial review is not an appeal against a decision. Judicial review is a review of the lawfulness of a decision, action or failure to act in relation to the exercise of a public function.[36]

18.53   The most common reasons for judicial review claims in community care cases are:

- failure or refusal to carry out an assessment;
- delay in carrying out an assessment;
- failure or refusal to provide interim services, including accommodation, pending full assessment;
- an assessment that is so inadequate as to be unlawful.

35   [2003] UKHL 57, 23 October 2003, at [10].
36   Civil Procedure Rules (CPR) 54.1(2)(a).

18.54 The following are examples of reasons why an assessment may be unlawful:

- *Failing to take account of relevant information/failing to make sufficient inquiries* This could include failing to follow statutory guidance.
- *Unfair procedure* This could include failing to follow an authority's own stated policy or procedure.
- *Error of law* Given the requirement to determine a person's immigration status and to carry out 'human rights assessments' there is an increased risk of errors of law when assessing the needs of migrants (see chapter 20).

18.55 The main advantage of using judicial review is that an application to the court can be made on an urgent basis. An interim order can be obtained at short notice to force an authority to commence an assessment and to provide services on an urgent basis.

Alternative dispute resolution

18.56 Before a claim for judicial review is issued parties should consider alternative ways of resolving the dispute.[37]

> In *Cowl v Plymouth CC*[38] the applicant issued a claim for judicial review to challenge the authority's decision to close a residential care home. The authority responded, proposing that the issue be dealt with as a complaint and the proceedings adjourned. The applicants rejected this proposal.
>
> The Court of Appeal held that the courts should not permit, except for good reason, proceedings for judicial review to go ahead if a significant part of the issues between the parties could be resolved outside the litigation process.

18.57 In a case of urgent need, however, the complaints procedure would not be appropriate unless the authority was prepared to offer assistance pending the resolution of the complaint.

Limits of judicial review

18.58 The disadvantage of judicial review is that the court's role is limited. The court is scrutinising the lawfulness of the local authority's

---

37 CPR Judicial Review Protocol, para 4.1.
38 [2001] EWCA Civ 1935, 14 December 2001.

decision or conduct, not considering the merits of the decision or making its own decision on the facts. See *P, W, F and G*[39] summarised at para 19.53.

Judicial review to obtain an assessment

18.59 Judicial review or the threat of judicial review is commonly used to force a local authority to carry out an assessment and to provide interim accommodation pending assessment. A precedent letter requesting an assessment is contained in appendix 1 to this chapter.

18.60 If the authority refuses to assess or fails to respond within the deadline indicated, the next step may be a judicial review protocol letter. A precedent pre-action protocol letter is contained in appendix 2 to this chapter.

18.61 In urgent cases, especially where a person has already approached the authority for help, it may be appropriate to send a judicial review protocol letter immediately.

Social services complaints

18.62 The limited scope of judicial review and the fact that judicial review is a 'remedy of last resort' means that in the following circumstances a complaint will usually be the most appropriate way of challenging a decision:

- where a person wishes to challenge a particular aspect of service provision, for example, the way services are delivered or the standard of accommodation provided;
- where services are being provided but there was delay in setting up the services (if services are still not being provided judicial review may be more appropriate);
- where the complaint is about the way a person has been treated, for example, rudeness or failure to keep a person informed.

18.63 An authority may decline to deal with a complaint if legal action is pending or is threatened (see para 18.70). However, where legal action or the threat of legal action results in an assessment and/or provision of services, this would not preclude a complaint being submitted about any delay or the initial refusal to assist.

39 [2004] EWHC 2027 (Admin), 19 August 2004.

Statutory complaints procedure

18.64 Local authorities must operate complaints procedures in relation to services to adults and children.[40] In April 2009 a new complaints procedure was introducted which covers all adult social care services provided by both social services and health authorities in England.

18.65 The Local Authority Social Services and National Health Service Complaints (England) Regulations 2009[41] set out how complaints about adult social care must be dealt with by social services, NHS bodies and private providers. The new procedure replaces a three-stage procedure which imposed clear time limits on social services (and was broadly the same as that which still applies in relation to children's complaints, see para 19.54). There is now a single stage which provides that the complaint must be acknowledged within three working days but the time limit for completing the investigation is six months, and even this is not a strict deadline.

Complaints procedure

18.66 'Responsible bodies' (which means local authorities, NHS bodies, primary care providers or independent providers) must have a complaints procedure so as to ensure that:

- complaints are dealt with efficiently;
- complaints are properly investigated;
- complainants are treated with respect and courtesy;
- complainants receive, so far as is reasonably practical:
  - assistance to enable them to understand the procedure in relation to complaints; or
  - advice on where they may obtain such assistance;
- complainants receive a timely and appropriate response;
- complainants are told the outcome of the investigation of their complaint; and
- action is taken if necessary in the light of the outcome of a complaint.

Complaints manager

18.67 A 'responsible person' to ensure compliance with the regulations and a 'complaints manager' must be appointed. For local authorities and NHS bodies the responsible person must be the chief executive

---

40 LASSA 1970 s7B.
41 SI No 309.

officer. The complaints manager may be the same or a different person. The complaints manager may also be someone not employed by the authority.

Who may complain

18.68 Usually this will be the service user but it could also be a person who is affected by the action, omission or decision of the responsible body (for example, a carer). Complaint may be made by someone acting on behalf of the complainant if that person has died, is a child or is unable to make the complaint himself or herself because of physical or mental incapacity. Or, a person may request a representative to act on their behalf. A complaint may be made orally, in writing or electronically.

Time limits

18.69 The stages of the complaints procedure and the time limits for each stage are summarised in the table below:

Making the complaint	Within 12 months of the issue arising or the complainant becoming aware of it. But this does not apply if the body is satisfied that the complainant had good reasons for not making the complaint within 12 months and it is still possible to investigate the complaint effectively and fairly.
Acknowledging the complaint	Not later than three working days after the day on which the complaint is received. This may be orally or in writing.
Offering to discuss the complaint	When the complaint is acknowledged the body must offer to discuss the complaint (at a time to be agreed with the complaint), how it is to be handled and the likely timescale for investigation and response.
Setting the timescale	If the complainant does not accept the offer of a discussion the responsible body must decide the period for investigation and response and inform the complainant in writing.
Recording the complaint	Before investigating the complaint the body must make a written record of the complaint and provide a copy to the complainant. No specific time limit.

Investigation	The investigation should be completed within six months of receiving the complaint. A longer period may be agreed between the parties before the end of six months. If the responsible body does not comply with this deadline, it must notify the complainant in writing and explain why and must send a response 'as soon as reasonably practicable after the relevant period.'
Report/ response	'As soon as reasonably practicable after completing the investigation' the body must send a written response including a report explaining how the complaint has been considered, the conclusion reached and whether any remedial action is proposed or has been taken. For local authority and health body complaints, details of the right to take the complaint to the Local Government Ombudsman or Health Services Commissioner must be given.
Conduct of the investigation	The complaint must be investigated in a manner appropriate to resolve it speedily and efficiently and the complainant should be kept informed, as far as reasonably practicable, of the progress of the investigation.
Exceptions	Oral complaints that are resolved to the complainant's satisfaction by the following working day do not have to be recorded or investigated.
Declining to deal with a complaint	Where the body decides that it is not required to consider a complaint (eg a complaint already dealt with or one about matters that occurred more than 12 months ago) it must notify the complainant in writing with reasons for its decision 'as soon as reasonably practicable.' This does not apply to oral complaints that have been resolved. See above.

The regulations also specify certain monitoring and reporting requirements about complaints generally.

18.70   It should be noted that a complaint to the Ombudsman must also be made within 12 months of knowledge of the matters complained of. However, the Ombudsman will not usually consider a complaint unless the authority has been given the opportunity to resolve the complaint. This is subject to exceptions, see para 19.56.

18.71   See paras 2.89–2.96 for further information about Ombudsman complaints.

APPENDIX 1

Letter requesting community care assessment (adult)

To:
Duty Manager
Assessment Team X Local Authority

Dear Sir/Madam,

Re: Mrs A

DOB: 01.01.1968

We are assisting Mrs A who is a failed asylum-seeker from [country]. We are referring her to your authority for an assessment under section 47 of the NHS & Community Care Act 1990.

[Reasons for possible community care services]

Mrs A suffers from depression which her GP describes as 'sometimes severe' (letter attached). She is receiving treatment for post traumatic stress disorder from the ... clinic. The claimant also has mobility problems caused by an historic hip fracture. This injury causes her pain and means that she cannot carry heavy bags and cannot walk far without additional pain and discomfort.

[Detail where she has been staying, why she can no longer stay there, how managing re food/support etc.]

Mrs A's claim for asylum was refused on [date] and her appeal refused on [date]. Mrs A was being supported and accommodated by NASS until [date]. Since then she has been homeless and destitute. For a period of two weeks she was street homeless but on [date] a friend, Mrs D of [address], permitted her to stay in her home for a maximum of two weeks. Mrs A has no financial support but has been provided with food by Mrs D for the past week. Mrs D has informed Mrs A that she must leave her home on [date].

Mrs A attended your offices on [date] seeking help but was advised that no help could be given as she was a failed asylum-seeker.

[Authority's possible duty to provide community care services]

We believe that your authority may be under a duty to provide support and accommodation to Mrs A under section 21 of the National Assistance Act 1948. Section 21 places a duty on a local authority to provide residential accommodation to an adult in need of care and attention because of age, illness, disability or other circumstance. Mrs A is in need of care and attention and her need does not arise solely from destitution.

[What local authority is being asked to do]

Please can you contact us so that the appropriate arrangements can be made for our client to be assessed. [Or, our client is delivering this letter to you. Please inform him/her of when and where he or she should attend for the assessment to be commenced].

[Deadline]

Please notify us/Mrs A no later than 4 pm on [date] of your agreement to carry out an assessment under section 47.

[In cases of urgent need]

Please also confirm that you will make arrangements to provide accommodation and financial support to Mrs A until the assessment has been completed.

[Consequences of failure to reply]

If we do not hear from you by 4 pm on [date] we will assume that your authority is refusing to carry out an assessment and will take appropriate action/ refer our client to solicitors with a view to taking legal action against your authority.

Yours faithfully,

APPENDIX 2

Pre-action protocol letter (failure to assess)

Proposed claim for judicial review

To
Director of Social Services X Local Authority
Address

The claimant
Mrs A
Of no fixed abode

Reference details

The claimant's advisers have spoken by telephone to Mr B, the Duty Manager of the assessment team.

The details of the matter being challenged:

(1) The failure/refusal of the defendants to carry out an assessment of the claimant's needs under section 47 of the National Health Service and Community Care Act (NHSCCA) 1990.

(2) The failure/refusal of the defendants to provide interim accommodation and support to the claimant pending an assessment under section 47 of NHSCCA 1990.

The issue

The claimant is a failed asylum-seeker who has been homeless and destitute since ... She has for the past two weeks been staying with a friend at ... but was told she must leave no later than ... as the premises are overcrowded. The claimant has no other friends with whom she can stay when she has to leave this accommodation. The claimant has no means of support.

The claimant suffers from depression which her GP describes as 'sometimes severe' (letter attached). She is receiving treatment for post traumatic stress disorder from the ... clinic. The claimant also has mobility problems caused by an historic hip fracture. This injury causes her pain and means that she cannot carry heavy bags and cannot walk far without additional pain and discomfort.

The claimant has attended the offices of the defendant's social services assessment team on two occasions. The first time was approximately two weeks ago when she was advised that the defendants could not assist her because of her immigration status. The second time was approximately one week ago when the claimant delivered a letter requesting a community care assessment (copy attached). The claimant was advised that she should apply to NASS for assistance.

The claimant's advisers spoke to the defendant's duty manager, Mr B, by telephone yesterday. He stated that the defendants could not assist the claimant as she was a failed asylum-seeker and that she should apply to NASS for section 4 support.

The defendants are acting unlawfully in refusing to conduct an assessment under section 47 of NHSCCA 1990. The claimant is clearly a person who may be in need of community care services that the defendants may provide. In particular, the claimant is in need of accommodation and support under section 21 of the National Assistance Act 1948 as she is destitute and in need of care and attention not otherwise available. Her need does not arise solely from destitution.

The details of the action that the defendant is expected to take

(1) Confirm that it will immediately commence an assessment of the claimant's needs;
(2) Confirm that it will arrange for the claimant to be provided with accommodation and support under section 21 of the National Assistance Act 1948 on an interim basis until the assessment is completed.

The details of the legal advisers, if any, dealing with this claim

CC and Company [address]

The details of any interested parties

There are no interested parties at present

The details of any information sought

If the defendants maintain that they have no duty to assess the claimant a full explanation is required.

The details of any documents that are considered relevant and necessary

The claimant requests a complete copy of her social services file under the Data Protection Act 1998. The claimant's signed authority is enclosed and a cheque in the sum of £10 is enclosed with the hard copy of this letter.

[If an assessment has been conducted request a copy of the assessment]

The address for reply and service of court documents

CC and Company [address]

Proposed reply date

By 4 pm on ... [two days before the claimant is due to be evicted from her current accommodation]

Yours faithfully,

CHAPTER 19

Community care: accommodation duties to children

continued

Key points

Children in need

- The main provisions regarding accommodation for children in need are sections 17 and 20 of the Children Act (CA) 1989.
- The section 17 duty is a 'target duty' owed to children and families generally. It includes a power to provide accommodation, or financial help to obtain accommodation. It does not create an enforceable duty.
- In contrast, the section 20 duty is an enforceable duty to provide accommodation to children in need who require accommodation for one of the reasons set out.
- Usually the first step will be to request a 'child in need' assessment. If the child is 'in the area' of a local authority, that authority has a duty to assess. The child need not be permanently resident or have a local connection.
- The primary duty to accommodate homeless 16- and 17-year-olds is the social services duty under section 20.
- In an emergency the housing authority can provide accommodation but it should immediately make a referral to social services for an assessment.
- Social services and housing authorities/departments should operate joint working agreements for homeless 16- and 17-year-olds.

Children leaving care

- Social services may also have a duty to accommodate someone aged 18 to 20 (or, in some cases, up to age 24) who has previously been in the care of the authority or accommodated under CA 1989 s20 for at least 13 weeks.
- Care leavers have automatic priority need for housing until they are 21.

Introduction

19.1   This chapter examines:

- the accommodation duties to children in need;
- the duty to assess children's needs;
- the duties to children leaving care;
- the recent cases on the duty under the Children Act 1989 s20.

Local authority duties to children: Children Act 1989

19.2   The Children Act (CA) 1989 consolidated previously fragmented legislation about children. It reformed and simplified child care law, particularly in relation to child protection. One of its central tenets is that children should, as far as possible, be looked after by their families. Part III of the Act deals with 'Local Authority Support for Children and Families' and contains the two main provisions that may result in a local authority providing accommodation for the benefit of a child: sections 17 and 20.

Children in need

19.3   The concept of a 'child in need' is central to the local authority duties set out in CA 1989 Part III.

19.4   Section 17(10) defines a 'child in need' in the following terms:

... a child shall be taken to be in need if:
(a) he is unlikely to achieve or maintain, or to have the opportunity of achieving or maintaining, a reasonable standard of health or development without the provision for him of services by a local authority under this Part;
(b) his health or development is likely to be significantly impaired, or further impaired, without the provision for him of such services; or
(c) he is disabled.

19.5   Section 17(11) provides further definition: a child is 'disabled' if he or she is 'blind, deaf or dumb or suffers from mental disorder of any kind or is substantially and permanently handicapped by illness, injury or congenital deformity or such other disability as may be prescribed'. 'Development' is defined as 'physical, intellectual, emotional, social or behavioural development' and 'health' means 'physical or mental health'.

General duty under CA 1989 s17

19.6   Section 17(1) provides that every local authority has a 'general duty':

(a) to safeguard and promote the welfare of children within their area who are in need; and
(b) so far as is consistent with that duty, to promote the upbringing of such children by their families, by providing a range and level of services appropriate to those children's needs.

19.7 The services may be provided for the family of the child or any member of the child's family, so long as they are provided with a view to safeguarding or promoting the child's welfare.[1]

19.8 The services may include providing accommodation and giving assistance in kind or, in exceptional circumstances, in cash.[2]

Accommodating children and parents under section 17

19.9 Since the Children Act 1989 came into force, many local authorities have used section 17 to provide accommodation, or to give financial help to obtain accommodation, to families who were homeless but unable to get accommodation by way of a homeless application or through the allocations scheme. However, after the House of Lords considered the nature of the section 17 duty in 2003, this has been less common.

> *R on the application of G v Barnet LBC, R on the application of W v Lambeth LBC and R on the application of A v Lambeth LBC (G, W and A)*[3] concerned three single parents seeking to compel the local authorities to provide accommodation under CA 1989 s17 for themselves and their children. G was excluded from housing and benefits because she was from Holland and was not 'habitually resident' (see para 14.133 above). W had been found intentionally homeless so was not entitled to housing under Housing Act (HA) 1996 Part VII. A had two disabled children and social services had carried out an assessment concluding that 'the family needs re-housing to an appropriate accommodation'.
>
> The House of Lords held, by a majority of 3:2, that section 17(1) does not impose a duty on social services in respect of the needs of a particular child. The duty is a general duty to safeguard and promote the welfare of 'children within their area who are in need' and to promote the upbringing of such children by their families:
>
>> A social services authority which provides a range and level of services appropriate to meet the various needs of children in its area has discharged its duty under section 17(1). This cannot be read as a duty to meet the needs of any particular child. It is

---

1 CA 1989 s17(3).
2 CA 1989 17(6) as amended by the Adoption and Children Act 2002. The words 'in exceptional circumstances' will be removed when the Children and Young Persons Act 2008 s24 comes into force.
3 [2003] UKHL 57, 23 October 2003.

> sufficient that the authority maintains services for which his particular needs make him eligible.[4]

19.10   The local authority in *A* and *W* had a general policy of offering to accommodate the children of a family faced with homelessness (ie take the children into voluntary care under CA 1989 s20, see below, paras 19.12–19.14) but not of accommodating parents and children together under section 17. The House of Lords held that operating a general policy in those terms was not unlawful although each case would have to be considered on its merits. An authority will always have to have regard to the right to respect for family life under article 8 of the European Convention on Human Rights (ECHR) when making a decision on a particular case, see paras 2.42 and 7.100.

19.11   ECHR article 8 will be particularly relevant when the parent is a person from abroad who is unable to work or claim mainstream benefits such as housing benefit. In a number of cases the courts have held that where such a person has an outstanding immigration application, to refuse to accommodate the family so that either the children would be taken into care or the family would be forced to return to their country of origin would be a breach of the family's human rights. These cases are considered in paras 20.43–20.44.

Accommodation duty under CA 1989 s20

19.12   Children Act 1989 s20 sets out the duty to provide accommodation for a child who has no parent or guardian or whose parent or guardian is unable to provide suitable accommodation or care. Section 20(1) provides that:

> ... every local authority shall provide accommodation for any child in need within their area who appears to them to require accommodation as a result of:
> (a) there being no person who has parental responsibility for him;
> (b) his being lost or having been abandoned; or
> (c) the person who has been caring for him being prevented (whether or not permanently, and for whatever reason) from providing him with suitable accommodation or care.

Children aged 16 or older

19.13   In relation to children who are 16 years or older a duty to accommodate a child in need arises if the authority considers that the child's

---

4 [2003] UKHL 57, Lord Millett at [109].

welfare is likely to be seriously prejudiced if it does not provide him or her with accommodation.[5]

Consulting the child

19.14 Before providing accommodation under CA 1989 s20 a local authority must:

> ... so far as is reasonably practicable and consistent with the child's welfare
> (a) ascertain the child's wishes regarding the provision of accommodation, and
> (b) give due consideration (having regard to his age and understanding) to such wishes of the child as they have been able to ascertain.[6]

Assessment of children in need

19.15 There is no specific duty to assess potential children in need equivalent to the duty in relation to adults, set out in the National Health Service and Community Care Act 1990 s47, see para 18.33. However, the Children Act 1989 places on a local authority a duty to take reasonable steps to identify the extent to which there are children in need in its area[7] and makes clear that this will involve assessing the needs of each child found to be in need. More often it will be an approach by the family of the child or a referral from an adviser or other agency that brings the potential 'child in need' to the notice of the authority.

Timescale

19.16 The *Framework for the Assessment of Children in Need and their Families* (FACNF)[8] is policy guidance issued under the Local Authority Social Services Act 1970 s7. It should be complied with unless there are exceptional reasons which justify a departure.[9] FACNF describes the response to an initial contact or referral as 'critically important' and lays down a timetable for the assessment process:

---

5 CA 1989 s20(3).
6 CA 1989 s20(6).
7 CA 1989 Sch 2 paras 1 and 3.
8 4 April 2000. It can be downloaded from the Department of Health website: www.dh.gov.uk.
9 *R v Islington LBC ex p Rixon* (1997–98) 1 CCLR 119, see para 18.7.

- *Decision about response.* Within one working day of a referral being received a decision should be made about what response is required. This may include a decision that no action is to be taken but the decision should be made promptly and recorded.[10]
- *Initial assessment.* A decision to gather more information constitutes an initial assessment, which should be undertaken within a maximum of seven working days. This could be very brief depending upon the child's circumstances. It should determine whether the child is a child in need, the nature of the services required, from where and within what timescales, and whether a further, more detailed, core assessment should be undertaken.[11]
- *Core assessment.* A core assessment is an in-depth assessment which addresses the central or most important aspects of the needs of a child. The timescale for completion of the core assessment is a maximum of 35 working days. A core assessment is deemed to have commenced at the point the initial assessment ended. Where specialist assessments have been commissioned by other agencies or independent professionals it is recognised that they will not necessarily be completed within the 35 working day period.[12]

Cases of emergency

19.17   FACNF provides that '*Appropriate* services should be provided whilst awaiting the completion of the specialist assessment'.[13] As with services to adults, in cases of obvious need the courts will readily order an authority to provide services on an interim basis pending full assessment.

Which authority?

19.18   A dispute may arise about which local authority is responsible for assessing the child in need and for providing the necessary services.

19.19   Unlike under the National Assistance Act 1948, there is no requirement under the Children Act 1989 for a child to be 'ordinarily resident' in the area of a local authority. The authority's duty is to children 'within their area.'

---

10 FACNF para 3.8.
11 FACNF para 3.9.
12 FACNF para 3.11
13 FACNF para 3.11.

In *R on the application of Stewart v Wandsworth LBC, Hammersmith and Fulham LBC and Lambeth LBC*[14] a dispute arose between three authorities as to which should carry out a child in need assessment. Hammersmith and Fulham had temporarily accommodated a woman and her two children in the area of Lambeth, following a homeless application. The children attended school in the area of Wandsworth LBC. The woman was found to be intentionally homeless and she then sought a child in need assessment with a view to obtaining accommodation under CA 1989 s17. Each of the three authorities denied that it had a duty to carry out the assessment.

The court held that Hammersmith and Fulham LBC did not have a duty, because the children were not 'within their area'. The fact that the authority had investigated a homeless application did not place it under a duty to carry out a child in need assessment. To establish a duty it was both necessary and sufficient for the children to be 'physically present' in an area. Both Wandsworth and Lambeth were under a duty to carry out assessments and were ordered to do so.

'Looked after' children

19.20　A child who is accommodated under CA 1989 s20 is a 'looked after' child. When a child is 'looked after' this means that the local authority is responsible for the child's accommodation and maintenance.[15] It also means that the local authority may have continuing duties to support the young person after the the age of 18. Whether or not a child is a looked after child does not depend on the authority deciding that the child needs to be looked after but on whether the conditions under section 20 are met. The cases on when the section 20 duty arises are discussed at paras 19.35–19.43 below.

14　[2001] EWHC 709 (Admin), 17 September 2001.
15　CA 1989 ss22A and 22B.

Children leaving care

19.21 The Children (Leaving Care) Act 2000 ('Leaving Care Act 2000') sets out the responsibilities of local authorites to certain children previously in their care, up to and beyond the age of 18.[16]

19.22 The leaving care duties apply only to young people who have been 'looked after' children for a minimum period of time. This means having been provided with accommodation by social services for a minimum of 13 weeks in total. The period must end after the child reaches the age of 16. It need not be a continuous period but the child must have been in the care of the authority for at least 13 weeks in total after the age of 14 years.[17] Accommodation provided under CA 1989 s17 or under the leaving care duties does not count towards the total.[18] Therefore the duties apply to children accommodated under CA 1989 s20 and to children subject to care orders under the child protection provisions of the Children Act 1989.

19.23 The powers and duties under the Leaving Care Act 2000 apply to 'eligible' children, 'relevant' children and 'former relevant' children. These are defined as follows:

- *Eligible child:* a child aged 16 or 17, who has been looked after for the minimum period, and is still being looked after.[19]
- *Relevant child:* a child aged 16 or 17, not presently being looked after by any local authority, but who has previously been a 'looked after child' for the minimum period.[20]
- *Former relevant child:* someone aged between 18 and 20 who was previously a 'looked after child' for the minimum period. Furthermore, a young person who, at the age of 21, is being supported by the responsible authority with education or training remains a 'former relevant child' until the end of the agreed programme of education or training even if that takes him or her past the age of 21. This 'extension' of duties can last only up to the age of

16 The Act amended the Children Act 1989 by introducing duties to children who are leaving or have left the care of the authority. Reference should also be made to Children (Leaving Care) (England) Regulations 2001 SI No 2874 (Leaving Care Regs 2001) and the Guidance issued under Local Authority Social Services Act 1970 s7 (LAC(2003)13). For Wales, see Children (Leaving Care) (Wales) Regulations 2001 SI No 2189.

17 See CA 1989 s22 and Leaving Care Regs 2001 reg 3. Periods of care in pre-planned placements of less than four weeks (ie, respite care) do not count towards the 13-week total.

18 CA 1989 s22(1), as amended by Adoption and Children Act 2002.

19 CA 1989 Sch 2 para 19B.

20 CA 1989 s23A.

24.[21] The duty to a former relevant child falls on the authority that was the last 'responsible authority'. This means the authority that most recently owed a duty under the leaving care provisions, or, if there is no such authority, the authority in whose care the child was under CA 1989.[22]

Duties to eligible children

19.24 The local authority must appoint a 'personal adviser' and carry out an assessment of the child's needs with a view to deciding what advice, assistance and support should be provided while the child is still looked after and afterwards. Following the assessment of need, a pathway plan must be drawn up.[23] The pathway plan must set out the way the authority proposes to meet the child's needs and must be recorded in writing, see para 19.33 below.[24]

Duties to relevant children

19.25 The authority must take reasonable steps to keep in touch with the child, whether or not he or she is still within its area. The authority must also appoint a personal adviser, carry out an assessment of need and prepare a pathway plan (if not already done). The pathway plan must be kept under regular review.

19.26 In relation to support and accommodation the authority has a duty to safeguard and promote the child's welfare and (unless satisfied that his or her welfare does not require it) support the child by:

- maintaining the child; and
- providing the child with, or maintaining the child in, suitable accommodation.[25]

19.27 The presumption therefore is that a local authority should provide accommodation and financial support to a 16- or 17-year-old who has previously been a looked after child. The authority must be satisfied that the child's welfare does not require such assistance to avoid the duty.

---

21 CA 1989 s24B(3). However, the Children and Young Persons Act 2008 will change this so that the age of 25 will be the cut-off point.
22 CA 1989 s23C.
23 CA 1989 Sch 2 para 19B.
24 Leaving Care Regs 2001 reg 8.
25 CA 1989 s23A.

19.28   If a local authority has lost touch with a relevant child it must consider how to re-establish contact and take reasonable steps to do so. This duty continues until contact is made or the child reaches the age of 18.

Duties to former relevant children

19.29   The authority must take reasonable steps to keep in touch with the young person, whether within its area or not and, if it loses touch, must take reasonable steps to re-establish contact. It must continue the appointment of a personal adviser and continue to keep the pathway plan under regular review.

19.30   In relation to support and accommodation, the authority must give assistance to the young person to the extent that his or her welfare, educational or training needs requires it. This may include contributing to living expenses to enable the child to be near employment, training or education. The authority must also give other assistance to the extent that the young person's welfare requires it.[26] This can include actually providing accommodation.[27]

19.31   Any duty to provide assistance with accommodation and living expenses therefore depends on the authority having assessed that the young person's welfare requires such assistance. This question should be addressed in the assessment of need and the pathway plan. A failure to prepare the needs assessment and/or the pathway plan may be challenged by judicial review. A failure to address the issue of accommodation in those documents may also be challenged (see para 19.33).

Accommodation in student vacations

19.32   Where the local authority is satisfied that a person in full-time further or higher education needs accommodation during a vacation, because the term-time accommodation is not available, there is a duty to provide suitable accommodation during the vacation or to pay the person enough to enable him or her to secure accommodation.[28]

---

26   CA 1989 s23C.
27   *R (SO) v Barking & Dagenham LBC* [2011] EWCA Civ 1101, 12 October 2010.
28   CA 1989 s24B(5).

The assessment and pathway plan

19.33 The Department of Health Guidance LAC(2003)13, sets out in detail the role of the personal adviser and the way the assessment of need and pathway plan should be prepared. The guidance states that:

> The Pathway Plan should be explicit in setting out the objectives and action needed to achieve [the child's needs]; this should include who is responsible for achieving each action and timescale for achieving it.[29]

In *R on the application of J v Caerphilly County Council*[30] the court considered a pathway plan prepared in respect of a child who was in the care of the local authority and ready for release from a young offenders institution. The pathway plan was criticised for containing little more than vague aspirations. In relation to the boy's accommodation on release the pathway plan recorded that the local authority would 'continue to explore accommodation options in preparation for [his] release'.

The judge held that the pathway plan was 'hopelessly inadequate': 'A pathway plan must clearly identify the child's needs, and what is to be done about them by whom and by when. Or, if another aphorism would help, a pathway plan must spell out who does what, where and when.'[31]

Accommodating 16- and 17-year-olds

19.34 Over the last ten years the courts have been called on to consider the nature of the CA 1989 s20 duty in a number of cases. The reasons why this is an important issue are:

- Duties under the Leaving Care Act 2000 apply when a child has been accommodated by social services under CA 1989 s20 but not where assistance has been given under section 17.
- Unaccompanied asylum-seeking children are the responsibility of local authorities under the Children Act 1989 and, if accommodated under section 20 will also, in most cases, be entitled to Leaving Care Act 2000 services after the age of 18;

29 LAC(2003)13: Guidance on accommodating children in need and their families, para 7.7.
30 [2005] EWHC 586 (Admin), 12 April 2005.
31 [2005] EWHC 586 (Admin), Munby J at [45].

- Since 2002, homeless 16- and 17-year-olds have had automatic priority need for homeless assistance, except where a duty is owed under CA 1989 s20 by social services. A potential accommodation duty is therefore owed by both social services and housing departments.

Relationship between the Children Act and the Housing Act

19.35   A homeless 16- or 17-year-old has priority need under HA 1996 Part VII unless he or she is owed an accommodation duty under CA 1989 s20 or under the Leaving Care Act 2000 (see para 14.199). So, when a homeless child first seeks help from a local authority he or she could present to the housing department or the social services department.[32] This raises the question of which department owes the primary duty. If this is social services, the second thing to consider is when might a homelessness duty arise in relation to a 16- or 17-year-old applicant.

> The Supreme Court considered these issues in *R (G) v Southwark LBC*.[33] G was 17 when he was asked to leave home by his mother. After a period of sleeping on friends' sofas and in friends' cars he presented himself to social services with a letter requesting accommodation immediately. The following day his solicitors wrote to Southwark asking for an assessment under CA 1989 s17 and for accommodation to be provided under section 20. Southwark's assessment was completed just over a week later and their legal department wrote a letter stating: 'Our client department has fully considered your client's needs and reached the decision that Section 20 is not appropriate as [G] has no identified need for social services support, and his needs can be satisfactorily met through the provision of housing and referrals to other support agencies.' The conclusion was: 'Our client department has fulfilled its duty to assess your client and reached the decision that he is not in need of Section 20 accommodation; he simply requires "help with accommodation".' G sought judicial review of that decision.
>   The Court of Appeal held that the authority's decision was lawful and G appealed to the Supreme Court. The question was identified

---

32 In non-unitary authorities these will be different authorities, not just different departments.
33 [2009] UKHL 26, 20 May 2009.

as being whether, when a child of 16 or 17 who had been thrown out of the family home presents himself to social services and asks to be accommodated under CA 1989 s20, it was open to that authority instead to arrange for him to be accommodated by the local housing authority as a homeless person. The answer was that it was not. The lead judgment was by Baroness Hale, who held that section 20(1) entails a series of questions:

(1) whether the applicant is a child; (2) whether the applicant is a child in need; (3) whether the child is within the local authority's area; (4) whether the child appears to the local authority to require accommodation; (5) whether that need is because of one of the reasons set out in section 20; (6) what the child's wishes and feelings are regarding the provision of accommodation; and (7) what consideration (having regard to the child's age and understanding) should be given to those wishes and feelings?

In this case there was no issue that the applicant was a child and was within the local authority's area. Furthermore, the parties agreed that, because he was homeless, G was a child in need. Nevertheless, the court held, it was possible that 16- or 17-year-old temporarily without accommodation may not be a child in need, for example, perhaps a child whose home has been temporarily damaged by fire or flood but who can well afford hotel accommodation while it is repaired:

> But it cannot seriously be suggested that a child excluded from home who is 'sofa surfing' in this way, more often sleeping in cars, snatching showers and washing his clothes when he can, is not in need.[34]

As to whether the applicant appeared to require accommodation:

> ... it is quite obvious that a sofa surfing child requires accommodation. But there may be cases where the child does have a home to go to, whether on his own or with family or friends, but needs help in getting there, or getting into it, or in having it made habitable or safe. This is the line between needing 'help with accommodation' (not in itself a technical term) and needing 'accommodation'.[35]

As to whether the reason for requiring accommodation was because 'the person who has been caring for him being prevented from

---

34 [2009] UKHL 26, Baroness Hale at [28(2)].
35 [2009] UKHL 26, Baroness Hale at [28(4)].

providing him with suitable accommodation or care', Baroness Hale held that this

> ... has to be given a wide construction, if children are not to suffer for the shortcomings of their parents or carers. It is not disputed that this covers a child who has been excluded from home even though this is the deliberate decision of the parent.

On the issue of the child's wishes and feelings and the consideration that should be given to those wishes and feelings,

> Some have taken the view that this refers only to the child's views about the sort of accommodation he should have, rather than about whether he should be accommodated at all ... This is supported by the opening words, which are 'before providing' rather than 'before deciding whether to provide.
>
> On the other hand ... it is unlikely that Parliament intended that local authorities should be able to oblige a competent 16- or 17-year-old to accept a service which he does not want. This is supported by section 20(11), which provides that a child who has reached 16 may agree to be accommodated even if his parent objects or wishes to remove him. It is a service, not a coercive intervention ... It is not an issue in this case, because [he] wanted to be accommodated under section 20. But a homeless 16 or 17 year old who did not want to be accommodated under section 20 would be another example of a child in priority need under the 2002 Order.[36]
>
> It follows, therefore, that every item in the list had been assessed in [his] favour, that the duty had arisen, and that the authority were not entitled to 'side-step' that duty by giving the accommodation a different label.[37]

19.36   Therefore, it is now clear that the primary duty to accommodate homeless 16- and 17-year-olds is a social services duty and the duty cannot be side-stepped by referring the child to the housing department for homeless assistance. Furthermore, in a number of cases the courts have held that, even when social services purported to assist a homeless child by way of some duty or power outside CA 1989 s20, as a matter of law the section 20 duty had arisen.

---

36   [2009] UKHL 26, Baroness Hale at [28(6)].
37   [2009] UKHL 26, Baroness Hale at [28(8)].

Establishing the section 20 duty retrospectively

19.37   In *R on the application of S v Sutton LBC*[38] a 17-year-old who was
ready for release from a young offenders institution (YOI) was
assisted by social services to make an application to be placed in a
hostel. The authority accepted that a CA 1989 s20 duty had arisen
immediately before the child was released from the YOI. However,
it claimed that the fact that a hostel placement was secured meant
that the applicant no longer required accommodation so that it
was no longer under a section 20 duty. At the time her solicitors
had written to Sutton, complaining that a hostel placement was
inappropriate for a child but the authority had claimed (wrongly)
that if it were to accommodate her under section 20 it could only be
by way of a foster placement or residential care.

The Court of Appeal held that Sutton 'was seeking to "side-step"
its duties under section 20(1) by having [the applicant] declare
herself homeless ... '.[39] There was no evidence that Sutton had
offered her the choices of accommodation that she should have
been offered, nor was there any evidence that it could not have
placed her in the hostel in under its CA 1989 duties. It was held that
the applicant was placed by Sutton at the hostel under the section
20 duty and that this obligation continued from the time of her
release. Therefore, having now turned 18, she was entitled to leaving
care services.

19.38   Establishing retrospectively that an authority was under a CA 1989
s20 duty may benefit the young person in two ways. First, provided
the authority was under the section 20 duty for the requisite 13 weeks
in total (see para 19.22 above) the young person will be entitled to
ongoing support under the Leaving Care Act 2000. Second, if the
young person is homeless after the age of 18 and before the age of
21 he or she will have automatic priority need for housing as a 'care
leaver' (see paras 14.250–14.251). Note that to establish priority need
as a care leaver it is not necessary to have been accommodated for 13
weeks; any period in care between the age of 16 and 18 is sufficient.

19.39   However, this is not the case if the child is accommodated by the
housing department and does not come to the attention of social
services.

38 [2007] EWCA Civ 790, 26 July 2007.
39 [2007] EWCA Civ 790, Hooper LJ at [50].

In *R on the application of M v Hammersmith & Fulham LBC*[40] a
17-year-old had presented to the housing department following
the breakdown of her relationship with her mother. She was given
interim accommodation under HA 1996 s188. There was some
dispute about exactly where she had lived over the next few months
but eight months after presenting she was sentenced to four
months in a young offenders institution and she turned 18 while in
custody. On her release it was argued that she should have been
treated as a child in need and accommodated under CA 1989 s20
by social services. On that basis she would have been entitled to
ongoing support as a child leaving care.

The House of Lords considered the relationship between local
authorities' housing duties and social services duties to homeless
teenagers:

> ... the statutory guidance given to both housing and social
> services departments stresses the need for joint protocols for
> assessing the needs of homeless 16- and 17-year-olds. This is
> needed, not only to avoid a young person being passed from
> pillar to post, but also to ensure that the most appropriate
> agency takes responsibility for her. The 2002 Priority Need Order
> clearly contemplates that, if the criteria in section 20 ... are met,
> social services rather than housing should take the long-term
> responsibility. Such a young person has needs over and above
> the simple need for a roof over her head and these can better be
> met by the social services.[41]

If (as in *S v Sutton*, above para 19.37) a local authority's social
services department provides or assists with accommodation in
circumstances where it should have taken action under section
20 it cannot side-step the further obligations that arose under CA
1989. However, this did not mean that the actions of an authority's
housing department should be categorised according to what its
social services department should have done if the case had been
drawn to its attention.

M's appeal was dismissed.

19.40   So, while it may be appropriate for the homeless persons unit to
arrange interim accommodation in an emergency, it should always
refer a potential child in need for an assessment by social services

40 [2008] UKHL 14, 27 February 2008.
41 [2008] UKHL 14, Baroness Hale at [31].

and the primary, long-term accommodation duty lies with social services.

Joint protocols – housing and social services

19.41 For many years there has been guidance requiring local authorities to develop joint working practices between housing and social services to avoid children being from passed from one agency to another.[42] The need for this was reiterated by the House of Lords in *R (M) v Hammersmith & Fulham LBC* (above, para 19.39). Following *R (G) v Southwark LBC* (above, para 19.35), new statutory guidance was published in April 2010: *Provision of Accommodation for 16- and 17-year-old young people who may be homeless and/or require accommodation.*[43] The guidance is issued under the Local Authority and Social Services Act 1970 s7, which means that it must be followed unless there is a good reason not to. It states that:

> It is therefore essential that services for homeless 16- and 17-year-olds are underpinned by written joint protocols which set out clear, practical arrangements for providing services that are centred on young people and their families and prevent young people from being passed from pillar to post.[44]

19.42 Despite the statutory requirement for such protocols, repeatedly highlighted by the courts, by the end of 2010 few local authorities were able to demonstrate that they operated a protocol.

In *R (TG) v Lambeth LBC*[45] a 16-year-old boy became homeless at a time when he was being supported by the youth offending team (YOT). A social worker who worked for the YOT had sent a letter to the homeless persons unit stating that TG was a child in need and requesting that the authority accommodate him, which it did. After reaching the age of 18, he argued that this had been in discharge of the CA 1989 s20 duty, entitling him to services under the Leaving Care Act 2000. The local authority denied that this was the case, arguing that TG's situation was like *R (M) v Hammersmith & Fulham LBC* (above, para 19.39) in that he had not been seen or assessed by

42 See FACNF, para 5.72 and the Homelessness Code of Guidance, paras 10.39 and 12.6.
43 This can be downloaded from the DoE website: www.education.gov.uk/publications.
44 Paragraph 5.2.
45 [2011] EWCA Civ 526, 6 May 2011.

social services. TG made a claim for judicial review of this decision. Initially his claim was dismissed, the court holding that a child only became a 'looked after' child (accommodated under section 20) if accommodated by a local authority in exercise of its social services functions and that the functions of the YOT team were directed to working with offenders and not ordinarily to be considered as social services functions.

TG's appeal was successful. The Court of Appeal held that the social worker was 'the eyes and ears of the children and families division of the Children and Young Persons Service' and that her actions could be deemed the actions of social services; the case fell on the social services side of the dividing line as set out in *R (M) v Hammersmith & Fulham LBC*. TG was therefore entitled to services under the Leaving Care Act 2000.

The Court of Appeal also considered evidence provided by Shelter, who had written to all 144 local authorities in England (apart from Lambeth LBC who were the defendants) to request a copy of their procedures for joint working between housing and social services for homeless 16- to 17-year-olds. Only 29 produced a copy of their protocol and in eight of these cases the protocol was in draft form. The Court of Appeal held that

> ... the facts of the present case will reveal a serious absence of co-ordination in relation to the appellant's case within Lambeth, including between its housing department and its children's services department ... such absence of co-ordination was positively unlawful.'

Furthermore, the evidence supplied by Shelter should serve 'to advertise the need for all local authorities to take urgent steps to remedy any such failure'.[46]

19.43   It is clear then that a local authority cannot avoid the CA 1989 s20 duty simply by asserting or recording that it was or is assisting under section 17. In almost all cases where a child is homeless, the child will be a child in need and will require accommodation rather than assistance with accommodation. Exceptionally, there may be situations where a homeless child either is not a child in need or does not require accommodation to be provided but only help in obtaining accommodation (see Baroness Hale's judgment at [28] in *R (G) v*

---

46 [2011] EWCA Civ 526, Walker LJ at [5].

Southwark LBC, above, para 19.35). Similarly, while an authority may not side-step the duty by 'persuading' a child to agree to receiving section 17 assistance instead of being accommodated under section 20, there may be instances where a 16- or 17-year-old refuses to be assisted by social services, in which case the homelessness duty may apply.

Other ways of avoiding the section 20 duty for children under 16

Cared for by family or friends

19.44   There are two other ways in which a local authority may seek to label its actions or services in such a way as to avoid the CA 1989 s20 duty. Both concern situations in which the child (under the age of 16) is cared for by family or friends.

19.45   In relation to discharging duties to looked after children, the Children Act 1989 provides that, if possible, arrangements should be made for the child to live with his or her parents or those with parental responsibility. If this is not possible, the Act recommends a placement with relatives, friends or other people connected with the child. This is to be given preference over other placements (such as with local authority foster parents or in children's homes) provided such a placement will safeguard and promote the child's welfare.[47] Such carers must be approved as foster parents by the authority and provision is made for an interim approval to facilitate emergency placements.

19.46   Alternatively, informal arrangements may be made for the child to live with family and friends without becoming a looked after child. The Department of Education issued guidance in March 2011: *Family and Friends Care: Statutory Guidance for Local Authorities.* This states that when a placement with family and friends is made, the authority must decide whether the child still requires accommodation under CA 1989 s20 and, if it decides not, the child would cease to be a looked after child.[48]

---

47   The provisions as to how an authority should provide accommodation and maintenance for looked after children are now found in CA 1989 s22A which replaced s23 as of 1 September 2009.

48   Paras 2.13 and 2.19. The guidance can be downloaded from the DoE website: www.education.gov.uk/publications.

Private fostering

19.47   Another situation when the duty under CA 1989 s20 does not arise is when the child is privately fostered. This is when the parent or person with parental responsibility arranges for someone else, who is not a close relative, to care for the child. Local authorities should be informed of such arrangements in their area and have a duty to ensure that the arrangements are satisfactory.[49]

Not a 'looked after' child

19.48   In cases of both informal 'family and friends' arrangements and private fostering arrangements the child is not a 'looked after' child. This means that the authority is not responsible for the provision of accommodation and maintenance (usually by way of a fostering allowance) although it may give assistance under CA 1989 s17 if the child is a child in need. Furthermore, the child will not be entitled to Leaving Care Act 2000 support after the age of 18. Any assistance under section 17 would fall to be provided by the authority in whose area the child lives, which may be a different authority than the one involved in making the arrangements.

19.49   There is obvious scope for dispute about whether a child placed by the local authority with a carer other than the parent is in fact a looked after child and this issue has been examined by the courts in a number of cases.

> In *R (D) v Southwark LBC*[50] the Court of Appeal considered a situation in which the authority tried to argue either that the child had not been in its care but had been privately fostered or that any duty under CA 1989 s20 had ended when they made arrangements for her to live with a family friend. 'S' had lived on and off with her father since coming to the England at the age of 11. Her mother lived in Jamaica. For several periods of time S had lived with ED,

---

49   CA 1989 Part IX deals with local authorities' duties to privately fostered children.

50   [2007] EWCA Civ 182, 7 March 2007. See also *R (A) v Coventry CC* [2009] EWHC 34 (Admin), 22 January 2009 and *SA v Kent County Council* [2010] EWHC 848 (Admin), which reached the same conclusion as the Court of Appeal in *R (D) v Southwark LBC*. An appeal to the Court of Appeal is pending in the Kent case. All of these cases concern CA 1989 s23. The Children and Young Persons Act 2008 s8 repealed CA 1989 s23 and replaced it with ss22A–22G. Section 22C contains the same distinction between a 'placement' with family and friends and informal arrangements for the child to live with family and friends.

initially when ED had been one of her father's girlfriends. At school S alleged that her father had been violent to her and the school contacted social services, who sent a representative to the school and instructed it not to let the father take S. A meeting at the school was held when S expressed a desire to live with ED. ED was contacted by the social services representative by telephone and agreed that S could live with her. The representative then took S to ED's home and later contacted the mother by telephone who agreed to the arrangement. A dispute arose when ED sought financial assistance from Southwark LBC, which argued that it had no obligation to assist on the basis that this was a private fostering arrangement.

S thrived in the care of ED and just over a year after she went to live with her, ED applied for and obtained a residence order, which had the effect of giving ED parental responsibility for S. ED then issued a claim for judicial review seeking a declaration that for the 16-month period before the residence order was made S was looked after by Southwark under CA 1989 s20. Southwark argued that it had simply facilitated a private fostering arrangement, admitting that if this was so it had failed to comply with its duty to notify the local authority (Lambeth) of the arrangement. Alternatively, it argued that if it had been under a duty under section 20, the duty had ended when arrangements were made for S to live with ED.

The Court of Appeal held that:

We are prepared to accept that, in some circumstances, a private fostering arrangement might become available in such a way as to permit a local authority, which is on the verge of having to provide accommodation for a child, to 'side-step' that duty by helping to make a private fostering arrangement. However, it will be a question of fact as to whether that happens in any particular case. Usually, a private fostering arrangement will come about as the result of discussions between the proposed foster parent and either the child's parent(s) or a person with parental responsibility. But we accept that there might be occasions when a private arrangement is made without such direct contact. We accept that there might be cases in which the local authority plays a part in bringing about such an arrangement. However, where a local authority takes a major role in making arrangements for a child to be fostered, it is more likely to be concluded that, in doing so, it is exercising its powers and duties as a public authority pursuant to sections 20 and 23. If an authority wishes to play some role in making a private arrangement, it must make the nature of the arrangement plain to those involved. If the authority is facilitating a private arrangement, it must make it plain to the proposed foster parent that he or she must look to the parents or person with parental responsibility for financial support. The authority must explain that any financial assistance from public funds would be entirely a matter for the discretion of the local authority for the area in which the foster parent is living. Only on receipt of such information could the foster parent give informed consent to acceptance of the child under a private fostering agreement.'[51]

In this case the local authority had taken a central role in making the arrangements for S to live with ED and 'Those factors are far more consistent with the exercise of statutory power by Southwark than the facilitating of a private arrangement.'[52]

Key features of CA 1989 s20 – a summary

19.50
- The primary duty to accommodate homeless 16- and 17-year-olds is under CA 1989 s20.
- Social services and housing should operate joint protocols and working practices to ensure that children are assessed quickly under section 20 and are not passed from one department to another.
- If the conditions under section 20 exist, the section 20 duty may arise even if social services deny that they are acting under the section.
- The courts may declare that an authority was under a section 20 duty in the past with the consequence that a young person may be entitled to leaving care services and may have priority need as a care leaver.
- If the child does not come to the attention of social services the section 20 duty cannot arise even if the authority was wrong in the way they dealt with the child.
- A child does not have to agree to become a 'looked after child' for the section 20 duty to arise.
- But section 20 is not intended to be coercive and services cannot be forced on an unwilling young person.

51 [2007] EWCA Civ 182, Smith LJ at [49].
52 [2007] EWCA Civ 182, Smith LJ at [50].

Remedies: judicial review or complaint?

19.51 Decisions made by local authorities about services to children may be challenged by judicial review. Also, local authorities must operate a complaints procedure in accordance with the Children Act 1989 Representations Procedure (England) Regulations 2006.[53]

19.52 As a general rule, where the dispute is about the provision of a service, including accommodation, and the service is needed urgently or when the issue is the legal nature of the duty owed by social services, a claim for judicial review will be appropriate. However, the courts will not generally supervise or monitor the way social services discharge their duties and where the dispute is about the detail of service provision or about such matters as delay, failure to inform or consult, a complaint may be more appropriate.

19.53 Judicial review is a remedy of last resort and the court may refuse permission if it finds that another remedy, including the complaints procedure, should have been used instead. See *R (Cowl) v Plymouth*[54] (para 18.56).

> In *P, W, F and G*[55] Munby J was considering challenges to a local authority decision to offer accommodation to children under CA 1989 s17 not s20 and stated:
>
> > I am here concerned with an area of decision-making where Parliament has chosen to confer the relevant power on the County Council; not on the court or anyone else. It follows that we are here within the realm of public law, not private law. It likewise follows that the primary decision-maker is the County Council and not the court. The court's function in this type of dispute is essentially one of review – review of the County Council's decision, whatever it may be – rather than of primary decision-making. It is not the function of the court itself to come to a decision on the merits. The court is not concerned to come to its own assessment of what is in these children's best

---

53 SI No 1738 and Guidance issued by the Department for Education and Skills: *Getting the Best from Complaints, Social Care Complaints and Representations for Children, Young People and Others.* The guidance is issued under Local Authorities and Social Services Act 1970 s7 and therefore should be followed unless there are exceptional circumstances which justify a variation. The guidance can be downloaded from the DoE website: www.education.gov.uk/ publications.

54 [2001] EWCA Civ 1935, 14 December 2001.

55 [2004] EWHC 2027 (Admin), 19 August 2004.

interests. The court is concerned only to review the County Council's decisions, and that is not a review of the merits of the County Council's decisions but a review by reference to public law criteria ... Although I am, in a sense, concerned with the future welfare of very vulnerable children, I am not exercising a 'best interests' or 'welfare' jurisdiction, nor is it any part of my functions to monitor, regulate or police the performance by the County Council of its statutory functions on a continuing basis.[56]

However, in relation to the the nature of the authority's legal duty the judge held that it was not open to a local authority to choose to provide a package of support under CA 1989 s17 if the conditions under s20 were met.

Statutory complaints procedure

19.54   The complaints procedure for children has three stages:

Stage of complaint	Timescale
Stage 1: Informal resolution by the authority.	Within 10 working days of receiving the complaint, extendable by 10 working days in exceptional circumstances.
If the complainant is not satisfied, he/she can refer to Stage 2.	Within 20 working days.
Stage 2: Formal investigation. Investigation by an independent officer who submits a report to an adjudication officer. The adjudication officer is employed by the authority and responds to the report, indicating which findings are accepted and which rejected, and setting out what action the authority will take.	Deadline: within 25 working days, extendable, in complex cases to a maximum of 65 working days.
If the complainant is not satisfied, he or she can request a Stage 3 review panel.	Within 20 working days.

56 [2004] EWHC 2027 (Admin), at [32]–[33].

Stage of complaint	Timescale
Stage 3: Review panel. Consists of three people, of whom two must be independent. The role of the review panel is to consider whether the authority adequately investigated the complaint at Stage 2, not to re-investigate the complaint. The complainant has a right to attend the panel hearing and be accompanied by a representative who should not ordinarily be a lawyer.	The panel should be held within 30 working days. It should notify the complainant of its findings within 5 working days. The authority should notify the complainant of its response within 15 working days of receiving the panel's report.
If the complainant is not satisfied, complaint to Local Goverment Ombudsman.	Within 12 months of awareness of subject of complaint.

Local Government Ombudsman

19.55　If the complaint is not resolved satisfactorily by the local authority complaint may be made to the Local Government Ombudsman (LGO).

19.56　Paragraphs 2.93–2.96 describe in more detail how the LGO deals with complaints. In relation to complaints by or on behalf of homeless young people it should be noted that the LGO operates a fast track procedure for complaints from children and young persons (this means up to the age of 21, or 25 if the young person is disabled). In addition, where a person is homeless the LGO will accept a complaint even though the complaint has not been investigated by the authority first.

19.57　The LGO website: www.lgo.org.uk contains further information about how complaints are handled and reports on all the investigations it has undertaken.

CHAPTER 20

Community care: accommodation duties to migrants

> ## Key points
>
> • Access to most adult community care services is restricted for certain migrants.
> • Most asylum-seekers are provided with accommodation and support ('asylum support') by the Home Office.
> • If the asylum claim is refused, asylum support ends unless there are dependent children.
> • Local authorities are responsible for asylum-seekers with a need for care and attention.
> • Local authorities are also responsible for unaccompanied asylum-seeking children and there is no restriction on services provided directly to children.
> • People in the UK in breach of immigration law (including most failed asylum-seekers) are excluded from all community care services unless necessary to prevent a breach of human rights.
> • Asylum support is a 'residual' form of support for those who are destitute. When an authority is deciding if it owes an an accommodation duty under community care law the potential availability of asylum support must be ignored.

Introduction

20.1   Restrictions on access to housing and benefits and the prohibition on employment[1] means that many migrants, including failed asylum-seekers, face destitution in the UK. Many destitute migrants have turned to local authorities for help under the safety net provisions of community care law described in chapters 18 and 19. This has led to significant developments in the scope of community care law. This in turn has resulted in two major pieces of legislation which restrict community care duties to certain migrants:

• the Immigration and Asylum Act (IAA) 1999; and
• the Nationality, Immigration and Asylum Act (NIAA) 2002.

20.2   This chapter examines these restrictions and the legal tests that must be applied when a migrant seeks help from a social services

---

1   Where an application for asylum has been outstanding for 12 months (and any delay is not attributable to the asylum-seeker) an application can be made for permission to work. Permission will only be granted for work that is on the National Shortage Occupation List. This can be found on the website of the UK Border Agency: www.ukba.homeoffice.gov.uk. The current version is dated 16 March 2011.

authority. A flow chart is included in the appendix to illustrate how the tests should be applied.

Asylum-seekers: history of support arrangements

20.3   Before 1996 asylum-seekers could get homeless assistance and social security benefits while awaiting a decision on their asylum claims. In 1996 access to benefits and housing was restricted for large numbers of asylum-seekers. This led to destitute asylum-seekers requesting support from local authorities. It was clear that a duty was owed to families with children under the Children Act (CA) 1989. It was also established through the courts that an authority could owe a duty to destitute asylum-seekers without children under the National Assistance Act (NAA) 1948.

> *R v Hammersmith & Fulham LBC ex p M, R v Lambeth LBC ex p P, R v Westminster CC ex p A and R v Lambeth LBC ex p X ('M, P, A and X')*[2] concerned four single, healthy asylum-seekers who applied for assistance under NAA 1948 s21. As a result of the Asylum and Immigration Act 1996 they were not entitled to benefits or homeless assistance because they had applied for asylum after entering the UK. They argued that because of their destitution they were in need of care and attention not otherwise available to them.
>
> The Court of Appeal held that destitute asylum-seekers were 'in need of care and attention' and were therefore eligible for residential accommodation under section 21(1)(a). Furthermore, even if they were not yet in need of care and attention their destitution would lead to an almost certain future need, and it was not necessary for social services to wait for that point before providing assistance.

20.4   As a result of this judgment, between 1996 and 1999 local authorities had to provide support and accommodation for large numbers of destitute asylum-seekers. Others (who claimed asylum at the port of entry) were able to claim homeless assistance and social security benefits until their asylum claims were decided.

Asylum support

20.5   One of the central aims of the Immigration and Asylum Act 1999 was to transfer responsibility for the support and accommodation of

2   (1997–98) 1 CCLR 85, CA, 17 February 1997.

asylum-seekers to the Home Office. The Act created a system of support administered by a branch of the Home Office: the National Asylum Support Service (NASS). NASS was officially disbanded in 2006 and asylum support is now administered by the UK Border Agency (UKBA, itself a part of the Home Office). However, the system of asylum support is still commonly referred to as 'NASS support'. Asylum support (accommodation and subsistence) is provided to asylum-seekers and their households, usually in areas outside of London and the South East. If the asylum claim is refused this support ends unless there are dependent children in the household, in which case it continues until the family leaves the UK or any children reach the age of 18.[3] Under IAA 1999 s122 local authorities are prevented from providing housing and financial assistance under CA 1989 s17 to anyone who is entitled to asylum support. However, asylum support is provided only for adults and families. Unaccompanied asylum-seeking children are the responsibility of local authorities under the Chidren Act 1989. For adults, the Immigration and Asylum Act 1999 amended the National Assistance Act 1948 to exclude those who are 'subject to immigration control' and whose need arises solely from destitution, see para 20.11 below.

Immigration and Asylum Act 1999

Persons subject to immigration control

20.6   IAA 1999 s115(9) defines a 'person subject to immigration control' (PSIC) as a person who is not a national of an EEA State[4] and who:

- requires leave to enter or remain in the UK but does not have it;
- has leave to enter or remain in the UK which is subject to a condition that he or she does not have recourse to public funds;
- has leave to enter or remain in the UK given as a result of a maintenance undertaking; or

---

3   This is subject to a provision contained in the Asylum and Immigration (Treatment of Claimants etc) Act 2004 under which a family can be 'certified' as failing to make sufficient effort to leave the UK. If this happens, asylum support will terminate. As with most decisions regarding asylum support, an appeal lies to the First-tier Tribunal (Asylum Support).

4   The EEA refers to the European Economic Area. For a complete list of EEA countries, see para 14.38 above.

- continues to have leave to enter or remain in the United Kingdom
  only as a result of an appeal against a decision to vary, or to refuse
  to vary, any limited leave.

Asylum-seekers

20.7 Asylum-seekers are PSICs: they require leave to enter or remain in
the UK. Temporary admission is often granted to asylum-seekers
pending a decision. Temporary admission is not leave to enter but is
an alternative to detention. Until a decision is made on the asylum
claim an asylum-seeker is in the UK lawfully but is nevertheless a
PSIC.[5]

20.8 If the claim for asylum is refused and no leave granted, the legality
of the person's presence in the UK will depend on whether the application for asylum was made 'on entry' or 'in country' (after entry)
into the UK. An asylum-seeker who claimed asylum after entering
the UK unlawfully will be in the UK in breach of immigration law
after the claim has been refused and all appeal rights exhausted. This
is relevant if the person seeks social services assistance as a 'failed
asylum-seeker' (see paras 20.27–20.29 below).

No recourse to public funds

20.9 Under the Immigration Rules people can be granted leave to stay in
the UK for limited periods under various categories, such as visitor,
student or spouse.[6] For most of these categories, leave is only granted
on the basis that the person will be supported and accommodated
without 'recourse to public funds'.[7] The condition therefore applies
to most forms of leave. It is not applied to refugees, asylum-seekers
or their dependants.

---

5 Persons subject to immigration control (as defined under IAA 1999 s115, see
  para 20.6) are also excluded from social security benefits including housing
  benefit.
6 A spouse will initially be granted leave for a limited period of time and, at
  the end of that period, indefinite leave to remain should be granted provided
  the marriage still subsists, and, since November 2010, subject to passing an
  English language test.
7 'Public funds' do not include assistance under community care duties, such as
  under NAA 1948 and CA 1989. It does include homeless assistance and social
  security benefits. A leaflet issued by the Home Office: *No recourse to public
  funds* lists all of the prescribed funds and can be downloaded from: www.bia.
  homeoffice.gov.uk.

Maintenance undertakings

20.10   These are generally required when an application is made for a dependent relative (other than spouse and children) to join family members in the UK. Such people are normally granted indefinite leave to remain and it is not possible for such leave to be conditional on having no recourse to public funds. Therefore the Home Office usually requires that a nominated 'sponsor' offer an undertaking to be responsible for supporting the applicant in the UK. This must be a formal written undertaking.

National Assistance Act 1948 s21 and PSIC

20.11   In relation to a PSIC, as defined in para 20.6, the duty under the National Assistance Act 1948 is restricted so that such a person may not be provided with residential accommodation under NAA 1948 s21(1A) if his or her need for care and attention has arisen solely:

(a) because he or she is destitute, or

(b) because of the physical effects, or anticipated physical effects, of his being destitute.[8]

20.12   The National Health Service Act 1977 and the Health Services and Public Health Act 1968 have also been amended in the same way. However, these Acts concern duties to those who are elderly or ill and whose need is less likely to be caused solely by destitution.

Need arising solely from destitution

20.13   In a number of cases the courts have considered the question of whether the need for care and attention has arisen solely from destitution.

> In *R v Wandsworth LBC ex p O* and *R v Leicester CC ex p Bhikha*[9] the claimants were persons subject to immigration control, as defined in IAA 1999 s115. Mrs O had serious mental health problems and Mr B was suffering from cancer. The local authorities argued that they could not provide services under NAA 1948 s21 because the applicants' need arose solely from destitution.

8   NAA 1948 s21(1A).
9   (2000) 3 CCLR 237, CA.

> The court rejected this, holding that if an applicant has a need for care and attention made more acute by something other than destitution then a duty arises which is not excluded because of a person's immigration status.

20.14 The test set out in *O* and *Bhikha* was subsequently confirmed by the House of Lords.

> In *Westminster CC v NASS*[10] the applicant was an asylum-seeker who had spinal cancer, used a wheelchair and needed assistance with transfers and with personal care. She lived with her 13-year-old daughter, and needed regular hospital treatment. Westminster contended that NASS should accommodate and provide financial support while the council would provide the necessary community care services.
>
> The House of Lords upheld NASS's argument that Westminster was responsible for providing accommodation and support as well as community care services under NAA 1948 s21. It was held that Parliament must have intended local authorities to retain responsibility for some asylum-seekers. Lord Hoffmann stated that the Asylum and Immigration Act 1996 created two distinct classes of asylum-seekers, the 'able bodied destitute' and the 'infirm destitute'. The infirm destitutes' need for care and attention arises 'because they are infirm as well as because they are destitute'. It was acknowledged that, if they were not asylum-seekers, section 21 would not be needed because accommodation would be provided under the housing legislation. However NAA 1948 s21(1A) is not stating that the need for *accommodation* must not arise solely due to destitution.

20.15 A person who is destitute and who has a need for care and attention may be entitled to accommodation under NAA 1948 even though the level of need is not high.

> In *R on the application of Mani v Lambeth LBC*[11] the applicant was also an asylum-seeker. He had a leg abnormality and required some help with housework and heavy shopping. He also had a history of mental health difficulties.

10 [2002] 1 WLR 2956, HL, 17 October 2002.
11 [2003] EWCA Civ 836, 9 July 2003.

> The Court of Appeal confirmed the test set out in *O* and *Bhikha*, and found that the applicant came within NAA 1948 s21. The fact that he would probably not have a need for care and attention if he were not an asylum-seeker (because he would be housed) did not disentitle him. On the contrary, the fact that he is an asylum-seeker means that care and attention 'is not otherwise available' to him. As in *Westminster v NASS* (see para 20.14), this meant that the local authority and not NASS were responsible for providing support and accommodation, under section 21.

20.16   Moreover, if a person seeking accommodation under NAA 1948 s21 is a destitute asylum-seeker or failed asylum-seeker, the authorities' usual 'eligibility criteria' set under the *Fair Access to Care Services* (FACS) guidance do not apply.[12]

> In *R on the application of N v Lambeth LBC*[13] the applicant had been provided with accommodation and support by the local authority for several years. Her appeals against the refusal of leave to remain in the UK had been exhausted in the UK courts but she was awaiting the outcome of an application to the European Court of Human Rights. The authority re-assessed her needs under its eligibility criteria and decided that they fell into the moderate and low bands. As the authority only provided for substantial or critical needs, it proposed to withdraw the services. N sought judicial review of the decision.
>
> The court held that the decision was unlawful because the authority had applied the wrong test. Walker J held:
>
>> There is ... nothing in the authorities to suggest that it is appropriate for the defendant to treat eligibility criteria formulated in accordance with [FACS] as eligibility criteria which answer the statutory question posed by section 21 of the 1948 Act.[14]

20.17   In all cases, however, there must be a need for care and attention. A person who has no such need but who has a health problem for which NHS treatment is available is not entitled to accommodation and support under the National Assistance Act 1948.

---

12 See para 18.40 above.
13 [2006] EWHC 3427 (Admin), 20 December 2006.
14 [2006] EWHC 3427 (Admin), at [60].

In *R on the application of M v Slough BC*[15] the House of Lords
considered the test in relation to a man who was HIV positive
but was taking medication and was physically well. He needed
continuing medical treatment and a fridge to store his medication.
The House of Lords held that, on the facts, M's needs did not
amount to a need for care and attention. The need for care and
attention was more than a need for accommodation. It meant a need
to be 'looked after' which meant doing something for the person
that the person could not do for him or herself. It did not matter that
if the person was housed the care and attention could be provided in
his or her home. But there had to be a need for care and attention (ie
looking after) as opposed to a need for medical care. Provided that
there was such a need the local authority should intervene before the
need became worse but the duty under NAA 1948 s21 did not arise if
there was no present need for care and attention.

20.18 Following *M v Slough* (above), many local authorities have sought to
refuse accommodation on the basis that the applicant did not have a
need for care and attention in the sense of a need to be 'looked after'
and the Court of Appeal has considered the issue in relation to an applicant who was blind and one who was suffering from depression.

In *R (Zarzour) v Hillingdon LBC*[16] Mr Zarzour was completely blind.
The local authority had assessed him as needing help with shopping
and laundry and with travelling safely outside, particularly when
in an unfamiliar area. It concluded, however, that this did not
constitute a need for care and attention. The authority decided that
the applicant's friends could continue to provide the assistance
they were currently providing and that accommodation would be
provided by NASS. On Mr Zarzour's claim for judicial review, the
court made a declaration that the authority was under an NAA 1948
s21 duty to accommodate.
  The Court of Appeal dismissed Hillingdon's appeal, holding that
Hillingdon's own assessment had established that Mr Zarzour had
a need for care and attention and, as was clear from *Westminster
v NASS*, above para 20.14, NASS support is intended to be
'residual' and would not be available to anyone who was entitled to
accommodation under section 21.

15 [2008] UKHL 52, 30 July 2008.
16 [2010] EWCA Civ 1529, 17 December 2009.

The Court of Appeal again considered the issue in *R (SL) v Westminster CC*[17] in relation to a failed asylum-seeker (who shortly before the hearing was in fact granted indefinite leave to remain in the UK). He had been diagnosed as suffering from depression and post-traumatic stress disorder and had received in-patient treatment. He was assessed by the community mental health team as needing continued support on discharge, including community support from a social worker and referrals for counselling and to a befriending service. The authority decided that this was not a need for care and attention and that it was not under an accommodation duty.

The Court of Appeal upheld SL's appeal, holding that: '... this court in *Mani* rejected the local authority's submission that care and attention in s21(1A) means "care and attention of a kind calling for the provision of residential accommodation".' While it was not the case that accommodation must be provided if 'it is reasonably required in order for care to be furnished in a way that fully meets the claimant's needs', the court approved the following test when asking whether there is a need for care and attention not otherwise available: 'care and attention is not otherwise available unless it would be reasonably practicable and efficacious to supply it without the provision of accommodation'.[18]

Disabled asylum-seekers with children

20.19   The local authority's duty to provide accommodation and support to a disabled asylum-seeker does not extend to the whole family. Where a parent is entitled to accommodation under NAA 1948 s21, the local authority must arrange for accommodation for the whole family but UKBA is responsible for paying for the children's support and a proportion of the accommodation costs.[19]

20.20   However, where it is the children of an asylum-seeker who are disabled, the responsibility for providing adequate accommodation and financial support falls on NASS.[20]

---

17   [2011] EWCA Civ 954, 10 August 2011.
18   [2011] EWCA Civ 954, Laws LJ at [39].
19   See *R on the application of O v Haringey LBC and Secretary of State for the Home Department* [2004] EWCA Civ 535, 4 May 2004.
20   *R on the application of A v NASS and Waltham Forest LBC* [2003] EWCA Civ 1473.

Failed asylum-seekers: section 4 support

20.21   In relation to failed asylum-seekers, The Immigration and Asylum Act 1999 also introduced a power to provide accommodation and support pending voluntary return or removal. This is referred to as 'section 4 support' (previously 'hard cases support') and is administered by the Home Office. To qualify for section 4 support the applicant must in all cases be destitute, or likely to become destitute within 14 days. Most section 4 support is provided outside London. It is available only if the failed asylum-seeker satisfies one of five criteria. These are:[21]

- the person is taking all reasonable steps to leave the UK;
- the person is unable to leave the UK by reason of a physical impediment to travel or for some other medical reason;
- the person is unable to leave the UK because, in the opinion of the secretary of state, there is currently no viable route of return available;
- the person has an outstanding application for judicial review of a decision in relation to his or her asylum claim; or
- the provision of accommodation is necessary to avoid a breach of the person's human rights.

20.22   In relation to failed asylum-seekers, issues often arise as to whether accommodation should be provided by a local authority under community care duties or by the Home Office under IAA 1999 s4. The courts have held, in relation to both the National Assistance Act 1948 and the Leaving Care Act 2000, that, where accommodation duties arise under those Acts, the authorities cannot take account of the availability of support under the Immigration and Asylum Act 1999 (under both section 95 and section 4) because asylum support is a residual form of support, available only to the destitute.[22]

---

21 See IAA 1999 s4 and Asylum and Immigration (Provision of Accommodation to Failed Asylum-seekers) Regulations 2005 SI No 930.

22 See *Westminster CC v NASS* [2002] 1 WLR, HL, 17 October 2002, at para 20.14 above, *R (AW) v Croydon LBC* [2007] EWCA Civ 266, 4 April 2007, at para 20.28, and *R (SO) v Barking & Dagenham LBC* [2011] EWCA Civ 1101, 12 October 2010, see para 19.30.

Nationality, Immigration and Asylum Act 2002

20.23   In January 2003 the Nationality, Immigration and Asylum Act 2002 came into force and introduced further restrictions on access to community care services by migrants.

20.24   The Act goes further than the Immigration and Asylum Act 1999: for certain people from abroad a local authority is prohibited from offering a service, except to the extent necessary to avoid a breach of a person's human rights or a person's rights under the European treaties.[23]

Who is excluded from services: Schedule 3

20.25   The list of people is set out in NIAA 2002 Sch 3. They are therefore often referred to as 'Schedule 3 people' and are:

- a person who has refugee status in an EEA state (see para 14.38 above), and the dependants of such a person (para 4);
- a national of an EEA state, and the dependants of such a person (para 5);
- a person who was, but is no longer, an asylum-seeker and who has failed to co-operate with removal directions issued against him or her, and the dependants of such a person (para 6);
- a person who is in the UK in breach of the immigration laws and who is not an asylum-seeker, and the dependants of such a person (para 7); and
- a failed asylum-seeker who, because of having a dependent child in the household, is eligible for asylum support but who has been certified as having failed, without reasonable excuse, to take reasonable steps to leave the UK voluntarily (para 7A).[24]

EEA nationals

20.26   EEA nationals are now rarely affected by NIAA 2002 Sch 3 because an EEA national who is exercising rights under the EU Treaty has a right to reside and is therefore eligible for housing under Housing Act (HA) 1996 Parts VI and VII, see chapters 14 and 17.

---

23   NIAA 2002 s54 and Sch 3.
24   This category was introduced by the Immigration and Asylum (Treatment of Claimants etc) Act 2004 s9. The making of such certificates was piloted in certain areas in 2005 but was not widely implemented thereafter.

Failed asylum-seekers

20.27   NIAA 2002 Sch 3 para 6 refers to failed asylum-seekers who have failed to co-operate with removal directions. When removal directions are issued a formal notice is served informing the person of the date and time of travel. The notice gives a right of appeal. This should not be confused with Home Office letters that state that the person is 'subject to removal'.

20.28   Paragraph 7 deals with people in the UK in breach of immigration law. This includes some failed asylum-seekers.

> In *R on the application of AW v Croydon LBC* and *R (A, D and Y) v Hackney LBC*[25] the Court of Appeal considered the position of failed asylum-seekers who had made their claims for asylum after entering the UK ('in country'). No removal directions had been set.
>
> The court held that the applicants fell within NIAA 2002 Sch 3 para 7. Prior to making their claims for asylum they were in the UK in breach of immigration law. This was also the position after their claims for asylum were exhausted. The situation is different for a person who claimed asylum 'at port'. A 'port applicant' may be detained or granted 'temporary admission'. Someone who is detained or granted temporary admission is not deemed to have entered the UK and is therefore not in the UK in breach of immigration laws. A failed asylum-seeker who claimed asylum at port only falls within Schedule 3 if removal directions are set and he or she fails to comply with them, or if he or she fails to comply with reporting or other conditions.[26]
>
> The court also decided that failed asylum-seekers awaiting a Home Office decision on a potential fresh claim should be accommodated and supported by the local authority under NAA 1948 s21 if they had a need for care and attention. The court rejected the authority's arguments that they should be accommodated and supported by the Home Office under IAA 1999 s4.

20.29   In relation to a failed asylum-seeker it is therefore crucial to know whether the claim for asylum was made 'at port' or 'in country'. The majority of asylum claims are made in country.

---

25 [2007] EWCA Civ 266, 4 April 2007.

26 Temporary admission is usually given subject to a condition that the person reports regularly to a police station.

What services are excluded

20.30   NIAA 2002 Sch 3 para 1 provides that 'Schedule 3' persons shall not be eligible for support or assistance under the following provisions:

Provision	What kind of services
National Assistance Act 1948 ss21 and 29	Local authority provision of accommodation and other services to those in need of care and attention
Health Services and Public Health Act 1968 s45	Local authority provision for the welfare of the elderly
National Health Service Act 1977 s21 and Sch 8	Local authority provision of services at home to avoid hospital admission
Children Act 1989 ss17, 23C, 24A and 24B	Local authority provision (including accommodation) to adults, including care leavers
Housing Act 1996 ss188(3) and 204(4)	Local authority interim accommodation pending review or appeal in homelessness cases
Local Government Act 2000 s2	Local authority power to spend funds promoting well-being in the local area
Any provision of the Immigration and Asylum Act 1999 or the Nationality Immigration and Asylum Act 2002	Asylum support. This includes mainstream asylum support and support under section 4 of IAA 1999 (hard cases support)

20.31   The equivalent duties contained in Acts specific to Scotland and Northern Ireland are similarly excluded.

British citizens and children

20.32   NIAA 2002 Sch 3 does not prevent support or assistance being provided to:

- a British citizen; or
- a child.

20.33   The duties and powers in the Children Act 1989 that are excluded are those that may be exercised in relation to adults. NIAA 2002 Sch 3 does not prevent services being provided to a child directly, under CA 1989 s17 or s20.

The test: possible breach of human rights or European treaty rights

20.34 NIAA 2002 Sch 3 para 3 provides that the exercise of a power or duty is not prevented 'if, and to the extent that' it is necessary to avoid a breach of a person's rights under the European Convention on Human Rights (ECHR) or under the European Community treaties.

20.35 The most likely ECHR rights that may be breached by a refusal of assistance are:

- article 3: the right not to be subject to torture, inhuman and/or degrading treatment or punishment;
- article 8: the right to respect for private and family life;
- article 6: the right to a fair and public hearing.

20.36 See chapter 2 for an explanation of these rights.

20.37 The European treaties confer the right of free movement to European nationals in order to exercise such rights as working, studying and setting up in business in another member state, see paras 14.30–14.120.

Travel Regulations 2002[27]

20.38 Local authorities have the power to make travel arrangements and to provide temporary accommodation for some Schedule 3 people.[28] Local authorities can make travel arrangements for EEA nationals and their dependants and EEA refugees and their dependants (ie, help them to return to the member state from which they came). Accommodation may be provided pending travel to such people only if they have dependent children. Accommodation may also be provided to a person who is in the UK in breach of immigration law, provided that he or she has not failed to comply with removal directions. Again this is only possible for those who have dependent children. There is no power under the Nationality, Immigration and Asylum Act 2002 and the Travel Regs 2002 to give travel assistance to non-EEA nationals and refugees but such assistance can be given under the Local Government Act 2000 (see *R (Grant) v Lambeth LBC*, below, para 20.41).

27 Withholding and Withdrawal of Support (Travel Assistance and Temporary Accommodation) Regulations 2002 (Travel Regs 2002) SI No 3078.
28 NIAA 2002 Sch 3 paras 8, 9 and 10.

20.39   There is no power to provide accommodation for any person who has failed to comply with removal directions.

20.40   Schedule 3 requires a local authority to inform the Home Office of any person 'in the authority's area' who is or may be a Schedule 3 person.[29]

20.41   The statutory guidance[30] on the Travel Regs 2002 stresses that only 'temporary short-term accommodation' can be provided 'pending departure from the UK'.[31] In reality, however, many people with outstanding applications to UKBA wait for years before a decision is made by UKBA and during that time may be excluded from housing, benefits and employment.

The Court of Appeal considered this issue in *R on the application of Grant v Lambeth LBC*.[32] The applicant was a Jamaican national in the UK unlawfully. She was awaiting the outcome of an application for leave to remain in the UK. Having become homeless with her three children she sought help from the local authority under the Children Act 1989. The local authority concluded that NIAA 2002 Sch 3 prohibited them from providing support under CA 1989 s17 and that a return to Jamaica was in the family's best interests. Ms Grant argued that the local authority were obliged to provide accommodation until her application for leave to remain was determined, and, if refused, until removal directions were set. Lambeth argued that any duty to accommodate was only up to the point that Ms Grant left the UK voluntarily and proposed to give financial assistance to enable her to do so under the Local Government Act (LGA) 2000 s2.

The Court of Appeal held that the local authority's decision was lawful: it was entitled to use the powers under LGA 2000 s2 to assist her to return to Jamaica. The Travel Regs 2002 provided a *power* to provide temporary accommodation but there was no *duty* to exercise the power, except to the extent necessary to avoid a breach of rights under the European Convention on Human Rights (ECHR). The authority was therefore entitled to use the powers under section 2 to assist with travel so as to avoid a breach of ECHR rights.

29   NIAA 2002 Sch 3 para 14.
30   NIAA 2002 s54 and Sch 3 and the Withholding and Withdrawal of Support (Travel Assistance and Temporary Accommodation) Regulations 2002, Guidance to Local Authorities and Housing Authorities.
31   Guidance (see note 30), para 28.
32   [2004] EWCA Civ 1711, 17 June 2004.

20.42   Therefore, a local authority may offer to pay for a person to travel to their country of origin outside the EEA using its powers under the Local Government Act 2000. If the person has dependent children, temporary accommodation may be arranged pending travel. An authority must, however, be satisfied that such a course of action would not mean that a person's human rights were breached.

20.43   It should be noted that in *Grant* the court was focusing on the local authority's powers and duties under NIAA 2002 Sch 3 and the Travel Regs 2002. Ms Grant's case was not argued on the basis of the family's rights under ECHR article 8. In a number of subsequent cases the courts have held that, where a person has an outstanding immigration application which relies on article 8, it would be a breach of the person's ECHR rights to refuse support if that would mean that he or she would be forced to leave the UK.

> In *R on the application of Binomugisha v Southwark LBC*[33] the applicant had been in the care of the local authority as an asylum-seeking child. As an adult he suffered mental health problems and the authority therefore had potential duties to provide accommodation both under the Leaving Care Act 2000 and the National Assistance Act 1948. Although his asylum claim had been refused, Mr Binomugishu had a pending application for leave to remain relying on article 8 of ECHR. The authority carried out a 'human rights assessment' to decide whether services should be provided despite him being a 'Schedule 3 person'. Its assessment rejected the opinion of two psychiatrists and concluded that there would be no breach of article 8 if Mr Binomugishu were to return to Uganda.
>
> The court held that it is a task for the immigration authorities and not local authorities to make such decisions and that 'a local authority ... should only make its decisions on the basis that a person such as the claimant is free to go back to his own country if an outstanding human rights claim to remain in the UK is manifestly unfounded'.[34] The decision was quashed.

20.44   Furthermore, many claims for leave to remain relying on ECHR article 8 will involve not only the right of the adults who are migrants

33 [2006] EWHC 2254 (Admin), 18 September 2006.
34 [2006] EWHC 2254 (Admin), Andrew Nicol QC at [13]. See also *R on the application of PB v Haringey LBC and Others* [2006] EWHC 2255 (Admin), 18 September 2006.

but the rights of their children who may have lived in the UK for years, often having been born in the UK.

> In *R (Clue) v Birmingham CC*[35] the applicant had been in the UK since 2000. She had four children, three of whom had been born in the UK. She applied for indefinite leave to remain under the 'seven year policy', which at the time was that leave would be granted save in exceptional circumstances where children had resided in the UK for at least seven years. The Immigration Rules also provided that if the person left the UK before a decision was made his or her application would be treated as withdrawn (although there was a discretion to continue to consider the application). Until the application was determined (which in the event took exactly two years) Ms Clue was in the UK in breach of immigration law and therefore fell within NIAA 2002 Sch 3. Following the breakdown of her relationship with the father of the three youngest children she applied to Birmingham for support and accommodation. The council refused support under CA 1989 s17 but offered financial assistance for the family to return to Jamaica. Its human rights assessment concluded that because the children were not in contact with their father or his family there would be no breach of their rights under article 8 because they could enjoy family life in Jamaica.
>
> The Court of Appeal held that this was unlawful: 'when applying Schedule 3, a local authority should not consider the merits of an outstanding application for leave to remain. It is required only to be satisfied that the application is not "obviously hopeless and abusive".'

20.45　So, where a person has an outstanding immigration application that is not 'manifestly unfounded' or 'obviously hopeless and abusive' an authority will usually be bound to provide support and accommodation under one of the community care duties, despite the person falling under Schedule 3. It should also be noted that the independent human rights of children whose parents are in the UK unlawfully have recently been given greater prominence: see *ZH (Tanzania) v Secretary of State for the Home Department*,[36] discussed at para 2.62.

20.46　　The appendix to this chapter contains a flow chart for assessing the relevant tests for a person whose immigration status means that a community care duties may be limited.

35 [2010] EWCA Civ 460.
36 *ZH (Tanzania) v Secretary of State for the Home Department* [2011] UKSC 4, 4 February 2011.

APPENDIX

Adults seeking support and accommodation from social services

Applying tests under Immigration and Asylum Act 1999 (1999 Act) and Nationality, Immigration and Asylum Act 2002 (2002 Act)

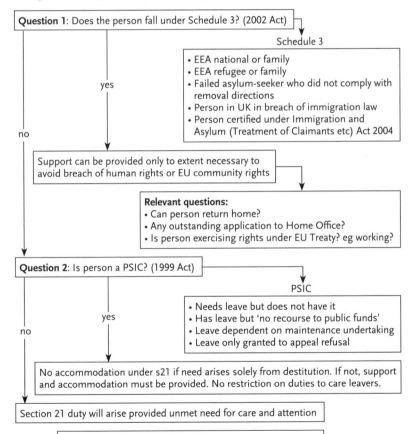

Question 1: Does the person fall under Schedule 3? (2002 Act)

Schedule 3

- EEA national or family
- EEA refugee or family
- Failed asylum-seeker who did not comply with removal directions
- Person in UK in breach of immigration law
- Person certified under Immigration and Asylum (Treatment of Claimants etc) Act 2004

yes

no

Support can be provided only to extent necessary to avoid breach of human rights or EU community rights

Relevant questions:
- Can person return home?
- Any outstanding application to Home Office?
- Is person exercising rights under EU Treaty? eg working?

Question 2: Is person a PSIC? (1999 Act)

PSIC

- Needs leave but does not have it
- Has leave but 'no recourse to public funds'
- Leave dependent on maintenance undertaking
- Leave only granted to appeal refusal

yes

no

No accommodation under s21 if need arises solely from destitution. If not, support and accommodation must be provided. No restriction on duties to care leavers.

Section 21 duty will arise provided unmet need for care and attention

NB Asylum-seekers and failed asylum-seekers
Asylum-seekers do not have leave, so are PSIC
Failed asylum-seekers may be Schedule 3 or PSIC:
- If claimed asylum in-country, will be Schedule 3
- If claimed on entry will be PSIC (unless failed to comply with removal directions, in which case will be Schedule 3)

Housing improvement and adaptation

Key points

- Mandatory grants for home improvements are no longer available. Instead local authorities have a wide discretion as to how assistance will be given to improve private sector accommodation. This may include giving grants and loans. Authorities must publish their policies.
- Disabled facilities grants (DFGs) remain mandatory for works costing up to £30,000 (£36,000 in Wales). Discretionary grants may be awarded for costs above this limit.
- There are clear statutory provisions, including time limits, regarding local authority decision-making in relation to DFGs. Despite this, many applicants face delays and other difficulties in obtaining grants.
- To qualify for a mandatory grant the works must be for a specified purpose to make the premises more suitable for the disabled person.
- The works must also be 'necessary and appropriate' to achieve the specified purpose and it must be 'reasonable and practicable' to carry out the works in the particular dwelling.
- DFGs are means-tested for adults but not where the disabled occupant is under the age of 19.
- DFGs are administered by local housing authorities.
- Adaptations may also be carried out by social services under the Chronically Sick and Disabled Persons Act 1970.

Housing improvement: grants and assistance

21.1   Until 2002 discretionary and mandatory grants administered by local authorities were available for the improvement of private dwellings. The Regulatory Reform (Housing Assistance) (England & Wales) Order 2002[1] ('2002 Order') replaced the system of discretionary and mandatory grants with a new scheme which gives to local authorities a general power to improve housing.

21.2   Under the 2002 Order local authorities may, for the purpose of improving living conditions in their area, give financial assistance to enable a person to:[2]

1 SI No 1860.
2 2002 Order para 3(1).

- acquire living accommodation, in or out of the area;
- adapt or improve living accommodation;
- repair living accommodation;
- demolish buildings comprising or including living accommodation; and
- where buildings have been demolished, construct replacement living accommodation.

21.3 The 2002 Order requires every authority to adopt and publish its policy as to how it intends to use these powers for the renewal of the private sector. Most authorities publish their policies on their websites and they are commonly referred to as private sector housing and/or renewal strategies.

Home improvement grants

21.4 A local authority must have a policy about home improvement grants. The policy may be available on the authority's website. If not, a copy should be requested from the authority.

21.5 Under the 2002 Order authorities have a wide discretion as to how to exercise their powers to improve standards in private sector accommodation. It is common for authorities to limit the availability of assistance by providing that grants are available only:

- to vulnerable groups, such as the elderly or disabled;
- for specific works, such as works to improve heating systems and thermal insulation;
- to those on means-tested benefits; and
- to owner-occupiers and not to tenants.

21.6 In addition to grants, some local authorities operate schemes whereby loans are made available through equity release schemes run by not-for-profit companies, such as the Home Improvement Trust.

21.7 While local authorities have a wide discretion about how much assistance they give to improve and repair private sector homes, they must act lawfully in devising and operating their policies, see paras 2.8–2.26.

Disabled facilities grants

21.8 The system of grants for disabled adaptations, known as disabled facilities grants (DFGs), is set out in the Housing Grants, Construction and Regeneration Act (HGCRA) 1996 ss19–24.[3] The DFG scheme provides that:

- grants up to a certain level are mandatory provided the necessary conditions are met; and
- decisions and payments must be made within a prescribed time period.

21.9   Despite the clear terms of HGCRA 1996 the administration of DFGs is problematic. This is reflected in the high proportion of Ombudsman complaints about DFGs. This chapter outlines the criteria for DFGs, examines some common problems and describes how decisions may be challenged.

Who can apply for a grant

21.10   An application may be made by:[4]

- an owner (or a person about to become an owner);[5]
- a tenant;[6]
- a licensee;
- an occupier of a houseboat or park home.

Qualifying conditions

21.11   To qualify for a mandatory grant the following conditions must be met (paras 21.12–21.21).

Disabled occupant

21.12   There must be a disabled occupant. This means:[7]

- a person whose sight, hearing or speech is substantially impaired;
- a person who has a mental disorder or impairment of any kind; or
- a person who is physically substantially disabled by illness, injury or impairment present since birth or otherwise.

---

3   The Act previously also set out the provisions for home improvement and regeneration grants but those provisions were repealed by the 2002 Order.
4   HGCRA 1996 s19.
5   This includes a landlord applying for the benefit of a disabled tenant.
6   This includes introductory tenants, agricultural occupiers and employees occupying tied accommodation: HGCRA 1996 s9(5).
7   HGCRA 1996 s100.

21.13 The following are taken as being disabled for the purpose of a DFG:

- any adult for whom social services have made welfare arrangements under section 29(1) of the National Assistance Act (NAA) 1948 or who is registered by the authority as such;[8]
- any child who is, in the opinion of social services, a disabled child as defined in the Children Act (CA) 1989, or who is registered as such.[9]

Only or main home

21.14 The disabled occupant must live in the premises as his or her only or main residence and it must be intended that he or she should do so for at least five years.[10]

Purpose of the works

21.15 The purpose of the works must one or more of the following:[11]

- to facilitate access by the disabled occupant to and from the dwelling or building;
- to make the dwelling or building safe for the disabled occupant and other persons residing with him or her;
- to facilitate access by the disabled occupant to the main family room, or to a bedroom, or to provide such a room;
- to facilitate access by the disabled occupant to a lavatory, a room with a bath or shower or wash-hand basin, or to provide such a room or facilities;
- to facilitate the preparation and cooking of food by the disabled occupant;
- to improve or install a heating system to meet the needs of the disabled occupant;
- to facilitate the use by the disabled occupant of power, light or heat by altering the position of the controls; or
- to facilitate access and movement by the disabled occupant around the dwelling to enable him or her to care for another person who is normally resident and in need of such care.

21.16 For an applicant to qualify for a mandatory grant the proposed works must be for one of the above purposes. However, a discretionary

8 See para 18.13 above.
9 See para 19.5 above.
10 HGCRA 1996 s22(2).
11 HGCRA 1996 s23(1).

grant may be awarded to make the dwelling more suitable generally for the disabled occupant.[12]

Need and practicality of works

21.17   The authority must also be satisfied that:[13]

- the proposed works are 'necessary and appropriate' to meet the needs of the disabled occupant; and
- 'it is reasonable and practicable' to carry out the works having regard to the age and condition of the dwelling or building.

21.18   In deciding whether the works are necessary and appropriate the authority must consult social services.[14] Most local authorities will obtain an occupational therapist's report to advise on whether the proposed adaptations will meet the disabled person's needs, increase independence and reduce the requirement for care or support.

21.19   The authority's resources cannot be taken into account in deciding whether the works are necessary or appropriate.[15]

21.20   To decide whether the works are 'reasonable and practicable' the authority will usually rely on an assessment by its own building experts.

21.21   The question of whether the purpose of the works falls into one of the specified categories is separate from the question of whether they are necessary and appropriate to meet the disabled occupant's need.

In *R on the application of B v Calderdale MBC*[16] the claimant was the father of four children, the eldest of whom (D) was autistic. The family lived in a three-bedroom house owned by a housing association. D shared a bedroom with his younger brother and was uncontrollably aggressive towards him, frightening him while he slept and attacking him when they were in the bedroom together. The claimant applied for a DFG to convert the loft into a separate bedroom for D. The occupational therapy reports obtained suggested that an extra bedroom would be helpful and would enable D to feel safe and to enable his condition to be managed more effectively. The authority refused the application, holding that the evidence related to D's behaviour generally rather than the physical

---

12   HGCRA 1996 s23(2).
13   HGCRA 1996 s24(3)(a) and (b).
14   HGCRA 1996 s24(3).
15   *R v Birmingham CC ex p Mohammed* [1999] 1 WLR 33.
16   [2004] EWCA Civ 134, 4 February 2004.

layout of the premises or the number of bedrooms. It decided that the works proposed did not fall within the criteria for a mandatory grant and the application was refused. The claimant sought judicial review of the decision.

Initially the application was dismissed: it was held that in deciding whether the purpose of the works was to make 'the dwelling ... safe for the disabled occupant and other persons residing with him' under HGCRA 1996 s23(1)(b), the authority was entitled to take account of the evidence that D's behavioural problems went beyond the issue of the shared bedroom and that his behaviour outside the home had improved. The decision was within the council's discretion on the basis of the material before it. The claimant appealed.

The Court of Appeal held that the correct approach was to separate the two questions: (1) whether the purpose of the proposed works fell within the criteria for a mandatory grant; and (2) whether the proposed works were necessary and appropriate to meet the needs of the disabled occupant. The council had erred in considering both questions at the same time. On the basis of the facts known to the council the case clearly fell within section 23(1): the purpose of providing a separate bedroom for D was to make the dwelling as safe as was reasonably practicable for D, and, more particularly, for his younger brother. The decision was quashed and it was directed that the council must go on to decide whether a loft conversion was necessary and appropriate to meet D's needs, including the need not to harm his brother. This was a matter for the council's judgment.

The means test

21.22 For disabled adults a financial assessment is carried out to determine eligibility.[17] However, if the disabled occupant is under the age of 19 there is no means test. Certain benefits such as disability living allowance and income support are generally ignored. Savings are taken into account but the first £6,000 is disregarded. The assessment does not take account of actual outgoings but makes standard deductions for items of expenditure, including rent or mortgage payments. The assessment may result in a decision that a contribution is payable. Above a certain level the contribution is 100 per cent.

17 HGCRA 1996 s30.

The maximum grant

21.23   The current maximum mandatory award is £30,000 in England and £36,000 in Wales.[18] If a person qualifies for a mandatory grant the authority *must* award a sum up to this amount and has a discretion to award a grant in excess of these limits where the works will cost more than the maximum. The grant may be paid in full on completion or by instalments.[19]

21.24   Where an authority does not exercise its discretion to pay a grant in excess of the statutory limit a person may be able to obtain a loan from the Home Improvement Trust to fund the excess, see para 21.6 above.

How to apply

21.25   Information on how to apply for a grant should be available on the local authority's website. General information is given on the 'Directgov' website[20] which should provide a link to the part of each local authority's website dealing with DFGs. Until October 2010 there was a prescribed form on which applications were made. Given the reluctance of many local authorities to deal with applications, advisers may experience difficulties in ensuring that an authority confirms that an application has been received. Unless the authority has its own application form, a letter stating clearly that it is an application and accompanied by the relevant documentation (see below, para 21.26) should be sufficient. Given the important deadlines that run from the date of the application it will be important to confirm receipt by the authority.

21.26   Applications must be accompanied by the relevant certificates.[21] An owner-occupier who applies must provide an owner's certificate and a tenant who applies must provide a 'tenant's certificate' confirming that it is intended that the disabled occupant will live in the dwelling as his or her only or main residence for at least five years. Unless the authority considers it unreasonable, where a tenant applies, an owner's certificate must also be provided from the landlord confirming his or her interest.

18   Disabled Facilities Grants (Maximum Amounts and Additional Purposes) (England) Order 2008 SI No 1189; Disabled Facilities Grants (Maximum Amounts and Additional Purposes) (Wales) Order 2008 SI No 2370.
19   HGCRA 1996 s35.
20   www.direct.gov.uk/en/DisabledPeople/HomeAndHousingOptions.
21   HGCRA 1996 ss19 and 22.

Home improvement agencies

21.27 Home improvement agencies (HIAs) assist homeowners and private sector tenants who are older or disabled to remain in their own home, living independently. HIAs advise on improvements and adaptations and help people to apply for grants or loans to carry out works. They also help identify reputable local contractors, oversee works and arrange payments. Many agencies also run schemes to provide handypersons to carry out small repairs or specific schemes to improve safety and security in the home, to improve energy efficiency or make homes suitable for people to return to after a stay in hospital.

21.28 HIAs are usually small, locally based not-for-profit organisations. Some are local authority agencies. Others are independent organisations and are often managed by a housing association or charity. They are often called 'care and repair' or 'staying put' agencies.

21.29 'Foundations' is the national co-ordinating body for HIAs in England and is appointed by the Department for Communities and Local Government (DCLG) to provide advice, training and support to HIA staff and managing organisations. A full list of all HIAs in England is contained on the Foundations website: www.foundations.uk.com.

Decisions and time limits

21.30 A local authority must notify an applicant in writing whether the application has been approved or refused as soon as reasonably practicable and, in any event, not later than six months after the date of the application.[22] If the application is approved, the decision letter must specify the works that are eligible for a grant and the amount of grant to be paid. If the application is refused, reasons must be given.[23]

21.31 Delays in dealing with applications are common. If action is to be taken to challenge delay, advisers must ensure that the application has been properly made and supported by the relevant certificates, see paras 21.25–21.26 above. Authorities 'shall not entertain' an application that is not accompanied by the relevant 'certificates'.[24]

21.32 Payment of the grant should be made no later than 12 months from the date of the application.[25]

22 HGCRA 1996 s34(1).
23 HGCRA 1996 s34(4).
24 HGCRA 1996 ss19 and 22.
25 HGCRA 1996 s36.

Common problems

Delays

21.33   Despite the fact that grants are mandatory and that there is a statutory time limit for decision-making, obtaining a DFG is often difficult and delays are common. In practice, it is often the case that the delay occurs before a completed application is submitted. The first step in obtaining a DFG will usually to be to request an assessment from social services (see para 18.33). The fact that authorities must carry out a means assessment and must take advice from social services and building experts about the proposed works means that decisions are rarely made within the six-month time limit.

21.34   Research conducted in 2005 by Bristol University revealed that the average delay before an occupational therapist assessment was completed in relation to a DFG was almost 20 weeks.[26] Further delays in the drawing up of plans, the obtaining of planning permission and building regulation approval are also common. The fact that applicants may have to fund part of the cost may also add to the delay if the funds must be raised by the household.

Funding

21.35   Central government funding for DFGs does not meet the full cost to local authorities, which means that many local authorities struggle to find the funding to meet their part of the costs.[27] Furthermore, funding for adaptations for those occupying local authority owned accommodation is not available from the central government grant but must be paid for from the authority's housing budget. Most local authorities therefore do not actively encourage applications.

Limits on maximum grant

21.36   The maximum mandatory grant of £30,000 may be insufficient to pay for substantial adaptations, such as an extension to a dwelling, which may be required for those with the most severe disabilities.

---

26   See *Reviewing the Disabled Facilities Grant Programme*, Bristol University, 2005. It is likely that the current delays are even longer.

27   In 2003/04, 47 per cent of all housing authorities had insufficient capital to meet valid DFG applications.

Private sector tenants – lack of security

21.37   Given that most private sector tenants have security of tenure for only the first six months of a tenancy, it will be difficult to establish that the disabled occupier intends to remain in the accommodation for at least five years. Moreover, a private landlord may be unwilling to consent to adaptations. A landlord does, however, have an obligation to make reasonable adjustments to premises, see paras 7.159–7.160.

Future proposals

21.38   In February 2008 the DCLG published *Disabled Facilities Grant – The Package of Changes to Modernise the Programme*.[28] Some of the proposed reforms, such as the increase in the maximum award from £25,000 to £30,000 (in England) and changes to the way means are assessed have already been implemented. However, given the current government's intention to reform local authority powers fundamentally through the Localism Act 2011, it is likely that in future local authorities will have greater discretion over the way DFGs are awarded.

Chronically Sick and Disabled Persons Act 1970

21.39   The Chronically Sick and Disabled Persons Act (CSDPA) 1970 lists a range of services that a local social services authority may be under a duty to provide in relation to a disabled person. The duty applies to both disabled adults and children. For the duty to arise the following conditions must be satisfied:

- the person must be disabled;[29]
- the person must be ordinarily resident in the area of the local authority; and
- the authority must be satisfied that it is necessary to make the arrangements to meet the person's needs.

21.40   Included in the list of services that may be provided under CSDPA 1970 to meet a disabled persons needs is:

28   Available as an archived publication on the website: www.communities.gov.uk.
29   This means persons who are blind, deaf or dumb or who suffer from mental disorder of any description or who are substantially and permanently handicapped by illness, injury or congenital deformity. See NAA 1948 s29 and CA 1989 s17(1).

... the provision of assistance for that person in arranging for the carrying out of any works of adaptation in his home or the provision of any additional facilities designed to secure his greater safety, comfort or convenience.[30]

21.41   Where an assessment of the needs of a disabled adult or child reveals a need for services under CSDPA 1970, the authority is under a duty to provide those services. An authority's duty to carry out an assessment is described at paras 18.33 and 19.15.

21.42   A social services authority may discharge the duty to 'assist' a disabled person in arranging for the carrying out of works of adaptation by assisting the person to apply for a DFG. However, there may be a delay in the application process, the application may be refused, or the DFG may not cover all of the necessary works. If this is the case, provided the social services authority is satisfied that the works are necessary to meet the disabled person's needs, it is under a duty to provide the services. See the Ombudsman complaint summarised at para 21.52 below.

21.43   In England minor adaptations that cost less than £1,000 should be provided free of charge.[31] In practice many local authority social services departments provide adaptations themselves if they cost less than £1,000 and provide assistance to apply for a DFG if the cost is likely to exceed this amount.

21.44   If services described in the CSDPA 1970 are provided by an authority for a disabled child, it is not open to the authority to maintain that the services are provided instead under the Children Act 1989.[32] The distinction is important since the courts have held that the duty to provide services under CSDPA 1970 is a specific enforceable duty but that the duty under CA 1989 s17 is a 'target duty': see para 19.9.

Means testing

21.45   There is no provision for local authorities to charge people for services provided under CSDPA 1970. However, it is not possible to avoid the means testing scheme under the DFG system by requesting that adaptations are carried out instead under the CSDPA 1970.

---

30 CSDPA 1970 s2(1)(e).
31 See the Community Care (Delayed Discharges etc) Act 2003 ss15 and 16.
32 *R v Bexley LBC ex p B* (2000) 3 CCLR 15, QBD.

In *R on the application of Spink v Wandsworth LBC*[33] it was held by the Court of Appeal that a local authority could decide that it was not satisfied that it was necessary to provide services for a disabled child under the CSDPA 1970 until it had been shown that, having regard to the parent's means, it was not reasonable for the parents to provide them.

21.46 Means testing does not now apply to adaptations for disabled children but the same principle will apply in relation to adaptations for adults.

Provision of equipment

21.47 In addition to adaptations, CSDPA 1970 s2 also provides for the provision of 'additional facilities' designed to secure the disabled person's 'greater safety, comfort or convenience'. Such facilities may include handrails, alarm systems and moveable baths.

Challenging decisions

21.48 Local authority decision-making is challenged principally by:
- judicial review proceedings; and
- formal complaints.

21.49 Both courses of action are described in more detail in chapter 2. The merits of judicial review and complaints in relation to social services are discussed at para 18.49.

21.50 One of the main causes of complaint in the administration of DFGs is delay. Some delay may be caused by the need for housing authorities to consult with social services, usually occupational therapists and building experts. Further delays may be caused by the need to obtain planning consent and building regulation approval for major works. However, the lack of funding for DFGs means that many authorities are reluctant to approve applications and several published Ombudsman investigations concern local authority procedures for dealing with DFGs. However, because the complaints procedure is itself very slow, advisers should consider an application for judicial review where an application has been made and the authority

33 [2005] EWCA Civ 302, 18 March 2005.

is delaying making a decision. Authorities should be reminded of the statutory time limits for decisions and payment and the duty to give reasons if an application is refused.

Judicial review

21.51   A claim for judicial review may be brought against an authority to:
- compel the authority to make a decision;
- give reasons for a negative decision; or
- challenge a refusal to award a grant, where it appears that the authority has applied the law wrongly.[34]

Local Government Ombudsman complaints

21.52   The following are examples of successful Ombudsman complaints concerning adaptations.

> *Ombudsman Complaint: 03/A/08718*
> The complaint was about the authority delaying making a decision, referring to possible start dates for works without informing the applicant that the authority might not fund the cost of works above £25,000 and deciding not to exercise its discretion to fund works above the mandatory limit without giving reasons. Following an appeal the authority decided to offer a final grant of £35,000 but this was three years after the applicant first applied for help and by then he had decided he could not afford to pay the non-funded costs and that he would move instead.
>
> The Ombudsman found that there had been maladministration because of the council's failure to advise the applicant about the policy on grants for extensions; to ensure adequate liaison between officers in processing the application; and to record reasons for the decision or to inform the applicant of the reasons.
>
> The Ombudsman recommended that the council should pay compensation of £2,000 because the applicant had spent two years longer than necessary in unsuitable accommodation; a £500 contribution to moving costs; and £150 for the applicant's time and trouble pursuing the complaint.

---

34 As in *R on the application of B v Calderdale*, see para 21.21 above.

Ombudsman Complaint: 05/C/13 157

A complaint was made by the husband of a woman who was seriously ill and profoundly disabled about the handling of a DFG application.

The Ombudsman found that the council had delayed in completing a financial assessment; had failed to review the grant section's position that a DFG could not be used to provide or retain a family room (which was wrong in law) and had failed to deal with the conflict between what was thought necessary by both the occupational therapist and the woman's husband, and what the grants section would fund. The council also failed to recognise its duties under CSDPA 1970 s2. As a result, for two years longer than necessary, the woman was confined to bed in the front living room and was unable to use a special wheelchair provided to relieve her pain and discomfort. She was unable to use a toilet, bath or shower and had to be strip washed by her carers. She was also unable to sit outside or with her family.

To remedy the injustice, the council agreed to pay £6,605 to the complainant; to establish a mechanism to resolve disputes about the adaptations required to meet a disabled person's needs; to ensure that all relevant officers were aware of the duty under CSDPA 1970 s2; and to produce a report about the lessons to be learnt from the complainant's experience and the changes it would make to its practice and procedures. Alternative accommodation was also identified which would be adapted to meet the woman's needs.

Civil proceedings

continued

Key points

- Most housing disputes are resolved in the civil courts, predominantly the county court. However, some housing disputes, including disputes about benefits and long leases, are dealt with by tribunals.
- The civil courts deal mainly with disputes between individuals, eg between a landlord and tenant. This includes disrepair and claims for possession.
- The civil courts also deal with challenges to the decisions of public bodies, including local authorities and government departments. Homeless appeals are dealt with by the county court and many housing decisions by public bodies can be challenged by judicial review in the High Court.
- A single set of procedural rules applies in both the county courts and the High Court: the Civil Procedure Rules (CPR).
- Fees must be paid to the court for starting a claim and at certain stages in the proceedings after the claim has been started.
- Legal aid is available for some civil claims, subject to financial eligibility and provided the claim has sufficient merit. Legal aid is not usually available for representation at tribunals.
- The general rule in the civil courts is that the unsuccessful party will be ordered to pay the legal costs of the successful party. However, legal aid provides a party with 'costs protection' which means that he or she does not usually have to pay the opponent's costs.
- The amount of legal costs that must be paid by one party to another is controlled by the court by way of assessment after the case has been decided. In some cases the costs recoverable are fixed or capped.
- After the court makes an order, the successful party may have to take further action to enforce the order.

The civil courts

22.1   The civil courts are distinct from the criminal courts in that they resolve disputes between individual legal persons (which may include a company or a public body such as a local authority). The criminal courts deal mostly with the prosecution by the state of individuals accused of committing criminal offences.

22.2   The civil courts comprise the county courts and the High Court. The civil division of the Court of Appeal hears appeals from the county court and the High Court. Appendix 1 to this chapter contains a diagram of the relationship between the various civil courts.

22.3   Housing litigation forms a substantial part of the business of the county court. It includes:

- possession proceedings;
- claims based on a landlord's failure to repair premises;
- claims based on unlawful eviction and harassment;
- homeless appeals;
- other disputes between landlords and tenants, for example, disputes about the rights of secure tenants and the recovery of deposits. The county court can make declarations, for example, to determine an occupier's status or the type of tenancy that has been granted if this is in dispute;
- applications for injunctions brought by local authorities and registered social landlords (RSLs) to restrain anti-social behaviour.

22.4   The jurisdiction of the county courts is local and possession claims must be brought in the court which covers the area where the premises are situated. Claims for money or other remedies may be started in any county court but it is advisable to bring such a claim in the court for the area in which the defendant lives or has its principal office.[1] The area covered by each county court is distinct from local authority boundaries. The court service website has a 'court finder' facility which indicates which court is responsible for a particular postcode. This can be accessed on www.hmcourts-service. gov.uk.

22.5   High value claims or claims that are complex may be brought in the High Court. Also, the High Court has exclusive jurisdiction for certain kinds of proceedings, including judicial review.

Organisation of the county courts

Judges

22.6   The county courts have two types of judges: district judges and circuit judges. In addition there are deputy district judges, who are usually lawyers who work part time as judges. District judges deal

---

1   A defendant may apply for the transfer of proceedings to his or her home court when filing a defence. If the claim is for a fixed amount this will automatically be done. Also, action to enforce court orders must usually be taken in the defendant's home court.

with most of the housing cases in the county court, including claims for possession. However, some housing cases can only be dealt with by a circuit judge. These include homeless appeals and most applications for committal for breach of injunctions.[2] Most long trials (more than one day) are heard by circuit judges. Circuit judges also deal with most appeals of decisions made by district judges. An appeal from the decision of a deputy district judge can be heard by a district judge.

Court staff

22.7   Much of the work of the county court is done not by the judges but by the court office staff. This includes the issuing of claims and bailiffs' warrants, the listing of hearings and the drawing up of orders. Most courts have different sections dealing with different stages of litigation, for example, issuing, listing and enforcement. When a claim is issued it is given a court reference number (the 'claim number') which is endorsed on all court documents. This must be quoted in all communications with the court.

Causes of action

22.8   To bring a claim in a civil court a claimant must have a recognised legal claim, known as a 'cause of action'. Furthermore, the claimant must be seeking some 'remedy' that the court is capable of granting, see paras 22.22–22.26.

22.9   Strictly speaking the term cause of action means the facts out of which the right to bring a legal action arises. However, the term is generally used to refer to a claim which is recognised in law as giving a person a right to sue.

22.10   In relation to housing litigation the relevant causes of action can be summarised as follows, see paras 22.11–22.21.

Breach of contract

22.11   A party to a contract has a legal right to compel the other party to comply with the contract and/or to be compensated if the contract is breached. The cause of action in such a claim is 'breach of contract'. In housing cases this includes:

2 See CPR Part 2, PD.

- tenants seeking compensation for disrepair and/or an order that a landlord carries out repairs;
- tenants seeking compensation for unlawful eviction and harassment and/or an order that the landlord allows them back into occupation and refrains from further harassment.

22.12   A landlord who claims that a tenant is in breach of the tenancy agreement could also seek compensation and/or an order restraining further breach. However, most landlords will instead claim possession, as one of the grounds for obtaining a possession order is that the tenant is in breach of the terms of the tenancy agreement.

Tort

22.13   Tort means a civil wrong which is independent of a contract. Tort is based on the principle that in certain situations a person has a duty to ensure that another person does not suffer harm or loss as a result of his or her actions. Some torts are 'common law' torts, recognised by the courts in previously decided cases. Other torts are 'statutory' torts set out in legislation. The torts which will commonly be alleged in housing cases are:

Common law torts

22.14   Nuisance and negligence are common law torts that may be alleged in cases involving harassment, unlawful eviction and disrepair.

Statutory torts

22.15   The Housing Act (HA) 1988 sets out the statutory tort of unlawful eviction for which damages are payable, calculated according to a statutory formula.

22.16   The Protection from Harassment Act 1997 created the statutory tort of harassment where a person is guilty of a course of conduct that causes another person alarm or distress.

22.17   In disrepair claims, the statutory torts set out in the Defective Premises Act 1972 and the Occupiers' Liability Acts 1957 and 1984 may be relied on.

22.18   All of these torts are discussed in more detail in chapters 8 and 10.

Claims for possession

22.19   Claims for possession make up a large part of the work of the county courts. The cause of action is the right to possession, which may be established on the basis that the tenant's right to occupy has ended or because one of the statutory grounds for possession is made out. Claims for possession are dealt with in detail in chapters 6 and 7.

Homelessness appeals

22.20   The jurisdiction of the county court to hear appeals about homelessness decisions is entirely statutory and is set out in the Housing Act 1996. The provisions are described in chapter 15.

22.21   The court's role in such cases is not the same as in most county court litigation because homeless decisions are administrative decisions made by a public body. Traditionally such decisions have been scrutinised by the High Court in judicial review proceedings. The volume of judicial reviews concerning homelessness decision-making during the 1980s and 1990s, however, led to the transfer of such cases to the county court. Homelessness appeals can only be heard by circuit judges who, when hearing appeals, are applying judicial review principles ie the court is examining the lawfulness of the decision rather than considering the merits of the decision. The principles of judicial review are explained in more detail in chapter 2.

Remedies

22.22   A remedy is what a person is asking the court to order, as distinct from the cause of action, which is the legal basis for the claim, see paras 22.8–22.9 above.

22.23   In a claim based on tort or breach of contract the claimant will be seeking one or more of the following remedies:

- damages (compensation); and/or
- an injunction (an order that a person does or refrains from doing something) or an order of specific performance (an order that a person must perform the obligations under a contract).

22.24   It is also possible to ask the court to make a declaration of a person's rights, for example, whether or not he or she is a tenant or the nature of the tenancy.

22.25   In a claim for possession, the applicant will asking the court to make a possession order. This authorises the claimant to take possession but, unless the defendant gives up possession voluntarily, must be enforced by court bailiffs. A social landlord may now also ask the court to make a demotion order in relation to a tenancy. The effect of this is to reduce the tenant's security of tenure, see chapters 6 and 7. If there are arrears of rent a landlord will usually also seek a money judgment.

22.26 In a homelessness appeal the claimant will be asking the court to make an order quashing (cancelling) the local authority's decision or varying the decision to a positive one.

The parties

22.27 In a civil claim the person who brings the claim is usually called the claimant and the person against whom the claim is brought is the defendant. A defendant may, at the same time as defending a claim, bring a counterclaim against a claimant.

22.28 In some kinds of cases the parties are instead known as the applicant and the respondent, for example, in applications for injunctions and committals.

22.29 In homelessness appeals the parties are referred to as the appellant and the respondent. The same terms are used in any appeal against an order made by a court.

Civil Procedure Rules

22.30 The Civil Procedure Rules 1998 (CPR) set out a complete code for the conduct of all civil claims and apply in the county courts and in the High Court.[3] The CPR can be accessed online at the Department of Justice website: www.justice.gov.uk. Most of the commonly used forms can also be downloaded from the same site.

22.31 Each part of the CPR deals with a specific aspect of procedure or type of claim. Each part contains the relevant rules with a practice direction (PD) setting out the more practical requirements.

Pre-action protocols

22.32 The CPR were designed to promote early exchange of information and to encourage the parties to settle disputes so as to avoid litigation. This is reflected in the use of pre-action protocols. These set out the steps parties should take before proceedings are commenced in particular kinds of cases. The following pre-action protocols are relevant to housing cases:

---

3 Previously, different rules applied in the county courts and in the High Court. Some of these rules are still in force, mainly in relation to enforcement, and are set out in a schedule to the CPR. They are known as the Rules of the Supreme Court (RSC) and the County Court Rules (CCR).

- Pre-Action Protocol for Possession Claims based on Rent Arrears;
- Pre-Action Protocol for Possession Claims based on Mortgage Arrears;
- Pre-Action Protocol for Housing Disrepair Claims;
- Pre-Action Protocol for Judicial Review Claims.

22.33   The pre-action protocols for rent and mortgage arrears, disrepair and judicial review are described in chapters 6, 10 and 2 respectively.

22.34   The CPR comprise the following parts:

The overriding objective	Part 1
Application and interpretation of the rules	Part 2
The courts' power to manage cases	Part 3
Forms and court documents	Parts 4–6
How to start and respond to proceedings	Parts 7–15
Drafting documents for court (statements of case)	Parts 16–17, 22
Applying for court orders	Parts 23–25
Case management and track allocation	Parts 26–30
Documents and evidence	Parts 31–35
Offers to settle claims	Parts 36–37
Costs	Parts 43–48
Enforcement	Parts 69–73

The overriding objective

22.35   The CPR came into being following a comprehensive review of civil procedure conducted by Lord Woolf. The aims of the review were:[4]

- to improve access to justice and reduce the cost of litigation;
- to reduce the complexity of the rules and modernise terminology; and
- to remove unnecessary distinctions of practice and procedure.

4 *Lord Woolf's interim report on access to civil justice* (June 1995). This and *Lord Woolf's final report on access to civil justice* (July 1996) can be downloaded from the old DCA website: www.dca.gov.uk.

22.36 This is reflected in rule 1.1, which is headed 'the overriding objective':

(1) These rules are a new procedural code with the overrriding objective of enabling the court to deal with cases justly.

(2) Dealing with a case justly includes, so far as is practicable:

    (a) ensuring that the parties are on an equal footing;

    (b) saving expense;

    (c) dealing with the case in ways which are proportionate:

        (i)   to the amount of money involved;

        (ii) to the importance of the case;

        (iii) to the complexity of the issues; and

        (iv) to the financial position of each party;

    (d) ensuring that it is dealt with expeditiously and fairly; and

    (e) allotting to it an appropriate share of the court's resources, whilst taking into account the need to allot resources to other cases.

22.37 The rule goes on to provide that the court must seek to give effect to the overriding objective when exercising its powers and interpreting rules and that the parties must help the court to further the overriding objective.

Active case management

22.38 The court has a duty to further the overriding objective by actively managing cases. This includes:[5]

- encouraging the parties to co-operate;
- identifying issues at an early stage;
- encouraging the parties to use an alternative dispute resolution procedure;
- helping the parties to settle the whole or part of the case;
- dealing with the case without the parties attending court;
- making use of technology; and
- giving directions to ensure that the case proceeds to trial quickly.

22.39 The ability of the judges to manage cases actively is limited by the fact that judges rarely have the time to examine cases other than when considering applications made by the parties. However, since the implementation of the CPR, judges do take a more active role in managing cases and, for instance, they are less willing to agree adjournments and extensions of time even if both parties are in agreement. Judges also take an active part in case management conferences to help clarify the issues and to expedite resolution.

5 CPR 1.4.

The usual steps in a civil claim

Claims other than possession claims

22.40   Most claims are brought under CPR Part 7 and, if defended, may involve the following stages:

- pre-action correspondence;
- issuing the claim;
- filing a reply/defence;
- track allocation and case management directions;
- parties complying with case management directions;
- off record negotiations to settle the claim;
- hearing/final order;
- enforcement – if defendant fails to comply with order.

22.41   CPR Part 8 provides an alternative procedure and is described below at para 22.104.

Pre-action correspondence

22.42   The CPR encourage early settlement and the aim of the pre-action protocols is to promote settlement so as to avoid proceedings. Even if no protocol applies, the parties are expected to act reasonably in exchanging information and documents relevant to the claim and generally in trying to avoid the necessity for the start of proceedings.[6]

22.43   Even before the CPR came into force, a party was expected to send a 'letter before claim/action' to the proposed defendant setting out the basis of the claim and inviting the defendant's proposals to settle the claim.

22.44   If a claim is issued without following the relevant protocol or (if no protocol applies) without first sending a letter before claim, the claimant may be unable to recover his or her costs even if the claim is successful.

22.45   If there is a protocol, the defendant is obliged to respond to the claimant's pre-action protocol letter, disclosing relevant documents, indicating whether the claim is admitted and, if so, making an offer to settle. Where a defendant fails to comply with a pre-action protocol, the sanction may be that costs are awarded to the other party on a more generous basis than usual.

---

6   CPR PD to Protocols, para 4.1.

Issuing the claim

22.46   To issue a claim, the claimant must draft the relevant papers (usually a claim form and particulars of claim) and send them to the court with enough copies for each defendant and a fee. The claim is issued when the court endorses the court seal. The papers are then posted by the court to the defendant(s).

Claim form and particulars of claim

22.47   The claim form is a court form (which can be downloaded) and is completed by the claimant.[7] In a simple case, the particulars of claim may be entered on to the claim form. In more complicated cases the particulars of claim will be a separate document. The particulars of claim should be a concise statement of the facts on which the claimant relies.[8] Both documents must be endorsed with a 'statement of truth' confirming that the contents are true to the best of the claimant's knowledge.[9] The form of the statement of truth signed by a party is:[10]

> I believe that the facts stated in this [claim form/particulars of claim] are true.

22.48   A statement of truth may be signed by a legal representative, in which case, the representative must ensure that the party believes the contents to be true and advise him or her of the consequences if this is not the case. The possible sanction for signing a statement of truth without an honest belief that the contents of the document are true is that contempt of court proceedings may be brought by the Attorney-General or with the permission of the court.[11]

22.49   If the statement of truth is signed by a legal representative the form is:

> The claimant believes that the facts stated in this [claim form/particulars of claim] are true.

22.50   If the particulars of claim is not verified by a statement of truth, it will stand as a summary of the claim but cannot be used as evidence. Furthermore, the court has the power to strike it out.[12] The court could,

---

7   Under CPR Part 7 this is form N1.
8   CPR Part 16 deals with the content of claims forms and particulars of claim.
9   CPR Part 22 deals with statements of truth. ·
10 CPR Part 22, PD para 2.1.
11 CPR 32.14.
12 CPR 22.2.

however, adjourn proceedings to permit a party to endorse the document with a statement of truth. If this means that the other party incurs unnecessary costs, the party in default will usually be ordered to pay those costs, regardless of the outcome of the claim, see para 22.152 below.

22.51 The court sends the papers to the defendant with a 'response pack' and notes as to how the defendant should respond.

Fees

22.52 Fees are paid to the court when issuing a claim, at certain stages throughout the process and when making applications to the court. When the claim is issued, the fee will depend on the value of the claim. For most other applications there is a set fee. Fees are usually increased each year and the most common fees are listed in the leaflet EX50 which can be downloaded from the Courts and Tribunals Service website: www. hmcourts-service.gov.uk. A full list of fees can be found in the relevant statutory instrument, a link to which is also on the website.

Fee exemption

22.53 Claimants on a low income can apply to the court for fee exemption. This will always be granted if the claimant is in receipt of certain benefits. Otherwise a court officer will assess the claimant's means before deciding whether the fee must be paid. Claimants must take to the court original documents to establish income (for example, letters from the Department for Work and Pensions or HM Revenue and Customs or bank statements showing receipt of benefit, wage slips etc). The fee exemption form (EX160) can be downloaded from the Court and Tribunals Service website. The same form can be used to apply for a refund of fees already paid.

22.54 Fee exemption does not apply if a party is formally represented by solicitors, ie the solicitors are on the court record as acting for the party. The solicitors pay any court fees and these are reimbursed by the Legal Services Commission.

Filing a reply/defence

22.55 The usual rule is that the defendant has 14 days from the date of service to file a defence.[13] However, if the defendant files an acknowledgement

---

13 Generally when documents are sent or taken to the court they are referred to as being 'filed' and when they are sent or delivered to the other party they are referred to as being 'served'.

of service, the period is extended to 28 days from the date of service of the claim form. In most cases the documents will be posted by the court to the defendant and the date of service is deemed to be the second day after posting. If the documents are delivered to the defendant's address the date of service is deemed to be the following day.[14]

22.56   The response pack sent to the defendant includes forms on which the defendant may admit the claim, admit part of the claim or dispute the claim. If the claim is defended it is sufficient to complete the defence form indicating the reasons. However, a defendant may instead file a defence as a separate document. In either case, the defence should deal with each allegation, stating whether it is admitted or denied. If an allegation is denied and the defendant intends to put forward a different version of events, this should be set out in the defence.[15] If the defence fails to deal with a particular allegation, that allegation will be treated as admitted, unless the defendant has set out the nature of his or her case relevant to the allegation. The form of defence must also be endorsed with a statement of truth and signed by the defendant or the defendant's representative.

22.57   There is no fee for the filing of a defence. However, if the defendant wishes to make a counterclaim a CPR Part 20 claim form must be completed[16] and the same fee will be payable as if it were a claim.

Track allocation

22.58   If the claim is defended the case will be allocated to one of three tracks. Allocation questionnaires are usually sent to the parties by the court and must be completed and filed so that the court has sufficient information to allocate to the appropriate track. If a claim is clearly within the small claims limit the court will usually allocate without requiring the parties to file questionnaires. Defended claims are allocated to one of three tracks:

- the small claims track;
- the fast track; or
- the multi-track.

22.59   This allocation depends mainly on the value of the claim but other factors such as complexity and the nature of the evidence are also taken into consideration. The small claims track is described in more detail below at paras 22.95–22.103.

14 CPR 6.7.
15 See CPR 16.5.
16 Form N211.

Case management directions

22.60   Case management directions set out the steps that each party must take before the claim can be listed for a final hearing. Standard case management directions are made for small claims and fast track cases. Usually multi-track cases will need more detailed and specific case management directions and these may be agreed by the parties or made at a case management hearing.

22.61   The usual case management directions require disclosure by each party of the documents in their possession and the evidence on which they intend to rely. This is to encourage the settlement of claims by ensuring that the parties can assess the relative merits of each other's case before the final hearing.

Disclosure of documents

22.62   Unless the claim is allocated to the small claims track, the parties must disclose *all* relevant documents, including those that are unhelpful to the party's case. Certain documents are excluded from disclosure because they are 'privileged'. This includes documents and correspondence relating to the legal advice given to the party. It also includes documents created for the purpose of the proceedings, for example draft statements and expert reports that the party does not intend to rely on.

Disclosure of evidence relied on

Factual witnesses

22.63   In most cases the parties must exchange written statements for all the witnesses whom they intend to call to give evidence. The statements are a summary of what the witness will say in court. At a final hearing the evidence will usually be given orally by witnesses. However, the parties may agree that certain uncontentious statements can be used as evidence so that the witness need not attend. Also, one party can serve notice on the other party that he or she intends to rely on hearsay evidence.[17] The other party can apply to the court for permission to call the witness so that he or she can be cross-examined. However, if the party on whom the notice is served does not object,

---

17 'Hearsay' means second-hand evidence. It includes a written statement if the maker of the statement is not present in court. It also includes one person's evidence about what another person has told him or her, if the evidence is given to prove that what the other person said was true: see Civil Evidence Act 1995 s1(2)(a). See also CPR Part 33.

the hearsay evidence can be used at the hearing. Hearsay evidence, however, will not have as much weight as direct evidence.

Expert witnesses

22.64 In some cases the parties rely on the opinion of experts such as doctors or surveyors. Expert evidence is different from that of witnesses of fact: expert witnesses' evidence may include a professional opinion. For example, a surveyor may express an opinion about the cause of dampness in a dwelling and a doctor may express an opinion about the effect of dampness on a person's health. CPR strongly encourage the use of single joint experts (SJEs). This means a single expert instructed by both parties, whose duty is to the court. If each party instructs a different expert, written reports must be disclosed in advance of the final hearing. The case management directions may order the experts to prepare a joint statement setting out what is agreed and what is at issue. If the experts do not agree on an issue, unless one party concedes the issue, the experts should attend court to give oral evidence. The use of expert witnesses is discussed in more detail in chapter 10. Expert evidence may be used only if the court gives permission.

Interlocutory applications and hearings

22.65 As the proceedings progress, the parties may be in dispute about procedural issues or may want to apply to the court for remedies available prior to the final hearing (for example, injunctions). Examples of procedural disputes would be where one party claims that another party has documents that should be disclosed or where one party wants to use a type of expert evidence and the other party does not agree that it is necessary. An interim remedy would include an application for an interlocutory (as opposed to a final) injunction or an application for an interim payment of damages.

22.66 Unless the parties reach agreement, such issues will be resolved by one party making an application to the court. The issue will be listed for a short hearing before a district judge (simple hearings can be arranged as telephone conferences). Applications for interim injunctions, however, are usually heard by circuit judges. Evidence is required in support of any interlocutory application and this will be in the form of written statements or affidavits.

22.67 The party who succeeds in making or resisting an interlocutory application will usually be awarded his or her costs of the application regardless of the final outcome of the claim (see para 22.125).

Settlement

22.68   One of the central aims of the CPR is to encourage settlement by ensuring that issues are clarified and evidence disclosed at an early stage. CPR Part 36 sets out a procedure that can be followed when attempting to settle claims. If this procedure is followed, certain consequences regarding the costs of the proceedings will usually follow automatically.

CPR Part 36 offers

22.69   CPR Part 36 encourages settlement by providing that penalties apply if a party refuses an offer to settle but subsequently fails to obtain a better outcome than under the proposed settlement.

22.70   A Part 36 offer must be made in writing, state that it is made under CPR Part 36, and the period during which, if accepted, the defendant will be liable for the claimant's legal costs. This must be at least 21 days, unless there are fewer than 21 days before the trial.

22.71   Either a defendant or a claimant can make a Part 36 offer. If the offer to settle is accepted, this will conclude the matter and the defendant will be liable for all of the claimant's costs (subject to assessment by the court, see paras 22.140–22.150 below).

22.72   If a defendant's offer is refused by the claimant and the claimant fails to obtain more in damages at trial (or if a non-monetary remedy is sought, fails to obtain a judgment 'more advantageous'),[18] the defendant will be liable for the claimant's costs up to the end of the period specified in the Part 36 offer. The claimant will be responsible for the defendant's costs, plus interest, from that date until the claim is decided by the court. As a large proportion of the costs of any case are incurred in preparation for and at trial, the claimant's costs liability will often exceed the defendant's liability.

22.73   If a claimant's offer is refused by the defendant and the claimant goes on to recover the same or more in damages, or obtains a judgment 'at least as advantageous',[19] the defendant will be liable for all of the claimant's costs plus interest. In addition, the court will usually order that the costs are assessed on a basis that is more generous to the claimant and can order that additional interest be paid on any damages.

18 CPR 36(1)(a).
19 CPR 36(1)(b).

Settlement outside Part 36

22.74 Offers to settle proceedings may be made outside the Part 36 procedure. A party can make an offer in whatever way he or she chooses but if it is not in accordance with Part 36, the costs consequences referred to above (paras 22.72–22.73) will not automatically apply.[20] The court will nevertheless always take account of the parties' attempts to settle when exercising its discretion in relation to costs.

'Without prejudice' communications

22.75 Whenever a party wishes to communicate an offer to settle a claim, any correspondence containing the proposals should be marked 'Without prejudice save as to costs'. This means that the correspondence will not be disclosed to the court until after the claim has been determined; settlement proposals are relevant to the issue of costs only. The most important points in relation to without prejudice communications are:

- Only genuine offers to compromise a claim should be marked 'without prejudice'.
- Offers to compromise may be treated as without prejudice even if not marked as such. However, this would require the agreement of the other party or a decision by the court.
- If a party refers to without prejudice communications at trial the judge may decide that the hearing must be abandoned and heard by a different judge. The party who has revealed the without prejudice communication may be ordered to pay the costs that have been wasted as a result (see para 22.152 below).
- Without prejudice discussions may take place by telephone (or sometimes at court). Both parties must agree that the discussion is on a without prejudice basis.
- Once agreement has been reached, the confirmation of the terms of that agreement should be confirmed in 'open' correspondence (ie not marked without prejudice). Usually the terms of the agreement will be incorporated into a 'consent order' (see para 22.88 and appendix 2 to this chapter).

20 CPR 36.1(2).

The hearing/final order

22.76   Unless the parties reach an agreement, the claim will be listed for a hearing. The claimant will usually be responsible for preparing a 'trial bundle' which comprises copies of all the relevant documents. The trial bundle will include: the statements of case (ie, claim, defence and any reply or counterclaim); the statements of the witnesses who will give evidence; expert reports; and all relevant documents. Copies of the bundle will be provided for the court and the other party or parties. Further copies should be available for the witnesses to refer to when giving evidence. The bundle should be organised chronologically and paginated for ease of reference.

The final hearing

22.77   Despite a move towards the use of written evidence at a final hearing, most evidence will be given orally, ie by witnesses who attend court and answer questions put by the parties' lawyers (or the parties, if unrepresented) and the judge. The format of a formal trial is as follows, paras 22.78–22.84.

Claimant opens

22.78   This will be a brief summary of the issues and reference to the evidence to be used, including the documents in the trial bundle.

Claimant calls evidence

22.79   All the witnesses (usually starting with the claimant) will be questioned first by the claimant's lawyer and then by the defendant's lawyer (cross-examination). To save time the witness may be asked to confirm that the witness statement in the trial bundle is true and then questioned only on certain issues. The defendant's lawyer must challenge any evidence that is at issue. The claimant's lawyer has the chance to re-examine only to clarify anything raised in cross examination. The judge may also ask questions of the witnesses.

Defendant calls evidence

22.80   The defendant's witnesses will be questioned in the same way, starting with questions from the defendant's lawyer.

Defendant closes

22.81   The defendant's lawyer makes a closing speech. This is a summary of the defendant's case and submissions as to why the court should find for the defendant.

Claimant closes

22.82   The claimant's lawyer also makes a closing speech.

Burden and standard of proof

22.83   In civil cases the claimant must prove the case 'on balance of probabilities', which means that the claimant is more likely to be right than the defendant; this is the 'standard of proof'. The 'burden of proof' is on the claimant, which means that, if the judge cannot decide between the parties, the claim will fail: the claimant will have failed to satisfy the judge on balance of probabilities.

Decision/order

22.84   In most county court cases the judge will give judgment immediately, indicating whether the claimant has proved the case and, if so, assessing the amount of damages and/or deciding the terms of the order, and dealing with the issue of costs. The judge will also give reasons for his or her decision. This enables the parties to know whether there are grounds to appeal the decision.

Rights of audience

22.85   The term 'rights of audience' refers to the right to represent a party at a hearing. The following people have a right to represent a party in county court proceedings:

- Qualified solicitors and barristers.
- In local authority possession proceedings before a district judge: any person authorised by the local authority.[21]
- Authorised employees of housing management organisations in relation to certain proceedings brought on behalf of local housing authorities before a district judge (possession claims on nuisance grounds, demotion claims and certain anti-social behaviour claims) and possession.[22]

21   County Courts Act 1984 s60.
22   County Courts Act 1984 s60A, inserted by Legal Services Act 2007 s191.

- Solicitor's employees only at a hearing 'in chambers' (the judge's room). In practice this means small claims hearings and inter-locutory procedural hearings. It does not include possession proceedings even though these are usually now heard in private.[23]
- Legal executives,[24] who have the same rights of audience as any person employed by a solicitor but, in addition, may appear in open court on unopposed applications for adjournments and applications for consent orders.
- Authorised employees of a company that is party to the proceedings.[25]
- 'Lay representatives' in small claims proceedings (see para 22.95 below).

22.86 If a party wants any other person to represent him or her at a hearing, the court must give permission.[26] This will usually be granted on a case-by-case basis. However, in possession proceedings some courts will effectively grant permission on a general basis to those assisting in duty advice schemes or employed by certain local housing associations.

McKenzie friends

22.87 Parties representing themselves are entitled to have someone assisting them in court. This means taking notes and (quietly) making suggestions and giving advice but not actually speaking for the party.[27] If the court refuses permission for a non-legally qualified person to represent a party he or she could assist in this role instead. A court may

---

23 Prior to the CPR coming into force there was a distinction between hearings in chambers and hearings in open court. Under CPR the distinction is between hearings in private and hearings in public. However, the rules regarding rights of audience still refer to hearings in chambers: Courts and Legal Services Act 1990 s27(1)(e).

24 Legal executives are regulated by the Institute of Legal Executives, which is a body authorised to grant limited rights of audience to its members.

25 CPR 39.6. A company employee needs the court's permission to represent the company but permission should be given by the court unless there is some 'particular and sufficient reason why it should be withheld': CPR Part 39 PD para 5.3.

26 The court has a broad discretion to do so under the Courts and Legal Services Act 1990 s27(2)(c).

27 The term 'McKenzie friend' does not denote any particular legal status. The term was coined following *McKenzie v McKenzie* [1970] 3 WLR 472 when the Court of Appeal ruled that it was in the interests of justice to allow an unrepresented party to have assistance from another person during a hearing. See also *R v Leicester City Justices ex p Barrow* [1991] 3 WLR 368.

refuse to permit a party to use a McKenzie friend. However, this will be rare and will usually be because of the conduct of the particular McKenzie friend. If permission is refused, reasons should be given.

Consent orders

22.88 The vast majority of defended claims are settled by the parties before a final hearing. If settlement is achieved after the claim has been issued the terms of the settlement will usually be incorporated into a 'consent order', which is then submitted to the court for approval. When the court approves the order, it will be stamped with the court seal and is enforceable in the same way as if the order had been made by a judge following a hearing. Where the terms of agreement are complex, the consent order will be in the form of a stay of proceedings, on the terms set out in a schedule. Either party has the right to apply to the court if the other party does not comply with the agreed terms. This is known as a 'Tomlin Order', an example of which is at appendix 2 to this chapter.

Undefended claims

22.89 If a defendant fails to respond to the claim by filing a defence, the claimant can ask the court to enter 'judgment in default'. A default judgment can be enforced against a defendant in the same way as an order made by a judge. CPR Part 12 sets out the rules for default judgments.

22.90 There are different procedures depending on whether the claim is for a fixed amount of money, for an amount of money to be decided by the court and/or when the claim is for some other remedy such as an injunction or order for works.

Claim for fixed amount

22.91 After the time for filing a defence has expired the claimant can apply for judgment by completing form N225[28] and sending it to the court with a fee. A court officer will draw up the judgment and will send it to the parties.

Claim for amount to be assessed by the court

22.92 This will be the case where the claim is for damages that have to be assessed by the court, for example, for disrepair or unlawful eviction

---

28 Form N205A can also be completed but it is not available online.

and harassment. In such a case the claimant applies for judgment to be entered against the defendant with damages to be assessed by the court at a later hearing. This can be done by completing form N227.[29] If judgment is entered this means that the defendant is liable to pay some damages but can attend the hearing to make representations about the amount (known as 'quantum'). He or she cannot argue about liability unless the default judgment is set aside.

Claim for non-money remedy

22.93   A hearing is also necessary where a claimant is asking the court to grant an injunction or an order for specific performance of a contract. Such claims are usually in addition to claims for damages. In this case, an application for judgment in default must be made under CPR Part 23.[30] The procedure under Part 23 requires the applicant to complete an application notice (form N244). The application is for two things: for judgment on liability to be entered immediately, without notice to the defendant, and for a hearing to be listed so that the court can assess the amount of damages and whether to grant the non-monetary remedy. The defendant will be notified of the hearing and may attend and make representations.

Possession claims

22.94   The procedure described above (paras 22.89–22.93) applies to most claims for money and other remedies such as for injunctions, but not to claims for possession. Most claims for possession are dealt with as follows:

- *Ordinary possession claims* A hearing is listed when the claim is issued and there is no procedure for obtaining judgment by default. A defendant can attend the hearing and argue against the making of a possession order.
- *Accelerated possession claims* The accelerated procedure is available to a landlord seeking a possession order against an assured shorthold tenant where there is a written tenancy agreement. A possession order can be made without a hearing if the judge decides that the claim is made out after looking at the papers.

Both procedures are described in detail in chapter 6.

29   Again, there is an alternative form: N205B, but this is not available online.
30   CPR 12.4(2). Part 23 concerns any sort of application made within proceedings.

Small claims

22.95　There is no separate small claims court within the civil system. Rather, defended claims below a certain value are allocated to the small claims track. This determines the type of case management directions that will be given and the way the final hearing will be conducted. CPR Part 27 sets out the rules relating to the conduct of small claims.

22.96　　It should be noted that if no defence is filed the claim is not allocated to track and the rules regarding default judgments described above (paras 22.89–22.93) apply.

Allocation to the small claims track[31]

22.97　The criteria for allocation are not limited to financial value but this is the main factor. The following claims will usually be allocated to the small claims track:

- money claims for not more than £5,000;
- personal injury claims for not more than £1,000;
- housing disrepair claims in which an order for works is sought, where the expected damages are not more than £1,000 *and* the estimated cost of works is not more than £1,000.

22.98　Claims above these values may be allocated to the small claims track only if both parties agree.[32]

22.99　　However, the following provisions apply to housing cases:

- claims in respect of harassment or unlawful eviction brought by a tenant against a landlord will not be allocated to the small claims track;[33]
- disputed claims for possession and demotion of tenancies are not generally considered suitable for the small claims track.[34]

Features of small claims cases

22.100　The main features of cases allocated to the small claims track are:

- only very limited legal costs can be recovered by the successful party;
- public funding will not usually be granted for representation;

31　CPR Part 26 sets out the criteria for allocation.
32　CPR 26.7(3).
33　CPR 26.7(4).
34　CPR Part 26 PD, para 8.1(c).

- simple case management directions will be made – these are usually limited to exchanging copies of the documents each party relies on;
- the hearing will usually be held in the judge's private room and will be informal;
- lay representatives have a right of audience provided the party is present at the hearing.[35]

Costs in small claims

22.101 The general rule is that legal costs incurred by a party in taking or defending a small claim cannot be recovered from the other party. However, the following costs can be recovered:[36]

- the court fee;
- any expenses incurred by a witness (including the successful party) in attending the hearing, including travel expenses and loss of earnings (up to a maximum of £50 per person per day);
- if a claim for an injunction or specific performance is made, legal costs of up to £260;
- expert witness fees, up to a maximum of £200.

22.102 Furthermore, if the claim exceeds the usual small claims limit but the parties have agreed to it being allocated to the small claims track the usual costs rules apply. See below at paras 22.119–22.133.

22.103   Also, in all cases, further costs may be awarded if a party behaves unreasonably.[37]

CPR Part 8 procedure

22.104 Most civil claims are brought under CPR Part 7, which is the procedure described above at paras 22.40–22.93. However, Part 8 provides an alternative procedure which should be used either:[38]

- where the court's decision is sought on a question which is unlikely to involve a substantial dispute of fact; or
- where the CPR require or permit the use of Part 8 for a specific type of claim.

---

35 Lay Representatives (Rights of Audience) Order 1992 SI No 1966 art 2.
36 CPR 27.14(2) and the PD para 7.
37 CPR 27.14(2)(g).
38 CPR 8.1(2) and (5).

22.105 The claims that *must* be brought under Part 8 are listed in the Practice Direction to Part 8, para 10.4. and Part 56. Tenancy deposit claims under HA 2004 s214 (see paras 4.142–4.163) must be brought under Part 8.

22.106 PD to Part 8, para 3 lists the claims that *may* be brought under Part 8. These include an application for the court's approval of a claim settled on behalf of a child or a protected person.[39]

22.107 The main features of the Part 8 procedure are:

- The claim is commenced by completing a claim form[40] with written evidence attached: it is not necessary to file particulars of claim.
- The defendant is not required to file a defence but must file an acknowledgment of service,[41] also attaching written evidence. If the defendant does not do so he or she may attend the hearing but can only take part if the court gives permission.
- There is no default procedure – the matter is usually listed for a hearing but may be dealt with by a judge without a hearing.
- A party may not use written evidence at the hearing unless it was served on the other party with the claim form or acknowledgement of service.
- The evidence at any hearing will mainly be written evidence but the court may order that oral evidence be given.
- At the hearing the court may decide the matter or give case management directions.
- The court may, at any stage, direct that the case proceed as if it had not been issued under CPR Part 8, and give directions for future conduct.

Enforcement

22.108 This section deals with the enforcement of money judgments and injunctions. The enforcement of possession orders is dealt with in chapter 6.

---

39 See CPR Part 21. A protected party is a person who lacks capacity, see para 7.171. Children and protected parties must have another person acting on their behalf: a litigation friend. A settlement reached before issue must be approved by a court.

40 Form N208.

41 Form N210.

Money judgments

22.109 A successful claim for damages or the repayment of a debt will result in the court making an order that the defendant ('the judgment debtor') pays to the claimant ('the judgment creditor') a sum of money ('the judgment debt') within a specified period. Unless the order states otherwise, payment should be made within 14 days.[42] The money is paid directly to the judgment creditor and not to the court.

22.110   Judgment debts are normally recorded in the Register of Judgments, Orders and Fines.[43] If the debt is paid within one month of the order the registration can be cancelled. If the debt is paid after one month the judgment will be recorded as satisfied. Applications for either cancellation or satisfaction are made by the judgment debtor to the court where the order was made and a fee is payable.

22.111   Apart from entering the judgment in the register, the court takes no further action after making the order. If the judgment debtor fails to pay, further action to enforce the judgment must be taken by the judgment creditor. The different types of enforcement action are described below.

22.112   In all cases a further court fee must be paid. Fee exemption is available for those on a limited income (see para 22.53). If a fee is paid and the enforcement action is successful the fee will be added to the judgment debt and must be paid by the judgment debtor.

Main methods of enforcing money judgments

22.113 The main methods of enforcing money judgments are shown in the following table.[44]

---

42 CPR 40.11.

43 The register is administered by a not-for-profit company: The Registry Trust Ltd. Searches of the register can be carried out online at its website: www.trustonline.org.uk.

44 References to CCR are to the County Court Rules and RSC to the Rules of the Supreme Court. These are rules retained from the old procedural codes which relate to proceedings in the county court and the High Court respectively. Those still in force are set out in a schedule to CPR.

Enforcement action	CPR/ authority	Effect/procedure
Warrant of execution (in the High Court called a 'writ of fi fa')	CPR Part 70 and CCR Order 26 (RSC Orders 46 and 47)	A warrant of execution authorises the court bailiffs to seize property belonging to the judgment debtor. A request is filed certifying the amount outstanding under the judgment. A warrant is issued by the court which authorises court bailiffs to levy execution (remove belongings) to be sold in order to satisfy the judgment debt. A warning notice is sent to the judgment debtor seven days before the proposed levy. Certain belongings are exempt. One limitation is that the bailiffs do not have the power to force entry on to premises in order to seize goods. The application must be made to the court for the area in which the debtor resides.
Attachment of earnings	CPR Part 70 and CCR Order 27 Attachment of Earnings Act 1971	An attachment of earnings order compels the employer of a judgment debtor to deduct an amount from his or her earnings until the debt is paid. Application should be made to the court for the area in which the debtor resides, unless this is not known in which case it is made to the court that made the order. The debtor is given notice of the application by the court with a form of reply. On receiving the reply a court officer may make an attachment of earnings order. A hearing may be listed if there is insufficient information for an order to be made. If an order is made without a hearing, both parties have the right to apply for a hearing within 14 days. Where a debtor fails to file a reply or attend a hearing an application may be made for the debtor to be committed to prison, provided service can be proved.

Enforcement action	CPR/ authority	Effect/procedure
Third party debt order	CPR Part 72	A third party debt order is an order that a person who owes money to the judgment debtor pays the amount of the judgment debt to the judgment creditor. It is generally used to obtain money directly from a person's bank or building society.
		The bank or building society is the third party. The court first makes an interim order without a hearing and without notice to the debtor. This order is served on the third party and specifies the amount of money that must be retained pending a final order. The interim order is served on the debtor after being served on the third party. The judgment creditor may apply for a hardship payment and, if he or she objects to the making of a final order, written evidence must be filed stating the objections. If no objections are made, or if the objections are not upheld, the order will be made final at a hearing and the third party must then pay the outstanding amount, plus the costs of the application, to the judgment creditor.
Charging order	CPR Part 73	A charging order may be appropriate when a judgment debtor owns property, including his or her own home or premises let to a tenant.[45] An interim order is requested without a hearing and without notice to the judgment debtor.
		This can be registered at the land registry to prevent the judgment debtor transferring ownership of the property.
		The interim order is served on the judgment debtor, who must file and serve written evidence if he or she objects to the making of a final order. If no objections are made, or if the objections are not upheld, the order will be made final at a hearing. A charging order is a form of mortgage and, if the judgment debtor does not pay, an application may be made for an order that the property be sold and the judgment satisfied from the proceeds of sale, see below.

45   This can be discovered by carrying out a Land Registry search. See para 4.139.

Enforcement action	CPR/ authority	Effect/procedure
Order for sale	CPR Parts 73 and 8	If a final charging order has been obtained and the judgment debt is still not paid, an application may be made under Part 8 for an order that the property be sold.
Appointment of receivers	CPR Part 69	A receiver may be appointed by the court to preserve or manage property pending the resolution of a dispute. Generally, other methods of enforcement will be more effective. However, in a disrepair action a receiver could be appointed to receive rents from a number of tenants to pay for essential repairs.

Oral examination

22.114 If the judgment creditor has insufficient information about the debtor's assets to decide on an appropriate method of enforcement an application may be made for an oral examination of the judgment debtor. This is summarised in the table below.

Action	CPR	Effect/procedure
Order that judgment debtor attend court	CPR Part 71	Application is made by request to a court officer. An order will be made without a hearing by a court officer. The order requires the judgment debtor to attend court to answer questions about his or her assets and income to enable the judgment creditor to choose the best way to enforce. The order should be endorsed with a notice warning the debtor that he or she may be sent to prison for contempt if it is not obeyed. The order should be served personally on the debtor by the creditor and travel expenses must be offered.
		At the hearing the debtor will be questioned by a court officer or a judge. If the hearing is before a court officer, the creditor *may* attend and ask questions. If the hearing is before a judge, the creditor *must* attend and conduct the questioning. If the debtor fails to attend the hearing the matter should be referred to a judge. The judge may make a committal order provided the order was served personally and an affidavit has been filed confirming service.

22.115 Each method of enforcement requires the creditor to make an application and pay a fee. If the application is successful, the creditor will usually recover the fee paid and a fixed amount towards any legal costs. Clearly, if the judgment debtor has no assets or cannot be traced, the creditor may be unable to obtain satisfaction of the judgment and it will be pointless to incur further court fees that are unlikely to be recovered from the debtor.

Enforcing injunctions and orders for specific performance

22.116 If a party does not obey an order that he or she must do or refrain from doing something, an application can be made for the person to be committed to prison for contempt of court. Committal proceedings are described in more detail at paras 10.172–10.177.

Judicial review proceedings

22.117 The above procedural rules relate to private disputes. The High Court also deals with challenges to administrative decisions made by public bodies. The procedure to challenge such decisions is judicial review.[46] Judicial review is explained at paras 2.4–2.30.

22.118 Claims for judicial review must generally be brought in the Administrative Court, which is a branch of the High Court. Some can be brought in the Upper Tribunal. The Administrative Court has a power to transfer judicial review claims to the Upper Tribunal.[47] At the time of writing the government has announced its intention to implement the Borders, Citizenship and Immigration Act 2009 s53 which will mean that fresh claim asylum and human rights immigration judicial reviews will be heard in the Upper Tribunal.

Costs

22.119 In civil proceedings the usual rule is that the losing party will be ordered to pay the legal costs of the winning party. The rules for criminal prosecutions (which may be brought by individuals) are different and are outside the scope of this book. The detailed rules about

---

46 CPR Part 54 sets out the procedure for judicial review claims.
47 See the First-tier Tribunal and Upper Tribunal (Chambers) Order 2010 SI No 2655 art 11(c)(ii) and Tribunals, Courts and Enforcement Act 2007 s15(1).

costs are contained in CPR Parts 43 to 48. This section examines the main issues that advisers are likely to encounter. These are:

- the circumstances in which a successful party may not recover costs;
- the nature of the 'costs' that can be recovered;
- what happens when one party is legally aided;
- how the amount of costs claimed is controlled;
- when costs can be ordered against someone who is not a party;
- when costs be ordered against a party's representatives.

When might a successful party not recover costs?

The general rule

22.120 Under CPR the court has a general discretion as to whether to make an order for costs at all.[48] If the court decides to make an order about costs, 'the general rule is that the unsuccessful party will be ordered to pay the costs of the successful party; but ... the court may make a different order'.[49] In deciding what order to make, the court must have regard to all the circumstances, including:

- the conduct of all the parties;
- whether a party has succeeded on part of his case, even if he or she has not been wholly successful; and
- any payment into court or offer to settle the case.

22.121 The court can order that one party pays a proportion of another party's costs; pays costs from or until a certain date; pays costs incurred before proceedings have begun; pays costs relating to particular steps taken in the proceedings; or pays costs relating to a distinct part of the proceedings.[50]

Conduct of the parties

22.122 This relates to conduct in relation to the proceedings, not generally. It would include such conduct as refusing to consider mediation as an alternative to litigation. However, there may be good reasons to refuse mediation and it is for the unsuccessful party to prove that it was unreasonable to refuse to mediate.[51]

48 CPR 44.3(1).
49 CPR 44.3(2). However, the general rule does not apply in Court of Appeal cases in relation to probate or family proceedings: CPR 44.3(3).
50 CPR 44.3(6).
51 *Halsey v Milton Keynes General NHS Trust* [2004] EWCA Civ 576, 11 May 2004.

Partial success

22.123 In some cases a party may succeed on one issue but not on another. In such a case the court may order that a proportion of the costs be paid by one party to the other or that each party recovers costs in relation to the issues on which they were successful. These are known as 'split costs orders'. Alternatively the court may order that each party pays their own costs or make no order for costs (which has the same effect).

Offers to settle

22.124 Offers made under CPR Part 36 will usually carry automatic consequences in relation to costs. These are described at paras 22.69–22.73 above. However, when deciding what costs order to make, the court will consider attempts to settle made by the parties, even if not made in accordance with Part 36. A party who has refused a reasonable offer to settle may be unable to recover all of the costs incurred even if successful.

Costs orders made before final hearing

22.125 Hearings may take place in relation to procedural issues before the final hearing. This can happen if the parties do not agree about the steps to be taken to prepare for the hearing. Also, in some cases, an urgent injunction may be sought. An application for an order made during the course of proceedings requires a further court fee to be paid. Also, each party may incur legal costs in making or opposing an application. In such a case, the court will usually make some kind of costs order relating to the application and hearing. The following is a list of the kinds of orders that may be made:

- *Costs in the cause (or case)* This means that the costs of the particular application/hearing will be paid by the unsuccessful party as part of the overall costs at the end of the case.
- *Costs of the defendant/claimant to be paid by the claimant/defendant (sometimes expressed to be 'in any event')* This means that the party who has been unsuccessful must pay the other party's costs of that particular application/hearing regardless of who is successful at the end of the case.
- *Costs reserved* This means that the costs of the particular application/hearing will be decided at the end of the case. This leaves open the possibility of arguing that the party who is ultimately

successful should nevertheless have to pay the other party's costs of the particular application/hearing.

- *No order for costs* This means that each party pays his or her own costs for the particular application/hearing. An order may also state expressly that each party should pay his or her own costs.

What costs can be recovered?

22.126 The costs that one party may be ordered to pay to another include:

- *Legal fees:* the legal fees paid by a party (or by the Legal Services Commission) to legal representatives (solicitors and barristers).
- *Disbursements:* fees paid to other professionals or agencies, including court fees and expert's fees.
- *Expenses:* the travel expenses and loss of earnings for the party and any witnesses attending court.

22.127 Other recoverable costs are the costs of a litigant in person (see paras 22.129–22.131 below), a 'success fee' charged under a conditional fee arrangement (although it is expected that from April 2012 success fees will no longer be recoverable)[52] and a 'reward' charged by a lay representative for acting in a small claims case.[53] All of these are explained below at paras 22.132–22.133.

Barristers' and solicitors' charges

22.128 Solicitors' costs are calculated on the basis of the amount of time spent and the number of routine letters and telephone calls made. Barristers usually charge a fee for each piece of work (for example, drafting a defence, attending a hearing) but this is also calculated on the basis of how much time the work takes. The court may reduce the amount recoverable because the rate is considered too high or the time claimed excessive (see paras 22.140–22.150 below).

Litigants in person

22.129 A person who conducts his or her own litigation is entitled to recover:

- the necessary disbursements and witness expenses; and
- an amount for the time spent preparing the case.

---

52 See Legal Aid, Sentencing and Punishment of Offenders (LASPO) Bill Part 2.
53 CPR 43.2(1)(a).

22.130   There are two possible ways for a litigant in person to calculate the amount to be claimed for his or her time. A person who can show actual financial loss (for example, a self-employed person who lost income as a result of time spent on litigation, or an employed person who had to take time off work) may recover costs on the basis of the lost income.[54] In the absence of actual loss, there is a prescribed rate of £9.25 per hour.[55] A litigant in person can claim this amount for each hour of his or her spare time spent preparing the case, subject to the court's overall discretion to disallow claims for excessive amounts of time.

22.131   Additionally, there is an overall limit to the amount of costs recoverable by a litigant in person: the costs allowed cannot exceed two-thirds of the amount that would have been allowed had a legal representative been instructed.[56]

Success fees

22.132   Representation in civil proceedings can be funded under a conditional fee agreement (CFA). A CFA means that the lawyers will only receive payment if the claim is successful and costs are recovered. It is usual that a success fee is charged under a CFA, which is a percentage increase on the usual level of fees to reflect the risk that no fees will be paid at all if the claim is not successful. At present the losing party will be responsible for paying the success fee provided the costs agreement has been disclosed at the start of the litigation. The court may reduce the amount claimed if it is considered excessive. This is expected to change in 2012: success fees will be chargeable under a conditional fee agreement but must be paid by the client not the opponent.

Rewards charged by lay representatives

22.133   Lay representatives may make a charge for representing a person at the hearing of a small claim. This charge is known as a 'reward'.

What happens when one party is legally aided

22.134   A party may be granted legal aid to bring or defend proceedings. The granting of a legal aid certificate means that, instead of that party being responsible for paying his or her own solicitor's costs, the Legal

---

54   CPR 48.6(4)(a).
55   CPR 48.6(4)(b). At the time of writing it is proposed that this rate be increased.
56   CPR 48.6(2).

Services Commission (LSC)[57] is responsible. However, the fact that one party is legally aided should not affect the court's decision when considering a costs order. The usual rule, with some exceptions, still applies: if the legally aided party is successful the other party should be ordered to pay his or her costs. However, the existence of the certificate does have implications for the way costs are assessed. The possible outcomes are described below at paras 22.135–22.139.

The legally aided party is successful and the other party is ordered to pay costs

22.135 In such a case the losing party may not be responsible for paying all of the winning party's costs. This may be because some of the costs are considered to relate solely to obtaining legal aid or because the court has previously made an order that both parties pay their own costs of a particular application or hearing. In such a case the solicitor can claim these costs from the LSC, while claiming the majority of the costs from the other party.

22.136 In all cases where the LSC pays costs to the legally aided person's solicitor this sum will be deducted from any damages or money awarded. This is known as the 'statutory charge'. See below at para 22.168.

The legally aided party is unsuccessful

22.137 Where the legally aided party loses the case, the court will usually make an order that he or she pays the costs of the successful party but the order will state that 'the order may not be enforced without the permission of the court'. This is referred to as 'costs protection'. Costs protection is given in recognition that the assisted person has limited means. However, it leaves open the possibility of a party seeking to recover costs in the future if the losing party is in a position to pay.

22.138 In certain circumstances the successful party may claim costs from the LSC.[58]

---

57 The LSC is to be abolished by the LASPO Bill and will be replaced by an executive agency of the Ministry of Justice.

58 The criteria for orders to be made against the LSC are complex and depend on when the certificate was issued. They are set out in the document *Costs Against the Commission Manual* which is available on the LSC website at: www.legalservices.gov.uk.

Partial success or case settled and court makes no order for costs

22.139 'No order for costs' means that each party is responsible for his or her own costs. In relation to an assisted person, this means that his or her solicitors claim the whole of the costs from the LSC. If the assisted person has been awarded money or property by the court, the statutory charge will apply.

Controlling the amount of the costs

22.140 There are three ways in which the amount of costs may be determined, see paras 22.141–22.150 below.

Fixed costs

22.141 Some applications and claims are subject to a 'fixed costs' regime. This means that a set amount can be claimed for solicitor's costs. This can only be claimed if a solicitor is actually instructed and is distinct from the fee paid by the party to the court. For example, there are fixed costs for an accelerated claim for possession brought against an assured shorthold tenant: the court fee is, at the time of writing, £175 and, provided the landlord instructs a solicitor to complete the claim form, an additional fixed amount can be claimed for the solicitors costs.[59] It should be noted that these fixed costs apply only if the matter is decided without a hearing. A defendant who raises an argument that results in a hearing being held risks being ordered to pay additional costs if unsuccessful.

22.142   The proceedings that are subject to fixed costs are listed in CPR Part 45.

Summary assessment of costs

22.143 In relatively straightforward cases a court may 'summarily assess' the costs of the successful party at the end of the final hearing (or in some cases at the end of an interim hearing).[60] A party who wishes the court to do this must serve a summary of the costs he or she is claiming on the other party at least 24 hours before the hearing.[61]

---

59 The amount varies depending on who serves the claim form.
60 CPR 44.7.
61 CPR PD to Part 45, para 13.5. The summary should be in a certain format – see form N260.

22.144   Costs being claimed by a legally aided party cannot be summarily assessed because the court must carry out a full, or detailed, assessment of the amount to be paid by the LSC.[62]

Detailed assessment of costs

22.145 In more complex cases the amount of costs to be paid by one party to another will be subject to 'detailed assessment' by the court. In all cases when a person has a public funding certificate the court must subject the solicitor's claim for costs against the LSC to detailed assessment.

22.146   As between the two parties there is a procedure to be followed to determine the amount of the costs. This involves the following steps, see paras 22.147–22.150 below.

Serving the bill

22.147 A bill is prepared setting out in detail the amounts claimed. This is served on the paying party with a notice informing him or her of the total amount that will be payable if he or she fails to respond or if the costs have to be assessed by the court.

Responding to the bill

22.148 The paying party's solicitors should respond within 21 days with 'points of dispute', setting out any objections to the costs, such as to the rate being charged, the time spent or particular items claimed. If they fail to do so, the receiving party's solicitors can apply to the court for a 'default costs certificate'. This entitles the receiving party to be paid the full amount of the costs claimed.

Assessment hearing

22.149 If points of dispute are served and no agreement about costs is reached, the receiving party's solicitors will apply to the court for an assessment hearing at which a judge will decide the amount to be paid in costs.

22.150   In practice, the parties usually negotiate 'without prejudice' to agree the amount of the costs. If an assessment hearing is necessary, additional costs will be incurred: the further court fee and the parties' costs of attending the assessment hearing. If the amount of the bill is reduced at the hearing by more than a certain proportion, the costs of the hearing will be paid by the receiving party, if not, by the paying party.

62 CPR PD to Part 45, para 13.9.

Costs against someone who is not a party

22.151   It is possible for the court to order a person who is not a party to the proceedings to pay the costs of one or all of the parties.[63] The person against whom costs are sought must be added as a party to the proceedings, for the purpose of costs only, and must be given a reasonable opportunity to attend a hearing at which the court will consider the matter. An order may be made where it is alleged that the proceedings would not have been necessary but for the actions or default of that party. An example is the county court case of *ASRA v Coke*[64] in which the London Borough of Newham was ordered to pay the costs of both parties in a claim for possession; the claim had been brought because of the authority's failure to deal with the tenant's claim for housing benefit.

Costs ordered against a representative/wasted costs orders

22.152   'Wasted costs' means any costs incurred by a party 'as a result of any improper, unreasonable or negligent act or omission on the part of any legal or other representative or any employee of such a representative'.[65]

22.153   The court may order that the legal or other representative must pay the whole or part of the wasted costs.[66] 'Legal or other representatives' are defined as those exercising a right of audience or right to conduct litigation. This includes solicitors, barristers and lay representatives exercising rights under the Lay Representatives (Rights of Audience) Order 1999.[67] However, the court clearly has the power under CPR 48.2 (costs orders against someone who is not a party, see para 22.151 above) to make an order against others who are informally representing a party. Many advice agencies assist people with litigation although they are not on the court record and do not have rights of audience or representation. Such agencies should ensure that they are not inadvertently placed on the court record as formally

---

63   CPR 48.2. The rule does not apply when the court is considering an order against the LSC or a wasted costs order: CPR 42.2(2).

64   Reported in June 2001 *Legal Action* 31.

65   Senior Courts Act 1981 s51(7). It also includes costs 'which, in the light of any such act or omission occurring after they were incurred, the court considers it is unreasonable to expect that party to pay': s51(7)(b).

66   Senior Courts Act 1981 s51(6).

67   SI No 1966.

acting for the party and should generally not agree to receive notices and correspondence from the court on behalf of a client. If notice of a hearing were sent to the agency direct and the client not notified, the agency could be ordered to pay any costs wasted as a result.

22.154   If the court is considering making a wasted costs order, it must give those against whom the order is to be made a reasonable opportunity to attend a hearing to give reasons why such an order should not be made.[68]

22.155   It is not necessarily 'improper, unreasonable or negligent' to act for a party whose claim is bound to fail. However, a representative who acts in a claim which is an abuse of process, or is dishonest may be at risk of a wasted costs order.[69]

Legal aid/public funding

22.156   The legal aid scheme was introduced to ensure that people with limited means could be represented in legal proceedings. The current system is administered by the LSC. This is expected to change in 2012 when the LSC is abolished and replaced by an executive agency of the Ministry of Justice. Also, the scope of legal aid will be dramatically reduced, with certain areas of law being taken out of the scope of legal aid entirely. These include welfare benefits, debt and non-asylum immigration claims.

22.157   In relation to housing cases, legal aid will remain available for possession claims (other than those made against trespassers), homelessness reviews and appeals, and for judicial review. It will be available for disrepair claims only if there is a serious risk to the health and safety of the occupiers and not for damages-only claims. In relation to unlawful eviction and harassment it will be available for injunctions claims but not for damages-only claims.[70] There will be a provision for exceptional funding to be granted if the lack of legal aid would lead to a breach of a person's rights under the European Convention on Human Rights or other international treaties.

22.158   It is also proposed that legal aid will only be available via a telephone gateway service and that the majority of legally aided advice will in future be given by telephone and email rather than by face-to-face advisers.

---

68   CPR 48.7(2).
69   *Tolstoy-Milosalvsky v Lord Aldington* [1996] 2 All ER 556.
70   See LASPO Bill clauses 7–9 and Sch 1.

22.159   Currently in relation to civil proceedings a person may be assisted in one of two ways: under the Legal Help scheme or under a public funding certificate. The following applies at the date of writing but will change significantly from 2012 onwards: see the LASPO Bill.

The Legal Help scheme

22.160   Under the Legal Help scheme advice and assistance can be given in relation to most legal issues. This covers advising orally and in writing, corresponding on the person's behalf and obtaining expert evidence. Since October 2007 the fees a solicitor or adviser can claim for assisting under the Legal Help scheme are fixed depending on the category of law. Expenses such as interpreter's fees and expert's fees can be claimed in addition to the fixed fee.

22.161   In most cases an adviser cannot represent a person in court under the scheme. However, the scheme does cover attending court to provide 'help at court' in possession proceedings for a tenant where the only issue is the amount of any arrears, the rate of repayment of arrears and whether a warrant of possession should be suspended or not.

22.162   All those on means-tested social security benefits qualify for Legal Help. For others, their disposable income and savings must be below a certain amount.[71] The means assessment is conducted by the adviser who must obtain proof of income or receipt of benefit.

Legal aid certificates

22.163   A certificate may be granted to cover representation in specific court proceedings. An application can be made on behalf of a prospective claimant to cover a civil claim against another person or by a person who is a defendant in a claim (but not in anticipation of being a defendant). The certificate is issued to a specific firm or organisation to represent the assisted person. To be eligible for a public funding certificate, the applicant must satisfy both a means test and a merits test.

22.164   The means test is similar to that applied in respect of Legal Help but people whose income is above a certain limit may be granted a certificate subject to payment of a financial contribution. The

---

71 The LSC website includes a calculator to assess eligibiity: www.legalservices. gov.uk.

contribution must be paid by the assisted person every month for as long as the certificate is in force.

The merits test

22.165 In addition to qualifying on the basis of income and capital, the case must have sufficient merit. A cost benefit test is applied, balancing the prospect of success and the likely benefit to the assisted person against the anticipated costs of the proceedings. The test differs according to what is at stake. For example, where a person's home is at stake the prospects of success need not be as high as where a person is claiming damages. In certain cases a certificate may be granted even though the benefit to the assisted person will be limited, if the case may result in wider public benefit, for example, a challenge by way of judicial review to a policy that affects a large number of people.

22.166 The merits test must be applied continuously as long as the certificate is in force. Any offers to settle a claim must be reported and if a person is considered to be acting unreasonably in his or her instructions the certificate may be terminated.

Emergency funding

22.167 An emergency certificate may be granted to cover urgent work such as an application for an injunction or to represent a person at an imminent hearing. Firms and organisations that have 'devolved powers' (most contract holders) can grant emergency funding as soon as the application forms are signed. The forms must then be submitted for the issue of a certificate within five working days.

Limits of certificates

22.168 Public funding certificates are limited to taking certain steps within proceedings and it may be necessary to apply for extensions of the scope at various stages as the litigation progresses. Similarly, a certificate will limit the costs that can be incurred under a certificate and for complex cases that are not resolved quickly it will be necessary to make several applications for the scope and costs limits to be extended. At all stages the LSC must be satisfied that the cost benefit test is met.

The statutory change

22.169 The statutory charge refers to the right of the LSC to recover the costs it has incurred funding litigation where the funding has resulted in an award of property or money to the legally aided person. If the person is successful in the litigation the court should order the other party to pay the assisted person's legal costs. If all of the costs are recovered from the other party there should be no claim for costs against the legal aid fund. Therefore the statutory charge will not apply, although it does mean that a solicitor cannot release damages to the client until all of the costs have actually been paid by the other side.

22.170 In some cases not all of the costs can be recovered from the other party (see para 22.135 above). If this happens and some of the costs are claimed from the LSC by the solicitor, the amount claimed will be deducted from any money recovered by the assisted person. Where property is recovered or preserved (for example, following a dispute about beneficial ownership or property transfer) the LSC may register the amount owed as a charge on the property and payment must be made when the property is sold.

Tribunals

22.171 Some housing disputes are heard not by courts but by tribunals. Tribunals are decision-making bodies set up by statute to resolve particular kinds of dispute. Public funding is not available for legal representation at most tribunal hearings.

22.172 Most tribunals are now incorporated into the First-tier Tribunal which has six chambers. Appeals from the First-tier Tribunal are generally made to the Upper Tribunal. However, the Residential Property Tribunal Service, which deals with several kinds of housing dispute, is an independent tribunal.

22.173 The Residential Property Tribunal Service includes:

- the Rent Assessment Committee, which deals with disputes about rent levels in the private sector, see paras 4.181–4.191;
- the Leasehold Valuation Tribunal, which deals with disputes between leaseholders and freeholders, for example, service charge disputes, see chapter 5;
- the Residential Property Tribunal, which deals with appeals by landlords and tenants in respect of statutory notices served by local authorities, see chapter 11.

22.174 The following First-tier Tribunals are also relevant to housing advisers:

- the Information Rights Tribunal (Part of the General Regulatory Chamber), which deals with disputes about access to information under the Data Protection Act 1998 and the Freedom of Information Act 2000, see paras 2.97–2.109;
- the Asylum Support Tribunal (Part of the Social Entitlement Chamber), which deals with disputes about asylum support, including accommodation;
- the Social Security and Child Support Tribunal (Part of the Social Entitlement Chamber), which deals with welfare benefit entitlement, including housing benefit.

APPENDIX 1

HM Courts and Tribunals Service

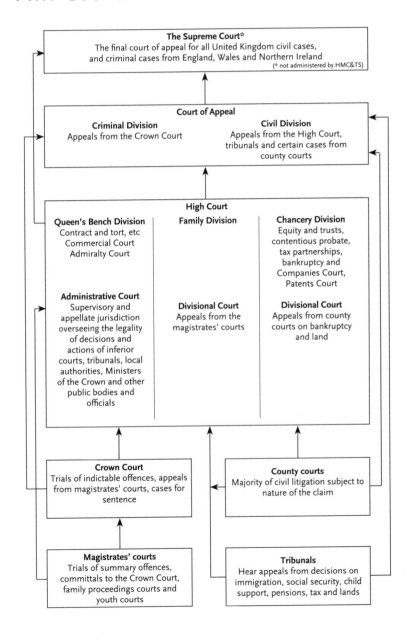

The Supreme Court*
The final court of appeal for all United Kingdom civil cases,
and criminal cases from England, Wales and Northern Ireland
(* not administered by HMC&TS)

Court of Appeal

Criminal Division
Appeals from the Crown Court

Civil Division
Appeals from the High Court,
tribunals and certain cases from
county courts

High Court

Queen's Bench Division
Contract and tort, etc
Commercial Court
Admiralty Court

Family Division

Chancery Division
Equity and trusts,
contentious probate,
tax partnerships,
bankruptcy and
Companies Court,
Patents Court

Administrative Court
Supervisory and
appellate jurisdiction
overseeing the legality
of decisions and
actions of inferior
courts, tribunals, local
authorities, Ministers
of the Crown and other
public bodies and
officials

Divisional Court
Appeals from the
magistrates' courts

Divisional Court
Appeals from county
courts on bankruptcy
and land

Crown Court
Trials of indictable offences, appeals
from magistrates' courts, cases for
sentence

County courts
Majority of civil litigation subject to
nature of the claim

Magistrates' courts
Trials of summary offences,
committals to the Crown Court,
family proceedings courts and
youth courts

Tribunals
Hear appeals from decisions on
immigration, social security, child
support, pensions, tax and lands

APPENDIX 2

Tomlin Order

TOMLIN ORDER

IN THE ...... COUNTY COURT

CLAIM No:

BETWEEN:

Claimant

and

Defendant

CONSENT ORDER

UPON the parties having agreed terms of settlement BY CONSENT

IT IS ORDERED that all further proceedings herein be stayed upon the terms set out in Schedule 1 hereto save for the purpose of enforcing or carrying into effect the said terms, with liberty to apply for that purpose.

IT IS FURTHER ORDERED that there be no order for costs save for the detailed assessment of the Defendant's public funding costs pursuant to the Community Legal Services (Costs) Regulations 2000.

SCHEDULE 1

1

2

3

We hereby consent to an order in the above terms:

Claimant   Defendant

or Claimant's solicitors   or Defendant's solicitors

Index